AMERICAN MILITARY AVIATION

NUMBER TWO

Centennial of Flight Series

Roger Launius, *General Editor*

AMERICAN MILITARY AVIATION

The Indispensable Arm

CHARLES J. GROSS

TEXAS A&M UNIVERSITY PRESS   COLLEGE STATION

Image on each chapter title page: Republic F-84 Thunderjets of the 182d Fighter Bomber Squadron, Texas Air National Guard. Taken from a photograph by Harold Beasley, courtesy of the Warren E. Thompson collection.

LIBRARY OF CONGRESS CATALOGING-IN-PUBLICATION DATA

Gross, Charles Joseph
American military aviation: the indispensable arm / Charles J. Gross.
p. cm.—(Centennial of flight series : no. 2)
Includes bibliographical references and index.
ISBN 1-58544-215-1 (cloth)
ISBN 13: 978-1-58544-255-3 (pbk.)
ISBN 10: 1-58544-255-0 (pbk.)
1. Aeronautics, Military—United States—History—20th century
2. United States. Air Force—History—20th century.
I. Title. II. Series.
UG633 .G767   2002
358.4'00973'0904—dc21   2002005334

TO CAPTAIN HARRY J. ZINSER,

USN (Retired),

naval aviator and friend,

whose quiet heroism

as a helicopter pilot

flying combat rescue missions

during the Vietnam War

was an inspiration

to all who knew him.

CONTENTS

List of Illustrations   ix

Acknowledgments   xi

List of Abbreviations   xiii

Introduction   3

Chapter 1. Brigades of Flying Horses   11

Chapter 2. A Golden Age of Innovation   48

Chapter 3. Armageddon   95

Chapter 4. An Age of Limits   142

Chapter 5. Cold Warriors   187

Chapter 6. The Renaissance of American Military Power   218

Chapter 7. The Empire Strikes Out   250

Epilogue   293

Notes   305

Bibliography   337

Index   355

ILLUSTRATIONS

Wright Brothers and Lt. Benjamin Foulois, 1909   19

Eugene Ely flying from the USS *Pennsylvania,* 1911   21

Major General George Owen Squier, chief signal officer, 1917–23   31

Captain Eddie Rickenbacker and pilots of the famed 94th
    Aero Squadron, France, 1918   43

Major Reuben Fleet and the first U.S. airmail, 1918   46

Captain Charles Lindbergh, ca. 1927   52

Major General Mason Patrick and Rear Adm. William Moffett   60

Trans-Atlantic flight of U.S. Navy NC-4s, 1919   62

USS *Langley* (CV-1), 1925   68

Army airmail, 1934   76

B-17s intercept the *Rex,* 1938   80

Generals Henry Arnold and George Marshall   106

L-4 observation plane on the USS *Ranger,* 1942   110

B-17s on a mission to Cologne, Germany   113

P-51 Mustangs in flight over Nazi territory   114

Aircraft on the USS *Enterprise* during the Battle of Midway   122

Atomic blast at Hiroshima   136

Major Gregory "Pappy" Boyington, USMC   140

Berlin Airlift, 1949   148

Convair RB-36D reconnaissance bomber in flight   154

Aircraft on the USS *Essex* during the Korean War   159

F-86 pilots in the Korean War   163

Wounded marines being evacuated by helicopter, Korea, 1951   167

Ensign Jesse Brown, first African American to fly in combat   170

F-104 being loaded aboard a C-124 during the Berlin crisis, 1961   192

P2V-7 inspects a Soviet freighter near Cuba, 1962   194

USS *Forrestal* aflame in the Gulf of Tonkin, 1967   198

Marine Corps close air support in Vietnam, 1967   200

Soldiers leap from a UH-1D "Huey" in Vietnam, 1967   202

Colonel Robin Olds and some of his pilots in Vietnam   214

C-141 unloads ECM pods airlifted to Israel during
    Operation Nickel Grass, 1973   231

Soviet "spy" ship off the stern of the USS *Franklin D. Roosevelt,* 1975   239

C-130 over the Egyptian pyramids, 1981   245

F-106 fires missile at William Tell competition   248

F-117As prepare to deploy to the Persian Gulf, 1990   255

KC-135 refuels F-16s during Operation Desert Storm   260

Aircraft carriers in the Red Sea during Operation Desert Storm   263

E-3 AWACS lands after completing a mission over Turkey   276

C-130 on a dirt strip in Somalia   278

Staff Sergeant Dixie Strom assembles a bomb during
    the Kosovo War, 1999   283

ACKNOWLEDGMENTS

This general history of American military aviation is based almost entirely upon the work of other historians. Without their hard work and perceptive analysis, which I have attempted to document in my endnotes and selected bibliography, this book would not have been possible. I am particularly indebted to Roger A. Launius, who suggested that I undertake this project and helped me develop its initial concepts and outline. My colleagues and friends have contributed an enormous amount of their time and valuable expertise to reviewing either all or portions of the manuscript and offering numerous suggestions to improve its factual contents, analysis, and organization. They included: Prof. Allan R. Millett, Perry D. Jamieson, Dan R. Mortensen, Edward J. Marolda, John D. Sherwood, Norman Polmar, Betty R. Kennedy, George W. Bradley III, Roy A. Grossnick, and Mark Evans. I am especially indebted to Gen. Charles A. Horner, USAF (Ret.), for his comments on the Persian Gulf crisis of 1990–91.

ABBREVIATIONS

AAA	Antiaircraft Artillery
ABM	Antiballistic Missile
AEC	Atomic Energy Commission
AEF	American Expeditionary Forces
AEFs	Aerospace Expeditionary Forces
AFRES	Air Force Reserve
ALCM	Air-Launched Cruise Missile
AMRAAM	Advanced Medium Range Air-to-Air Missile
ANG	Air National Guard
ASC	Air Service Command
ASW	Antisubmarine Warfare
ATC	Air Transport Command
ATO	Air Tasking Order
AWACS	Airborne Warning and Control System
BAP	Bureau of Aircraft Production
CENTCOM	Central Command
CIA	Central Intelligence Agency
CINC	Commander in Chief
CNO	Chief of Naval Operations
COMAIRSOLS	Air Command Solomons
CRAF	Civil Reserve Air Fleet
DEW	Distant Early Warning
DMA	Division of Military Aeronautics
DOD	Department of Defense
DSP	Defense Support Program
ECM	Electronic Countermeasures
FEAF	Far East Air Forces
GHQAF	General Headquarters, Air Force
GPS	Global Positioning System
HARM	High-Speed Antiradiation Missile
ICBM	Intercontinental Ballistic Missile

IFF	Identification, Friend or Foe
JCS	Joint Chiefs of Staff
JFACC	Joint Force Air Component Commander
JOC	Joint Operations Center
JSTARS	Joint Surveillance Target Attack Radar System
KLA	Kosovo Liberation Army
KTO	Kuwaiti Theater of Operations
MAC	Military Airlift Command
MACV	Military Assistance Command Vietnam
MAD	Mutually Assured Destruction
MATS	Military Air Transport Service
MRC	Major Regional Contingency
NACA	National Advisory Committee on Aeronautics
NAF	Naval Aircraft Factory
NATO	North Atlantic Treaty Organization
NOE	Nap of the Earth
NORAD	North American Air Defense Command (later North American Aerospace Defense Command)
NSC	National Security Council
OSRD	Office of Scientific Research and Development
PGM	Precision-Guided Munitions
PLAAF	Peoples Liberation Army Air Force
PLO	Palestine Liberation Organization
POW	Prisoner of War
PPBS	Planning, Programming, and Budgeting System
RAF	Royal Air Force
RCAF	Royal Canadian Air Force
ROTC	Reserve Officers Training Corps
SAC	Strategic Air Command
SALT	Strategic Arms Limitation Treaty
SAM	Surface-to-Air Missile
SIOP	Single Integrated Operational Plan
SLBM	Submarine-Launched Ballistic Missile
SPEAR	Strike Projection Evaluation Research
SRAM	Short-Range Attack Missile
START	Strategic Arms Reduction Treaty
TAC	Tactical Air Command
TACC	Tactical Air Control Center
TAR	Training and Administration of Reserves
TOW	Tube-Launched, Optically Tracked, Wire-Guided Missile

UAV	Unmanned Aerial Vehicle
UN	United Nations
UNC	United Nations Command
USAAF	U.S. Army Air Forces
USAF	U.S. Air Force
USAFE	U.S. Air Forces, Europe
USMC	U.S. Marine Corps
USN	U.S. Navy
USS	United States Ship
WAACS	Women's Auxiliary Army Corps
WACS	Women's Army Corps
WASPS	Women Airforce Service Pilots
WAVES	Women Accepted for Voluntary Emergency Service

AMERICAN MILITARY AVIATION

Introduction

n the years since Orville and Wilbur Wright made their first flight at
Kitty Hawk, North Carolina, in 1903, aviation has emerged as the
indispensable arm of American military power. Like many other technological revolutionaries, the Wrights believed their invention would insure international peace and prosperity. However, they soon turned to
the armed forces because there was no commercial market for their fragile
contraptions. Beginning in World War I, many senior American civilian and
military officials turned to aviation as a potentially decisive, inexpensive, and
relatively bloodless solution to complex and dangerous national security
problems. Because of their growing speed, range, and flexibility, aircraft proved
to be an enormously powerful tool of statecraft and war. Air power was attractive
because of its glamorous, high technology, modern image—which reflected
America's view of itself.

Military aviation has had a significant impact on warfare as well as the American culture and economy. Yet, despite its importance, there has never been a
comprehensive scholarly study of the subject that concentrates on developments
in the United States. Robin Higham's classic *Airpower: A Concise History* (1972)
surveys the international development of military and civil military aviation
from the Wright brothers to the Vietnam War with an emphasis on the United
Kingdom and the United States. Unlike most aviation historians, he concentrated on ideas instead of personalities and hardware. Higham, who served in
the Royal Air Force during World War II, rejected strategic bombing as an

independently decisive factor in armed conflict. Instead, he emphasized that air power has only been effective when used in conjunction with land and sea power.

Other international surveys of military aviation exposed the biases and narrow preoccupations of their authors. Alexander P. de Seversky's *Airpower: Key to Survival* (1950) was a parochial propaganda tract intended to advance the air force's cause in its bureaucratic struggles with the army and navy. De Seversky, a Russian émigré and leading aeronautical pioneer before World War II, argued that strategic bombardment had relegated the established surface forces to distinctly secondary roles. Basil Collier, a British scholar, took an opposite approach. Seldom straying from the Royal Air Force, his *A History of Airpower* (1974) concluded that the World War II strategic bombing campaigns were an enormous waste of resources that should have been devoted to providing tactical air support to the Allied armies. Other early military aviation histories have concentrated on individual services, specific wars or campaigns, colorful and important individuals, or individual aircraft.

This study analyzes the evolution of American military aviation from the cultural and technological antecedents of the Wright brothers through recent operations in the Persian Gulf and the Balkans. It relies upon published scholarly works on the general history of American military policy, institutions, and operations, as well as more specialized monographs. In particular, it draws heavily on highly regarded general interpretive histories such as Allan R. Millett's and Peter Maslowski's *For The Common Defense: A Military History of the United States of America* (1984, 1994), and Russell F. Weigley's *The American Way of War: A History of United States Military Policy* (1973). More specialized works—including Kenneth Hagan's *This People's Navy: The Making of American Sea Power* (1990), Millett's *Semper Fidelis: The History of the United States Marine Corps* (1991), Weigley's *History of the United States Army* (1967, 1983), and John B. Rae's *Climb to Greatness: The American Aircraft Industry, 1920–1960* (1968)— illuminate critical themes and events. Archibald D. Turnbull's and Clifford D. Lord's *History of United States Naval Aviation* (1949) remains the standard work on the pre–World War II period.

Charles H. Gibbs-Smith's *Aviation: An Historical Survey from Its Origins to the End of World War II* (1970) is especially valuable for its coverage of the prehistory of flight, including the technological developments exploited by the Wright brothers. The reasons for the triumphs and controversies associated with the Wrights are analyzed in Thomas Crouch's superb biography *The Bishop's Boys: A Life of Orville and Wilbur Wright* (1989). Lee Kennett's *The First Air War, 1914–1918* (1991) is a comprehensive analytical account that avoided the well-worn path of focusing on romanticized visions of the exploits of individual combat pilots. Departing from the dominant tradition of most of the earlier literature on the Great War, he suggested that aviation played a significant role in the conflict. John H. Morrow Jr.'s *The Great War in the Air: Military Aviation from 1909 to 1921* (1993) provides an encyclopedic international survey of the early development of military aviation. James J. Hudson's *Hostile Skies: A Combat History of the American Air Service in World War I* (1968) is a lively, well-researched account of the combat flying experiences of the army's infant air arm in Europe during World War I. Irving B. Holley Jr.'s *Ideas and Weapons: Exploitation of the Aeripon by the United States in World War I: A Study of the Relationship of Technological Advance, Military Doctrine, and the Development of Weapons* (1953, 1971) examines American efforts to create, virtually from scratch, a large military aviation program after the nation entered the conflict.

Much of the early writing on military aviation during the interwar period focused on the colorful and controversial Brig. Gen. William "Billy" Mitchell. Alfred F. Hurley's *Billy Mitchell: Crusader for Airpower* (1964, 1975) remains the best scholarly treatment of Mitchell's career. Recent scholarship has shed light on other significant personalities and topics. Two of the former are Rear Adm. William A. Moffett and Maj. Gen. Mason M. Patrick, the true postwar builders of aviation in their respective military services. William F. Trimble's *Admiral William A. Moffett: Architect of Naval Aviation* (1994) focuses on Moffett's successful efforts to build air power into an integral part of fleet operations. The best analysis of Patrick's role is Robert P. White's *Major General Mason M. Patrick and the Fight for Air Service Independence* (2001). These two works are complemented by two excellent biographies of key but even more obscure officers: Clark. G. Reynolds's *Admiral John H. Towers: The Struggle for Naval Air Supremacy* (1991) and John F. Shiner's *Foulois and the Army Air Corps, 1931–1935* (1983). In *The Wings of Democracy: The Influence of Airpower on the Roosevelt Administration, 1933–1941* (1991), Jeffrey S. Underwood examines how Air Corps leaders abandoned the politically confrontational approach of Mitchell to win influence and resources during the New Deal.

Richard J. Overy's *The Air War, 1939–1945* (1980) provides a superb general historical analysis of why the Allies won the war in the air against the Axis. Ronald H. Spector's *Eagle Against The Sun: The American War With Japan* (1985) is an acclaimed survey of the war in the Pacific, including the central role air power played on both sides. *A War to be Won: Fighting the Second World War* (2000), by Williamson Murray and Allan R. Millett, is a comprehensive single-volume study of combat operations on land, sea, and in the air that encompasses all of the major combatants. It also examines politics, strategy, tactics, military doctrine, weapons, and science.

James L. Stokesbury's *A Short History of Airpower* (1986) is a very readable overview of the international history of air power through the Falklands War in

1982. Roger E. Bilstein's *Flight in America, 1903–1983: From the Wright Brothers to the Astronauts* (1984) reviews the broad development of military, commercial, and private aviation in the United States, as well as its industrial base. Joseph Corn's *The Winged Gospel: America's Romance with Aviation* (1983) provides seminal insights about aviation's impact on American culture through the early days of the Cold War. Updating the better-known World War II studies, the official history programs of the armed forces provide a treasure trove of invaluable recent scholarship, including such works as Edward J. Marolda and Robert J. Schneller's *Shield and Sword: The United States Navy and the Persian Gulf War* (1998) and *Winged Shield, Winged Sword: A History of the United States Air Force* (1997), edited by Bernard C. Nalty. Under the guidance of editor in chief, John Whiteclay Chambers II, *The Oxford Companion to American Military History* (1999) provides an excellent collection of short interpretive essays incorporating the latest scholarship on a broad spectrum of military topics ranging from civil-military relations to the evolution of stealth technology.

From its inception, military aviation has focused on the development of several key missions. All of them except aerial refueling were developed in at least some preliminary form during World War I. Aircraft at first were used for reconnaissance purposes. They kept track of enemy ground forces and served as spotters to gauge the accuracy of friendly artillery fire. Although reconnaissance remains an important mission, more and more of it is being performed by space-based satellites and unmanned aerial vehicles. When it became apparent in 1914 that it would be a good idea to deny enemy aircraft unobstructed opportunities for reconnaissance of friendly forces, aircraft with armed pilots and observers were sent up to shoot them down. Thus was born the idea of air superiority or controlling the airspace over the battlefield. Air defense, a doctrinal cousin of air superiority, employed fighter aircraft to prevent armed enemy long-range bombers, airships, and fighters from attacking a combatant's homeland, especially the civilian population and economic infrastructure. Britain's Royal Air Force was established during World War I to defend England against attacks by German zeppelins. A consensus quickly emerged within the military services that air superiority was a critical mission that, when achieved, helped ground, sea, and air forces accomplish other missions. Nevertheless, air defense has never been a popular mission with airmen, who have always stressed that the speed, flexibility, and range of aircraft favor the attacker.

Strategic bombing became an enormously important mission in the United States because it provided the rationale for the creation of an independent air force, although its results in combat have been decidedly mixed and extremely controversial. It has been used to destroy enemy production capabilities and transportation networks as well as government centers. It has also been used, usually without success, to terrorize enemy civilians into forcing their leaders to capitulate. Aerial interdiction seeks to cut off or reduce the flow of enemy troops and materiel to the battlefield. Like strategic bombing, however, its results have been mixed. It appears to have worked best when employed against islands that can be isolated by friendly air and naval forces. Both bombers and fighters have been used for interdiction. Ground attack and close air support missions employing aircraft in direct support of ground troops are very popular with ground commanders but are extremely dangerous and demand close coordination between air and ground forces. Only Marine Corps and army aviators put this mission at the top of their respective priority lists. Beginning with the Vietnam War, both the Marine Corps and the army employed helicopters to help accomplish this mission. Although it occasionally fielded superb aircraft like the P-47 Thunderbolt and the A-10 Warthog, the air force and its predecessors have never given ground attack and close air support forces a high priority.

Airlift is another critical element of air power, but it has usually been taken for granted and given relatively low priority—especially in the allocation of resources. In recent decades it has been broadened into the concept of air mobility by including aerial refueling aircraft. The ability to move troops, combat aircraft, and materiel quickly anywhere in the world has become a key element of American military power and diplomatic influence. Naval aviation has developed its own variations of most of these key aviation missions as part of the navy's effort to control the seas and to project power ashore from the fleet. Technologies associated with what we now call command, control, communications, and intelligence (C3I) have supported the successful use of U.S. military aviation. Close cooperation between the aviation industry, the armed forces, government labs, and university researchers have provided the wherewithal to develop the advanced technologies and hardware that have made American air power a formidable force in the modern world.

The history of American military aviation suggests five major conclusions. First, aviation has become an indispensable element of America's military force and diplomacy. As a highly industrialized modern nation that relies on advanced technology to offset superior enemy numbers and minimize its own casualties while promoting its global interests and security, the United States simply cannot afford to leave home without it. However, military aviation has usually failed to provide an independently decisive force in modern warfare capable of winning quick and relatively bloodless victories against determined and innovative foes. Air power still works best in conjunction with armies and navies. Recent U.S. military triumphs in the Persian Gulf and Kosovo came at the expense of weak and diplomatically isolated states whose armed forces and civilian populations clearly had little stomach for war with the world's only remaining superpower. While military aviation played the leading role in Operations Desert Storm and Allied Force, ground troops were needed to secure fragile and incomplete victories in both cases.

Second, political and military leaders have consistently overestimated the potential of military aviation to solve the nation's national security problems with a minimum expenditure of American blood and treasure. From Woodrow Wilson to William J. Clinton, presidents and their senior advisers have frequently turned to air power for quick and relatively cheap solutions to difficult diplomatic and security problems. Military leaders have often shared the exaggerated hopes and expectations of civilian leaders. Indeed, airmen have often promoted those expectations in the first place. Once it became apparent that the airplane could be an extremely useful weapon in the crucible of combat, the U.S. military services and their civilian allies did not neglect aviation. Starting in World War I, each of the armed forces rushed to develop its own powerful air arm. Each of them wanted a piece of the action. The real argument was over who would control aviation assets and for what purposes they would be used. The emphasis on strategic bombardment, especially by the air force and its predecessors, often retarded and overshadowed the development of other military aviation missions that turned out to be far more important. The navy's post–World War II efforts to develop supercarriers as launching platforms for fighter-bombers that could deliver nuclear bombs on Soviet targets had a similar impact. Controversies associated with strategic bombardment tended to obscure the enormous contributions that air power had made in conjunction with armies and navies.

Third, air mobility forces consisting of airlift and air refueling aircraft have been the neglected stepchildren of air power. Their growing range and capabilities have added enormous flexibility to American military power and diplomacy. They have enabled the United States to respond to a variety of threats in an enormously effective manner. In some special circumstances, including the Berlin airlift and the Yom Kippur War as well as various humanitarian operations in Africa and the Soviet Union, they provided senior American civilian policy makers with tools that were simply unavailable elsewhere. They also remain critical to the rapid projection of American combat power to the far corners of the globe.

Fourth, air power has transformed warfare by extending the range and destructiveness of combat operations for military personnel and civilians alike. Those developments paralleled what happened on the ground and at sea. Military aviation extended the horrors of combat from the trenches to homes, factories, and offices, thus contributing to the fact that the twentieth century was the bloodiest hundred years in recorded human history. Prior to the advent of precision-guided munitions, air power, especially the nuclear-armed variety, had become so destructive that some theorists forecast that it would either destroy civilization or end warfare altogether. Neither of those predictions proved to be accurate. Because of their enormous destructive power, nuclear weapons probably prevented a catastrophic war between the United States and the Soviet Union, but they have not proven to be very useful for anything else. It is also fair to note—as demonstrated by developments in the Persian Gulf, the Balkans, and Afghanistan—that those who predicted air power would be largely irrelevant to the national security challenges of the post–Cold War world clearly missed the mark.

Finally, aviation, including its military component, has had a significant impact on American culture and the economy. Like developers of the telegraph in the nineteenth century and the Internet in the late twentieth, aviation pioneers encouraged the growth of millennial expectations about the imminent arrival of universal peace and unending prosperity because human beings had finally achieved powered flight. Aviation became something of a secular religion in America during the interwar period. Aviators epitomized the rugged individualism, technological progress, and democratic freedoms so prized by Americans. Men like Eddie Rickenbacker and Charles A. Lindbergh became heroes of the emerging mass popular culture. Books, movies, magazines, and newspapers were permeated with stories and images about flying. However, dreams that aviation would establish heaven on earth were shattered by the searing images of places like Dresden and Hiroshima during World War II. Nevertheless, the aviation industry has become a cornerstone of the American economy, and military aviation has been the industry's most important customer since World War I. Military spending and operational requirements, supplemented by research at government laboratories and universities, provided the stimulus for much of the industry's technical progress. As a matter of necessity and policy, the armed forces have sustained that critical industry and underwritten its technical advances. Wars, both cold and hot, have been responsible for its most intense periods of growth.

CHAPTER 1

Brigades of Flying Horses

The idea of flight is nearly as old as human imagination. Inspired by birds and religion, virtually every epoch of recorded human history includes references to flight in its art, music, and literature. The ancient Egyptians worshipped winged gods, the Greeks recounted the legend of Icarus's risky business, and formidable Teutonic maidens celebrated the ride of the Valkyries in song. Despite all of that, ancient civilizations left almost no credible records of attempts to actually achieve mechanical powered flight. The exceptions are few and far between. In about 400 B.C., the misty historical figure of Archytas of Tarantum may have built and flown a wooden dove powered by a steam jet. Armin Firmen, an Arab savant, actually attempted a flight at Cordoba, Spain, in 852.

Four centuries later, Roger Bacon, an English Franciscan friar, made vague references in his writings to an ornithopter, a man-powered machine that duplicated the flapping motion of birds. However, since human muscles are not strong enough to enable a man to fly, that contraption was doomed to failure. Others who replicated his machine in one form or another achieved equally unsatisfactory results. Leonardo da Vinci (1452–1519) was the first man of scientific renown to turn his attention to flight. He designed a helicopter and a parachute, but kept his work secret. It thus had no real impact on aeronautics even after it was discovered in the late nineteenth century. In 1638, two books published by clergymen in England speculated on the possibilities of flying to the moon with the help of angels and wild swans. These and other early literary speculations testified to the continuing interest in flight but had no practical effect on the science and technology needed to get the job done.

BALLOONS, GLIDERS, AND AERONAUTICS

Because there was no adequate source of mechanical power available, man had to rely on the wind to fly. The earliest known reports of gliding are dated about 1000. In that year, an English Benedictine monk named Elmer fashioned a pair of wings and launched himself from a tower at Malesbury Abbey. After a floundering glide of about six hundred feet, Elmer crashed, breaking both his legs. Structural and stability problems frustrated any real progress in gliding by intrepid clerics, cranks, and other adventurers until the nineteenth century.[1]

Where human muscles and primitive early gliders failed, hot air finally succeeded. On June 4, 1783, Etienne and Joseph Montgolfier, French papermakers, publicly demonstrated the first small hot-air balloon at Annonay, France. That September, at Versailles, a full-size version of their invention made the first recorded balloon ascent. The device carried a sheep, a rooster, and a duck aloft to test whether or not they could survive in the unknown atmosphere above the earth. The barnyard denizens lived, so the brothers moved on to experiments with humans. After a series of tethered flights, they launched the first free balloon flight on November 21, 1783, with a doctor and a French infantry major aboard. It lasted twenty-five minutes. Throughout the flight, the heroic major doused burning holes in the balloon's fabric with a wet sponge.

The Montgolfiers' success stimulated a wave of balloon mania in Europe. It was a very dangerous pursuit. Often relying on burning straw to heat the air, early balloons were floating firetraps. Hydrogen-filled balloons, which were much safer, made their debut in France shortly after the Montgolfiers' initial success with passengers. In 1793, Frenchman Jean-Pierre Blanchard demonstrated the first hydrogen-filled balloon in the United States at Philadelphia. That public display failed to generate any official government interest. The young republic's fledgling military-industrial complex was content to focus on producing frigates and muskets with interchangeable parts. But the private exploits of men like Blanchard inspired a growing coterie of "aeronauts" on both sides of the Atlantic.

The French Revolution produced the first military use of balloons. In 1794, the French formed an "Aerostatic Corps" that served in the field for several years. Many pamphlets published during the Napoleonic wars contained detailed proposals for employing balloons for military purposes, including drawings showing huge devices flying units of the *Grande Armée* across the English Channel complete with horses and artillery. Apparently the balloons were not very useful; Napoleon abandoned them after he came to power in 1798.

Intensive balloon activity continued in Europe during the nineteenth century. The Austrians attempted the first bombing raid with balloons in June, 1849. They sent pilotless hot-air balloons against Venice with bombs released by timing devices. The raid was a failure: no lives were lost and little damage was done. The real problem was that balloons remained at the mercy of the winds and other unpredictable weather conditions. That difficulty was partially solved in 1852 by Frenchman Henri Giffard. He designed and successfully flew a cigar-shaped airship equipped with a propeller and lightweight steam engine for seventeen miles at a speed of five miles per hour. That configuration gave Giffard's device directional control.

Ballooning mania hit the United States in the mid-nineteenth century. By 1859, Americans had made an estimated three thousand balloon ascents carrying some eight thousand passengers. However, the flights were essentially for entertainment rather than serious scientific experiments. The army rejected proposals to take balloons along during the Seminole and Mexican Wars, but civilian balloonists finally got the chance to show their stuff during the Civil War. A handful of volunteers on both sides offered their services. In April, 1861, Rhode Island militiamen James Allen and Dr. William H. Helm took two balloons to Washington, D.C., and made the U.S. Army's first trial captive balloon ascent on June 9. The most significant ballooning effort was made by a Union contingent led by Thaddeus S. C. Lowe. That same year, he supervised the construction of seven balloons and a dozen mobile hydrogen generators. Once in the field, balloons normally operated tethered to the ground. Each carried an observer in a wicker basket who either telegraphed or dropped messages. The balloonists achieved some success in observing Confederate troop movements and spotting artillery fire in the Richmond campaign of 1862. Some of Lowe's balloons were also used in the western theater. Many Union officers remained skeptical of the value of Lowe's balloons, however. His organization's civilian volunteer status placed Lowe constantly at odds with military authorities over resources that it needed to operate in combat zones. Changes in Union commanders in 1863 settled the matter. The new leaders were not interested in Lowe's balloons, and the Army of the Potomac's balloon corps was disbanded in June. Although free-flight civilian ballooning briefly regained its popularity in America after the war's end, the U.S. military ignored it until the 1890s.

Despite progress in ballooning, mankind's ancient dreams of mechanical-powered flight remained frustrated until the science of aerodynamics and structures evolved, effective flying methods were developed, and modern technology produced a reliable, light, and powerful engine. That process—which culminated with the Wright brothers' success over the windy sand dunes at Kitty Hawk, North Carolina, in December, 1903—took a little over a century. It can be traced to Sir George Caley, a Yorkshire aristocrat who was the true originator of the modern airplane. Caley's interest in flight was inspired during his boyhood by the initial ascents of the Montgolfiers' balloons. Caley invented a model helicopter in 1796. After studying birds and concluding that ornithopters would not work, Caley advocated designs for heavier-than-air vehicles that separated the power source from the source of lift. They featured angled wings and tail assemblies with horizontal and vertical stabilizers. In 1799, he produced a drawing of a fixed-wing glider and built a successful model five years later. Caley next produced a full-size glider that was first flown unmanned and then carried a boy for a few yards at a time in 1809. Based on those experiments, he published a scientific paper that laid the foundations of aerodynamics and flight control upon which the modern science of flying is based. However, the scientific community did not take his work seriously before his death in 1857.

During the remainder of the nineteenth century, dozens of experimenters built gliders based on Caley's ideas while searching for an efficient lightweight power source. Steam engines were too heavy and cumbersome for full-sized flying machines. Although they did not realize it at the time, a French engineer named Lenoir, who invented the gas engine in 1860, suggested the solution to their problem. His work led to the Otto and Daimler petrol-powered engines in Germany during the 1870s. The latter were light and powerful enough to propel heavier-than-air machines.[2]

Aeronautical research and experimentation had begun to attract the attention of formally trained scientists and engineers by the mid-nineteenth century. In the 1860s, professional scientific societies devoted to the study of aeronautics were established in France and Great Britain. They became primary forums for disseminating information on aeronautical progress during that era. The Franco-Prussian War in 1870–71 and the general expansion of technology in Europe during the 1870s stimulated significant progress. Aeronautical developments in the 1870s were dominated by Alphonse Penaud, a Frenchman who ranks with Caley and the Wrights. In September, 1871, Penaud flew a model monoplane 131 feet in eleven seconds. Powered by a twisted rubber band attached to a two-bladed propeller mounted in the rear, it was the first inherently stable airplane ever seen in public. Penaud's crowning achievement was the design in 1874 of a full-size, two-seated monoplane. His design, which was patented but never actually built, featured twin front-mounted propellers, elliptical wings with curved surfaces, twin rear elevators, a vertical fixed fin with a rear rudder, a retractable undercarriage and tail skid, flight instruments, a glass-domed cockpit, and a single control stick that operated the elevators and rudder. Penaud's work became widely known and was one of the most significant formative influences in aviation history.

In Germany, Otto Lilienthal pursued the dream of flight carefully and systematically. He made more than two thousand successful glider flights before being killed in a crash in 1896. A trained engineer, he contributed enormously to the store of available knowledge of materials, design, construction, and piloting of gliders. Since photography had advanced to the point where it could show objects and people in motion, illustrated articles about his flights were printed all over the world, inspiring unknown numbers of enthusiasts and scientific researchers. Among those he directly influenced were Orville and Wilbur Wright, wallflower brothers from Dayton, Ohio, who were self-educated high school dropouts.

The work of Caley, Lilienthal, and others was discussed at scientific meetings and published in various professional journals and popular magazines. In the latter half of the nineteenth century, dozens of researchers were pursuing the goal of powered flight. In the United States, Octave Chanute played a key role as both a researcher and conduit for European aeronautical developments. A French-born civil engineer, Chanute finalized the Lilienthal-type hang glider in biplane form in 1896. He also published the first accurate history of aviation in 1894, providing a major vehicle for disseminating practical information on European technical progress to American researchers. Chanute became a close friend and encourager of the Wright brothers.

The leading figure in American aeronautics in the late nineteenth century was Samuel Pierpont Langley. A patient researcher and a good writer who exaggerated his own modest scientific accomplishments, Langley initiated serious aeronautical research in 1887—the same year he became secretary of the Smithsonian Institution. He began with a series of technically dubious tests of stuffed birds and model airplanes financed by a private benefactor. He then built a series of gliders and model aircraft powered by steam engines. While serving as assistant secretary of the navy, Theodore Roosevelt recognized the military potential of Langley's work. Although he could not convince the navy to subsidize it, Roosevelt became a great aviation enthusiast and persuaded the army to spend $50,000 in 1898 on Langley's proposal to build a man-carrying aircraft.

THE WRIGHT STUFF

Directly inspired by published accounts and photos of Lilienthal's glider flights, the Wright brothers had become enthralled by the challenge of achieving controlled, powered flight with heavier-than-air craft. They grew up in the stimulating atmosphere of an inquisitive and well-read family. Their father was a well-known minister and Methodist bishop in Dayton. The brothers were known locally as tireless tinkerers and builders of high-quality bicycles. What they lacked in professional scientific and engineering training, they made up for with mechanical aptitude and voracious reading. They wrote to the Smithsonian for aviation literature and began an extensive correspondence with Chanute, who remained in contact with other aeronautical researchers in Europe and the United States.

It took the Wrights a mere six years to progress from their first experiment with a box kite until they achieved immortality at Kill Devil Hill, North Carolina in December 1903. Along the way, they built their own small wind tunnel to compile data on wing shapes and lift. The Wrights then designed and built their own gliders and mastered the art of flying them in periodic trips to Kill Devil Hill, a location they had carefully selected because of its favorable wind conditions. They developed the technique of wing warping (bending) so their gliders could bank in flight and linked its controls to a movable rudder that enabled them to make controlled turns. The Wrights also installed forward elevators so they could control glider climbs and descents. Unable to purchase an adequate engine, they built their own twelve-horsepower model. After studying existing propellers and compiling additional data from a wind tunnel they built for testing, the brothers produced their own aeronautical propellers, which were the most efficient ones in existence at the time.

Orville and Wilbur packed up their equipment and returned to North Carolina in December, 1903. Men from a nearby lifesaving station were invited to witness the event. Orville provided one of them with a camera to record it. At exactly 10:35 A.M. on December 17, 1903, the Wright brothers became the first to achieve sustained controlled flight by a human in an airplane. With Orville at the controls, their "Flyer" traveled 120 feet in twenty seconds. They made three more successful flights that day before wind damaged the Flyer. It never flew again. It never had to. After dreaming of powered flight since ancient times, mankind had finally taken to the sky.

Following their triumph at Kill Devil Hill, Orville and Wilbur spent the next two years perfecting their invention. Although convinced that the airplane would guarantee international peace and stimulate prosperity, the Wrights finally turned to the only profitable market available to them: the military. The American armed forces had shown no official interest in the Wrights' invention in the years immediately after 1903. The brothers, determined to protect their pending patent, had tried to convince the services to buy an aircraft sight unseen. The army was already leery of the whole subject of aviation. It had been seriously embarrassed in the autumn of 1903 when Langley's experimental "Aerodome" twice burrowed into the muddy bottom of the Potomac River while attempting to make its maiden flight. The army had invested $50,000 in the project, and Langley's failure prompted screams from Congress and the press that the service was wasting public money on harebrained inventions that lacked military value. The Langley controversy convinced many senior officers that the armed forces should avoid risking their reputation and limited funds on such highly speculative ventures.[3]

Instead, the army was more comfortable with its small but entrenched ballooning program. In the early 1890s, its newly established Signal Corps laid claim to aeronautics as a natural extension of the communications mission granted to it by Congress. Its leaders realized that successful development of military aeronautics could help ensure the Corps's survival. Beginning with Brig. Gen. Adolphus W. Greely, the chief signal officer from 1887–1906, heads of the Signal Corps brought the army into contact with the work being done on powered flight and ballooning by civilian scientists and inventors. Because of the success of dirigibles in France and Germany, their efforts initially focused upon lighter-than-air equipment. The army took its first organizational step to recognize the importance of aeronautics when it organized the Aeronautical Division of the Signal Corps on August 1, 1907. The division, which emphasized ballooning, was also responsible for aircraft. Initially, it consisted of one captain and two privates.[4]

The army was finally compelled to take a serious look at the Wrights' invention by a civilian special interest group, the Aero Club of America and pressures from within the Signal Corps. Organized by members of the Automobile Club of America in 1905, it consisted of businessmen, sportsmen, army officers and inventors—including the Wright brothers and Octave Chanute. Like similar groups in France and Great Britain, they wanted to promote aeronautics.

In 1907, the club's president, millionaire Corlandt Bishop, asked his brother-in-law, Rep. Herbert Parsons, to intercede with the War Department on behalf of the Wright brothers. Instead, Parsons took the issue directly to President Theodore Roosevelt. The president asked Secretary of War William Howard Taft to have the army reconsider the Wrights' invention. During the same period, Brig. Gen. James Allen had directed his assistant, Maj. George Owen Squier, to perform a detailed study of aeronautics and its potential military applications. The two officers made plans to publicize aeronautics in an effort to win War Department and congressional support. They also worked behind the scenes to get the army to take another look at the Wrights' invention. The combination of external and internal pressures bore fruit. The Board of Ordnance and Fortification remained skeptical but changed its mind following a personal appeal by Wilbur Wright in November, 1907. Acting on the board's recommendation, the chief signal officer issued specifications for the world's first military aircraft and advertised for bids the following month.

The Signal Corps drew up Specification No. 486 for the first experimental military aircraft with the help of a number of scientifically trained individuals interested in the advancement of aeronautics. Major Squier played a key role in that process. After graduating from West Point in 1887, he apparently became the first officer with a doctorate in the army after completing his doctoral studies in electrical engineering at Johns Hopkins University in Baltimore in 1893. Squier represented an emerging class of uniformed military technocrats who played a key role in securing the future of U.S. military and naval aviation during and after World War I. They recognized that the fate of military and naval aviation was tied to vigorous research and development programs, government organizations that promoted and applied such advances, and a strong commercial aviation industry that included manufacturers as well as airlines.[5]

Squier, who had helped convince the Board of Ordnance and Fortification to allot $50,000 to Professor Langley's Aerodrome experiments, drew upon his extensive studies of aeronautics to develop a draft of Specification No. 486. He then tapped the advice of aeronautically minded friends and colleagues in the American scientific community on an informal, ad hoc basis. The army received twenty-four bids to build an airplane in response to the specification, including one from an inmate in a federal prison. The latter offered to build a flying machine if the government would release him from solitary confinement. Only three of the proposals actually met army specifications. The Wright brothers' submission was one of them. Although, the Signal Corps clearly preferred to deal with the Wrights, their $25,000 bid was the highest of the three. This placed them last on the list of potential contractors under the procurement practices of the day. The army's only other viable alternative was to buy from all three successful bidders, but the Board of Ordnance and Fortification lacked the money to do it. That problem was solved when additional money was obtained from a special fund maintained by President Roosevelt. The extra funds turned out to be unnecessary when only the Wrights were able to fulfill the terms of the contract.[6]

Orville Wright delivered an aircraft to the army on August 20, 1908, and tests were scheduled at Fort Myer, Virginia. Major Squier headed a board appointed by the chief signal officer. The navy also sent two official observers, and President Roosevelt, his cabinet, and members of Congress turned out for the event. Thousands of ordinary citizens, responding to sensational newspaper stories, braved the heat and humidity of late summer to join them. However, tragedy soon darkened the proceedings. Lieutenant Thomas Selfridge, a veteran balloonist who had volunteered to serve as an observer at the acceptance trials and ride as a passenger with Orville, was killed when the aircraft crashed on September 17. Orville was seriously injured and his machine was

Wilbur, *left,* and Orville Wright, *right,* confer with 1st Lt. Benjamin D. Foulois, *center,* on July 30, 1909, during their successful military aircraft trials at Fort Myer, Virginia. (U.S. Air Force photo collection, National Archives.)

badly damaged. The army delayed the final aircraft tests until the following summer.[7]

The Wright brothers came to the nation's capital in June, 1909, with an improved version of their aircraft. In late July, Orville completed the official trials at Fort Myer. Airplane No. 1 met all of the army contract's requirements. The remaining provisions were fulfilled later that year when Wilbur trained two army officers as pilots at a temporary flying field established near College Park, Maryland.[8]

A GAME FOR FOOLS AND NITWITS

The navy had been even more reluctant than the army to become involved in aviation. The Naval Board of Construction had rejected Theodore Roosevelt's initiative in 1898 to sponsor Langley's experimental airplane despite the endorsement of a small committee of junior-ranking army and navy officers convened to evaluate the proposal. Composed of conservative senior officers of the battleship-oriented "Gun Club," the board saw no reason to spend money on a device that had not even been invented. It concluded that such machines were the army's business, if anybody's in the federal government. The navy later rejected overtures from the Wright brothers, and Orville's crash at Fort Myer in September, 1908, confirmed its resolve. However, technical progress, lobbying by technically oriented naval officers, and pressure by an outside interest group eventually overcame institutional resistance.[9]

In August, 1909, the acting secretary of the navy rejected a Bureau of Equipment request to advertise for construction of two aircraft on the grounds that aeronautical technology had not advanced far enough to be of value to the service. The following year, John B. Ryan, who headed an unofficial civilian group known as the U.S. Aeronautic Reserve, wrote to the navy secretary asking him for the name of an officer his organization might contact on aviation matters. In response, the secretary's office designated Capt. Washington Irving Chambers that September as the person responsible to monitor aeronautical developments. Chambers, an engineer and a Naval Academy graduate, was not a pilot. He had no stated formal authority over aeronautics. The situation became even more confused in October, 1910, when the secretary directed the Bureau of Construction and Repair to monitor aviation developments. That splintered authority was maintained until the navy established the Bureau of Aeronautics in 1921.[10]

Chambers proved to be an effective champion of naval aviation in its infancy. He closely followed developments in aviation in the U.S. and abroad. Chambers also fostered interest in naval aviation by jawboning senior officers, civilian officials in the executive branch of government, and members of Congress. He arranged to have the first aircraft ever launched from an American warship. Eugene Ely, a civilian pilot, flew a Curtiss biplane from the deck of the cruiser USS *Birmingham* on November 14, 1910. Ely achieved another historic first when he landed a Curtiss machine on the USS *Pennsylvania* on January 18, 1911. Chambers also brought talented officers, including Lt. (j.g.) John H. Towers, and Lt. Comdr. Henry C. Mustin, into naval aviation. Like Squier, he insisted that vigorous technical and developmental research was the key to designing useful aircraft for the armed forces.[11]

Aviation advocates in the U.S. armed forces faced an uphill battle prior to America's entry into World War I. The nation's military was dealing with instability on its southern border caused by the Mexican revolution, operations against Muslim Moro holdouts on the islands of Mindanao and Jolo in the Philippines, and vicious guerrilla wars with rural terrorists in Haiti and the Dominican Republic. However, the United States was at peace with the great powers. Its security seemed assured by large oceans and a strong navy. Most senior army and

Eugene Ely, a civilian pilot employed by Glenn H. Curtiss, flying from the USS *Pennsylvania* in San Francisco Bay on January 18, 1911. Earlier that day, Ely landed on a specially built platform on the *Pennsylvania*. On November 14, 1910, Ely launched a Curtiss plane from a wooden platform on the USS *Birmingham* (CL-2) at Hampton Roads, Virginia. His flights, designed to demonstrate that aircraft could operate from warships, were intended by Curtiss to help sell aircraft to the U.S. Navy. (U.S. Air Force photo collection, National Archives.)

navy leaders were at least skeptical of military aviation. Before April, 1917, there was little detailed planning for massive American military intervention in Europe, and U.S. aviation technology progressed slowly in the absence of any significant domestic military or commercial market.

Congress had rejected the chief signal officer's appeals in 1908, 1909, and 1910 to appropriate funds for aeronautical development before finally granting appropriations for that purpose in March, 1911. The Signal Corps obtained $25,000 for the purchase of five aircraft. Largely because of Chambers's effective lobbying, the navy received an equal grant that month for buying two land planes and an amphibian. In May, the sea service ordered its first aircraft, a Curtiss A-1 Triad that could operate on land or water. Nevertheless, money shortages remained a severe problem for the struggling U.S. military aviation programs.

Across the Atlantic, the situation was dramatically different. Motivated by an escalating arms race and the fear of war, European states poured funds into anything they thought might give them an edge in a future conflict, including aviation. During 1908–13, the United States spent only $435,000 of the estimated $85 million lavished on military and naval aviation around the world. At least thirteen other nations had spent more than the United States by the latter year, including Bulgaria and Brazil. It was not until 1916, however, that growing fears of American involvement in World War I sparked a significant expansion of spending on U.S. military aviation.[12]

Europeans had been quick to realize the value of trained engineers and scientists working in well-equipped national aeronautical laboratories. Against the backdrop of mounting international tensions and the threat of war, Britain, France, Germany, Austria-Hungary, Russia, and Italy launched major aeronautical research and development programs after 1910. There was little government support for such a program in the United States. There was, however, a strong commitment to it among a small group of well-placed men that Paul Wilson Clark labeled the "invisible establishment of aeronautics." Those individuals, largely friends of Langley, were devoted to science and convinced of the potential importance of powered flight. They included Alexander Graham Bell, Dr. Charles D. Walcott, aircraft designer Glenn H. Curtiss, and Major Squier.

Bell and Walcott led the drive for a national aeronautical laboratory in America. In 1912, Pres. William Howard Taft appointed a commission to study the matter. The body, which included representatives of the army and navy, recommended a national laboratory, but Congress ignored its advice. Three years later, with Europe engulfed in war, Walcott again asked the government to establish an aeronautical laboratory. President Woodrow Wilson approved the proposal and Congress authorized the creation of the National Advisory Committee for Aeronautics (NACA) on March 3, 1915, in a rider to a naval appropriations act. A month later, the president appointed the committee's members, including two army and two navy officers.[13] The NACA's explicit purpose was the "scientific study of problems of flight with a view to their practical solution."[14] Although it served a valuable advisory role during its early years, the organization did not actually begin to make its own substantial contributions to American aeronautics until it inaugurated its first full-scale program of aeronautical research in 1920 at the organization's new Langley Memorial Aeronautical Laboratory in Hampton, Virginia.[15]

American aerial technology remained primitive and unreliable. Clear military roles had yet to be established for U.S. aircraft, and trained pilots were in extremely short supply. Since aviation was not recognized as a separate branch of either service, only a handful of army and navy officers could be temporarily detailed to flying. Army aviation had no legal status until Congress passed legislation in July, 1914, which established the Aviation Section of the Signal Corps. The navy established a separate office for naval aviation in September, 1910, by administrative fiat, but it resisted a provision in a 1916 naval appropriations bill that authorized the establishment of a separate naval flying corps.[16]

Despite institutional resistance, meager budgets, and the absence of doctrinal guidance, a handful of army and navy aviators explored the operational possibilities of their primitive machines. In August, 1910, at the Sheepshead Bay racetrack near New York City, Lt. Jacob E. Fickel, a passenger in an aircraft piloted by Glenn Curtiss, had made the army's first attempt to fire a rifle while airborne. Live bombs were dropped from an aircraft for the first time in January, 1911, by their designer, Lt. Myron Crissy of the Coast Artillery. He was a passenger in a Wright aircraft flying above the Tanforan racetrack near San Francisco. In October, 1911, Riley E. Scott, a former Coast Artillery officer, invented a bombsight and tested it at College Park. In June, 1912, Col. Isaac N. Lewis, inventor of an air-cooled machine gun, had it test fired from an aircraft flying from that same field.[17]

Like the army, the navy dispatched a handful of young officers to pioneering civilian aviators to learn the art of flying. Lieutenant Theodore G. Ellyson, the first naval officer to become a trained pilot, was ordered to report to Glenn Curtiss at North Island in San Diego in December, 1910. The following March, Lieutenant John Rodgers traveled to Dayton, Ohio for instruction by the Wright brothers. Lieutenant (j.g.) John Towers began his flight training with Curtiss at Hammondsport, New York, in June, 1911. In January, 1913, four naval aircraft under the command of Lieutenant Towers were sent to Guantanamo Bay, Cuba, to make their debut with the fleet during the latter's annual maneuvers. Towers played a key role in the development of naval aviation. He was a very conventional junior officer who became interested in using aircraft to spot the fall of shells that could hit targets up to twenty-one thousand yards from the battleships that fired them, far further than the human eye can see. He requested aviation training in November, 1910, even before the navy had acquired an aircraft or developed a formal requirement for trained pilots. Later, based upon his hands-on experience, Towers was convinced that aircraft would play an important naval role in the future, although he did not see them as miracle weapons capable of rendering other forms of military power obsolete. As a result, he worked quietly within the system to convince the navy, members of Congress, senior civilian government leaders, and the public to integrate aircraft in the fleet.

When they were not busy scouting for mines, submerged submarines, and a "hostile fleet," Towers's four aircraft gave rides to curious officers from the warships gathered at Guantanamo Bay for the 1913 fleet exercise. He had a huge selling job on his hands. The fleet commander, Rear Adm. Charles J. Badger, "considered aviation a game for fools and nitwits and wanted no part of it."[18] Towers made quite a few converts anyway.

The marines had been watching the navy's experiments with growing interest. Convinced that aircraft might play a role in the Corps's future, the commandant, Maj. Gen. William P. Biddle, sent two lieutenants to Annapolis for flight training. The first of them, Alfred A. Cunningham, reported on May 22, 1912. That date became the official birthday of Marine Corps aviation. The leathernecks continued training with the navy until January, 1914, when several pilots, enlisted mechanics, and their equipment was sent from Annapolis to Puerto Rico to join the Corps's advance base force for the annual Atlantic Fleet exercises. The advance base force was based on a new concept that called for marine units to occupy undefended harbors and secure them for the navy's use in the early stages of a sea campaign in the Caribbean or the Pacific. Flying a Curtiss C-3 flying boat, they concentrated on scouting and reconnaissance missions. The 1914 exercise marked the debut of an all-marine aviation contingent operating with that service's ground forces. However, when they returned to the continental United States, the unit was disbanded and incorporated in the overall naval aviation establishment.[19]

While the U.S. armed forces' tiny aviation programs were struggling to establish themselves, several important aeronautical advances had emerged from private designers in Europe and America. Open-frame, pusher-type aircraft like those first built by the Wrights were being replaced by more efficient tractor designs with enclosed fuselages. Pushers, with the engines located behind the wings and pilot, were unstable and extremely dangerous. Frequent crashes and numerous deaths had caused army pilots to lose faith in them. In 1914, an army board condemned all pushers and recommended adoption of the Curtiss tractor design. The latter featured an engine mounted in front of the wings and pilot. Another major development was the availability of relatively reliable and powerful engines like the Gnome from France. A more effective device, the aileron, supplanted wing warping as a means of lateral control, and the relatively simple control stick replaced the earlier profusion of flight controls.[20]

The National Guard was a hotbed of early grassroots interest in aviation. As with the army, its enthusiasm had been foreshadowed by ballooning. In April, 1908, a group of guard enthusiasts organized an "aeronautical corps" at the Park Avenue Armory in New York City to learn ballooning. In 1910, members of the unit raised $500 in private contributions to buy their first aircraft. The investment disappeared when the plane crashed on takeoff during maneuvers that same year. In 1911, the Curtiss Aeroplane Company loaned it an aircraft and a pilot named Beckwith Havens. Havens later joined the unit as a private and was recognized as the guard's first aviator. Several states tinkered with a handful of pilots and aircraft. However, Capt. Raynal Cawthorne Bolling, a prominent attorney, established the first real National Guard aviation unit in New York in

1915 with the active encouragement of the state's adjutant general, Maj. Gen. John O'Ryan. Although those early efforts to build flying units floundered because of poor funding, unreliable aircraft, and War Department neglect, the National Guard became an important source of pilots and air leaders during World War I.[21]

BANDITS, REVOLUTIONARIES, AND PREPAREDNESS

The Mexican civil war provided the first opportunity to test the fledgling U.S. military aviation programs in combat. In February, 1913, revolutionary general Victoriano Huerta seized power in Mexico. The United States refused to recognize his regime and concentrated troops along the border between the two nations. The army hastily assembled a provisional air unit in Texas to support its ground forces, but hostilities were averted before it could be tested in battle. Frequent accidents and poor leadership caused morale to plummet. Flyers on the border were so dissatisfied that they sent the chief signal officer a round-robin letter demanding major changes in the aviation program, most of which were granted. Meanwhile, the squadron had been transferred to San Diego in June, 1913, once the crisis cooled. It spent most of the following two years training and testing aircraft on the West Coast.

The next major incident with Mexico took place at Tampico. On April 9, 1914, Mexican police arrested a navy shore party at that port, provoking an international confrontation. President Wilson decided to defend American honor from that insult and teach the Mexicans a lesson. He sent the navy to occupy the ports of Tampico and Veracruz. Lieutenant Towers and Lieutenant Commander Mustin convinced their superiors to embark aircraft on the warships sent to Mexico. On April 25, a floatplane scouted the harbor at Tampico for mines. At Veracruz, two floatplanes scouted inland. During one flight, enraged Mexicans fired on the aircraft, scoring at least two hits. The pilot responded by hurling a bar of laundry soap at his assailants. Despite its comic-opera quality, U.S. military aviation had made its combat debut. More importantly, naval aviation had demonstrated that it had some operational value to the fleet.[22]

Aviation had only a limited impact on army doctrine before the United States entered World War I. In November, 1915, the General Staff modified army doctrine by officially acknowledging the airplane's role in reconnaissance and airborne direction of artillery fire. By accepting the principle that friendly forces had to retain control of the air over the battlefield, the General Staff also officially endorsed the concept of air superiority.[23]

American aeronautical technology failed to keep abreast of changing doctrine, however, and the next crisis with Mexico produced a major disaster for army aviation. In March, 1916, Pancho Villa, a Mexican bandit and erstwhile revolutionary, raided Columbus, New Mexico. His forces killed seventeen U.S. citizens during the attack. President Wilson responded by ordering Brig. Gen. John J. Pershing to chase Villa into Mexico and break up his army. The 1st Aero Squadron was dispatched to New Mexico to support Pershing's expedition. Although its mission was not clearly spelled out at the time, it soon became evident that the squadron would be used for reconnaissance and courier duties.[24]

The debut of the first formally constituted army tactical air unit to be tested under realistic field conditions was a fiasco. Although not a shot was fired, six of the squadron's eight Curtiss JN-3s were rendered useless within two weeks. Two of them collapsed in the relentlessly dry desert heat and four needed repairs. Their engines were too weak to fly over the Mexican mountains, and they lacked the range needed to support Pershing's forces as they searched fruitlessly for Villa in the vast wastelands of northern Mexico. The pilots complained of their plight to a reporter, whose sensational stories encouraged Congress to appropriate $500,000 for the Signal Corps to purchase twenty-four new aircraft. None of them were delivered in time to be useful in Pershing's campaign against Villa.

By the summer of 1916, Americans had begun to move away from the idea that the United States should remain strictly neutral in the so-called Great War that had erupted in Europe two years earlier. The troubles with Mexico, strong American economic ties with the Allies, and increasingly effective British propaganda contributed to this change in public and elite political opinion. Private groups like the National Security League and the American Defense Society, prominent Republican politicians like Theodore Roosevelt, and army and navy officers were all calling for stronger defense measures. The burgeoning military preparedness movement and the troubles with Mexico forced the federal government to take action.[25]

Congress passed the National Defense Act of 1916, which created a system of manpower and economic mobilization for modern war. Among other provisions, the legislation raised the authorized peacetime strength of the regular army to 175,000 (expandable to 286,000 in wartime), increased the National Guard to over 400,000 while tightening federal supervision of it, and gave the president the power to place mandatory defense orders with industry. The legislation also created a federal Officer Reserve Corps and an Enlisted Reserve Corps for the army.

Federal reserve programs for the army had gradually emerged since the Spanish-American War in 1898. The Army Appropriations Act of 1912 created the Army Reserve by changing the terms of enlistment in the regular force to seven years, with three or four to be served on active duty and the balance consisting of a furlough to the new reserve program. Previously, the army had relied on militia (now known as the National Guard), wartime volunteers, and, in the Civil War, conscription, to expand its personnel strength in a crisis. Although criticized by military professionals, the older system had been consistent with America's strategic interests, cultural values, and emerging democratic institutions. Utilizing it as their basic military institution, the English colonists had secured a foothold along the Atlantic seaboard, survived repeated onslaughts of Indians and hostile European powers, won and maintained their independence from Britain, acquired a vast continental domain, survived a terrible civil war, and ended slavery while developing an increasingly liberal and affluent society. They had accomplished all that without creating a large and expensive standing army that could pose a threat to personal freedom and democratic government. Those forces had often been poorly prepared at the outbreak of hostilities, however, and thus learned to fight at a high cost of blood and treasure.

Revolutionary changes in technology and America's emergence as a world power late in the nineteenth century had weakened the citizen-soldier's central role. Modern warfare demanded military forces that were well trained and equipped according to professional standards before the outbreak of hostilities. The National Defense Act of 1916 played a key role in moving U.S. national security policy and institutions in that general direction. The legislation established a Reserve Officers Training Corps (ROTC) at universities and summer camps to prepare junior line officers and technical specialists for wartime service with the army. It also authorized a reserve corps of 2,300 officers and enlisted aviators for the army. During the war, the reserve program provided approximately ten thousand pilots, who served as Reserve Military Aviators. In 1917, the War Department organized two Aero Reserve Squadrons and mobilized them for active service shortly afterward.

Sea power remained the bulwark of the American defense program in 1916. Congress passed legislation that year designed to build a "Navy second to none" and authorized a $300 million shipbuilding program. The goal of the legislation was to build a fleet to assure the United States strategic independence regardless of which side won the war. It was not intended as preparation for U.S. military intervention in that conflict. A rider to the Army Appropriations Act of August 29, 1916, established the Council of National Defense, an advisory body that studied the problems of economic mobilization. After years of ignoring warnings that American military aeronautics was falling dangerously behind other powers, the legislators appropriated $13.28 million for the army and $3.5 million for the navy. Those were enormous sums by American standards, but they soon proved to be totally inadequate.

The 1916 appropriation provided the Signal Corps with the funds it needed to develop a real air program, not just a modest experimental activity.[26] Secretary of

War Newton D. Baker had moved to help prepare the army's fledgling air arm for the possibility of America's entry into the European conflict. Under his auspices, a technical board of officers and engineers conducted a thorough study of the U.S. aircraft industry during fiscal year (FY) 1916 to assess its productive capacity and encourage improved military aircraft designs. In May, Baker had placed Squier, by then a lieutenant colonel, in charge of the Signal Corps's aviation section. Although not a pilot, Squier had just spent four years in London as the U.S. military attaché. Having secretly observed the air war over the western front, he knew that American military aeronautics lagged far behind the major European combatants. Squier convinced Baker that the technological gap could not be closed unless the nation mobilized the immense technical resources of science and industry.

Lieutenant Towers played a similar role for naval aviation. He had served as an observer with the British beginning in 1914, and secretly saw combat over the western front. Returning to America in September, 1916, he was placed in charge of the naval aviation desk in the Office of the Chief of Naval Operations. Towers found naval aviation in a neglected and chaotic condition. The navy's battleship-oriented leaders did not consider aviation an important element of sea power. They agreed to buy only a few seaplanes for battleships and reluctantly decided to rely on naval reserve officers instead of Annapolis graduates as the primary source of pilots for the expanded aviation program. Those reserve aviators were to be supplied by a Naval Reserve Flying Corps authorized by Congress in 1916, makeshift preparedness organizations like the "First Yale Unit" financed by well-heeled civilians, and a training program at Pensacola, Florida, which had been established in January, 1914.[27]

The tiny American aviation industry was unable to keep pace with the modest (by European standards) expansion program that had been set in motion in 1916. Like other American industries, it was already flooded with orders from the warring European powers. Although Congress had appropriated the unprecedented sum of nearly $19.5 million for army aeronautics in 1916 and early 1917, the nation's aviation industry was able to deliver only 314 aircraft during that period. When the United States declared war in April, 1917, only one of the planned army aviation squadrons was fully equipped, albeit rather marginally by European standards.[28]

The American aviation industry consisted of a few small, struggling firms most of whose military aircraft designs were hopelessly out of date by the rapidly advancing standards of the major European belligerents. It was starved for resources because of the lack of a viable civilian market and the extremely limited aviation procurement budgets of the military services before 1916–17. The army and the navy, limited by small budgets, manpower shortages, and the uncertain legal status of their aviation programs had made tentative efforts to explore the operational and technological frontiers of flight.[29]

AN INSTANT AIR ARMADA

Like the rest of its armed forces, America's military aviation programs were totally unprepared for combat on April 6, 1917, when Pres. Woodrow Wilson asked Congress for a declaration of war against Germany. The president took the nation to war after Kaiser Wilhelm's government announced that it would engage in unrestricted submarine warfare against all vessels in a war zone around Europe, including those flying the American flag. At that point, the Signal Corps Aviation Section consisted of just 131 officers and 1,087 enlisted men. Only twenty-six of those officers were considered qualified aviators. None of them had ever been trained for combat. Most of its aircraft were obsolete because of the rapid development of technology in the crucible of aerial combat. Naval aviation (navy and Marine Corps) was in a similar state. Consisting of forty-eight officers and 239 enlisted men, its handful of aircraft and lighter-than-air vehicles were completely out of date. The gigantic expansion of wartime aviation programs would depend primarily on civilian volunteers, members of the newly authorized federal reserve programs, and guardsmen instead of career officers. That pattern, which had been established by necessity, would be sustained until the Vietnam War.

Despite its minuscule military air arms, the United States embraced the incredible notion that one of its key contributions to victory would be a gigantic aviation program. Overwhelmed by the problems of raising a massive land force, the army's General Staff largely ignored aviation in the spring of 1917. Aeronautical enthusiasts inside and outside the armed forces moved to fill the vacuum. The tiny Signal Corps Aviation Section had begun promoting the concept of a large wartime air force. However, compared to what was eventually accepted, its initial proposal, which called for the appropriation of $54 million to equip a force of sixteen reconnaissance squadrons and the same number of balloon companies, was quite modest. That force was designed to provide reconnaissance units for the combat divisions the army was planning to field. In June, 1917, Congress appropriated $43.45 million for the program.[30]

The German U-boat threat was the real stimulus for U.S. naval aviation during the war. Contrary to the navy's prewar plans and assumptions, U.S. battleships played no significant role in the war since Britain's Royal Navy had checkmated Germany's surface fleet. Instead, the U.S. Navy's real challenge was to improvise a fleet of small warships and aircraft that could help neutralize the submarine menace. Lieutenant Towers developed a proposal for a chain of air stations to defend coastal shipping after Germany announced that it would resume unrestricted submarine warfare on January 31, 1917. However, nothing was done to implement his program until after the United States declared war on April 6. Towers had to quickly improvise a huge expansion of personnel, facilities, and equipment. Although he was promoted to lieutenant commander effective July 1, 1917, Towers was too junior in rank to stay on as the wartime chief of naval aviation. Consequently, Capt. Noble Irwin was appointed to the position in May, 1917, with Towers as his assistant. In practice, Irwin concentrated upon administration while the more experienced Towers ran the operation.

Meanwhile, Vice Adm. William S. Sims, the commander of U.S. forces in European waters, had called for establishing naval air bases in Britain and France and equipping them with long-range flying boats to help counter German U-boats. The navy's ambitious initial wartime program focused on building seven hundred seaplanes. Congress, which had appropriated $3 million for naval aviation on April 17, added another $11 million on June 15, and an additional $45 million on October 6. On September 18, the navy adopted an extraordinarily ambitious program to build seventeen hundred seaplanes. Eventually, naval aviation grew to 2,107 aircraft, fifteen dirigibles, and 215 kite and free balloons. A total of 6,716 officers and 30,693 men in navy units, as well as 282 officers and 2,180 men in marine units, manned the force. Of those totals, eighteen thousand personnel and 570 aircraft were sent overseas. During World War I, navy and Marine Corps aviation units operated from air stations in the United States, Canada, Europe, the Panama Canal Zone, and the Azores. A few pilots flew with British squadrons. In future conflicts, they would operate from both land bases and warships.[31]

While the Signal Corps Aviation Section was struggling to gain approval for a relatively modest aerial reconnaissance program, Premier Alexander Ribot of France dropped a bombshell on the U.S. government. Apparently prompted by a then-obscure lieutenant colonel named William "Billy" Mitchell, who Squier had sent to Europe as an air observer, the premier wired President Wilson in May, 1917, asking the United States to create a gigantic air force.[32]

Seizing the opportunity, Squier—who had been assigned as the chief signal officer and promoted to major general in 1917—directed Maj. Benjamin D. Foulois to head a Joint Army-Navy Technical Aircraft Committee and develop a bold plan for a huge American aviation program. Foulois, who began his military career as an enlisted man, was one of the first army officers to fly. Working quickly, his committee, which included Lieutenant Towers, called for a production program that would build forty-nine hundred training planes, twelve thousand combat aircraft, and twenty-four thousand engines by June 30, 1918. It also called for 6,210 pilots to be trained by July 15, 1918. Although specific

Major General George Owen Squier, chief signal officer, U.S. Army, 1917–23. Squier was a leading proponent of military aviation who stressed the need for a strong industrial base and extensive aeronautical research and development programs to nourish it. He was in the forefront of those who brought science and engineering into the army. His influence played an important role in shaping the development of two of the key technological innovations of the early twentieth century: aircraft and radios. (U.S. Air Force collection, National Archives.)

aircraft types were not spelled out due to the absence of current technical and operational information from Europe, the planners estimated that the program's combat aircraft complement should consist of 6,667 pursuits, four thousand reconnaissance planes, and 1,333 bombers.[33]

The War Department General Staff, appalled by the stunning proposal to sink an enormous amount of money into a new and, in its opinion, peripheral technology, refused to act on it. Frustrated by the General Staff's hostility and foot-dragging, Squier ignored normal procedures. In an act of considerable courage for a career officer, the air enthusiast bypassed the General Staff and took the proposal directly to Secretary of War Baker. Baker approved it and obtained President Wilson's permission to send it directly to Congress without the General Staff's endorsement.[34]

Meanwhile, Howard Coffin, chairman of the Aircraft Production Board, put together an extensive public relations campaign to build popular support for an American aviation program. Coffin, an engineer and automobile manufacturer, courted some of the most influential newspaper editors in the country. He convinced them that an American military aircraft program could end the war. Officers from Allied military missions and prominent industrialists echoed that same basic message. Editorials soon began appearing around the nation urging Congress to authorize a gigantic American air armada.[35]

Coffin also arranged to have top government officials issue periodic press releases on behalf of the aviation program. Exaggerated claims were soon pouring forth from men who should have known better. For example, in June, 1917, Squier urged the public to back "building an army in the air . . . brigades of flying horses . . . [that will] sweep the Germans from the sky, blind the Prussian cannon, and the time will be ripe to release an enormous number of flying fighters to raid and destroy military camps, ammunition depots, military establishments of all kinds."[36] Soon afterward, Secretary Baker publicly endorsed the aircraft program. He also released a letter from the president that firmly committed Wilson to it. It would not be the last time senior American civilian officials and military officers exaggerated air power's potential.

Propelled by a groundswell of popular wartime enthusiasm and great expectations about America's industrial ability, the House and Senate quickly appropriated some $640 million for the aviation program. There was no significant debate or opposition to the measure on Capitol Hill. President Wilson signed the legislation—the largest appropriation for a single procurement program in American history up to that time—into law on July 24, 1917. All the while, the General Staff had never officially passed its professional military judgment on it.[37]

Since little was known on the banks of the Potomac about the specific equipment the United States would need for its air program, a special aeronautical mission led by Maj. Raynal C. Bolling was dispatched to Europe in June at the suggestion of the Joint Army-Navy Technical Aircraft Committee.[38] Bolling's mission to Europe in 1917 included several army and navy officers as well as civilian mechanics and industrial experts.[39] After examining European aviation programs, the group concluded that the United States would have to depend heavily upon them, at least initially, to fulfill its aircraft needs. Under the immense pressures of combat, pursuit aircraft, the key to air supremacy in the World War I, were changing rapidly. Bolling's mission concluded that it would be very difficult to design and produce them in significant numbers and then ship them to Europe before they became obsolete. Consequently, they recommended that the United States concentrate on producing training aircraft and engines as well as certain European service aircraft and engines whose designs were not changing so quickly. The latter would include observation aircraft and bombers. They urged that single-seat pursuit aircraft be purchased directly from the Europeans. Although it emphasized that the United States must first obtain aircraft that would support the ground forces, the mission also called for development of a strategic air force to conduct independent bombing operations.[40]

It was apparent by early 1918 that America's vaunted air armada was not going to materialize in Europe's skies on schedule to drive the Germans back to Berlin. Instead, the Central Powers had expanded their own aircraft production. Army aviators, equipped with second-rate aircraft obtained from the Allies, did not even begin flying combat missions in their own units until that April. The first American-made land-based plane, a De Havilland DH-4, flew in France in May, and it was August before a plane built in the United States actually flew over the trenches. Aircraft production had fallen well behind schedule in the United States. The public and press sensed a scandal. Acrimonious charges of waste mismanagement, corruption, and even sabotage by German sympathizers were rampant. Wilson's congressional opponents, sensing political vulnerability, tried unsuccessfully to strip the president of his powers to manage the war effort. The program had stalled, along with the rest of the nation's wartime economic mobilization.[41]

Institutional confusion and top-level mismanagement within the War Department also troubled the air production effort. Secretary Baker, convinced that only the auto industry had the management expertise and manufacturing capacity to mass-produce aircraft, turned to businessmen like Howard Coffin and Edward Deeds, to run the aviation program. Like Baker, they had virtually no practical experience in aviation. The secretary of war then compounded his error by refusing to exercise strong supervision over the inexperienced men he had appointed.[42]

American aircraft production in World War I was also slowed by the fragile nature of the nation's technical-industrial base in aeronautics. There was no functioning national program of aeronautical research and development when President Wilson took America to war. Neither the military services nor the universities had established significant aeronautical research programs before April, 1917. In 1915, only twenty-five colleges reported even having aviation courses. Furthermore, there was virtually no commercial airline industry in the United States from which to draw skilled pilots, mechanics, and managers. America's aircraft manufacturers were tiny, technologically backward, and poorly funded. Initial War Department plans had identified no more than ten or eleven plants for the wartime production of military aircraft and engines. Their annual production capacity had been set at an exaggerated seventy-two hundred aircraft. The industry's prewar capitalization was $15 to $20 million, and it employed some eight thousand workers.[43]

Established aircraft plants were divided between the army and the navy early in the war. Although there were exceptions, the general policy was that each plant would produce aircraft for only one of the armed services. The ambitious aviation production program approved by Congress in July, 1917, demanded the vast expansion of America's aircraft manufacturing capacity. Lured by one of the largest pork barrels in American history, the Aircraft Production Board and the Signal Corps had been inundated by unsolicited proposals from charlatans and dreamers as well as legitimate businessmen anxious to obtain lucrative contracts for building aircraft. The official policy, however, was to award contracts to the limited number of companies that either had aircraft production experience or the general capacity for mass production. Curtiss and the newly established Dayton-Wright Aeroplane Company got the lion's share of aircraft orders. Several automakers, including Fischer Body and Packard, also produced substantial numbers of aircraft during the war. The government encouraged a few firms to build plants specifically for wartime aircraft production. Contracts for spare parts and components were placed widely with smaller companies. Government officials hoped that these orders would prepare some of the firms to produce entire aircraft if additional capacity was needed in the future.[44]

Patent infringement lawsuits had slowed the technical progress of the American aviation industry even before the United States declared war. The Wright-Martin and Curtiss companies claimed most of the key patents needed to build aircraft in the United States, and they sued each other and any other firms that attempted to build aircraft in America without first obtaining licenses from them. The impasse had threatened to cripple technical innovation and production. To help break that legal logjam, acting–Secretary of the Navy Franklin D. Roosevelt turned to NACA in January, 1917. After several months of quiet negotiations, NACA was able to convince the manufacturers to form an association and pay a set fee for each aircraft produced. The proceeds of that cross-licensing agreement were then divided between Wright-Martin, Curtiss, and the association. The accord ended the patent troubles that had plagued the aircraft industry.[45]

By the end of World War I, more than three hundred plants employing some two hundred thousand people were involved in aircraft and engine construction in the United States. The capacity of prewar plants had been expanded many times. Many of the firms that became involved in the wartime aviation program were not used to the fine tolerances, specific manufacturing processes, and demanding inspection methods needed to produce military aircraft. Skilled labor was hard to find, and machine tools were in short supply. Fundamental differences between European and American manufacturing methods also hindered aircraft production. American industry relied on the mass production of standardized (or interchangeable) components of a final product like an automobile. That approach required tedious preparation of detailed drawings for parts, dies, tools, jigs, and fixtures. The Europeans emphasized the talents of highly trained mechanics who virtually handcrafted aircraft. Consequently, the

United States found it difficult to mass-produce European designs. The latter's blueprints and technical specifications were usually not detailed enough for the demands of Yankee mass-production methods. This required the Americans to undertake the time-consuming process of disassembling European prototypes, making meticulous measurements, completing detailed drawings, and then fabricating the tools needed to build them.[46]

In April, 1918, President Wilson appointed John D. Ryan, a mining engineer from the copper industry, to supervise aircraft production. Although lacking experience, Ryan proved to be a good choice. He had a solid business background and was untainted by even the hint of corruption.[47] Despite General Squier's strong objections, Wilson issued an executive order removing the Aviation Section from the Signal Corps on May 21, 1918. The order created two new organizations in the War Department: the Division of Military Aeronautics (DMA) and the Bureau of Aircraft Production (BAP). The former, headed by a military officer, was responsible for organization and training. It also developed requirements for aircraft and other equipment. The latter, under civilian leadership, was responsible for aircraft production. At first, both the DMA and the BAP acted independently of each other, reporting directly to the secretary of war. The two organizations found it hard to reconcile their differences. Finally, in August, 1918, the president brought them together under Ryan, who he appointed assistant secretary of war and director of the Air Service.[48]

Pressing wartime needs and slow progress in building the NACA laboratory prompted the armed forces to establish their own separate technical organizations for aeronautics. The sea service had been conducting experimental activities at several locations. In July, 1917, it had authorized construction of a Naval Aircraft Factory (NAF) in Philadelphia. Several factors drove the NAF's creation: the army's indifference to the navy's requirements for relatively small numbers of aircraft; the perceived shortcomings of private manufacturers in designing and producing specialized aircraft for service with the fleet; and, finally, the idea that a government plant would help hold prices down by providing competition with private firms and establishing a yardstick for gauging costs and production data. Originally conceived as a facility capable of all phases of aircraft production, the vast wartime expansion of the navy's flying-boat program forced it to radically reorient its function. The NAF became a final assembly plant that controlled the civilian contractors producing most of the major airframe components.

During the war, the NAF produced 137 H-16 and thirty-one F-5-L flying boats plus four experimental N-1 aircraft designed to carry lightweight artillery for use against surfaced submarines. Glenn Curtiss designed the H-16, and the F-5-L represented significant British improvements to his basic design. The output of F-5-Ls peaked at eight a week before the navy began to apply the breaks in November, 1918. The NAF's wartime performance vindicated those who had championed the creation of a government factory to meet the navy's special needs and remained a force in naval aviation until after the Korean War.

Like the navy, the army established its own aeronautical research and development organization as a temporary wartime expedient. Located at McCook Field near Dayton, Ohio, the organization eventually became known as the Engineering Division. It began operating in December, 1917, and consolidated the army's fragmented aeronautical engineering activities. In less than a year, the Engineering Division made substantial contributions to the nation's troubled wartime aviation program. Several experimental aircraft were designed and built there. However, it primarily adapted European aircraft designs to American production methods, developed ancillary equipment, and then tested them.

Unlike the NAF, production and final assembly of service aircraft and equipment for the army remained in the hands of civilian contractors. The Engineering Division worked out a system of government and industry cooperation during the war to develop and produce aviation equipment for military use. It demonstrated the importance of a strong centralized research and development organization to the progress of military aviation, firmly establishing those functions within the army. Although McCook Field was closed in the 1920s, Wright-Patterson Air Force Base in the Dayton area plays a major role in aeronautical research and development for military purposes to the present day.[49]

THE GREAT WAR IN THE AIR

Many American pilots were trained and given their initial combat experience by one of the Allies before the Air Service of Gen. John J. Pershing's American Expeditionary Forces (AEF) could bring its weight to bear in the spring of 1918. The Air Service, for example, drew some combat leaders from France's famed Lafayette Escadrille. Although it existed for less than eleven months and its flying roster consisted of just thirty-eight American volunteers and four French officers, the Escadrille gained an enduring international reputation far larger than its own proud record. In January, 1918, the AEF began to commission the Lafayette Escadrille's pilots into the Air Service.[50]

Billy Mitchell and a handful of other army aviators who had not been trained by the Europeans were already in Europe when Pershing arrived. Energetic and aggressive, Mitchell had volunteered to be sent to Europe to observe the air war. It helped that his boss, General Squier, was just as eager to get him out of Washington because of the friction Mitchell had caused within the Signal Corps staff. Once abroad, Mitchell sent a steady flow of reports on the air war back to

Squier, including proposals for an American air force on the western front. When Pershing arrived in France, Mitchell presented him with a proposal for an air force featuring two kinds of combat organizations: one to be tied directly to the needs of the ground forces and another for strategic operations against the enemy, well behind the latter's front lines.

Pershing dismissed Mitchell's scheme. Instead, he formed a board of officers that included Mitchell to recommend the makeup of an Air Service for the AEF. Mitchell dominated the board's proceedings. It recommended a strategic force of thirty bomber groups and an equal number of pursuit groups, as well as a second force based upon the size of the American ground forces to which it would be attached. Pershing again rejected the proposal for a strategic air force. Instead, he opted for an air arm tied directly to the needs of the AEF's ground forces and the availability of Allied aircraft. His decision was largely based on the Allies' experiences during the first three years of the conflict.

The AEF commander was convinced that the war's outcome would be decided on the ground by the infantry and artillery. Aircraft would support that effort by serving as the army's eyes and attacking enemy ground forces. Aviation was an important component of the AEF's plans, and Pershing devoted a significant amount of resources and a good deal of his own time to it. He did not, however, accept the view that aviation, especially bombers, would be a decisive force in World War I. Mitchell was never given permission to establish a separate American strategic bombing force during the conflict. However, the arguments over the Air Service's force structure and missions in France during the summer of 1917 marked the beginning of a debate that continues to the present day.[51]

Pershing's airmen had to build an organization from scratch while training personnel, building airfields, and securing aircraft—all under the intense pressures of war. After a brief tenure as the AEF's ranking air officer, Mitchell was given control of aviation in front-line areas known as the zone of advance. Colonel Bolling, who had remained in Europe after completing the work of his aeronautical mission, was placed in charge of aviation in the rear areas. The absence of a single overall air commander generated an enormous amount of conflict and confusion, as did the fact that the Air Service's pilots were relatively inexperienced junior officers who were poorly prepared for senior military posts. Intense personal jealousy and friction within the air arm further complicated matters.

Air and ground officers were also frequently in conflict. Pershing appointed Brig. Gen. William L. Kenly, a field artillery officer, as his chief aviation officer in September, 1917, to provide experienced overall senior leadership to the floundering aviation program. Bolling, the production expert, was placed in charge of supplies, but friction persisted between him and Mitchell. Pershing reorganized his Air Service again that fall, bringing in Brig. Gen. Benjamin Foulois and a staff from Washington, D.C., to replace Kenly in November. Mitchell called them "carpetbaggers."[52]

The AEF commander was appalled by the bickering and slow progress in building an effective Air Service. In May, 1918, he assigned his old West Point classmate, Brig. Gen. Mason M. Patrick, to supply some badly needed adult leadership to the young airmen. Patrick, a seasoned Engineer officer who had well-developed administrative and organizational skills, wasted no time straightening out his new command. His no-nonsense approach quickly ended the chaos that had engulfed it. The fact that Pershing had to reach outside the Air Service underscored a key weakness that would plague the army's fledgling air arm until the 1930s: the lack of seasoned senior leaders. Patrick later noted in his diary that Pershing might have fired both Mitchell and Foulois in 1917 if experienced senior air officers had been available to replace them.

Patrick appointed Foulois as chief of the Air Service in the AEF's First Army, and Mitchell became the latter's subordinate. Despite Mitchell's insubordination and poor knowledge of logistics, Foulois recognized his leadership abilities and recommended him for the prestigious job of leading the First Army's air component. Foulois then arranged to be reassigned as Patrick's assistant. That reshuffling resolved the last of the major personality issues plaguing the Air Service and paved the way for Mitchell to become the war's outstanding American tactical air commander.[53]

While Mason Patrick and his airmen were sorting out plans, personalities, and organizational relationships in France, Squier's Signal Corps Aviation Section had launched a huge accelerated training program back in the United States. Instead of the highly personalized prewar methods, flight training was standardized in three stages—ground, primary, and advanced—along Canadian lines. After individuals entered flight training, they were exposed to general-purpose trainer aircraft and then moved on to specialized instruction in observation, pursuit, or bombing aircraft. Initially, most of the advanced flight training was conducted overseas, where experienced foreign instructors and more advanced aircraft were available. Although the phased system of flight instruction was retained throughout the war, responsibility for the conduct of various stages of training bounced back and forth across the Atlantic, so the program never settled into a constant pattern. Ground schools were conducted at leading American universities. Primary training had quickly fallen behind schedule because American airfields had to be built first and Canadian facilities could not bridge the gap. It took six to eight weeks for aviation cadets to earn their wings once airfields in the United States became operational in late 1917. Some eighty-six hundred pilots were awarded the Reserve Military Aviator rating after completing stateside primary training. Another fourteen hundred received that training overseas. Instruction of American pilots abroad was limited by the lack of facilities and the more pressing needs of the Allied air services.

The AEF began building its own air schools in August, 1917, because the French could not handle all the expected American trainees. Approximately eight thousand pilots and observers obtained some form of flight training in France, with the AEF responsible for nearly 1,750 fully trained pilots and 850 observers. Nearly five hundred Americans received all or some of their flight training in Great Britain.

Pilots and observers represented only a small fraction of the Air Service personnel that had to be trained. Mechanics, engineers, supply specialists, and a host of other support personnel were needed in order to field an effective air force. It quickly became apparent that the Air Service would not be able to obtain enough trained mechanics and other technical personnel from civilian life. Then the emphasis shifted to training them at U.S. factories and northern airfields that had to be closed in the winter because of severe weather conditions. That approach simply could not keep up with the growing demands for skilled personnel, and in late 1917 the Air Service began to rely heavily on large civilian technical institutions to train such personnel. By May, 1918, some ten thousand Air Service mechanics had been trained, more than half of them in civilian technical institutions. A month later, the Air Service concentrated most of its mechanical training at St. Paul, Minnesota, and Kelly Field, Texas. By the war's end more than seventy-six hundred men had been trained at those two installations. Some mechanics were trained at Scott Field, Illinois, and other bases. In addition, the British trained many American mechanics and other ground personnel in the United Kingdom. Large numbers of ground support personnel were trained in French factories and in the AEF's own Air Service schools.[54]

Balloons played an important role in the war, serving as the eyes of the AEF along with observation aircraft. The term "when the balloon goes up" entered the American lexicon during that conflict. For the doughboys, it originally meant that a maelstrom of artillery fire was about to begin once the spotters' balloons were raised. When the United States entered the war, the army had no organized balloon companies and only a handful of experienced balloon officers. One of them was Maj. Frank P. Lahm, a West Point graduate who became one of the first balloon pilots and the second military aviator in the U.S. Army. Lahm, who had been trained to fly aircraft by the Wright brothers after he became an accomplished balloonist, organized the AEF's Balloon Section in November, 1917. The balloon force in the United States and overseas had grown to seventeen thousand officers and men by the war's end.[55]

The AEF and its Air Service had to travel to Europe by sea. With the German surface fleet bottled up by the Royal Navy, the principal threat to that deployment was U-boats, which were taking a terrible toll of Allied shipping after resuming unrestricted submarine warfare in 1917. Working with the Allies, the U.S. Navy's principal mission in the war was to make sure that General Pershing's army got safely to France. It did this primarily by quickly building a fleet of destroyers and smaller warships to protect convoys of troopships and merchant vessels. Convoys, a British innovation, were also aided by Allied and U.S. naval aviators.

As it had in Europe, the war stimulated rapid progress in American naval aviation. The first U.S. air unit to fly combat missions in Europe belonged to the navy. Responding to a French request to help shore up sagging public morale, Lieutenant Towers had scraped together a token force of seven officers and 122 mechanics and sent them to the continent in June, 1917, under the leadership of Lt. Kenneth Whiting. Although lacking their own aircraft, they were the first organized U.S. combat unit to arrive in France. Without authorization from Admiral Sims, Whiting negotiated with the French for bases and aircraft. When Sims got wind of Whiting's actions from the British admiralty, he summoned him to London to explain. The admiral congratulated Whiting on his initiative, approved his existing plans, and ordered him to submit future recommendations through proper channels. That fall, naval aviators flew the first U.S. operational air missions in the European war zone: antisubmarine patrols over the Bay of Biscay in French Le Tellier flying boats. The intrepid Americans flew their first aerial coastal patrol on November 18, 1917, from Le Croisic Naval Air Station. Four days later, in response to a report of a German U-boat, they conducted their first armed patrol in European waters.[56]

After arriving safely in Europe and preparing for combat, the AEF's Air Service had only a very short time to prove its mettle in battle. It compiled its combat record between April and November, 1918. Starting almost from scratch, it had taken a year to develop and deploy the first army aviation units on the western front. Aircraft production and procurement as well as organizational, training, and logistical problems delayed their combat debut, as did Pershing's insistence that they fight as part of an independent American army in France. However, the Allies' desperate manpower needs had forced Pershing to compromise. In the autumn of 1917 he allowed U.S. battalions and regiments to serve with the British and French until they could be integrated with AEF divisions and its First Army in the summer of 1918.

Army aviators followed a similar pattern. The French and British trained a majority of the American pilots, observers, and mechanics available for duty in 1917. Some had joined the Royal Flying Corps in Canada or through service in the British army. Others had joined the French army and joined flying units, including, as mentioned earlier, the famous Lafayette Escadrille. Most of them eventually found their way into the AEF's Air Service. As a temporary expedient, Pershing allowed some aspiring U.S. Army aviators to be trained by the Allies in 1917 and then serve as individuals in their units. The Europeans had both the most advanced aircraft and the combat experience the Americans so desperately needed. Army aviation squadrons began to trickle into France during September.

After training at French schools, the 1st Aero Squadron was given French aircraft and additional training as an observation unit. Other U.S. Army air units went through a similar process. Once they received their aircraft and advanced training, Air Service units were gradually concentrated in a relatively quiet area near Toul, on the eastern end of the front. On April 14, 1918, the first Air Service unit made its combat debut.[57]

Other American air squadrons began flying in the Toul sector later that month. Balloon squadrons had begun operating with an American division near Toul in March and April. The air squadrons grew to groups and wings. By mid-June, the Air Service was operating pursuit, observation, bombardment, and balloon units in that area. The inexperienced U.S. fliers were soon severely tested. In March, the Germans launched their last great offensive of the war, which reached a climax in the Marne-Champagne campaign in July. In late June, American ground and air units were moved to the vicinity of Château-Thierry to destroy a huge salient that the German offensive had driven into the French lines. Mitchell organized and commanded the 1st Air Brigade, consisting of American and some French units, to counter German air units. The numerically superior and more experienced German fliers taught the Americans some hard lessons in that battle. Essentially, Mitchell's unit found itself on the defensive while supplying information to the ground forces from its observation aircraft.

The Allies and the Americans launched an offensive against the Germans in August after the latter's last great effort to win the war fizzled out. That month, Patrick placed all U.S. air units under the Air Service, First Army, with Mitchell in command. He organized them, with some French units, into three wings for pursuit, observation, and bombing operations. Altogether, Mitchell was able to mass nearly fifteen hundred aircraft against an estimated 295 German planes. Their mission was to support the AEF ground forces in wiping out the Saint-Mihiel salient, a bulge in the front lines that had existed since 1914. Mitchell worked out a comprehensive air attack plan designed first to gain air superiority over the battlefield and then attack the enemy forces. The campaign, which began on September 12, was hailed as a huge success. It was helped by the facts that, for the first time, the Americans enjoyed numerical superiority in the air and that the Germans, who were taking a terrible pounding elsewhere, were already abandoning the salient when the attack began.

Pershing wanted to just keep on going into Germany after the Saint-Mihiel salient was destroyed, but the Allied high command had other ideas. With the Germans being pushed back all along the front, the AEF was tasked with forming the bottom prong of a giant pincer in the Meuse-Argonne offensive. The objective was to destroy German forces in France. Operations associated with the offensive began on September 26 and lasted until the armistice on November 11. Mitchell again commanded the AEF's air component. Although his force was smaller than the one he had commanded during the previous campaign, fresh American units augmented it. American pilots flew approximately six hundred of his eight hundred aircraft. As he had done during the Saint-Mihiel offensive, Mitchell sent large groups of pursuit aircraft strafing over the lines.

On October 9, he concentrated two hundred bombers and a hundred fighters for an attack on enemy troop concentrations. He increased U.S. fighter patrols to blunt German units at the point of American ground attacks. Following the British and French practice, Mitchell had sent small formations of three to six virtually unprotected day bombers on raids six to twelve miles behind enemy lines during the earlier offensive. The resulting heavy casualties forced him to adopt much larger formations protected by pursuit aircraft during the Meuse-Argonne offensive.[58]

Despite the heroics and publicity associated with pursuit pilots like Capt. Eddie Rickenbacker, the crews of observation aircraft had the most dangerous and difficult mission in the Air Service. Sometimes flying at treetop level, often in terrible weather conditions, they had to keep pace with the advancing infantry in addition to their critical artillery-spotting mission. Eventually, eighteen observation squadrons served the ground forces.[59]

American aircraft production during the war reached impressive levels after much confusion, delay, and scandal. Although only 750 planes had been completed in January, 1918, the trickle became a flood as 1,207 planes were being built each month by September. During the war's final full month, the flood turned into a raging torrent as American factories produced 1,651 aircraft. From President Wilson's war message to the armistice, the United States produced 11,754 aircraft and 28,500 engines. During the twelve months before April, 1917, American industry had produced fewer than 800 aircraft, most of them trainers manufactured for export. The Allies supplied 5,198 aircraft to America during the war. Overall, the U.S. government had contracted for some 101,000 engines and 23,000 planes during the conflict. From its entry into the conflict until the end of the war production program in December, 1918, the United States produced 12,571 aircraft. More than 8,500 of those planes were trainers—a prudent

World War I fighter pilots were accepted by the public as a glamorous new breed of individual heroes who transcended the senseless slaughter in the trenches. Some of the most dashing American aviators were members of the 94th Aero Squadron. Shown here in France on October 18, 1918 are, *left to right*, Lt. Joseph Eastman, Capt. James Meissner, Capt. Edward V. Rickenbacker, Lt. Reed Chambers, and Lt. Thorn C. Taylor. Rickenbacker, a Medal of Honor recipient with twenty-six aerial victories, was the top U.S. ace of the war. Meissner and Chambers were also aces. (U.S. Air Force photo collection, National Air and Space Museum.)

first step in developing a large air force by a nation that had never built a modern land-based combat aircraft. Altogether, the United States expended over $848 million on military aeronautics during FYs 1917–19.[60]

The U.S. Army's air arm grew to 183,000 officers and men in flying and ground support roles during the war, including twelve thousand pilots. About 58,000 airmen served in France. The actual burden of combat fell on some fifteen hundred aviators in forty-five flying squadrons that engaged the enemy beginning in the spring of 1918. Concentrating on observation and air superiority missions, the American airmen destroyed 781 German aircraft and seventy-three balloons at a cost of 583 casualties and 289 of their own aircraft destroyed.

Aviation played a limited but important role in the Great War. No major power, including the United States, could have conducted significant operations without it. Observation was aviation's most important mission. Aircraft forewarned senior commanders of gathering enemy forces and, with few exceptions, helped guarantee their failure. Artillery was the war's top killer, but aircraft and balloons directed its fires. Once the western front stabilized, aerial reconnaissance inhibited the movement by armies and largely kept them in their trenches. That was a significant contribution to the stalemate on the western front. The role of pursuit (later known as fighter) aircraft was ambivalent. Their biggest contribution was protecting observation planes and denying enemy aircraft the opportunity to observe what friendly ground forces were doing. The bombing force's contribution was also ambivalent. Bombers appeared to be most profitable when acting as an extension of artillery. Strategic bombing aimed at enemy morale and war-making capabilities produced meager results. Close air support was the last function to evolve, but it disappeared quickly in most air forces after the war—probably due to the heavy casualties it produced among airmen. In the United States, the postwar Army Air Service retained ground-attack units and Marine Corps aviation staked its very existence on that role.

Because aircraft were totally new machines, it proved tremendously difficult for armies and navies to integrate them into battle systems during World War I. They required thinking in a new dimension and proved difficult to coordinate with the surface combat arms. However, those fragile flying machines ultimately altered attitudes, especially among the men who flew them. Flight changed the mind-set of pilots and set them apart from all others. The war produced an era of enthusiasm for aircraft, especially in the civilian population. Encouraged by government propaganda organs and a compliant press, aviators came to be seen as glamorous heroes who transcended the anonymous slaughter on the ground. Pilots lived on in folklore, myth, and song after the war. Some, like Eddie Rickenbacker and Hermann Göring, became major national figures.[61]

Martin Van Creveld has observed that, despite the relatively primitive flying machines that were available during the Great War, aviators "not only fought with each other but carried out a variety of other tasks which have not been improved upon since. . . . The intensive utilization of aircraft helped to develop a thorough understanding of their strengths and weaknesses which, for the most part, have persisted to the present day in spite of all technological improvements. The principal strengths were speed, flexibility, the ability to reach out and hit any point . . . and a great potential for achieving surprise, a potential that was frequently exploited, from 1939 on, to get in a devastating blow from the air."[62] Although seldom discussed publicly, their weaknesses were also very significant. Probably the most important ones were their increasing dependence on sophisticated land bases and ships, vulnerability to attack when not airborne, limited endurance, relatively small load capacity, and an enormous decrease in their combat effectiveness at night or during bad weather conditions.[63]

American naval aviation also experienced enormous growth in 1917–18. Highly successful seaplanes, based upon the designs of Glenn Curtiss, were a major exception to the American dependence on the Europeans for combat aircraft during the Great War. In the fall and winter of 1917, naval aviators had begun flying antisubmarine patrols from a series of air stations established along the U.S. East Coast, as well as in France, England, Ireland, and Italy. Like the army, the navy relied on wartime volunteers to fly its aircraft and airships because its prewar aviation program had been so tiny and ill prepared for the challenge it faced in 1917–18. Approximately 95 percent of the naval aviators who flew during the war were reservists.

Navy pilots were joined by a small contingent of marine aviators who, after being rebuffed by the army in their efforts to support their fellow leathernecks fighting with the AEF in France, concentrated on the antisubmarine campaign. One marine unit flew patrols in its Curtiss R-6 floatplanes from Cape May, New Jersey, from October, 1917, until January, 1918. It then departed for the Azores, where it conducted antisubmarine patrols with meager results. Frustrated by the army's refusal to accept land-based marine aircraft in France, Capt. Alfred Cunningham won approval from the navy in February, 1918, for his innovative proposal to establish a "Northern Bombing Group" in Europe. The unit would attack German U-boat bases. Previously, the navy had only attacked them at sea. Consisting of a night wing of naval aviators and a day wing of marine fliers, formation of the group was slowed by interservice squabbles over the allocation of aircraft and other resources. By the time it launched its first attacks in the fall of 1918, the Germans had evacuated most of their submarine bases along the Channel coast due to the pressure of the Allied ground offensive. Instead, the marines focused most of their energy on operating with Royal Air Force (RAF) units supporting British and Belgian forces against the German army.

Allied and U.S. aircraft and airships discouraged attacks on convoys by forcing U-boats to remain submerged during daylight. Actual encounters between German submarines and enemy aircraft or airships were comparatively rare. Kills by aircraft were even more unusual. Clearly, the Royal Navy carried the main burden of the antisubmarine campaign. Its ships and aircraft destroyed the vast majority of the 132 U-boats sunk in 1917–18. American escort ships, aircraft, and airships played a limited role in the antisubmarine campaign, achieving only five confirmed kills. Regardless of the paucity of hard data on wartime contacts, much less actual sinkings of German submarines by aviation assets, the U.S. Navy was impressed by its presumed deterrent effect on them. It continued, for example, to use small, nonrigid airships in that role until 1961.[64]

Major Reuben H. Fleet, an army officer during World War I, inaugurated the first U.S. airmail service on May 15, 1918. Fleet, a former National Guardsman, successful businessman, and Washington state legislator, founded the Consolidated Aircraft Corporation after he left military service. His career illustrated the close ties between politics, the armed services, and the aircraft industry that played a critical role in the development of American commercial and military aviation. (Signal Corps photo courtesy National Guard Bureau.)

Despite its limitations and disappointments, aviation had won a firm place in the U.S. military establishment by the war's end. As in Europe, pilots had emerged as a breed apart. They were individual heroes who inspired the popular imagination and influenced mass culture. It was clear to all but the most thickheaded American reactionaries in uniform that aircraft would play an integral role in any future conflict. Each of the services included cadres of talented and energetic officers like Billy Mitchell, John Towers, and Alfred Cunningham, who were dedicated to advancing the future of military aviation. Moreover, key senior officers like Pershing and Sims valued and supported a growing role for it. Because technological progress had been an essential element of combat success during World War I, aeronautical research and development had been institutionalized within both the army and the navy.

Senior leaders in both services also recognized the necessity to maintain a strong and technically progressive domestic aircraft industry as well as foster commercial aviation. Although dramatically reduced after the war, the American aircraft industry was grounded in modern science and engineering. As it would in World War II, American military aviation during the Great War had demonstrated an awesome ability to make enormous progress quickly in a crisis. Technical developments in European aviation, adapted and improved by Americans, would continue to exercise a significant impact on air power in the United States.[65]

CHAPTER 2

A Golden Age of Innovation

The two decades following World War I were a golden age of innovation in American aviation. They were a period of enormous progress in civil and military aviation. Technology advanced rapidly while numerous speed and distance records were made and broken because of those technological improvements. Heroic flights spanned the oceans and explored remote regions of the globe. Air shows, races, and long-distance flights captivated the public. They provided extraordinary publicity and public recognition for the military's fledgling air arms. They also tested technological innovations in aircraft and engines to some extent. Military funding and operational requirements were critical forces driving the development of a strong and technologically progressive American aviation industry. The interwar years also witnessed an enormous amount of doctrinal and organizational innovation by the armed services that laid the foundations of American air power in World War II.

KNIGHTS OF THE SKY

As soon as the guns fell silent on the western front in November, 1918, America reasserted its historic pattern. It rapidly demobilized most of its massive wartime military establishment and dismantled the formidable armaments industry that had sustained it. As doughboys, sailors, and marines rushed home to civilian life, the military foundations of U.S. power drained away while Pres.

Woodrow Wilson negotiated at Versailles. Disillusioned by the results of the peace treaty, America rejected the League of Nations and sought a return to "normalcy"—a new term for familiar ways of thinking. The public turned inward once again. Isolationist sentiment was strong in the nation at large and influential on Capitol Hill. Yet American foreign policy, despite its rejection of Wilsonian idealism and the League of Nations, was hardly isolationist. Instead, it stressed America's traditional unilateral approach to foreign and military affairs. In the absence of any credible threats to U.S. security until the mid-1930s, military spending was slashed dramatically and Americans relied upon the nation's geographic isolation and a strong navy to protect them from potential foes. As it had for most of its history, the nation would call upon citizen-soldiers to fill out the army should there be another war. Those circumstances shaped the fierce postwar debate over U.S. defense policy, including the role of military aviation.[1]

The emergence of the airplane as a dangerous weapon complicated the development of defense policy more than any other issue between World Wars I and II. It blurred established boundaries between the armed services' missions. Because it devoured scarce personnel and financial resources that might otherwise have gone to the established surface forces, it stimulated sharp internal power struggles within the army and navy. Aviation inspired visionaries who believed it would either deter future wars or decide them quickly and cheaply. It created an increasingly influential coalition of military fliers, scientists and engineers, aircraft and engine builders, politicians, and entrepreneurs inspired by the airplane's commercial and military potential.

While often overshadowed by the controversies associated with the colorful career of Brig. Gen. Billy Mitchell, military aviation made enormous advances in the United States during the interwar period. Although frustrated in their efforts to achieve a separate air force, army airmen acquired greater bureaucratic influence and a viable organizational framework. They sustained a strong industrial base, fostered technological progress, and promoted the development of commercial aviation. After acquiring significant numbers of modern aircraft in the late 1920s, they began evolving a distinctive doctrine for their employment. During the 1930s, they acquired the mission, organization, weapons, and political support needed to produce an effective fighting force.

Naval and marine aviators experienced a similar pattern. Some argued for independent offensive operations with the fleet instead of the dominant predilection after World War I for shore-based patrol work and dirigibles. A few believed, like Mitchell, that aviation offered the most effective means of defending the nation—even at the expense of more traditional modes of warfare. Naval aviators benefited enormously from the establishment of a separate Bureau of Aeronautics in 1921, which championed their cause at the sea service's highest levels and developed effective long-range plans to integrate aircraft with fleet operations. The navy established a second major flight training center in San Diego, California, to augment its Pensacola, Florida, operation. The fine points of maintenance were taught in Chicago, while Lakehurst, New Jersey, specialized in dirigibles. Naval aviators promoted a healthy industrial base and continuous technological progress in aviation. They developed the doctrines, equipment, and operational techniques that produced the fast-carrier task forces of World War II.

Although burdened with castoff army and navy aircraft, marine fliers began to make their mark in the Caribbean after World War I. They developed their distinctive approach to aviation in the crucible of combat operations. Marines employed aircraft to transport troops and supplies to remote locations, evacuate sick and wounded leathernecks to hospitals, and scout for enemy troops. Marine and naval aviators also perfected dive-bombing attacks against ships and shore installations. The Germans were probably the first to employ dive-bombing during World War I. Marine pilots used the tactic in Haiti in 1919 to bomb hostile forces in close proximity to their own ground troops. They went on to perfect the tactic and made it a central aspect of their approach to air warfare. Well before World War II, the flying leathernecks had won themselves a significant role in the infantry-oriented Marine Corps.[2]

Aviation enthusiasts, including Mitchell and Rep. Fiorello H. LaGuardia of New York, championed a radical approach to postwar defense after World War I. They were convinced that the airplane had revolutionized warfare, necessitating a radical overhaul of American military policy and institutions. The colorful and outspoken Mitchell was clearly the most influential air-power radical. He believed that wartime breakthroughs in aeronautical technology had destroyed the assumption that the United States could rely on geography, a small standing army that was expandable in wartime, and a strong navy for its defense. To protect America from aerial attack, he argued, an independent air force was needed. The new military service would be cheaper than the battleship-oriented fleet. Free of control by surface-oriented army and navy officers, it could focus on developing the most effective doctrines, tactics, organization, and equipment needed for aerial combat. Although originally an advocate of air supremacy as the primary role of military aviation, Mitchell had gradually come to see strategic bombing as its key mission in future wars.

Mitchell recognized that neither American public opinion nor aviation technology was ready for strategic bombing. Nevertheless, he was convinced that a separate air force must possess an independent offensive capability and campaigned for the establishment of a defense department to direct the activities of all of the armed services. According to Timothy Moy, Mitchell and other senior army airmen "carefully and deliberately wedded their institutions to visions of warfare that were based on new technologies and then staked their institutional survival on those images."[3]

Mitchell found the public to be a receptive audience in the 1920s. Many Americans believed that aviation fostered such societal virtues as economy, efficiency, and technical innovation. It would also help reduce federal spending and enable America to defend itself without becoming mired in another bloody European ground war. The 1920s and 1930s were the heyday of American technological enthusiasm. Air power advocates fed on the public's increasing disillusionment with the results of World War I and the widespread image of the prewar naval arms race as a major cause of the war. In the public mind, the best case for an independent air force was that it was an economical and inherently defensive alternative to a large fleet and standing army. Champions of air power, especially its army variety, cultivated the romantic image of airmen as elite knights of the sky—a vision that had somehow emerged unscathed from the gruesome realties of World War I air combat. That perception merged in the popular culture with the futuristic high-technology image of fictional movie hero Buck Rogers.

Aviation's benign and technologically progressive image made it especially attractive to reformers. Flying had a significant impact on American culture during the interwar period. Barnstormers, who were mostly former military pilots, actively promoted "air mindedness" at fairs, air shows, and impromptu events all over the country. That attitude meant that the public was enthusiastic about aircraft, believed in their ability to improve human life, and supported the general development of aviation. The peacetime exploits of army, navy, marine, and National Guard pilots also played a key role in developing a benign image of air power during that era. The media lavished coverage on air races and record-setting long-distance flights. Hollywood also discovered aviation. Flying had become popular with members of the film community. Cecil B. de Mille learned to fly and bought his own airplane. Dozens of films were produced about flying, and movies like *Wings, Dawn Patrol,* and *Hell's Angels* became extremely popular.

Movies and magazine and newspaper articles portrayed pilots as reformers and heroic individuals in the traditional American mode. They stood against bureaucracy and militarism aligned with private economic greed. Those positive cultural images were reinforced by Charles A. Lindbergh's solo flight across the Atlantic in 1927. However, appearances could be misleading. Although celebrated as the "Lone Eagle," Lindbergh was financed by a group of wealthy St. Louis businessmen. His aircraft was designed and built with Lindbergh's input by the Ryan Aircraft Corporation, a medium-sized airframe manufacturer in San Diego with a sophisticated design and manufacturing capability. The army taught Lindbergh to be a pilot, and he flew the airmail for a private firm under government contract and was an aviator in the Missouri National Guard at the time of his historic flight. The American public, entranced by the Lone Eagle's undaunted courage and superb flying skills, overlooked the fact that Lindbergh's achievement was the end product of a large and complex partnership between government and the private sector.[4]

Contrary to the claims of Mitchell and other air-power radicals, military aviation was hardly neglected after World War I. No fewer than eight different bills calling for the creation of an independent air force were introduced in Congress in 1919 and 1920. Numerous official groups grappled with difficult

Captain Charles A. Lindbergh, *center*, shown with members of his Missouri National Guard aviation unit after he became the first pilot to fly solo across the Atlantic in 1927. Lindbergh became an American cultural icon who represented the nation's "can do" spirit and faith in technology. In popular mythology, he accomplished an incredibly difficult feat alone while other, better-funded efforts, backed by large bureaucracies, failed. Although his involvement with army and National Guard aviation as well as his civilian job flying the airmail suggested more complex realities, Lindbergh remained a quintessential American hero. (Photo courtesy 131st Fighter Wing, Missouri Air National Guard.)

questions posed by the evolution of military aeronautics. Despite all of this interest, the National Defense Act of 1920 rejected both a large standing army and a separate air force. Instead, it called for a small regular army that would be augmented by citizen-soldiers to be drawn from the National Guard and organized reserves. In the event of war, a big navy, held in a relatively high state of peacetime readiness, would defend America's sea approaches while the nation raised a massive land force. The War Department's plan for maintaining a large active-duty army was cut by almost 50 percent, to 280,000 men. Congress did, however, authorize each of the services to maintain significant aviation programs.

The navy was sharply divided about how to develop aviation after World War I. Most of its air arm had been demobilized after the armistice. By the early summer of 1919, it carried only 580 officers and 4,879 enlisted men on its rolls, and Congress appropriated a paltry $25 million for it in 1920. What remained of the program was weakened by factional infighting over its best course for the future. The most controversial idea was to establish a separate Naval Flying Corps akin to the Marine Corps—a move that was rejected out of hand as an extremist measure that would divorce aviation from the navy's mainstream.[5]

Reflecting the fact that the wartime force had been primarily a shore-based antisubmarine force of flying boats, the dominant group within naval aviation advocated patrol work. They sought long-range seaplanes that could operate from land bases or seagoing tenders, which would give them strategic mobility. There were also strong advocates of lighter-than-air craft in the navy. They contended that the enormous range of rigid airships offered great potential for reconnaissance in the vast reaches of the Pacific, and pointed to the antisubmarine capabilities of nonrigid airships, known as blimps. Others stressed the development of floatplanes that could be launched from battleships and cruisers at sea. They were convinced that such aircraft could be put to sea quickly and serve in a variety of roles, including gunfire spotting, scouting, and air defense of the fleet.

The other major naval aviation faction pinned their hopes on aircraft carriers, which Britain's Royal Navy had experimented with during World War I. Experience gained in that conflict suggested that carrier aircraft were excellent for tactical reconnaissance and spotting gunfire for the battle line. It also was obvious to observers that maintaining air superiority over fleet engagements would be critical. Finally, they envisioned that carriers might also employ their aircraft against submarines and in independent attacks on surface ships.

As World War I drew to a close, the navy began to cautiously explore each of those major avenues for aviation. In October, 1918, naval leaders asked Congress to fund the construction of four rigid airships and two hangars. The following year, Congress authorized the sea service to convert a collier into an experimental aircraft carrier and two merchant vessels to become seaplane tenders. Only one of the latter, the USS *Wright,* was commissioned. Capitol Hill also approved the purchase of two airships from the British and funding for the construction of an airship hangar at Lakehurst. However, those preliminary steps foundered because of tight budgets, doctrinal confusion, and the absence of a strong organizational champion for aviation at the highest levels of the battleship-oriented navy.[6]

The National Defense Act of 1920 recognized the growing importance of military aviation. It made the Air Service a permanent combat arm of the army and authorized it 1,516 officers and sixteen thousand enlisted men (including twenty-five hundred aviation cadets) within the army's overall manpower ceiling of 280,000. Unlike other combat arms, it would administer its own research and development and weapons procurement programs. The Air Service would also control its own supply, personnel, and training activities. The chief of the Air Service, a major general, remained subject to General Staff direction and could not exercise command of tactical air units. The latter were subordinate to ground forces' commanders at division and corps level. The bill also authorized the Air Service to form reserve formations that would fight in wartime as intact units instead of serving as manpower pools to augment the regulars.

Despite those gains, air-power radicals like Mitchell were bitterly disappointed by the aviation provisions in the 1920 legislation. They were convinced that the army did not understand the airplane's full military potential. Mitchell, frustrated by his unsuccessful efforts to build the case for military aviation within the government, turned to the public for support. He was determined to demonstrate the independent offensive capabilities of land-based military aircraft. Aware of the limitations of available Air Service equipment and sensitive to the national mood, he dropped his previous calls for offensive air capabilities. Instead, he said military aircraft could defend the United States against attacking hostile fleets. To prove his point, Mitchell challenged the navy, which had begun testing the effects of bombs on warships in 1920, to accept Air Service participation in those experiments. The confident navy brass, believing that Mitchell's airmen could never sink a battleship, accepted.

To the dismay of sea power advocates, army airmen, assisted by their navy counterparts, sank three former German vessels, including the battleship *Ostfriesland,* anchored off the mouth of Chesapeake Bay. Two years later, Air Service bombers sank two old U.S. battleships, the *Virginia* and *New Jersey,* in tests near Cape Hatteras, North Carolina. Those tests, conducted against stationary and undefended warships, generated spectacular headlines. Mitchell crowed that they proved battleships and other surface combatants were obsolete. The navy responded that maneuvering warships closed up at battle stations and firing antiaircraft guns would have easily defended themselves. Nevertheless, navy leaders moved vigorously to strengthen the fledgling carrier program in an effort to protect the battle line against the growing threat posed by enemy aircraft.

In one sense, Billy Mitchell was the "deadbeat dad" of naval aviation. His irresponsible charges and inflammatory rhetoric may have saved it. Although proposals to create a separate aviation bureau in the Navy Department had remained in limbo for years, the admirals, alarmed by Mitchell's onslaught, closed ranks in 1921 and supported legislation to establish the Bureau of Aeronautics, which consolidated the fragmented responsibilities for developing naval aviation.

THE INSIDERS

Rear Admiral William A. Moffett, a Naval Academy graduate and respected military insider who was popular on Capitol Hill, became the bureau's first chief. A skilled administrator with a real flair for publicity, the former battleship skipper earned a rating as a naval observer after assuming his new duties. He took the ad hoc wartime infrastructure needed to administer, train, and supply aviation and placed it on a solid permanent footing. While his vigorous advocacy of aviation at the expense of battleships was not always welcome in the navy, Moffett's skill at countering Mitchell's attacks was highly valued. However, his greatest contribution was to convince the navy that the fleet needed a strong aviation program.[7]

Aside from prompting the navy to strengthen its own aviation program and generating enormous public controversy, Mitchell's bombers had little impact. The bombing tests failed to convince either senior government officials or the public that America needed to base its national security on a separate air force built around long-range bombers.

Limited resources also frustrated Mitchell's dreams. War Department expenditures nose-dived after the war. The Air Service, like the rest of the army, never came close to reaching its authorized personnel strength. By March, 1923, it only had 9,279 personnel, less than 53 percent of its planned peacetime force. Its material shortcomings were even more serious. That year, 1,531 of the army's 1,970 aircraft had been built during the recent war. Official policy, shaped by the nation's desire to limit government spending and strong antiwar sentiments, forced it to rely on war surplus aircraft. Those obsolete weapons were expensive to maintain and increasingly dangerous to fly.[8]

The fight over the future of air power was also undercut by strife within the Air Service. General Mitchell was at the center of that storm too. In December, 1918, Maj. Gen. Charles T. Menoher had been appointed director of the Air Service. But, Menoher, an artillery officer, had been unable to control the public outbursts of Mitchell who openly coveted the former's job. In 1921, Mitchell was openly critical of Congress for cutting the Air Service's appropriations request and demanded its separation from the army. Menoher was so infuriated that he gave Secretary of War John W. Weeks an ultimatum: either he or Mitchell would have to go. Menoher was removed but Mitchell did not replace him. Instead, Gen. John J. Pershing, the army chief of staff, asked his old friend Maj. Gen. Mason M. Patrick to rescue army aviation once again.

Like Moffett, Patrick was a service academy graduate and a respected military insider. He agreed to take on the challenge of preventing the Air Service from self-destructing. With little more than two hundred officers and less than twenty-eight hundred mostly aging aircraft on hand, it was a mere shadow of its wartime strength. Patrick discovered that the Air Service was in near chaos— just as it had been in France in 1918. Most of its huge and expensive wartime infrastructure was still in place. Mountains of surplus material had to be disposed of, and little, if any, tactical training was being accomplished. No settled policies for administration and training had been adopted, and ignorance about and jealousy of the Air Service were widespread in the War Department.[9]

Mitchell was at odds with Patrick at the outset. When the latter assumed his new post, Mitchell lectured him on how to run the Air Service. When Mitchell threatened to quit after Patrick suggested that command responsibility was his, not Mitchell's, Patrick called his bluff and the younger man stayed on.[10] In April, 1925, at the end of Mitchell's War Department tour, Patrick reduced him to his permanent grade of lieutenant colonel and exiled him to San Antonio, Texas. Following several highly publicized naval aviation disasters later that year, Mitchell charged that incompetence, negligence, and near-treasonous management by the army and navy were responsible. His rash public outburst led to a court-martial conviction. The affluent Mitchell resigned and continued his crusade for a separate air force from his Middleburg, Virginia, estate until he died in 1936.

Although celebrated as a prophetic martyr in air force myth, Mitchell's quest for air power was a failure. His flare for publicity had only a modest influence on public policy during his lifetime. General Henry H. "Hap" Arnold, leader of the Army Air Forces during World War II and one of Mitchell's strongest supporters, admitted that the latter's tactics did more harm than good. Mitchell's primary contribution was to create a group of dedicated disciples, including

Arnold, who carried on the crusade for a separate air force. Mitchell's doctrinal prescriptions proved to be tragically flawed in World War II. More significantly, Mitchell and his disciples focused the army's air arm on strategic bombing at the expense of a broader and more effective conception of air power. Their foolhardy and incorrect belief that air power, especially strategic bombing, is an all-purpose military and political tool has persisted to the present day despite the fact that it has repeatedly fallen short of its overly ambitious objectives. Occasionally it generated the even sillier and more dangerous notion that air power has been a failure and should be deemphasized in favor of more conventional approaches to military policy that would restore the primacy of surface forces.[11]

Unlike Mitchell, Patrick was successful in promoting the development of air power during his military career. He saved army aviation from a variety of self-inflicted wounds and laid the groundwork for a separate air force. Although he came to agree with many of Mitchell's views, Patrick avoided public confrontations and sensational headlines. Instead, he orchestrated behind-the-scenes maneuvers that promoted the development of military aviation. From 1921–27, he guided the army's air arm to a realistically achievable degree of autonomy. Patrick was an able administrator who placed the Air Service's operations on a more professional and economical basis. He oversaw the rapid disposal of surplus material and excess infrastructure, and consolidated training at a handful of installations. New experimental facilities were established at Wright Field in Dayton, Ohio. To better understand the needs of his young aviators and gain their respect, Patrick earned his pilot's wings when he was nearly sixty years old.

The new chief of the Air Service was a professionally trained engineer with a long-term plan that included building a viable commercial aviation industry, officer professionalism, the development of sound air-power doctrine, and legislative initiatives that would set the Air Service on the road to independence. Because of his high standing with Congress and the War Department, Patrick had much more freedom than Mitchell to push for significant improvements in army aviation.

Like Patrick, Moffett charted a long-term course for aviation. The central problem that he faced was how to take air power to sea with the fleet to scout for enemy ships and protect the navy's battle line from hostile aircraft. The Washington naval treaties of 1921–22 placed significant limits on warship construction. The navy faced the daunting task of preparing for war in the vast reaches of the western Pacific against the Japanese without an adequate battle line and access to fortified bases. Moffett pressed for a balanced naval aviation program that included carriers, shore-based patrol aircraft, lighter-than-air vehicles, and floatplanes on major warships. His organization played a critical role in the evolution of aviation operations and doctrine. However, the Bureau of Aeronautics functioned as much more than a mere technical organization. Yet, despite Moffett's best efforts, it was only able to share control of aviation personnel policy with the powerful Bureau of Navigation.[12]

Patrick had gained War Department acceptance of the idea that part of the Air Service should be concentrated on offensive operations. He proposed the creation of an air organization within the War Department whose status was similar to that of the Marine Corps. Patrick's ultimate goal was a separate air force. Unlike Mitchell, he had a legislative road map for getting there. His proposal, along with Mitchell's court-martial and separate investigations of military aviation by congressional and presidential boards—heavily influenced the Air Corps Act of 1926.[13]

That legislation reflected a consensus in the government that, although military aviation needed to be strengthened, there was no justification for a separate air force because it lacked an independent mission in warfare. The act also fell short of the complete autonomy Patrick sought for aviation. Nevertheless, it was an important milestone along the road to a separate air force. To give aviation more prestige and influence within the army, the Air Service was renamed the Air Corps and given special representation on the General Staff. The act also created a new civilian assistant secretary of war for air and authorized a five-year expansion and modernization program for army aviation.

The Air Corps's goal under the five-year program was a force of 1,650 officers, fifteen thousand enlisted men (including up to fifteen hundred aviation cadets) and eighteen hundred serviceable aircraft. When the law was passed, army aviation consisted of 919 officers, 8,725 enlisted men, and some 344 aircraft, most of which were obsolete. Because of government-wide budget cuts and the onset of the Great Depression in 1929, the army was unable to buy all of the aircraft authorized under the five-year program. Nevertheless, it provided the impetus for major improvements in the Air Corps. From 1927–32, Congress provided $147 million in direct appropriations for army aviation. The total number of Air Corps personnel and aircraft grew by about 50 percent during that period.

Although the Air Corps never received all the money it requested, it was significantly strengthened at the expense of the rest of the army. Between 1920 and 1934, it spent an average of 18.2 percent of the army's annual budget although it comprised only about 11 percent of the service's strength. In the early 1930s, while the Air Corps was being equipped with sleek new all-metal bombers like the Martin B-10, which were among the best in the world, the rest of the army relied on World War I vintage tanks, artillery, and rifles. Air Corps manpower was increased under the five-year program by transferring personnel from other army branches. By 1929, the army had deactivated five infantry battalions and most of an artillery regiment because of those transfers. Army leaders did the best they could to build up their air arm, but they refused to sacrifice their entire service to fund one visionary branch. There is little in the historical record that suggests the airmen would have won greater funding as a separate service in the depths of the Great Depression, especially after the navy-oriented Franklin D. Roosevelt became president.[14]

By 1925, the navy had only a little over two hundred operational aircraft. Many were still World War I vintage machines, and about half were shore-based. Moffett exploited that situation and the furor over the status of American military aviation created by Mitchell's court-martial to convince Congress to authorize a long-term naval aviation modernization program in 1926. Its estimated cost was $85 million over five years. Congress eventually appropriated enough money for the navy to achieve its goal of a thousand modern aircraft by the end of 1931.

The chief of the Bureau of Aeronautics also convinced Congress to mandate that only aviators be given command of carriers, seaplane tenders, air squadrons, air stations, and aviation training units. That policy strengthened the aviators' control of their own program and created a pool of senior command assignments that made aviation a much more attractive career choice. It brought a number of talented and ambitious midcareer officers, including Capts. Ernest J. King and William F. Halsey into the field. Although resented by some aviators, those "Johnny-come-latelys" played important roles in making aviation an integral part of the fleet. They filled a gap in senior positions until career aviators like John Towers could rise to the top. The 1926 legislation also created a new civilian assistant secretary of the navy for air position whose responsibilities paralleled that of its War Department counterpart.[15]

Marine Corps aviation also had to struggle to survive after World War I. It disbanded its overseas wartime force of 282 officers and 2,180 enlisted men, disbursing the remaining assets to stateside marine bases in September, 1919. Largely due to the lobbying of Maj. Alfred A. Cunningham, Congress placed Marine Corps aviation on a permanent footing. In 1920, it authorized the Corps a force of 27,400 officers and men, including a hundred officers and 1,020 enlisted personnel assigned to aviation duties. Capitol Hill also provided funds for marine air stations in Quantico, Virginia; Parris Island, South Carolina; and several locations around San Diego. An aviation section was established at Marine Corps headquarters to oversee training and personnel matters as well as coordinate with the navy's air organization on equipment and supply matters. The latter supplied aircraft to the marines—primarily army and navy castoffs.

Major General Mason M. Patrick and Rear Adm. William A. Moffett, shown with an unidentified civilian, were the chief architects of robust aviation programs in their respective military services during the interwar period. They were highly respected military insiders who effectively promoted the advancement of aviation in their dealings with Congress, the executive branch of government, and industry, as well as line officers of the army and navy. (U.S. Air Force photo collection, National Archives.)

During the 1920s, the bulk of marine aviation strength was concentrated at Quantico and San Diego.

Marine fliers—during actual combat operations in the Dominican Republic, Haiti, and Nicaragua—developed their own techniques for supporting ground forces without any particular guidance or doctrine from higher authority. Although they had been outsiders searching for a mission during World War I, the flying leathernecks had clearly defined their ground-support role by the mid-1920s. Like the rest of U.S. military aviation, however, they suffered from severe shortages of resources during that decade. Trained aviators were in especially short supply. To meet increased requirements for pilots, the marines began training enlisted men as fliers and planned to commission them in wartime. In 1928, they revived the wartime Marine Aviation Reserve.[16]

Patrick and Moffett both understood that the future of their respective air arms was inextricably linked with the general development of American aviation. Commercial aviation was virtually nonexistent in the United States, and the infant aircraft industry was struggling to survive after World War I. To stimulate interest in flying, build a strong manufacturing base, expand the frontiers of aeronautical technology, and encourage the development of commercial aviation, they adopted what was, in effect, an industrial policy. Military needs and funding remained the dominant factors shaping the development of American aviation throughout much of its history.

To win support for their respective programs while encouraging technical progress, army and navy pilots competed for headline-grabbing aviation "firsts." These included long-distance and high-altitude flights, races, aerial fire fighting, aerobatics, and border patrols. Inspired by foreign efforts and his desire to publicize naval aviation, Lt. Comdr. John Towers had convinced his service to sponsor the first successful transatlantic flight. On May 27, 1919, one of four navy flying boats that had departed from Naval Air Station Rockaway, New York, reached Lisbon, Portugal. Its arduous nineteen-day journey included a ten-day layover in the Azores. That same year, Mitchell had sponsored a "Round-the-Rim Flight" during which army pilots circumnavigated the border of the continental United States.[17] However, his "Coast-to-Coast Army Reliability Race" in 1919 backfired. Of the forty-nine pilots who began it, only nine completed the transcontinental contest. Another nine died during the effort. In May, 1923, army lieutenants Oakley G. Kelly and John A. Macready, piloting a T-2 transport developed by Dutch designer Anthony Fokker, made the first nonstop flight across the country. The twenty-five-hundred-mile trip from New York to San Diego took nearly twenty-seven hours.[18]

The most famous military aviation exploit of the period was the first aerial circumnavigation of the globe, a trip made in 1924 by two of four aircraft specially designed for the Air Service by the Douglas Corporation for that flight. Their twenty-six-thousand-mile journey lasted nearly six months. In May, 1926, Lt. Comdr. Richard Byrd, piloting a Fokker trimotor, became the first man to fly over the North Pole. In November, 1928, he achieved that same distinction over the South Pole. Although such long-distance flights generated banner headlines and an enormous amount of public interest, they failed to produce substantial increases in either political support or funding for military aviation. They had only a marginal impact on technological progress.

Closed-circuit air racing was a different matter. The army and the navy engaged in a fierce competition to win the race for speed supremacy, national

On May 8, 1919, three navy NC-4 flying boats launched an attempt to cross the Atlantic Ocean from Naval Air Station Rockaway, New York. On May 27, an NC-4 landed in Lisbon Harbor, Portugal. Commanded by Lt. Comdr. Albert C. Reed, it was the first aircraft to fly across the Atlantic. The NC-4 ended its flight in Plymouth, England, on May 31, 1919. The flight was part of a determined effort by army and navy flyers to publicize aviation in their respective services and win increased support through participation in headline grabbing races, long-distance and high-altitude flights, and aerobatic displays at air shows. (U.S. Air Force photo collection, National Archives.)

honor, and service advantage during the 1920s. The Gordon Bennett, Schneider, and Pulitzer races contributed to the explosive international growth of aircraft technology during that decade, especially the development of more powerful and reliable engines as well as more streamlined aircraft.

The victory of a Curtiss CR-3 flown by a U.S. Navy pilot in the 1923 Schneider Trophy Race marked the emergence of superior postwar American aviation technology before a stunned European audience. Rival army and navy teams dominated closed-circuit racing until they withdrew from competition in the late 1920s due primarily to reduced budgets inspired by the Great Depression. In the meantime, race-bred Curtiss fighters and engines gave the U.S. a brief international lead in that critical aircraft category during the 1920s. By 1931, closed-circuit air racing had produced, in embryonic form, the designs of the fighters that would rule the skies in World War II.

Nevertheless, some informed observers—including famed test pilot, air racer, and World War II army air combat leader James H. "Jimmy" Doolittle—were convinced that such races had outlived their usefulness. During the 1930s, racing was dominated by civilians who concentrated on increased engine power while largely neglecting improvements in aerodynamics. Their exploits during that decade had little impact on the technological progress of aviation.

The industrial base upon which American military aviation depended had been in deplorable condition after the armistice in 1918. According to one contemporary account, it "was hanging on by its eyelids."[19] Most of the industry had been created during the war and depended almost entirely on military contracts. By 1919, approximately 90 percent of it had either disappeared or turned to other lines of business. Boeing, for example, built wooden furniture until the aircraft market revived.[20]

To assist the struggling aviation industry, Patrick and Moffett minimized two sources of direct competition, the Air Service's Engineering Division and the Naval Aircraft Factory. Products of the World War I aviation program, they had designed and built prototypes of new aircraft and engines. Patrick ordered that practice stopped altogether by the Engineering Division. Instead, it focused on helping develop military requirements for new equipment, and then testing aircraft and engine prototypes developed by the manufacturers.[21] Moffett was also determined to sustain the critical aviation industrial base and foster technological progress. Under his direction, the NAF performed the same basic functions as its army counterpart. Unlike the Engineering Division, the NAF continued developing aircraft prototypes to serve as yardsticks for gauging industry costs. It also performed maintenance on naval aircraft.

The armed forces primarily relied upon NACA and a handful of universities like the Massachusetts Institute of Technology (MIT) for fundamental and applied research in aviation. The former, established during World War I, acquired a reputation as the world's premier aviation research organization after its Langley Memorial Aeronautical Laboratory was dedicated in June, 1920. A joint body of civilians and military officers that included the senior army and navy aviators controlled its work. The NACA's research, especially in aerodynamics, was one of the major reasons why American commercial and military aircraft were among the world's most advanced by the early 1930s.[22]

To maintain as large an industrial base as possible, Patrick and Moffett built alliances with congressmen and aircraft manufacturers as well as senior civilian and military officials in the executive branch. They negotiated contracts with those few companies that had the capability to design and actually produce the advanced aircraft and engines the armed forces needed. That practice enabled Patrick and Moffett to circumvent the existing legal requirement that manufacturers sell their design rights to the government. Production contracts were then supposed to be awarded to all qualified firms based upon their estimates of what it would cost to actually build those designs. Consequently, the firms that had devoted a great deal of time, talent, and money to developing advanced designs risked losing the relatively lucrative contracts to actually produce aircraft.

Congress, which maintained strong control of military procurement practices, insisted that the aircraft industry be preserved as a bastion of free market, laissez-faire capitalism. That ideological commitment—which flew in the face of a consensus among aircraft makers, army and naval aviators, and executive-branch officials—created a difficult business environment that inhibited technological innovation. Patrick and Moffett ameliorated the problem by obtaining administrative rulings from their departments that enabled them to negotiate the production contracts with the firms that actually developed the winning designs.

Those contracting practices were attacked on Capitol Hill during the mid-1930s. The army and the navy were forced to revert to costly and time-consuming price competitions because Congress remained firmly wedded to nineteenth-century notions of laissez-faire capitalist competition and was under intense pressure to spread government contracts as widely as possible during the Great Depression. Furthermore, many of its members feared that so-called aircraft and other armament trusts would draw the nation into another world war. Negotiated military aircraft contracts were seen as proof of the continuing insidious influence of "the merchants of death." Many Americans blamed the latter for drawing the United States into World War I. Nevertheless, the armed services were usually able to continue awarding production contracts to the firms that had actually produced the winning designs. That was primarily because production of the increasingly sophisticated aircraft of the period required machinery and skills that were far beyond the resources of all but a handful of manufacturers.

The emergence of long-range commercial aircraft in the early 1930s provided army and navy flyers the technology they needed to realize their dreams. There was a phenomenal change in international aircraft design between the late 1920s and mid-1930s that became known as the airframe revolution. This aeronautical transformation culminated in the emergence of the modern prejet airplane, epitomized by the first flight of the Douglas DC-3 in December, 1935. The new breed of airliners consisted of low-wing monoplanes with streamlined, all-metal airframes built of aluminum alloy. They were powered by air-cooled radial engines that burned high-octane aviation gas. Their other major design features included: low-drag engine cowlings, controllable-pitch and constant-speed propellers, retractable landing gear, and enclosed cabins. These sleek new aircraft rendered obsolete old-fashioned biplanes with open cockpits, cloth-covered frames, fixed landing gear, external braces, and boxlike fuselages.[23]

During the interwar period, designers, the armed forces, and commercial airlines widened their requirements for speed, range, altitude, carrying capacity, and the ability to fly in various weather conditions, thus stimulating technical improvements in aircraft. Those changes, in turn, encouraged higher expectations and additional progress. Aircraft were complicated flying machines consisting of smaller machines and systems including engines, airframes, control surfaces, cockpit controls, and pilots' instrument panels among others. Advances in any of the major components of modern aircraft promoted progress in other areas. For example, increasingly "powerful engines permitted more powerful hydraulic systems, larger airframes, and greater speeds. Greater airspeeds encouraged (and later required) all-metal cantilever-wing monoplanes without external bracing . . . greater airspeeds ultimately required engineers to retract the landing gear."[24] There are many other examples of this phenomenon. For instance, monocoque fuselages were metal structures in which an aircraft's outer skin carried a major portion of the plane's stresses. They were far stronger than wooden and canvas fuselages of comparable weight. When combined with metal cantilevered wings that supported their own weight by internal bracing, monocoque fuselages significantly reduced drag and made possible much faster aircraft. The introduction of high-octane aviation gasoline was another example of that process. It meant more power per pound of fuel. When married to air-cooled radial engines, high-octane gasoline saved significant aircraft weight while substantially increasing horsepower.[25]

The technologies incorporated in those modern designs came from many different sources in Europe and the United States. The all-metal monoplane, for example, was a European innovation that predated World War I. It had evolved into effective aircraft designs on the continent in the decade after the armistice. Although it had begun to emerge during the war, instrument flying became practical chiefly due to the work of an American, Lawrence Sperry. Variable-pitch propellers were patented in the United Kingdom in 1924 and put into practical production in the United States in the 1930s. Igor Sikorsky, who fled to America after the Bolshevik Revolution, had formed his own aircraft company in 1923. It built a series of huge flying boats and developed the first practical helicopter in 1939. Adolph Rohrbach and Herbert Wagner, who both immigrated to the United States in 1927, pioneered research on stressed-skin fuselages in Germany. The navy initiated the development and purchase of a two-hundred-horsepower advanced air-cooled radial engine in January, 1920, from the Lawrence Aero Engine Corporation. S. D. Heron, an Englishman, also conducted pioneering development work on radial engines while working for the army at Wright Field in the 1920s.

As a result of such technical developments, there was rapid improvement in the international performance records of military aircraft between 1918 and 1939. For example, the top speed of pursuit aircraft jumped from about 155 to more than 469 miles per hour during that period. Altitude records increased from twenty-five thousand to over fifty-six thousand feet. The combat radius of bombers grew from thirteen hundred to over thirty-five hundred miles. Moreover, military aircraft carried far more devastating armament by the late 1930s than did their World War I counterparts.[26]

The explosive growth of military and commercial aviation in the United States in the 1930s and the technical skill of American aircraft designers created an environment where technical advances associated with the airframe revolution could be synthesized in revolutionary new aircraft. A combination of factors—a booming economy prior to 1929, the vast geographic dispersion of American urban centers, research by the NACA, and sound federal policies adopted in the mid-1920s to promote and regulate commercial aviation—contributed to that development.

The U.S. armed forces played central roles in promoting the development of the technology incorporated in advanced commercial airliners. Prior to the five-year expansion program authorized by Congress in 1926, Patrick had explicitly sacrificed the operational capabilities of the Air Service in favor of aircraft research and development programs because of severe funding shortages. Examples of direct military contributions to the technical progress of American aviation included the Air Corps's research on more powerful engines, variable-pitch propellers, and high-octane aviation fuels, plus the navy's promotion of air-cooled radial engines.[27]

From its origins through the 1940s, the American aviation industry enjoyed and suffered from a symbiotic relationship with the armed forces. The boundary between the two institutions was blurred. Military pilots often shuttled between the armed forces and private industry, as did engineers. The army and navy relied on industry for the bulk of their aeronautical research and development. A major source of tension between the two sides involved the sale of top-of-the-line military aircraft to foreign customers. After 1924, when it was discovered that the Curtiss Corporation had sold aircraft engines to the British without even notifying the army, all foreign military contracts required War Department approval. With sales significantly reduced during the early 1930s due to the Great Depression, the industry sought government permission to sell state-of-the-art aircraft overseas. Military aviation leaders did what was necessary to protect their industrial base in tough times. For example, in 1934 the chief of the Army Air Corps approved a request to sell B-10 and B-12 bombers abroad to protect the economic health of their manufacturer, the Glenn Martin Corporation. Senior airmen "believed that the threat of state-of-the-art aircraft in the hands of potential enemies was less grave than the threat of losing any of the large aircraft companies to economic ruin."[28]

The American aviation market during the interwar period was dominated by the military. Although the industry usually sold fewer military than civilian aircraft in any given year, the dollar value of the former was almost always significantly larger. For example, the industry sold 1,219 military and 3,542 commercial aircraft valued at $19 million and $17 million respectively in 1928. By 1937, those figures were 949 military and 2,281 commercial aircraft with respective price tags of $37 million and $19 million. The unrelenting requirement for improved performance made the military market the most difficult one to enter in the technical sense, so it was concentrated in a relatively small number of firms. While the Aeronautical Chamber of Commerce reported that its membership included thirty-four airframe firms in 1938, only eighteen of them actually produced military aircraft. Measured by the cost and weight of aircraft produced, the vast bulk of military contracts had gone to four firms: Douglas, Boeing, Curtiss-Wright, and North American. Because of low profit margins, rapid technological advances, high development costs, and the conservative procurement practices of the armed forces, there were only two significant additions to the ranks of American military aircraft manufacturers during the 1930s: Seversky and Bell.[29]

AIR POWER GOES TO SEA

The navy made significant progress in integrating aviation with the fleet between 1921 and 1933 under Admiral Moffett's leadership. Only gradually did he realize that the aircraft carrier would dominate that development. In 1922, the USS *Langley*, a former collier, was commissioned as the navy's first carrier and began a series of experiments on the employment of aircraft at sea with the fleet. The *Langley* was slow and usually carried no more than seventeen relatively fragile biplanes. That same year, naval aviation acquired a powerful friend when Adm. William Simms, the commander of U.S. naval forces in Europe during World War I and a leading battleship advocate, was converted to the value of air power at sea during war games at the Naval War College.

Beyond scouting and maintaining air superiority over the battle line, the navy was uncertain about how best to employ its aircraft. Naval aviators began

The USS *Langley* (CV-1), under way with biplanes embarked, in 1925. Converted from the collier *Jupiter,* she was commissioned as the U.S. Navy's first aircraft carrier on March 20, 1922, at Norfolk, Virginia. (U.S. Air Force photo collection, National Archives.)

their own experiments with dive-bombing and quickly discovered that pointing a plane at a ship and releasing a bomb during a dive was similar to aiming it at a hostile aircraft as the most effective technique for destroying the latter with a machine gun. Unlike the army, the navy considered horizontal bombing against moving targets ineffective. The forward pitch and long flight times of one-thousand- to two-thousand-pound bombs dropped from between five thousand and ten thousand feet usually caused them to miss maneuvering ships. Captain Joseph M. Reed began developing naval dive-bombing tactics in connection with amphibious warfare at San Diego in 1925. Naval aviators conducted dive-bombing experiments against battleships the following year. In 1928, it was formally accepted as a naval tactic.

By the early 1930s, navy dive-bombers were capable of attacking at angles of seventy degrees or more and released their one-hundred- to five-hundred-pound bombs at altitudes of fifteen hundred to two thousand feet. The technique was extremely accurate with well-trained pilots, but ordnance that light could not penetrate the armored decks or turrets of battleships. The development of more powerful dive-bombers capable of carrying heavier bombs in the late 1930s solved that problem and dive-bombing was used with devastating effectiveness in World War II.

The navy concentrated on developing specialized fighters, torpedo and dive-bombers, and scouting aircraft for carrier operations in order to maximize the performance of each individual type. It also pioneered the development of powerful air-cooled engines in the 1920s. They were less vulnerable to battle damage than heavier, maintenance-intensive liquid-cooled power plants, and enabled carrier aircraft to rival the performance of land-based planes. In 1927, the navy commissioned the carriers USS *Lexington* and USS *Saratoga,* which were built on converted battle-cruiser hulls under the terms of the Washington naval treaties. At thirty-three thousand tons each, embarking eighty-one aircraft apiece, and capable of thirty-three-knot speeds, those giant ships stimulated rapid advances in carrier aviation. Existing doctrine called for such ships to remain in protected positions behind the battle line in fleet engagements. Initially, their primary roles were to provide air cover for the fleet, locate the enemy, and then spot the gunfire of American warships. The latter enormously increased the potential power of warships by enabling them to accurately engage targets far beyond the horizon at the full range of their main batteries.

Since carriers were the only capital ships that could be added to the fleet under the five-power treaty, there was heated debate over how to apportion the remaining sixty-nine thousand tons after the *Lexington* and *Saratoga* were commissioned. Moffett initially argued for building three twenty-three-thousand-ton ships because they could embark more aircraft than smaller vessels. However, he gradually became convinced that four or five fourteen-thousand-ton carriers would be a better choice. The doctrinal issue that changed his thinking was how best to maintain air superiority over the fleet. The bigger carriers of the day could not launch and recover aircraft any faster than smaller ones such as the *Langley.* Naval planners concluded that the number of flight decks available, not the total number of aircraft embarked, was the key to generating higher aircraft launch and recovery rates. They believed that more flight decks meant more aircraft over the fleet in a hurry. However, actual fleet operations showed that inexperienced crews and inadequate ship designs, among many other factors, contributed greatly to low sortie rates. On the negative side, the planners knew that smaller carriers would have less staying power in a prolonged campaign than the *Lexington* and *Saratoga* because they could accommodate less fuel, munitions, and supplies, as well as fewer aircraft.

Knowing that aircraft and speed were a carrier's best defense, Moffett also proposed eliminating heavy guns and deck armor on any new vessels. They would, however, carry large numbers of antiaircraft guns. The General Board approved his proposal for a 14,500-ton flush-deck carrier with a top speed of twenty-nine knots capable of carrying up to eighty current aircraft. In 1928, Congress authorized construction of the USS *Ranger,* the first U.S. Navy vessel to be designed from the keel up as a carrier. The lawmakers were impressed by the fact that the proposed ship would be cheaper to operate and cost less than half to build than either the *Lexington* or the *Saratoga.* Because of its limited size, the *Ranger* would be unable to embark an entire air group of the heavier second-generation naval aircraft set to join the fleet in the 1930s. Construction was begun in 1931 and the carrier was commissioned three years later.

During the annual fleet exercise in 1929, which featured a simulated attack on the Panama Canal, Capt. Joseph Mason Reeves tested an idea that eventually radically transformed carrier aviation doctrine. He won permission for a daring experiment with the *Saratoga.* On the last night of the war games, the ship sortied beyond the battle line and penetrated the screen of defending warships. Umpires ruled that its aircraft, launched before sunrise, had rendered the canal inoperable and destroyed many of the defending army aircraft on the ground. The attack showed that independent carrier operations against land targets could be devastating.

They could also be dangerous gambles. During joint army-navy maneuvers in 1930, a fleet that included battleships and three aircraft carriers equipped with full aircraft complements attacked San Francisco Bay. The defenders included a small number of warships and Coast Guard cutters plus army antiaircraft artillery. Major Carl A. Spaatz's Air Corps bomber unit, greatly outnumbered by naval aircraft, formed the heart of the defense. On the first day of the exercise, his bombers absorbed an initial thrust by naval aircraft with minimal losses and then shadowed the attackers back to their carriers. The army airmen surprised the carriers with their decks full and no significant combat air patrols aloft. Umpires ruled that the army airmen had "destroyed" all three vessels. Spaatz's airmen repeated the feat the next day when all participating forces were resurrected for another round of war games. The exercise underscored something that naval aviators had already been worried about privately: that it could be suicidal for carrier aircraft to take on large concentrations of land-based air power before the latter had been significantly weakened through well-planned surprise attacks. That could be an especially daunting task because the aircraft of the day could be widely dispersed and hidden on primitive airstrips.[30]

Naval aviators also struggled to overcome the "defensive" carrier policy favored by the Gun Club. The navy's more traditional elements believed that carriers were too vulnerable to surface attack and had to be protected by battleships. Moreover, they wanted carriers to remain near the battle line to control the air over it and protect their own spotting planes during fleet engagements. Proponents of an "offensive" policy believed that the navy's 1929 war game demonstrated that carriers could be more than an appendage of the battle line. Moreover, because U.S. Navy carriers were capable of speeds over thirty knots and its battleships were much slower, some officers believed a defensive policy limited the carriers' potential and made them sitting ducks for an aggressive enemy.

Undaunted by their setback at Spaatz's hands and the conservatism of the Gun Club, navy flyers solidified their concept of independent carrier air operations during fleet exercises in 1931 and 1932. Naval aviation continued to demonstrate its growing versatility during the remainder of that decade. Carriers conducted cold weather operations first off New England and then the Aleutians. Mass flights of standard service aircraft to remote stations demonstrated the mobility of air power. Although battleships were still seen as the most critical element of sea power, the concept of the independent fast-carrier task force had emerged and was becoming firmly embedded in naval doctrine.[31]

Despite the growing importance of carriers, Moffett pursued a balanced air program. He pushed to place as many float planes as possible on battleships and cruisers. In addition, he insured that the navy also developed a series of long-range flying boats for use as patrol bombers. Either shore-based or supported by seagoing tenders, that program culminated in the introduction of Consolidated's PBY "Catalina" in the mid-1930s. With a range of over two thousand miles, it did yeoman service during World War II.

The most controversial element of Moffett's program involved rigid airships. Altogether, the navy purchased five of the giant lighter-than-air craft in an effort to increase its long-range reconnaissance capabilities. Moffett's penchant for publicity influenced airship operations from the start. Publicity flights tended to dominate their schedules, making it difficult for them to train adequately with the fleet. Moffett, for example, had planned a grandstanding polar flight for one of the navy's rigid airships, but Pres. Calvin Coolidge canceled it in February, 1924. Nonetheless, their technical flaws and operational shortcomings sealed their fate. Three of the giant airships crashed with considerable loss of life, including Moffett, who was killed when the *Akron* was destroyed during a thunderstorm off the New Jersey coast in 1933. The navy was never able to effectively integrate its costly and vulnerable airships into fleet operations. After the *Macon's* destruction off the California coast in 1935 due to structural failure, the navy stopped purchasing rigid airships. However, the service retained its lower profile and less expensive blimp program. The navy's first J-1 blimp had been built in 1922. Intended primarily as training craft, the J-1s proved to be highly serviceable, remaining in the inventory until 1940. More advanced navy blimps played a significant role in the campaign against German submarines during World War II.[32]

The quest for a separate air force preoccupied army airmen throughout the interwar years. Army aviators emerged from World War I relatively young, inexperienced in managing large organizations, and junior in rank. Aside from Billy Mitchell and Benjamin Foulois, most of their key leaders were West Point graduates. They were part of the army's institutional culture that still found it difficult to grapple effectively with the implications of some radical new technologies, especially aviation. Influenced by Maj. Gen. Hugh M. Trenchard of the Royal Air Force, Count Gianni Caproni and Giulio Douhet in Italy, and the strategic bombing attacks mounted by the Royal Navy's Air Service on critical German industrial targets during World War I, influential army aviators came to view the airplane not as a new weapon that would gradually alter the way their service did business, but as a revolutionary technology that would radically transform warfare.

Over time, more and more of them became convinced that such a change first required a separate military service that would concentrate its energies on developing air power's full potential. Not coincidentally, a separate air force would also advance their careers while bringing the professional standing they craved. All of this preceded the development of the official doctrines, technologies, validated international threats to American security, and national policies needed to make their dreams of a separate air force with an independent role in warfare a reality.

Mason Patrick, the most significant army aviation leader of the interwar period, pursued a gradual approach to achieving a separate air force. Although he did not agree with all of the ideas emerging from the Air Corps Tactical School at Langley Field, Virginia (moved to Maxwell Field, Alabama, in 1931), about the paramount role of strategic bombing, he strongly endorsed the school's educational and professional benefits for Air Corps officers. Some of them advocated daylight precision bombing against strategic targets as the decisive factor in future wars. If adopted as official policy, their ideas would have implied a radical reallocation of defense resources and provided the rationale for a separate air force. But those proposals were largely based upon unproven theories and futuristic dreams. While Patrick appreciated the resource implications of that doctrinal position, he did not neglect the army's ground forces. Throughout his tenure as chief of the army's air arm, Patrick strongly supported the development of doctrine that included the attack, pursuit, and observation missions.

Army aviation achieved significant increases in autonomy after the establishment of the Air Corps in 1926. Within the protective umbrella of the army,

airmen quietly built the doctrinal, organizational, and technological foundations of a strong aviation program. Except for the top two positions in the Air
Corps, army airmen controlled their own promotions. Eschewing the flamboyant public confrontations of the Mitchell era, more sophisticated leaders like
Patrick, Frank Andrews, and Henry H. "Hap" Arnold struggled within the War
Department's existing structure to forge the military capabilities that might
eventually justify their longstanding goal of a separate military service. They
recognized that the heart of their task would be to acquire offensive and defensive missions that were not controlled by ground force commanders, develop
aviation doctrine, and field the equipment needed to implement it. They also
developed great skill in using the growing operational capabilities of army aircraft to forge political alliances that assured the Air Corps would play a larger
role in national defense as the threat of war grew in the late 1930s.[33]

Leading Air Corps officers in flying units and at the Air Corps Tactical School
had developed their own distinctive theory of air warfare. Air power, they reasoned, could bypass conventional armies and navies to directly attack enemy
nations. They dismissed earlier concepts featuring terror bombing of enemy populations and the destruction of opposing air forces on the ground as ineffective.
For similar reasons, they rejected the concept of night bombing of enemy cities
and military installations. By 1935, they were espousing a well-developed theory
that mass formations of heavily armed long-range bombers, unescorted by friendly
fighters, could destroy an enemy's will and ability to fight with high-altitude
precision daylight bombing attacks on selected economic and military targets.[34]

Airmen justified strategic bombers as practical and humane instruments of
war capable of surgical precision that would bring victory quickly and cheaply
with minimal risks to the American heartland. Large armies and navies would
be unnecessary. The Air Corps never actually worked out in detail how high-
altitude precision strategic bombing might achieve the promised results even
after it began to receive aircraft that might perform such missions. It lacked the
money and expertise to study the economic vulnerabilities of potential enemies
in detail. The swift pace of technological change and the primitive bombing
campaigns directed against civilians in Ethiopia, Spain, and China during the
1930s allowed Air Corps officers to ignore the apparent shortcomings of their
theories. They discounted the vulnerability of bombers to a new generation of
high-performance fighters and were largely unaware of the implications of a
revolutionary new technology: radar. Above all, they completely underestimated
the resiliency of civilian populations and modern industrial economies in the
face of massive bombing campaigns.[35]

Air Corps funding had flowed into long-range bomber research and development at the expense of other aircraft types. Major General James E. Fechet,

chief of the Air Corps, ordered that bombers be given the highest research and development priority in 1927. Emerging air doctrine and institutional self-interest pointed in that direction. Furthermore, army pilots and engineers doubted the ability of the new monoplane designs associated with the airframe revolution to withstand the stresses of high-speed combat maneuvering by pursuit aircraft. They believed that pursuit aircraft needed external wing braces to perform such sharp turns. Fechet's decision reversed a steady decline in the priority that had been accorded the development of new army bombers in favor of pursuit aircraft since the early 1920s. It helped pave the way for sleek new high-speed bombers in the 1930s. The operational capabilities of those aircraft suggested to Air Corps officers like Hap Arnold that strategic air power would at last possess the weapons it needed to become the decisive form of warfare.

Bombers, which were not called upon to execute such violent combat maneuvers, could be monoplanes. Lacking external braces, which increased drag, gave the new monoplane bombers an added speed advantage over pursuit aircraft. Streamlined fuselages and retractable landing gear further widened the speed gap between bombers and pursuits. The Air Corps's preference for bombers was also encouraged by the growing interest of major American aircraft manufacturers in building long-range commercial airliners. The Boeing B-9, built in 1931, and the Martin B-10, first flown the following year, pioneered the new breed of modern bombers. Their technologies were subsequently incorporated in airliners developed by those firms.

In 1931, the Air Corps secured a mission that justified its enormously expensive efforts to develop modern long-range bombers. Under presidential pressure, Gen. Douglas MacArthur, the army chief of staff, and his navy counterpart, Adm. William V. Pratt, temporarily resolved a ticklish interservice issue when they agreed that the Air Corps would be responsible for mounting all land-based air attacks against enemy invasion fleets. It was something Air Corps leaders had been quietly pressing for since the late 1920s. Although that defensive mission was real enough, army airmen used it as a pretext to develop long-range bombers that could implement their emerging offensive bombardment doctrine.

In 1933, MacArthur gave his airmen more ammunition in their fight to obtain additional bombers. He directed them to establish long-range patrol and bombing squadrons to help defend the Philippines, Hawaii, and the Panama Canal. The Air Corps conducted numerous bombing exercises that refined its operational techniques and influenced its doctrine for coastal defense. Coastal defense also encouraged the Air Corps to obtain long-range navigation equipment and the Norden bombsight for high-altitude precision strikes on key enemy economic, governmental, and military targets.[36]

In the mid-1930s, the General Staff, with navy approval, decided to curb bomber development by deemphasizing the Air Corps's coastal defense role. The navy promptly repudiated the MacArthur-Pratt agreement after the latter retired in 1933. By then, however, multiengine bomber programs were too far advanced to be eliminated entirely, even though the army wanted the Air Corps to refocus its energies on smaller planes that could directly support the ground forces.[37]

Most Air Corps leaders had become convinced that bombers would always be superior in performance to fighters. Coastal defense and other bombing exercises suggested to them that modern bombers organized in tight defensive formations could penetrate enemy defenses and attack their targets with acceptable losses. A small band of officers still championed fighters. Their most outspoken member was Capt. Claire Lee Chennault, who later commanded the famed "Flying Tigers" in China before the United States entered World War II. He bitterly criticized the Air Corps's bomber advocates, claiming that they had ignored the lessons learned about the proper defensive deployment of fighters during maneuvers at Fort Knox, Kentucky, in 1933. As a result of his uncompromising opposition to the bomber orthodoxy of the Air Corps as he saw it, the partially deaf Chennault retired as a bitter and frustrated captain in April, 1937. The Chinese Nationalist government hired him as an aviation adviser later that year and he took command of the American Volunteer Group in 1941. Chennault was recalled to active duty in April, 1942, and commanded the China Air Task Force and, later, the Fourteenth Air Force.[38]

Despite significant organizational and technological strides, the progress of army aviation was called into question in 1934. President Roosevelt, responding to charges that commercial airlines were monopolizing airmail contracts, canceled existing agreements that year and asked the Air Corps to fill the gap. Without first consulting his superior, General MacArthur, or his principal operational deputy, Colonel Spaatz, Air Corp's head Maj. Gen. Benjamin D. Foulois accepted the new mission. He wanted to showcase the capabilities of his airmen and build support for larger Air Corps appropriations. The result was a bloody fiasco. Air Corps's pilots were ill trained and poorly equipped for night and instrument flying. The winter of 1934 was the worst on record in the United States. After numerous crashes and twelve deaths, the Air Corps was relieved of the airmail assignment in May.

Congress and the media concluded that Foulois was personally responsible for the noncompetitive nature of the Air Corps's aircraft procurement and that those practices had led to the sorry performance of army aviation. Despite heroic lobbying efforts by its leaders, the Air Corps's 1926 expansion program had never been fully funded. A shortage of procurement funds, not a lack of proper management or personal integrity, was responsible for the Air Corps's poor

An Army Air Corps pilot accepts a letter from a civilian at March Field, California, in 1934. Despite the smiles in this publicity photo, the Air Corps's effort to carry the mail at the request of Pres. Franklin D. Roosevelt's administration was a bloody fiasco that exposed many shortcomings in army aviation. (U.S. Air Force photo collection, National Archives.)

showing, flying the mail in the winter of 1934. As a result of the airmail debacle, a congressional subcommittee was appointed to investigate the War Department's aircraft procurement programs. The committee ignored audited evidence that the aviation industry was not making excessive profits on army contracts, and instead retreated to the traditional Capitol Hill explanation for military aircraft procurement troubles: conspiracy, collusion, and violation of free competition. Progressives and isolationists ravaged the politically weak aviation industry during the early New Deal. For them, the airmail crisis symbolized the corrupt manipulation of the American economy by a few wealthy corporations and the dashed popular hopes that aviation would rescue the mythic American individualist from the inroads of modern industrialism.[39]

Foulois had seriously undermined his own cause. Over the years, his intemperate claims, constant complaints, and willingness to appeal to Congress and the public outside the chain of command had alienated much of official Washington. He was blamed for the airmail fiasco and forced to retire. In April, 1934, Secretary of War George H. Dern appointed a special board headed by Newton D. Baker to investigate the Air Corps's performance in the airmail crisis. President Roosevelt subsequently appointed a Federal Aviation Commission, led by newspaper editor Clark Howell, to examine all aspects of American aviation policy. Both bodies endorsed negotiated military aircraft procurement contracts. Because of the Great Depression, there was enormous pressure to spread federal funds around as widely as possible. Furthermore, isolationists had portrayed negotiated aircraft procurement contracts as proof of the continuing insidious influence of the "merchants of death," which the former blamed for America's entry into World War I. The president was well attuned politically to all those political currents and was unwilling to swim against them. The result was that the army and navy were forced to conduct separate costly and time-consuming price competitions for prototypes and production aircraft.[40]

Rear Admiral Ernest J. King, chief of the Bureau of Aeronautics from 1933–36, estimated that, because of the small number of aircraft being ordered each year during the mid-1930s, manufacturers were probably making less than 10 percent profit on their planes. Nevertheless, the Air Corps and navy were generally able to manipulate the system to get the aircraft they wanted within the limits of congressional appropriations.[41] Brigadier Gen. Benjamin S. Kelsey, who headed the development of Air Corps fighter aircraft from 1934–43 stressed that the new system "satisfied Congress and worked quite well [for the military services]. We were never forced to buy whatever was cheapest, and, in general got the best."[42]

The Baker Board also rejected the idea that an independent air force would solve the problems revealed by the airmail crisis. However, it endorsed a proposal approved by the War Department in 1933 to establish a separate air headquarters that would supervise the training and operations of air combat units not directly tied to the army's ground forces. The organization, which Patrick had proposed in the early 1920s, pleased army flyers because it placed a consolidated air striking force under the command of a senior aviator. The General Staff was satisfied because it preserved War Department control over aviation while mollifying the restless aviators. The new organization was established on March 1, 1935, at Langley Field, Virginia, as the General Headquarters Air Force (GHQ Air Force) under Brig. Gen. Frank M. Andrews, a highly respected aviator. All Air Corps pursuit, bombardment, and attack units in the continental United States were assigned to it.[43]

In August, 1935, an aircraft appeared that promised to make the GHQ Air Force's independent air power mission a reality. That month, Boeing's Model

299 competed for an Air Corps long-range bomber production contract. Although the four-engine Model 299 was clearly superior to its twin-engine rivals, the Boeing entry lost after it crashed on takeoff during a test flight at Wright Field, Ohio. The Douglas B-18 won the award, but the Air Corps had been so impressed by the Model 299's performance that it ordered several aircraft for experimental purposes. Later designated the B-17 "Flying Fortress," it became one of the mainstays of the Army Air Forces' strategic bombing campaigns during World War II.[44]

After Gen. Malin Craig became chief of staff in October, 1935, he rejected the Air Corps's request to spend most of its procurement funds on long-range bombers like the B-17. Instead, Craig stressed the procurement of smaller, less expensive aircraft for use in the ground support and air defense roles.[45] A limited number of experimental B-17s was obtained from 1936–38. Nevertheless, army airmen believed that the aircraft's debut marked the turning point in the doctrinal battle. It gave army airmen a plane that was actually capable of testing their strategic bombardment ideas and justifying a separate air force because of its independent role in warfare.[46]

The General Staff continued to emphasize the need for aircraft that could directly support the ground forces, while the navy sought to reassert its monopoly on long-range coastal patrol activities. Congress and the public had little enthusiasm for weapons that suggested America might adopt an offensive strategy that could kill large numbers of unarmed civilians. Consequently, only thirteen B-17s had been delivered to the Air Corps when war erupted in Europe.[47]

In the Air Corps, General Foulois's forced retirement in 1935 had placed officers with more sophisticated ideas about promoting air power into positions of authority. They avoided public confrontations with senior army and navy leaders. Convinced that an independent air force was unrealistic and unattainable at that time, they focused on developing an effective unified air strike force under the GHQ Air Force. Possessing a sophisticated understanding of politics and the media, they took every opportunity to garner positive publicity for the Air Corps by displaying its growing capabilities and professionalism. They also worked hard to build close personal and professional ties with industry leaders including Donald W. Douglas Sr., Glenn Martin, Robert Gross, and Jack Northrop. Arnold was especially adept at cultivating personal relationships with key aviation and movie-industry leaders and members of the press.

President Roosevelt had begun speaking openly about the need for the United States to be prepared to fight against two potential enemies, Germany and Japan, so the GHQ Air Force prepared to defend both of the nation's coasts simultaneously. In 1938, Lt. Col. Ira C. Eaker played a central role in publicizing maneuvers intended to demonstrate the army air arm's growing coastal defense capabilities. To impress the public and top government officials, the GHQ Air Force dispatched three B-17s to intercept the Italian passenger liner, *Rex* seven hundred miles off the East Coast. Eaker arranged for a live radio broadcast of the event by an NBC announcer, as well as photographs and newspaper coverage.

The navy, which had claimed that nobody could find ships that far from shore, pressured the army to drastically curtail such flights. General Craig limited them to a hundred miles beyond America's coastlines in May, 1938, hurting the case for buying additional B-17s. Undaunted, the GHQ Air Force staged long-distance demonstration flights to Latin America. Although the Air Corps was desperate to purchase additional B-17s, the War Department rejected its requests, focusing instead on shorter-range bombers and fighters designed to support the ground forces. Consequently, only forty B-17s were on order in 1938, and none of them were due to be delivered until the following year.[48]

GATHERING STORMS

The Great Depression and the rise of totalitarian states destroyed the postwar international order undermining the assumptions upon which American military policy was based. Japan's military-dominated government established a puppet state in Manchuria in 1931 and invaded China six years later. Adolf Hitler came to power by constitutional means in 1933. In 1935, he renounced the Treaty of Versailles and declared that Germany would rearm. Hitler remilitarized the Rhineland in 1936, annexed Austria in 1938, and gobbled up Czechoslovakia in 1938–39. The Italians extended their empire in Africa and teamed up with the Germans to support the fascists in Spain's civil war. The Axis coalition of Germany, Italy, and Japan undermined the existing world order while the Western democracies and the Soviet Union unsuccessfully attempted to appease them.

President Roosevelt's cautious efforts to awaken the American people to the dangers of the gathering storms overseas were largely unsuccessful at first. Reflecting the public's aversion to foreign wars, Congress passed a series of neutrality acts in the mid-1930s to prevent government and private assistance to potential belligerents. Driven by the fiscal orthodoxy of his day, Roosevelt, like his predecessor Herbert Hoover, had initially cut government spending to erase the budget deficit caused by the depression. As late as 1938, military planners concluded that there was no political support and precious little money for any strategy except hemispheric defense. While the threat of global war mounted, the United States held to its traditional unilateralism, neutrality, and defense of the Western Hemisphere.

Army Air Corps B-17s based at Mitchell Field on Long Island, New York, intercept the Italian ocean liner *Rex* at sea, on May 12, 1938. By successfully locating the ship 725 miles east of New York City, army airmen sought to demonstrate that their sleek new bombers could intercept and destroy hostile fleets far from the nation's shores. Widely covered by the press and radio, the flight was seen by senior army and navy leaders as an effort to create public and congressional pressure to purchase more Flying Fortresses at the expense of conventional surface forces. (U.S. Air Force photo courtesy Air Force Historical Support Office.)

The development of air power had little impact upon American strategic planning until the second half of the 1930s. Prior to that time, military planners had focused on combined arms assaults, not air attacks, on the United States. In 1938, army and navy planners began considering the threat of attacks on the American homeland from either ocean or both simultaneously due to the increasing militancy of Germany and Japan. They feared that the Germans might establish air bases in South America that could threaten vital U.S. interests, including the Panama Canal and the New England–New York–Norfolk area. On the West Coast, aircraft factories were considered especially vulnerable to attacks by Japanese naval aviation. In 1939, American military officers started developing a series of color-coded "Rainbow" war plans to deal with the various contingencies the nation might face. The critical roles played by the Luftwaffe and the RAF in the European war, which began when Germany attacked Poland on September 1, 1939, greatly intensified the growing American emphasis on air power. In 1942–43, a plan called "Rainbow 5" became the basis of the U.S. strategy of fighting a global coalition war against Germany, Italy, and Japan.

Regardless of the state of war planning, budget cuts inspired by the depression had undermined the U.S. Navy's fleet operations, maintenance, and personnel levels in the early 1930s. Warship tonnages also remained below authorized treaty limits to save money. The army found itself in an even more precarious position. It was held at half strength and all of its elements were in a sorry state of readiness as it entered the 1930s. The United States launched a modest rearmament effort in 1933 that focused on shipbuilding and aircraft construction. Roosevelt sought to use those programs to deter Japanese adventurism. However, as usual, they were also driven by domestic political and economic considerations.

The initial pressure for increased military spending came from Capitol Hill, not the White House. Carl Vinson, an influential Georgia congressman, ensured that the navy and Air Corps received significant sums from the National Recovery Administration (NRA) and the Works Projects Administration (WPA). Naval aviation was given a major boost in March, 1934, when Congress passed the Vinson-Trammel Act. Designed primarily to build the navy's surface warships and submarines up to treaty limits by 1942, the legislation permitted the sea service to add 650 planes to its existing thousand-aircraft program.[49]

The United States began a serious naval rearmament program in January, 1938, in response to Japan's renunciation of naval arms limitation treaties in 1936 and its invasion of China the following year. Prodded by President Roosevelt and Representative Vinson, Congress passed the Naval Expansion Act, which approved spending $1.1 billion over ten years to expand the fleet beyond treaty limits. Among other things, the legislation approved the construction of two more carriers and several seaplane tenders. It also authorized naval aviation to expand to three thousand aircraft, nearly doubling its size. Meanwhile, the aircraft carriers USS *Yorktown* and USS *Enterprise* had been commissioned in 1937 and 1938 respectively. Construction of both vessels had been initiated in 1934 with WPA funds.[50]

While a political triumph for the navy, the legislation was a slap in the face for the army, which had to make do with an increased authorization of only $17 million. The Air Corps got nothing at all. That enraged army airmen who were convinced that their new B-17 bombers were superior to battleships and aircraft carriers as the nation's first line of defense. They argued that the naval rearmament program was designed to promote an interventionist foreign policy but failed to sidetrack it on Capitol Hill.[51]

By 1938, a new generation of naval aircraft was in service that reflected the technological strides associated with the airframe revolution. Like the latest army aircraft, they were all-metal monoplanes with enclosed cockpits, retractable landing gear, and powerful engines generating nearly a thousand horsepower. Among them was the Douglas TBD "Devastator." The Devastator marked the return of torpedo bombers as a major component of U.S. carrier air groups. Although torpedoes had been the main weapons of strike aircraft in the early 1920s, the dive-bomber had largely eclipsed them by the decade's end. The Devastator was the first all-metal, low-wing monoplane assigned to American naval aviation. Armed with a thousand-pound torpedo, it could severely damage and possibly destroy a battleship if its "fish" struck below the waterline.

The modernization of carrier aircraft had proceeded more slowly than the navy desired for several reasons. They were unique aircraft requiring specialized designs so they could operate at sea, and the service purchased relatively small numbers of them each year. The aircraft were designed to carry heavy loads and required extensive testing and some modifications. The new monoplane designs featured retractable or semiretractable landing gear that had to be adapted for the heavy stresses of carrier landings. The navy's policy of purchasing only small numbers of a particular aircraft model or series also delayed the delivery of planes to operational squadrons. However, that policy was intentionally applied so that the service could promote continuing technological progress in the industry while keeping some of the most modern aircraft in the fleet at all times.

The strategic assumptions behind the 1938 naval rearmament program were that, in the event of a future war with Japan and Germany, the United States would concentrate on a blockade of the Japanese home islands. The Royal Navy would control the Atlantic while Britain and France would handle a resurgent Germany on the continent. However, the rearmament program failed to give the U.S. Navy any real superiority over its most likely adversary, Japan. The latter had authorized its first carrier, the *Hosho,* prior to the Washington Naval Conference. In the late 1920s, the Japanese had completed converting two battle-cruiser hulls into carriers, just as the United States had done. During that same period, the Japanese had begun employing their own aircraft designs in fleet operations rather than relying on foreign types. They also deployed shore-based naval aircraft and embarked floatplanes on battleships and cruisers.

By 1930, Japan boasted as many carriers as the United States, although its were slower and carried fewer aircraft. The Japanese naval air force began to expand early in the decade, keeping pace with the United States. An additional carrier was launched in 1933. After renouncing its adherence to all treaty limitations in 1936 so that it could overcome its inferiority to the U.S. and British fleets, Japan embarked on a major naval expansion program. It launched two additional carriers in 1936 and 1937. Four seaplane tenders joined those warships between 1936 and 1939. Borrowing from the U.S. Navy, the Japanese consolidated all of their carriers into one organization in 1938. During the late 1930s, a series of sleek new aircraft also entered service with the Japanese Imperial Navy including the *Kate* (Type 97) and *Val* (Type 99) torpedo and dive-bombers.

The American military establishment had closely monitored the progress of Japanese naval and military aviation through intelligence reports that were reasonably accurate and generally free of racial stereotypes beginning in the mid-1930s. Lieutenant Commander Ralph A. Ostie began reporting from Tokyo in 1935 that Japanese flyers were very capable.[52] Claire Chennault, who Chiang Kai-shek had employed to train the Chinese air force, wrote that flight tests of a captured Japanese Type 96 demonstrated it was "one of the most up-to-date pursuit airplanes in the world."[53] But such reports had little impact on military planners and senior leaders. In 1937, Rear Adm. Harry E. Yarnell, commander of the U.S. Asiatic Fleet, boasted that Japanese "aviation is strictly inferior to ours. A few of our well-trained squadrons would drive their planes out of the air . . . in a short time."[54] Intelligence officers were poorly regarded within the U.S. armed forces. More significantly, myths about Japanese racial inferiority were deeply entrenched in the minds of many American officers.[55]

The emergence of naval aviation in Japan and the United States had a major international impact on conventional warship designs. With the expiration of the Washington naval treaties in 1936, the leading naval powers began replacing their aging battle fleets. While none of them considered building more carriers at the expense of battleships, new warships were designed with defense against air attack in mind. American and British battleships featured thick armored decks and heavy complements of antiaircraft guns. Cruisers were designed with antiaircraft guns as their main armament to help protect fleets against air attack. New destroyers mounted dual-purpose guns capable of use against both ships and aircraft. Fleet exercises by the U.S. Navy from the mid-1930s onward produced valuable experience in conducting carrier strikes against shore bases and in defending against them. Carriers also learned to operate behind inner screens of heavy cruisers armed with antiaircraft guns defending against air attacks and outer screens of light cruisers protecting them from surface threats. The crews of patrol aircraft were trained to detect enemy submarines soon enough to force them to remain submerged if they did not destroy them.

Throughout its long history, the Marine Corps had learned to identify new missions in order to survive. Its aviators were strongly influenced by the institutional culture produced by that history. They firmly linked themselves in the 1930s to the Corps's emerging mission of seizing and holding enemy bases during amphibious operations. However, the emergence of high-performance fighters equipped with inadequate two-way radios made it increasingly difficult to provide effective close air support for the ground forces. Since they had to obtain aircraft and related equipment from the navy, marine aviators had to accept the secondary missions of preparing for carrier operations and defending naval bases. As a result, preparation for the primary amphibious mission suffered. The necessity of balancing the competing demands of their own ground-oriented generals and the carrier admirals retarded the development of marine aviation. It remained a poor relation to its more glamorous naval cousin.[56]

NEUTRALITY AND HEMISPHERIC DEFENSE

While the navy began to rearm in response to the deteriorating international situation, Air Corps modernization programs failed to keep pace. When Maj. Gen. George C. Marshall became head of the army's influential War Plans Division in the summer of 1938, the airmen found him to be receptive to their ideas about air power, including strategic bombing. They also educated him on the realities of America's limited aircraft production capacity and other factors slowing the development of military aviation. Marshall became convinced that air power would play a critical role in the war he was sure was coming, and soon. He became a strong supporter of Air Corps expansion and modernization.

Marshall also gained an appreciation of the outstanding abilities of some of the Air Corps's leaders before he became army chief of staff in September, 1939. Two years later, he gave Frank Andrews command of all air and ground units in the Caribbean Defense Command, which was responsible for the most important U.S. overseas possession: the Panama Canal. For a brief time in early 1942, an airman held every major overseas army command. Those critical assignments illustrated the significance that Marshall attached to air power and the abilities of his senior aviators as the United States went to war.

The Munich crisis in September, 1938, marked a turning point for the Air Corps. When Hitler threatened to use the German air force against his opponents, the British and the French caved in to his demands and forced the Czechs to accept them. The Germans annexed the Sudetenland in western Czechoslovakia, which was home to a large ethnic German population, leaving what was left virtually defenseless. Hitler seized the remainder of that hapless nation the following March. The Luftwaffe demonstrated that air power had become a potent factor in international relations—at least as an instrument of blackmail.

Charles Lindbergh was skeptical about any nation's ability to defeat Germany. He enjoyed an enormous international reputation as an aviation expert. Working with the U.S. military attaché in Berlin, he had begun sending detailed secret reports to Washington in 1936 describing the alarming technical and operational strides the Luftwaffe was making. But Lindbergh failed to grasp that the German airmen were building a tactical organization designed to support the army, not a strategic bombing force. The Germans, meanwhile, encouraged such exaggerated estimates of their military strength, especially air power. The French and British governments began pressuring the United States to increase its military aircraft production rapidly to deter Hitler or, if war came, to enable them to defeat him without U.S. military intervention.

Journalists had given extensive coverage to the role of air power during wars in Ethiopia, Spain, and China, as well as air raid preparations in European capitals earlier in the decade. Air raid precautions had become a part of daily life. European elites became increasingly preoccupied with the concept of an aerial "knockout blow" by bombers in a war's opening stages, despite abundant evidence that this had never happened and was unlikely to occur in the foreseeable future. Aviation carried a special mystique that contributed to a tendency to exaggerate its role in warfare. Many of the era's popular heroes, like Rickenbacker and Lindbergh, were aviators. Moreover, there was a widespread belief, encouraged by both the airmen and pioneer aircraft makers like Glenn Curtiss and Donald Douglas, that the nature of war and the relationship of civilian populations to it had changed dramatically because of the bomber's emergence as a potent weapon. In fact, only Great Britain and the United States were actually committed to developing strategic air forces that could lay waste to large cities and modern industrial complexes.

As the threat of another world war increased, American attitudes about air power remained ambivalent. Its advocates were convinced that a strong military aviation program could deter aggression against the United States and insure a quick, relatively bloodless, and decisive victory if war came. Detractors believed that air power's limited utility would insure restricted use in the event of an armed conflict. The possibility of a serious aerial attack on the American mainland was seen as unlikely by both sides.[57]

President Roosevelt, a former assistant navy secretary, yachtsman, and avid collector of ship models, had long championed a strong fleet as the nation's primary military arm. However, influenced by elite political opinion on both sides of the Atlantic about the growing potency of military aviation, FDR became more air power conscious. The president, certain that the Anglo-French capitulation at Munich had been caused by fear of the Luftwaffe, decided that aviation was the panacea for America's growing security problems. He was convinced that it could serve as a powerful instrument of deterrence and diplomacy. Consequently, Roosevelt convened a secret meeting of his top civilian and military advisers at the White House on November 14, 1938, to consider the nation's aviation needs in the wake of the Munich crisis. The president shocked some of his military advisers when he announced that, for the sake of hemispheric defense, the Air Corps would expand its inventory of eight hundred modern aircraft to twenty thousand at a cost of $500 million. He wanted to increase the American aviation industry's production capacity to twenty-four thousand military aircraft a year. The president was also determined to allocate a significant portion of those aircraft to strengthen the British and French against Hitler, to the dismay of some U.S. military leaders, especially Maj. Gen. Hap Arnold, who had been appointed chief of the Air Corps in September, 1938.

The president, meanwhile, virtually ignored the far more serious shortcomings of the ground forces and the fact that an effective air force required a great deal more than a lot of shiny new planes. For its part, the Air Corps was desperately short of trained personnel, bases, supplies, and support equipment. Roosevelt rejected the idea of building up the ground forces. In January, 1939, Congress significantly scaled back FDR's request, appropriating $300 million for the Air Corps while authorizing it to raise its inventory to fifty-five hundred aircraft, including 3,251 new ones. The Air Corps's authorized pilot strength was increased by three thousand. Those changes were justified by growing fears that Germany might establish air bases in South America.

By most measures of modern air power, the Air Corps was well behind the other major powers, which had launched rearmament programs in the mid-1930s. The most immediate problem limiting Air Corps expansion in 1939 was a severe shortage of trained personnel. Its strength was approximately 26,000 men. At that point, the RAF had approximately 100,000 personnel while the Luftwaffe boasted more than 500,000. The Air Corps's inventory of modern aircraft stood at about 800 versus 1,900 for the RAF and 4,100 for the Luftwaffe. The qualitative inferiority of most of its aircraft exacerbated the numerical gap. Only its B-17 bombers were superior to their foreign counterparts, but the Air Corps had few of them in its inventory. That technical superiority had been gained at the expense of fighters and attack aircraft.[58]

Spearheaded by coordinated air and armored attacks, Germany invaded Poland on September 1, 1939, and quickly overwhelmed the Poles. Great Britain and France then declared war on Hitler's Third Reich. The Soviet Union grabbed what was left of Poland from the east while the German's were making short work of her in the west. World War II had begun. Then Europe lapsed into several months of relative military inactivity known as the "phony war." The United States responded with cautious declarations of neutrality, then gradually shifted to support of those nations actively opposing Germany and Japan. President Roosevelt also ordered the navy to establish a "neutrality patrol" in the Atlantic with its ships and aircraft. He then declared a limited national emergency that extended those patrols into the Caribbean and around the Philippines. Convinced that the American public would not support any more sweeping measures and that the western European democracies could defeat Hitler without U.S. military involvement, the president asked Congress only for funds to improve the readiness of the regular army and navy so that they could defend the Western Hemisphere.

In November, 1939, Roosevelt convinced Capitol Hill to revise the neutrality acts to permit arms sales to European belligerents on a "cash-and-carry" basis. That had favored the British and French at the expense of the Germans because the latter could not contend with the Royal Navy. In March, 1941, the president persuaded Congress to pass the Lend-Lease Act, which enabled the United States to send massive munitions aid to Britain despite the fact that she could no longer pay for it. Lend-lease assistance subsequently was extended to China, the Soviet Union, and other nations that fought against the Axis alliance of Germany, Japan, and Italy that was formed in September, 1940. America supplied more than forty-two thousand American aircraft to Allied nations during the war.[59]

While the United States was mobilizing its industrial resources to aid those resisting the Germans while officially remaining neutral, General Arnold moved to develop an air defense system because of the Luftwaffe's early combat successes. Air defense had not been a priority in the bomber-oriented Air Corps before the war. In 1930, the Air Corps had conducted inconclusive experiments at Aberdeen, Maryland, with a rudimentary air defense warning system that relied on ground observers using radios or telephones to relay aircraft sightings to a central command post. Another round of inconclusive tests employing ground observers was conducted at Fort Knox, Kentucky, three years later. Both sets of exercises were hindered by the reliance on ground observers and the absence of reliable two-way airborne radios.

Experiments were also conducted with acoustical, infrared, and radio-wave detectors. Radar (short for radio detection and ranging) ultimately emerged as the technological response to the early warning problem. It was based on German scientist Heinrich Hertz's discovery in the 1880s that a radio beam striking a dense object is reflected. If a receiver located at the beam's origin captures the beam, it can then be analyzed to determine how far away the object is because radio waves travel at the speed of light, which does not vary. The direction from which the radio energy was received is then used to determine the distant object's bearing. Guglielmo Marconi, an Italian, developed the first radio device for detection purposes in the 1920s. By the early 1930s, the United States, Germany, and Great Britain were conducting radar research and development programs. The Germans initially deployed superior radar devices on surface warships, and the British began deploying radar in a network along the English Channel in 1937. The RAF radar stations were effective because they were integrated into an air defense system that brought together relevant data in centralized command posts. There, trained experts analyzed it, made informed decisions about which threats were the most dangerous, and then directed the appropriate fighter and antiaircraft artillery units to deal with them.

Two-way radios were critical components of integrated air defense systems. The U.S. Army Signal Corps began experimenting with voice radio in 1907. It sent its first radio message from an aircraft in 1910 and began experimenting with airborne communications by the end of the decade. In 1916, the navy began experimenting with aircraft radios but did not order them for single-seat fighters until 1932. Motivated by General Mitchell's interest in cross-country flying, the army had begun to build a system of radio ground stations in 1923 that provided air-to-ground as well as point-to-point land communications and weather information. However, only thirty-three of those stations had been built by 1933, and the system for linking them together was extremely poor. Pilots were reluctant to use existing radios because of their poor quality and weight. Until aircraft engines were modified in the mid-1930s to prevent ignition interference, airborne radio reception was difficult and frequently impossible. Complex radio wiring often caused aircraft fires, and early radios were so heavy that they were responsible for significant reductions in aircraft payloads and fuel supplies. Consequently, many pilots became so hostile to radios that they actually tossed them overboard in flight and later reported that the sets had been lost in accidents. Nearly all of those problems were solved during the 1930s. By 1939, most U.S. combat aircraft were equipped with reliable two-way radios that enabled them to communicate with each other, their bases, and surface forces. Improved communications did as much as anything else to change the conduct of air operations during the interwar period.

By the end of the 1930s, Air Corps leaders had concluded that a limited air defense system was feasible and could hinder, if not defeat, a strong bombing campaign. However, because they failed to understand the offensive and defensive implications of the emerging radar technology and were wedded to the strategic bomber, the United States had not even begun to build a continental air defense system when war erupted in Europe. In February, 1940, fearing that the Germans might somehow find a way to attack the U.S. mainland with aircraft launched from submarines or bombers based in the Western Hemisphere, General Arnold established a command to deploy and test air defense systems in the northeastern United States. Severe shortages of aircraft, antiaircraft artillery, radar, radios, and trained personnel undercut the effort to build a unified system.

GERMANY FIRST

Meanwhile, the "phony war" in Europe had not lasted long. In the spring of 1940, Germany rapidly conquered Norway, Denmark, Holland, Belgium, Luxembourg, and France. The stunning Nazi "blitzkrieg" galvanized American public opinion to support radical improvements in the nation's defenses. Military leaders realized that the tacit assumption that the major European democracies could defeat Germany without direct American military intervention had been shattered. Nevertheless, the American people remained deeply divided over the issue of armed U.S. intervention overseas. A majority were still isolationists. Limited by deep divisions in public opinion, FDR and Congress moved cautiously ahead.

The most controversial defense initiatives were designed to expand the army's ground forces. From September, 1940, through June, 1941, the National Guard, consisting of nearly three hundred thousand men, was mobilized. At the beginning of the call-up, Congress authorized the nation's first peacetime draft. Draftees, volunteers, and recalled guardsmen and reservists swelled the army's strength to 1.2 million personnel by the summer of 1941.

Underscoring his faith in air power, Roosevelt also called for the annual production of fifty thousand military aircraft in 1940. The army would get 36,500 of them, while the rest would go to the navy and Marine Corps. The president apparently pulled that number out of thin air. It was a dramatic gesture rather than a concrete goal based upon a careful consideration of the needs of the U.S. armed forces and Great Britain. Although it appeared to be hopelessly unrealistic at the time, Roosevelt's initiative stimulated popular support for the military buildup, pressured industry to rapidly expand production, and compelled conservative military planners to think big. The long-term effect of the president's initiative was to commit the nation early on to a massive wartime aviation program that enabled it to adopt a general air-power strategy that played a crucial role in securing victory. Instead of primarily concentrating on strategic bombing or tactical support of armies and navies as other major powers did during World War II, the Anglo-American Allies fielded air forces that accomplished both missions on a global scale while devoting enormous resources to airlift, reconnaissance, air defense, and antisubmarine warfare.

Roosevelt was determined to furnish significant numbers of new American aircraft to the British to help keep them in the war. General Arnold strongly opposed that policy because it undermined his efforts to eliminate severe shortages of modern equipment in the army's rapidly expanding air arm. The president, whose strategic instincts proved to be sound, warned Arnold that he could be replaced if he continued to resist. That year the American aircraft industry had barely begun to expand. After much foot-dragging, the major aircraft manufacturers agreed to begin enlarging their production facilities. The federal government financed most of that plant construction.[60]

Congress, meanwhile, appropriated $4 billion in the summer of 1940 for a massive shipbuilding program that included eighteen of the new *Essex*-class aircraft carriers. It also raised the navy's authorized strength to 14,500 aircraft. The Marine Corps was allocated 10 percent of that figure. At the time, the navy had only 2,965 pilots and 1,741 aircraft. America's growing emphasis on air power was also underscored by governmental approval that year of the army's request to increase the authorized strength of its air arm to seventy-eight hundred combat aircraft.

Before war erupted in Europe, the Army-Navy Joint Planning Committee had begun examining existing national strategy in light of the deteriorating international situation. They had developed a series of five color-coded Rainbow plans to deal with a range of contingencies instead of merely focusing on defending the Western Hemisphere against a single enemy. From January to March, 1941, the planners met secretly with their British counterparts to develop the broad outlines of a coalition strategy against the Axis if the United States entered the war. The Americans had already concluded that Germany must be defeated first because it was the most powerful member of the Axis. The British shared that judgment. The resulting "ABC-1 Staff Agreement" presented a coalition military strategy that was consistent with the policies of both nations. Although the president never formally approved the agreement, army and navy planners used it to work out the details of a "Germany First" strategy in Rainbow 5, a war plan that emerged during the summer of 1941.

Air power had not played a major role in earlier Rainbow plans. However, Germany's conquest of France radically changed things. The planners recognized that, for the time being, strategic bombing and a naval blockade would be the only ways to weaken Germany prior to an invasion of continental Europe. According to Rainbow 5, U.S. air forces would contain Japan in the Pacific, protect the Western Hemisphere, and help defeat Germany before engaging in offensive operations against Japan. Under the pretext of defending neutral rights,

Roosevelt had expanded the U.S. Navy's surface and air patrols in the Atlantic after the ABC talks. As a result, American sailors found themselves in an undeclared war against German submarines in late 1941.[61]

Meanwhile, the frenzied expansion of military aviation had to rely on training and equipping young men who had no intention of making the armed forces a career. Many of them had never been far from home, and most had never even ridden in an airplane. The vast majority of airmen who shouldered the burdens of combat during World War II would be citizen-soldiers, not professionals. By July, 1945, only some 4,000 of the army air arm's approximately 374,000 rated officers were members of the regular army. The rest were reservists, guardsmen, and wartime volunteers. Reservists also played an important role in the rapid prewar expansion of naval aviation. When Rear Adm. John Towers took charge of the Bureau of Aeronautics in 1939, naval aviation, like its army counterpart, had far too little equipment and trained personnel to deal with the growing challenges to U.S. security. Recognizing that it would have to rely on reservists to build up naval aviation if the deteriorating international situation brought America into the war, Congress passed the Naval Reserve Act of 1939 based on proposals submitted by Towers. By war's end, 83 percent of the fleet's manpower, including the vast majority of its aviators and support ratings, were reservists.[62]

Following France's defeat in the spring of 1940, Hitler wanted to invade England. However, the Luftwaffe failed to overcome the RAF in the Battle of Britain that summer, making a cross-channel invasion impossible. The führer then turned his attention to the east. Convinced that Germany could quickly dispatch Joseph Stalin's communist empire, his armed forces invaded the Soviet Union in June, 1941. The bulk of Germany's air and ground forces were concentrated on the eastern front for the rest of the war. Hitler's strategic miscalculation gave Britain and the United States time to mobilize their superior economies and build up their armed forces. His blunder also afforded them the freedom of action to seize the initiative in the west.

Hitler's fundamental error led to an equally disastrous set of Japanese blunders. Freed of the threat of war with the Soviet Union, Japanese leaders prepared to conquer the resource-rich European colonies in Southeast Asia. They knew that this would put them on a collision course with the United States, but Japanese leaders reasoned that after they had won their own short war of conquest, they could build an impregnable chain of air and sea bases in the Pacific while the Americans and British exhausted themselves against Germany. The Japanese plans included surprise attacks on U.S. military forces and possessions in the Pacific.

After Germany invaded the Soviet Union, President Roosevelt asked the army and navy to prepare estimates on what resources would be needed to destroy the Axis. The resulting "Victory Program," completed in September, 1941, served as a blueprint for the military force the United States built when it went to war. The army's estimates called for a wartime force of 8.7 million uniformed personnel, including 2 million in the air arm. Air Corps planners had hastily prepared an aviation supplement to the plan. Known as AWPD-1, it proposed a huge aviation program that spelled out the details of a general air-power strategy for the United States. Although emphasizing strategic air bombardment, the army's air arm would also support the ground forces during an invasion of Europe, provide for defense of the Western Hemisphere, and help block further Japanese aggression in the Pacific. To accomplish this, the airmen asked for 61,799 aircraft, including 37,000 trainers and 11,800 combat aircraft organized in 239 combat groups.

The navy's parallel planning effort to the Victory Program, developed in isolation from the army, was essentially a rehash of its 1940 plan with additions that were made the following year. However, the naval planners changed the rationale for their proposed force structure. Although the 1940 plan had been predicated on the navy's ability to conduct offensive operations in one ocean while staying on the defensive in another, its 1941 version advocated a fleet strong enough to conduct simultaneous offensives in both the Atlantic and the Pacific. Those estimates included thirty-two battleships and twenty-four aircraft carriers, plus numerous destroyers, submarines, and cruisers. The authorized ceiling of fifteen thousand naval aircraft remained in effect.

To keep pace with its explosive prewar growth and foster greater control of its own destiny, the Air Corps was reorganized and officially renamed the U.S. Army Air Forces (USAAF) on June 20, 1941.[63] That change was part of a larger reorganization of the entire army. Then, on March 9, 1942, the army was reorganized again, this time putting the USAAF on an equal footing with the ground and service forces. Generals Marshall and Arnold agreed that, in return for the airmen suspending their behind-the-scenes lobbying for a separate air force until the war was over, the USAAF would enjoy organizational autonomy within the army. Arnold was convinced that greater freedom from control by ground generals was essential to mounting effective air campaigns against the Axis. He also believed it would enable airmen to build a stronger case for their own separate service once victory was won.

America gradually edged toward armed confrontation after Germany invaded the Soviet Union. By September, 1941, the navy found itself in an undeclared shooting war with German submarines in the Atlantic after it began escorting merchant ships as far east as Iceland. The following month, German submarines attacked the USS *Kearny* and sank the USS *Reuben James*. To help counter the growing German submarine threat, individual Coast Guard cutters and units were assigned to the navy during the spring of 1941. On November 1, the rest of the Coast Guard was assigned to the navy, including nine air stations and fifty-six aircraft.

In the Pacific, President Roosevelt moved the fleet from the West Coast to its unfinished base at Pearl Harbor in 1940 to deter the Japanese. The president removed the navy's senior operational commander, Adm. James O. Richardson, after the latter complained too strongly that the fleet was dangerously exposed to attack at its unfinished base in Hawaii. Ignoring American warnings, the Japanese occupied portions of French Indochina in mid-1941. The president immediately froze Japanese assets, embargoed oil shipments to Japan, and strengthened America's Philippine defenses. The Japanese responded by planning a daring attack on the U.S. Pacific Fleet by carrier-based aircraft of its Combined Fleet.

Prompted by ambiguous political reports and radio intercepts, U.S. officials feared a Japanese attack in the Pacific but they were uncertain about when and where it might occur. The dangers posed by that ambiguity were compounded by the army's and navy's unwillingness to cooperate on building an effective joint air defense system for Hawaii. The destruction of most of the U.S. battle fleet and land-based air power in Hawaii on a quite Sunday morning in December, 1941, removed the uncertainty about Japan's intentions. Fortunately, the Pacific Fleet's aircraft carriers were at sea when its battleships settled into the Pearl Harbor mud. The following day, in a disaster that still defies understanding, the Japanese destroyed most of Gen. Douglas MacArthur's air force in the Philippines on the ground. Hitler made things easy for Roosevelt by declaring war on the U.S. several days later.[64]

Army, navy and marine flyers built strong aviation programs in their respective services during the interwar period. They actively encouraged technological progress, fostered a healthy industrial base, and encouraged the American people to be air-minded. Contrary to popular belief, the armed forces' conservative leaders devoted an enormous amount of their limited resources to military aviation—although never enough to satisfy the insatiable appetites of their growing air arms. Nor did the civilian leaders in the federal government neglect military aviation. The real issues were always how much was enough for national security, how would those resources be allocated, and who would control the resulting combat assets? The United States faced no real threat to its national security through much of the interwar period. Its defense budgets and military policies, coupled with disarmament treaties, were reasonable responses to that reality. This began to change in the early 1930s. America was slow to react to the rising threat to international peace and its own security posed by aggressive authoritarian regimes in Germany and Japan.

Nonetheless, the United States proved to be what Richard Hallion called a "fast second" to the other major combatants, even though they had gone on a war footing years earlier. It rapidly surpassed them in the production of aircraft. In every major category except jet fighters and bombers, U.S. combat aircraft equaled or exceeded their foreign counterparts well before the war's end. Every major combat aircraft employed by the U.S. armed forces during World War II was either in service, under production, or on the drawing board before December, 1941. Overall, American military aviation made enormous strides during its golden age of innovation, and it went on to play an indispensable role in the war against the Axis. On its own, however, it could not provide a cheap, humane, or decisive way to defend the nation.

CHAPTER 3

Armageddon

orld War II began in earnest for the United States with a devastating attack by Japanese naval aviators and ended with the Americans launching one of the most deadly air campaigns in history. From start to finish, aviation played a critical role in America's only truly global war. In the process, it achieved unprecedented levels of coordination between armies, navies, and air forces. Richard Overy observed that, along with Great Britain, the United States "embraced air power as one of the most important instruments for achieving victory. . . . [T]he Allies opted for the general use of air power in bombing, blockade, land support, and the naval war" while their enemies followed more limited air strategies.[1]

Although America's military aviation program had fallen well behind those of the other major belligerents in the late 1930s, it rapidly surpassed them in most areas after the United States entered the war in December, 1941. That broad application of air power depended on the wartime mobilization of the world's largest economy, the nation's strategic circumstances, and an unprecedented degree of collaboration between America's military, industrial, scientific, and political elites. It rested upon the strong technological and industrial foundation the armed forces had developed with the aviation industry during the interwar years. Yet, although critical to victory, air power proved not to be the military panacea that some had predicted before the nation went to war. The aerial Armageddon unleashed by Anglo-American air power caused so much death and destruction that it called warfare's utility as a rational tool of state-craft into question while threatening the very existence of civilization.[2]

GLOBAL AIRLIFT

President Roosevelt's massive aircraft production program, technological progress, and military circumstances encouraged the U.S. armed forces to develop applications of air power to which they had devoted little or no resources in the past. Airlift was a prime example. As early as World War I, aircraft had been used to transport key personnel, vital supplies, and wounded troops. During the interwar years, army aviators had recognized that the geographic mobility of their operational flying units was a key dimension of air power. The extremely short range of military aircraft and the army's reliance on relatively slow surface transportation to deploy critical support units and their equipment, severely limited its mobility.

In the 1930s, the Army Air Corps had begun transporting supplies to its maintenance and repair depots around the United States in a handful of aircraft dedicated to that purpose. It experimented with using transports and bombers to support air units deployed on exercises. The Air Corps also conducted a few tests with parachutists during the interwar period while monitoring airborne warfare developments in Germany and the Soviet Union. However, it devoted few resources to either airlift or airborne operations before World War II. Because the British were extremely short of pilots, Air Corps aviators were pressed into service in November, 1940, to ferry American-built aircraft to overseas pickup points. The following May, the Air Corps established a ferrying command to run the operation and created an international airlift network for carrying key personnel, high-priority cargo, and diplomatic correspondence abroad. It functioned for about a year before General Arnold reorganized the army's airlift operations. He established the Troop Carrier Command in June, 1942, to conduct airborne operations and ad hoc airlift within operational theaters. Arnold formed a separate support organization, the Air Transport Command (ATC) that same month. It flew combat aircraft and key U.S. and Allied personnel all over the world. In the process, the ATC developed an international system of airfields, communications facilities, and weather stations that spanned six continents. The navy established the Naval Air Transport Service (NATS) in December, 1941, because it was convinced it could not rely upon the army to meet all of its global airlift needs.[3]

While the vast bulk of personnel, equipment, and supplies were moved from the United States to the combat theaters overseas by ship, airlift made enormously significant contributions to military operations. At its wartime height, "an ATC cargo or combat plane crossed the Atlantic at an average rate of one every 13 minutes and traversed the wider Pacific Ocean once every 90 minutes. The personnel and equipment of civil airlines in the United States contributed significantly to ATC's success."[4] By the war's end, ATC's approximately 209,200 military and 104,600 civilian personnel operated more than thirty-seven hundred aircraft. Its naval counterpart consisted of 431 aircraft and approximately 26,100 military personnel. The ATC carried some 339,000 sick and wounded personnel. During the war, "the command's ferrying operations delivered 282,537 aircraft. Its air transport operations, both military and contract carriers, flew over 8.5 billion passenger- and 2.7 billion ton-miles."[5]

The nation's commercial airline industry supplied executives, pilots, navigators, and operations specialists who played critical roles in the wartime military airlift program. Arnold appointed American Airlines president C. R. Smith to serve as a general officer and as ATC's second in command. His role epitomized "the unlimited knowledge of airports, cargo handling, and meteorology, which only the airlines could contribute, [and which] made the difference between success and failure."[6] After the war, Smith and other airlift veterans drew heavily on their military experience and the global airlift network they had developed to establish American commercial carriers as the dominant force in international airline competition.[7]

MOBILIZING THE NATION

The Japanese attack on Pearl Harbor and Hitler's subsequent declaration of war on the United States removed the remaining political restraints on the mobilization of American resources for a long global war. The world's most powerful economy was fully tied to the Allied cause, and America quickly became the "Arsenal of Democracy." It would rather spend treasure than blood to field forces employing weapons that were qualitatively and quantitatively superior to those of its enemies. That approach worked. The United States spent $350 billion on its war effort—more than any of the other major powers expended—while suffering 405,399 war-related military deaths, the fewest of the major belligerents.

America placed the smallest proportion of its population in uniform of any of the major combatants. Some 16 million Americans served in the armed forces during the war. Separated geographically from the fighting fronts, it experienced trivial civilian casualties and virtually no damage to its economy due to enemy action. American industry lavishly supported the nation's own armed forces. It also played a major role in sustaining the Allies while building a huge merchant marine fleet. Unlike other major belligerents, the war actually strengthened the nation's economy.

By the end of 1941, America's aircraft industry was already outproducing every other major power except Great Britain. It manufactured 19,433 military planes that year. Germany, which had yet to fully mobilize its economy for a long war, produced 11,776 aircraft in 1941, while Japan turned out only 5,088. Great Britain produced 20,094.

Unlike Germany and Japan, where the military controlled industrial production decisions, the United States relied on cooperation between industrialists, military officers, and civilian government officials to shape economic mobilization.[8] Industry and the armed forces had experimented with various methods to expand aircraft production. To achieve Roosevelt's ambitious goals, aircraft makers converted from handcrafting to mass production. Factories began operating around the clock, seven days a week. Building on the momentum of European military orders beginning in the late 1930s, industry sold stock and borrowed money from government agencies for expansion. However, most of the wartime increase was achieved by direct government funding of new plants operated by the aircraft manufacturers, greater reliance on subcontractors outside the aircraft industry, and the eventual conversion of segments of the automobile industry to aviation production.

Both the aircraft and automobile industries were reluctant to embrace such a conversion. Aircraft manufacturers feared that Detroit, with its far larger financial resources, would steal their technology and swallow them up after the war. The automakers, who had experienced a boom in private car sales and government contracts in 1940–41 primarily due to increased defense spending, were reluctant to plunge into military aircraft production. The Roosevelt administration eventually forced a significant segment of the auto industry to convert to aircraft production through its control of critical raw materials.

America's enormous wartime aircraft production program required a huge expansion of the industry's labor force that, for the first time, tapped large numbers of women, minorities, and other unskilled workers. Aviation industry employment grew from sixty-three thousand in 1939 to a wartime peak of more than 2 million in 1944. The new workers had to be trained quickly and integrated into constantly changing production programs. To accommodate the huge influx of unskilled workers and mass production requirements, aircraft firms divided production responsibilities into simple repetitive tasks and adopted an unprecedented degree of mechanization.

World War II dramatically illustrated the importance of feedback from the combat theaters as well as intensified research and development that responded to rapidly changing combat needs and exploited technical opportunities for improved weapons performance. Beginning in 1940, the army and the navy sent observers to the United Kingdom to gather critical operational and technical data on air combat in Europe. Borrowing from the British example, modification centers were established to incorporate those and other changes in American aircraft. According to one estimate, 25 to 50 percent of the labor devoted to manufacturing military aircraft was performed at modification centers. It was 1944 before the services mastered block modifications that incorporated the latest design changes in aircraft as they were produced in the primary assembly plants.

American aircraft production accelerated in 1942, reaching a wartime peak of 96,318 in 1944. Germany, the most formidable member of the Axis, increased its aircraft production from 11,776 to just 39,807 during the same period. While it was producing astounding numbers of planes, the United States was also building progressively larger, more technically complex, and increasingly capable aircraft.

Aviation experts generally agreed that the overall weight of national airframe production offered a rough measure of qualitative progress except for jet aircraft. The nation's airframe production soared from 81.5 million pounds in 1941 to 951.6 million in 1944. The latter figure was larger than the combined 518 million pounds produced by Britain, Germany, and Japan. The Soviet Union claimed that it produced forty thousand aircraft in 1944 with a weight of 200 million pounds. Japan, Germany, the Soviet Union, and Great Britain together produced less than 700 million pounds, or less than two-thirds of U.S. output that year. From 1939, when it began its first major production expansion, until 1945, the United States built more than 324,000 military aircraft. The U.S. Army Air Forces received 231,000 of them; the navy, Marine Corps, and America's Allies got the rest.

In addition to outstripping the other major belligerents in volume of aircraft production, the United States rapidly eliminated the prewar aircraft quality gap. All the combat planes flown by the U.S. armed forces in World War II were either in production or under development before December 7, 1941. Many of them were being produced in quantity and had already entered operational service when the Japanese struck Pearl Harbor. Before the war ended, the army, navy, and Marine Corps fielded aircraft that were at least the equal of and often superior to every class of foreign military planes except jet fighters and bombers.[9]

The main aeronautical innovations undertaken by American industry during the war were gliders, helicopters, and jet engines. Nearly sixteen thousand gliders were produced for the U.S. military use during the conflict. Igor Sikorsky, a Russian émigré, produced the first practical helicopter, which was test-flown in April, 1939. The helicopter's wartime production run was limited to four hundred aircraft because of its poor performance. Although the Germans used them widely during the war, the helicopter did not come into its own in the

U.S. armed forces until after the conflict ended. The same was true of American jet engines, which were based on a British design transferred to America after General Arnold observed them during a trip to the United Kingdom in the spring of 1941. The first U.S. jet aircraft, the Bell XP-59A, flew in October, 1942, but its performance fell far short of expectations. The USAAF then asked Lockheed to build an airframe for another jet. It designed and produced the XP-80 in 143 days. After its first successful test flight in January, 1944, the aircraft was redesigned to accommodate a more powerful engine. Altogether, 243 P-80s were produced during World War II, but none flew combat missions during that conflict. However, it did see extensive combat during the Korean War.

Ryan Aeronautical Corporation built the navy's first jet-powered aircraft, the XFR-1, which made its maiden flight on June 25, 1944. Because of the requirement for short takeoffs from aircraft carriers, it was a composite aircraft with both a piston engine and a jet power plant. Its operational version, the FR-1, was fielded in March, 1945, but only sixty-six were produced before the contract was terminated. The FR-1 never saw combat and was withdrawn from service in 1947. The navy had several pure jet fighters under development during the war and one of them, the FD-1 Phantom, made its first flight before the war ended.[10]

The unprecedented wartime mobilization of Anglo-American science and engineering played a key role in achieving a balance between quantity and quality in aircraft and other weapons. The United States stressed applied research and development rather than basic research to improve existing equipment and help solve operational problems. The USAAF and the navy relied on industry, the National Advisory Committee on Aeronautics, and military laboratories to improve their aircraft, engines, and related support equipment during the war. They emphasized practical improvements that increased the range, firepower, and reliability of aircraft. Relatively little attention had been devoted to revolutionary new technologies like radar, jet propulsion, and atomic fusion by the American armed forces before the war.

To apply science and technology beyond the immediate needs of aircraft and their related equipment, the government turned to the National Academy of Sciences. When that body proved to be unresponsive to pressing military requirements, FDR established the National Defense Research Committee in June, 1940. Chaired by MIT's Vannevar Bush, it operated mainly through contracts with colleges, universities, and private laboratories. In January, 1941, Roosevelt incorporated it in the new Office of Scientific Research and Development (OSRD), which reported directly to him. Bush also won a critical early bureaucratic battle, getting some ten thousand scientists and engineers exempted from the draft. Under his leadership, OSRD played a key role in fostering the successful development of such high-technology armaments as proximity fuses, computers, radar, and rockets during the war. The OSRD ensured that there was close collaboration between the military and civilian scientists and engineers in the development of wartime equipment.

The war stimulated especially important gains in electronics and rocketry. While the Germans and Americans had achieved significant progress in the development of radar since the mid-1930s, the British advanced even more rapidly while building an air defense network to blunt the growing threat posed by the Luftwaffe. As mentioned earlier, ground-based radar played a critical role for the RAF during the Battle of Britain in 1940. That same year, Henry Tizard led a British mission to the United States that persuaded the Americans to devote more of their resources to the development and production of improved radar systems. At about the same time, the British achieved a technical breakthrough that led to smaller and more effective airborne radar sets that improved navigational and targeting techniques and were used by RAF and USAAF aircraft in all of the combat theaters. In the Atlantic, radar played an important role in the defeat of German U-boats. On the other side of the world, radar-directed U.S. naval gunfire helped defeat the Japanese in several surface engagements.

The USAAF and the navy also successfully employed radio-guided bombs launched from aircraft as far as twenty miles away against key targets such as bridges and warships. Work on these weapons provided a useful foundation for the development of guided missiles after the war. The Allies also fielded solid-propellant rocket devices, including jet-assisted boosters to help aircraft on take-off. The Luftwaffe made even more successful use of such devices, employing guided bombs to sink a battleship and several smaller vessels.[11]

While industry and science were gearing up for war, the U.S. armed forces struggled to acquire and train personnel for the massive wartime expansion needed to conduct a global war against the Axis powers. The USAAF and naval aviation were much smaller and more selective than the established surface components of their parent services. Because aerial combat made much greater demands on individuals than surface combat, aircrew members required more extensive training. Since their duties were more technical, they were also taught aeronautics. Generally, only men who met high physical, intellectual, and educational standards were selected for flying duties.

The huge expansion of wartime aviation forced the USAAF and the navy to reorganize their training programs. Preflight training was initiated at civilian schools. In the USAAF, flight training had taken one year to complete before the war. That was compressed to twenty-seven weeks plus nine weeks of preflight training. Army Air Forces pilots continued to receive some three hundred hours in the air before going into combat, three times what novice German aviators received after the United States entered the war. The training of naval aviators went through a similar compression, because the sea service was more interested in preparing them for combat than careers. The prewar requirement that each naval aviator qualify on every major type of aircraft in the navy's inventory was dropped in favor of specializing in one. When volunteering was eliminated in December, 1942, the military air arms had to compete with the other branches for personnel from the selective service system. Draftees and other enlisted men were allowed to apply for aviation training including flight school. Unlike the Germans and the Japanese, who kept veteran pilots flying until they were captured or killed, the Americans rotated experienced aviators stateside for training and other key support assignments once they had completed their prescribed combat tours.

Women also played an important supporting role in wartime U.S. military aviation. Female civilian volunteers began ferrying aircraft overseas for the USAAF in 1942. Later, they served as flight instructors. Altogether, 1,074 Women Airforce Service Pilots (WASP) flew during the war. While women did not serve as naval or marine aviators during the war, they were recruited for volunteer service in administrative and other support positions beginning in 1942 in order to release more men for combat duty. Unlike the WASPs, the navy's Women Accepted for Voluntary Emergency Service (WAVES), and their army counterparts in the Women's Army Auxiliary Corps (WAAC) eventually held military rank. The WAAC was redesignated the Women's Army Corps (WAC) in 1943. At their peak in May, 1945, 99,388 WACs were in uniform. They included twenty aircrew members and over seventeen hundred aircraft mechanics. Some twelve thousand WAVE officers and seventy-five thousand enlisted women served in the navy during the war. They were concentrated in support and training activities at shore installations in the continental United States. Women also served in the Coast Guard and Marine Corps during the war.[12]

Pressure on the Roosevelt administration from civil rights groups compelled the armed forces to increase the number of blacks on active duty and expand the enlisted occupational specialties open to them. However, they remained barred from flying duty in the navy and Marine Corps. In the USAAF, Negroes were limited to 6.1 percent of all personnel despite agreements by the armed forces to recruit 10.6 percent of their personnel from the black population. Although accepted for flight training in the army's air arm, they were restricted to segregated flying units in line with War Department policy. The mechanics and other support personnel in those organizations were also black. They were trained at a segregated installation: Tuskegee Field, Alabama. During the war, more than two thousand Negro pilots earned their pilot's wings. The USAAF established eight segregated flying squadrons—four fighter and four medium bomber—during World War II. Although the bomber units did not see combat, the fighter squadrons compiled an outstanding record against the Germans in North Africa and Italy. The exploits of the Tuskegee airmen did not, however, obscure the fact that the vast majority of black servicemen in World War II were relegated to menial tasks by a highly segregated military establishment.[13]

STRATEGY AND SUBMARINES

While the United States was mobilizing its industrial, scientific, and human resources, American and British military leaders were planning how to defeat the Axis. They agreed before the United States declared war on Japan that Germany was the most dangerous enemy and had to be defeated while the Japanese were held at bay. The Americans were convinced that the best way to defeat Germany was to launch a cross-Channel invasion of Europe from Britain as soon as possible. However, before they could amass the forces and supplies to do that, they had to overcome several enormous challenges—not the least of which was that the attack on Pearl Harbor had convinced many Americans that the United States should first seek revenge on the Japanese.

To stem the rapid advance of Japanese forces across the Pacific, President Roosevelt had to devote enormous military resources to that theater early in the war, despite his agreement with British prime minister Winston Churchill on the Germany first strategy. More U.S. forces were dispatched to the Pacific than to Europe in 1942, delaying efforts to amass sufficient strength in Britain to invade the continent in 1943, as originally proposed by General Marshall. Churchill's fascination with a Mediterranean strategy and FDR's determination to have U.S. ground troops in action against the Germans before the congressional elections in 1942 led to campaigns in North Africa, Sicily, and Italy that devoured critical resources and delayed the day when the Allies faced the Germans head-on in western Europe.

General Arnold and other senior USAAF leaders hoped that a cross-Channel invasion would prove unnecessary. Inspired by prewar Air Corps doctrine and determined to make the strongest possible case for a separate postwar air force, they prepared to mount a strategic bombing campaign against German economic and military targets from Britain, which they hoped would drive Hitler out of the war before Allied soldiers were ready to invade France. Williamson Murray and Allan Millett concluded that, despite the fact the army airmen watched the first two years of the European war from the sidelines, "the Americans learned little from the experience of their Allies. There is no evidence that the additional time had any impact on the American airmen's conceptions of the campaign they aimed to wage; in their minds, only a large precision bombing force could destroy the Nazi war economy by attacking the electric grid, transportation network, and key industries such as oil."[14]

General Arnold commanded the USAAF during World War II. A pioneer military aviator who had been trained to fly by the Wright brothers and a disciple of Billy Mitchell, he was a pragmatic leader who developed the full spectrum of air power missions—including those like airlift, which had been neglected by the prewar Air Corps. Although not a combat veteran, he led the USAAF throughout the war and built it into the world's most powerful air force. At its peak, the USAAF consisted of 2.5 million personnel and 243 combat groups operating more than sixty-three thousand aircraft from airfields around the globe. Arnold was the chief spokesman for land-based American air power, serving as a member of the Anglo-American Combined Chiefs of Staff and its U.S. counterpart, the Joint Chiefs of Staff (JCS). John W. Huston observed that while he was "neither a superb organizer nor a formulator of strategic thought, Arnold was best known as an innovator with a ready smile and a dedication to hard work. . . . He had vision and an appreciation of the role of technology in air power. . . . Concerned with the future, he rotated his most promising staff officers between staff and combat assignments, thus seeking a cadre of versatile leadership for the postwar air force."[15] Arnold was an impetuous, volatile, and dedicated officer with keen political and public relations skills. Although he retired in June, 1946, while the USAAF was still part of the army, Arnold has been quite properly honored as the true father of the U.S. Air Force.[16]

Before the United States and Britain could mount a serious challenge against Germany on the continent, they first had to defeat its submarine force in the Atlantic. If anything came close to being a war-winning weapon during World War II, it may have been the German U-boat. Despite the valiant efforts of the Royal Navy, the RAF, and their Canadian counterparts, Germany's submarines appeared to be on the verge of winning the Battle of the Atlantic in December, 1941. The world's other major navies had drawn the wrong conclusions from the first Battle of the Atlantic in 1914–18 and technological advances during the interwar years. They initially planned to employ submarines as escorts and scouts for their battle fleets. Grand Admiral Karl Dönitz drew radically different conclusions. He became convinced during the 1930s that German submarines, if properly employed against merchant shipping, could strangle Britain's seaborne lifelines and drive the British out of the war. Despite having only fifty-six U-boats available when the war began, Dönitz nearly succeeded.[17]

Beginning in January, 1942, German U-boats launched an unparalleled campaign against coastal shipping near the eastern and southern United States. The Kriegsmarine by then had two hundred submarines, although only forty of them could be on foreign stations at any one time. The U.S. Navy lacked the ships, aircraft, equipment, and trained personnel, as well as a plan and an effective organization, to tackle the onslaught. Consequently, the Germans enjoyed a "merry massacre" of merchant shipping, often within sight of American shores. In November, 1942, alone, they sent seven hundred thousand tons of Allied commercial shipping to the bottom.

The navy, with grudging support from the USAAF, rapidly overcame shortages of antisubmarine warfare (ASW) ships and patrol aircraft in 1942. That April, it organized coastal convoys and escorts. The navy also established "Sea Frontier" commands to coordinate ASW operations and training. Cities along America's coastlines were blacked out at night. Growing numbers of escort vessels accompanied convoys. The Royal Navy shared information on tactics and technology, as well as intelligence derived from broken German radio codes known as Ultra. However, for much of the time between January, 1942, and October, 1943, that information was sporadic at best.

Navy blimps also escorted coastal convoys in the Atlantic, Pacific, Gulf of Mexico, and the Mediterranean. They employed radar to find submarines on the surface and magnetic detectors to locate submerged ones. With only ten airships of all types in its inventory on December 7, 1941, the sea service's wartime lighter-than-air program peaked at 119 craft in March, 1944.

Aircraft played a critical role in the campaign against the U-boats. Like airlift and air defense, ASW had received little or no attention during the 1920s and 1930s by either army or navy flyers. Army airmen had joined their naval counterparts and civilian volunteers flying improvised ASW patrols along the East Coast in December, 1941, because of the severe shortage of long-range patrol aircraft in the sea service. They were neither trained nor equipped to conduct such operations. In January, 1942, Adm. Ernest J. King, the chief of naval operations (CNO), asked the USAAF to transfer two hundred heavy and two hundred light bombers to the navy for ASW operations. General Arnold refused but countered by strengthening some East Coast USAAF units and placing them under the navy's operational control. Nevertheless, Admiral King persisted in his efforts to obtain brand new bombers. In June, 1942, General Marshall's direct personal intervention forced Arnold give the navy 187 factory-fresh B-24s equipped with radar for use against German U-boats.[18]

While the slaughter of merchantmen continued, USAAF and navy officers argued over the proper allocation of long-range aircraft and how best to employ them against German submarines. Army airmen wanted to centralize control of all ASW air assets and use strategic bombers to attack known U-boat concentrations as well as bomb their European bases and factories. Army airmen considered the navy's emphasis on escorting convoys and decentralized command

General Henry H. Arnold, left, commanding general of the U.S. Army Air Forces, and Gen. George C. Marshall, U.S. Army chief of staff, shown at a meeting of the Anglo-American Combined Chiefs of Staff in Cairo, Egypt, on December 4, 1943. Both officers played key roles in the development and global employment of land-based U.S. airpower in World War II. (U.S. Air Force photo courtesy Air Force Historical Support Office.)

wasteful and ineffective. Naval officers resisted the establishment of a centralized ASW command urged on them by the British and the USAAF. It violated the navy's doctrinal tradition of decentralized command and suggested a larger role for land-based air power than they were prepared to acknowledge. Nevertheless, by the summer of 1942, U.S. warships and air patrols had driven the U-boats to the mid-Atlantic, the Gulf of Mexico, and the Caribbean, where the pickings were easier.

The arrival of radar-equipped RAF B-24s in Ireland and PBY Catalinas in Iceland temporarily ended sinkings in the mid-Atlantic. However, the U-boats recovered the initiative when they were equipped with radar-warning receivers. In October, 1942, the USAAF created its own antisubmarine warfare command whose units flew under navy operational control. By year's end, the navy had established a land-based air umbrella over the sea approaches to the Western Hemisphere that extended from Iceland to Brazil.

The decisive phase of the Battle of the Atlantic took place during the first five months of 1943 when the navy began employing small escort carriers that provided seagoing air cover for convoys. Prior to the start of the war in Europe, naval leaders had not even seriously contemplated such vessels. However, faced with the necessity to train unprecedented numbers of aviators and growing requirements to ferry aircraft overseas, Rear Adm. William F. Halsey, as well as other officers and civilian officials in the navy, proposed converting merchant ships to small aircraft carriers. Nothing came of that proposal until President Roosevelt intervened. In June, 1941, the navy commissioned the USS *Long Island,* the first of eighty-six escort carriers constructed during World War II. They varied in size from seventy-eight hundred to 11,400 tons. Their top speed was eighteen knots. Each embarked a composite air group consisting of nine fighters and twelve torpedo bombers. In March, 1943, escort carriers began operating with convoys. As more became available, they were formed into hunter-killer groups with surface warships that aggressively hunted down German submarines.[19]

Improved detection and cryptographic analysis of German radio traffic helped pinpoint the location of U-boat wolf packs and learn many important details of their operational orders. In May, 1943, Admiral King established the Tenth Fleet, nominally under his direct personal control. Its mission was to conduct all American ASW operations. Prior to that point, the British and Canadians had provided a majority of the ASW ships in the North Atlantic. Moreover, the Tenth Fleet nullified General Marshall's proposal to create a joint ASW command reporting directly to the JCS.

The cumulative effect of all those developments devastated the Germans. In the summer of 1943, Admiral Dönitz withdrew his U-boats from the North Atlantic because he could no longer replace his escalating losses. Moreover, American factories and shipyards quickly replaced the dwindling number of Allied merchant ships being sunk.

Rather than continue to submit to continued navy operational control of its prized heavy bombers, the USAAF abandoned the ASW mission in August, 1943. In return for seventy-six B-24s configured for antisubmarine warfare, the USAAF obtained an equal number of the navy's production allocation of those bombers and regained control of the bomber units that had been assigned to ASW duty.[20]

Although German submarines remained a potential threat until the war's end, the crisis passed for the Allies in mid-1943. In October, Admiral King declared, "Submarines have not been driven from the seas, but they have changed status from a menace to a problem."[21] By defeating the U-boats, the Allies established control of the Atlantic, saved Britain, and made possible the invasion of Nazi-occupied Europe. Fortunately for the United States, the Japanese never attempted to mount a serious submarine campaign against American shipping in the Pacific. A Japanese submarine offensive could have severely challenged the American war effort and drained away some of the U.S. Navy's limited ASW resources from the critical struggle against the Germans.[22]

AN INDIRECT APPROACH

While the Battle of the Atlantic hung in the balance, the army was struggling to build up its air and ground forces in Britain to prepare for a cross-Channel invasion against the Germans. This was especially important for General Arnold, who expected the USAAF to begin a daylight high-altitude precision bombing campaign against economic and military targets in enemy-occupied Europe as soon as possible. However, early attacks on targets in France produced only marginal results. American inexperience and aircraft shortages accounted for many of those disappointments. Arnold also complained about having to divert scarce resources to the Pacific and the campaign against German U-boats. He received another setback when President Roosevelt and Prime Minister Winston Churchill agreed that Allied forces would invade North Africa before the end of 1942.

Churchill was convinced that following a strategy of encirclement and blockade that avoided a head-on clash across the English Channel could defeat Germany. His indirect approach also was designed to preserve important British interests in the Mediterranean region. Roosevelt, on the other hand, was determined to get American ground forces into combat in the European theater of operations before the November congressional elections to shore up popular support for the Germany first strategy.

The Operation Torch landings began on November 8, 1942. The USS *Ranger* and three escort carriers provided ASW patrols and air cover for the invasion because no airfields were available to the Americans. Another escort carrier ferried seventy-eight USAAF P-40s to North Africa. Although the operation encountered little French opposition, carrier-based naval aviation played a critical role in its execution because naval and ground commanders had demanded that the entire operation, including troop convoys from Britain and the United States, be provided air cover.[23]

Once ashore, the USAAF's initial support of the ground forces was poor. The inexperienced Americans had few combat aircraft at first, and they operated from dirt strips that became muddy quagmires during the autumn rains. Command arrangements were decentralized and ineffective. Reflecting longstanding arguments within the U.S. Army, ground commanders wanted an air umbrella subject to their direct orders over their units at all times. The airmen argued that such tactics were ineffective and hopelessly out of date. They insisted that air and ground forces must be coequal and that each should operate under a single commander who reported directly to the theater commander. War Department doctrine—FM 100-20, *Command and Employment of Air Power,* adopted in July, 1943—supported the airmen's notion of centralized command as learned in the battles of North Africa, and led to more effective cooperation between army air and ground forces for the remainder of the war.

Army Air Forces leaders in North Africa stressed that gaining air superiority over the Luftwaffe was their first and most important task. Once that was achieved, they wanted to concentrate on interdicting the flow of enemy troops and supplies to the battlefield and then provide close support to Allied troops in contact with the enemy. Gradually, the USAAF built up its forces, mastered the demands of maintenance in the harsh desert environment, and learned how to overcome the Luftwaffe. With the help of their British colleagues, they sold their air power concepts to ground commanders and established an Anglo-American command for all air units in the theater. British airmen also played a critical role in teaching their USAAF counterparts how to organize and train for desert warfare. Lieutenant General Dwight D. Eisenhower, the theater commander, acknowledged the independent basis of air-ground relations in modern warfare early in the campaign.

Like the RAF, the Americans stressed the offensive uses of air power. They mounted continuous attacks on enemy airfields and supply depots by fighters and bombers to secure air superiority. While the Anglo-American air forces fought to seize control of the skies, they also allocated sorties to disrupting enemy supply convoys and providing close support to Allied ground troops in contact with the enemy. With the aid of Ultra intelligence, they cut the flow of men and materiel to German and Italian forces in North Africa by air and sea. Running low on supplies, cornered by Allied air and ground forces, 270,000 enemy troops surrendered in Tunisia on May 12, 1943.[24]

In practice, the army had not actually centralized all of its theater aviation assets under a USAAF commander. The army ground forces had a small force of light aircraft that performed observation and liaison functions the USAAF had abandoned. In the summer of 1940, the Piper Aircraft Corporation had agreed to supply a light aircraft and a pilot to observe artillery fire at maneuvers in Louisiana. Although its performance was impressive, opposition by senior USAAF and ground commanders had prevented the development of aviation units integral to infantry, armor, and artillery formations until after the United States entered the war. In June, 1942, Secretary of War Henry L. Stimson approved the creation of organic aviation for the field artillery that would be assigned to the ground forces instead of the USAAF.

The USAAF purchased light aircraft and provided basic flight training for the ground forces' new light aviation units. The latter supervised tactical training for

2,630 pilots and technical instruction for 2,252 mechanics during World War II. Supply and maintenance arrangements for the almost sixteen hundred aircraft in the ground forces' own air corps by 1945 were improvised. Beginning on November 8, 1942, when three L-4s were flown from the deck of the *Ranger* during the invasion of North Africa, the army's organic aviation force provided invaluable support to U.S. soldiers in every operational theater.[25]

While Allied forces were struggling to defeat the enemy in North Africa, their top political and military leaders met at Casablanca in January, 1943, to chart strategy for the next year. Roosevelt and Churchill decided to launch an Anglo-American Combined Bomber Offensive against Germany, strengthen the antisubmarine campaign in the Atlantic, and invade Sicily and Italy. The latter seemed to make sense at the time. It would relieve pressure on the Russians by attracting German forces to the Mediterranean theater, secure bases closer to Germany for bomber attacks on the Third Reich, and eventually drive Italy out of the war. It also took advantage of the forces and infrastructure the Allies had already built up in the region.

At Casablanca, the broad lessons of the North African campaign were adopted for the remainder of the air war in Europe. Gaining and maintaining air superiority would be a prerequisite to Allied victory over Hitler's Germany. The Anglo-American air forces would wage a continuous campaign to wear down the Luftwaffe through attrition rather than conduct a short series of strikes that would cripple it and the Third Reich's economy in short order. It was also clear

Captain Ford Allcorn flies his L-4 aircraft from the deck of the USS *Ranger* during the U.S. invasion of Morocco in French North Africa in November, 1942. World War II saw the rebirth of army aviation units flying light aircraft that were organic to the ground forces. A separate organization from the Army Air Forces, those units performed a wide variety of invaluable functions—including artillery spotting, reconnaissance, and personnel transport—in every theater of war. (Photo courtesy U.S. Army Aviation Command.)

that a large tactical air force would be needed to help the ground forces master the Wehrmacht. The flexible system of close cooperation between air and ground forces developed during the desert campaign was adopted for the rest of the war in Europe. All of this was complemented by the Combined Bomber Offensive, which was intended to pave the way for a cross-Channel invasion by weakening German morale and undermining its industrial output, especially aircraft and submarine production.[26]

Air power played a central role, both good and bad, in the Anglo-American invasions of Sicily and Italy in the summer of 1943. Bombers based in North Africa pounded enemy transportation hubs before each of those operations. Ground commanders would not land their troops on Sicily until the Luftwaffe had been neutralized. Land-based Allied fighters lacked the range to support the invasion from North Africa. Only two Royal Navy fleet carriers and a U.S. Landing Ship Tank (LST) manned by Coast Guard personnel and fitted with a very small flight deck were available for Operation Husky. Consequently, General Eisenhower's forces seized two small islands near Sicily and established airfields there to provide additional air cover for the invasion.

Allied fighter pilots and antiaircraft gunners in the invasion fleet fought off waves of German aircraft attacks during the operation. A large drop of paratroopers in Sicily was a bloody fiasco. Nervous sailors shot down more American and British troop transports than they did enemy fighters. The paratroopers who survived the flight were widely scattered. Naval gunfire support, directed by spotter aircraft launched from warships, helped destroy furious German counterattacks on the invasion beaches. Once established ashore, however, the Allied forces were plagued by poor air-ground cooperation. Aircraft were slow to hit enemy targets and sometimes attacked friendly forces while the latter often fired on their own aircraft. Despite Allied air superiority, the Germans were able to evacuate their troops to Italy over the narrow Straits of Messina.[27]

The U.S. landing in Italy at Salerno in September, 1943, was also constrained by the range of Allied fighters. That consideration resulted in a landing south of Naples instead of north of that city, where it might have cut off more Germans. Ground commanders demanded fighter cover for the invasion despite the fact that Italy had signed an armistice and there were few Germans initially available to contest the landing. Royal Navy carriers supported the operation. Allied armies were on the verge of annihilation by a strong German counter attack when a combined air and naval bombardment coupled with a pinpoint drop on the beaches by American paratroopers saved the day.

Unfortunately, the decision not to order Italian forces to resist the Germans, who intervened massively and quickly disarmed them, resulted in one of the greatest debacles of the war. Instead of a cakewalk through Europe's "soft underbelly," the Allies faced a grinding campaign against a determined enemy who skillfully used the peninsula's mountain and river barriers to turn the invasion into a bloody and increasingly pointless battle of attrition. Air power played an important role in the Italian campaign. Bombers based at Foggia in southern Italy struck key targets throughout the Balkans and southern Germany. They also supported ground troops in contact with enemy. Drawing on the lessons of earlier Anglo-American operations in North Africa and Sicily, radio-equipped air liaison officers called "rovers" traveled in jeeps with the ground forces and coordinated air strikes by fighter-bombers overhead. During the campaign, black combat pilots of the 332d Fighter Group performed superbly in missions over Italy and central and southeast Europe, overcoming the low expectations of the USAAF.

Although Allied aircraft were able to dramatically limit the Germans' ability to resupply their forces in Italy by attacking railroads and highways, their interdiction efforts were unable to force the enemy out of the peninsula. The last major Allied effort to circumvent German defenses and capture Rome, the Anzio landing on January 22, 1944, quickly bogged down after achieving initial surprise. The assault forces were too small to achieve the operation's objectives without a high degree of risk. Air strikes were unable to block German reinforcements from reaching the high ground that dominated the beachhead. As the Allies prepared for the cross-Channel invasion of France, the bloody Italian campaign faded into the background until Germans forces surrendered there just before the war ended in Europe.[28]

DESTROYING THE THIRD REICH

While Allied forces struggled to overcome the Germans in Italy, the Anglo-American Combined Bomber Offensive was pounding away at enemy targets in France and Germany. Strategic bombing had been a part of Allied strategy against Germany since Pearl Harbor. The offensive formally sanctioned 'round-the-clock bombing of the Third Reich. The RAF had been forced to adopt night attacks on cities because of the heavy losses it sustained during daylight raids early in the war. The USAAF, however, persisted in its daylight attacks against industrial and military targets. Although fighters escorted the American bombers over France, their losses still averaged 10 percent. The ability of those attacks to have a decisive impact on the war's outcome remained a matter of faith on the part of USAAF leaders and their political masters.

Target selection and strategy turned out to be huge problems. The early campaign against the German submarine construction yards, approved at the Casablanca conference, failed and was dropped in May, 1943. Attacks on the

Army Air Forces B-17s raid Cologne, Germany, during World War II. Although the centerpiece of prewar Air Corps doctrine, high-altitude precision attacks on enemy industrial targets achieved mixed results while exacting an enormous cost in blood and treasure. (U.S. Air Force collection, National Archives.)

German aircraft industry were then given top billing in order to weaken the Luftwaffe's fighter strength. Other priority targets included enemy morale as well as the ball bearing, oil, and synthetic rubber industries.

Senior USAAF leaders were convinced that they had accumulated enough strength in Britain by 1943 to test their preferred strategy: daylight high-altitude precision bombing attacks on German industrial targets. In practice, "precision" meant an entire bomb group releasing its ordnance simultaneously on the signal of the unit's lead bombardier. That was a far cry from the accuracy associated with individual precision-guided munitions attacks on enemy targets by American military aviators in the 1990s. During World War II, army airmen thought that their B-17s carried enough firepower to defend themselves against determined attacks by the Luftwaffe. However, the catastrophic losses suffered by unescorted American B-17s and B-24s during attacks on targets in the Third Reich threatened the USAAF's entire strategic bombing campaign. Sustaining losses of 30 percent among his bomber crews each month, the Eighth Air Force commander, Lt. Gen. Ira Eaker, temporarily halted deep penetrations of Germany in the fall of 1943. Long-range escort fighters were desperately needed to protect the bombers, but the P-47s and P-38s in the theater lacked the necessary range even when equipped with external fuel tanks that could be jettisoned during combat. A disastrous raid against Schweinfurt, Germany in October, on which sixty B-17s were lost, gave the final push to extend the range of U.S. escort fighters and intensified efforts to get North American's new P-51 Mustang into quantity production.[29]

The balance in the air campaign finally tipped in the Americans' favor in February, 1944, when large numbers of P-51s appeared in the skies over Germany. Those sleek aircraft illustrate how foreign influences continued to play a major role in American military aviation during the war. The North American Aviation Corporation developed the Mustang in response to a British request for a new fighter in 1940. Its chief designer was German-born and -educated engineer Edgar Schmued, who had worked on military aircraft projects in the Third Reich during the 1930s. Marrying American airframe technology with Schmued's conception of an angular wing and tail, and a two thousand horsepower Rolls Royce–Packard Merlin engine, the P-51 became one of the war's best fighter aircraft. Its deployment to the United Kingdom accelerated enemy

North American P-51 Mustangs escort Eighth Air Force bombers on a mission over Nazi-occupied Europe. The availability of long-range, high-performance fighters like the P-51 helped tip the balance in the European air war against Germany's Luftwaffe. (U.S. Air Force photo collection, National Archives.)

fighter losses while protecting the growing numbers of USAAF heavy bombers that were able to attack German industry. Escorted on long-range missions into the heart of the Third Reich by their "little friends," the heavy bombers became flying magnets that attracted Luftwaffe fighters and enabled American fighters to destroy them.

During the so-called Big Week that began on February 10, 1944, the RAF and the USAAF severely jolted German production and won control of the skies over Europe. The Luftwaffe lost more than eight hundred day fighters over France and Germany in February and March. More importantly, it began to run out of trained pilots. Despite Allied air superiority, furious air battles continued over western Europe for the rest of the year. Although the Americans continued to lose aircraft and crews, albeit at a much lower rate than in 1943, unlike the Germans, they could more than replace their losses. Nevertheless, the illusion of a quick and relatively easy victory through strategic bombing died hard in the skies over Hitler's Germany. The planned blitzkrieg had become an aerial Verdun, a long and bloody World War I–style battle of attrition.[30]

As the Allied air forces were gaining mastery of the skies over Germany in early 1944, the rest of the war caught up with the bomber generals. Against their better judgment, General Eisenhower forced the USAAF's and RAF's strategic bomber commanders to employ their forces to support the invasion of France, Operation Overlord. Allied air power played a central role in the invasion by achieving air superiority over western France and isolating the battlefield, making it enormously difficult for the Germans to reinforce and resupply their troops at Normandy. Eisenhower stressed that Overlord would have been impossible without the Allies' overwhelming air superiority.

Eisenhower's deputy, Air Marshal Sir Arthur W. Tedder and the latter's chief scientist, Dr. Solly Zuckerman, developed an air campaign plan designed to hobble the German army's ability to reinforce its units in the planned invasion area. Unlike most other senior RAF leaders during the war, Tedder took a broad joint perspective that saw beyond the narrow parochial needs and interests of his own service. With Zuckerman's considerable help, he designed a transportation plan that sought to destroy the railroad network and cripple highway traffic by wrecking bridges on main routes in western and central France. Bombing and sabotage reduced rail traffic in France and western Germany by 70 percent during the three months before D-Day. The Germans lost the race to reinforce Normandy even before the invasion began.

The three airborne divisions—two American and one British—dropped by Allied transports behind the Normandy beachheads helped delay German reinforcements, as did relentless attacks by Anglo-American fighters and medium bombers. But air power had its limitations against a resourceful and well dug-in foe. Despite the Allies' overwhelming mastery of the skies, the Normandy invasion required nearly two months of bloody ground combat before the Germans were finally defeated and pushed out of the region.[31]

Some twenty-five hundred USAAF aircraft paved the way for the breakout from the Normandy beachhead by Lt. Gen. Omar N. Bradley's forces at Saint-Lô in late July by blasting a whole through the German lines. Although the air attack helped prepare for the success of Bradley's offensive, errant bombs killed 102 American soldiers, including Lt. Gen. Lesley J. McNair. McNair was the senior U.S. Army general killed in action during the war. After clearing the Normandy hedgerow country, Americans perfected the air-ground coordination techniques they had developed in North Africa. German resistance stiffened in the fall of 1944 as Allied ground forces, advancing on a broad front, outran their logistical base. Field Marshal Sir Bernard Law Montgomery's ambitious plan to end the European war by a concentrated airborne-armored thrust across the Rhine River into the north German plain, was a bloody fiasco. Some two thousand transports and approximately six hundred gliders dropped thirty-five thousand airborne troops along a narrow, sixty-five-mile-long corridor during Operation Market-Garden in September, 1944. Unexpectedly strong German opposition and poor weather that nullified air support caused the operation to begin to unravel. Brutal fighting in the Hürtgen Forest and the Battle of the Bulge later that year underscored the limits inclement weather and difficult terrain could impose on tactical aviation.[32]

While aircraft carriers had not been needed at Normandy because of the proximity of British air bases, they played an important role in Operation Anvil, the Allied invasion of southern France on August 15, 1944. That little known campaign, designed to help trap German forces west of the Rhine, employed seven Royal Navy escort carriers and two of their U.S. Navy counterparts. Naval aircraft covered the amphibious assault against light German opposition and supported ground forces ashore until temporary airfields could be established in France. The capture of the intact port of Marseille and the relatively undamaged French transportation network in the Rhone River valley played a critical role in providing badly needed logistical support to Allied forces following the Normandy breakout. Because Eisenhower's air forces had destroyed the railroads and river bridges in central and western France during Operation Overlord, access to the Rhone valley transportation network proved to be a godsend to the Allies.[33]

American strategic bombers had resumed their attacks on the German economy after the Allies were firmly ashore at Normandy, concentrating on oil refineries and aircraft plants. Then German secret weapons designed to terrorize enemy populations and win back control of the skies over the Third Reich became priority targets. The first of these was the V-1 "buzz bomb," a small, unmanned, pulse-jet-powered aircraft filled with high explosives. Allied bombers had begun attacking experimental facilities, factories, and launch sites linked to the program the previous August. They intensified their bombing campaign after the first V-1 was launched against Britain on June 12, 1944, with little effect. About twenty thousand V-1s were fired from fixed ramps and Luftwaffe bombers before Allied ground forces overran the areas from which they could hit the United Kingdom and the port of Antwerp in Belgium. Allied fighters and anti-aircraft artillery managed to shoot down about 20 percent of the V-1s. On September 8, 1944, the first V-2 rocket hit England. The V-2 was a ballistic missile against which there was no defense except frantic bombing attacks on its mobile launching sites. The Germans launched some three thousand V-2s against targets in Britain, France, Belgium, and western Germany before their attacks ended in March, 1945, because of the progress made by Allied ground forces. Between them, the German missiles killed about nine thousand people. Pure terror weapons, they had no impact on the war's outcome but they did provide a terrible vision of future warfare. Allied bombing had little effect on the V-2 campaign. The last of the German wonder weapons to debut in 1944 were jet- and rocket-powered fighters. However, like the V-1s and the V-2s, they were too little and too late to affect the war's outcome.[34]

Air Marshal Tedder proposed a plan in September, 1944, to destroy the Third Reich's railroad network, canals, and waterways to prevent raw materials, finished goods, and parts from being moved. Despite the strong resistance of Allied air commanders, the attacks began that September and had a major impact almost immediately. While their offensive in the Ardennes region showed that the second transportation plan had not hobbled the German army by late fall, the Third Reich's economy was beginning to falter. Its collapsing transportation system soon strangled the war effort and economy by disorganizing the flow of materiel to combat units. Starting in January, 1945, the German military collapse began in the east against the Soviets. It was followed a month and a half later in the west. The Wehrmacht's final breakdown as a functioning military machine was caused by the fact that the transportation offensive had successfully destroyed the war economy. It no longer had the weapons, the ammunition, and especially the fuel needed to keep fighting. Not even blind fanaticism could sustain an effective resistance to the Allies in such circumstances.[35]

Strategic bombing continued into 1945 as Allied ground forces fought their way into Germany. Running out of viable economic and military targets, the USAAF increasingly struck at civilian population centers in an effort to destroy German morale. That thinking led to the controversial bombing of Dresden in cooperation with the RAF. Although it boasted few militarily significant targets, the city was incinerated by waves of bombers that killed 135,000 people. The strategic air campaign against Germany essentially ended in mid-April when the bomber units were ordered to provide direct assistance to the land campaign.[36]

Strategic bombing was only one element of the broad air power strategy the Allies employed against Hitler's Third Reich. American and British aircraft, working in conjunction with warships, had played a critical role in winning the Battle of the Atlantic. Developed into an effective air-ground team in North Africa, tactical air forces had made possible the Allied invasions of Europe and eased the progress of ground troops across the continent when weather and terrain conditions permitted. Airborne operations had enjoyed varying degrees of success against the Germans. In general, lightly armed paratroopers proved to be most effective when they surprised the enemy and were then quickly reinforced by rapidly advancing infantry and armored forces.

The brunt of USAAF tactical air operations in Europe had fallen on the Ninth Air Force. Established in October, 1943, in Great Britain, it became arguably the most powerful tactical air force in the war by the time of the Normandy invasion. Although it had initially focused on escort missions for RAF and USAAF strategic bombers attacking Germany, it gradually switched its emphasis to training with the ground forces for the invasion of Europe and attacks on the Belgian and French transportation systems prior to D-Day. During the Normandy landings, its medium bombers struck invasion beaches while its fighters supplied air cover. Fighter-bombers made daylight movement by German ground forces almost impossible and completely thwarted Luftwaffe tactical operations.

After assisting American ground forces and heavy bombers with breaking through the German resistance at Saint-Lô on June 25, 1944, the Ninth Air Force worked closely with General Bradley's ground units. A tactical air command was assigned to each numbered ground army. Experienced Army Air Forces pilots rode in the turrets of the most advanced American armored spearheads so that they could call in air strikes on German forces whenever they were needed. The tactical air commands adhered to the principle of cooperation with the ground forces that they supported. Neither the air commands nor the armies were subordinate to each other. Attacks were either preplanned or diverted from scheduled missions to handle emergencies. Pilots on the ground often controlled air strikes. Frequently, Maj. Gen. Elwood R. "Pete" Quesada, commander of the IX Tactical Air Command, and Brig. Gen. Otto P. Weyland, commander of the XIX Tactical Air Command, would devote several fighter-bomber units to supporting a specific division on a given day. That practice reflected the vast air superiority enjoyed by the Allies in the skies over Europe by mid-1944 and was not seen as conflicting with USAAF doctrine because airmen remained in charge. On December 16, 1944, the Germans launched their Ardennes counteroffensive in poor flying weather in hopes of negating American and British air power. When the weather cleared a week later, the Allied tactical air forces helped blunt the German advance and then supported the final push into Germany during the spring of 1945.

The Combined Bomber Offensive played an important but still controversial role in defeating Germany. It helped cripple the Luftwaffe by the summer of 1944 and forced Germany to spend 30 percent of its war effort on air defense. German morale never cracked, although about three hundred thousand civilians were killed by the bombings. Spurred by Albert Speer's economic reforms, German industry continued to produce tanks, aircraft, and weapons until late in the war but could not send materiel to the fighting fronts because the Third Reich's petroleum industry and transportation network had been destroyed. In the process of indirectly weakening the German army, the bomber forces paid a terrible price. The Americans alone lost over forty thousand airmen and forty-nine hundred heavy bombers in a narrow triumph that contributed to Germany's final collapse and surrender in May, 1945, after U.S. ground forces linked up with the Soviets at the Elbe River. In the end, tactical air power working in conjunction with ground and naval forces, not strategic bombers, made the most significant contribution to Allied victory.[37]

CHECKING JAPAN

While the United States was mobilizing for the assault on Hitler's Third Reich, the Japanese raced to one quick victory after another during the first six months following Pearl Harbor. The Allied strategy was to conduct a vigorous defense in depth against further Japanese advances, strengthen Chinese resistance through economic and military aid, and preserve crucial Pacific supply lines. Air power, to an even greater extent than in Europe, dominated the war with Japan. According to Ronald Spector: "Despite all these false starts and exaggerated expectations, Air Corps officers were fundamentally right: air power was to prove the decisive element in the Pacific war. Unfortunately, they were fundamentally wrong about the ways in which air power would be applied. . . . Big guns, big ships, the big battle—these dominated navy thinking during the years between the world wars. Aircraft and torpedoes were important, but they were distinctly secondary weapons."[38]

Early Japanese victories changed all that. Aircraft carriers and submarines, not battleships, dominated the American naval war with Japan. As in Europe, the side that was prepared to wage a long battle of attrition won the air war in the Pacific. The United States eventually overwhelmed Japanese military aviation with significantly larger numbers of superior aircraft, better-trained aircrews, superior tactics, and bountiful logistics.

Before they could take the offensive against the Japanese, however, the army and navy had to sort out command arrangements for the new kind of coordinated air, sea, and ground warfare that was emerging. Both agreed in principle that a single theater commander was needed. But, unlike in Europe and the Mediterranean, neither was willing to entrust significant numbers of its own forces to command by a senior officer from the other service for long periods of time. The navy, which had been planning for a decisive battle against the Japanese in the western Pacific since Theodore Roosevelt was president, adamantly refused to entrust its fleet and its future to an army officer.

The army based its claim to theater command on the fact that it had more than a hundred thousand air and ground personnel in the Pacific early in the war. To shore up public morale while counteracting pressure by the Republican Party and the media in the dark months after Pearl Harbor, President Roosevelt and General Marshall decided that the nation needed a hero. They selected Gen. Douglas MacArthur to play the role. MacArthur, who had been training Philippine troops for the commonwealth's government, was recalled to active duty in the U.S. Army and given command of all U.S. forces in the islands.

By evacuating General MacArthur to Australia and awarding him the Medal of Honor before the Japanese completed their conquest of the Philippines, they created an enormous problem. The navy found itself with a formidable rival. No naval officer on active duty was senior to MacArthur or approached him in public stature or talent for self-promotion. Nonetheless, Admiral King adamantly refused to entrust the navy's Pacific forces to an army general. He pressed instead for an offensive through the central Pacific that would feature the navy's aviation, amphibious, and submarine forces. MacArthur, on the other hand, clamored for command of all U.S. forces in the Pacific. His plan was to advance on Japan through the Southwest Pacific, liberating the Philippines along the way.

Unable to resolve their differences, senior army and navy leaders in Washington, D.C., reached a compromise. Against both logic and sound military doctrine, they agreed to launch *two* major offensives across the Pacific. MacArthur would command forces in the Southwest Pacific Area (SWPA) from Australia, and Hawaii-based Vice Adm. Chester W. Nimitz was given responsibility for the Pacific Ocean Areas. Complicating matters even further, the boundary between the two theaters bisected the Solomon Islands. Because Admiral King refused to entrust aircraft carriers to MacArthur for use against Japanese strong points in the Solomons, the JCS designated them the South Pacific Area. The latter was placed under a naval commander who cooperated with MacArthur while remaining under Nimitz's command. Although rationalized as being mutually supporting, the multiple offensives could have been disastrous had the Japanese taken full advantage of opportunities available to them to defeat their widely separated enemies in detail. Like the Confederates in the American Civil War, the Japanese attempted to defend all along their outer perimeter but were unable to do so in the face of rapidly escalating American military power.[39]

During the early part of 1942, inferior American forces remained on the defensive and were mauled by the Japanese. The only significant exceptions were hit-and-run carrier air strikes against enemy bases in the Marshall Islands by Vice Adms. William F. "Bull" Halsey and Wilson Brown Jr., and Lt. Col. Jimmy Doolittle's raid on the Japanese home islands with USAAF B-25s launched from the USS *Hornet*. While Doolittle's raid did little damage, it caused the Japanese to strengthen their air defenses by withdrawing badly needed fighter units from their outer defensive perimeter and set in motion an effort to lure U.S. aircraft carriers into a trap near Midway Island. The raid also provided an enormous boost to American morale on the home front after a series of stunning Japanese victories.

Carriers had emerged as the weapon of expediency for the U.S. Navy after the Japanese destroyed its battle fleet at Pearl Harbor. Neither doctrine nor combat performance had entitled either U.S. or Japanese carriers to serve as the primary capital ships of their respective navies before the war. Battleships were still considered the principal combatants. Nevertheless, Japanese carriers early in the conflict were probably the finest naval weapons in the world with the possible exception of the German U-boats. They vastly outnumbered the United States in early 1942, with ten carriers against four American flattops in the Pacific (and three others in the Atlantic). Japanese aircraft and pilots were also far better trained than those of their enemies. American carriers were larger and carried more aircraft, which, although slower and less maneuverable than Japanese planes, were more rugged and could absorb greater punishment because of their armor. Like the Germans, the Japanese kept most of their best pilots flying until they died. As noted previously, the Americans rotated their veterans between operational and training duties, thus passing on recent combat experience to fledgling aviators while providing a continual flow of veteran flyers to training assignments and leadership positions in front-line units.[40]

Aided by electronic intelligence, the U.S. Navy checked Japanese expansion for the first time during the great carrier battles at the Coral Sea in May, 1942, and Midway early the following month. Although the Japanese lost four carriers and scores of highly skilled aviators during the latter battle, they retained

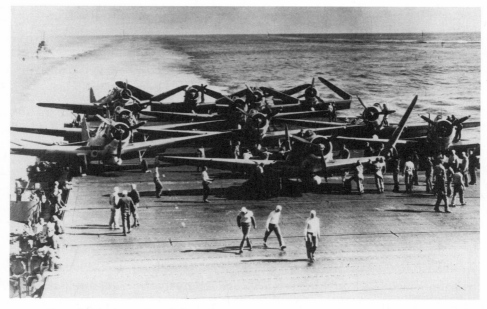

Torpedo bombers aboard the USS *Enterprise* prior to takeoff during the Battle of Midway in June, 1942. Although few of those aircraft survived, U.S. Navy dive-bombers sank four Japanese aircraft carriers during the battle, effectively ending enemy military expansion in the Pacific. (U.S. Navy photo.)

enough forces to resume the offensive. However, they reverted to their defensive strategy and became mired in a battle of attrition in the Solomon Islands. Like the Germans, they allowed the Allies to dictate the timing and location of major offensives. American shipbuilding, aircraft production, and pilot training programs begun in 1940–41 rapidly changed the military balance in the Pacific after Midway.[41]

Underscoring the growing odds against them, the Japanese attempted to increase their aircraft production but they could not keep pace with an enemy that devoted only 15 percent of its total war resources to the Pacific. A major bottleneck was engine production. Like the Germans, the balance of Japanese production between bombers and fighters swung sharply to the latter in a vain effort to blunt growing American superiority in the air. The Japanese, because of growing petroleum and aircraft shortages, also found themselves increasingly unable to adequately train pilots to replace the growing number being lost.[42]

To check the Japanese threat to American lines of communication with Australia, U.S. Marines landed unopposed on Guadalcanal in the southern Solomons in August, 1942. They quickly seized a Japanese airfield under construction there that military planners believed was the key to the entire region. Marine air squadrons aided by other land-based aviation contingents from the navy, USAAF, and Royal New Zealand Air Force won a six-month campaign for air superiority. Control of the air gave the Americans a tremendous advantage in the months of bloody ground and naval surface battles that lay ahead. Although the "Cactus Air Force" flying from Henderson Field dominated by day, the Japanese surface fleet owned the night at the beginning of the campaign. The Americans lost twenty-four warships, including two aircraft carriers, and an estimated ten thousand sailors in numerous engagements before emerging victorious in early 1943.[43]

MACARTHUR'S AIRMEN

Meanwhile, General MacArthur had begun an overland offensive in September, 1942, with American and Australian troops in the mountainous jungles of southern New Guinea. Allied aircraft achieved air superiority there by November. MacArthur's new air commander, Maj. Gen. George C. Kenney, waged a brilliant campaign of land-based aerial improvisation in the Southwest Pacific. MacArthur had lost most of his original air force on the ground when the Japanese attacked the Philippines on December 8, 1941, and Allied air forces had been largely ineffective against the Japanese before Kenney assumed command in the SWPA. Their morale was at rock bottom. Kenney focused on training, maintenance, supply, and developing new tactics to fit the situation in the Southwest Pacific. Above all, he won MacArthur's trust and convinced him to rely on innovative uses of air power to support his ground and naval forces.

High-altitude bombing, a dismal failure when confronting maneuvering ships in the terrible weather conditions of the Southwest Pacific, was scrapped. Primitive airstrips were hacked from the jungle. Ground forces were deployed and resupplied by transport aircraft while Japanese supply lines were interdicted by air in a mad scramble to improvise an effective strategy with available forces and equipment. Kenney shook up MacArthur's air forces and turned them into an invaluable tool of war. Propelled by Kenny's aggressive leadership, the airmen wrote their own tactical manual in the Southwest Pacific. Prewar Air Corps doctrine, with its emphasis on high-altitude precision strikes against critical industrial targets, was almost totally irrelevant in that theater of operations.[44] Another key to Kenney's success was signals intelligence. "Magic" (the code name given to decrypted Japanese naval radio messages) permitted him to concentrate his air forces when and where they could have the greatest impact on the Japanese. But Kenney was hardly unique in that regard. Information gleaned from Magic intercepts contributed significantly to Allied victories at Midway and in other great air battles in the war with Japan. They also played an important role in the shooting down of Adm. Isoroku Yamamoto's aircraft by USAAF P-38 Lightnings and in the devastating submarine campaign against Japanese shipping.

Perhaps Kenney's greatest shortcoming was his generally adversarial relationship with naval officers. Like other army airmen, he had had little contact with naval aviators before the war and was largely unschooled in warfare at sea. He also clashed with the navy over key operational issues. The most longstanding controversy focused on how to conduct air operations during amphibious landings. The navy preferred to maintain air cover over convoys and to begin landings at dawn to hide the ships under cover of darkness. Kenney argued that standing air patrols were wasteful and inefficient. He pressed for later landing times so that his pilots could attack enemy forces near the beaches just before Allied troops stormed ashore. Kenney remained distrustful of the navy throughout the war. While growing American materiel superiority obscured many of the problems caused by interservice conflicts, Kenney's aggressiveness did little to improve cooperation between the army and the navy.

Except for refineries in Indonesia that supplied petroleum products to the Japanese war machine, there were no strategic targets in the region. Long-range bombers eventually destroyed the refineries, but for the most part, Kenney's was a tactical air force. Gaining air superiority was his top operational priority. After that, his airmen developed skip- and parachute-bombing techniques while packing the noses of B-25s with machine guns and cannons with which they destroyed small ships. Aerial attrition was a key element of the SWPA campaign. After destroying enough enemy aircraft to ensure air superiority, MacArthur's forces would bypass Japanese strong points and build more airfields to cover the next amphibious landing.

Naval and marine forces under Admiral Halsey, the South Pacific Area commander, were temporarily assigned to MacArthur in early 1943 to launch a parallel drive through the treacherous narrow waters of the Solomons. Against all expectations, the two "grandstanders" got along wonderfully well and cooperated effectively during the campaign. Halsey had only a handful of fleet carriers to risk in those dangerous seas. To deal with that dangerous situation, he established the Air Command Solomons (COMAIRSOLS). Consisting of land-based navy, marine, USAAF, and Royal New Zealand Air Force aircraft, it was one of the hardest hitting air forces of the Pacific war.[45]

In many respects, World War II was an engineer's war. Nowhere was that truer than in the Pacific. Naval Construction Battalions, the famed "Seabees," and their less well-publicized USAAF counterparts, the Aviation Engineers, played a critical role in the air campaigns as they quickly hacked out and repaired dirt airstrips covered with pierced-steel planking in some of the harshest conditions on earth. Planning for future assaults and the acquisition of new airfields was dominated by the overlapping range arcs of Allied fighters and bombers.[46]

The strengths of the Aviation Engineers and the Seabees magnified Japanese weaknesses. The enemy was seriously burdened by a lack of heavy equipment and labor for airfield construction and repair. Because they were unable to disperse their aircraft around the perimeter of an airfield or construct more bases, the Japanese clustered their aircraft together. That situation made it comparatively easy to destroy large numbers of enemy aircraft in a single attack. According to Ronald Spector, "The entire progress of the war in the South and Southwest Pacific and, to a lesser degree, the Central Pacific, was keyed to the rate of development of air bases in newly captured areas from which allied planes could neutralize and isolate targets in the next objective area."[47]

Halsey's COMAIRSOLS and General Kenney's airmen concentrated primarily on air superiority and interdiction. Close air support of ground troops was not well developed in the region. That mission had enjoyed the lowest combat priority in the prewar Air Corps. The marines, although committed to the concept of supporting ground forces with aircraft, had not worked out the details of close air support, and it would be late 1943 before they began to train for it. The navy had done even less than the army or the marines to prepare for that mission. Close air support developed as a series of ad hoc responses to the needs of the ground forces. It enjoyed limited effectiveness because of the difficulty of locating targets in dense jungles, poor radio communications, inadequate training, and competing demands on tactical aircraft, which enjoyed higher priority. It was 1944 before these problems were systematically overcome in the Pacific war.

Under the cover of land-based air power, MacArthur's and Halsey's forces moved up the New Guinea coast and the Solomons in 1943, leapfrogging around and isolating large concentrations of enemy forces. By the end of the year, American troops were pointing at the big Japanese base at Rabaul on the island of New Britain off the New Guinea coast.[48] The Southwest and Central Pacific campaigns competed with each other and with the European theater for troops and equipment in 1943–44. MacArthur opposed the navy's Central Pacific campaign entirely. In late 1943, he announced his intention to invade the Japanese fortress of Rabaul but was forced to bypass it by the Joint Chiefs of Staff, who directed the bulk of Pacific-bound resources to Nimitz. Air superiority over Rabaul was achieved by COMAIRSOLS.[49]

In the process, Halsey, learning from code breakers that the Japanese planned a surface attack with cruisers on American forces landing on Bougainville, attacked Rabaul with his small carrier force. Lacking heavy warships to protect the flattops, Halsey took an enormous risk and won. Although celebrated as a brilliant success, the real significance of the operation was that he lacked heavy warships to protect his carriers in the narrow waters of the Solomons. Such vessels were not available because the Americans had divided their Pacific forces. By February, 1944, it was over. Rabaul had been neutralized by American air power and bypassed. The Japanese had lost the Southwest Pacific and the American focus shifted to the Central Pacific Area, where the navy had launched its campaign of choice to defeat Japan.[50]

THE CENTRAL PACIFIC OFFENSIVE

Against the initial opposition of Nimitz and Halsey, who were convinced that it would divert badly needed resources from the Solomons, King had won Marshall's support for a navy–Marines Corps offensive in the central Pacific. It would rely on the burgeoning force of *Essex*-class carriers that began to reach the fleet by mid-1943 and amphibious assaults by marines. But the potency of carrier aviation for sustained offensive campaigns had yet to be established. Land-based tactical aviation dominated the Southwest Pacific after aircraft carriers had proven to be extremely vulnerable there. The Japanese sank three U.S. flattops and heavily damaged a fourth in MacArthur's theater. In the central Pacific, King expected to demonstrate the war-winning potency of carrier aviation.[51]

The new *Essex* fleet carriers were faster and more maneuverable than most of their predecessors. Bristling with antiaircraft guns, they each carried up to a hundred aircraft each. By the fall of 1943, six of the ships had joined the fleet, along with an equal number of *Independence*-class light carriers that embarked fifty aircraft apiece. Both classes of warships were capable of steaming at speeds up to thirty knots. A force of eight new fast battleships, seven cruisers, and thirty-five destroyers protected them. Their air units were equipped with the sturdy new Grumman F6F Hellcat fighter, which could outperform the Japanese Zero.

The navy had adapted radar technology and the centralized fighter direction techniques developed by the RAF in the Battle of Britain and Royal Navy carrier operations in the Mediterranean to the war in the Pacific. Those developments eliminated the need for a large aircraft scouting force to protect the fleet and increased the complement of strike aircraft that could be embarked on carriers. Radar also enabled American carrier task forces to maneuver at high speeds at night and in bad weather. The navy developed techniques for multicarrier task force operations that concentrated their air power for defense and offensive strikes. In addition, eight escort carriers had joined the Pacific fleet in 1943. They had a top speed of about nineteen knots. Operating separately from the fast carriers, they ferried aircraft and supported amphibious operations.

Logistics, which had been a relatively neglected field in the prewar navy, was a vital factor underpinning operations in the vast reaches of the Pacific. Aside from Hawaii, Australia, and New Zealand, the U.S. fleet lacked access to good ports in the region. To sustain fast carrier task forces at sea, Nimitz organized a system of mobile logistical and repair bases. Ships, barges, floating dry docks, and lighters would anchor in protected harbors away from enemy planes and submarines. Oilers and supply ships would replenish warships while under way at sea. According to Norman Polmar, "the most critical logistic factor for U.S. offensive operations in the Pacific was the use of underway replenishment of carrier task forces."[52]

The navy launched its central Pacific drive with an attack on tiny Tarawa atoll in the Gilberts. Because King did not want to give the British time to back away from their support for that offensive, the attack was moved up one month from December, 1943, when tide conditions would have been much more favorable for an amphibious assault. The result was a bloody mess. Front-page newspaper photos of the carnage shocked the American public, which was used to viewing the war through the lens of favorable propaganda. After several days of horrific combat, the marines prevailed. Next, Nimitz's forces attacked the Marshall Islands. Aircraft from the fast carriers destroyed Japanese planes and ships, attacked their bases, and then isolated their island strong points. In the process, they perfected a coordinated system of amphibious assaults by marines supported by carrier aircraft.

The marines depended heavily on air support during that campaign. However, it proved difficult to reintegrate aviation with the operations of the Fleet Marine Force. Marine aviation had been a major contributor to land-based air power in the Southwest Pacific and was not prepared for carrier operations when the central Pacific drive began. It remained under navy control until the autumn of 1944. Navy close air support left a lot to be desired according to the leathernecks. The marines experimented with operating from carriers and improved navy close air support during the central Pacific drive, but with only limited success at first.

Marine Corps aviation had mushroomed to ten thousand pilots and 126 squadrons with a hundred thousand support personnel by 1944. After the giant Japanese base at Rabaul was isolated and their forces in the Marshalls neutralized, marine aviation units were underemployed. Furthermore, the navy needed to find more pilots to man its growing fleet of escort carriers, which, among other important roles, provided critical air support to amphibious operations.

The navy had stopped qualifying marines for carrier operations, and it was late 1944 before they were allowed to resume that training. In early 1945, eight marine squadrons embarked on escort carriers. In addition, ten leatherneck F4U Corsair squadrons were transferred to fast carriers due to the need for more fighter aircraft to counter the growing threat posed by Japanese "kamikaze" suicide air attacks. For administrative purposes, marine air units were placed under the Fleet Marine Force, Pacific.[53]

After the Marshalls, the navy moved on to the Mariana Islands. With its defensive perimeter broken, the Japanese fleet came out to fight. The ensuing battle of the Philippine Sea in June, 1944, became famous as the "Great Marianas Turkey Shoot." It was the largest carrier battle in history. Japanese naval aviation, which had been rebuilt following its enormous losses in 1942, proved to be no match for its rivals. American naval aviators shot down 475 Japanese aircraft, sank one enemy carrier (submarines sank two more), and heavily damaged four. Although the Americans lost a hundred aircraft, they were able to rescue all but sixteen pilots and twenty-three other aircrew members. Outnumbered, inexperienced, and equipped with inferior aircraft, the Japanese were simply overwhelmed. The battle broke the back of Japanese carrier aviation. Vice Admiral Raymond Spruance, the cautious nonaviator victor at Midway, commanded the Fifth Fleet during the Marianas campaign. Afterward, he and a team of his senior officers were sent home to rest and plan future operations. His forces were redesignated the Third Fleet and placed under command of the aggressive and flamboyant Halsey.[54]

The prospect of acquiring the Marianas was extremely important to General Arnold, who wanted to base the army's giant new Boeing B-29 Superfortresses there for a strategic bombing campaign against the Japanese home islands. The Air Corps had begun developing the B-29 before America entered the war. By far the world's most advanced bomber, it could carry sixteen thousand pounds of bombs fifty-eight hundred miles at a cruising speed of 225 miles per hour. It featured pressurized cabins and remotely controlled gun turrets equipped with electro-optical sights.

Arnold was so impressed with the B-29's potential that he had ordered production to begin before its first test flight in September, 1942. Fearing that theater commanders like Nimitz and MacArthur would use it for tactical instead of strategic purposes, he convinced the JCS to grant him personal command of the B-29s for use against Japan. That extraordinary arrangement was exercised through the creation of the Twentieth Air Force, headquartered in Washington, D.C. Detailed planning and operations would be controlled by the XX Bomber Command in the China-Burma-India theater and later the XXI Bomber Command in the Pacific.

BACKWATER

The USAAF had already begun B-29 raids on Japan from bases in China in June, 1944, while others, based in India, attacked enemy targets in Southeast Asia. The China-Burma-India theater proved to be a backwater of the Allied war effort. The overriding goals there were to keep China in the war, thereby tying down enormous Japanese military resources on the Asian mainland and preserving India as the crown jewel of the British Empire. Most of the volunteers in Maj. Gen. Claire L. Chennault's China-based "Flying Tigers" became pilots in the USAAF, navy, or Marine Corps after the United States declared war. Originally organized as a small force equipped with P-40 fighters, the Flying Tigers enjoyed great success against the Japanese by employing hit-and-run tactics. His forces acquired medium bombers and then B-29s as the war progressed. Chennault's B-25s virtually choked off the river transport of vital raw materials bound for Japan from China's interior. The B-29's mechanical problems and difficult relations with both the Chinese and Chennault's U.S. military superior, Lt. Gen. Joseph W. Stilwell, complicated the bombing campaign. Above all, logistics problems made China a poor base for bombing Japan.

Impenetrable jungles and the towering mountain passes of the Himalayas, coupled with Japanese advances on the ground in Burma, forced the Americans to rely on supplies airlifted from India to sustain Allied operations in China. Begun in April, 1942, the "Hump" airlift over the Himalaya Mountains struggled against terrible weather, dangerous high-altitude flights through mountain passes, shortages of aircraft and crews, inadequate maintenance, and occasional attacks by Japanese fighter aircraft. During the first two months, it airlifted 196 tons of cargo to China. By the end of 1943, Air Transport Command aircraft and crews finally reached their goal of moving ten thousand tons each month.

To improve flight safety and increase tonnage, Brig. Gen. William H. Tunner, who had successfully run ATC's enormous global aircraft-ferrying operation, assumed command of the operation in mid-1944. Under his able leadership, morale, safety, and cargo tonnages improved dramatically. By war's end, his aircraft inventory had increased from 369 to 722, while its assigned personnel had grown from twenty-six thousand to more than eighty-four thousand. Accident rates fell more than 50 percent. In July, 1945, Tunner's force delivered a wartime peak of seventy-one thousand tons to China. Nevertheless, the Hump airlift operation had been extremely dangerous, with losses of 460 aircraft and 792 men.

Yet neither the fabled Hump airlift nor the reforms instituted by a hard-driving strategic bombing expert imported from Europe, Maj. Gen. Curtis E. LeMay, could overcome the huge difficulties posed by Chinese political and military weakness, an enormously long and slender supply line, and a complicated set of military command arrangements dominated by feuding generals. Long-range B-29 operations were curtailed in China in late 1944 as new bases became available in the Marianas and advancing Japanese ground forces threatened the Chinese airfields. The airlift to China, despite demonstrating the potential of air transport in warfare, was never able to generate enough cargo tonnage to sustain major air and ground offensives against the Japanese. Like Italy, the China-Burma-India theater sucked up enormous Allied resources while failing to achieve results commensurate with the blood and treasure expended there.[55]

CLOSING THE NOOSE

Regardless of the frustrations experienced by the Allies in the China-Burma-India theater, it was clear by the summer of 1944 that Japan was losing the war. The main debate concerned how the Americans would close the noose and finish the Japanese off. Admiral King wanted to extend the navy's central Pacific offensive to Formosa and then to the China coast, bypassing Luzon in the northern Philippines. Once enemy forces on Formosa and the China coast were defeated, those areas would serve as bases for imposing a tight blockade on the Japanese home islands. Determined to redeem his pledge to liberate all of the Philippines and remain a major player in the final victory, General MacArthur objected strongly to the navy proposal. To hear both sides of the argument firsthand, Roosevelt met with MacArthur and Nimitz at Pearl Harbor in July, 1944. However, a final decision had not been made by the time the president met with Prime Minister Churchill in Quebec two months later.

Logistics played a major role in resolving the debate. The Americans lacked the amphibious forces and shipping required for operations near China and Japan at that time. In addition, Halsey's carriers discovered that Japanese air power in the central Philippines was astonishingly passive during raids in early October, 1944. The Americans, with more than a thousand planes embarked on their carriers, possessed as many aircraft as the RAF's Fighter Command had at the height of the Battle of Britain.

At Halsey's urging, MacArthur's scheduled invasion of Leyte in the southern Philippines was advanced by two months to October. That gave MacArthur a much stronger case for U.S. forces following up with an invasion of Luzon rather than Formosa. It also produced the last major surface fleet action of the greatest sea war in history. However, Halsey's fast carriers missed the Battle of Leyte Gulf (October 23–26) when a decoy force of Japanese carriers lured them three hundred miles north of the main engagement. Disaster on the invasion beaches was narrowly averted when the commander of a strong Japanese battle-ship force apparently lost his nerve and retired from the action on the verge of victory. His only opposition was a collection of U.S. submarines, destroyers, old battleships, and escort carriers. When it was all over, Japan's Combined Fleet had been reduced to a few scattered remnants. It lost four large carriers, three battleships, nine cruisers, eleven destroyers, and five hundred aircraft during the battle. Reflecting their growing desperation, the Japanese launched their first kamikaze suicide attacks during that engagement.[56]

By the time of Leyte Gulf, navy flyers had won their own private war with the Gun Club. Vice Admiral John Towers, the senior naval aviator, had been assigned to Nimitz's headquarters in October, 1942, to oversee the growth of the navy's mushrooming Pacific air forces. Growing resources and the success of the fast carriers gradually strengthened the position of Towers and other senior naval aviators. Increasingly, flyers dominated key fleet and carrier task force leadership positions. By the summer of 1944, Admiral King had "ruled what aviators had considered long overdue, that all nonaviator fleet and task force commanders would have aviator chiefs of staff."[57]

Despite their fleet's destruction, the Japanese continued to bring troops and supplies into Leyte through December, 1944, because of the weakness of American air power in the region. The fleet carriers had been withdrawn from the area for replenishment after the battle for Leyte Gulf, and the escort carriers were too battered to provide effective support to the troops ashore. In addition, heavy monsoon rains slowed the construction of airfields ashore.

In December, the JCS ordered MacArthur to invade Luzon. Marine aviators flew almost half of the U.S. sorties during that army-dominated campaign, which did not end until April, 1945. The flying leathernecks employed air liaison parties attached to ground units to request and direct air strikes. This was quicker, safer for friendly troops, and more flexible than the more centralized approach favored by army and navy aviators. Before, the campaign was over, army fighter-bomber units and the Sixth Army had adopted the marines' methods. Nevertheless, the battle for Luzon turned into a bloody slugging match against skillful Japanese defenders well entrenched in the island's northern mountains. As in Italy, geography sometimes minimized the impact of air power, no matter how skillfully employed.[58]

By early 1945, U.S. forces were closing in on Japan. Whether or not an invasion of the home islands would be needed depended on the success of American submarines and B-29s. Before the war, the United States had condemned unrestricted submarine warfare and the indiscriminate bombing of civilians. The navy, however, initiated an unrestricted submarine campaign against the Japanese shortly after the Pearl Harbor attack. Although initially

unprepared for a war against commerce, by the end of 1944 American submarines had destroyed approximately half of Japan's merchant fleet and two-thirds
of its tankers. At that point, oil deliveries from the East Indies were almost
completely eliminated and general bulk cargo imports had fallen by nearly 40
percent.[59]

Strategic bombing of the home islands by B-29s was the USAAF's main hope
for bludgeoning the Japanese into surrender. In late 1944, the XXI Bomber
Command began gearing up for operations from its new bases in the Marianas.
Senior naval officers were simultaneously skeptical and wary of the B-29 campaign. Above all, some feared that their carrier and amphibious operations in
the western Pacific would turn into auxiliary support of the USAAF, placing the
latter in position to claim the credit for beating Japan.

The strategic bombing campaign from the Marianas was plagued by mechanical difficulties, inexperience with long over-water flights, and foul weather.
Employing high-altitude, radar-guided precision strikes through bad weather
against the Japanese aircraft industry, B-29 crews encountered the jet stream's
two-hundred-mile-per-hour winds, which often blew their bombs off target.
Their accuracy was terrible. To revive the failing effort, Arnold sacked the commander, Brig. Gen. Haywood S. Hansell Jr., and replaced him with LeMay in
January, 1945. Meanwhile, the navy diverted some carrier strikes from support
of the hard-pressed marines on Iwo Jima to targets in Japan's home islands to
reduce the number of kamikaze attacks on the fleet and landing forces. Iwo
Jima, a small volcanic island about midway between the Marianas and Japan,
had been invaded on February 19 to serve as a haven for damaged B-29s and a
base for their P-51 escorts.

Iwo Jima was the first test of a new marine arrangement that transferred
some control of air operations from the amphibious force commander to the
landing force leader, enabling the latter to control air strikes during extended
operations ashore. Contrary to navy and army doctrine, the marines also began
targeting enemy positions close to friendly troops. Such attacks were directed at
targets within hundreds rather than thousands of yards of American forces.

Despite naval gunfire and improved navy-marine close air support, Iwo Jima
cost the leathernecks more than six thousand dead and approximately twenty
thousand wounded before the campaign ended on March 26. The Japanese
were so deeply entrenched in caves and bunkers away from the landing beaches
that marine infantry had to root them out. In the process, almost all of the
twenty-one thousand enemy soldiers defending the island perished.

The island never became a major offensive base and P-51s were not really
needed to escort B-29s because the Japanese air defenses of their homeland
proved to be very weak. Nonetheless, Iwo became a haven for crippled B-29s,

which made some twenty-four hundred emergency landings there before the war ended. It is estimated that as many as twenty thousand airmen flying all types of damaged American aircraft were saved because they could land on the island.[60]

While the marines were securing Iwo Jima, General LeMay struggled to breathe life into the faltering B-29 bombing campaign. As in Europe, the pre-war Air Corps doctrine of high-altitude precision attacks against the enemy's industrial base eventually had to be junked. High winds and poor visibility because of rain and heavy cloud cover minimized bombing accuracy. Only 10 percent of the bombs dropped landed within a thousand feet of their targets. LeMay turned to low-level incendiary attacks on Japanese cities at night in March, 1945. That change in tactics produced enormous death and destruction. To reduce weight, he stripped the B-29s of their defensive machine guns and ammunition. City after city was burned to the ground. The largely civilian death toll was estimated at 330,000, with another 476,000 injured. The primary precision target of the bombing campaign was the aircraft industry, but it accounted for only 9 percent of the bombs dropped. Although carrier aircraft dropped just 4.2 percent of the bomb tonnage, they were more accurate than the B-29s due to their low-level dive-bombing techniques.[61]

Despite the hopes of senior USAAF leaders to defeat Japan with B-29s, the JCS saw the bombing as a useful technique for weakening the Japanese in preparation for an invasion of their home islands. To secure a staging area for that assault, 180,000 American soldiers and marines invaded Okinawa on April 1, 1945. Some twelve hundred ships, including forty large and small aircraft carriers, supported them. During the central Pacific campaign, the fast carriers would neutralize Japanese air bases within range of their objectives before D-Day. However, there were too many enemy airfields in Japan and on Formosa, and their aircraft were too well dispersed, to neutralize them all—even with the help of B-29s. The Japanese made widespread use of kamikazes during the Okinawa campaign. Although most of the attacking Japanese aircraft were shot down, those that did get through wreaked havoc on the invasion fleet.

Ashore, the soldiers and marines encountered the same fanatical resistance that had bloodied the Americans on Iwo Jima. Employing marine concepts that stressed the direction of strikes from the front lines by pilots accompanying the infantrymen, a joint command of leatherneck, navy, and USAAF airmen provided some of the war's best close air support. By the time organized resistance ended on June 21, some 5,000 sailors, 7,000 soldiers and marines, 70,000 Japanese troops, and 80,000 civilians had been killed. The Japanese lost over seventy-eight hundred aircraft. In return, the kamikazes sank thirty-six ships and damaged 368 others, including carriers and cruisers. Like the German terror weapons, the kamikazes reflected the desperation of the Japanese position. They had equally little impact on the overall military situation and, since most of them were training aircraft, their wastage and the extreme shortage of petroleum due to the submarine campaign meant that the Japanese could not reconstitute their air forces.[62]

Meanwhile, the blockade of the Japanese home islands had been tightened. Submarines were able to cut off the flow of most raw materials and petroleum to Japan, accounting for 60 percent of the 8.1 million tons of Japanese shipping sunk during the war. The B-29s played a major supporting role in the blockade by dropping aerial mines in Japanese waters from March through August, 1945. Yet even before LeMay launched his bombing campaign, the submariners had largely eliminated the flow of raw materials to Japanese industry. Although the big bombers finished off the economic destruction begun by the submarines and severely damaged civilian morale with their fire raids, they did not directly cause the surrender of an authoritarian society ruled by the military. Before the latter would lay down their arms, however, the Americans felt compelled to introduce an untried weapon that revolutionized warfare and threatened to destroy civilization itself.

LETTING THE GENIE OUT OF THE BOTTLE

The decision to employ atomic bombs against Japan was made by the new and untried American president, Harry S. Truman, who had succeeded Franklin D. Roosevelt when the latter died in April, 1945. Roosevelt had established an ad hoc panel of scientists to examine the feasibility of building such weapons after Albert Einstein warned him in late 1939 that the Germans were working on them. Little progress was made until 1941, when the British secretly reported that the Germans might develop a practical bomb before the war was over. Galvanized by that information, FDR launched an all-out U.S. effort to build the first atomic bomb. More than 120,000 people, including some of the nation's top scientists, mathematicians, and engineers, were employed on the supersecret "Manhattan Project."

The first atomic bomb was successfully tested in New Mexico on July 16, 1945. With the bomb in hand, the United States no longer needed the Soviets to enter the war against Japan, but it had no way to keep them out if Stalin decided to enter the fray. The USAAF's 509th Composite Group prepared its B-29s and aircrews at Wendover Field, Utah, through the winter and spring of 1945 to drop atomic bombs on Japanese targets if needed. Under the command of Col. Paul W. Tibbets Jr., the 509th deployed to Tinian in the Marianas that summer and began dropping practice bombs on Japan.

A dissident group of American scientists opposed use of the atomic bomb, but the JCS and an interim committee of civilian officials both recommended employing the weapon if the Japanese refused to surrender. Despite their faltering economy, the Japanese still retained strong ground forces on their home islands. Some 2.3 million soldiers and 4 million paramilitary fighters were ready to die for their emperor. After seeing the fanatical Japanese resistance on Iwo Jima and Okinawa, Truman and his military advisers believed they would fight to the end. Extrapolating from the bloody Okinawa campaign, the joint chiefs told the president to expect 280,000 American dead and wounded in the invasion of Kyushu, the rugged and mountainous southernmost Japanese island, set for November, 1945. Faced with that appalling prediction, Truman gave the order to use the two completed bombs unless the Japanese agreed to unconditional surrender. Although he publicly maintained that he lost no sleep over it, Truman later privately confided to his sister that it was a "terrible decision" for him.

Truman's decision remains controversial. Critics claim that use of atomic bombs was unnecessary because Japan was already beaten and would have surrendered soon without it. Others seeking to buttress their opposition to the use of those weapons cite much lower casualty estimates for the planned invasion of Japan than were furnished by the joint chiefs. But the sneak attack on Pearl Harbor, atrocities in prisoner of war camps and occupied Asia, and the kamikazes all combined to strengthen the prevalent American attitude that the Japanese were savage fanatics who cared nothing for human life. The bloody resistance of the last-ditch defenders of Iwo Jima and Okinawa only hardened that attitude.

On August 6, the "Enola Gay," a B-29 named for Colonel Tibbets's mother, dropped a lone bomb on Hiroshima. At least 60,000 civilians and several thousand troops died instantly. Another 60,000 perished later from injuries and radiation poisoning. The bomb destroyed 81 percent of Hiroshima's structures. Whatever its operational merits at the time, the nuclear genie had been let out of the bottle, setting a dangerous precedent for the postwar world. The Soviets declared war on Japan two days later. That same evening, another atom bomb laden B-29 left Tinian bound for Nagasaki. At least another 35,000 people were killed by the August 9 detonation, but Japanese military leaders still adamantly opposed surrender. Subsequently, 40,000 more human beings died in Nagasaki as a result of injuries and radiation sickness. Emperor Hirohito took the unprecedented step of directly intervening in a political matter. He used his moral authority to sanction the Japanese government's acceptance of Allied peace proposals with the sole exception that the imperial institution be preserved. Japan announced on August 10 that it would surrender if the emperor were retained. The Americans waffled, however, and four days later a group of fanatic Japanese officers attempted a coup. Hirohito, who was considered a divine being and had never been heard or seen by most of his people, broadcast a radio message saying that all Japanese must lay down their arms. The war was over. On September 2, General MacArthur accepted the formal surrender aboard the battleship USS *Missouri* anchored in Tokyo Bay.[63]

During the ceremony, nearly a thousand carrier aircraft and B-29s soared overhead, symbolizing the critical role that military aviation had played during the Pacific war. But that was only part of the story. Kenneth Werrell concluded that "Japan was not defeated by air power or the atomic bomb alone; it was defeated by the combined actions of American and Allied ground, sea, and air forces. In the final analysis, this joint effort caused the rising sun to set."[64]

An atomic bomb delivered by an Army Air Force B-29 nicknamed the *Enola Gay* was detonated over the Japanese city of Hiroshima on August 6, 1945. Together with another atomic bomb dropped on Nagasaki three days later, those weapons destroyed both cities and helped to end World War II. (U.S. Air Force collection, National Archives.)

AIR POWER'S IMPACT

American air power came of age during World War II. It played a central role in defeating the Axis powers—but often not in the ways that its prewar advocates had anticipated. Airplanes did not supplant the army, navy, and Marine Corps. Driven by its strategic circumstances as an island nation that needed to project power globally to defeat its enemies, and determined to maximize it's immense economic strength, the United States had adopted a broad military aviation strategy for a long global conflict before the Japanese attack on Pearl Harbor. That strategy enabled it to produce enormous numbers of increasingly capable aircraft and well-trained aircrews that eventually surpassed the numbers and capabilities of their Axis foes. Unlike Germany and Japan, the wartime development of American air power was not dominated by the needs and perceptions of military elites. Instead, it was based on the collaborative efforts of science, industry, the armed forces, and the civilian government. Foreign technological influences continued to play an important role in the development of American military aviation during the conflict.

Aviation became the navy's primary combat arm, assured a critical role for itself in the infantry-oriented Marine Corps, and achieved coequal wartime status with the army's ground forces while ensuring the creation of a separate postwar air force—all during World War II. Contrary to the expectations of some prewar advocates, air power did not provide a quick and relatively blood-less panacea to the military challenges the United States faced after Pearl Harbor. Although strategic bombing played an important role in achieving Allied victory, the prewar doctrine advocated by the Air Corps was a ghastly failure. Air campaigns against modern industrial powers like Germany and Japan turned out to be protracted battles of attrition rather than quick, decisive bombing raids against a few critical industries. Before heavy bombers could even begin to have a real impact, German submarines had to be defeated in a long combined arms operation in the Atlantic. In North Africa, the Mediterranean, and western Europe, fighters had to achieve air superiority before other forms of air power could be brought to bear effectively. Allied airmen worked closely with their ground and naval comrades to defeat the well-armed and experienced German military machine.

Like Britain, the United States pursued a broad air power strategy employing military aviation in all of its major roles simultaneously. Some of them, such as airlift and antisubmarine warfare, had received little prewar attention or resources. Tactical aviation facilitated the advance of ground troops in North Africa and the Mediterranean and supported them on the continent. Strategic bombers forced the Germans to devote a major share of their total war effort to air defense and eventually contributed to the Luftwaffe's destruction by undermining its industrial base, destroying its oil supplies, and serving as bait to lure its fighter forces into battle, where they suffered catastrophic losses. Despite the enormous destruction and huge number of casualties that it was responsible for, strategic bombing did not win the war in Europe on its own. Nevertheless, air power broadly applied as a force coequal with ground forces was an indispensable element of Allied victory over Germany.[65]

Although Allied airmen had created false expectations by making exaggerated claims for aviation before and during the war, the strategic bombing campaign complemented the efforts of Allied ground and naval forces. However, its cost was extremely high, and the campaign was often waged unimaginatively. Senior airmen sometimes failed to adapt to the true conditions of the war, thereby restricting air power's potential.[66] Nevertheless, all wars have been fought with such misconceptions and failures of imagination. Regardless of its many shortcomings, the strategic bombing campaign was essential to the defeat of Nazi Germany. It was not humane and it was not quick, but it worked.[67]

Aviation played an even more important role in the Far East. According to Richard Overy: "America had from the start placed a great emphasis on a general air strategy . . . as the fastest and surest way of containing Japan until forces could be released from the European area. Secondly, the geography of the region placed a premium on air power combined with powerful naval support in the form of floating aerodromes."[68] He added that American air power was even more significant there than in Europe "because of the relative strength of the two main combatants. Japan's air force was outnumbered; its economy was weakened by American blockade strategy; its industrial homeland was poorly defended and provided an ideal target for firebombing which the Americans practiced with greater ruthlessness and efficiency in the east than against the better-defended and less flammable targets in Europe."[69] Overy concluded that "Perhaps most important of all, the Allies developed a strategy for the decisive exploitation of the advantage in the air without which the combat with Japan would have been far longer and less predictable."[70]

Aviation emerged as an indispensable element of America's global military effort during World War II. However, as Overy observed: "There can be no definite conclusion about how decisive air power was. There was too much inter-dependence between the services and between strategies to produce a list of components that were either more or less decisive. Just as an aircraft could not be flown without a propeller nor a propeller fly without its aircraft, so was air power related to the war effort."[71] He added that "The only conclusion that the evidence bears is . . . that victory for either side could not have been gained without the exercise of air power."[72]

The war created a large permanent defense industry with strong ties to scientific researchers in colleges, universities, and commercial laboratories. Military spending became a major continuing source of scientific and engineering innovation after the victory over Japan. Employment in the high-paying aviation industry encouraged many women and nonwhite males to look for better jobs and be more assertive about their economic prospects after the war. Wartime training and aircraft testing generated an enormous expansion of the civilian aviation infrastructure especially in the Sun Belt states of the south and west.[73]

The war also had an enormous impact on commercial aviation technology. It accelerated or expanded trends that already had been under way or were the object of serious study before America went to war. Every large commercial transport that flew during the conflict—the Douglas DC-4, the Lockheed Constellation, and the Boeing Stratoliner—was either in service or on the drawing boards by 1939. Military necessity rushed their development far faster and farther than would have been likely in peacetime commercial service. Transcontinental and transoceanic flights by land-based American four-engine aircraft became routine during World War II. They took over the world's air transport routes virtually overnight and, after the war, drove the less efficient flying boats from the commercial airways. Long-distance air travel, a novelty before the war, became routine. Civilian airliners equipped with pressurized cabins for high-altitude flights were being introduced into commercial service before the conflict began. The war diverted that development to military needs but intensified research and development, making far superior systems available when peacetime operations resumed.

Instrument landing and ground-control approach systems developed during the war to control large numbers of military aircraft returning from missions were applied immediately after the conflict to control traffic around large commercial airports. Without those systems, airport congestion would have seriously threatened the rapid development of commercial air traffic. The war enormously accelerated jet engine development and its adaptation to commercial use. Although the "gas turbine in due course would have replaced the piston engine, its [commercial applications] would have been markedly delayed by its high developmental cost and by the elaborate aerodynamic research needed to build planes designed for jet propulsion."[74] The helicopter's development was also promoted by the war, but not nearly as decisively as either jets or air traffic control systems.

World War II underscored and magnified the critical role that the military had played in the development of American aviation technology. In John Rae's view, "The bulk of the research and development work in aviation has been supported by military sources and undertaken for military objectives, with commercial benefits accruing as a byproduct."[75] One of the leading American aircraft makers, Donald Douglas, echoed the point: "If it were not for military expenditures, commercial aircraft would cost more than twice as much, would be less advanced, and would cost more to operate."[76]

Wartime American military aviation also influenced the larger society and culture. Richard Overy concluded that air combat "assumed a significance in the popular mind out of all proportion to the contribution of air forces to victory or to the technical capabilities of the air weapon."[77] Images and accounts of the Japanese surprise attack on Pearl Harbor were employed as powerful propaganda tools to justify taking a once reluctant people into war and punishing their treacherous attackers. Movies, magazines, and books celebrated the exploits of air combat commanders like Jimmy Doolittle plus aces such as Joe Foss, Dick Bong, and Gregory "Pappy" Boyington to help mobilize popular support for the war. It was easy to focus on pilots because of the individualist

Major Gregory "Pappy" Boyington, a U.S. Marine Corps ace, Medal of Honor recipient, and commander of the famed VMF-214 "Black Sheep" fighter squadron. Boyington scored twenty-two kills while flying marine F4U Corsairs in the South Pacific during World War II. Piloting a P-40 with the Flying Tigers in China, he became an ace with six kills before America officially entered the war. Boyington personified the rough-and-tumble image of hard-fighting, hard-drinking American fighter pilots during the war. (Defense Department photo.)

nature of air combat. But such wartime heroes did not resonate with the post-war popular culture the way that Eddie Rickenbacker and Charles Lindbergh had a generation before. Instead, if individual World War II airmen are remembered at all, they tend to be commanders like Halsey, LeMay, and Chennault. Nevertheless, the military flyboy image retained a glamorous niche in the popular culture despite being nameless and faceless.

The public understood that air power played a major role during the war. Movies such as *12 O'Clock High* and *The Flying Tigers* celebrated the airmen's heroics and anguish. But with the firebombing of enemy cities and the advent of atomic weapons, military aviation had become so large, impersonal, and destructive that some began to fear its ultimate implications. According to Joseph Corn, the wartime aerial Armageddon had dimmed earlier naive millennial hopes that aviation and "air-mindedness" would insure peace and prosperity. During World War II, and with increasing velocity afterward, disillusionment grew "as the airplane was seen as an instrument of mass destruction at its worst and merely another means of transportation at best."[78] Regardless of the ambiguity and skepticism about it in the popular culture, aviation continued to play an important role in America's postwar economy and military establishment.

CHAPTER 4

An Age of Limits

T he American experience in World War II suggested that air power had emerged as the decisive factor in modern war. The atomic bombing of Japan reinforced that opinion among those who were convinced aviation had revolutionized warfare. However, as the Cold War emerged, the limits of military aviation gradually became apparent. Nuclear forces did not play a central role in U.S. and Soviet strategy until the mid-1950s. Although they probably prevented a war between those superpowers, such forces often did not provide the diplomatic leverage and military deterrent expected of them at other levels of military and political competition. Stimulated by Cold War tensions, nuclear weapons helped to create a dangerous and expensive arms race between the two superpowers. Paradoxically, the dangers of nuclear war encouraged limited conventional wars and guerrilla conflicts all over the globe. While air power and nuclear weapons may have kept those bloodlettings from escalating into World War III, they were powerless to resolve them. The heavy emphasis placed on strategic forces, as well as the move to conventional and guerrilla conflicts, repeatedly undermined air power's position during the Cold War. According to John Buckley, "far from emerging from the ruins of World War II as the supreme and omniscient force, air power has struggled to assert itself and its impact has been patchy and far short of what many in 1945 might have expected. . . . [I]n many ways it has failed to adapt to an age when total war has become less and less likely."[1]

Despite its limitations, aviation remained an indispensable element of the nation's technological, diplomatic, and military strength. Air forces had been at the cutting edge of technological advances since V-J Day. Their requirements drove much of the development of America's first large peacetime military-industrial complex. Although it no longer required the broad mobilization of the nation's industrial resources that had been essential to win World War II, air power required unprecedented continuing access to scientific and technological resources in peacetime. Alex Roland concluded that the conflict "transformed the relationship between war and the military on the one hand and science and technology on the other. What had been a fitful and uncomfortable relationship before the war became continuous and consistent thereafter. Important ties existed before 1941, but they were nothing like the intimate connection of those two fields in the last half of the twentieth century."[2]

A REVOLUTION IN MILITARY AFFAIRS

During the immediate postwar years, the U.S. armed forces took major steps to institutionalize scientific and technical assistance. Although many American military officers had been skeptical of technological innovation in the past, they had come to embrace research and development as a key to national security. While industrial production had been critical to the Allied victory over the Axis, revolutionary innovations including ballistic missiles, jet aircraft, and the atomic bomb led many officers to believe that quality would be more critical than quantity on future battlefields.

In the late 1940s, the United States faced a radically changed international security environment. Its principal adversaries, Germany and Japan, had been utterly defeated and were occupied by the victorious Allied powers. Much of Europe and Asia lay in ruins. Soviet armies occupied most of central Europe. Except for America, the economies of the victorious powers had been terribly weakened by the conflict. Independence movements were beginning to stir in European colonies. Atomic weapons, long-range aircraft, and ballistic missiles threatened to eliminate the established barriers of time and space that had long protected the United States. After V-J Day, most of America's armed might had melted away as the nation rushed to bring the troops home.

Although Pres. Harry Truman attempted to cooperate with the Soviets, conflicting ideologies and clashing national interests gradually hardened into open hostility. Winston Churchill coined the phrase "Iron Curtain" in reference to the separation of Western and Eastern Europe during a speech in Fulton, Missouri, in early 1946. The following year, Truman promised aid to Greece and Turkey when the British were no longer able to do so. The president then sponsored the Marshall Plan—named after his secretary of state, retired army general George C. Marshall—to rebuild the shattered economies and promote political stability and pro-American democratic governments in Europe. After the Soviets sponsored a communist coup that overthrew Czechoslovakia's democratic government that same year, the Cold War was on in earnest.

The collapse of European colonialism after World War II added another dangerous dimension to the Cold War. Generally, the indigenous leadership of anticolonial movements had been captured either by communists or those sympathetic to their goals. However, the Truman administration was unwilling to accept communist victories in a series of guerrilla wars that broke out against colonial rule in Indochina, Malaya, Burma, the Philippines, and the Dutch East Indies. Although the United States opposed restoration of colonial empires in principle after V-J Day, it needed the support of Western European nations in its emerging global competition with the Soviet Union.

The containment policy, first publicly articulated in an anonymous article published in July 1947 by diplomat George F. Kennan, initially emphasized political and economic measures. Gradually, however, the Truman administration concentrated on military solutions to the challenges posed by the Soviet Union and international communism. Consequently, the United States disregarded George Washington's advice and developed a series of "entangling alliances" that sought to contain Soviet-inspired expansionism without starting another world war. The most important of them, the North Atlantic Treaty Organization (NATO), was established in 1949 to keep "the Russians out, the Americans in, and the Germans down."[3]

To make that work, the Americans built a large peacetime military force for the first time in the republic's history and stationed much of it overseas. Professionals and draftees—augmented by guardsmen, reservists, and wartime volunteers—would deter aggression and fight the nation's wars if containment failed. To equip that force with modern weapons, the armed services developed an unprecedented set of long-term domestic alliances with defense contractors, university-based scientific researchers, private think tanks, and members of Congress, plus a host of state and local politicians. The federal government eventually built the interstate highway system and began to play a significant role in education at all levels in the name of national security because of the Cold War. The armed forces, which had been historically relegated to the fringes of American society, culture, and the economy except in wartime, became major actors on the national stage.

It took several years of bitter arguments and political infighting after World War II to sort out U.S. national security policy and institutions. Unresolved questions about the roles of air power and atomic weapons were central to those struggles. Amid demobilization and dramatic declines in military spending, the armed services fell into their usual habit of arguing about resources and national strategy. Some officers, mostly in the army, had long favored unifying the services under an overall military commander. Those opposed, led by the navy, usually voiced their opposition as a fear of "Prussianizing" the armed forces.

Joint operations during World War II had strengthened the hand of those who supported unification. After several years of military boards and congressional hearings punctuated by name-calling and backroom political maneuvering, Capitol Hill and the White House decided on a relatively weak federation instead of a strong centralized military system. The National Security Act of 1947 established the basic framework for the postwar American defense organization. It created the National Military Establishment (renamed the Department of Defense [DOD] in 1949), which was presided over by a secretary of defense who had a small staff and very little real power. The legislation also gave legal standing to President Roosevelt's wartime expedient, the Joint Chiefs of Staff. The president would formulate policy in consultation with a new National Security Council (NSC). He would draw upon another new agency for information about threats to American security: the Central Intelligence Agency (CIA).

Achieving what many army airmen had been struggling for since the end of World War I, the Army Air Forces were transformed into a new military service, the U.S. Air Force (USAF), in September, 1947. The army, navy, and air force were separate military departments, each with their own secretary, staff, and seats in the president's cabinet. The marines fought off a strong coalition in the War Department, the White House, and Congress that wanted to strip the Corps of its amphibious assault mission and transfer its aviation assets to the air force. The legislation specified service roles and missions, a provision that saved all naval aviation functions and the Fleet Marine Force. Interservice relations remained bound to the JCS system of military negotiation. It did not even establish a formal chairman of the nation's highest military body.

The legislation was largely a victory for the navy, which—under the leadership of its civilian secretary, James V. Forrestal—had fought the original army plan for a centralized postwar defense organization to a standstill. He understood well the assumptions of the War Department's proposal for the postwar military establishment: Sea-based naval aviation would be reduced dramatically, land-based naval air assets would be given to the air force, and the doctrinal heirs of Billy Mitchell would monopolize nuclear weapons. The Marine Corps, in turn, would be reduced to minor peacetime security functions like those it had exercised in the nineteenth century. No major naval campaigns were envisioned in any future war with the Soviet Union. The sea service's primary mission thus would have been to secure the sea lanes against Soviet submarines while transporting army troops overseas to seize advanced bases from which the air force would launch atomic strikes against the Soviet Union.

It took the armed forces years to digest the implications of atomic weapons and the postwar international security environment for their own doctrines and force structure. American national security would be based upon two new concepts: strategic nuclear deterrence and forward collective defense. During World War II, the army made plans to maintain a strong professional postwar cadre that would mobilize a mass citizen force if the need arose. That force was to be supplied by universal military training. Army leaders reluctantly yielded to budgetary and political realities, however, and settled for a regular force of some six hundred thousand troops. Although such a force was historically high for the United States in peacetime, it was inadequate to meet the service's global responsibilities after V-J Day. The army also grudgingly agreed to retain the politically potent National Guard as its primary reserve combat force. When Congress refused to enact universal military training for able-bodied males, the army in 1947 supported adoption of the first peacetime draft in the nation's history.

Because of tight budgets and occupation duties in Germany and Japan, army training and weapons modernization programs languished. Nevertheless, the service expanded its organic aviation capabilities after the war's end. Division aviation companies performed observation, liaison, and communications functions, and Transportation Corps aviation battalions were assigned to field armies. Although it obtained its first helicopters in 1946, the army was only beginning to understand the potential of those versatile aircraft in the late 1940s. Small fixed-wing planes thus continued to dominate the service's aircraft inventory.

During World War II, USAAF planners had stressed the need to build the largest standing postwar force possible and hold it in a high state of readiness so that it could undertake offensive combat operations immediately at the outset of hostilities. In their opinion, there would be no time to mobilize the nation's scientific, industrial, and manpower resources after the next war began. Although they wanted it to be a balanced organization with tactical aviation, airlift, and air defense units, the air force would be built around the long-range strategic bombardment mission that most senior army airmen since Billy Mitchell had considered the key to attaining a separate service and winning modern wars against first-rate industrial powers. Army Air Forces planners pressed for about a million men to man 105 combat air groups after the war. They expected that force to relegate the other military services to minor supporting roles. They had little faith in guard and reserve units, which historically had required a good deal of time to train and reequip after mobilization. General Marshall, however, understood that Americans were unlikely to accept such a grandiose and expensive active duty force after World War II. He forced the USAAF to scale back its plans to seventy groups manned by four hundred thousand personnel. A combination of pressure from him and the politically influential National Guard Association compelled senior army airmen to accept proposals for a large dual-component postwar reserve program consisting of the Air National Guard and the Air Force Reserve.

Like military unification, defense spending became a highly contentious issue in the immediate postwar era. The United States spent $350 billion dollars on manpower and materiel during the war. President Truman's defense budgets averaged only $10–14 billion annually in the late 1940s. Because of the severe constraints imposed by those budgets, the armed forces were unable to achieve their ambitious force structure goals before the Korean War.[4]

A STEPCHILD SAVES A CITY

The first big postwar test of American air power was far removed from the doctrinal mainstream of the bomber-oriented USAF. As the United States, Britain, and France began merging their occupation zones to build a separate West German state, Soviet dictator Joseph Stalin retaliated in June, 1948, by initiating a ground blockade of those sectors of Berlin controlled by the Western Allies. Instead of risking a global war by forcing the blockade with ground troops, the United States and Britain cobbled together an airlift to sustain the city. Airlift was at best the stepchild of Billy Mitchell's disciples who dominated the brand-new U.S. Air Force. The decision to launch the airlift was made by President Truman and Gen. Lucius D. Clay, the U.S. military governor of Germany, without even consulting the JCS. With a population of 2.5 million, Berlin had only enough food on hand to last thirty-six days, and coal stocks that might last up to forty-five days. Military planners did not expect the airlift to be a long-term diplomatic countermove that would last through the winter. Air force leaders initially opposed the extended airlift because it would tie up scarce transports, which would be vulnerable to Soviet air attacks. The question of whether or not Berlin was worth fighting for if the airlift failed was never answered.

Quickly overcoming the doubts of its senior leaders, the USAF moved vigorously to deal with its first major international crisis. Under the command of Lt. Gen. Curtis E. LeMay, the U.S. Air Forces in Europe (USAFE) collected worn-out C-47s in Germany. Air force, navy, and RAF transports with much larger cargo capacities later replaced them. In Berlin, contractors built two new runways at Tempelhof Airport and a third one at Tegel, a new airport in the French sector. Major General William Tunner, who had gained fame overseeing the

Navy airmen celebrate the news that the Soviet Union lifted its land blockade of Berlin on May 12, 1949. Primarily a U.S. Air Force operation, the Royal Air Force and the U.S. Navy also participated in the Berlin Airlift. Conducted without resorting to combat, the operation was one of the greatest triumphs of American air power after World War II. (U.S. Air Force collection, National Air and Space Museum.)

Hump airlift in the China-Burma-India theater, was brought in to complete the operation. Round-the-clock flights by ground-controlled aircraft were instituted, along with new maintenance and traffic management procedures needed to sustain the grueling pace of operations regardless of weather conditions.

When the Soviets threatened to disrupt the operation, President Truman dispatched a wing of B-29s to Britain that were called "atomic bombers" for public consumption. The B-29s were not actually armed with atomic weapons, but the Soviets could not really be sure. Having boasted that they could force the Americans, British, and French out of Berlin, they looked sillier and sillier the longer the airlift lasted. Joseph Stalin, the Soviet dictator, quietly ended the blockade on May 12, 1949. Although the airlift continued until the following September, the United States and its allies had won one of the first great victories of the Cold War. The western zone of Berlin remained in allied hands, becoming a symbol of human freedom and a flash point for Cold War tensions. During the Berlin airlift, the fledgling USAF employed an undervalued stepchild of military aviation to achieve a vital national policy objective without firing a shot.[5]

The Berlin blockade was a disaster for Stalin's foreign policy objectives. According to John Lewis Gaddis, the Soviet leader "brought about many of the things he feared most: an American commitment to defend Western Europe; a revived West German state closely tied to his adversaries; the beginning of fragmentation within the international communist movement; and a conviction on the part of Western leaders that, because the Soviet Union could not be trusted, negotiations with it . . . could only be approached with the greatest caution and from positions of strength, if they were able to take place at all."[6] The blockade was directly responsible for the creation of NATO and the establishment of the Federal Republic of Germany, both in 1949. Nevertheless, airlift continued to languish in the financially strapped air force, which was firmly wedded to the doctrine of strategic bombardment.[7]

ROLES, MISSIONS, AND HIGH TECHNOLOGY

Meanwhile, another kind of crisis had been boiling over back in the United States because of the unification of the armed forces. James Forrestal became the first secretary of defense. While serving as navy secretary from 1944–47, Forrestal had strongly resisted President Truman's plans to unify the postwar armed forces. Ironically, while running the navy, he was instrumental in obtaining legislative amendments that severely weakened his authority as defense secretary. When the president's top choice for the post declined, he turned to Forrestal. The latter reluctantly accepted, but he soon found that he lacked the staff and authority to control the bitter rivalries between the armed forces. The allocation of service roles and missions, especially aviation, were the thorniest issues he faced.

The air force and navy remained at odds about the future of military aviation. The controversy was rooted in Billy Mitchell's old assertion of the indivisibility of air power. The navy wanted the air force confined to the tactical use of air power on land and to strategic bombing. The air force, on the other hand, wanted every mission that air power could perform and did not like the navy poaching on its strategic bombing preserve with carrier-based aviation. However, those roles and missions could not be clearly defined. Despite Forrestal's best efforts, the issue culminated in a B-36 versus supercarrier political struggle better known as "the revolt of the admirals."[8]

The navy and Marine Corps had sought to integrate conventional and nuclear war preparations with their established ideas about sea power after Nagasaki and Hiroshima. The sea service was determined to acquire atomic weapons, but it had no well-developed concept for employing them and lacked the wherewithal to do so. It lobbied hard for new supercarriers that would be capable of launching aircraft that could deliver atomic bombs to inland targets. The latter mission trespassed on the air force's monopoly of atomic weapons. Meanwhile, naval officers remained privately skeptical about how useful such weapons would actually be in combat. More significantly, the Strategic Air Command (SAC), the air force's new atomic strike organization, remained a "hollow threat" that lacked enough trained crews, atomic bombs, and properly equipped bombers to mount a serious air campaign against the Soviet Union until the early 1950s. However, the weakness of the nation's atomic strike force was not widely understood at the time.

General LeMay was given command of SAC in October, 1948, and ordered to turn the struggling organization around. In addition to being a superb organizer and problem solver, he was one of the leading proponents of strategic bombing. The Strategic Air Command profited from strong JCS as well as air force support of LeMay's efforts to strengthen it. During his unprecedented nine years at the helm, he built a dispirited command into an elite all-jet bomber force supported by air refueling aircraft that gave them global range. Armed with nuclear weapons and trained to unprecedented levels of peacetime readiness, LeMay's SAC served as the centerpiece of American military power into the 1960s—well after he left the command's headquarters at Offutt Air Force Base (AFB), Nebraska, for the Pentagon. However, his success at SAC—which was sustained by and reinforced his service's doctrinal emphasis on strategic bombing—had been achieved at the expense of other critical dimensions of air power including tactical aviation and airlift.[9]

Nuclear weapons were the key to SAC's awesome power under LeMay. After World War II, Secretary of War Henry Stimson and government scientists had urged President Truman to provide a system of strict controls to prevent the future use of atomic bombs. Congress passed legislation in 1946 that established the Atomic Energy Commission (AEC), a civilian research and development agency outside military control that also maintained custody of atomic weapons. The bombs themselves were stored apart from their other components at a site near Albuquerque, New Mexico. Under the pressure of postwar economizing, fewer than two hundred bombs could have been assembled in a crisis as late as 1949. Moreover, SAC did not have a single team capable of assembling a bomb until 1948. That same year, the command possessed only fifty bombers equipped to handle atomic weapons. However, when LeMay first tested his new command, he discovered that none of his aircrews could place a weapon on target under wartime conditions. It was April, 1951, before Gen. Hoyt S. Vandenberg, the air force chief of staff, was able to convince President Truman to instruct the AEC to transfer nine bombs and their atomic cores to his service because of growing fears of a global conflict with the Soviet Union following Communist China's intervention in the Korean War.

Atomic weapons underscored the central role that research and development played in the postwar American military establishment. Each of the armed forces was convinced in varying degrees that its future was tied to technological advances. The army, navy, and air force each claimed major roles in the deployment of nuclear weapons. Previously known for their technological conservatism, the armed forces embraced innovation and devoted substantial shares of their budgets to research and development in order to secure their futures.

Unlike prewar American aircraft design practices, the postwar period saw the general abandonment of incremental model improvement in favor of striking advances in performance based upon improved jet engines and advanced aerodynamic designs. Captured German aerodynamic research data for high-speed jet aircraft had an enormous impact on postwar American aviation. It prompted North American and Boeing to incorporate swept wings into plans for some new aircraft. North American's design for a straight-wing navy fighter became the air force's F-86 Sabre, one of the greatest fighters of its day. Boeing's proposal for a jet bomber was revamped as the swept-wing B-47 Stratojet, a speedster that became the mainstay of SAC's nuclear deterrent force in the 1950s. The B-47 influenced the firm's subsequent bomber designs, including the B-52 Stratofortress, and was a precursor of that corporation's phenomenally successful commercial airliners.

Despite the impressive performance gains represented by those jet fighters and bombers, public attention was riveted on the quest for supersonic speed by a series of experimental aircraft financed by the armed services in the immediate postwar period. The most famous of them was Bell's rocket-powered X-1. On October 14, 1947, with air force captain Charles E. Yeager at the controls, it became the first aircraft to break the sound barrier. Working with NACA and aircraft makers, a series of air force and navy experimental planes helped solve a number of high-speed flight problems and enhanced the designs of future jet airliners and supersonic fighter aircraft.[10]

Less spectacular than the supersonic tests but equally important to the future of American air power, in-flight refueling was transformed from an experimental oddity and a headline-grabbing stunt into a practical technique that promised to achieve truly intercontinental reach with bombers based in the continental United States. Army aviators had first demonstrated the feasibility of aerial refueling in the 1920s. The emergence of modern prejet airplanes in the 1930s apparently overcame the range limitations with which those early experiments had grappled. Promising British tests of various military and commercial applications of aerial refueling during the 1930s were aborted by the outbreak of World War II, and wartime air-to-air refueling experiments took a backseat to more pressing developmental and production priorities in Britain and the United States.

The need to be able to strike targets in the Soviet Union with relatively short-ranged B-29s and B-50s drove the air force to adopt air-to-air refueling systems as Cold War tensions increased. The service equipped a number of B-29s with a British-developed looped-hose system and activated its first air refueling squadrons in 1948. On February 26, 1949, a B-50 named "Lucky Lady II" took off from Carswell AFB, New Mexico. It returned some ninety-four hours later, after completing the first nonstop flight around the globe. Although General LeMay told reporters that the flight showed the air force could now deliver atomic bombs anywhere in the world, technical problems prevented extensive aircrew training with the air refueling systems until the mid-1950s. By the end of 1949, the air force had successfully flown several F-84E fighters nonstop across the Atlantic with the aid of in-flight refueling.[11]

To some observers, atomic weapons, jet fighters, and in-flight refueling of strategic bombers appeared to have rendered much of the navy's postwar force structure obsolete. An economy-minded Congress and strategic air power proponents argued that it was largely irrelevant. A presidential air policy commission and a similar congressional body concluded that the threat of nuclear retaliation provided by combat-ready intercontinental air forces was the cornerstone of America's defense. The Soviet Union was a land power with no significant navy. Consequently, Navy Secretary Forrestal and senior naval aviators had to expand the navy's missions and modernize its equipment after

World War II. The navy wanted aircraft and carriers that could not only maintain control of the seas, but also launch atomic attacks on the Soviet Union. However, no existing carrier aircraft could carry early versions of the atomic bombs, which weighed at least ten thousand pounds. The postwar weakness of the Royal Navy meant that its American cousin would have to expand its geographic role to protect against a new continental adversary, the Soviet Union.

Postwar atomic tests in the Pacific had forced the Marine Corps to reexamine its own amphibious doctrine. It decided that "vertical envelopment" by helicopters was the best way to avoid dangerous exposure to enemy atomic weapons while concentrations of leathernecks were embarked on landing craft preparing to assault defended beaches. Helicopters would land at weak points behind enemy forces and clear the way for the landing craft. It was an intriguing idea, but the marines had no helicopters in the early postwar period with which to test the concept. The navy, meanwhile, had already established a close working relationship with pioneer helicopter makers. Drawing on those ties, the Marine Corps obtained several helicopters and began testing their troop-carrying potential in 1948. Helicopter advocates faced strong resistance from fixed-wing marine aviators wedded to the close air support mission and navy planners concerned about the costs of heavy-lift helicopters capable of transporting significant numbers of troops. Slender postwar budgets slowed the development of such helicopters before the Korean War.

In 1943, the navy had convinced Congress to authorize construction of two new forty-five-thousand-ton *Midway*-class carriers that were launched in 1945. They were joined by a third vessel of that class in 1947. *Midway*-class carriers could launch the AJ-1 Savage, a hybrid propeller-and-jet-powered aircraft capable of delivering an atomic bomb, which joined the fleet in 1949. The navy developed the A3D, a twin-jet bomber weighing about seventy thousand pounds and capable of carrying an atomic bomb. The aircraft flew in squadron strength from Midway-class carriers and in three- or four- plane detachments from modernized *Essex*-class ships. To accommodate hundred-thousand-pound aircraft, the navy proposed a sixty-five-thousand-ton supercarrier to be named the *United States*. The sea service argued that its proposed jet bombers could deliver the heavy nuclear weapons of the day from carriers more reliably and more effectively than unescorted long-range air force bombers.

As secretary of defense, Forrestal was unable to reconcile the armed forces' budget requests, which totaled about twice what Truman would allow. He convened meetings of the JCS at Key West, Florida, and Newport, Rhode Island, in 1948 to hammer out agreements on roles and missions that would help resolve those budget issues. When the discussions were finished, the JCS

Convair's jet-augmented RB-36D Peacemaker reconnaissance bomber. This mammoth aircraft was equipped with cameras and electronics for conducting strategic reconnaissance, mapping, and bomb damage assessment missions for the air force. First flown in December, 1949, it did not enter operational service until June, 1951, and was phased out of the air force's inventory in 1956–57. Although the B-36 symbolized the Strategic Air Command's nuclear deterrent and war-fighting missions early in the Cold War, air-refueled pure-jet bombers like the B-47 and B-52 soon surpassed it. (Defense Department photo.)

and Forrestal had determined that the navy could develop atomic weapons for naval campaigns but not acquire a strategic air force. The marines, on the other hand, would maintain their air-amphibious force but not attempt to develop into a second ground army. However, the defense secretary could not create a consensus to implement those decisions in the face of growing pressure from the services and Congress. Frustrated by his inadequate authority as secretary of defense and unwilling to support the additional cuts in military spending demanded by the president, Forrestal was forced to resign in March, 1949. Plagued by fatigue, psychiatric problems, and the burden of caring for a bedridden alcoholic wife, he plunged to his death from the Bethesda Naval Hospital in May. Louis Johnson, a strong supporter of Truman's tight budget policies and the air force, replaced Forrestal on March 28. Five days after the keel of the *United States* was laid down in April, the new defense secretary canceled it.

Navy partisans cried conspiracy. The whole future of carrier aviation and, by extension, the navy's role in the U.S. military establishment appeared to be in jeopardy. The same organization that had cried wolf about the dangers of Prussianizing the armed forces during the military unification struggle, sought to undermine the authority of the Truman administration's civilian leaders and discredit the air force by charging that the B-36 long-range bomber would be no match for Soviet jet fighters.

This so-called revolt of the admirals was decided in the political arena. During the ensuing fracas, the B-36 was characterized as a "billion-dollar blunder" and Johnson was, in effect, accused of being bribed by Convair, the firm that designed and produced it. The admirals charged that strategic bombing had been a failure in World War II and that the air force was largely propaganda. It was an outburst of service hostility and parochialism seldom seen in public. Congress held hearings while air force and navy partisans hosted dueling press conferences.[12]

In the short run, the navy was discredited when it was revealed that anonymous and unsubstantiated charges against the air force had originated with a senior civilian official in the Department of the Navy. Navy Secretary John Sullivan resigned in protest and the chief of naval operations, Adm. Louis E. Denfeld, was forced to retire. The navy regained some ground during its public testimony before Congress in 1949, when senior naval officers raised troubling fundamental questions about the atomic blitz strategy championed by the air force. According to Jeffrey G. Barlow, the congressional hearings "went far to convince important members of the House Armed Services committee . . . that naval aviation remained a vital part of the country's defense capabilities. . . . [I]f the Navy had not taken a public stand in the congressional hearings, it is unlikely that the navy would have seen the new, highly-capable *Forrestal*-class carriers after the mid-1950s that have played such an important part in increasing the capabilities of carrier aviation."[13]

The navy was unable to discredit the Truman administration's austere military budget or to convince Capitol Hill that the air force had a narrow view of the nation's security needs in 1949. Nevertheless, the whole controversy contributed to a growing consensus that the National Military Establishment needed major modifications. That realization produced a series of amendments to the National Security Act in 1949 that strengthened the secretary of defense and created a single Department of Defense with three component military departments. The legislation also eliminated the military department secretaries from the NSC and the cabinet to curb service rivalry. Congress also approved creating the post of chairman of the Joint Chiefs of Staff. While the chairman did not have a vote on the JCS, he became the principal military adviser to the defense secretary and the president.[14]

The revolt of the admirals encouraged a trend toward greater centralization of policy making and budgeting in the Office of the Secretary of Defense (OSD). It also stimulated fears that interservice rivalries were carrying the armed forces farther away from a proper appraisal of the nation's strategic military needs. Those concerns were strengthened when Mao Tse-tung's communists won control of China after a long civil war and Secretary Johnson responded to the Soviet Union's explosion of its first atomic bomb by proposing that the United States launch a crash program to develop an even more powerful weapon, the hydrogen bomb. Those developments prompted Secretary of State Dean Acheson to call for an overall review of the Truman administration's military and diplomatic policies. A team of planners from the State Department and the JCS conducted a three-month study beginning in January, 1950. Their findings were presented that spring as NSC Memorandum 68. The planners concluded that the Soviet Union posed a long-term threat to U.S. security and the maintenance of world peace. They recommended that the best way to deal with that situation was to build up the military power of America and its allies in order to deter the Soviets. The estimated price tag for that policy was $40 billion a year. President Truman did not act on their recommendations because he was convinced that there would be no public or congressional support for sharply increased military spending in the absence of a grave international crisis. Such a crisis began in the early morning hours of June 25, 1950, when communist North Korean troops invaded South Korea.

The aggression caught Washington by surprise and unprepared for a conventional military conflict. Korea had been split between the Soviet Union and the United States at the 38th Parallel after World War II in order to disarm the Japanese forces occupying the peninsula. A communist government headed by Kim Il Sung had been installed in the north by the Soviets. In the south, the autocratic Syngman Rhee had emerged victorious after an internal power struggle. Both the Soviets and the Americans had withdrawn their occupation forces in the late 1940s, leaving behind relatively small numbers of military advisers. Agreements to reunify the country and hold free elections were never honored. Aggressive rhetoric, border skirmishes, and reciprocal efforts at subversion marked the strained relationship between the two Koreas. The United States, fearing that Rhee's aggressive intentions to reunify the country by force might start a war, had only provided enough military aid to lightly equip a small army in the south. Public statements by senior Truman administration officials and JCS war plans had placed Korea outside the U.S. defense periphery before the war began. The North Koreans, who were well trained and equipped with tanks and other heavy weapons by their Soviet sponsors, rapidly overwhelmed the lightly armed South Koreans.

President Truman believed that the Kremlin was behind the invasion. Although top U.S. civilian and military officials feared the crisis might be a feint designed to divert American power to the Far East before a Soviet invasion of Western Europe, they were determined to repel communist aggression through collective action under the United Nations charter. Although the president could have gotten a declaration of war from Congress, he was convinced that he had sufficient authority to take military action under UN auspices. Fortuitously, the Soviets boycotted the UN Security Council, thus avoiding a certain veto of a U.S.-sponsored resolution authorizing the use of armed force if necessary to repel the invasion and restore peace to the area. Truman easily obtained overwhelming support from Capitol Hill for emergency measures, including supplemental defense appropriations, guard and reserve mobilization, and an extension of the draft to support the "police action" in Korea.

General Douglas MacArthur, operating from his headquarters in Tokyo, was given command of UN forces in the Korean theater of operations. In addition to the use of U.S. Army units, he was authorized to employ American air and naval forces against the North Koreans. Back in the United States, General Hoyt S. Vandenberg, the air force chief of staff, and Adm. Forrest P. Sherman, the CNO, seriously miscalculated the situation. They believed that air and sea power could halt the invasion without the introduction of ground troops. MacArthur ignored their advice. He dispatched the few available army units to the peninsula, but they proved to be no match for the North Koreans, who quickly pushed them back to a bridgehead around the port of Pusan in the southeastern portion of the peninsula. Only desperate ground fighting supported by Allied air and naval forces prevented the Americans and South Koreans from being pushed into the sea.[15]

Korea was not the kind of war that either air force or navy leaders had expected to fight in 1950. Instead of nuclear strikes on the Soviet heartland, they faced a war of attrition against a numerically superior enemy. Both sides operated from untouchable sanctuaries and neither wished to expand the conflict beyond the Korean peninsula. Led by Lt. Gen. George E. Stratemeyer, the Far East Air Forces (FEAF) was the largest air component in MacArthur's United Nations Command (UNC). In the summer of 1950, FEAF was prepared to defend Japan from air attack and to conduct a strategic bombing campaign against Russian and Chinese targets. It was not, however, ready for an extended conventional air war. Stratemeyer's forces included nearly four hundred combat aircraft assigned to bases in Japan, Okinawa, Guam, and the Philippines. Strategic bombing was not a major factor in the war because the major economic sources of the enemy's military power were in the People's Republic of China and the Soviet Union—both off limits to allied air strikes. The FEAF did conduct a brief strategic bombing campaign against North Korean targets, but it lasted a mere eight weeks. LeMay fought tooth and nail against sending any SAC bombers to what he considered to be a sideshow in Asia while the threat of nuclear war with the Soviet Union seemed to be a real possibility. Vandenburg, was not swayed by LeMay's arguments and ordered him to dispatch two groups of B-29s to the Far East. MacArthur believed that the public announcement that SAC was supporting the UN cause would deter Chinese communist military intervention. Overriding strong objections from LeMay and the Air Staff, the JCS and the Truman administration agreed to MacArthur's request and ordered ten nuclear-capable B-29s and their nonnuclear bomb components to Guam in July. The bombers remained there until the crisis passed in Korea and returned to the United States in September. Between, August 1 and September 27, FEAF's conventionally armed B-29s destroyed every strategic target of any significance in that hapless nation.

However, fighters, not strategic bombers, carried the burden of the air war in Korea. Stratemeyer's most advanced jet fighter, Lockheed's F-80 Shooting Star, lacked the range to operate effectively from their bases in Japan and were not configured for ground missions at the beginning of the conflict. His fighter units had little practice in supporting ground troops because of the recent air force decision to merge the tactical and air defense missions plus the absence of space for large-scale military training in Japan. The only base in Korea that could take jets was Kimpo near Seoul. It was quickly overrun by rapidly advancing North Korean forces.[16]

Vice Admiral Turner C. Joy commanded the Naval Forces Far East. His main striking force was the *Essex*-class carrier USS *Valley Forge*. When the war began, the *Valley Forge* and its escorts were dispatched from the Philippines to Okinawa, where they were joined by a contingent of Royal Navy warships that included the carrier HMS *Triumph*. MacArthur then dispatched the Anglo-American squadron, designated Task Force 77, to the Yellow Sea off Korea's west coast. The *Valley Forge* carried two squadrons of F9F Panther jet fighters, two squadrons of World War II–vintage F4U Corsairs, and a squadron equipped with the new Douglas AD Skyraider, a propeller-driven attack aircraft. The *Triumph* carried squadrons of Fireflies and Seafires, nonjet fighters primarily employed in the fleet air defense and antishipping roles.

The FEAF launched combat operations over Korea on June 27. It was joined on July 3 by Task Force 77, which began attacking targets around Pyongyang, the North Korea capital. By the end of July, most of North Korea's combat aircraft had been destroyed, giving MacArthur's UNC total air superiority—as

The USS *Essex,* carrying a mixed group of jet and propeller-driven combat aircraft, is shown off the coast of Korea in January, 1952. Aircraft carriers adapted successfully to the demands of the jet age and limited warfare during the Korean "police action," providing mobile platforms for attacking enemy troop concentrations and lines of communications. (U.S. Navy photo courtesy of the Fiftieth Anniversary of the Korean War Commemoration Committee.)

long as neither the Chinese nor the Russians chose to massively intervene in the air campaign. But air attacks against enemy forces, supply lines, and installations were initially unable to halt the North Korean advance. The North Korean People's Army (NKPA) neutralized much of the FEAF's firepower by seizing its airfields in South Korea and forcing it to withdraw its short-ranged, gas-guzzling F-80s to Japan. To help improve close air support for the hard-pressed GIs in the shrinking Pusan perimeter, the air force repossessed F-51s from Air National Guard units in the United States and rushed them to the Far East, where they operated from primitive airstrips close to the front lines. B-29s were also pressed into service against North Korean lines of communications and, briefly, frontline positions.[17]

To provide immediate relief to Pusan, Task Force 77 launched emergency strikes against the NKPA forces besieging the UN perimeter. This triggered an interservice controversy over close air support and control of tactical air power that festered for the rest of the war. The air force approach to close air support was quite different than that of the navy and Marine Corps. Influenced by its World War II experiences and its doctrinal imperatives as a separate service, the former had adapted a highly centralized approach that featured a Joint Operations Center (JOC) manned by air force and army personnel. It was colocated with an air force Tactical Air Control Center (TACC). Tactical air control parties, each usually manned by a pilot and two enlisted men with a radio-equipped jeep, would spot likely targets at the front and then radio there location up through the army chain of command to the JOC. The air force saw close air support as a weapon augmenting artillery. Strikes were seldom closer than a thousand yards to friendly ground forces. Tight post–World War II budgets and the doctrinal emphasis on strategic nuclear deterrence had robbed the air force of the resources it needed to provide effective close air support.

Senior air force officers wanted command of all tactical air assets operating over the battlefield, regardless of which service owned them. They were especially sensitive to criticisms that inevitably found their way into the press that the air force had neglected its close air support responsibilities and that its jet fighter-bombers were unsuited to that role. For them, it was more of a public relations crisis than a military problem. The friction in the theater between air force and army commanders on the most effective use of air power continued throughout the war.

The navy and the air force agreed that air superiority in the theater of operations was the top priority. Unlike the air force, however, the navy saw close air support and battlefield interdiction as equally valuable from a doctrinal perspective. The navy, and especially the Marine Corps, employed a decentralized close air support system that placed a premium on rapid response and accurate delivery of ordnance. They allocated the money, manpower, equipment, and training time needed to make the system work. The marines employed aircraft on a relatively narrow front as a substitute for heavy artillery. Controlled by frontline tactical air control parties, marine and navy airmen routinely conducted strikes within fifty to two hundred yards of their own troops. Because of decentralized control, the practice of orbiting fighter-bombers over friendly ground forces, and the close proximity of carriers offshore, they could be more responsive to requests for emergency fire support than their FEAF counterparts. Navy and marine leaders insisted on retaining command of their air assets.[18]

Regardless of the merits of both approaches to tactical air support, it was clear that allied airmen played a critical role in preventing the Eighth Army from being destroyed at Pusan during the summer of 1950. The air force greatly improved its close air support system during the defense of Pusan and the remainder of the war, but it had to be satisfied with largely meaningless "coordination control" of navy and Marine tactical air assets for most of the rest of the conflict. Regardless of doctrinal differences and flawed command arrangements, poor communications was the most critical problem blocking effective centralized control of tactical air power.[19]

In some respects, MacArthur fought the rest of the Korean War as if it was a replay of his highly successful island-hopping campaign in the Southwest Pacific during World War II. To destroy the North Koreans, he conceived a brilliant and highly risky amphibious end run that was opposed by most senior American officers in the Far East and the Pentagon. Spearheaded by the 1st Marine Division, U.S. forces organized as the X Corps, landed at Inchon on Korea's west coast, bypassing the enemy's strength in the south. Four fleet and two escort carriers provided air cover for the invasion, which was launched on September 15, 1950. The North Koreans soon found themselves caught between the landing force and the Eighth Army, which had broken out of its perimeter at Pusan. Fighter-bombers savagely attacked retreating enemy units, and the remnants of the NKPA were quickly pushed north of the 38th Parallel.

Ignoring hints of possible Chinese communist military intervention, President Truman announced the fateful decision to reunify all of Korea by force of arms. Although the idea to change the war's basic aims originated in Washington, not Tokyo, MacArthur eagerly endorsed it. United Nations forces were soon racing north toward the Yalu River, which divided North Korea from China. Less than a third of the one hundred thousand NKPA soldiers fleeing ahead of them escaped the allied pincers.

Transport aircraft parachuted supplies to advancing UN troops and carried as many as a thousand passengers and a thousand tons of cargo a day from Japan to Korean airfields. B-29s attacked bridges over the Yalu on November 8, but failed to drop them. During the operation, Russian-made MiG-15 jets secretly manned by Soviet pilots based in China attacked the Americans. The MiGs pounced on the escorting F-80s and then darted back into their Manchurian sanctuary after losing one of their own aircraft to a Shooting Star. Navy fighter-bombers, which had been concentrating on close air support and interdiction strikes against the fleeing North Koreans, attacked the bridges with limited success the following day. Navy F9F Panthers shot down three of the MiGs that came up to meet them. The victories by American fighter pilots reflected their superior training and experience because it was obvious that the MiG-15 was a far more capable aircraft than either the F-80 or the F9F.

No responsible official in either the air force or MacArthur's command was prepared to meet the challenge posed by the MiG-15. Not for the last time, Americans had seriously underestimated Soviet technological skills. The sudden emergence of the MiG-15s posed a grave threat to the air superiority taken for granted by MacArthur's forces. The immediate result of the MiG-15s' appearance was to deny the FEAF effective air reconnaissance as Chinese communist ground forces were preparing to enter the war. The MiGs also made daylight raids by B-29 bombers prohibitively expensive, forcing them to concentrate on nighttime attacks for the rest of the war.

The Soviets had dispatched substantial air assets to China's northeastern and coastal regions between October and December, 1950, to provide air defense and help train Chinese pilots. By the spring of 1951, the Soviets had moved three air divisions and approximately two hundred MiGs into Chinese bases north of the Yalu River. During the remainder of the war, at least twelve air divisions manned by some seventy-two thousand Soviet airmen were rotated through China. Although Soviet pilots regularly engaged American airmen south of the Yalu, their primary role was to provide for the air defense of North Korea and northeast China.

The air force responded to the MiG-15s' appearance by deploying its most advanced jet fighter to Korea, the North American F-86 Sabre. Matching up very well with the MiG-15, it entered combat in mid-December. In the hands of skilled USAF pilots, the F-86s dominated the skies over North Korea. MiG-15s and Il-28 jet bombers also posed a serious problem for fleet air defense. Navy radar was inadequate, and its Identification Friend or Foe (IFF) systems were too unreliable to deal with those fast-moving aircraft. The navy did not deploy a better fighter than the F9F to its carrier air wings until after the war ended. Instead, it had to rely on its pilots' superior skill and the enemy's unwillingness to attack its carrier task forces.

While American fighter pilots were encountering their first MiG-15s, MacArthur's ground forces continued to race north. The ground units were widely split by the nearly impassable Taebeck Mountains, which ran down the center of North Korea. Compounding the problem, Eighth Army in the west and the X Corps in the east reported separately to MacArthur in Tokyo. Neither he nor senior civilian and military officials in the Pentagon thought the Chinese were likely to enter the war. Confident of his air power, the United Nations commander was convinced he could isolate the Chinese People's Volunteers forces and destroy them if Mao Tse-tung's government chose to make good on its veiled threats. MacArthur's confidence was largely based on his experiences in the Southwest Pacific during World War II, where his air and naval forces had successfully isolated Japanese garrisons.

Korea, however, was a peninsula attached to the Asian mainland, not an island in the Pacific that could be isolated by overwhelming air and naval forces. When limited numbers of Chinese troops appeared in combat during October,

Air force F-86 pilots assigned to the 4th Fighter Wing pose during the Korean War. *From left to right,* they are: 1st Lt. James F. Lowe, Maj. Robinson Risner, Col. Royal N. Baker, and Capt. Leonard W. Lilley. Superior training and aggressiveness, not better aircraft, gave American fighter pilots a critical edge over their Soviet and Chinese adversaries during the conflict. (Photo courtesy John D. Sherwood.)

MacArthur dismissed them as inconsequential. Moving at night through the mountains during worsening winter weather, some three hundred thousand Chinese light infantrymen launched devastating attacks on Eighth Army and X Corps. The 1st Marine Division, supported by 1st Marine Air Wing (MAW) strikes, staged an epic fighting retreat from the Chosin Reservoir in northeast Korea to Hungnam for evacuation by sea. Meanwhile on the other side of the Taebeck range, the Chinese sent Eighth Army units reeling back to the 38th Parallel.[20]

It was a brand-new war. MacArthur was stunned. Fearing that UN forces would be pushed off the peninsula entirely, the UN commander ordered his airmen to isolate the battlefield by destroying all of the Yalu bridges without violating Chinese airspace. Some of the spans were dropped, but the river soon froze over and enemy troops and supplies were able to cross it at any point. MacArthur asked the president to consider various options ranging from evacuating his forces from the peninsula to launching nuclear attacks on the Chinese. Truman responded by declaring a national emergency, accelerating guard and reserve mobilizations, and speeding up rearmament programs with another supplemental defense appropriation.

Nevertheless, Truman, the JCS, and America's NATO allies were determined not to widen the war beyond Korea or use atomic weapons, thereby risking a military confrontation with the Soviet Union in Europe. General LeMay vigorously resisted the use of nuclear weapons unless they were part of a general campaign against China. Truman did, however, order nuclear weapons and additional SAC bombers to the Far East in April, 1951. Control of those weapons remained with SAC, not the theater commander. This move was in response to the buildup of Chinese forces for a spring offensive in Korea, as well as the massing of additional Soviet units in the Far East. However, since the United States was concentrating on rearming for a possible global war with the Soviets, no major ground reinforcements were provided to the beleaguered UNC. The president decided to return to his administration's original war aim, preserving an independent South Korea, and directed MacArthur to continue the fight. But the theater commander was unwilling to accept that decision and was relieved of command in April after he tried to publicly subvert the president's policy. His actions threatened to undermine civilian control of the military and the professional standing of the JCS.

Galvanized by the leadership of Lt. Gen. Matthew B. Ridgway, Eighth Army fought the Chinese forces to a standstill and launched a series of limited counteroffensives. The Chinese began what turned out to be their last major offensive of the war in April, 1951. This time, the Eighth Army conducted an organized retreat, fought the communist forces to a standstill, and then counterattacked with massive artillery and air support. Enemy units began falling apart.

To fight the war in Korea while building up America's military might for a possible confrontation with the Soviet Union required a massive and rapid expansion of the U.S. armed forces. The number of personnel on active duty grew from 1.458 million in June, 1950, to 3.528 million by 1953. Mobilizing 806,000 guardsmen and reservists and drafting 585,000 men accounted for much of that increase.

The armed forces' aviation components relied heavily on guardsmen and reservists to fill their expanding ranks. For example, more than 146,000 air force reservists and some forty-five thousand guardsmen were mobilized. The call-up included all of the Air Force Reserve's flying units and approximately 80 percent of the Air National Guard's. In Korea itself, a Fifth Air Force survey conducted in 1951 revealed that approximately 80 percent of its personnel were guardsmen and reservists who had been recalled to active duty. They included three reserve and two Air National Guard wings that saw combat service in the Far East. Large numbers of guard and reserve pilots flew as individual replacements in active duty air force units.

The Naval Air Reserve mobilized more than thirty thousand personnel and eighty-four squadrons. Like their air force counterparts, many had to trade in obsolete aircraft for modern ones and participated in the global U.S. military buildup far away from the Korean peninsula. Most Naval Air Reservists were mobilized as individuals and assigned to active duty navy units. They played a major combat role in the Korean War. At times, reservists flew 75 percent of navy combat sorties during the war. The Marine Corps mobilized twenty of its thirty reserve fighter squadrons. All but five Marine Corps Reserve air units were immediately deactivated following the recall, and individual reservists were assigned to regular Marine organizations. Reservists flew 48 percent of the 1st MAW's combat sorties during the war.[21]

The partial industrial mobilization required by the Korean conflict was relatively easy compared to obtaining the manpower needed to wage it. The nation's economy was so large that there was little difficulty producing enough guns and butter to satisfy all of its civilian and military needs. Increased defense spending and an initial splurge in consumer spending produced some inflation. However, higher taxes, wage and price controls, and a significant increase in the gross national product stimulated by military spending kept inflation below 3 percent. Early in the war, the Truman administration assumed that the conflict would not last longer than a year and could handled by rushing mothballed equipment to the front. But the Chinese intervention forced the president to declare a national emergency and call for the production of fifteen thousand aircraft. Although Congress was willing to provide the $17 billion needed to meet that ambitious goal, the JCS was unable to develop a realistic program to implement it. The cautious expansion of military production was undertaken in ways that deliberately avoided dislocating the civilian economy. The aircraft industry experienced enormous shortages of men, materials, and machine tools in struggling to meet a scaled back program and embraced subcontracting to avoid overexpanding its production capacity. The auto industry began producing aircraft again. Despite switching to complex and technologically advanced jets that included sophisticated electronic gear, military aircraft production grew from three thousand in 1950 to twelve thousand in 1953.

Meanwhile, the Korean War itself was largely fought with World War II relics and new weapons from the immediate postwar period. The bulk of the brand-new aircraft, like the B-47 and B-52, were earmarked for use in a possible conflict with the Soviet Union. While several of its older *Essex*-class carriers were engaged in combat operations in the Far East, the navy kept its newer and larger *Midway*-class carriers on the East Coast and in the Mediterranean in anticipation of a possible Soviet attack on Western Europe.

As high-technology jet bombers girded for war with the Russians, helicopters and light aircraft made significant contributions to the real thing in Korea. Choppers became firmly entrenched in each of the armed forces as a result of their Korean War service. The navy and the air force used them to rescue downed fliers at sea and behind enemy lines. They also flew emergency supply missions supporting hard-pressed ground troops. The marines employed utility helicopters for observation and emergency medical evacuation from the earliest days of the war. They gradually began employing them to carry supplies and small numbers of troops in unopposed landings, and then started ferrying entire battalions.

Although Generals MacArthur and Ridgway both pressured Washington to obtain modern helicopters, relatively few reached army units in Korea before the war ended. Except for a small number of helicopter evacuations of the wounded celebrated by the television series *M.A.S.H.,* army aviation functioned as it had during World War II. There were more light fixed-wing airplanes than during the previous conflict. They continued to perform artillery spotting, reconnaissance, and personnel transportation missions.[22]

Fixed-wing transport planes also made substantial contributions to the allied war effort. In the fall of 1950, rapidly advancing UN forces relied primarily on them for resupply. After the Chinese intervention, transports were widely employed to evacuate troops and wounded servicemen. Shorter-range transports like the C-47 and C-119 conducted resupply, troop carrier, and airdrop missions within Korea. Longer range transports including C-54s, C-97s, and C-124s carried troops, cargo, and the wounded between Korea and Japan. The Military Air Transport Service (MATS) delivered 214,000 passengers and eighty thousand tons of cargo to Japan from the United States during the war. Commercial carriers flew over 40 percent of the trans-Pacific airlift missions. Altogether, the strategic and theater airlift systems moved some 391,700 tons of cargo, over 2.6 million passengers, and more than 310,000 patients during the conflict.

Aerial refueling made its combat debut in the Far East during the war. To improve their range, KB-29 tankers refueled a limited number of air force and Air Guard jets on an experimental basis. The wing tanks of some fighters were fitted with probes that could be flown into a basketlike drogue that trailed behind each KB-29 on a rubber hose. However, the tanker's limited performance capabilities forced jets to operate at low altitudes and dangerously slow speeds while refueling. The air force preferred the more stable and controllable flying-boom system developed by Boeing and wanted all of its receiver aircraft modified

Marines wounded in Korea are evacuated by helicopter and flown to a hospital in a rear area for treatment on May 23, 1951. The Korean War marked the first widespread use of helicopters by the U.S. armed forces in a combat theater. (Photo courtesy of the Fiftieth Anniversary of the Korean War Commemoration Committee.)

for single-point refueling instead of multiple off-loads to wing tanks. In late 1952, two wings of F-84Gs equipped for single-point refueling deployed non-stop from the West Coast to Japan with the aid of KB-29 tankers.[23]

The air war had entered a dangerous new phase with the appearance of large numbers of MiG-15s flying from sanctuaries in Manchuria. With the ground war stalemated, air combat intensified. The MiGs clearly outclassed the American fighters originally deployed to Korea, but the debut of the F-86 turned the tables on the Russian "volunteers." Moscow was very careful to prevent the air campaign from escalating into a wider war.

The Korean War also stimulated the rapid expansion and training of the Chinese People's Liberation Army Air Force (PLAAF) by the Soviets. The PLAAF expanded from virtually nothing in June, 1950, to one of the world's largest air forces when combat operations ended some three years later. To accelerate the training of their inexperienced pilots, the Chinese began flying combat missions with Soviet squadrons in late December, 1950. In April, 1951, the PLAAF fielded its first operational MiG squadron. Although very large by the war's end, the Chinese air force was not especially effective in dealing with American air power.

To retain control of the skies over Korea, the FEAF's fighter pilots had to abandon the air superiority doctrine based on the USAAF's experiences in World War II. That doctrine stressed that air superiority was not to be won primarily through aerial combat. It was best achieved by destroying enemy aircraft on the ground and then occupying or bombing enemy military installations and factories. However, air force fighter pilots in Korea were compelled to wage a war of attrition through aerial combat against a numerically superior foe because enemy airfields and factories outside Korea were officially off limits. For their part, the Chinese and the Soviets respected allied sanctuaries. They never attempted to mount a campaign with bombers against the airfields and ports in Japan and South Korea that sustained the flow of troops and supplies to UNC forces on the peninsula.

The Chinese increased their overall fighter strength to some one thousand aircraft during the course of the war, nearly three times the number of F-86s available in the theater. But FEAF bombers and fighter-bombers and navy attack aircraft closed enemy airfields in North Korea that could have hosted the relatively short-ranged MiG-15s. In thirty months of combat, F-86 pilots claimed the destruction of 792 MiGs and eighteen other enemy aircraft. The FEAF lost 1,466 aircraft during the war, including 139 in air-to-air combat. The latter losses included seventy-eight Sabres. The command endured 1,466 personnel killed and 309 wounded in aerial operations.

While the F-86 was an outstanding fighter, the MiG-15 was well matched against it. The Sabre's enormous success resulted primarily from its superior pilots, many of whom were World War II combat veterans. That conclusion represented a reversal of the prewar air force assumption that youthfulness, rather than experience and maturity, would be critical to victory in jet fighter combat. Victory in the air superiority campaign, which included denying the communist air forces use of airfields in North Korea, was critical to the success of UN ground forces. If MiG-15s had been able to operate freely over the entire peninsula from bases in North Korea, the UNC would have been deprived of the air support it needed to offset the enemy's manpower advantage.

While the air superiority campaign was taking center stage and the ground war was stalemated, U.S. airmen intensified the campaign to interdict the flow of manpower and supplies to the communist armies in Korea. Operation Strangle, which borrowed its name from a similar air interdiction campaign in Italy during World War II, was packaged as an effort to surmount the skepticism of some senior ground officers who doubted that it could achieve its announced goal of paralyzing the enemy's approximately 150-mile-long transportation network from the Yalu River to the 38th Parallel. Beginning on May 31, 1951, the Fifth Air Force—assisted by Task Force 77, the 1st MAW, and, to a limited extent, the

FEAF's Bomber Command—attacked railroads, roads, bridges, and tunnels during the daylight hours. Air force F-80s and F-84s conducted most of those strikes. They were joined at night by air force B-26s and Marine Corps fighters, which concentrated on the highway network. However, the deadlock on the ground reduced the enemy's consumption of materiel, undermining the operation's effectiveness. Since the communist forces were not challenged by major UN ground attacks, they adjusted their logistical efforts to exploit Operation Strangle's main weakness: its inability to sustain pressure at night and in poor weather.[24]

Task Force 77, usually consisting of three fleet carriers on station with a fourth in Japan, played a major role in the interdiction campaign. A typical carrier air group consisted of eighty-one aircraft. The vast majority of them were propeller-driven Corsairs and Skyraiders, which carried the burden of the navy's air campaign in Korea. However, the proportion of jets embarked on carriers grew from 25 to 40 percent as the war progressed. Between the winter of 1950 and mid-1952, naval aviation gradually shifted its emphasis from close air support to interdiction because of the stalemate on the ground. Responsibility for the former mission was shifted to the 1st MAW, which operated from bases ashore and from escort carriers. Relations between the navy and air force steadily improved during the course of the war, but this was due more to operational necessities and the personalities of senior leaders rather than doctrinal changes or improved command arrangements.

Although unable to cut off the flow of supplies and reinforcements to the communist armies in Korea, the interdiction campaign helped insure they never accumulated enough resources to launch a major offensive. Its main cost was weakening the close air support provided to UN ground forces. The air force retained its centralized close air support system and prevented the decentralized navy–Marine Corps system from being adopted outside of X Corps. The air force's doctrinal position prevailed because senior army leaders in the Far East chose not to press the issue in the Pentagon. Marine and navy leaders who did so received little support. Instead, marine leaders in the nation's capitol were satisfied with obtaining legislative protection for a Fleet Marine Force of three divisions and three air wings. At the same time, navy leaders obtained more carriers, additional carrier air wings, and land-based air squadrons. Although the army did not like the air force system, it chose not to fight it. Following the war, air force interest in close air support waned, and both the army and the air force repudiated their joint agreement regarding such operations. Essentially, they agreed to disagree on what role close air support would play in future wars.[25]

With the war stalemated on the ground, both sides recognized early on that they could not win militarily in Korea without dangerously escalating the

Ensign Jesse L. Brown poses in the cockpit of an F4U Corsair fighter on the USS *Leyte* (CV-32). Brown was the first African American naval aviator to fly in combat. On December 4, 1950, his aircraft lost power and crashed while on a close air support mission for the 1st Marine Division near the Chosin Reservoir in North Korea. Despite the heroic efforts of his wingman and the pilot of a marine helicopter, who both landed to rescue him, Brown could not be freed from his aircraft and died at the crash site. (U.S. Navy photo courtesy of the Fiftieth Anniversary of the Korean War Commemoration Committee.)

conflict. A negotiated settlement was increasingly attractive to them. After three months of preliminary peace talks in North Korea, a small demilitarized zone was established and formal truce negotiations began at Panmunjom, just south of the 38th Parallel, in October, 1951. Ferocious battles continued sporadically as the communist and UN forces struggled to gain the advantage at the sporadic peace talks. During the summer of 1952, Gen. Mark W. Clark, who had assumed command from General Ridgway in May, approved a FEAF proposal to employ air power to force the communists to accept peace terms favorable to the United States and its allies. To break the deadlock at Panmunjon while avoiding the casualties of a major ground offensive, he approved a Fifth Air Force proposal to launch an "air pressure" campaign to destroy North Korea's hydroelectric plants. In June, air force and navy fighter-bombers destroyed eleven of seventeen hydroelectric generating complexes in North Korea. When the bombing failed to end the impasse at the negotiating table, the target list was expanded to major towns and cities containing large concentrations of enemy troops and military supplies. B-29s joined the fighter-bombers in those attacks.

The bloody stalemate in Korea became an issue in the 1952 presidential election. The Republican candidate, retired army general and World War II hero Dwight D. Eisenhower, promised that he would go to Korea if elected, implying he would find a way to end the war. He kept his word. After the election, Eisenhower visited the peninsula and returned to the United States determined to end the fighting. His trip confirmed what he already knew: the war had to be ended as quickly as possible under the best terms that he could obtain. Once inaugurated in January, 1953, the new president signaled that he might widen the war with the Chinese communists. Nuclear-capable U.S. aircraft were sent to Okinawa. B-29s and fighter-bombers began destroying North Korea's irrigation dams during the spring. Stalin's death in March may have weakened Soviet support for the war while contenders for his leadership position maneuvered to replace him. The most important issue during truce negotiations was the fate of UN-held prisoners of war (POWs). The communists finally agreed that POWs would be voluntarily repatriated. With that sensitive issue resolved, representatives of the United States, China, and North Korea signed an armistice on July 27, 1953.[26]

United Nations forces suffered some 450,000 killed and wounded, including 33,686 Americans killed in action and another 2,830 who died from accidents or disease. The United States spent approximately $40 billion to fight the so-called police action in Korea. The communists lost between 1.5 and 2 million soldiers. Reliable figures are not available on how much money they spent on the war. Allied air operations were incredibly destructive. The FEAF estimated that it killed nearly 150,000 North Korean and Chinese troops while destroying more than 950 aircraft and numerous vehicles, trains, bridges, and buildings. Allied air operations cost the lives of twelve hundred airmen and 750 aircraft. United Nations airmen destroyed virtually every major town and city in North Korea and obliterated its irrigation system. Estimates of the number of North Korean civilians killed during the war remain sketchy and unreliable.[27]

Air power again proved to be unable to win a war by itself, but it did offset the communists' tremendous manpower advantage, thus preventing the UN's defeat. Gaining and maintaining air superiority over the Korean peninsula and adjacent seas was critical to the success of other allied air and ground missions. It enabled the allies to conduct ground operations and other air missions undisturbed by communist air power. The aerial effort to interdict communist supply lines ended with disappointing results. The largely static nature of the war after 1950 limited the enemy's supply requirements. However, interdiction did prevent the communists from accumulating a large enough stockpile of supplies to launch a major offensive with any realistic chance of driving UN forces from the peninsula during the last two years of the war.

With the exception of the air pressure campaign and attacks on North Korean airfields, strategic bombing played a limited role in the war because nuclear strikes were rejected and the key targets for such attacks were off limits in China and the Soviet Union. Unlike World War II, the air force was restricted by serious controls imposed by the White House, the JCS, and the theater commander. In the opinion of senior air force leaders, those restrictions caused confusion at the operational level and limited the bombing campaign's effectiveness. Close air support, the most contentious air power issue of the war, played a critical role in supporting UN ground forces throughout the conflict. Just as it had in World War II, air power appeared to work best in conjunction with surface forces.[28]

REFORM AND REARMAMENT

There was a significant cultural split within the air force over the implications of the Korean War. The dominant bomber-oriented senior leadership of World War veterans was convinced "that war would not have occurred if SAC had received greater funding; hence, it would have been stronger before the war and thus offered a more credible deterrent. . . . Senior Air Force leaders 'chafed under the prospects of political constraints' that reduced the decisiveness of air power and surrendered initiative to the enemy."[29] They were convinced that the high costs to the enemy of the air pressure campaign, coupled with President Eisenhower's threat to use nuclear weapons, were responsible for the armistice. They argued that the "shoestring Air Force" had been decisive in Korea despite all the restrictions and limitations it had faced. Somehow, they interpreted the Korean War experience as vindication of their prewar policy that proper preparation for a general war with the Soviet Union was the most effective way to ready the service for lesser conflicts.

However, some younger leaders in the fighter community saw matters differently. Raised in the uncertainties and ambiguities of limited war in Korea, they tended to be more pragmatic than the bomber generals. According to Col. Michael Worden, a serving air force officer, they realized that "War contained rivalries, conflicting interests, changing priorities, distractions, and complexities that demanded patience. . . . Pragmatists favored relative interests over absolute values, and the air pragmatists were more comfortable with alliances and working with other services."[30]

The air force's fighter community believed that the Tactical Air Command (TAC) ought to be put on an equal footing with SAC in terms of funding and its contributions to the air force's missions. However, their call for parity was not realized until the 1960s. Meanwhile, TAC developed a composite air strike force to deploy quickly to limited wars and began preparing its fighter-bombers to deploy nuclear weapons to support NATO in a general war with the Soviet Union and its Warsaw Pact allies. But the bomber-oriented generals and their absolutist views dominated the air force during the Eisenhower administration. Viewing the Korean War as an aberration, they saw no reason to change the air force's doctrine, force structure, and development programs. Instead, the introduction of increasingly powerful nuclear weapons, electronics, and missiles drove changes in air force doctrine during the remainder of the 1950s.[31]

The Korean War confirmed the navy's fundamental conceptions about the changed role of carrier air power. Unlike World War II, carriers were not employed in short raids designed to destroy an enemy fleet and supporting shore installations on islands that could be readily isolated once control of the air and sea around them had been achieved. Instead, they were used as mobile airfields to support friendly ground forces by attacking the frontline positions and supply lines of a large enemy army well entrenched on the Asian mainland. This power projection role, which had little relation to the established concepts of a naval campaign designed to win control of the seas by destroying an enemy's fleet, was reminiscent of nineteenth-century gunboat diplomacy. Although naval leaders were convinced that any future armed conflict with the Soviet Union would require nuclear weapons, a lesson of the Korean War for them was that such a global struggle would be protracted and involve all of America's conventional forces. Korea compelled the navy to accelerate the deployment of long-range land-based early warning aircraft and improved shipboard radar aircraft, develop high-performance swept-wing jet fighters that could compete with MiGs, and speed up guided missile development. It also encouraged naval aviation to acquire an all-weather ground attack aircraft that could operate around the clock.

As part of the general military buildup aimed at the Soviet Union, the White House and Capitol Hill approved a significant expansion of naval aviation and the construction of supercarriers. Navy leaders were determined to build enormous flattops that could launch large and heavy nuclear-armed jet bombers. With the Cold War growing dangerously hot in the Far East and defense dollars flowing freely again, Congress and the Truman administration agreed. Shortly after the Korean War began, Secretary of Defense Johnson approved Admiral

Sherman's request to fund a supercarrier. Featuring such British innovations as an angled flight deck, steam catapults, and mirror landing systems, the first of the seventy-eight-thousand-ton behemoths, the USS *Forrestal,* was commissioned in 1955. The navy laid down five more of them at the rate of one a year through the remainder of the decade. Their complement of eighty-five aircraft included the nuclear-capable North American AJ-1 and AJ-2 Savage. Beginning in 1953, the navy modified AJ-1s to serve as carrier-borne aerial tankers as AJ-2s became available. The Savage's original combat radius was about seven hundred nautical miles.

After 1956, the AJ-2 was replaced by the jet-powered Douglas A3D Skywarrior, which had a combat radius of approximately nine hundred nautical miles. With in-flight refueling, the A3D's combat radius could be extended beyond fourteen hundred nautical miles. To protect the fleet from MiGs, missile-armed escort ships, improved radar, and a new generation of swept-wing jet interceptors were developed. The first of these, Grumman's Cougar—a swept-wing version of the company's successful F9F Panther—entered the fleet in 1952. Five years later, the navy began to take delivery of Chance-Vought's F8U Crusader, which was capable of supersonic performance. However, the original strategic bombing mission of the *Forrestal* and its complement of bombers was out of date by the time it joined the fleet because air-refueled air force B-52s could devastate targets in the heart of the Soviet Union operating from bases in the United States. The navy kept building larger and more expensive carriers anyway. In 1961, it commissioned its first nuclear-powered carrier, the USS *Enterprise.* The warship displaced eighty-six thousand tons and embarked a hundred aircraft. It also cost 50 percent more than its conventionally powered counterparts.[32]

The basic naval strategic concept in the 1950s was to deploy hunter-killer submarines and *Essex*-class ASW carriers in front of attack carriers as the latter advanced into the eastern Mediterranean and Norwegian Seas with their nuclear-capable bombers in the event of a war with the Soviet Union. The attack carriers would then launch their bombers against Soviet naval forces, bases, and associated industries. However, despite a large investment in heavy attack aircraft since 1945, none of them could conduct long-range, high-speed deliveries of the most lethal high-yield nuclear weapons until the A3D joined the fleet. The Skywarrior could hit almost any target in the Soviet Union. Because the fear of placing nuclear weapons on warships was very strong early in the decade, the plan was to fly the bombs from stateside installations to advanced overseas bases and then transfer them to the attack carriers in the event of an international crisis. With the huge expansion of America's nuclear stockpile and its growing reliance on such weapons later in the decade, atomic bombs were routinely stored on attack carriers when they deployed from their home ports.[33]

The Truman administration spent 60 percent of its FY 1951–53 defense budgets on general military programs, and the remaining 40 percent on waging the Korean War. Defense outlays rose to consume two-thirds of all federal spending.[34] American rearmament was based on the assumption that, if the Russians were not deterred from attacking the West, then a war might open with nuclear weapons. It would, however, require a long struggle employing conventional forces to win it. During that period, the United States also developed and tested a hydrogen bomb while dramatically reducing the size and weight of its nuclear warheads. That paved the way for a dramatic expansion of the nation's nuclear inventory as well as the number and variety of its delivery systems, including fighter aircraft, missiles, and heavy artillery.

The air force, especially SAC, was the principal beneficiary of the rearmament program. As the nation's principal striking arm, its $20.6 billion funding for FY 1952 was well ahead of the navy's $12.6 billion and the army's $13.2 billion. The newest service fielded its first all-jet strategic bomber, the B-47, in 1952. The air force also reestablished its Air Defense Command as a major air command on January 1, 1951, and began developing an integrated system of radar, interceptors, antiaircraft artillery, and surface-to-air missiles (SAMs) to protect the continental United States from nuclear-armed Soviet bombers. In 1952, the Truman administration directed the air force to build a radar picket fence across the top of the North American continent. This series of arctic radar stations became known as the Distant Early Warning (DEW) line. The air force saw continental air defense primarily as a way to protect its strategic nuclear forces from Soviet attack. To help defend Europe, the Truman administration also approved a significant expansion of tactical aircraft, including nuclear-capable ones.[35]

Like the navy, the air force pushed ahead after the Korean War with the development of a new family of fighter aircraft designed to maintain air superiority, blunt the growing Soviet strategic bomber fleet, and deliver tactical nuclear weapons. They evolved into the "century series" of fighters. This series debuted with North American's F-100 Super Sabre. Initially tested in 1953, it was the first U.S. fighter designed for extended supersonic flight. Convair's F-102 Delta Dagger and F-106 Delta Dart were supersonic interceptors equipped with advanced fire control systems. Armed only with missiles, they entered active service in 1956 and 1959 respectively. The increasing size, sophistication, and cost of the century series fighters were hallmarks of that period.

The air force relied on improved versions of the slower B-52 for nuclear attacks on the Soviet Union. The B-52G and H models, for example, were modified for low-level nuclear attacks to avoid improved Soviet radar and missile systems. Incremental advances in fan-jet engines borrowed from the civilian sector, as well as advanced electronics, greatly improved the capabilities of the late-model Stratofortresses.[36]

Each of the air force's strategic bombers carried from one to four high-yield nuclear weapons during the late 1940s and early 1950s. To confuse Soviet Union defenses, the plan was for them to fly alone, usually without fighter escort, following widely separated routes to their targets. This tactic differed radically from the huge, tightly massed, fighter-escorted formations of heavy bombers employed in Europe in World War II. The Strategic Air Command's prevailing targeting philosophy during that period was "One plane, one bomb, one city (destroyed)."[37]

THE NEW LOOK

After President Eisenhower's inauguration in 1953, his administration embraced nuclear deterrence as the basis of American strategy to an even greater extent than its predecessor had. Eisenhower came into office determined to maintain international peace, achieve a balanced federal budget, end inflation, and cut taxes. Achieving those goals would require a significant reduction of defense spending. There was, however, more to Eisenhower's ideas than just slashing the Pentagon's budget. The new president wanted a strong military force equipped with modern weapons and bolstered by vibrant allies to deter the expansion of global Soviet power. He was determined to avoid involving U.S. ground forces in limited wars like Korea that were marginal to the nation's critical interests. Fundamentally conservative in his economic views, Eisenhower was determined not to bankrupt the nation with his military program. Because it was less costly than maintaining a balanced force across the entire spectrum of modern military capabilities, the United States would rely primarily on nuclear-armed, long-range aircraft and missiles supported by strong naval forces. The nation's conventional ground forces would be scaled back. Like Woodrow Wilson and Franklin Roosevelt, Eisenhower believed that air power offered a better solution to the nation's security problems than balanced military forces. Billy Mitchell's doctrinal heirs again felt vindicated.

If deterrence failed, the United States reserved the right to respond with an all-out nuclear attack on the Soviet Union. That nuclear spasm strategy became known as "massive retaliation." The president formally approved his "New Look" defense policy during an NSC meeting in October, 1953. The air force, especially SAC, was the principal beneficiary of this policy. The nation deployed tactical nuclear weapons to Europe to bolster NATO's conventional ground forces against the threat of a Warsaw Pact attack. Substantial sums were also devoted to developing and fielding advanced new weapons systems.

The New Look strategy enabled Eisenhower to cut the defense budget by some $8 billion dollars a year. Averaging about $40 billion a year, military spending during the Eisenhower years dropped from 64 to 47 percent of the federal budget. Although extraordinarily high by normal peacetime standards, that spending was sustained by a strong foreign and military policy consensus in the United States that supported the need to contain, mainly through military means, what was then perceived as a monolithic international communist threat directed from Moscow. On the diplomatic side, the Eisenhower administration attempted to build a strong system of international alliances outside of Europe, including the Southeast Asia Treaty Organization (SEATO) and the Baghdad Pact to hold the communists in check. It also had the CIA wage aggressive covert campaigns against communist sympathizers and other revolutionaries who threatened the status quo in countries like Iran and Guatemala.

To complement its massive retaliation strategy, the Eisenhower administration strengthened the nation's continental air defenses under the mistaken assumption that the Russians were also building a large force of long-range, nuclear-equipped bombers. But air defense proved to be a costly and frustrating effort for both the air force and the army. Although exact figures are not available, one scholar has estimated that the Defense Department probably spent $40 billion on air defense during the 1950s. Bureaucratic battles between the air force and the army over that mission, as well as the huge amount of money tied to it, gave the whole undertaking a sour flavor. The air force stressed the need to defend SAC bases, while the army argued that its "Nike" conventional and nuclear surface-to-air missiles could provide effective air defense if assisted by air force fighter interceptor aircraft.[38]

Deployment of the air force's BOMARC air defense missile program complicated matters, which became even more confused when U.S. officials determined that the main threat was ballistic missiles rather than bombers. The United States and Canada established the North American Air Defense Command (NORAD) in 1957 to provide an integrated air defense of the two nations. By the end of 1961, NORAD controlled an enormous force of more than a hundred fighter-interceptor squadrons as well as BOMARC and Nike surface-to-air missiles. Those forces were tied together by a computerized command and control system with over three hundred ground-based radar sites plus navy picket ships, offshore "Texas Tower" radar platforms, and EC-121 early warning aircraft.[39]

Massive retaliation also reinforced the navy's earlier decision to build the fleet around supercarriers equipped with nuclear-capable bombers. It remained European-oriented until Adm. Arleigh Burke, who became CNO in 1955, began to shift more flattops to the Pacific. Its operating expenses were high because the navy and Marine Corps gradually evolved their overseas "presence" mission of compelling better behavior by Third World nations. Done under the American nuclear umbrella with conventional weapons, that policy shift led to confusion over the aircraft carrier's real purpose.[40]

For the marines, the New Look was an unwelcome development because of the Corps's continuing emphasis on conventional warfare. They used their strong ties with Congress to minimize the impact of the Eisenhower administration's budget-cutting activities. Nevertheless, they had to adapt to changing times, and aviation played an important role in that process. In 1955, Gen. Lemuel C. Shepherd Jr., the marine commandant, approved a proposal for a division that could be airlifted into combat by helicopter. Although it rejected the use of armed helicopters on the assumption that fixed-wing aircraft would provide the fire support needed in landing areas, the proposal worried close air support advocates who—working within an established ceiling of 1,425 marine aircraft of all types set by the navy—viewed it as a potentially dangerous drain on pilots, aircraft, and other scarce resources. Budgetary and technological problems impeded the concept's full development. Because of their growing appeal to the marines' ground-oriented senior leaders, helicopters had made significant strides within the Corps by the early 1960s. They grew from 33 percent to 50 percent of its lowered total ceiling of 1,050 aircraft. After 1960, the marines, like the navy, shifted to the F8U Crusader, an air superiority fighter poorly suited to close air support missions. The Marine Corps considered the F8U to be a stopgap aircraft while it awaited the McDonnell F-4 Phantom II.[41]

A critical but often overlooked element of the New Look strategy was the effort to strengthen guard and reserve programs to save money while helping to compensate for a smaller active duty establishment—especially conventional ground forces. Prompted by the mobilization fiasco during the Korean War, Congress had already moved to strengthen the reserve components. It had passed the Universal Military Training (UMT) and Service Act of 1951, which required each man inducted into the armed forces to serve on active duty for twenty-four months and then transfer to the reserve components for six years. Those individuals who volunteered for the guard or reserves could be released from their active service commitment as soon as their basic military and job-specialty training was completed.

The Armed Forces Reserve Act of 1952 required the services to maintain three categories of reserve programs—ready, standby, and retired—each liable to different degrees of involuntary recall to active duty. The legislation also allowed individual guardsmen and reservists to volunteer for active duty when the regulars needed help. The air force was especially active in employing volunteerism to integrate guardsmen and reservists into peacetime operations for relatively short periods of time. In larger contingencies, it provided a "silent call-up" option that enabled the air force to employ the resources of its citizen airmen without requiring the president to resort to a politically and diplomatically complicated mobilization.

The armed forces, stimulated by the political and military costs of the botched Korean War mobilization, had also moved on their own to strengthen reserve programs. For the first time, the air force included specific mobilization requirements for guard and reserve units in its war plans. Guard and reserve officers were integrated into planning and budgeting activities in the Pentagon. As air force budgets and procurement programs swelled, more modern aircraft became available for the reserve components. The number of full-time support personnel was increased, and additional flight training periods were mandated for aircrews. In 1953, the air force reluctantly agreed to an ANG proposal to test the feasibility of using several of its fighter squadrons to augment the former's air defense runway-alert program. The experiment was the first broad effort to integrate reserve units into the services' ongoing peacetime missions on a continuing basis. Against air force expectations, it succeeded and was adopted as a regular program the following year. In the late 1950s, the same concept was applied to the Air Force Reserve's airlift units. The navy transferred jet fighters into its air reserve flying squadrons and established the Training and Administration of Reserves (TAR) program to provide full-time personnel for continuity in such organizations. The Marine Corps retained a reserve air wing after the Korean War. It served as a training organization to provide individual replacements for the active force during mobilization rather than as an organized tactical unit for wartime.[42]

Despite the Eisenhower administration's emphasis on strategic nuclear forces, air defense, and stronger guard and reserve programs, it soon became apparent that the New Look could not provide an all-purpose answer for America's security problems after the Korean War. Although it probably prevented a direct military clash between the United States and the Soviet Union, nuclear deterrence proved to be irrelevant in dealing with a whole series of international crises during the 1950s. America's capacity for massive retaliation was unable to rescue the French from a crushing defeat by the Vietminh at Dien Bien Phu in 1954 or prevent the Russians from crushing a Hungarian uprising against their communist masters two years later. When Lebanon erupted in civil war in 1958, the president dispatched fifteen thousand U.S. marines and army troops to Beirut to stabilize the situation and force a negotiated settlement. They were supported by navy fighters from three carriers and an air force composite strike force dispatched to Turkey at the outset of the crisis.

During the decade, the Nationalist Chinese and Chinese communists clashed several times over the tiny islands of Quemoy and Matsu near the mainland's coast. Held by the nationalists, conflicts over the islands threatened to escalate into full-scale war until the United States dispatched naval and land-based tactical air units to the region. In 1954, the Eisenhower administration began rotating air force fighter squadrons to Taiwan as a show of force to defuse growing tensions in the area following attacks on Quemoy. The following January, hostilities intensified. Eisenhower responded by sending three aircraft carriers and a wing of air force fighter-bombers to Taiwan. Although war between the United States and the People's Republic of China was avoided, the air force continued to rotate fighter units to the area to demonstrate American resolve.

Another major crisis flared up over Quemoy in 1958. Eisenhower again was reluctant to use nuclear weapons and determined to avoid war. This time he dispatched six carriers, an air force composite strike force, and fifty-six marine aircraft to Taiwan to deter the Communists, but refused to threaten to employ nuclear weapons against them. According to an official air force history, once more "the forces deployed by the United States did not meet the needs of the situation. President Eisenhower insisted that the aviation units respond with conventional firepower, except possibly in the event of an invasion, but the carrier groups and the composite air strike force had been trained principally for nuclear war. . . . Air Force and Navy commanders hurriedly adjusted their planning to reflect this attitude."[43] General Lawrence C. Kuter, commander in chief of the Pacific Air Forces, was gravely concerned "that American airmen were at a disadvantage because of a critical shortage of conventional munitions and because the communists enjoyed a numerical advantage in aircraft."[44]

Eisenhower consistently rejected the actual use of nuclear weapons to deal with international crises short of a general war with the Soviet Union. Stephen E. Ambrose observed that "In mid-1953, most of his military, foreign-policy, and domestic political advisors were opposed to accepting an armistice in place in Korea. . . . Five times in 1954, virtually the entire NSC, JCS, and State Department recommended that he intervene in Asia, even using atomic bombs against China. . . . Five times in one year the experts advised the President to launch an atomic strike against China. Five times he said no."[45]

THE MISSILE AGE

Rapid Soviet military advances undermined the New Look's strategic deterrent value in the 1950s. The Russians built an extensive air defense system featuring large numbers of radar sites, jet interceptors, and surface-to-air missiles (SAMs) to help blunt the threat posed by growing American nuclear forces. They exploded their first hydrogen bomb in 1953, far sooner than expected by U.S. military and intelligence officials. In 1954, the Soviet Union unveiled advanced long-range jet bombers and gave the impression they had a large number of them by repeatedly flying a single small group of the aircraft over Western observers at a military celebration in Moscow. That episode, coupled with exaggerated estimates of Soviet aircraft production, gave rise to the "bomber gap" controversy of 1954–56, which the air force used to bolster its own long-range aircraft and air defense programs at a time when the Soviet Union had actually decided to invest heavily in ballistic and cruise missiles instead of strategic bombers.

President Eisenhower awarded the development of ballistic missiles the highest national priority in 1955 because of alarming intelligence reports about Soviet progress in developing those critical weapons. Although the air force was initially reluctant to depend on them as its primary strategic weapons system, the U.S. military had already become heavily reliant on other types of missiles. Various tactical missile systems had become commonplace in the armed services for bombarding land targets, defending ground installations against air attack, and conducting air-to-air combat operations. Those weapons were relatively short ranged (seven hundred miles or less), comparatively slow by later standards, and subject to control after launch. The dawn of the missile age suggested a military revolution at least as significant as the changes produced by the airplane. Since they could perform tasks traditionally assigned to either aircraft or artillery, missiles furthered blurred the already unclear boundaries between services creating additional friction between them. Some observers predicted that SAMs and long-range ballistic missiles might eventually eliminate the need for fighter and bomber aircraft.

The emergence of intercontinental ballistic missiles (ICBMs) was especially disconcerting to the air force. It was very comfortable with bombers and emphasized the development of cruise missiles, which its pilot-dominated senior leadership saw as logical extensions of manned aircraft. Air force leaders feared that ICBMs might drain money away from strategic bomber programs. They did not push for the development of solid-fuel missile boosters to replace relatively vulnerable liquid-fueled ones like the Atlas until threatened by the success of the navy's Polaris submarine-launched ballistic missile (SLBM) program. Eventually, the range and improved reliability of ballistic missiles, coupled with sharp declines in the size and weight of nuclear warheads, created a mad scramble between the army, navy, and air force for control of those weapons systems. Convinced that competition would speed development, Eisenhower allowed the armed services to pursue four separate ICBM projects simultaneously.

In 1960, Secretary of Defense Thomas S. Gates and the Joint Strategic Planning Staff sought to meld SAC's nuclear war plan with its navy counterpart. At a minimum, he wanted the staff to eliminate or reduce the possibility of fratricide by uncoordinated air force and navy air strikes during a nuclear attack. The first Single Integrated Operational Plan (SIOP), produced by the joint planners in 1961, reflected the air force's emphasis on targeting Soviet nuclear forces. But no massive American nuclear strike could have avoided destroying many Soviet cities. More significantly, military planners could not predict which threats would actually deter the Soviets. Contrary to the administration's intent, the planning staff was unable to assess the relative merits of various nuclear delivery systems and provide a mechanism for slowing their growth.[46]

Meanwhile, the Soviet launch of its *Sputnik* space satellite in 1957 had created a panic in the United States. Weighing less than two hundred pounds and carrying no scientific or military equipment, the earth's first artificial satellite shattered the complacency of the American people about their nation's supposed scientific and military superiority over Russia. The air force had begun investigating the possibility of developing reconnaissance satellites in 1946, but it did not actually sign a contract for that purpose until October, 1956.

The armed services began flying regular medium- and low-level reconnaissance missions near Soviet borders in 1946 to collect intelligence information on communist military activities. Those dangerous flights sometimes deliberately penetrated Russian airspace. A number of American aircraft were shot down, resulting in significant casualties. However, even after the high-flying U-2 spy plane began operating in 1956, the medium- and low-level flights continued. Satellites promised to provide a much richer and safer harvest of information on the Soviets than the spy planes.

President Eisenhower, dissatisfied with the early results of the initial satellite effort, known as Samos, approved Project Corona in February, 1958. The latter was a collaborative effort between the CIA and the air force to place a camera-equipped satellite capable of ejecting film containers that could be retrieved on earth into orbit. After numerous failures, the program hit its stride on August 18, 1960. The launch that day provided intelligence analysts with a gold mine of intelligence about the Soviet Union. Eventually, regular Corona launches revealed that the Americans were ahead of the Russians in the escalating race to field ICBMs.

Based on a slim flow of hard information from refugees and high-flying U-2 spy planes, the CIA had already estimated that by 1961 the Soviets would deploy five hundred operational ICBMs. *Sputnik* and the CIA's estimates of Soviet ICBM progress created the great "missile gap" scare, which stimulated a $1.5 billion increase in the FY 1959 defense budget and led directly to the 1958 Defense Reorganization Act. The latter vastly strengthened the secretary of defense's authority to assign weapons development programs and operations, consolidate or transfer service functions, and exercise command of military forces through the JCS—all at the expense of the individual services.

Senator John F. Kennedy and other democratic presidential candidates in 1960 attacked the Eisenhower administration and its defense policies by citing the so-called missile gap and *Sputnik* as examples of their failure. Kennedy argued that overreliance on nuclear-armed strategic aircraft and missiles had crippled the conduct of American foreign and military policy. Because of the neglect of its conventional air, ground, and naval forces, the United States faced the untenable choice of capitulation or nuclear war in any future confrontation with the Soviet Union. Civilian defense intellectuals and disgruntled army officers had been making that argument for years. Such criticisms were not limited to lower-ranking officers. While serving as army chief of staff in the mid 1950s, General Ridgway had argued that the United States had designed its military and foreign policies to fit its weapons, not the reverse. He feared that it could trap the president into having to use nuclear weapons when it could be extremely dangerous to do so. The spectacular growth of the nation's stockpile of nuclear warheads during the Eisenhower years underscored those concerns. Although exact figures are difficult to obtain, Stephen Ambrose has estimated that "Eisenhower inherited an arsenal of about fifteen hundred weapons ranging from the low-kiloton yield to bombs of many megatons. If there were six thousand or so weapons by 1959, then the AEC had built about forty-five hundred weapons during the first six years of the Eisenhower Administration, or more than two per day."[47]

THE MILITARY-INDUSTRIAL COMPLEX

Frustrated by his inability to adequately control the military and a spiraling arms race involving ballistic missiles, aircraft, and nuclear weapons, Eisenhower warned about the dangers of a "military-industrial complex" as he prepared to leave office in January, 1961. He noted that until after its victory over the Axis powers, the United States had no permanent defense industry. In earlier times, "American makers of plowshares could . . . make swords as well."[48] However, the rapid progress of technology and the requirements of the Cold War meant that the United States had "been compelled to create a permanent armaments industry of vast proportions."[49] The president observed: "This conjunction of an immense defense establishment and a large arms industry is new in the American experience. . . . The total influence-economic, political, even spiritual—is felt in every city, every statehouse, every office of the federal government."[50]

Eisenhower warned that "we must guard against the acquisition of unwarranted influence, whether sought or unsought, by the military-industrial complex. The potential for the disastrous rise of misplaced power exists and will persist."[51] His primary concern was that the overlapping interests of arms makers and the military services made it difficult, if not impossible, to impose the administration's will on them during the annual struggle over military spending despite the additional authority conferred on the secretary of defense by Congress in 1958. With the concentration of major defense contractors in a few states and congressional districts, their senators and congressmen became, in effect, representatives of those firms. They were often members of key congressional committees that could heavily influence military procurement decisions. As a result, the military-industrial complex evolved into an "iron triangle" of congressional committees, military services, and military contractors.

After the Korean War, the gradual decline in military aircraft production was offset by civilian aircraft sales—especially those of commercial jet airliners. More and more emphasis was placed on research and development as increasingly sophisticated and expensive military aircraft entered the armed forces' inventories. That critical development was mirrored in the changing nature of the aerospace industry's workforce. Between 1954 and 1962, the percentage of hourly-wage workers in its ranks dropped from 71.6 to 40 percent while the numbers of scientific and engineering employees increased correspondingly.

The demand for the industry's products was reinforced by the U.S. policy of providing military assistance to its allies and promoting foreign sales of American weapons, including advanced fighter aircraft. Sometimes an arms maker promoted overseas sales as an essential element of its corporate strategy for ensuring the profitability of a particular weapons system. Lockheed's F-104 Starfighter was a prime example of that phenomenon. Although it was sold to the German air force in large numbers, it became notorious as a pilot killer.

Following the Korean War, U.S. military aircraft development and production costs accelerated rapidly. Specialized tools and costly lightweight alloys contributed to the upward spiral, as did the increasing complexity of aircraft. By the early 1960s, avionics comprised 25 percent of military aircraft costs and 35 percent of those of missiles. Military requirements that mandated complicated designs and advanced performance requirements contributed to the growing cost of aircraft and missiles. Industry costs were often excessive. Congress also imposed requirements that added layers of bureaucrats and reams of paperwork to the armed forces and manufacturers. Moreover, powerful individuals on Capitol Hill continued to pursue the time-honored American practice of pork-barrel politics, which increased defense costs beyond what the Pentagon and the White House concluded were necessary.[52]

By the end of the 1960s, the size and presumed influence of the aerospace industry were impressive. In 1969, two of the nation's four largest defense contractors were aerospace firms: Lockheed, with $2 billion in annual sales, and McDonnell Douglas, with $1 billion. The two other top firms, General Electric and General Dynamics, were leading suppliers of engines, missiles, and aircraft. Their military sales that year were $1.6 billion and $1.2 billion respectively. However, concerns about the influence of the military-industrial complex were exaggerated, despite scandals involving cost overruns, occasional technological failures, influence peddling, and even outright bribery.

The Defense Department remained the aerospace industry's most important customer by far. Although members of Congress and special interests could influence military procurement decisions from time to time, military requirements formulated by the Defense Department dominated the weapons acquisition process. Industry profits were not excessive by contemporary standards. Nevertheless, the rush to develop and field competing new weapons systems that often were on the cutting edge of various technologies in order to stay ahead of the Soviets while securing the competing organizational interests of the individual military services drove up costs enormously.

Defense purchases, which represented 14 percent of the gross domestic product at the peak of the Korean War, fell to 10 percent during the Vietnam War in the 1960s. During the 1950s and 1960s, military spending accounted for about 50 percent of federal spending. Aerospace, electronics, shipbuilding, and computer industries benefited substantially from defense spending during those years, as did the interstate highway system and higher education. Most of America's largest corporations, however, derived only a small portion of their revenues from defense expenditures during that period. James L. Clayton concluded that the "military-industrial complex was and is only one of numerous and powerful interest groups with conflicting goals in the American system. . . . [C]areful studies of congressional voting patterns in heavily defense-oriented districts show that the representatives of those districts were not more hawkish than those with little defense spending. . . . [B]ig spenders in both parties tended to be those who were in Congress the longest."[53]

AIR POWER STRUGGLES TO ADAPT

During the early decades of the Cold War, air power proved to be something less than the panacea for American national security problems that its most ardent advocates had predicted. While it probably prevented World War III with the Soviet Union, American military aviation could neither deter a whole series of international crises in places like the Taiwan Straits nor win a limited war on its own in Korea within the constraints established by U.S. presidents. Once the Soviet Union developed its own nuclear weapons and the means to deliver them, they were far too dangerous to be actively employed in any situation short of a direct attack upon the continental United States that threatened the nation's survival. Mutual fears and competition for global influence, coupled with growing inventories of nuclear weapons systems, precipitated a costly and increasingly dangerous arms race between the two superpowers.[54] Despite the dangers posed by the nuclear arms race, aviation, working in conjunction with ground and naval surface forces, remained an indispensable element of American military power after 1945. Air mobility forces and conventionally armed fighter aircraft working closely with surface forces provided the most effective employment of U.S. air power in the early decades of the Cold War.

In the face of moral, political, technological, and operational limitations that undercut its potential decisiveness, American military aviation struggled after 1945 to adapt to an era characterized by ambiguous national goals and military operations short of total war. John Buckley summed up the changing role of air power in the early decades of the Cold War with the observation that its impact had decreased after World War II "largely because mass industrial war has, in effect become obsolete. . . . Nevertheless, air power, in conjunction with nuclear weapons, played a major part in shaping the Cold War. . . . War was not made obsolete by nuclear armed air forces . . . but it had become so potentially destructive that war had to be conducted by other means. When so constrained, air power has been less effective."[55]

CHAPTER 5

Cold Warriors

U nlike his predecessor, John F. Kennedy was not especially concerned about either controlling military spending or curbing
the political machinations of the armed forces and defense
contractors when he became president in 1961. Kennedy's
advisers were convinced that increased defense spending and
tax cuts would spur the sluggish economy the new administration had inherited from Eisenhower. They also believed that the military stalemate in Europe
and the nuclear balance of terror had driven the military competition between
the United States and the Soviet Union to lower levels in other parts of the
world. Such ideas fit well with Kennedy's own streak of romantic liberalism,
which encouraged him to promote democracy and economic progress in nonwhite developing nations of the "Third World." His administration adopted a
"flexible response" military strategy that sought to deter or defeat the communists with appropriate levels of matching force.

Coupled with defense budgets that grew from $44.2 billion in 1958 to $54.1
billion in 1964, the new strategy gave the president a wider variety of military
options for dealing with communist challenges ranging from guerrilla insurgencies in the Third World to nuclear confrontations in Europe. In effect, that
meant a return to the Truman administration's emphasis on building balanced
forces capable of executing a broad range of military responses, especially combined arms operations. Although nuclear weapons would not be neglected, conventional air, ground, and sea forces capable of conducting extended combined

arms operations on a global scale would be substantially strengthened. Kennedy intended to actively employ America's economic, diplomatic, and military resources to get the nation moving again in the international arena. His muscular vision of America's Cold War role contributed to dangerous confrontations with the Soviet Union over Berlin and Cuba as well as a debilitating war in Southeast Asia.

FLEXIBLE RESPONSE

To implement his administration's new military strategy, Kennedy recruited Robert S. McNamara, head of the Ford Motor Company, to be his secretary of defense. McNamara set out to reorganize the Defense Department and assert strong central civilian control of its competing military fiefdoms. He installed the planning, programming, and budgeting system (PPBS) being promoted by elite East Coast business schools as his most powerful Pentagon management tool. Employing PPBS, he reorganized the defense budget around outputs such as strategic deterrence that crossed military service lines while junking the existing system, which focused on inputs from each of the armed forces such as manpower.

The defense secretary also supported the application of "commonality" as an efficiency tool that justified the creation of new organizations like the Defense Intelligence Agency (1961) and the Defense Supply Agency (1961) as well as the development of fighter planes for use by both the air force and navy. Commonality had its ups and downs. The navy's F-4 Phantom II and A-7 Corsair II were successfully adapted to air force use. However, since the services' requirements for the air force's F-111 were fundamentally incompatible, that aircraft failed as a navy fighter before it ever reached the fleet. After overcoming developmental and operational problems, the aircraft enjoyed a long and successful air force career. After the naval version of the F-111 was canceled in July, 1968, the sea service proceeded to develop its own next-generation fighter, the F-14 Tomcat.

McNamara sought to assert civilian control of DOD procurement programs from the individual armed services while making them more cost effective by streamlining the weapons acquisition process and switching to fixed-cost contracts with bonuses for good contractor performance. He eliminated the requirement for developing and flight testing competing aircraft prototypes, and began selecting contractors on the basis of competing design proposals instead. The most notorious example of that approach was the C-5A Galaxy transport program, which many observers considered to be an expensive, underperforming disaster. Although the Pentagon scrapped most of his major acquisition reforms after McNamara left office in 1968, civilian officials retrained control of weapons procurement decisions. His revolutionary management and budgeting reforms "gave 'Flexible Response' a life that outlived Kennedy, for it brought such disarray to the armed forces and Congress that it took another war and a decade of learning and political infighting to devalue its assumptions."[1]

McNamara also directed a major buildup of American military capabilities in the early 1960s. He strengthened the survivability and second-strike capacity of U.S. strategic nuclear forces, accepting a force with three times as many delivery vehicles as Eisenhower's, but the military wanted still more. Convinced that ballistic missiles and improved Soviet SAM's had turned manned bombers into costly white elephants, the defense secretary questioned the need for the existing fleet of such aircraft. He also canceled the air force's high-flying, supersonic B-70 bomber and the Skybolt cruise missile development programs. During his second term, Eisenhower had attempted but failed to cancel the costly and technologically obsolete B-70 because he had been undercut by the air force on Capitol Hill. McNamara, with Kennedy's strong support, enjoyed more success—at least initially. He scuttled various antiballistic missile (ABM) programs being promoted by the armed services on the grounds that they were ineffective, expensive, and could easily be overwhelmed by adding a few more enemy warheads and decoys. The Kennedy administration's flexible response strategy was predicated on the notion that the ability to deter and fight with conventional forces would reduce the probability of nuclear war.

Despite a steady stream of technological innovations and growing numbers of deployed strategic nuclear weapons systems, it became apparent by the mid-1960s that neither the Americans nor the Russians could achieve a first-strike capability that would enable one side to attack the other without being destroyed in retaliation. That realization forced U.S. leaders to think in terms of maintaining a stable nuclear balance as the central objective of American strategy. That stability could only be achieved if both sides enjoyed the capability of mutually assured destruction—a phrase that entered the language as the acronym "MAD." McNamara realized that America could no longer maintain massive nuclear superiority over the Soviet Union. Consequently, the two superpowers began to negotiate in November, 1969, to limit the numbers and types of strategic nuclear forces they fielded.

Under McNamara's leadership, active duty military manpower was increased by 250,000. Approximately 80 percent of the defense budget increase, some $10 billion per year, was devoted to strengthening conventional forces. He allowed the navy to modernize its aircraft inventory and continue to maintain twenty-four carriers while approving an amphibious force building program that gave the Marine Corps the capability of deploying two full division–air wing teams. The defense secretary also authorized a major expansion of the air force's tactical aviation assets, and permitted the army to add two divisions. At President Kennedy's behest, the army expanded its Special Forces, popularly known as the "Green Berets," to help friendly governments plagued by subversion and guerrilla warfare.[2]

The air force's airlift component languished following the Korean War. It had been nearly squeezed out of business by an overemphasis on massive retaliation and pressure from the commercial airline industry to acquire more military business during the Eisenhower administration. Although a series of international crises, including Lebanon and the Taiwan Straits in 1958, had demonstrated the growing importance of dedicated long-range military transports, the Military Air Transport Service's fleet was dominated by inadequate numbers of old and slow propeller-driven aircraft possessing a limited cargo-carrying capacity—especially when compared to jets like the Boeing 707, which were then entering commercial airline service.

The nation's military airlift shortfall also aroused Capitol Hill's interest. In 1960, the House Armed Services Committee formed a special subcommittee to investigate military airlift capabilities. The subcommittee concluded that the nation's strategic airlift capacity would be seriously inadequate in the event of war. To overcome that shortcoming, the subcommittee members recommended the air force develop a new long-range jet cargo aircraft and buy a hundred off-the-shelf long-range commercial jets, including Boeing 707s. They also suggested that the air force obtain additional advanced turboprop transports with extended range capabilities.

Procurement of a modernized and significantly expanded airlift fleet did not occur until after President Kennedy took office. His administration's flexible response strategy required the armed forces to be able to move a large conventional force quickly to any of a number of trouble spots all over the globe. Kennedy and McNamara planned to increase military airlift capacity by 400 percent. To provide a relatively quick increase in strategic airlift capabilities, Congress approved the procurement of forty-five C-135 Stratolifters. A military version of Boeing's 707 jetliner, the Stratolifter began to enter the air force inventory in 1961.

As an interim partial solution to its airlift shortfalls, the air force also began taking delivery of C-130E Hercules turboprop transports in 1962. An updated version of the Hercules, which the air force had first acquired in the early 1950s to support army airborne operations, the aircraft proved to be versatile in a variety of airlift roles. However, Lockheed's C-141 Starlifter, which began flying operationally in 1965, was the primary instrument for expanding and modernizing strategic airlift. Capable of carrying either two hundred fully equipped troops or 150,000 pounds of cargo more than twenty-one hundred nautical miles, 284 C-141As were produced for the air force. In 1969, the C-5 Galaxy entered operational service. Designed to carry oversized equipment such as army tanks, it could carry more than a hundred thousand pounds of cargo fifty-five hundred nautical miles. Altogether, the air force obtained 131 C-5s between 1969 and 1989.[3]

Many air force generals found it difficult to adapt their thinking to the Kennedy administration's flexible response strategy and emphasis on conventional warfare. They were highly suspicious of civilian officials. Insisting on arguing with McNamara about new weapons programs on the basis of their military experience instead of facts and figures, they lost most of the time. LeMay and other bomber generals were convinced that only the preservation of overwhelming nuclear superiority over the Russians would ensure the nation's security. Colonel Mike Worden concluded that the doctrinal preeminence conferred by the massive retaliation strategy and generous funding of the service's strategic nuclear systems in the 1950s had hardened into "conservatism and dogmatism by the early 1960s. . . . As the bomber-dominated Air Force became increasingly dogmatic, the new John F. Kennedy administration championed change and favored a choice other than holocaust or humiliation."[4] As a result, Kennedy and his military advisers increasingly turned a deaf ear to the air force regarding major weapons acquisition decisions, strategy, and the military implications of its foreign policy initiatives.

SUPERPOWER CONFRONTATIONS

The president's determination to conduct an activist foreign policy against international communism received an early test close to home. In April, 1961, Cuban exiles trained by the CIA launched an ill-fated invasion of their homeland designed to topple Fidel Castro's revolutionary regime. Originally conceived by the Eisenhower administration, the Bay of Pigs invasion failed when neither a popular uprising nor American air cover appeared to aid the exiles. The fiasco intensified political pressure on Kennedy to achieve a major foreign policy success as did the next major crisis, Berlin. Soviet premier Nikita Khrushchev revived the longstanding Soviet campaign to force the Western allies out of that city deep inside East Germany. At a June summit meeting in Vienna, Khrushchev renewed his public calls for the allies to get out of Berlin and threatened to sign a separate peace treaty with East Germany's communist regime. Offering to negotiate, Kennedy rejected the Soviet premier's demands as well as the nuclear war option while accelerating the pace of the conventional U.S. military buildup.

The growing crisis received a new sense of urgency when the Soviets began constructing a wall around their zone in Berlin on August 13. Kennedy then dispatched additional air force aircraft to Europe, mobilized some 146,000 guardsmen and reservists, and appointed Gen. Lucius D. Clay, the symbol of American determination to stay in Berlin during Stalin's blockade, as his personal representative to the city. Although the mobilization revealed shocking readiness problems in the Army National Guard and Army Reserve, the air force and naval reserve component programs performed reasonably well. Naval air units flew antisubmarine patrols along the nation's coasts while eleven Air National Guard fighter squadrons deployed to European bases in the fall of 1961 to strengthen NATO's conventional firepower. The latter returned home and were demobilized the following summer. By that time, the crisis had run its course as Khrushchev abandoned his effort to drive the United States and its allies out of Berlin. The wall, however, remained.[5]

A far more serious test of flexible response began in September, 1962. American U-2 spy planes and navy reconnaissance aircraft discovered Soviet SAM and ballistic missile sites as well as Il-28 jet bombers in Cuba. Khrushchev,

Air Force loadmasters carefully move an F-104 Starfighter of the South Carolina Air National Guard's 157th Fighter-Interceptor Squadron into a C-124 Globemaster in November, 1961. During the Berlin crisis, 276 jet fighters from mobilized ANG units were deployed to Europe. Since they were not equipped or trained for aerial refueling at the time, ANG fighter aircraft either island hopped across the Atlantic Ocean or were carried by Military Air Transport Service transports. (U.S. Air Force photo.)

making a dangerous gamble, had secretly placed them on to the island to protect Castro from another invasion and offset America's growing strategic nuclear advantage. Unknown to U.S. intelligence at the time, the Soviets had already stockpiled nuclear warheads on the island for tactical rockets. In the end, Kennedy decided that he could not accept the political and military risks of Soviet nuclear forces stationed ninety miles off Florida's coast.

In one of the most dangerous superpower confrontations of the Cold War, the president imposed a "quarantine" on Cuba. A euphemism for blockade, which is an act of war, it enabled the navy to stop and search all vessels suspected of transporting additional offensive weapons to Cuba. Kennedy also placed U.S. strategic nuclear forces on heightened alert while preparing its conventional naval, air, and ground forces for an invasion of the island if his demands were not met. Faced with America's overwhelming conventional military superiority in the region, Khrushchev ordered Soviet merchant ships carrying additional missiles and bombers to Cuba to return home. Kennedy in turn agreed not to invade Cuba if the weapons already on the island were removed. The Soviet premier kept his end of the bargain, ending the crisis.

The navy relied on large numbers of small and relatively inexpensive ships, including the ASW carrier *Essex,* to impose the blockade. They were backed by an overwhelming array of land-based warplanes and conventional ground forces in the southeastern United States. Because of their greater speed and range, plus their larger complement of aircraft, the larger attack carriers patrolled the vast expanses of the Atlantic, Pacific, and Indian Oceans.[6]

Although both sides backed off after the Cuban missile and a period of relative calm between the two global superpowers followed, the increasingly dangerous arms race in which they were engaged continued unabated. The United States and the Soviet Union "continued to exhibit the messianic tendencies that had led them into confrontation in the first place, and both continued an arms-building program that was quantitatively and qualitatively unprecedented in human history. . . . [T]hey distrusted each other, and therefore found it extraordinarily difficult to reach any agreements on arms limitation."[7] The result was a nihilistic balance of terror in strategic nuclear delivery systems. By 1972, the United States fielded 1,054 ICBMs, 656 SLBMs, and 522 long-range bombers. The Soviets, meanwhile, had deployed some 1,530 ICBMs, 560 SLBMs, and 140 strategic bombers. Those forces were augmented on both sides by a huge array of nuclear-capable fighter-bombers and shorter-range missiles.

The missile crisis also contributed to Khrushchev's fall from power in 1964 and accelerated the Soviet navy's rise into a global force to be reckoned with by the 1970s. Paradoxically, Kennedy administration officials redoubled their efforts to make arms control a central national security goal while directing a massive

A U.S. Navy P2V-7 Neptune of Patrol Squadron 18 inspects a Soviet freighter carrying crated aircraft from Cuba on June 12, 1962. Air force and navy reconnaissance aircraft played critical roles in monitoring Soviet actions during the Cuban Missile Crisis. (U.S. Navy photo.)

expansion of strategic nuclear forces. In 1963, their efforts led to the establishment of a hotline between Moscow and Washington, as well as the signing of a limited test-ban treaty that prohibited all but underground nuclear explosions. The president and his top advisers concluded that their flexible response strategy, coupled with cautious threats of nuclear escalation during the missile crisis, had restored American initiative during the Cold War. This encouraged them to make a fateful strategic gamble of their own in Southeast Asia.[8]

THE QUAGMIRE

The United States had reluctantly supported the restoration of French colonial rule in Indochina after World War II in return for France's active participation in NATO. Washington supplied arms, ammunition, and supplies to the French in their war against communist-dominated Vietnamese nationalists known as the Vietminh, which erupted in 1946. Ironically, the communists were the leaders of a nationalist insurgency against the Japanese occupation during World War II. President Eisenhower had resisted French pleas for the United States to intervene with combat units, and the French military effort collapsed at Dien Bien Phu in early 1954. A few months later, the Geneva Accords ended French colonialism in the region and created Laos, Cambodia, and Vietnam as separate nations.

Although he rejected direct U.S. military intervention to bail out the French, Eisenhower was determined to contain the spread of communism in Southeast Asia, as Indochina came to be called. To that end, the president approved the SEATO pact in September, 1954, which pledged the United States to defend South Vietnam. The administration also provided substantial economic and military assistance to the regime in the south. The latter's president, Ngo Dinh Diem, tried to build a strong national government while dealing with corruption and inept leadership, military coups, religious strife, a civil war with a gangster army, and the turmoil of a war-ravaged people. Ho Chi Minh, the popular nationalist leader of the Vietminh's war against the French, headed North Vietnam's communist government. His overriding goal was to reunite all of Vietnam under his control. As the level of violence and chaos escalated in the south, Ho and the rest of the communist leadership in Hanoi decided it was time to resume their deferred war of national liberation. As a result, the Vietminh, renamed the Vietcong or Vietnamese communists, were clearly in a guerrilla war with the South Vietnamese by the end of 1958. President Kennedy and his advisers were determined to prevent any more Cold War victories by what they mistakenly believed to be Soviet or Chinese communist proxies.

Confronted with a serious decline in Diem's position in the fall of 1961, Kennedy substantially increased the level of support to South Vietnam, including more military advisers, equipment, and limited numbers of combat troops. Aviation played a major role in that escalating effort. Army helicopters began carrying South Vietnamese troops into action. Demonstrating both the flexibility of air power and the limitations of its own fixation with the strategic nuclear bombing mission, the air force established a scratch counterinsurgency unit of aging propeller-driven aircraft that conducted airlift, reconnaissance, psychological warfare, and bombing operations. After the Korean War, it had quietly turned its special operations responsibilities over to the Air National Guard. The American military role in Vietnam essentially shifted "from advice to partnership" in those expanded counterinsurgency operations during the early 1960s.

Diem's precarious grip on power continued to weaken and the campaign against the Vietcong faltered as American military involvement grew. In November, 1963, a clique of South Vietnamese generals seized power and murdered

Diem. The plotters had received tacit approval for the coup from the Kennedy administration, which had lost confidence in Diem. Within months, the political and military situation in South Vietnam deteriorated even further.

Vice President Lyndon B. Johnson—who succeeded Kennedy after the latter was assassinated within three weeks of Diem's death—had little enthusiasm for the war, and none at all for rivals whom he feared would ravage him politically if Vietnam fell to the communists during his watch. Johnson's overriding objectives were to block a Vietcong victory and preserve his "Great Society" domestic programs while holding America's alliances together. To achieve them, his administration evolved a strategy of carefully controlled escalation of military pressure against the communists. Known as "graduated response," the strategy was designed to send political signals to Hanoi that its war was not worth the sacrifice of blood and treasure it entailed. Based upon rational cost-benefit analyses and social science game theories, it failed to take into account the fact that national reunification was an absolute goal for Vietnamese communists that transcended all other considerations except losing power. It also ignored the fact that the Saigon government was an extremely weak ally.[9]

In August, 1964, the North Vietnamese inadvertently gave Johnson an opportunity to rally American support for the faltering war effort in Southeast Asia by attacking two U.S. destroyers on patrol in the Gulf of Tonkin. One of the warships, the USS *Maddox,* had been conducting electronic surveillance along the coast. Secretary McNamara recommended that the United States launch retaliatory air strikes. He ignored the fact that South Vietnamese gunboats had recently shelled a nearby North Vietnamese island as part of an American plan to apply low-level military pressure on the communists, as well as follow-up reports from the skipper of one of the U.S. warships that weather effects and overeager sonar operators had made the initial reports of hostile enemy action unreliable.

The Johnson administration, determined to reassert the traditional freedom of the seas that had been a hallmark of American policy since the early days of the republic, wanted to retaliate against what it saw as an attack against U.S. warships in international waters. The president authorized the air strikes McNamara had recommended. On August 5, aircraft from the carriers USS *Ticonderoga* and USS *Constellation* bombed North Vietnamese torpedo boat bases and fuel dumps in Operation Flaming Dart. One pilot was killed, and another was taken prisoner. The president then obtained the fateful "Gulf of Tonkin Resolution" from Congress, which authorized him to take "all necessary measures to repel any armed attacks against the armed forces of the United States and to prevent further aggression."[10]

Johnson retained two carriers in the Tonkin Gulf, organized as Task Force 77, to conduct additional air strikes against North Vietnamese military installations. Believing that the North Vietnamese would abandon their aggression in the face of U.S. air and sea power, senior naval leaders—including Adms. George W. Anderson and David L. McDonald, both chiefs of naval operations, and Adm. Harry D. Felt, commander of U.S. forces in the Pacific, had all pressed for more forceful military measures against Hanoi before the Gulf of Tonkin incidents. But both the admirals and their civilian leaders were mistaken. Sporadic bombings by carrier aircraft failed to deter the North Vietnamese and Vietcong, although those strikes did substantially enhance Johnson's stature with the voters during his landslide victory in the November, 1964, presidential election.[11]

After Johnson's inauguration, he escalated U.S. military involvement in the Vietnam quagmire. In February, 1965, the president approved a bombing campaign against North Vietnamese military, industrial, and transportation targets known as "Rolling Thunder." It was a weak version of the all-out air assault plan pushed by the air force chief of staff, General LeMay, and approved by the JCS. Fearing domestic political opposition and intervention by the Soviet Union and Communist China, Johnson dramatically scaled back the target list and intensity of the planned air assault. The Vietcong responded to the bombing campaign by attacking American air bases in South Vietnam. In a series of fateful decisions between April and July, 1965, the president shipped the equivalent of five divisions of American ground troops to Vietnam. Their missions were to defend U.S. air bases and take the field against communist forces, which appeared poised to defeat the Army of the Republic of Vietnam (ARVN) in 1965. General William C. Westmoreland, commander of the U.S. Military Assistance Command, Vietnam (MACV), intended to win the war by sending large American ground units on massive search-and-destroy operations that would drive the communist forces out of urban areas into the remote jungles and mountains along South Vietnam's border, where they would be destroyed by superior firepower. Rebuilt South Vietnamese forces would then regain control of the countryside and rural villages behind a shield provided by the Americans.

Meanwhile, the bombing campaign in the north waxed and waned. Rolling Thunder had been undermined by numerous problems ever since it was launched in 1965. Deep divisions in the Johnson administration prevented it from fully testing anyone's strategic vision of how to successfully prosecute the war. Carefully calibrated bombing attacks and halts were employed in a vain effort to pressure Hanoi to negotiate while strengthening the morale of America's allies in Saigon.

Crewmembers battle flames and smoke on the flight deck of the USS *Forrestal* in the Gulf of Tonkin on July 29, 1967, after ordnance exploded while aircraft were being prepared to launch combat missions over North Vietnam. The accident underscored the inherently complicated and dangerous nature of carrier operations, especially in wartime. (U.S. Navy photo by PH2 S. A. Shepherd.)

The North Vietnamese used the bombing halts to repair damaged facilities and build the world's most formidable air defense system. Featuring heavy concentrations of radar-directed antiaircraft artillery (AAA) and SAMs designed to drive U.S. aircraft to lower altitudes where they were vulnerable to fire from smaller weapons, the North Vietnamese defenses exacted a growing toll on American aircraft and flyers. The ground-based defenders were augmented by small numbers of MiGs, whose bases were sometimes off limits to the attackers. Sporadic MiG attacks sometimes forced U.S. fighter-bombers to jettison their ordnance prematurely and adopt tactics that increased their vulnerability to either AAA or SAMs.

The services themselves were not especially well prepared for the air campaign against North Vietnam. There was no overall air commander and joint staff to direct Rolling Thunder. To prevent air force and navy aircraft from interfering with each other, North Vietnam was divided into six geographic areas known as route packages. Each service was assigned responsibility for conducting operations within its designated route packages. With the exception of the navy's A-6, most U.S. fighters were poorly prepared to bomb through the poor weather conditions that often plagued air operations in Southeast Asia. Designed to deliver tactical nuclear weapons, Republic's F-105 shouldered the burden of air force bombing attacks early in the campaign. Their employment as bombers and the air force's insistence that MiG killing was primarily the responsibility of the McDonnell Douglas F-4 Phantom II, limited the F-105's air-to-air combat effectiveness. Although it emerged as a fighter-bomber without equal during the war, the F-4 suffered from poor cockpit visibility and left a trail of black smoke that could be seen for miles. Early versions of the Phantom II lacked internal cannons and machine guns. When their guided missiles proved to be ineffective against close-in hit-and-run attacks by MiGs, air force F-4s were modified to carry guns. The aircraft were also vulnerable to ground fire.

Despite the limitations imposed by the organizational and technological shortcomings of air force and navy air units involved in Rolling Thunder, the biggest obstacle to its success remained the tight controls imposed from Washington, D.C. The airmen were prevented from conducting an all-out campaign to destroy North Vietnam's air defenses and capacity to wage war. Instead, they had to learn how to penetrate North Vietnam's airspace in a self-defeating battle of attrition to destroy targets of limited value to the enemy. As the list of killed and captured aviators grew, so did the bitterness of American flyers.

According to John D. Sherwood, U.S. airmen continued to risk their lives "not because they believed in the cause but because they took pride in their service, their units, and their unique fast-mover culture."[12] They were sustained by the stimulation of war and a respect for the others with whom they flew combat missions. To gain the acceptance of his peers, "a pilot did not have to believe in the war. . . . He did need to be patriotic and love the U.S. military. Even more important, he had to be willing to make his squadron and its well-being his number one priority in life."[13]

Although attacks on North Vietnam with high-performance air force and navy jet fighters dominated the headlines and the attention of scholars, it was only one of four separate but related air campaigns conducted by the Americans during the war. The second and arguably most important campaign was waged within the borders of South Vietnam itself. While fixed-wing aircraft played an important role in it, the ubiquitous helicopter emerged as the universal image of the conflict in the American popular mind. The army and Marine Corps increasingly relied on helicopters after the Korean War to enhance battlefield mobility and firepower. Initially, the marines had stressed the troop transport role for helicopters because they already possessed their own strong contingent of fighter-bombers for close air support of ground troops.

In the army, a small cadre of insurgent officers at the aviation and infantry training centers had opposed their own senior civilian and military leaders as

Marines of the 3d Battalion, 5th Marine Regiment, receive close air support from an F-4 Phantom II of the 1st Marine Air Wing ten miles northwest of Tam Ky, Vietnam, on May 6, 1967. (Defense Department photo.)

well as the air force in order to rebuild the air corps their service had lost after World War II. Often working on their own free time, and relying on equipment scrounged from other military units and private firms, army aviators had begun developing armed helicopters at Fort Rucker, Alabama, in 1955. In 1962, the army convened a high-level board to examine the feasibility of using more fixed-wing aircraft and helicopters to enhance battlefield mobility and fire support.

Following the approach taken by naval aviators during the interwar period, the goal of army aviation advocates was to put the mainstream foot soldier into the air as an integral part of a combined arms team while at the same time removing the "flyboy" onus from army aviators. In addition to lobbying members of Congress, they gave aircraft and helicopter rides to senior generals and established a short orientation course to provide them a greater appreciation of aviation's potential in the army. Packed with aviation proponents, the board's conclusions were predictable. It strongly supported the creation of airmobile units and the development of armed helicopters.

Despite air force opposition and doubts whether Secretary McNamara would support greater air mobility for ground forces, the army began testing the air assault division concept in 1962. Discussions about the issue became so heated within the JCS that General LeMay personally challenged Gen. Harold K. Johnson, the army chief of staff, to an aerial duel between an F-105 and a Bell UH-1 Huey helicopter to see which aircraft would survive. A nonaviator, Johnson agreed to take up the challenge after he learned to fly. Finally, Gen. Earle G. Wheeler, the JCS chairman, intervened to cool off the situation. The aerial duel was canceled and, following a series of successful tests, McNamara approved the creation of an airmobile division in 1965. That same year, the 1st Cavalry Division (Airmobile) was activated and then dispatched to Southeast Asia to participate in the Vietnam War.

Army aviation grew rapidly in Vietnam. Beginning with twenty-one helicopters dispatched in December, 1961, to increase the mobility of South Vietnamese troops and evacuate wounded soldiers, it mushroomed to some four thousand fixed- and rotary-wing aircraft a decade later. They provided airlift for troops and performed resupply, reconnaissance, direct fire support, and medical evacuation missions. Unlike air force and navy tactical aircraft, army helicopters and fixed-wing aircraft seldom carried out independent air operations. They virtually always operated in conjunction with ground units.[14]

Helicopters in particular provided ground commanders with enormous flexibility. Roger Bilstein observed that their widespread employment meant that "Infantry, artillery, or both could be shifted in the midst of an engagement startling the enemy by the sudden appearance of fresh troops or subjecting them to an artillery barrage from an unexpected quarter. In the dense jungles, helicopters constituted an instantaneous logistics capability and eliminated long, vulnerable supply routes to remote outposts. . . . [R]apid evacuation of wounded personnel kept down combat deaths and became a strong morale factor."[15]

Members of a 1st Cavalry Division (Airmobile) reconnaissance platoon rapidly depart from a UH-1D helicopter hovering above a ridgeline three kilometers west of Duc Pho in Quang Ngai Province during a search-and-destroy mission on April 24, 1967. The ubiquitous helicopter became the symbol of the U.S. military's role in the war in South Vietnam. (U.S. Army photo by S.Sgt. Howard Breedlove.)

Helicopters, principally the UH-1, also served as heavily armed gunships providing direct fire support to ground troops with a variety of automatic weapons and rockets. They provided firepower that often proved decisive in jungle fighting where artillery and fixed-wing aircraft support was not available. However, even in the relatively permissive combat environment in South Vietnam, helicopters proved to be vulnerable to enemy fire. The United States lost over four thousand helicopters during the war, including more than two thousand to hostile fire despite the fact that the enemy had only a primitive air defense capability in South Vietnam.

While invaluable, helicopters could never begin to approach the level of firepower and airlift capabilities supplied by fixed-wing aircraft. However, much of the air campaign in the south had to be improvised as U.S. involvement in the conflict deepened. The air force was only just beginning to adjust to the requirements of flexible response. Many of its bomber-oriented senior leaders were reluctant to become involved in counterinsurgency operations in the first place. If compelled to become involved in the conflict, they believed that an intense strategic bombing campaign aimed at North Vietnam would achieve a quick and relatively cheap victory. For conventional conflicts, the predominant view in the air force was that close air support should rank behind air superiority and interdiction. The air force also lacked adequate stocks of conventional munitions to arm its high-performance jet fighters and bombers, which had been designed for nuclear war with the Soviet Union.

But the youngest of America's military services adapted quickly to the requirements of the Vietnam War. For example, air force B-52 bombers conducted devastating conventional bombing attacks on communist staging areas and supply routes. Confronted by growing Soviet strategic nuclear forces, SAC had resisted using B-52s in a conventional warfare role. The giant bombers finally joined the fight in June, 1965. In some respects, their missions represented the trump card of American air support in South Vietnam. North Vietnamese Army (NVA) POWs consistently reported their "fearsome effect." Nevertheless, their employment in a tactical role against elusive enemy troop concentrations from bases as far as two thousand miles away raised troubling issues of cost, efficacy, and morality. Another air force innovation that proved to be particularly effective in the relatively permissive air environment of South Vietnam was equipping aging transports, designated AC-47s, with automatic weapons. Starting in late 1968, those gunships poured withering streams of fire on ground targets while circling overhead. After about three years, the AC-47s gradually gave way to more heavily armed AC-119s, which operated mainly in South Vietnam, and AC-130s, which were employed principally on interdiction missions in southern Laos. The latter were Hercules transports modified with sensors, radar, flares, miniguns, and a 105-mm cannon to provide even more deadly gunships. They were especially useful in blunting night attacks by enemy units, providing close air support in many battles, and in destroying enemy trucks in southern Laos.[16]

Vietnam marked the debut of American space capabilities to support air combat operations. Weather and communications satellites provided crucial near real-time data for mission planning and execution. Weather satellites were especially valuable because air power in Southeast Asia often depended on the absence of clouds and heavy rainstorms for low-level fighter, tanker, and gunship operations. During the war, the U.S. armed forces also began relying on commercial satellites to communicate routine administrative and logistical messages while focusing dedicated military systems on sensitive command and control matters. Satellites established their operational value for future defense combat support and peacetime operations.[17]

The most controversial wartime innovation was the spraying of 19.22 million gallons of defoliants by air force transports on six million acres of South Vietnamese farmland and jungle. Vietnam's dense jungle hid enemy supply routes and made it difficult to detect storage sites, troop movements, and ambushes. The air force sprayed hundreds of square miles of countryside with defoliants to deprive communist forces of effective cover. Spraying decimated trees in rubber plantations and damaged the ecology of vast areas within Vietnam.

Following the war, many veterans exposed to the defoliants claimed that those toxic substances were responsible for cancer and other ailments they had contracted. In 1984, a class-action lawsuit against the producers of Agent Orange, the most dangerous and widely used defoliant, was settled out of court for the relatively modest sum of $180 million. Although the appeal of the legal settlement was rejected by the federal courts, the parallel political controversy over the government's responsibility for dealing with veterans' health problems linked to Agent Orange remained alive until the Veterans Administration finally agreed to compensate certain illnesses related to exposure to dioxin, one of the most toxic substances in the defoliant. The long-running controversy exposed "a deep bitterness among those who had fought in Southeast Asia, including Adm. Elmo Zumwalt, whose son died from exposure to Agent Orange in Vietnam."[18] While commanding U.S. Navy forces in Vietnam, Zumwalt had approved spraying chemical defoliants along riverbanks where American sailors, including his son, operated armed patrol boats.[19]

Despite technological innovations and tragically unforeseen results, old problems persisted. Colonel John Schlight observed that "Since the end of the Korean war, the Air Force had given little thought to close air support and had dismantled the tactical air control system that had successfully directed strikes from the battlefields of World War II and Korea."[20] As in previous conflicts, it pressed for centralized management of all air assets in the combat theater regardless of which military services they belonged to and stressed preplanned strikes—both in the name of efficient use of scarce resources. Eventually, it accepted the fact that the army and navy would remain outside its rebuilt air control system. Except for certain designated free-fire zones frequented by the enemy, all air force fighter strikes had to be controlled by airborne forward air controllers in order to minimize the accidental killing of friendly forces and noncombatants.

The marines operated their own distinctive air-ground system in Vietnam as they had done during the Korean War and World War II. Their 1st Marine Aircraft Wing (MAW), consisting of helicopter and fighter-bomber squadrons, concentrated on supporting ground operations in the northern portions of South Vietnam. They emphasized on-call strikes by orbiting aircraft for large-unit operations backed up by other jets on quick-reaction ground alert for emergencies. Because marine ground units carried far less heavy artillery than their army counterparts, they received twice as many close air support sorties.

As in Korea, the air force tried to gain control of marine tactical air assets, precipitating another major interservice controversy. Heavy fighting in the northern part of South Vietnam during late 1967 and early 1968 brought the issue to a head during the siege of the isolated marine combat base at Khe Sanh. Fearing that air force "mission control" of their aircraft could undermine ground operations and set an unhappy precedent for future amphibious campaigns, marines fought the issue all the way to the White House. President Johnson ruled for the air force, but marine commanders in South Vietnam persuaded MACV to return control of 70 percent of their fighter sorties to them as early as May, 1968. In 1970, MACV preserved the single air management system in name only while allowing the marines to return to their pre-1968 practices.

Westmoreland's force grew to five hundred thousand American troops in 1967. By the end of that year, they had turned the tide of battle in South Vietnam. Blessed with vastly superior firepower and mobility, they were winning a battle of attrition against a relatively primitive but determined foe. Initially, the Americans held the cities and the highways while the guerrillas controlled the villages and footpaths. When the Americans took those, the guerrillas withdrew to the jungle. Eventually, the Americans took the jungle, too, and the guerrillas literally were forced underground. The basic difference between the French and the Americans was air power. Because of it, the Americans owned the battlefield.

Nationwide elections that year had given the South Vietnamese government at least a veneer of democratic respectability and popular support. Westmoreland's large unit search-and-destroy campaign forced the North Vietnamese on the defensive and MACV's pacification program stalemated the Vietcong insurgency. Consequently, Ho Chi Minh and the rest of the communist leadership in Hanoi decided to take a big gamble to regain the initiative. Avoiding U.S. forces along South Vietnam's borders, they infiltrated large numbers of NVA troops into the south for a massive surprise attack. The Vietcong would stimulate a popular uprising by seizing South Vietnamese civilian government and military installations while attacking relatively vulnerable American administrative and logistical posts.

The North Vietnamese siege of Khe Sanh in January, 1968, partially distracted the U.S. commanders, who had evidence of the planned communist offensive. By the time the siege was broken in late March, two NVA divisions had been destroyed. Air power played a critical role in defending and resupplying the base. Meanwhile, the communists launched their main offensive in late January while many South Vietnamese soldiers were on leave for the annual Tet lunar new year celebration.

The offensive was a military disaster for the communists. South Vietnamese army and police units as well as ad hoc formations of U.S. military support personnel fought with unexpected fierceness. There was no urban uprising by disaffected elements of the civilian population. Air strikes and allied ground force counterattacks kept most NVA reinforcing units from entering the fray in the cities. Before it was over, the communists lost at least 50 percent of the eighty thousand troops they committed to the offensive, including invaluable Vietcong cadres.

However, the catastrophic communist battlefield defeat was transformed into a political victory for them in the United States. Misled by the Johnson administration's overly optimistic assessments of military progress in the war and shocked by television images of the slaughter during the Tet offensive, American public opinion turned against the war. The president responded by rejecting General Westmoreland's request for an additional 206,000 troops. Instead, he dispatched less than a tenth of the troops requested—twenty thousand—to the war zone, and further restricted the scope of the air campaign against North Vietnam without imposing conditions on Hanoi in an unsuccessful effort to stimulate meaningful peace talks with Hanoi.

Johnson also approved a limited reserve mobilization. A North Korean patrol boat seized the USS *Pueblo,* an electronics surveillance vessel, as it cruised off the Korean coast on January 23, 1968. Fearing the incident was a prelude to a North Korean attack on their country, South Korean officials threatened to pull their troops out of South Vietnam. In response, the president dispatched 350 air force tactical aircraft to South Korea and ordered fourteen thousand reservists and guardsmen to active duty. Another 22,200 were mobilized in response to the Tet offensive. Although most remained in the United States to strengthen the nation's strategic military reserve, four Air National Guard F-100 squadrons were dispatched to South Vietnam, where their performance was indistinguishable from that of their active duty counterparts. Virtually unnoticed by the media and the public, thousands of air force reservists and guardsmen flew airlift missions to Southeast Asia between 1965 and 1972 serving as volunteers. Nevertheless, Vietnam marked the first time that the major burden of aerial fighting was borne by professionals rather than wartime volunteers and citizen airmen mobilized for active duty during a crisis.

On March 31, Johnson shocked the nation by announcing that he would not seek reelection. Ho Chi Minh launched another major offensive in May, losing an additional fifty thousand troops. The war split the Democratic Party wide open. Richard M. Nixon narrowly won the White House, and Capitol Hill was overrun with antiwar advocates and repentant hawks as a result of the November, 1968, elections.[21]

Johnson essentially halted Rolling Thunder bombing operations in the north during October, 1968, in return for Hanoi's agreement to negotiate. Except for infrequent strikes in response to violations of those agreements, the air campaign shifted to intensifying the existing effort to interdict the flow of enemy troops and supplies through the panhandle of North Vietnam and southern Laos into South Vietnam.

Begun in December, 1964, the Laotian air campaign was the third of four major air campaigns conducted by the United States during the Vietnam War. It focused on destroying trucks, storage and bivouac areas, bridges, and AAA sites. As time passed, the North Vietnamese carefully camouflaged a steadily expanding network of trails, roads, waterways, and storage facilities to minimize the impact of American bombing on what became known as the Ho Chi Minh Trail. Troops and supplies moved at night in small, dispersed groups. Bicycles, oxcarts, boats, and hordes of porters augmented trucks. The North Vietnamese also strengthened their antiaircraft gun defenses, added more SAMs, and employed occasional MiG forays to threaten attacking U.S. aircraft. The deployment of advanced electronic sensors along the Ho Chi Minh Trail and the intensification of American bombing efforts transformed the operation from basically a dry season effort into a year-round campaign. Overall, although the air interdiction campaign cut some supplies, it was a failure.[22]

Meanwhile, the United States had been waging a separate but related air campaign in northern Laos. Enjoying the lowest priority of the four American air campaigns in Southeast Asia, that effort sought to protect radar sites in Laos that directed the bombing of North Vietnam and tie down enemy resources that might be used to greater effect elsewhere. The American air campaign in northern Laos effectively began in June, 1964 when, air force F-100s attacked a Pathet Lao AAA site after a navy F-8D reconnaissance jet was shot down. Aging but effective propeller-driven air force B-26s and A-1s, augmented by jet fighter-bombers, carried out strikes on Pathet Lao forces.[23]

While campaigning for the presidency, Nixon vowed that he had a secret plan to achieve "peace with honor" in Vietnam. But that claim lacked any basis in fact. Nixon was determined to either win the war or avoid losing it as long as possible. He was convinced that an unconditional American withdrawal would seriously damage the nation's international standing and hand his domestic political rivals a huge victory. After taking the oath of office, he accelerated a program begun by LBJ to train and equip the South Vietnamese forces to take over the war. Nixon's "Vietnamization" program was accompanied by U.S. troop withdrawals and negotiations with the Soviet Union and Communist China designed to undermine their support for North Vietnam. Before Nixon agreed to the Paris peace agreement in 1973, another twenty-one thousand Americans and an estimated six hundred thousand Vietnamese were killed.

Under Vietnamization, air power would provide a shield for disengaging U.S. ground forces while stiffening South Vietnamese resistance to the communists. Unfortunately, peace negotiations with Hanoi stalled and the war ground on. A U.S. raid on North Vietnamese bases in Cambodia in May, 1970, intensified the antiwar movement in the United States despite inflicting considerable damage on the enemy supply network. In April, 1972, the North Vietnamese gave Nixon an opportunity to regain the initiative. They committed twelve of their fifteen army divisions to a conventional invasion of South Vietnam. The so-called Easter Offensive produced another devastating defeat for the communists. South Vietnamese units, aided by American advisers, fought the NVA to a standstill. American air power destroyed the enemy's mechanized formations and ravaged his supply lines. The North Vietnamese suffered twice as many casualties as they had during their abortive offensive four years earlier. To interdict the flow of North Vietnamese troops and supplies during the Easter Offensive, as well as pressure Hanoi to negotiate seriously, Nixon removed many of the restraints that had hobbled American air power during Rolling Thunder. Commanders in the war zone were allowed to run the operation as they saw fit within broad limits established by the Nixon administration.

One of the most significant actions of that entire operation was the mining of Haiphong Harbor on May 8, 1972, by three marine A-6s and six navy A-7s flying from the USS *Coral Sea*. It was the first time during the war that mines were used to block the logistically critical port. Almost 85 percent of North Vietnam's supplies moved through Haiphong. In conjunction with attacks on missile storage facilities, radar, and communications systems, the mining of that port helped to convince the North Vietnamese to return to the negotiating table. One of the supreme achievements by U.S. naval air power during the entire war, much of the initial mining was done by marine reservists. They displayed enormous professional skill and courage, like other members of their "fast-mover" jet pilot culture, despite the fact that none of them enjoyed the advantage of a service academy degree or expected to make the military a career.

From May to October 1972, air force, navy, and marine fighter-bombers conducted an intense aerial assault. Renamed Operation Linebacker, it ruined North Vietnam's economy, reduced its imports by 80 percent, wrecked its transportation system, and exhausted its air defenses. Fighter-bombers employing precision guided missiles (PGMs) and B-52s equipped with conventional ordnance intensified the bombing's impact.

The Easter Offensive marked the first time U.S. forces employed significant numbers of PGMs. They were weapons with terminal guidance systems used to destroy North Vietnamese bridges that had withstood years of conventional bombing by American aircraft. In addition, U.S. helicopters and South Vietnamese infantry used tube-launched, optically sighted, wire-guided (TOW) missiles to devastate attacking NVA armor. The navy, meanwhile, had developed the "Walleye" PGM, which was basically a small television camera mounted in a bomb's nose. After the bomb was dropped, a weapons officer guided it to its target by controlling its tail fin while watching a television monitor in his fighter-bomber. The air force opted for a different technical approach in its "Paveway" laser-guided bomb. After locating a target with a television camera and then illuminating it with a laser, the bomb, which had a seeker unit located in its nose, followed the beam to the target. While the Paveway required only one aircraft, operational experience in North Vietnam showed it was more effective with two. One aircraft would designate the target with a laser while a second dropped the bomb. Although PGMs were expensive, they were much more efficient than conventional bombing because their accuracy was much greater. Moreover, advanced PGMs increased the safety of aircrews because they could be fired outside the effective range of most land-based enemy air defenses. Both Walleye and Paveway munitions were used to destroy key North Vietnamese bridges in 1972 during Linebacker.

Although there were some civilian casualties, the bombing did not target urban populations. Nevertheless, both Hanoi's new communist leadership (Ho Chi Minh died in 1969) and South Vietnamese president Nguyen Van Thieu refused to negotiate seriously after Nixon halted the operation in October. The president was furious. He ordered an even more intense bombing campaign and secretly promised Thieu that U.S. air power would crush any future NVA invasion. American air attacks concentrated on the Hanoi-Haiphong area, but the final bombing plan prepared by SAC headquarters at Offutt AFB near Omaha, Nebraska, bore little resemblance to the proposals put forward by air force and navy planners in Southeast Asia. B-52s, not faster and more nimble fighter-bombers, were given the primary role in the attack.

Strategic Air Command's headquarters retained control of the giant bombers as well as their target selection, routes, altitudes, and timing. Stereotyped and predictable tactics imposed from Omaha on the B-52 crews produced heavy losses. After a Christmas bombing halt, overall control of the operation was shifted to the Pacific theater commander in Hawaii. Bomber losses dropped significantly as local commanders familiar with the changing tactical situation and weather conditions gained the initiative in planning and conducting missions. B-52s attacked targets from different directions within much more compressed time periods and greater emphasis was placed on destroying enemy air defense sites.

Operation Linebacker II destroyed Hanoi's will to continue fighting. Following another round of talks, the belligerents signed agreements that ratified the American withdrawal but left all other issues to be settled by the Vietnamese. But the peace was only temporary. A cease-fire went into effect in January, 1973, freezing the battle lines in South Vietnam, enabling the last U.S. combat forces to leave the country, and resulting in the release of 591 American POWs by the North Vietnamese.

The remaining U.S. combat forces were withdrawn from South Vietnam in 1973. In March, 1975, the NVA launched another conventional invasion of the south. Congress denied a request for emergency military aid, and the South Vietnamese military and government crumpled under the communist onslaught. Hordes of terrified Vietnamese tried to escape with the Americans as North Vietnamese forces approached Saigon. Escorted by air force and navy fighter-bombers as well as Marine Corps helicopter gunships, helicopters rescued over six thousand persons from the defense attaché's office and the U.S. embassy.[24] George C. Herring observed that "The spectacle of U.S. marines using rifle butts to keep desperate Vietnamese from blocking escape routes and of angry ARVN soldiers firing on departing Americans provided a tragic epitaph for twenty-five years of American involvement in Vietnam."[25]

REPERCUSSIONS

Elsewhere in Southeast Asia, some but not all of the dominoes fell to communist control. The Americans launched a secret bombing campaign in Cambodia in 1969 as a smaller scale extension of their interdiction efforts in southern Laos. Although the air attacks were halted in the summer of 1973, both the communist Khmer Rouge and Cambodia's nominally neutral government continued to receive military aid from their respective patrons in Hanoi and Washington, D.C., to sustain a civil war. In April, 1975, the Khmer Rouge emerged victorious and renamed Cambodia the People's Republic of Kampuchea. The communists subsequently slaughtered and starved their countrymen in numbers that are mind-numbing even by the twentieth century's bloody standards. Over a million Cambodians died. In Laos, the communist Pathet Lao won their own civil conflict by December 1975. Not long afterward, the last U.S. troops were required to leave Southeast Asia.

Losing the Vietnam War was a military and diplomatic disaster for the United States despite that fact that its forces never suffered a major battlefield defeat.

The cost was staggering. The United States spent $150 billion to fight the war while suffering 47,000 servicemen killed in action. Another 10,000 died from accidents or disease in the war zone. Its South Vietnamese allies suffered over 200,000 killed in action and probably more than a million civilian casualties in a population of approximately 17 million. The butcher's bill for the North Vietnamese victory was some 800,000 people killed. The war crippled the power of the U.S. presidency, split the Democratic Party, and destroyed the bipartisan domestic political consensus on the need for a strong, forward collective defense that had prevailed since World War II. While U.S. military spending grew from $47 billion to $74 billion between 1965 and 1974, inflation cut the actual purchasing power of the defense budget by 33 percent. As a direct result of opposition to the war, the United States ended the draft in 1973. The conflict also contributed to growing doubts about America's reliability among its European and Asian allies. The war in Southeast Asia "made a major contribution to reducing the United States' ability to protect itself and its allies. . . . It also crippled the American armed forces, which found themselves deprived of the draft for raising manpower and stripped of money to buy new weapons and improve readiness. The war brought no end to the Cold War, but ended twenty-five years of American military superiority."[26]

As in previous conflicts, it was difficult to assess the role of U.S. air power in the Vietnam War. Evaluations of the impact of military aviation during that conflict have usually focused on the bombing of North Vietnam to the exclusion of virtually everything else. However, as noted earlier, the bombing effort was only one of four separate but related air campaigns waged by the United States during the conflict. Each should be evaluated individually when assessing the impact of American military aviation on the overall war effort. The first campaign, involving the application of air power within South Vietnam, was a great success despite some initial doctrinal, organizational, and technological problems. Helicopters and fixed-wing aircraft gave U.S. and allied forces insurmountable advantages in firepower and mobility over their ground-bound communist foes.[27]

The interdiction campaign waged in southern Laos and Cambodia was essentially a failure. In the absence of significant involvement by friendly ground forces in that area, American aircrews could not overcome the challenges posed by weather, dense jungle canopies, strengthened air defenses, camouflage, and a highly decentralized logistical system. Except for several conventional invasions by the North Vietnamese, enemy requirements for additional troops, ammunition, and supplies were relatively low, further complicating the challenges faced by the attacking aviators.

The relatively low-priority air campaign in northern Laos was basically a war between relatively weak proxies of the North Vietnamese and the Americans.

Bargain basement American air power held the Pathet Lao and their North Vietnamese allies at bay but could not secure victory for either the royal government of Laos or the neutralist factions that opposed the communists. Although waged on a comparatively economical scale, the air campaign in northern Laos had little impact on the outcome of the main event in Vietnam.

The most controversial and important air campaign of the war was the bombing of North Vietnam. It failed to secure America's main objective: the preservation of South Vietnam as an independent noncommunist nation. Opponents of the war charged that bombing the north not only failed to achieve its primary objective, it presented mankind with the terrible spectacle of the world's most powerful nation employing high-technology weapons against the civilian population of a poor Third World nation. That portrait had little or nothing to do with reality. With the help of the Soviet Union and Communist China, North Vietnam developed one of the world's most sophisticated and deadly air defense systems. American aircrews and their political masters in Washington attempted to minimize civilian casualties in North Vietnam, and they were generally effective. But that goal had the unfortunate effect of placing many valuable military targets off limits. Nevertheless, the bombing of North Vietnam helped to generate growing hostility to the war and the counterculture movement in the United States.

Many American supporters of the war had a diametrically opposed view of the air campaign against North Vietnam. They argued that the restrictions placed on aircrews during Rolling Thunder needlessly exposed them to capture or death while attacking trivial targets in a piecemeal fashion that could not possibly force Hanoi to halt its aggression. The wartime hawks advocated an all-out aerial assault designed to force the communists to the peace table or destroy their regime.

Air force and navy leaders had initially shared the same overconfidence in the efficacy of American power as their political masters. Lacking any real understanding of North Vietnamese culture and history, they became convinced that air power could achieve U.S. political goals quickly, cheaply, and with relatively little loss of life. Their main quarrel with Johnson and McNamara involved the restrictions placed on bombing North Vietnam. Those restrictions clearly hobbled U.S. air power during Rolling Thunder, as did the inability of the services to agree upon a unified command structure and integrated operational plans for bombing North Vietnam.

At the operational level, the air force and navy drew significantly different conclusions about air-to-air combat over the north after Rolling Thunder's termination in 1968. Unlike the air campaigns in South Vietnam and Laos, those conclusions had major implications for a high-intensity, advanced-technology war against the Soviet Union and its allies because the North Vietnamese had deployed such a sophisticated air defense system. Early on, air force leaders had hurriedly added guns to the most advanced U.S. fighter, the F-4, after they discovered that the Phantom II's air-to-air missiles were unreliable against low-level, maneuvering enemy aircraft. That change only temporarily restored the American advantage in air-to-air combat. Then the MiGs, directed by highly skilled ground controllers, altered their tactics, gaining the upper hand from late 1967 until the end of Rolling Thunder.

Concluding that its tactics and formations were sound, the air force essentially turned to technological improvements and deemphasized air combat training after LBJ halted Rolling Thunder in 1968. However, the navy decided that, although its tactics were sound, it had to make significant improvements in air combat training for its fighter crews. The result was that it inaugurated its "fighter Ph.D." training program in late 1968. That effort paid off when President Nixon resumed the intense U.S. bombing of North Vietnam in April, 1972. By June of that year, the MiGs stopped engaging navy aircraft and began concentrating on air force fighters instead. North Vietnamese and air force fighters fought on more or less even terms until the end of Linebacker II, while navy aircrews ran up a 12:1 kill advantage. Those results led to the establishment of the navy's more formalized "Top Gun" Fighter Weapons School at Miramar Naval Air Station, California, in 1972.

While critical, improved pilot training was not the only reason for higher navy kill ratios against the North Vietnamese air force. Because they operated in a relatively confined area near the coast, naval aviators enjoyed better radar and ground-controlled intercept support than their air force counterparts. They also were much less vulnerable to surprise attacks by MiGs. Aging North Vietnamese MiG-17s were the primary fighter opposition the navy flyers faced. Meanwhile, air force pilots had to deal with a tougher area of operations than their navy counterparts. They were much farther from their home bases, had less effective radar coverage, and faced the more capable MiG-21.

The air force acknowledged that inadequate fighter aircrew training and ineffective tactics were major problems. Led by veterans of the conflict in Southeast Asia, the service made significant changes in tactical training at Nellis AFB, Nevada, by creating "aggressor" squadrons that mimicked Soviet tactics in 1972, and initiating the "Red Flag" training program in 1975. The latter included both air-to-air combat and mass strike package training for ground-attack missions. Although instituted too late to have any impact on the air force's performance in Southeast Asia, Red Flag went beyond Top Gun because it integrated air-to-air and air-to-ground tactics.

Although navy and marine units participated in Red Flag, they did not really match its total spectrum of training until they later established their own

Colonel Robin Olds, *seated*, plans a mission with aircrews of the 555th Tactical Fighter Squadron at their base in Thailand. Olds, who commanded the squadron's parent 8th Tactical Fighter Wing, shot down four North Vietnamese MiG fighters during the war while flying the F-4 Phantom II. He led by example, flying many dangerous combat missions over North Vietnam. (U.S. Air Force photo.)

advanced ground-attack programs. The marines created their "postgraduate" air warfare training program at Yuma Marine Corps Air Station, Arizona, to sharpen their air-ground coordination. Spurred by Secretary of the Navy John Lehman's extreme dissatisfaction with the performance of naval aviation during a disastrous attack on Syrian positions in Lebanon in retaliation for SAMs fired at low-flying reconnaissance aircraft the previous year, the service established a Strike Warfare Training Center at Fallon Naval Air Station, Nevada, in 1984. The creation of "Strike University" addressed the last major shortfall in institutionalized tactical air training in the U.S. armed forces.[28]

Despite the frustrations of the war and the heavy losses they sustained, American fighter pilots as a group considered their wartime service in Southeast Asia to be the high point of their military careers, if not their lives. According to John Sherwood, "They participated in the war for the sake of their comrades, their units, their service, and to demonstrate their unique skills in an air-combat environment. . . . Very few aviators 'gave a damn' about the fate of South Vietnam or the rise of communism in Southeast Asia, In fact, most felt that nothing over there was 'worth one American life.' . . . [T]he Vietnam War offered fast movers the best available opportunity to test their unique skills, live up to their reputations as Naval, Air Force, and Marine aviators, and partake in a challenging struggle with a like-minded brotherhood of comrades."[29]

Although many analysts were convinced that Vietnam showed that the U.S. military would lose confidence in a war if the American people did, the experience of those flyers suggested a different conclusion. According to Sherwood: "An elite group of military professionals like the fast movers will go and fight wherever they are lawfully ordered, regardless of what the public opinion polls say. The challenge of war, combined with the pride of enjoying a uniquely high status within the military culture, is all the motivation they need."[30]

At the time, American military and civilian leaders viewed Operation Linebacker II as a success because it ended the war, at least temporarily, enabling the United States to disengage militarily from the Vietnam quagmire. However, that victory proved to be illusory. It only delayed the communist triumph. Major Mark Clodfelter observed: "Because most air chiefs think political limitations prevented air power from gaining a victory in Vietnam, they have not revamped the fundamentals of strategic bombing doctrine. Their unspoken belief is that since Linebacker II demonstrated bombing's effectiveness, political leaders must realize that bombing can win limited wars if unhampered by political controls."[31]

Clodfelter stressed that they did not "understand that the 'Eleven-Day War' was a unique campaign for very limited ends, and its success stemmed from the destruction wrought by the previous Linebacker, the diplomacy of Nixon and Kissinger, and North Vietnamese fears that further bombing would paralyze the army with which they persisted in waging a conventional war to gain territory."[32] On the operational level, the bombing of North Vietnam showed that air-refueled fighter-bombers equipped with PGMs, air-to-air missiles, and other conventional munitions had demonstrated greater versatility, survivability, and ability to conduct precision strikes than heavy bombers. In an era of limited war, the former has become the weapon of choice for American national security policy makers. Air force leaders, still wedded to the interwar strategic bombing theories that had provided the rationale for a separate military service, were slow to recognize the ascendancy of the fighter-bomber.

Senior naval aviators were comfortable with the growing importance of such aircraft as instruments of national power because it apparently validated their carrier aviation concepts and programs during the Vietnam War. However, they were concerned that using aircraft carriers as floating airfields near enemy coastlines to attack targets deep in hostile territory made no use of those warships' prime advantage: their mobility. They feared that employing carriers as fixed airfields made them sitting ducks for any nation capable of mounting credible aircraft or submarine threats.

Air refueling and airlift made enormous contributions to the mobility and flexibility of allied military operations. Air force KC-135 jet tankers operated over the Gulf of Tonkin and portions of Southeast Asia that were free of enemy SAMs and MiGs. Their refueling operations made it possible for B-52s to bomb targets in Southeast Asia from Guam, over twenty-five hundred nautical miles away, while enabling air force fighters to attack targets in the heart of North Vietnam from bases in Thailand and, initially, South Vietnam. During the war, air force KC-135s flew 194,687 sorties, delivering nearly 1.4 billion gallons of fuel to airborne receivers. Although occasionally helped by the air force, the navy refueled its own fighters and attack aircraft with KA-3 and KA-6 tankers based on carriers.

Tactical airlift by fixed-wing C-7, C-123, and C-130 transports focused on delivering goods and people to critical areas within the theater of war. In some respects, it was the glue that held the war effort together in South Vietnam and served as a critical element of the strange proxy conflict in northern Laos. Tactical airlift allowed the allies to rapidly concentrate troops and materiel at remote airstrips for ground offensives against communist forces. It also enabled them to defeat widespread enemy attacks during the Tet offensive by quickly moving forces to isolated areas where the ground lines of communications had been cut.

Strategic or intertheater airlift played a key role in transporting U.S. military personnel and critical supplies to Southeast Asia. Air force airlifters, principally C-141s, concentrated on moving cargo. Leased commercial jetliners carried most U.S. military personnel to the theater of war. They were augmented by reserve and guard volunteers who flew thousands of missions in Southeast Asia in their aging C-97s, C-121s, and C-124s. Vietnam was the first time that most American servicemen flew to a theater of war as passengers.[33]

The helicopter clearly came into its own during the Vietnam War. Choppers carried assault troops into combat, served as gunships to escort troops, and provided close air support to them when engaged in combat. They also scouted for enemy forces, provided flying command posts for commanders, evacuated the wounded, and resupplied troops in remote or otherwise inaccessible areas. Rotary- and fixed-wing aviators made stunning contributions to the army's war effort in Vietnam, earning their branch a permanent place among that service's elite combat arms. Based upon its performance in Southeast Asia, the army began to envision a key role for its organic aviation assets, including attack helicopters equipped to destroy tanks around the clock in all weather conditions in high-intensity combat against conventional armies like those of the Soviet Union and other members of the Warsaw Pact.[34]

Regardless of the firepower, mobility, and flexibility that the helicopter and other elements of air power provided U.S. forces, the communists won the Vietnam conflict. North Vietnam fought a total war for national unification while the United States engaged in a limited conflict for marginal strategic goals that increasingly undermined its ability to successfully prosecute its Cold War struggle with the Soviet Union. Beset by corruption and inefficiency, the South Vietnamese government was unable to rally enough popular support to emerge victorious in the long, bloody struggle with North Vietnam once U.S. military power was withdrawn from the region. Air power, no matter how destructive and brilliantly employed at times, could not overcome poor strategy, flagging national will, and a weak ally to secure America's political objectives in Southeast Asia.

Despite the dangers posed by the continuing nuclear arms race, conventional military aviation, working in conjunction with ground and naval surface forces, remained an indispensable element of American military power during the 1960s after President Kennedy took office. Technological advances during the Vietnam War—especially the employment of precision-guided munitions and airborne electronics, as well as the widespread use of in-flight refueling—led to the emergence of the fighter-bomber as the dominant aerial weapons system for both tactical and strategic missions. Helicopters evolved as a vital part of the ground forces during the conflict in Southeast Asia.

CHAPTER 6

The Renaissance of American Military Power

Aviation, especially its conventionally armed fighter and airmobility components, emerged as the dominant element of a resurgent U.S. military establishment after the Vietnam War. Airmobile infantry and helicopter gunships equipped to kill tanks in high-intensity warfare scenarios became firmly imbedded in the ground components of the armed forces. Nuclear weapons, though retained for their deterrent effect, lost much of their theoretical appeal as active instruments of statecraft and military operations. Emerging technologies associated with precision guidance, low observables, and space, as well as advanced infrared and radar sensors, encouraged the rebirth of old claims that air power no longer really needed conventional surface forces.

Following the Vietnam War, American policy makers and military leaders refocused the armed forces on preparing for a NATO war with the Soviet Union and its Warsaw Pact allies in Europe. Under the "Nixon Doctrine," the United States would contribute air and naval but not ground forces to deal with communist-sponsored wars of national liberation outside that continent. Inflation reduced the spending power of the defense budget by 33 percent during the 1965–74 period. Congress, exploiting growing public disenchantment with the war and a politically weakened presidency, reasserted its role in formulating national security policy. Through legislative vetoes and new laws, it restricted the flexibility of the executive branch. A reform movement on Capitol Hill changed the political environment dramatically for the worse for the national security establishment. Congressional reformers concerned with foreign policy intervened frequently in the executive branch's military policy decisions and savagely attacked the intelligence community.[1]

REBUILDING THE ARMED FORCES

While struggling against antimilitary attitudes in America, declining congressional defense appropriations, weak civilian and military leadership, and unsettling policy innovations like the all-volunteer force and the incorporation of large numbers of blacks and women in the armed forces, the military services totally rebuilt their aviation programs between the Vietnam War and the mid-1980s to meet the growing challenges posed by the Soviet Union and its surrogates. They modernized their aircraft and missiles systems, adopted highly realistic air combat training programs, and adjusted their doctrine and tactics to deal with the changing conditions of modern warfare. The incorporation of advanced technologies associated with target acquisition, precision guidance, and radar-evading "stealthy" design features of aircraft was a key element of their improved capabilities.

The armed forces also increased their airlift and air-refueling assets. Airmobility assets were recognized increasingly not only as force multipliers for the rest of the armed forces, but also as national assets that could play a critical role in achieving the government's key foreign policy objectives. Strategic bombers and ballistic missile systems were modernized to strengthen the nation's nuclear deterrent. This was coupled with a growing emphasis on achieving significant arms control agreements with the Russians in order to halt and reverse the momentum of the strategic arms race that threatened the security of both sides.

America's post-Vietnam military renaissance was aided by a significant increase in defense spending begun during the waning years of Jimmy Carter's presidency and greatly expanded under his successor, Ronald Reagan. Equally important, the U.S. armed forces regained their self-confidence and sense of professional pride by concentrating on mastering the operational art of warfare and reinvigorating military thought. Ironically, this rebirth of American military power reached its apogee just as the chief reasons for its existence, the Cold War and the Soviet Union, ceased to exist.[2]

Providing adequate manpower and budgets to implement the Nixon doctrine proved to be virtually impossible at first. To undermine the antiwar movement, Pres. Richard Nixon announced in 1971 that his administration would end the draft. Two years later, an all-volunteer force replaced conscription. But the services were unprepared for the end of the draft. Congress decreed that military and civil service pay should be comparable, tripling the cost of each serviceman by some estimates. Moreover, the overall quality of people entering the armed forces dropped significantly. Integrating the growing numbers of black and female recruits into organizational cultures dominated by white males created new problems. Violence associated with drugs and racial tensions permeated the junior enlisted force. Neither hard-line enforcement nor a permissive approach to discipline was especially effective. Demoralized career officers and sergeants either left the service in droves or sought duty away from combat units.[3]

To help compensate for declining budgets and lower numbers of active duty personnel, the Defense Department placed greater reliance on National Guard and reserve forces under the auspices of the "Total Force" concept. Secretary of Defense Melvin Laird adopted the Total Force in August, 1970, at the urging of Theodore Marrs, his senior assistant for reserve component programs. Marrs, a former air guardsman and air force reservist, based his proposals largely on the air force's own reserve programs. The Total Force sought to rebuild public confidence in the guard and reserves, which had been badly undermined during the Vietnam War because of their reputations as draft havens. It committed the nation to use guardsmen and reservists instead of draftees as the first and primary source of manpower to augment the active duty forces in any future crisis. The Nixon administration found the Total Force concept useful on Capitol Hill. Sensitive to the intensity of antimilitary congressional feeling in the early 1970s, the administration stressed that a much larger share of the nation's scaled-back defense budgets was going to the reserve components.[4]

Guard and reserve long-range transports began flying missions to Southeast Asia in the mid-1960s as either volunteers or to meet their annual overwater training requirements. Because the air force lacked enough tankers in its active duty fleet to satisfy SAC's nuclear alert requirements and prosecute the war in Southeast Asia while fulfilling all of the U.S. Air Force in Europe's needs, an even more interesting innovation was implemented on the other side of the world. In April, 1967, Air National Guard KC-97L tankers initiated Operation Creek Party from Rhein-Main Air Base, Germany. The operation pioneered a new dimension of the Total Force by using contingents of Air National Guard volunteers and full-time support personnel to help fulfill continuing air force operational requirements overseas in peacetime. By the time Creek Party ended in April, 1977, it had demonstrated that the Air National Guard could sustain a significant operational rotation overseas in support of the air force without resorting to a politically sensitive mobilization. Back home, Creek Party provided significant recruiting and retention incentives for participating units. The operation set a precedent for other sustained overseas rotations by the Air Force Reserve and Air National Guard, including Operation Volant Oak (originally

Operation Coronet Oak), a C-130 airlift rotation based in Panama that was shared by both organizations beginning in 1977.[5]

In addition to building a smaller active force manned by volunteers and placing greater reliance on the reserve components, the Nixon administration strengthened nuclear stability between the United States and the Soviet Union through weapons modernization and arms control agreements. By 1970, SAC planners had concluded that the Soviet Union could damage the United States more heavily with a first strike than it could with a retaliatory blow in response. President Nixon immediately endorsed several key programs that had been approved by his predecessors, including developing an ability to retarget ICBMs; mounting multiple, independently targeted (MIRV'd) warheads on new ballistic missiles; and developing air-launched cruise missiles (ALCMs) for SAC's bombers. Work was also begun on a new manned strategic bomber for the air force, capable of penetrating deep inside the Soviet Union. The new bomber was eventually designated B-1A, and the first of four prototypes flew in 1974. However, President Carter canceled its production three years later, although he permitted research and development to continue. In 1981, President Reagan approved production of a hundred B-1B Lancers, an improved version of the original aircraft designed to deliver nuclear weapons at high subsonic speed and low altitude.

The future of expensive strategic bombers like the B-1 was challenged by the maturation of the cruise missile. The latter, which traced its origins to World War I, suffered more from political than technological problems during the Cold War. Kenneth P. Werrell characterized it as "a miniature, self-guided, unmanned, armed, one-way aircraft which is dependent on air for lift and as a source of oxygen. In short, it is an unmanned kamikaze."[6] During the 1950s and 1960s, the air force and navy deployed several different cruise missile systems, but they were plagued with serious technical problems and were soon eclipsed by ballistic missiles. The miniaturization of nuclear warheads, development of smaller and more efficient jet turbofan engines, and the evolution of miniaturized electronics and computers built into a small aircraft fuselage produced a weapon that had enormous potential. Guided by satellite mapping, it had great accuracy, could be launched from a variety of air and surface platforms, was capable of long ranges, was relatively small and cheap, and was difficult to defend against. However, the senior leadership of the air force and navy not only failed to embrace the cruise missile, they actively worked to kill it. They were convinced that it threatened the established roles of their services' major weapons systems, including manned long-range bombers, aircraft carriers, and attack submarines.

Arms control considerations played a major role in the cruise missile's eventual rebirth in the United States. The Soviets had continued to improve their own versions of the weapon and resisted American attempts as early as 1970 to negotiate it out of existence. It survived because senior civilian officials in the Defense Department and the White House came to understand that the cruise missile was not only a useful bargaining chip in arms control negotiations, it also provided a cost-effective standoff weapon that could penetrate increasing lethal Soviet air defenses without putting the lives of aircrews at risk. Incorporating the new generation of cruise missiles into the navy and the air force provided new offensive capabilities while suggesting novel challenges for each service. For example, American warships were vulnerable to enemy cruise missiles and sea-launched U.S. cruise missiles redistributed some of the navy's offensive power to its long-neglected surface warfare branch. Air-launched cruise missiles threatened the future of the air force's long-range bombers.[7]

Meanwhile, to slow down the strategic arms race with the Soviets, the Nixon administration negotiated an antiballistic missile (ABM) treaty and an interim agreement on land- and sea-based ICBMs. Those accords attempted to scale back the Russian's first-strike counterforce potential while ensuring that both nations retained the ability to destroy each other's cities. The Strategic Air Command's bomber force and its MIRV'd ICBMs escaped treaty limitation. The SALT I treaty, signed in May, 1972, temporarily modified the strategic arms competition. Additional negotiations between the superpowers produced the Vladivostok Accords in 1974, established a mutual ceiling of twenty-four hundred nuclear delivery vehicles, including bombers, and 1,320 MIRV'd ICBMs.[8]

In addition to a strong desire to prevent the development of a first-strike capability by either side, arms limitation agreements were encouraged by the growing understanding within policy-making circles on both sides that "strategic nuclear weapons played a largely peripheral role in the development of Cold War strategies. Little of advantage was ever gained out of the possession of nuclear weapons, other than the avoidance of suffering the disadvantage of not possessing them."[9]

The growing challenges posed by ballistic missiles, coupled with a belated appreciation that the Soviet Union had never actually fielded a large strategic bomber fleet like SAC's, had encouraged DOD and the air force to deemphasize continental air defense. The Air Defense Command (renamed the Aerospace Defense Command in 1968) was abolished in 1979 as U.S. priorities shifted from bomber defense to missile warning and space surveillance. The Strategic Air Command temporarily assumed responsibility for missile warning and space surveillance systems before they were transferred to the air force's new Space Command, which was established on September 1, 1982. Meanwhile, TAC had taken over the control centers and radar sites as well as the steadily shrinking fighter-interceptor force structure responsible for continental air defense. After peaking at approximately twenty-six hundred aircraft, including U.S. Air Force, Royal Canadian Air Force (RCAF), and Air National Guard fighters in the early 1960s, that force had steadily declined to a handful during the following decades.[10]

Because of the nuclear stalemate that emerged between the United States and the Soviet Union in the early 1960s, the development of precision-guided munitions and sophisticated airborne electronic countermeasures (ECM) packages, and changing national defense policies, the emphasis shifted toward fighter aircraft at the expense of long-range strategic bombers. Within the air force, SAC's share of the budget and force structure declined significantly while its tactical forces gained in relative importance. Those developments in turn drove a growing requirement for general officers with significant fighter experience after the Vietnam War. Defense Secretary Melvin Laird's determined efforts to bring more youth and fresh thinking into senior military leadership positions magnified the importance of fighter generals in the service's upper echelons. By 1982, there were no longer any bomber generals in senior Air Staff positions. However, air force doctrine was slower to change. Many influential officers believed that their service should return to its established emphasis on preparing for a general war with the Soviet Union involving strategic bombers and ICBMs. They were convinced that limited conventional wars like those in Korea and Vietnam were anomalous distractions from their main Cold War task of dealing with the Russian threat.

But the future of American air power lay in tactical aviation and airmobility forces, not a return to the glory days of the Eisenhower administration's bomber-oriented New Look strategy. Drawing on the lessons of Vietnam and a 50 percent increase in the size of Soviet air forces between 1967 and 1977, the air force and navy emphasized more rigorous air combat training and the acquisition of a new generation of tactical aircraft with advanced electronics systems to deal with the growing threat posed by improved enemy aircraft, SAMs, and AAA. Soviet air doctrine stressed seizing air superiority and then supporting a ground offensive in Europe. While relying more on conventional weapons than their NATO adversaries because of their superior numbers, the Soviets also had the ability to deliver tactical nuclear weapons. By the late 1980s, the Warsaw Pact enjoyed a massive advantage over NATO forces deployed in Europe. For example, it fielded 8,250 combat aircraft versus NATO's 3,977. In ground forces, the Pact deployed 3,090,000 troops compared to the Western alliance's 2,213,593. Soviet-led forces boasted 16,424 tanks compared to the West's 15,500. Faced with such overwhelming odds, NATO air commanders had grave doubts the alliance could achieve even local air superiority over the battlefield.

To offset numerically superior Warsaw Pact air and ground forces, NATO adopted a new air doctrine based on the "AirLand battle" concept developed by the U.S. Army in cooperation with but never formally approved by air force after the end of the Southeast Asia conflict. Published as FM 100-5, *Operations*, in 1982, it stressed that NATO air power would concentrate on cutting the flow of Warsaw Pact units and supplies to the battlefield in the event of a Soviet-sponsored Warsaw Pact invasion of Western Europe. Relying on the new technology of tactical air power, including PGMs and advanced ECM, the United States and its NATO allies planned to blunt any invasion without resorting to either nuclear weapons or a massive buildup of their conventional ground forces.

For its part, the air force would maintain air superiority while launching deep air strikes on Warsaw Pact armies to isolate them on the battlefield, interrupt the flow of enemy forces and supplies to the front, and furnish close air support to NATO ground forces engaged with the leading enemy echelons.[11] The service's newly dominant fighter community "sought decisiveness against a formidable enemy through cooperation with the Army and through the traditional refinement of technique and technology. At risk stood a balanced and holistic concept of air power. It remained to be determined if the TAF (tactical air forces) emphasis was any better than the previous SAC emphasis."[12]

In May, 1984, the army and the air force announced that they had agreed upon a number of initiatives that would become the framework for cooperating on air support doctrine and planning. Unlike the periods after World War II and the Korean War, both services had cooperated to develop a coherent body of thought on the employment of tactical air power to support the ground forces, and the planning mechanisms needed to turn it into reality. Although NATO air forces had not developed an overwhelming firepower advantage over the Warsaw Pact by the end of the 1980s, they had acquired the means to ensure that the Pact would be unlikely to defeat them.[13]

Prior to that point, the air force's conventional bombing doctrine had changed little since the 1930s, despite three wars and revolutionary technological advances. It focused on achieving decisive military victories with air power through saturation bombing of enemy choke points with industrial targets as the key objectives. Colonel John Warden sought to radically overhaul that doctrine. Warden emphasized the use of "precision munitions to attack an expanded list of targets. He viewed the enemy's war-making capacity in five concentric rings. The center ring consisted of its civilian and military leadership, the first ring out, its production sources, the second ring out, its transportation and communication infrastructure, third ring out, the will of its population, and, the last ring its military forces."[14]

Warden was a disciple of Billy Mitchell, a true believer in the ability of air power to achieve decisive victories in modern wars without significant involvement by conventional ground and naval forces. He advocated air attacks on rings of enemy targets that "would be 'inside-out' warfare, starting from the center and working outward. The first objective of an air campaign would be to seize air superiority followed by attacks on an enemy's leadership and other vital centers."[15] Warden stressed that in planning any air campaign, the enemy's "center or centers of gravity" must be identified and attacked. They were the point or points where an enemy was most vulnerable and an attack would have the greatest opportunity to be decisive. Of course, the real question is whether such key points actually exist or can be identified and destroyed if they do.[16]

It took well-trained aircrews and highly sophisticated modern weapons to turn such doctrinal musings into military victories. Realistic combat training and sophisticated weapons were the key elements in the reform of American air power. Employing Red Flag exercises and aggressor squadrons designed to mimic Warsaw Pact tactics, the air force significantly strengthened its combat aircrew training after the Vietnam War. Those initiatives complemented several important weapons development programs that came to fruition after the end of active U.S. military involvement in Southeast Asian combat operations. Senior air force fighter leaders who became general officers in the 1960s, as well as more junior officers known as the "Fighter Mafia," did not want another generation of fast, low-level, deep-penetrating aircraft designed to deliver tactical nuclear weapons. Instead, they emphasized the need for more agile aircraft armed with guns and missiles that would serve primarily as fighters.

To seize and maintain air superiority, the air force pinned its hopes on the McDonnell Douglas F-15 Eagle, which was first flown in 1972. An all-weather fighter, the F-15 was a highly maneuverable aircraft equipped with a cannon, air-to-air missiles, and a sophisticated radar system that can track small, fast-moving objects from seventy thousand feet down to treetop level. To provide larger numbers of lightweight and relatively inexpensive general-purpose fighters, the service funded General Dynamics's F-16 Fighting Falcon. Although many of its components are interchangeable with those of the F-15, the F-16 also featured several innovative technologies, including a "fly-by-wire" system that employs electrical signals to actuate mechanical linkages that move control surfaces, and a high-visibility cockpit that minimizes the impact of g-forces in combat maneuvers.

To help the army overcome the Warsaw Pact's massive advantage over NATO in tanks and other armored vehicles, it turned to Fairchild to develop the A-10 Thunderbolt II. Designed as a close air support aircraft, the A-10 is relatively slow but employs various design features to enhance its survivability against enemy ground fire. It can carry up to sixteen thousand pounds of bombs, napalm, and rockets externally. In addition, it is armed with a 30-mm multibarreled gun that fires depleted uranium rounds capable of penetrating any known Soviet-designed armor. Its large bubble canopy provides good vision for the pilot, who is protected by titanium cockpit armor.

In the strategic arena, the air force decided to extend the B-52's service life following President Carter's cancellation of the B-1 bomber in 1977. The venerable Stratofortress was equipped with improved electronics and short-range attack missiles (SRAMs). Carter wanted to use savings from the B-1 to free up funds for the MX ICBM and the ALCMs he hoped would become bargaining chips for a SALT II agreement with the Soviets while the air force developed a stealth bomber. F-111As modified with electronic gadgets were employed to find gaps in enemy air defenses and jam hostile radar. F-4E Wild Weasels were equipped to destroy enemy radar systems. Because of the growing costs of acquiring and maintaining major new weapons systems, as well as those needed to sustain the all-volunteer force during the 1970s, logistical requirements were shortchanged, contributing to significant readiness problems in operational units.[17]

One of the most important new aircraft of the post-Vietnam period was the Boeing E-3 Airborne Warning and Control System (AWACS), a modified version of the firm's 707 commercial jetliner that serves as a long-range radar station and airborne command post for air defense and tactical air forces. Airborne warning aircraft were first developed in response to Japanese kamikazes in World War II when the U.S. Navy modified B-17s by replacing their bomb bays with belly-mounted radar. A whole series of aircraft were subsequently modified to perform such missions. The most notable was Lockheed's C-121 Constellation, an aircraft with a large radar dome mounted atop its fuselage, which helped to direct U.S. air operations over North Vietnam. The AWACS began as a controversial and unpopular program. In the cash-strapped 1970s, many of the air force's senior leaders were initially skeptical about its value. Some of them saw it as nothing more than a tall and expensive flying antenna. If it could not drop bombs or fire guns and launch missiles, they did not think it was worth spending much money on. Nevertheless, the AWACS program survived and its first prototype flew in 1972. The initial production aircraft was delivered to the air force five years later. Altogether, thirty-four AWACS aircraft were delivered to the air force, and additional advanced models have been produced for NATO, France, Great Britain, and Saudi Arabia.

The most advanced versions of the aircraft are capable of maintaining all-weather radar coverage from the earth's surface to the stratosphere at a distance of more than two hundred miles over land and water. In addition to its radar, the air-refuelable AWACS is equipped with a secure voice communications system, advanced IFF radar, and the Navstar satellite Global Positioning System (GPS). During operations, E-3s can be linked to other aircraft, ground stations, and warships. They demonstrated their enormous value while helping the Saudis protect their oilfields during the 1980–88 Iran-Iraq War and in contributing to Iraq's defeat during the Persian Gulf War in 1991.[18]

While the air force reshaped itself for a conventional conflict featuring tactical aviation with the Warsaw Pact in Europe, the navy concentrated on strengthening its established air-maritime forces, which had proven to be an effective means for dominating limited areas on the periphery of Asia since the beginning of the Cold War. The longstanding argument by advocates of land-based air power, that aircraft carrier task forces were overly expensive "white elephants" that had been relegated to the ash heap of history by atomic weapons and other technological developments after World War II, had been debunked by America's experience in Korea and Vietnam. Carriers have provided a highly flexible military presence to deal with a wide range of conventional armed conflicts and international crises short of war. Nevertheless, the navy was aware of their limitations. According to John Buckley, it had concluded "that its carrier groups are not suited to full scale war environments and are best deployed as symbols of intent in low intensity situations."[19]

The navy's material condition had declined visibly during the 1960s and early 1970s because of the demands placed upon it by the Vietnam War. Like the other military services, shrinking budgets, deferred weapons modernization programs, racial strife, and rampant drug abuse had complicated the service's postwar tasks. Ships were wearing out and sailors were exhausted by endless deployments. At the strategic level, the navy had been challenged by the fact that the Soviets had begun building a substantial oceangoing surface fleet. Although internal politics brought a halt to that historical deviation by the late 1970s, when the Soviet Union returned to coastal defense as its navy's main role, the Soviet buildup had appeared to menace U.S. naval supremacy at the time. Russia's nuclear submarine fleet and long-range bombers equipped with antiship cruise missiles had posed a growing challenge to American carrier battle groups. For the first time since 1945, war at sea seemed to be a real possibility.

Admiral Elmo R. Zumwalt tackled those problems while the navy was withdrawing from Southeast Asia. A reform-minded surface warfare officer who served as CNO for four years beginning in July, 1970, he was determined to thoroughly reform the navy, restore its pride and sense of mission, and insure that its personnel enjoyed a real sense of equity—regardless of their race or gender. Zumwalt's programmatic and strategic innovations were equally far-reaching. The CNO retired the fleet's aging and increasingly expensive to operate ASW

Essex-class carriers. Their antisubmarine warfare function was transferred to the heavy attack carriers. Since neither Congress nor the White House was willing to rebuild the carrier force to pre–Vietnam War levels, Zumwalt based some of those vessels overseas to reduce their transit times for overseas deployments. Noting the established dual mission of U.S. naval forces, sea control and overseas power projection, the CNO prescribed a different kind of fleet to accomplish those responsibilities. Zumwalt stressed that sea-control forces—ASW planes and their carriers, as well as patrol and escort ships—had been allowed to become obsolete and then were retired without replacement during the Korean and Vietnam Wars. Instead, money had been poured into heavy carriers and ballistic-missile submarines for power projection.

To deal with that imbalance and the budget reductions associated with the scaling back of America's active combat role in Vietnam, Zumwalt proposed a "high-low" mix of warships that would enable the navy to meet its global commitments in conditions other than nuclear war. As the centerpiece of that new thinking, he proposed a small, conventionally powered "sea-control ship" carrying fourteen helicopters and three AV-8 Harrier fighters to show the flag in dangerous waters like the Mediterranean Sea in peacetime while the large attack carriers remained in the broad oceans beyond the Soviets' reach. In wartime, the sea-control ship would escort convoys across the oceans while the carriers operated closer to land. Zumwalt's proposed sea-control ship displaced seventeen thousand tons—less than a World War II–vintage *Essex*-class carrier—and cost about 12.5 percent of a new, nuclear-powered supercarrier. A hard-line cold warrior, Zumwalt warned about the threats posed by the buildup of the Soviet blue-water navy.

But Zumwalt's reform proposals courted disaster, and it found him. A coalition of entrenched carrier aviators, Adm. Hyman G. Rickover—who dominated the navy's nuclear power program—key members of Congress, and powerful representatives of the shipbuilding, aircraft, and electronics industries allied with them, combined to delete funding for sea-control ships from the navy's budget submission in December, 1973. Zumwalt's successors rejected his vision of a different kind of fleet to accomplish the navy's sea control and power projection missions. Instead, they pressed for large nuclear-powered carriers, escort vessels, and submarines. In 1977, they ran afoul of Jimmy Carter, the first and only U.S. Naval Academy graduate to occupy the White House. Carter's administration, drawn mainly from groups outside Washington, D.C.'s established elites, was determined to reduce defense spending after it took office. But President Carter lost the "great carrier war" inside the "beltway" when Congress resisted funding cuts for the nuclear-powered warships the navy brass wanted and refused to allocate funds for a smaller, nonnuclear ASW carrier proposed by the administration. Like the battleship and the strategic bomber, the nuclear-powered heavy attack carrier had emerged as its champions' "sacred vessel."[20]

While the old guard scuttled reforms in the fundamental structure and operating concepts of the fleet, enormous progress was made in naval aviation technology. Faced with extremely limited space aboard its carriers, the navy placed a great emphasis on developing multirole aircraft. Although satisfied with their A-6 and A-7 ground-attack aircraft, aviation admirals pressed for a premier new air superiority fighter: the Grumman F-14 Tomcat. Designed to replace the F-4, the F-14 had emerged as the navy's top fighter program after the service convinced Congress to terminate the naval F-111B program in 1968. The Tomcat, which first flew in 1970, was designed primarily to protect the fleet with Phoenix air-to-air missiles. Operated by a two-man crew consisting of a pilot and weapons officer, the aircraft is capable of performing other combat missions, including attacking surface ships and ground targets.[21]

Soaring costs and mismanagement forced the navy to cut back its planned F-14 buy from 1,336 to about seven hundred aircraft. Meanwhile, like the air force, the navy had begun looking for a less expensive, lightweight aircraft to augment its top-of-the-line fighter. Although the McDonnell Douglas F-17 lost the air force's lightweight fighter competition to the General Dynamics F-16, the former corporation had spread subcontracts around enough congressional districts to place strong pressure on the White House to buy its own aircraft, which became known as the F/A-18 Hornet. Harold Brown, the secretary of defense from January, 1977, to January, 1981, forced the navy to buy the F/A-18 as a replacement for the A-7 Corsair II and to compensate for its reduced F-14 buy. Following considerable "teething" problems, production of the Hornet began in 1980. However, while the F-14 could barely cope with the greatest threat to the fleet, Soviet Backfire bombers equipped with antiship missiles, the Hornet could not. The F/A-18 considerably reduced the overall strike range and payload of the fleet's attack squadrons. Robert Love concluded that "Brown's decision to buy the F/A-18 Hornet eroded the fleet's defenses against the Soviet air threat and its capability to deliver conventional ordnance against land targets."[22] For ASW, the navy acquired the light airborne multipurpose system, which combined shipboard electronics and the SH-2D helicopter. By the end of the 1970s, a new heavy-lift helicopter, the CH-53E, was ready for acceptance by the navy and Marine Corps.[23]

Because of the serious readiness problems that surfaced during the 1968 mobilizations, the Naval Air Reserve program was overhauled in the 1970s. To mirror the fleet, two reserve carrier air wings and two carrier ASW groups were established that could be called to active duty as functioning units ready to deploy quickly in emergencies. Twelve patrol and three transport squadrons augmented them. By the mid-1970s, the reserve carrier air wings began to receive more modern aircraft, including F-4Bs and A-7Bs. Patrol wings started converting to P-3A Orions, and transport units also obtained more modern equipment. The carrier units began performing their required annual active duty training as integrated organizations. In 1976, one of them embarked on the USS *Ranger* for a week to assume the role of the warship's dedicated air unit. That deployment encouraged Naval Air Reserve wings to participate in more exercises and to travel farther from home to do so.

Naval Air Reserve units benefited from another major round of aircraft modernization in the 1980s designed to bring them into closer parity with active duty units. Among others, it brought F-14s, F/A-18s, and E-2Cs into their inventories. Augmentation units were established during that decade to create pools of trained reservists who could augment the fleet in wartime or other emergencies. The augmentees either trained with their assigned reserve units or parent active duty squadrons while flying the latters' aircraft to maintain operational proficiency. In addition, reserve patrol squadrons began occasionally filling operational requirements for navy units on a temporary basis, sometimes as far away as Japan and Spain. Encouraged by post-Vietnam reorganization and equipment modernization, the hopes and expectations of Naval Air Reservists grew. At a minimum, they were convinced that their established image as a flying club for airline pilots was changing.[24]

One of the most serious problems navy and air force pilots faced during the Vietnam War was the poor performance of their air-to-air missiles. The radar-guided or infrared versions of the AIM-4 Falcon, the radar-homing AIM-7 Sparrow, and the infrared AIM-9 Sidewinder missiles had been under development since the early to mid-1950s. They had been designed primarily to destroy gently maneuvering large targets such as Soviet Bear, Bison, and Badger nuclear-armed bombers. The 'one missile, one kill' expectation that had governed their acquisition was junked during the conflict in Southeast Asia.[25]

Fighter crews had watched in frustration as they fired their missiles at fast, small, and highly maneuverable North Vietnamese MiGs, only to see many of those high-technology munitions "go stupid." Some failed because they were launched outside their operational performance parameters, whereas others failed to track targets for no apparent reason. Subsequent investigations concluded that a combination of inadequate quality control during production and poor maintenance and handling procedures in the field contributed to the missiles' unreliability. Developers responded by both improving Vietnam era air-to-air missiles and developing totally new ones. Sparrows and Sidewinders were continuously upgraded. In addition, the AIM-54 Phoenix was developed for the navy, while the air force pressed ahead with the AIM-120 advanced medium

Electronic countermeasures pods are unloaded from a C-141 Starlifter at Lod International Airport in Israel in 1973 during Operation Nickel Grass. The massive arms resupply effort, mounted from the United States by the Military Airlift Command, played a key role in preventing Israel from being defeated by its Arab neighbors. (U.S. Air Force photo.)

range air-to-air missile (AMRAAM). Both missiles were designed to be fired from well beyond a pilot's visual range. The Phoenix was designed to destroy Soviet bombers and antiship cruise missiles over a hundred miles away from the navy fighters that launched them. The AMRAAM, which carried its own radar, was developed to operate in a "fire-and-forget" mode—which meant that a pilot would not have to continue illuminating a target after launching it.[26]

Realistic testing and evaluation under simulated combat conditions proved to be a critical element of the subsequent success of those new weapons. There had been few attempts to test prototype missiles in a mock combat environment in the 1950s. Significant advances in electronics and solid-state physics played a major role in improving American missiles after the Vietnam War. In addition, the evolution of comprehensive, well-instrumented test ranges in the 1970s to support more realistic air combat training provided developers with opportunities to test missiles as fully integrated elements of fighter weapons systems in situations that approximated combat conditions to the greatest extent possible. Because of their growing complexity, the development of the new missiles and improved versions of the older ones took anywhere from ten years for the AIM-7 Sparrow to fifteen for the AIM-120 AMRAAM. However, the combat potential of the complex, realistically tested, and costly new missiles proved to be very real indeed. The advanced versions of the AIM-7, AIM-9, AIM-54, and AIM-120 demonstrated the one-shot, one-kill performance their champions had claimed for them, but which earlier versions of those weapons had lacked.[27]

The high-threat environment of interlinked SAMs, AAA, radar, and fighters that U.S. aircraft faced over North Vietnam had forced planners to include increasing numbers of electronic countermeasures aircraft in strike packages. Despite heavy losses during operations like Linebacker II, the extensive ECM effort proved invaluable. The air force estimated it saved 25 percent of attacking aircraft, whereas the navy believed 80 percent were saved. Regardless of whose calculations of the value of ECM are more valid, it was clear that U.S. tactical air forces could no longer afford to leave home without them. The Vietnam experience stimulated an expansion of research and development that produced, among others, the air force's EF-111A Raven standoff jammer and F-4G Wild Weasel SAM-suppresser aircraft. The navy deployed the EA-6B Prowler to the fleet to jam enemy communications. The Prowler was armed with more lethal antiradar munitions like the AGM-88 high-speed antiradiation missile (HARM).[28]

A major air force response to high-threat environments was to protect its aircrews by developing ultrasecret and highly expensive "stealth" technology. Stealth is the term commonly used in public to refer to aircraft and missiles that are difficult for modern radar systems to detect. More accurately, the armed forces and defense industry refer to them as "low observables." The SR-71 Blackbird strategic reconnaissance aircraft was delivered to the air force starting in 1966. It was the first operational system designed to have a greatly reduced radar signature. According to Richard Hallion: "It made use of the three major means of radar cross-section reduction: shaping, structural absorption via special materials, and specialized coatings. During the Vietnam war, such technology was also exploited on small jet-propelled drones launched over North Vietnam on photo reconnaissance and electronic intelligence missions."[29] He added that the Vietnam "experience coupled with the lessons from the 1973 Arab-Israeli war (which demonstrated the vulnerability of conventional aircraft to radar-guided missiles and gunfire as well as heat-seeking missiles) greatly encouraged development of larger special-purpose radar-defeating 'stealth' aircraft."[30]

As has so often been the case throughout the history of American military aviation, foreign influences played an important role in the emergence of stealth aircraft. Although the Soviet Union failed to exploit it, a critical scientific break-through in the development of low observables came from theoretical studies by Pytor Ufimtsev, chief scientist at the Moscow Institute of Radio Engineering. Lockheed engineer Denys Overholser, who recognized that they could have an enormous impact on the radar reflectivity of future aircraft, studied his ideas.[31]

Lockheed's "Skunk Works" development team designed a stealth technology demonstrator aircraft that first flew in 1977. The following year, the air force signed a contract with that corporation to design and produce what became known as the F-117 Nighthawk. The latter's maiden flight took place in June, 1981, and it entered service in 1983. Lockheed produced fifty-nine of the aircraft, which fly at night and are capable of delivering laser-guided bombs with great accuracy. The progress of the F-117 encouraged the air force to acquire Northrop's B-2 Spirit bomber, which entered service in December, 1993. The B-2 is a flying wing with masked engine intakes and exhausts and no vertical surfaces. Its bomb bay can carry up to sixteen nuclear weapons or as many as eighty five-hundred-pound conventional bombs. Stealth capability is considered an important advantage for U.S. combat aircraft because it makes them almost impossible to detect and destroy. Although only the United States has fielded such aircraft, other nations are reportedly working on countermeasures.[32]

Extracting themselves from the Vietnam quagmire, the marines adopted a very different approach than the high-tech air force and navy. They wanted to cultivate their image as elite infantry ready to go to war on a moment's notice and rebuild the Marine Corps to its 1965 posture, including an inventory of 1,004 aircraft that was evenly divided between helicopters and fixed-wing planes. However, there was little public and political support during the 1970s for either the military generally or its elite organizations. Post-Vietnam budget cuts caused significant reductions in marine aviation and its support establishment. Readiness suffered and modernization programs lagged.

The status of aviation was one of the Marine Corps's most difficult challenges coming out of Southeast Asia. The navy was still responsible for acquiring new aircraft for the marines. Hard-pressed for funds, it was reluctant to purchase aircraft that could not operate from carriers and was determined to rotate marine fighter units on flattop deployments. Marine leaders knew that carriers might not linger long in dangerous amphibious operational areas in future conflicts. Consequently, they would have to seize and hold austere airfields from which to provide aviation support for marine ground units ashore. This issue came to a head with the F-14. The navy wanted the marines to buy the Tomcat in order to reduce the fighter's soaring unit cost. Under great pressure from the navy, they agreed—but then backed out in 1975 because of its high cost, complex maintenance requirements, and primary air superiority mission.

Instead, the Marine Corps waited for the development of the F/A-18, a multirole fighter, to replace its aging F-4s.

Based upon their Vietnam experience, the marines began purchasing AV-8A Harriers for their light attack force. The Harrier was especially attractive to them as a close air support aircraft because it is capable of vertical takeoffs and landings in primitive front-line combat areas. Designed by a British firm, Hawker, the AV-8A was manufactured under license in the United States by McDonnell Douglas and began to enter the marine inventory in 1971. The aircraft initially was plagued by crashes, poor maintenance, and doubts about its vulnerability to enemy fire. Those problems were overcome during the early 1980s when an advanced version of the Harrier, the AV-8B, which had evolved into an air superiority fighter with interdiction and close air support capabilities, entered active service with the leathernecks. Advanced avionics, improved maintainability, and the development of improved tactics stressing high-speed delivery of weapons at low altitude all helped to overcome skepticism about the Harrier.

During the 1970s and 1980s, the marines had also stressed improvements of their Vietnam era helicopter workhorses, including the UH-1E, AH-2 Cobra, CH-46, and CH-53. Helicopters had become the backbone of the marine infantry's tactical mobility and cost about 33 percent of the fixed-wing aircraft force. If provided with adequate artillery and fixed-wing close air support, the Marine Corps leaders believed that helicopter-borne forces would remain combat effective except in the firepower-intensive mechanized warfare associated with central European combat scenarios. To dramatically extend its over-the-horizon amphibious assault capability, it proposed to buy the experimental V-22A Osprey, a costly tilt-rotor aircraft, to replace the CH-46. However, the Osprey ran into numerous barriers. Developmental problems and budget reductions in the late 1980s plagued the program. Nevertheless, over the objections of a series of defense secretaries, the Marine Corps and its Capitol Hill supporters were able to keep the program alive until the political prospects for production funding improved.[33]

The army, meanwhile, pressed forward with the development of helicopters as transports, reconnaissance vehicles, and gunships based upon their success in Vietnam. It planned to use them in combat areas for carrying cargo, airlifting troops, and attacking enemy forces.[34] Abandoning the medium altitude diving attacks favored by U.S. helicopter pilots in Vietnam, army aviators stressed nap-of-the-earth (NOE) flying. This technique involves helicopters moving cross-country at treetop level and below while following routes that reduce their exposure to enemy fire. Army pilots reassigned to Germany from Vietnam learned those techniques from their NATO colleagues.[35]

Army aviators struggled to secure a firm place for the air cavalry and armed attack helicopter in the NATO-oriented post-Vietnam army. Aviation was not formally recognized as a separate combat branch in the army until 1983. Many officers, including some senior generals, doubted that helicopters could survive on medium- and high-intensity European battlefields against Soviet armored forces liberally endowed with mobile AAA and shoulder-fired SAMs. In addition to those concerns, tighter budgets reinforced the intense competition between the combat arms for money and personnel. Some officers resisted major new investments in aviation because they feared that such initiatives would come at the expense of the army's older armor, infantry, and artillery branches.

To help resolve those doubts, Gen. James H. Polk, commander of U.S. Army forces in Europe, authorized a series of tests in 1970 to determine the effectiveness of helicopters in the NATO environment. Conducted in the spring of that year, the trials suggested that air cavalry units could be effective on the continent against Soviet forces. However, doubts persisted in the army about the helicopter's ability to destroy tanks. A follow-on series of exercises that summer at Ansbach, Germany, verified that attack helicopters could be successfully employed against enemy armor. The experiments proved that helicopters, especially attack helicopters, would add combat power to NATO forces. Furthermore, they dramatically highlighted the fact that NOE flying techniques would have to become integrated in all aviation training.[36]

Aviation had secured a firm place for itself in the army's post-Vietnam force structure, and by 1980 it boasted 490 fixed-wing and 7,952 rotary-wing aircraft—not far below the air force's total inventory of 9,070 planes. The centerpiece of the army aircraft inventory was a fast, low-flying helicopter that could kill tanks—a requirement that had not even existed on a formal basis during the war in Southeast Asia, although some UH-1B Huey gunships destroyed eight North Vietnamese tanks with rockets during the latter stages of the war. While the AH-1G Cobra had lacked an antiarmor capability prior to the air cavalry tests in Germany, it was subsequently equipped with a 20-mm cannon, as well as the TOW and Hellfire (helicopter-launched, fire-and-forget) missiles. Both army and marine units were equipped with Cobras.

In 1972, the army announced a new attack helicopter program that was subsequently designated the AH-64A Apache. It was one of the "big five" technologically superior weapons systems that the army began developing in the 1970s to help offset the numerical advantages enjoyed by Warsaw Pact armies in Europe. The others were the M1 Abrams tank, the M2 Bradley infantry fighting vehicle, the UH-60A Black Hawk utility helicopter, and the Patriot air defense missile. Developed by Hughes, the Apache incorporated the Cobra's combat experience and technological advances from the AH-65A Cheyenne development program that had been canceled in 1969. Advanced night-vision and target-sensing devices enable pilots to fly Apaches using NOE techniques even at night. The AH-64A can be armed with a combination of eight Hellfire missiles and thirty-eight rockets. It also has a 30-mm, single-barrel chain gun in its nose. The army received its first production aircraft in December, 1983.[37]

THE AEROSPACE INDUSTRY

The U.S. armed forces continued to rely heavily on the aviation industry to develop new weapons systems that would give them a technological edge over the Soviets. However, by the late 1950s, military aircraft had ceased to be the industry's main product. Missiles, electronics, space systems, and commercial airliners accounted for the majority of its revenues. Officials began calling it the aerospace industry. The staggering costs of producing sophisticated new weapons systems had encouraged another round of corporate mergers and product diversification, as well as efforts to balance military and commercial production. For example, McDonnell acquired Douglas in 1967 after pursuing a merger for several years. The new firm produced a broad range of aerospace products, including airliners, fighter aircraft, and space systems. Lockheed, which had come to dominate the air force transport market, floundered badly in its efforts to reestablish itself in the commercial airliner market in the 1970s. The corporation had already begun making helicopters, electronics equipment, space systems, and ships. Huge financial losses from its C-5 Galaxy transport program nearly bankrupted the corporation. Only a special emergency government loan of $250 million approved by Congress in 1971 kept it from going out of business. The legislation authorizing the loan emphasized that Lockheed's survival affected not only a number of key national defense contracts, but also employment rates in several congressional districts across the nation.[38]

The immediate impact of the Vietnam War on the industry had been more qualitative than quantitative. With the exception of helicopters, military aircraft were not mass-produced during that conflict. Several thousand helicopters delivered troops and supplies, evacuated wounded personnel, and provided direct fire support to U.S. and allied forces in Southeast Asia. Bell, Sikorsky, and Boeing were the primary American helicopter producers during that conflict. Industry helped make major improvements in the electronics and missiles used by fixed-wing U.S. combat planes during the war.[39]

The growth of space systems also had a major impact on the aerospace industry after the Vietnam War. By 1990, they totaled $28.9 billion. The Defense Department claimed the largest share of that amount, $15.4 billion, while civilian orders—led by NASA's $12.3 billion—accounted for most of the rest. Ballistic missiles, which also served as launch vehicles for space systems, encouraged the development of microcircuitry that has had an enormous impact on American life.

The post-Vietnam generation of U.S. fighters—including the F-14, F-15, and F/A-18, along with their associated missiles, electronics, and ECM devices—gave the United States a convincing qualitative lead over both the Soviet Union and America's NATO allies. The costs of those weapons systems and associated equipment skyrocketed even as the total production of American military aircraft declined. The budget for U.S. military engines alone in the 1970s was $10 billion. Despite its technological virtuosity and growing revenues, the aerospace industry was haunted by sensational stories of bribery and other corrupt practices associated with military contracts. Much of the attention focused on Northrop's efforts to sell its F-20 Tigershark to foreign customers. Developed with $1.2 billion of the corporation's own funds to meet the Carter administration's goal of providing less-sophisticated weapons to foreign customers, Northrop's efforts to sell the F-20 abroad foundered when the USAF refused to purchase it. Despite the corporation's desperate attempts to recover its investment by selling the aircraft overseas, foreign governments refused to purchase a weapon the U.S. armed forces had already rejected.

Lockheed, Boeing, and McDonnell Douglas were also accused of paying tens of millions of dollars overseas to ease the way for foreign sales. Although such practices were common in other businesses and in some foreign cultures, the high-profile aerospace industry became the target of many exposés in the American media. The furor over these events led to the Foreign Corrupt Practices Act, enacted by Congress in 1977 to halt bribery overseas by U.S. firms. Nevertheless, allegations of shady practices by the aerospace industry persist.[40]

In addition to charges of widespread fraud and corruption, civilian critics associated with the defense reform movement during the 1980s charged that the aerospace industry and the military services collaborated to field weapons systems that were too costly, complex, and sophisticated to offset the Warsaw Pact's large numerical advantages in a real war. The underlying concern of those reformers was to convince the federal government to adapt its military policies and organizations to what they perceived as an overall decline in global American power. However, except in the very broadest sense, it was difficult to identify a unifying goal of the reformers.

Samuel P. Huntington observed that the "Two central points in the reform critique . . . are the desirability of shifting emphasis in military doctrine from attrition to maneuver and of shifting the emphasis in military procurement from a smaller number of highly sophisticated (and expensive) weapons to a larger number of proven, less sophisticated (and cheaper) weapons."[41] He found it difficult to understand "why maneuver should imply larger numbers of simpler weapons or why highly sophisticated weapons are tied in with attrition doctrine. If anything, one would think that just the reverse would be true: that a maneuver doctrine would require highly advanced sophisticated weapons for rapid movement and effective command and control, while an attrition doctrine would demand overpowering numbers of simpler, cheaper weapons that one could afford to lose in battle."[42]

THE YOM KIPPUR WAR

While the strategic arms competition with the Soviet Union and preparations for a combined arms war with the Warsaw Pact dominated the attention of the aerospace industry and Pentagon planners, events in the turbulent Middle East provoked an unexpected Cold War crisis. Egypt and Syria had been determined to even the score with Israel ever since their humiliating defeat by the latter in the Six-Day War of 1967. While Israelis celebrated the Jewish holy day of Yom Kippur on October 6, 1973, those two nations launched a joint attack that caught Israel largely by surprise. With Soviet help, the invaders had modernized their armed forces. They also had learned some hard lessons from the Israeli Air Force during the previous war. For their part, the Israelis knew that something was brewing, but they were preoccupied with a terrorist campaign being mounted by the Palestine Liberation Organization (PLO). They also seriously underestimated their enemies but decided to forego a preemptive strike.[43]

Air power played a key role in the Israeli decision. During the first hours of the Six-Day War, Israel's air attacks had crippled its enemies. The air force had dominated the rest of the conflict. By 1973, the situation had changed dramatically. Moscow had supplied the Arab states with six hundred advanced surface-to-air missiles, three hundred MiG-21 jet fighters, and twelve hundred tanks—plus hundreds of thousands of tons of consumable war supplies. Egypt and Syria had significantly strengthened their air defenses, acquired modern Soviet aircraft, and provided better training for the men who would fly them. More significantly, they had developed a significant surface-to-air missile capability built around new Soviet missiles that far surpassed anything in their earlier experience.[44]

The Arab states quickly gained the initiative when they attacked across the Suez Canal and into the Golan Heights in October, 1973. Through a combination of new equipment and ingenious tactics, they almost overwhelmed the overconfident Israelis. The most significant new element on the battlefield was the incredible attrition rate of personnel and weapons. Both sides employed

A Soviet intelligence collection ship closes on the stern of the USS *Franklin D. Roosevelt* underway in the Mediterranean Sea in April, 1975. Soviet and U.S. military units closely monitored each other's forward-deployed forces during the Cold War. (Photo courtesy Air Force Historical Support Office.)

guided missiles against tanks and aircraft. Despite their use of electronic and other countermeasures, the new missiles were incredibly effective.[45]

The fantastic expenditures of munitions, tanks, and aircraft shocked both sides, who pleaded with their respective backers to restock their inventories. The Soviets were quick to respond. They soon had transports flying military materiel into Egyptian and Syrian airfields. However, the United States was slower to react because of both Vietnam War finger pointing and the Nixon administration's domestic political difficulties. Vice President Spiro Agnew had resigned from office after being implicated on charges of petty graft and corruption while governor of Maryland, and some of the president's aides had been indicted in the growing Watergate scandal. More importantly, the White House and the Pentagon had assumed that the war in the Middle East would produce another quick Israeli victory, and they were astounded by the extent of the Jewish state's early losses. Initially, the U.S. government provided only token aid to its Middle East ally as Nixon tried to strike a balance between the competing demands of maintaining the fragile détente with the Soviet Union and supporting Israel.

The result was confusion and delay on the banks of the Potomac. While Nixon fiddled, Israel burned. Finally, heeding the personal pleas of Prime Minister Golda Meir, the president decided on October 9 to resupply Israel by air and sea. However, it quickly became apparent that only an airlift would be timely enough to save Israel from a catastrophic military defeat. After determining that neither Israeli nor American commercial air carriers could handle the job, the president directed on October 12 that the Military Airlift Command (MAC) undertake the entire airlift. Because the oil-producing Arab nations had threatened to impose an oil embargo on any nation that aided Israel, America's NATO allies in Europe—whose economies depended on imported petroleum—denied the air force use of their bases to support the aerial resupply effort. The lone exception was Portugal, which Washington successfully pressured into allowing U.S. military aircraft to use its mid-Atlantic airfield at Lajes in the Azores. That bit of major league diplomatic arm twisting was critical, because the distance from MAC's main East Coast staging point at McGuire AFB, New Jersey, to Tel Aviv was about five thousand nautical miles. Other airfields in the United States would have to be employed in order to complete the airlift before it was too late. Their use raised the maximum distance to 6,450 nautical miles. However, the air force had only a limited ability to resupply Israel from the United States without landing to refuel en route because military airlift had taken a backseat to the development of combat aircraft during the first two decades after World War II.

The air force's primary long-range transports were the jet-powered C-141A and C-5A. The air force had 268 Starlifters when the Yom Kippur War began. Although they could each lift thirty-one tons of cargo over a distance of thirty-six hundred nautical miles, the C-141As were not equipped for aerial refueling. The giant C-5A, which could lift fifty tons of cargo over fifty-eight hundred nautical miles, was equipped for in-flight refueling. However, because air force planners feared that flying in a tanker's downwash would further shorten the life span of the C-5A's defective wings, MAC had not conducted refueling operations with its fleet of seventy-seven Galaxies. Although the C-5As could fly nonstop to Tel Aviv with reduced payloads, it was out of the question for the C-141As. Access to Lajes was critical for them.

The U.S. military airlift to Israel, code-named Operation Nickel Grass, began on October 14 and lasted thirty-four days. American pilots, refueled by air force KC-135 tankers, ferried F-4s and A-4s to Israel during the war to replace the latter's combat losses. A resupplied Israel finally regained the military advantage and fought the war to the edge of victory. Secretary of State Henry Kissinger negotiated a fragile cease-fire on October 22, but fears that an Egyptian army east of the Suez Canal might still be destroyed or captured by an

Israeli force that had already encircled it prompted the Soviets to threaten to intervene with their own troops to establish a joint peacekeeping force with the United States. President Anwar Sadat had kicked Soviet forces out of Egypt in 1972, and President Nixon was determined to keep Moscow from restoring its influence in the region. He did not want the already dangerous situation there to degenerate into another war. American forces, including SAC, were placed on a heightened state of global alert to back the administration's diplomacy. The Soviets subsequently backed down and agreed to allow a UN peacekeeping force deploy to the Sinai Peninsula.[46]

The Yom Kippur War had significant diplomatic, economic, and military implications for the United States. The Soviets were clearly supplanted by the Americans as the dominant foreign influence in the region. President Sadat cut his remaining bonds with the Soviet Union, and Egypt began negotiations with Israel that enabled it to regain territories lost in the 1967 conflict and eventually ended the state of war that had existed between the two nations since 1948. Without Egypt, there was virtually no chance U.S. forces would not have to intervene militarily to save Israel from a conventional attack by any coalition of Arab states. Egypt, in effect, became a regional ally of the United States. However, the war also stimulated the rise of anti-Western Islamic fundamentalism and led to a huge increase in the cost of imported oil from Organization of Petroleum Exporting Countries (OPEC) in retaliation against those nations that supported Israel in 1973. Although a ban on exports to the Jewish state's supporters was canceled in 1974, the cost of annual OPEC oil exports to Western Europe, Japan, and North America increased by $40 billion.

As a result of the airlift to Israel in 1973, MAC ensured that its entire strategic airlift fleet of C-5s and C-141s was trained and equipped for in-flight refueling. In conjunction with the lessons learned from the Southeast Asia airlift, Operation Nickel Grass led to the consolidation of all air force airlift assets under MAC and its designation as a specified command reporting to the Joint Chiefs of Staff on February 1, 1977. The crisis in the Middle East had also highlighted the need to incorporate cargo-convertible aircraft in an expanded Civil Reserve Air Fleet (CRAF) and the critical importance of maintaining airfield facilities at Lajes. The airlift to Israel also led to a program to lengthen the fuselage of each C-141 by more than twenty-three feet. Nickel Grass showed the need for additional long-range airlift resources. Coupled with other events in the Middle East in the late 1970s, Nickel Grass stimulated the development of the C-17 jet transport, which entered full-scale development in 1985.[47]

The airlift to Israel also had a major impact upon the laws governing the employment of the guard and reserve. Because of the enormous stresses placed upon its airlift capabilities in 1973, the air force asked that ten thousand additional personnel be assigned to MAC. An economy-minded Congress rejected the request. Instead, it urged the air force to make greater use of guard and reserve personnel in future emergencies. However, federal laws mandated either a declaration of war or national emergency before those individuals and their units could be recalled involuntarily to active service. The Vietnam War heightened the reluctance of both the president and Congress to take the political risks associated with mobilizations.

Congress responded in 1976 by authorizing the president to recall up to fifty thousand guardsmen and reservists for as long as ninety days without either a declaration of war or a national emergency. On his own authority, the chief executive could double the mobilization service period if he determined that circumstances warranted it. Later, Congress increased the number of reserve components personnel who could be called up under that basic legislation to two hundred thousand. Although it continued to rely on volunteers from the guard and reserve to temporarily expand the armed forces in the 1970s and 1980s, the White House began to employ that enhanced mobilization authority on a fairly regular basis beginning in 1990.[48]

The Yom Kippur War's most startling implication for the U.S. armed services was the destructive power of the new smart weaponry and the enormous materiel loss rate it generated. Planners realized that their weapons inventories would have to be increased enormously if their forces participated in sustained combat operations. But the American military, struggling with a post-Vietnam budget squeeze intensified by the soaring costs of oil and weapons modernization programs as well as the growing personnel budget of the all-volunteer force, lacked the resources to expand its stocks of weapons and spare parts to adequate levels. According to many critics, it had become a "hollow force" that lacked the wherewithal to project power globally and sustain combat operations against its major adversary, the Soviet Union. Those circumstances did not change significantly until events in Afghanistan and Iran created a sense of crisis in Washington that changed the direction of American defense policy and stimulated major increases in military spending.[49]

REASSERTING AMERICAN POWER

Although the armed forces had taken significant steps toward military reform and weapons modernization even before the United States extricated itself from Vietnam, their civilian political masters had to provide significant increases in the defense budget before those changes could be translated into substantial increases in U.S. military capabilities. Furthermore, Presidents Nixon, Ford, and Carter had pursued a national security strategy that was driven by the desire to control defense costs, negotiate with the Soviets to reduce tensions and craft arms control agreements, and avoid another limited war like Vietnam. To help counter Soviet power and end decades of antipathy, President Nixon visited Communist China in February, 1972, and normalized diplomatic relations with the People's Republic. America's NATO forces were strengthened for a possible short war with the Soviet Union and its Warsaw Pact allies in Europe. Under those conditions, the Pacific-oriented power projection and sea control missions of the navy and Marine Corps were marginalized. The army and the air force would fight on Western Europe's central front with units and equipment already stationed there and reinforcements that could be airlifted quickly from the United States. Tactical nuclear weapons would be employed if NATO conventional forces could not keep the aggressors at bay. The two superpowers' vast nuclear arsenals would deter any conflict on the continent from escalating into all-out war. Based on the assumption that a Soviet invasion in Europe could be stopped within weeks, relatively little attention was paid to the possibility of military operations in the North Atlantic, the Mediterranean, or the Pacific. Plans for a strategy that would shift U.S. naval forces from the Pacific to European waters were not taken seriously because they would take too long to implement and there was no role for carriers in NATO war plans anyway. Although the navy was assigned the responsibility for antisubmarine warfare and convoy escort in the North Atlantic, those missions were meaningless in a short war with the Soviets.

After a halting start, Pres. Jimmy Carter launched critical changes in American national security policy that were accelerated during Ronald Reagan's administration. When Carter took over the Oval Office in January, 1977, he was committed to transforming American national security policies. The new president was convinced that his administration could curb nuclear weapons proliferation, keep America at peace, pursue détente with the Soviet Union, reduce defense spending, shift the burden of maintaining international security to the nation's allies, and expand the role of "human rights" in diplomacy.

When he left office four years later, Carter had abandoned the policies of the 'peace phase' of his presidency.[50] His initial policies reflected both post-Vietnam public opinion and the president's own noninterventionist ideals. He knew that there was little public and congressional support for military spending beyond preserving nuclear deterrence and strengthening NATO. His first two defense budgets included real cuts in military spending. Carter canceled the B-1 bomber, reduced shipbuilding programs and the procurement of tactical aircraft, and cut back on operations and maintenance funding for the armed forces. Congress restored some of his cuts, especially in major shipbuilding programs, but acquiesced to others.[51]

However, events in the Persian Gulf region changed the president's mind about defense spending and American national security policy. Iranian revolutionaries seized American hostages in the U.S. embassy in November, 1979, after they overthrew the Shah's pro-Western regime. That outrage led Carter to impose diplomatic and economic sanctions on the regime in Teheran led by the Ayatollah Ruhollah Khomeini. The following April, a joint service attempt to rescue the hostages in Iran was aborted after several helicopters failed and they were spotted by Iranian civilians. Another helicopter collided with a C-130 transport at a desert rendezvous point during the withdrawal, killing eight servicemen. The debacle, which dramatized lingering U.S. military and diplomatic weakness in the wake of Vietnam, strengthened Carter's domestic political rivals and was a key factor in his loss in November, 1980. The hostages were not released until after Ronald Reagan replaced Carter as president.

Before his presidency ended, however, Carter had taken important steps to reassert American power and influence. He slowed and then canceled scheduled U.S. troop withdrawals from South Korea. American troops were committed to policing the Sinai Peninsula. To counter Soviet intervention in the Horn of Africa and a Russian occupation of Afghanistan in December, 1979, his administration launched a U.S. military buildup, reversing the decline of defense spending since America's withdrawal from Southeast Asia. Carter approved construction of a new ICBM, upgraded existing B-52s and equipped them with cruise missiles, gave the go-ahead for the development of stealth technology, accelerated the development of Trident nuclear submarines, and resumed compulsory draft registration. He strengthened NATO and publicly committed the United States to protect the oil-rich Persian Gulf region and established a rapid deployment military force to honor that pledge.[52]

From the outset of his presidency, Ronald Reagan's foreign policy was "defined by his antipathy to the Soviet Union, which he called the 'evil empire.' He and his security advisers, especially Defense Secretary Caspar Weinberger, called for preparedness for war with the Soviet Union and its allies on a global scale. . . . Reagan presided over the largest military buildup in peacetime U.S. history; probably around $2.4 trillion on the armed forces, of which an estimated $536 billion represented increases over previous projected trends for the decade."[53] Reagan's defense budgets peaked at $296 billion (inflation-adjusted constant dollars) during FY 1985. After that, Congress, concerned by soaring federal deficits and the revival of détente with the Soviets, forced significant reductions.

The Reagan military buildup featured a massive investment in new weapons systems, increased readiness through intensified training and increased purchases of spare parts and munitions, and the initiation of the Strategic Defense Initiative (SDI) or "Star Wars" program to defend the nation against ballistic missile

A C-130 Hercules from the West Virginia Air National Guard flies over the Egyptian pyramids in 1981. By the early 1980s, American air units deployed regularly to the Middle East, demonstrating the region's growing importance to the nation's global interests. (Photo by MSgt. Michael K. Pitzer, 130th Tactical Airlift Group, Charleston, West Virginia.)

attacks. To stabilize the strategic competition with the Soviets, the president accelerated the fleet ballistic missile submarine and cruise missile programs, and revived the B-1 bomber. He also decided to deploy a hundred new air force MX ICBMs and extended the U.S. commitment to live within the terms of the unratified SALT II treaty. While strategic mobility programs were strengthened, Reagan left the structure and personnel levels of the armed forces largely untouched. The president also secretly funded highly classified stealth fighter and bomber projects.[54]

The Reagan administration pressured America's allies for greater participation in the global military buildup against communist powers and emphasized developing greater U.S. capabilities to intervene outside NATO's central front in Western Europe. The president added Latin America as a crisis region requiring deeper U.S. involvement and proclaimed the "Reagan Doctrine," which committed the administration to active support of anticommunist insurgencies in the Third World. Within Europe, the army and the air force pushed NATO toward acceptance of a high-technology, air-power-oriented, deep-battle concept relying on precision-guided munitions that would attack all Warsaw Pact echelons simultaneously, especially follow-on forces, in the event of a war. Although the United States never actually fielded a force capable of implementing the army's AirLand Battle doctrine properly, the Soviet hierarchy believed that it demanded a major reorganization of their defense system and weapons acquisition programs. That decision helped to set in motion a series of broad-ranging economic and political reforms the Soviets were ultimately unable to handle.[55]

Fueled by soaring defense budgets and anticommunist rhetoric, Reagan's dynamic secretary of the navy, John F. Lehman Jr., sponsored a dramatic expansion of U.S. naval power that rivaled the importance of changes tied to AirLand Battle doctrine and associated force structure improvements in the army and air force. Like Theodore Roosevelt, Lehman was a geopolitical realist whose ideas were colored by a strong strain of military romanticism. He was determined to strengthen carrier aviation and revamp naval strategy to highlight the role of large, nuclear-powered flattops in modern warfare. Lehman pushed for construction of a six-hundred-ship fleet designed to insure American command of the seas against all potential enemies.

His signature "maritime strategy" advocated attacks by carrier aircraft on the Soviet maritime heartland from the Baltic, Norwegian, and North Seas. The essence of that strategy was that the navy would attack the Soviet Union from the start of a general war in order to turn it into a protracted, global, nonnuclear struggle that would exploit the inherent strengths of the United States. The maritime strategy required a larger, more modernized fleet capable of conducting global operations. Its advocates claimed that it was a much more flexible and useful strategy than the existing NATO-oriented plan for a conflict with the Soviets in the heart of Europe that would almost invariably involve tactical nuclear weapons. However, critics charged that Lehman's highly risky approach to superpower conflict would come at great cost while achieving marginal strategic gains at a time when the Soviets had already begun backing away from their efforts to develop a true blue-water fleet.

Undaunted by his opponents, the navy secretary also stressed the value of large carriers in limited wars and contingencies. His acquisition policies favored large, electronically sophisticated aircraft like the F-14 fighter and the night-flying A-6 attack plane at the expense of the lighter A-4, precision-guided munitions, and stealth bombers. Carrier aircraft equipped with air-to-air missiles were deployed to defend against Soviet aircraft as far away from battle groups as possible. To protect its carriers against the growing challenge posed by Soviet missiles, the navy also deployed cruisers, frigates, and destroyers equipped with the Aegis combat system. Developed during the 1970s in response to the threat of a saturation missile attack by the Soviets, Aegis employed an advanced radar and computer system that could track hundreds of targets simultaneously. Aegis could destroy multiple aircraft and missile targets at the same time with its antiair missiles. In an ostensible effort to reduce the navy's vulnerability to Soviet nuclear strikes on the American homeland, Lehman proposed to significantly expand the number of home ports the fleet operated from in the continental United States. His critics, emphasizing the obvious domestic political implications of that policy, dismissed it as "home porking."[56]

Outside Europe, the Reagan administration aggressively engaged Soviet-sponsored governments, Islamic fundamentalists, terrorists, Arab nationalists, and others with decidedly mixed results. Sponsoring a largely covert war against communist revolutionaries, it achieved relative success in Latin America. The administration feared that a recently installed communist government was going to turn the small island of Grenada into a major base for exporting terrorism and more conventional forms of aggression in the Caribbean. Using the pretext of rescuing American medical students trapped on the island, a force of some six thousand U.S. servicemen invaded Grenada in October, 1983, and overwhelmed its defenders. Fighters from the USS *Independence* provided air support and marines staged a helicopter assault. Air force transports, supported by tankers, moved troops and supplies to the island while E-3A AWACS aircraft monitored Cuba for any signs of a hostile response to the American operation. Problems of command, control, planning, spotty intelligence, and interservice cooperation plagued the hastily assembled operation. Although successful, Operation Urgent Fury was controversial. Bernard Nalty observed: "Despite overwhelming numbers, it took U.S. forces several days to beat down the

An F-106 Delta Dart from the 144th Fighter-Interceptor Wing of the California Air National Guard fires a missile at the Air Force's 1980 William Tell aerial weapons meet. The "Golden Bears" won overall honors in the competition, an indication of the growing competence and importance of the service's reserve components under the auspices of the Total Force policy. (Photo courtesy National Guard Bureau.)

opposition. Because of the tight time frame for planning, the execution of the various phases of Urgent Fury was too often mishandled or poorly coordinated. Most seriously, poor intelligence led to poor decisions. . . . One critic later stated 'We won Grenada in spite of ourselves.'"[57]

Attempts to deal with threats to Israel's security, Islamic fundamentalists, and other Middle Eastern problems produced less satisfactory results. The Reagan administration turned to air power in August, 1981, when U.S. Navy jets shot down two Libyan fighters in the Gulf of Sidra. Libya's leader Muammar Qadhafi claimed that the gulf fell within the limits of his nation's territorial waters and airspace, a stance that the United States rejected. In October, 1985, navy jets, supported by air force intelligence and refueling aircraft, forced a commercial airliner that had been hijacked by Palestinian terrorists to land in Sicily. The terrorists were turned over to Italian authorities, but the latter released them.

The president also approved a clandestine war against terrorism after Middle East terrorist activities escalated. His administration linked to Qadhafi the destruction of an airliner bound for Athens and the bombing of a Berlin nightclub in which several American soldiers were killed and others were wounded. In April, 1986, Reagan authorized a massive retaliatory air strike on high-value Libyan political and military targets by air force F-111s based in England and navy fighters from two carriers in the Mediterranean Sea. The administration asserted that the devastating raid would deter further terrorist assaults in the Middle East. However, the explosion of a car bomb that killed 239 U.S. military personnel at a marine barracks in Beirut in October, 1983, and the destruction of a Pan American Airlines Boeing 747 over Scotland in December, 1988, by Palestinian terrorists linked to Iran and Libya cast doubt on such conclusions.[58]

Nevertheless, when Ronald Reagan departed from the White House in January, 1989, he left behind a far more capable military establishment than he had found when he was inaugurated eight years earlier. Despite a 10 percent reduction during the FY 1986–FY 1989 period, military spending still remained high by Cold War standards in the face of a growing détente with the Soviet Union and exploding federal deficits. The personnel of the active duty military force looked outstanding by every measure of skill, commitment, and trainability. A Congressional initiative, the Goldwater-Nichols Reorganization Act of 1986, gave more authority to the JCS chairman and regional theater commanders in chief while compelling the services to train their leaders and forces for more effective joint operations.[59]

Aviation, spearheaded by fighters equipped with PGMs, attack helicopters, and airmobility forces, emerged as the cutting edge of the post-Vietnam renaissance of American military power. Confronted with the growing numerical superiority of Soviet Union and Warsaw Pact forces, the U.S. armed forces revamped their doctrine, training, and technology. The American approach to combined arms warfare relied increasingly on interservice cooperation, joint command structures, and advanced technologies associated with computers, infrared and radar sensors, and low-observable platforms. A smaller and more consolidated aerospace industry supplied the armed forces with aircraft, missiles, electronics, and space systems that were decidedly superior to those of the nation's allies and rivals. Nuclear weapons declined in relative importance as both the United States and the Soviet Union sought to increase their own security by negotiating arms control agreements for missiles and bombers

Driven by the military defeat in Vietnam and the growth of Soviet military power, America's rejuvenated military forces confronted an unexpected challenge by 1990. It was becoming increasingly clear that the Soviet Union was in political and economic disarray as the last decade of the twentieth century dawned. In Congress, the mood was shifting from international engagement and strong budgetary support of the armed forces to military and fiscal retrenchment.[60]

CHAPTER 7

The Empire Strikes Out

With the sudden and unexpected collapse of the Soviet Union in 1991 and the demise of communist rule in Eastern Europe, air power served as the military instrument of choice for national policy makers. They had to deal with a world increasingly marked by communal violence, terrorism, international drug trafficking, the proliferation of weapons of mass destruction, global economic integration, the emergence of the information economy, and uncertainty about America's proper role in it. Eliot A. Cohen observed that air power was "an unusually seductive form of military strength because, like modern courtship, it appears to offer the pleasures of gratification without the burdens of commitment."[1] In the tradition of Billy Mitchell, its most passionate advocates were convinced that it could be applied with almost surgical precision to achieve national policy objectives without exposing American troops to the bloody uncertainties of ground combat.

America's success in short wars against Iraq in 1991 and Yugoslavia in 1999 made air power appear to be spectacularly effective and relatively bloodless. However, in other post–Cold War situations—including the U.S. military interventions in Somalia, Haiti, and Panama—air power played a distinctly supporting role. Although there were substantial reductions in the size and budgets of the U.S. armed forces after the Cold War, both remained historically high by peacetime American standards. Substantial portions of them remained either forward deployed or were rotated overseas for short periods of time to maintain American power and influence. Policy makers again had to grapple with the basic questions of how much was enough and for what purposes did the republic maintain its armed forces? Tighter defense budgets and a growing unwillingness to risk casualties in faraway places where vital national interests were not at risk enhanced air power's appeal as a tool of statecraft. No broad consensus was reached on when and how the armed forces should be employed. Lacking a major threat to American security like the former Soviet Union, downward pressure continued on the military budget, and the defense industrial base shrank to alarming levels.

MIDNIGHT FOR MOSCOW

As Ronald Reagan flew off to retirement in southern California, his underrated former vice president, George Herbert Walker Bush, grappled with the challenges of holding the nation's highest office on his own. Bush, a navy combat pilot in World War II and the scion of a wealthy East Coast family, had enjoyed a long career in Republican politics before winning the 1988 presidential election. His administration immediately plunged into a dizzying period of changes in the international environment that affected virtually every aspect of American national security policy.[2]

During the Bush presidency, the United States and its allies enjoyed an unexpected triumph of historic proportions. Communism in Eastern Europe and the Soviet Union unraveled and collapsed. The clock struck midnight for Moscow. The game was over. While president, Reagan had attacked the Soviet Union as an "evil empire" bent on world domination that had to be opposed at all costs. He had used strong anticommunist rhetoric to justify the largest increase in peacetime military spending in American history. However, quite unexpectedly, the empire struck out after Reagan left office. Soviet leaders tried to match Reagan's military spending increases. While their war against Muslim rebels in Afghanistan deteriorated, the Kremlin's aging leaders discovered that the Soviet Union's ailing industry and economy could not keep pace with the Americans. In 1985, a dynamic young politician named Mikhail Gorbachev became premier. He had instituted a series of reforms designed to preserve communist rule by opening up society and restructuring the nation's economy.[3]

The Soviet Union had largely conceded the contest for supremacy in the Third World to the West by the late 1980s. During the Reagan years, East-West relations had improved dramatically despite the president's harsh talk and deep anticommunist convictions. On December 8, 1987, Reagan and Gorbachev signed a treaty eliminating intermediate-range American and Russian nuclear weapons, including ground-launched cruise missiles, worldwide. A year later, Gorbachev announced unilateral cuts in his nation's armed forces during a speech at the United Nations.

Civil unrest along the rim of the "evil empire" had spread from the Baltic States to the rest of Eastern Europe in 1989. Poland was the first domino to fall. On September 13, the Polish Communist Party voluntarily relinquished power after losing the first partially free election in a Soviet bloc country. On November 9, East German protesters tore down the Berlin Wall. Within a year, Germany had been peacefully reunified. Other communist regimes had already begun to fall from power throughout Eastern Europe. Governments dedicated to democracy and free markets replaced them. The Baltic States declared their independence from the Soviet Union. Unlike earlier upheavals in the region, Soviet tanks did not roll in to save unpopular communist rulers. North Atlantic Treaty Organization and Warsaw Pact members agreed to reduce conventional weapons in Europe by 40 percent, and the Warsaw Pact disbanded in July, 1991. On the last day of that year, the Soviet Union formally dissolved as a unitary communist state. The Cold War was finally over.[4]

The Cold War's end provided no easy answers to the traditional American defense questions of "How much is enough?" and "Enough for what?"[5] Regardless of their political party affiliation, every U.S. president and Congress since the late 1940s had supported a robust military establishment, thus helping to contain the expansion of Soviet power after World War II and contributing to its collapse. In the final analysis, "the exhaustion of the Russian people, the patriotic endurance of national minorities in the Soviet Union, the rebelliousness of the member states of the Warsaw Pact, and the greed and moral poverty of the communist party brought the Soviet Union down."[6] The post-Vietnam renaissance of the U.S. military may have provided an unanswerable challenge to the Soviets and reassurance to America's allies. Dramatic improvements in American air power, especially those associated with tactical aviation and stealth technology, played a central role in that military revival.[7]

With communism dead in Europe and the Soviet Union, the American electorate and the nation's political and media elites lost interest in foreign and defense issues. Congress pressed for major reductions in U.S. defense spending. In 1990, Capitol Hill ordered 13 percent annual cuts over each of the next five years. The White House, resting its case for smaller reductions on the unsettled international environment outside Europe, proposed much smaller spending cutbacks. Led by the chairman, army general Colin Powell, the JCS proposed cutting spending and force structure by as much as one-third.[8]

A crisis in Central America underscored the argument that mobile, combat-ready armed forces were still useful instruments of American foreign policy, despite the ailing condition of the Russian bear. In Panama, Manuel Noriega established a dictatorship after his patron, Omar Torrijos, died in a plane crash in 1981. After ignoring an election in 1989 where the voters rejected his candidate, Noriega launched a campaign of abuse of Americans in Panama that culminated in the murder of a marine officer. Pushing his luck too far, the dictator thumbed his nose at the Yankees and declared war on the United States. In retaliation, an outraged President Bush "ordered the execution of Operation Just Cause, the largest military posse in recent memory, which was organized to serve a Florida indictment against Noriega for drug dealing."[9]

The biggest U.S. combat engagement since the Vietnam War, Just Cause was a joint undertaking that involved ground, naval, air, and special operations forces. Although the primary air force role was to employ a large fleet of transports to deliver ground troops and supplies to the combat zone, it also provided covering fire with fighter aircraft. Air force reservists flew AC-130 gunships and Air National Guard units, on scheduled volunteer rotations to Panama, operated A-7s against Noriega's forces. In a controversial aspect of the operation, two supersecret air force F-117 stealth fighters made their combat debut against an enemy that had no appreciable air defenses. Critics of the stealth fighter program used that episode to publicize their allegation that the F-117 was an expensive and unnecessary white elephant.

Operating from bases in the Canal Zone and the United States, a joint force of some twenty-six thousand U.S. troops subdued the Panamanian military in an eight-day war in December, 1989. They then arrested the fugitive Noriega after he surrendered to them from his sanctuary at the official residence of the Papal Nuncio. The deposed Panamanian strongman was flown to Florida, where he was tried, convicted, and imprisoned for his drug offenses. Although Just Cause was considered a successful military operation, innocent Panamanians paid a high cost in death and property destruction for the American triumph. Estimates of civilian deaths ranged from two hundred to three hundred, and as many as three hundred Panamanian soldiers and members of paramilitary organizations may have lost their lives.[10]

The invasion of Panama was launched against a convenient enemy. It was easy and accurate to portray Noriega as a drug-dealing thug who ruled through fear and intimidation. The operation was undertaken in "uniquely favorable conditions: in a country where U.S. military forces had been stationed for years and were able to train for their D-Day assignments under the noses of the soon-to-be defenders, in a country whose people strongly favored the overthrow of their leader, and against a weak military force."[11] As in all other combat operations, mistakes were made. Poor security "gave the Panama Defense Force warning of the impending attack, bad weather delayed the airborne assault, Noreiga escaped initial attempts to capture him, friendly fire caused 'blue on blue' casualties, and some Rangers and paratroopers and their equipment did not land exactly as intended. Overall though . . . Just Cause was professionally and efficiently executed."[12]

While some optimists claimed that Operation Just Cause laid to rest lingering public doubts about the post-Vietnam competence of the U.S. armed forces, a more formidable test of that proposition awaited them in Southwest Asia. On August 2, 1990, President Bush announced that the United States would shift the focus of its military planning from a global war with the Soviet Union to regional conflicts with lesser powers. That same day, Iraqi dictator Saddam Hussein sent his armed forces across the border to seize and annex Kuwait, his nation's tiny, oil-rich neighbor. In less than a week, the Iraqis crushed all conventional military resistance. That aggression threatened the access of the United States and its allies to the vital oil resources of the Persian Gulf region. On August 6, Saudi Arabia's King Fahd agreed to accept American military aid following a meeting in Riyadh with a delegation of senior U.S. officials led by Defense Secretary Richard B. Cheney. Protected by a modern air defense and communications systems that included Saudi F-15s and AWACS, U.S. and coalition military units began pouring into the kingdom through an extensive infrastructure of modern airfields and ports.[13]

American civilian and military officials had long viewed the Persian Gulf region as a strategic backwater. However, the growing dependence of the United States and its allies in Western Europe and Japan on imports of Persian Gulf oil following World War II had gradually changed that situation. The U.S. military establishment, confronted with the global Cold War challenge of the Soviet Union, as well as hot wars in Korea and Indochina, had been reluctant to devote significant resources to Southwest Asia until the 1980s. Instead, it had preferred to rely on the British to maintain security in the Gulf, a role the latter had played since the early nineteenth century. In January, 1968, the British announced that they would be withdrawing all their forces from east of the Suez Canal by 1971. To compensate for the British withdrawal and the growing Soviet naval presence in the region, the American and British governments announced an agreement in 1972 to expand the U.S. military facilities on the tiny island of Diego Garcia in the Indian Ocean to include a runway extension, anchorage improvements, and construction of fuel storage tanks. In 1974, Defense Secretary James Schlessinger and Admiral Zumwalt agreed to keep an aircraft carrier battle group permanently in the Indian Ocean.

Air Force F-117As prepare to depart Langley AFB, Virginia, in 1990 to participate in Operation Desert Shield. Along with cruise missiles, these "stealth" fighters were employed to attack critical, heavily defended targets in Iraq during Operation Desert Storm in 1991. (U.S. Air Force photo.)

The only permanent U.S. military presence in the Persian Gulf region after World War II had been a small flotilla of warships based at Bahrain beginning in 1949. Instead of military force and formal alliances, the United States had relied on trade and diplomacy to advance its interests in that troubled area. The Army Air Forces opened a base at Dhahran in 1946 to advance American diplomatic and commercial interests in Saudi Arabia. Before it was closed in 1962 due to growing political opposition in the region, the base had served as a stopover point for U.S. military airlift aircraft transiting the Persian Gulf area, and as the forward location for nuclear-armed bombers targeted against the Soviet Union. Moreover, Dhahran had also served as the headquarters of the U.S. military mission that administered security assistance programs for the Saudis. Aid in the form of weapons and equipment, training, and construction was arguably the most important postwar tool of American diplomacy in the desert kingdom. Until the 1970s, those security assistance programs were very small and generally ineffective in building a Saudi military force capable of defending the kingdom against a serious regional military challenge.

That situation changed dramatically with the British withdrawal and the explosion of oil revenues in the early 1970s. America, sensitive to the political and military limits of its power as a result of the Vietnam War, adopted a "twin pillars" strategy of supporting Iran and Saudi Arabia as its military surrogates in the Gulf. Intent on building their own defense capability against regional rivals and internal unrest, the Saudis had begun spending large amounts of money on U.S. arms. When Washington failed to provide the desired weapons, they turned to Western European suppliers. At the urging of the American government, the Saudis focused on developing a modern air force as the cornerstone of their defense system beginning in 1974. Air power was attractive to the Saudis for several reasons. The kingdom's large and desolate landmass, coupled with its small population, precluded the development of an army capable of protecting it from bigger and often hostile neighbors. Furthermore, the long track record of armies overthrowing civilian regimes in the Middle East troubled the Saudi royal family. A modern air force did not pose such risks and offered a relatively inexpensive method of defending the kingdom, especially if backed by private promises of U.S. military intervention in the event of aggression by regional rivals.

With the overthrow of the Shah's regime in Iran and the Soviet invasion of Afghanistan, both in 1979, America's "twin pillars" strategy collapsed. American defense planners began preparing to project massive U.S. power directly into that region to protect Western access to its vital oil supplies, block the expansion of Soviet influence, and defend conservative Arab states against the spread of radical Islamic fundamentalism. President Carter responded by declaring the "Carter Doctrine" in his January, 1980, State of the Union address. Basically, it meant that the United States would view any attempt by an outside power to gain control of the Persian Gulf region as an assault on its vital interests. Carter also inaugurated a significant military rearmament program that was accelerated and expanded by his successor, Ronald Reagan.

Following the Iraqi seizure of Kuwait in August, 1990, U.S. air, naval, and ground units moved rapidly into the Arabian Peninsula and surrounding waters. They quickly began operations with a coalition of forces from NATO and Arab nations. The U.S. forces were able to draw upon supplies from prepositioned logistics ships berthed at Diego Garcia. American aviation units occupied air bases in Saudi Arabia that had been built to NATO specifications. Most of those facilities were far larger than any military installations the Saudis would have ever needed, and U.S. air units found large stocks of spare parts, fuel, lubricants, and munitions that were compatible with their needs. As a result of the U.S. foreign military sales program, their Saudi counterparts flew American-made aircraft, including F-15 fighters and the E-3 AWACS. Many of the Saudi pilots had been trained in the United States. Because of nearly continuous airborne radar surveillance of the northern Persian Gulf from 1981–88 by air force AWACS aircraft based in Riyadh during the Iran-Iraq War, and AWACS support of navy convoys protecting reflagged Kuwaiti supertankers from 1987–

90, there was an established communications, early warning, and air defense data network linking the Saudis, other friendly states in the region, and U.S. Navy ships in the Persian Gulf.

For several decades, the army's Corps of Engineers and the air force had been collaborating closely with the Saudis and other conservative Arab regimes in the Persian Gulf to manage the growing U.S. foreign military sales and facilities construction programs in the region. By improving interoperability, it eased the development of an integrated air campaign plan designed to protect the rest of the region from further Iraqi aggression and then to expel them from Kuwait. Although often overlooked during the buildup of U.S. and coalition forces during the fall of 1990, efforts begun in the 1970s to build an infrastructure of logistics, basing, and training on the Arabian Peninsula played a key role in preparing for the successful American military intervention in the Persian Gulf in 1990–91. Without them, the "over-the-horizon" rapid air reinforcement strategy the U.S. Central Command (CENTCOM) developed for the region after its creation in 1983 could have been much riskier and far slower to unfold.[14]

The 1990 Persian Gulf crisis tested American air power, logistics, and joint command arrangements. Although Iraq's air force, which consisted of more than six hundred combat planes provided by the Soviet Union and France, was the world's sixth largest, the quality of its pilots was suspect. Iraq's extensive air defense network was more formidable, at least on paper. Following the pattern established by Iraq's Soviet patrons, it consisted of a closely linked, redundant, and centrally controlled network of radar, AAA, and SAMs in addition to fighter aircraft. Those ground-based air defenses were seven times as dense as Hanoi's before the Linebacker II operation. Iraq also had a million-man army. With a population only 33 percent the size of Iran's, it had fought the latter to a stand-still during the bloody 1980–88 war. Iraq also possessed the largest supply of chemical weapons in the Third World, as well as the means to deliver them: modified Soviet-built "Scud" ballistic missiles. Intelligence estimates placed as many as 450,000 Iraqi troops equipped with four thousand tanks and three thousand artillery pieces in the Kuwaiti theater of operations (KTO)—which consisted of Kuwait and southern Iraq—alone. However, many of those men were poorly trained reservists and draftees. Saddam Huessin's best troops, his Republican Guard divisions, were held in reserve in the northern KTO. Finally, because it was a virtually landlocked nation, Iraq had a small navy.[15]

But those weaknesses were not readily apparent as the Bush administration worked feverishly to cobble together a loose military coalition of twenty-four nations to oppose the Iraqis while trying to convince Congress and the American people that Kuwait was worth going to war for if Saddam could not be persuaded to withdraw his forces. Through skillful diplomacy, Iraq was diplomatically isolated. Unlike North Korea and North Vietnam earlier in the twentieth century, there were no powerful allies that the Iraqis could turn to for support. Although there was no real danger of nuclear war between the United States and the collapsing Soviet Union, the Americans had to prevent the Iraqis from using their own chemical and biological weapons of mass destruction. To preserve Arab support for the coalition, it was essential for the United States to keep Israel from responding to Iraqi attacks on the Jewish state with nuclear or conventional weapons. Diplomacy also played an important role in persuading Turkey to allow the air force to base combat aircraft there for a second front in the event the Kuwait crisis could not be ended peacefully.[16]

The United Nations approved economic sanctions enforced by a coalition naval blockade against Iraq to pressure it into leaving Kuwait. But that operation had little apparent effect on Saddam or his nation's military capabilities, aside from preventing them from stockpiling additional stocks of weapons and ammunition. The basic U.S. military response to the crisis, Operation Desert Shield, was to assemble an overwhelming force in the Persian Gulf region to protect Saudi Arabia from an Iraqi invasion and convince Saddam to withdraw his army from Kuwait. Air power played a critical role in the rapid American response. On the heels of the Iraqi invasion, Defense Secretary Cheney had ordered two aircraft carrier battle groups to proceed to the region. F-15C fighters, supported by E-3B AWACS, flew from the United States and arrived in Saudi Arabia at almost the same time as aircraft from the carriers *Independence* and *Eisenhower*. An airlifted brigade from the 82d Airborne Division followed them. On August 16, marines began arriving in Saudi Arabia by air. Their heavy weapons, vehicles, tanks, artillery, and much of their supplies arrived later by sea. While airlift put most of the U.S. troops on the ground during the Persian Gulf crisis, approximately 95 percent of their weapons, vehicles, ammunition, supplies, and fuel moved to the region by sea.

By September, coalition air strength consisted of more than twelve hundred mostly land-based aircraft. Although ground troops and their equipment poured rapidly into the region, it was eight weeks before CENTCOM concluded that it had the forces in place to deter or defeat an Iraqi invasion of Saudi Arabia. In the meantime, MAC and the commercial airlines mounted a huge strategic airlift operation. The Civil Reserve Air Fleet, activated for the first time ever, provided passenger airliners and cargo aircraft. Tanker aircraft also moved passengers and cargo to the Persian Gulf as they deployed to the region. Air refueling served as a "force multiplier" that accelerated the pace of the coalition's military buildup. Before the crisis ended in 1991, aircraft moved almost half a million troops and six hundred thousand tons of supplies to the Gulf. It was the largest military airlift in history.

Less publicized but equally valuable, intratheater airlift delivered supplies, equipment, spare parts, fuel, munitions, and personnel throughout the Arabian Peninsula after they arrived in theater. The workhorses of this effort were 149 air force, Air National Guard, and Air Force Reserve C-130s, as well as smaller numbers of coalition aircraft. As in Vietnam, the C-130s were extremely versatile. Air refueling also played a critical role in the success of Operations Desert Shield and Desert Storm. It facilitated the rapid movement of large air forces to the region and enabled commanders to employ them in extremely complex combat operations. Air refueling extended the range of attack aircraft and allowed coalition air forces to conduct massive aerial strikes on Iraqi targets while maintaining continuous airborne control and surveillance of battle areas.[17]

While the coalition military buildup continued during the fall of 1990, senior American officers were reluctant to plan a ground offensive to eject the Iraqis from Kuwait. Their forces were too small and lightly armed to provide the margin needed for a quick victory with few friendly casualties. Such an operation was the only post–Vietnam War standard for a regional conflict outside the NATO–Warsaw Pact scenario that they believed the American people would support. Following the November congressional elections, the president announced that U.S. forces deployed to the Gulf would be doubled to more than five hundred thousand in order to provide an offensive option. That policy decision forced a massive increase in mobilized guardsmen and reservists from the forty thousand called up in August, 1990, to some 227,800—plus more than ten thousand volunteers—by January, 1991. The call-up highlighted the strengths of the Total Force as it had been implemented by the air force. The performance of Air Force Reserve and Air National Guard units was indistinguishable from that of their active duty counterparts. The two reserve components provided fighter, tanker, airlift, special operations, and support units to the operation. Those units mobilized quickly, deployed rapidly, and merged effectively into active operations.

Aviation units from the Naval Reserve and Marine Corps Reserve also played an important role during the Persian Gulf crisis. Naval Reserve air units flew helicopters, P-3s, C-9Bs, and DC-9s that were significant to underway replenishment, maritime patrol, and cargo missions. Marine Corps Reserve units flew attack and cargo helicopters as well as aerial refueling aircraft during Operations Desert Shield and Desert Storm.

Many senior members of the guard and reserve community were convinced that the Persian Gulf call-up would also demonstrate that a major policy error of the Vietnam War had been corrected. They believed that if President Johnson had authorized a massive mobilization of guard and reserve forces during that conflict, broad public support for the conflict in Southeast Asia would have

An Arizona Air National Guard KC-135 tanker refuels an air force F-16 Fighting Falcon while another F-16 waits its turn for gas during Operation Desert Storm in 1991. The immense air-refueling capability of America's armed forces played a critical role during the Persian Gulf crisis. (U.S. Air Force photo by S.Sgt. Lee F. Corkran.)

been maintained. They argued that such call-ups in future wars would rally American public opinion behind U.S. military involvement. However, the U.S. military intervention in the Persian Gulf in 1990 was a very contentious issue that split the nation along politically partisan lines. That situation was exacerbated by the opinion held by some senior active duty officers, as well as a number of retired officers and civilian officials from previous administrations, that Saddam's troops would eventually be forced out of Kuwait by the economic embargo that was already in effect. Although the public rallied behind President Bush in August when he announced the American military intervention, popular support for his Persian Gulf policies soon fell sharply. The mobilization of large numbers of guardsmen and reservists had no impact on that precipitous drop in public support. Opinion polls showed that the American people's support for Bush's Persian Gulf policy was not restored until U.S. forces began combat operations.[18]

In planning for a possible war against Iraq, U.S. political and military leaders sought to erase the stigma of the defeat in Vietnam. President Bush was determined to apply a massive dose of military force to achieve primary political goals that were clear and realistic: drive Iraqi forces out of Kuwait, restore the sheikdom's legitimate government, protect the lives of American citizens in the region, and promote the security of the Persian Gulf. Boiled down, however, the administration's response to the Iraqi seizure of Kuwait was about access to the region's vast oil resources. That was the most critical reason for the U.S. military response. The economic health of the Western World and Japan depended on the availability of oil. However, the president's public position was muddled by ambiguous statements, which suggested that another important U.S. goal was to remove the Iraqi dictator, who he compared to Adolf Hitler, from power. Although military planners had to work within the framework of the primary stated goals, any overall assignment of the war's outcome would be complicated by Bush's evident desire to eliminate Saddam's regime without fracturing the coalition, especially its Arab members.

As in Vietnam, air power played a central role in U.S. strategy in the Gulf. However, unlike the former conflict, civilian and military officials had little say in planning the air campaign and in picking targets. Those responsibilities were exercised by the air force's Lt. Gen. Charles A. Horner, the joint force air component commander (JFACC), for Gen. H. Norman Schwarzkopf, the army officer who served as the overall commander of U.S. and coalition forces. Because of the reforms instituted by the Goldwater-Nichols Act of 1986, "jointness" had become a much stronger force within the American military establishment. As CENTCOM's commander in chief, Schwarzkopf exercised authority to plan and conduct joint operations in the Gulf that would have been unthinkable for Gen. William Westmoreland in Southeast Asia. There were significant frictions in those relationships. Major General Royal N. Moore Jr., commander of the 3d Marine Air Wing (Reinforced) fought Horner's control of his unit all the way to the Pentagon and lost. Powell and Schwarzkopf stood behind the JFACC's authority. Most importantly, Lt. Gen. Walter Boomer, the overall marine component commander in the Persian Gulf, supported Horner's position as air boss.

To its regret, the navy had resisted building adequate long-term command relationships with CENTCOM after the Goldwater-Nichols legislation was passed. Consequently, when the crunch came in August, 1990, the navy was not well positioned to shape critical force deployment and employment decisions. Several other problems complicated the navy's contributions to the air campaign. The CNO, Adm. Frank B. Kelso II, and Vice Adm. Henry M. Mauz, the Seventh Fleet commander, who was nominated by the former to head Schwarzkopf's naval forces, both saw the assignment as more of a temporary fleet command rather than a critical position as the leader of CENTCOM's naval component. Mauz compounded the problem by sending a representative to Riyadh who lacked the rank and carrier experience needed to have any real impact on Horner and Schwarzkopf. Kelso then authorized Vice Adm. Stanley R. Arthur to replace

Mauz in December, 1990, on the eve of hostilities. Arthur was an able commander and a vigorous champion of naval aviation, but he needed time to familiarize himself with the evolving situation in the Persian Gulf and establish relationships with key figures in the joint command structure. The result was that air force officers who had taken CENTCOM far more seriously filled the resulting leadership and planning voids. Aviation became the fulcrum of the resulting controversy. Unlike his predecessors in World War II, Korea, and Vietnam, Horner had control of virtually all coalition air assets and could use them as he thought necessary because of his authority as the JFACC. Although joint in name, his staff was dominated by air force officers.[19]

Some naval aviators advocated a geographic division of effort that reminded General Horner of the route package system employed in Vietnam. Navy flyers were unhappy with the concept of an overall air commander, especially since it appeared to favor the air force in the allocation of missions. The potential contributions of naval aviation were also limited by the fact that its carriers lacked the computer systems needed to most quickly receive the air tasking orders (ATOs) that Horner's staff employed to disseminate the voluminous daily assignments for the massive joint air campaign. Instead, paper versions of those huge documents had to be flown from Riyadh to the carriers each day. Lastly, like many of the air force's fighter-bomber units, few of the navy attack squadrons had a sufficient supply of precision-guided munitions.[20]

Those circumstances produced mixed results for naval aviation during the war. Carriers in the Red Sea were well established in the theater before the war began. They relied on air force tankers and AWACS aircraft and worked closely with their air force counterparts before the war to fit naval operations into the joint air campaign. Those factors minimized friction between Battle Force Yankee and the air force when Operation Desert Storm was launched.[21] However, carriers operating in the Persian Gulf were less well prepared to participate in the joint air campaign. The commander of Battle Force Zulu carried out unilateral training exercises in the northern Arabian Sea during much of Operation Desert Shield and had less face-to-face contact with military leaders and planners in Riyadh than did his Red Sea counterpart. Naval leaders, rightly concerned about threats to carriers in the Persian Gulf's narrow waters, were reluctant to deploy there before the war. They were especially worried about the threats posed by missile-armed Iraqi aircraft, shore-based Silkworm missiles, and fast attack vessels, as well as Iran's potential for causing harm. Battle Force Zulu's limited training for joint service air operations complicated its participation in the air war.[22]

Naval aviation adapted to the centralized ATO process out of necessity. It was the only mechanism available that could handle twenty-five hundred sor-

Portions of three navy carrier battle groups involved in Operation Desert Storm come together in the Red Sea for a "photo opportunity" on February 9, 1991. Pictured abreast *from left to right* are the USS *Thomas S. Gates,* USS *Saratoga,* USS *San Jacinto,* USS *John F. Kennedy,* USS *Mississippi,* USS *America,* USS *William V. Pratt,* USS *Normandy,* USS *Philippine Sea,* and USS *Preble.* (U.S. Navy photo by PH3 Chester O. Falkenhainer.)

ties daily in a coordinated air campaign against Iraq. Horner, who was not an air power ideologue, accommodated the needs of the naval services. He allowed Arthur to direct overwater operations, especially the assault on the small Iraqi navy, and provide for the fleet's air defenses. Naval aviation also protected the coalition's entire right flank, including the vulnerable allied nations of the Gulf Cooperation Council. Unarmed tankers and merchantmen continued to operate in the Persian Gulf. Virtually all of the coalition's war materiel poured into the region through three ports on the south side of that body of water.

Horner also permitted the marine's air commander, General Moore, to manage most of the 3d MAW's missions in Kuwait, where the leathernecks would attack if President Bush authorized an invasion. Nevertheless, controversy dogged the relations between the air force and navy staffs managing the air campaign. While the carriers in the Red Sea worked reasonably well with Riyadh, relations between those in the Persian Gulf and Horner's headquarters remained strained.

Edward J. Marolda and Robert J. Schneller Jr. stressed that "The causes were many: inadequate prewar Battle Force Zulu preparation for joint air war, different service doctrines, parochialism on both sides, poor communications, a shortage of Navy officers in Riyadh with sufficient authority, and the small number of Navy personnel on the JFACC staff."[23] Battle Force Zulu depended on air force tankers to conduct strike missions into Iraq. It was especially concerned that its carriers did not receive their fair share of tanker support in the early stages of the air campaign. However, that problem was worked out as Desert Storm progressed and the carriers moved closer to the KTO, where they were able to rely more heavily on navy refueling aircraft.[24]

Nevertheless, the navy and Marine Corps made an enormous contribution to the air campaign. Naval and marine aircraft flying from land bases and six carriers—the USS *Midway*, USS *Theodore Roosevelt*, USS *America*, USS *John F. Kennedy*, USS *Ranger*, and USS *Saratoga*—contributed approximately 28 percent of coalition combat air assets in theater and flew roughly 28 percent of their combat sorties. Carrier aircraft destroyed Iraq's small navy and helped decimate its army in the KTO. Cruise missiles fired from battleships, cruisers, destroyers, and submarines were a critical element of the strikes on Baghdad. Aegis cruisers managed the Persian Gulf airspace so well that there was not a single engagement between coalition forces.[25]

While American commanders and their coalition partners prepared massive air and ground assaults on the Iraqis if the latter refused to leave Kuwait promptly and unconditionally, the Bush administration continued its struggle to maintain domestic political and international support for its Persian Gulf policies. Congressional, media, and public opinion vacillated as the crisis stretched on unresolved through the end of 1990. The UN Security Council, prodded by American diplomacy, authorized the use of force if Saddam did not withdraw his troops from Kuwait by January 15, 1991. Congress did not actually vote to support a war until January 12, on the eve of that UN deadline. The Russians were vague and waited until January to signal that they would not intervene on behalf of their Iraqi client.[26]

Air power provided the cutting edge of the military juggernaut that had been assembled in the Persian Gulf region and Turkey. Neither side fully understood the capabilities of the massive air armada of twenty-six hundred coalition aircraft, including nineteen hundred U.S. planes, poised to attack Iraq. Trained rigorously since the Vietnam War, American "aircraft and munitions themselves had been electronically mated with their targets with new precision. Based on terminal guidance systems that gave precise thermal or visual aim points, strike aircraft could find their targets under the direction of airborne air control (AWACS) and airborne ground target acquisition (JSTARS) systems, and they could be assisted by a fleet of aerial refuelers and electronic warfare aircraft."[27] The navy's ship-launched Tomahawk cruise missile, capable of precision attacks at night and in bad weather conditions through the use of an internal terrain-following navigation system, was prepared to make its combat debut. The air force's F-117 radar-evading stealth fighter was also primed to make a significant contribution in its first real war.[28]

The war against Iraq began on January 17, 1991, after President Bush's January 15 deadline for the Iraqis to withdraw from Kuwait passed uneventfully. Desert Storm opened with a strategic air campaign. The initial round was a massive coordinated nighttime assault against the enemy's air defense system, much of it based on an outstanding analysis of that system by the Naval Intelligence Command's Strike Projection Evaluation Research (SPEAR) group. The attack was led by a trio of air force MH-53J Pave Low special operations helicopters equipped with advanced navigational systems. They guided nine army AH-64 Apache gunships into Iraq, where the latter destroyed several enemy early warning radar sites with their missiles. F-15Es then dashed through the gap in radar coverage to attack fixed Scud missile launch sites while F-117As, accompanied by EF-111A jamming aircraft for the only time in the war, exploited that same hole to attack the heart of Iraq's air defense command and control system. Navy and marine E-6B Prowlers provided critical ECM support for allied and coalition strike packages throughout the war.

Tomahawk cruise missiles, fired from surface ships and submarines, struck additional targets, including the electrical power plants upon which the entire Iraqi military relied. Within minutes, Baghdad lost all commercial electric power. General Horner also employed navy air-launched decoys and USAF-operated navy drones to fool the Iraqis into wasting SAMs on phantom aircraft. Without radar, the defenders fired their SAMs and antiaircraft artillery blindly. Within hours, waves of coalition aircraft and cruise missiles were able to destroy Iraq's air defense system. Saddam chose to hide his air force in shelters, but when coalition pilots began destroying those sites, he evacuated the remaining planes to Iran and they sat out the rest of the conflict. The opening round of the air campaign "was a brilliant piece of operational planning that wrecked Iraq's complex air defenses over the course of the opening night, all at the cost of a single coalition aircraft. Stealth, precision weaponry, and the extraordinary capabilities of coalition aircrews destroyed Iraq's capacity to defend herself in the first hours of the war."[29]

The problems facing Iraqi defenders were complicated by the fact that, in addition to the enormous concentration of enemy forces in the Persian Gulf region, they also had to deal with a formidable concentration of air power based in Turkey. Joint Task Force (JTF) Proven Force usually concentrated on attacking targets north of the 35th Parallel. Although JTF Proven Force's aircraft were not included in the daily ATO, Horner exercised tactical control of them and supplied their targets. Consisting of about 120 aircraft, they generated a considerably smaller number of sorties than the coalition aircraft in the south, but nevertheless made a significant contribution to the air campaign against Iraq.[30]

The ambitious goals of the strategic air campaign's original planners in the Pentagon had been to force the Iraqis out of Kuwait without a ground offensive and, even better, to topple Saddam's regime in Baghdad. Those objectives had been significantly modified and continued to evolve throughout the Persian Gulf crisis because of the needs and perceptions of the various senior military leaders, including Generals Horner, Schwarzkopf, and Powell. The original air plan called for an intense, round-the-clock air assault against Iraq's "strategic centers of gravity," including its leadership, strategic air defenses, weapons of mass destruction, and electrical system. Although the original plan sought to undermine enemy morale, it did not advocate directly attacking the Iraqi civilian population. The planners estimated that the strategic air campaign might last five or six days. Subsequent air plans completed by Horner's staff in Riyadh added additional tasks, including defending Saudi Arabia against an Iraqi armored thrust, wrecking enemy forces in the KTO in preparation for a ground war, and supporting the latter. The original estimates of how long the various phases of the air campaign would last were provided to army officers so they could see where Horner expected the relative emphasis would be at any given point. He realized that each of the air campaign's various tasks would overlap and probably continue throughout the war. The ambiguity of President Bush's political goals, as well as the various needs of the military commanders in the combat theater, led to a split air campaign in which the strategic assault against Baghdad was waged almost entirely separately from the tactical onslaught against the enemy's army hunkered down in Kuwait and southern Iraq.[31]

The strategic air campaign quickly destroyed Iraq's air defenses and electrical system. Since damage to the latter was difficult to assess, many facilities were attacked several times. Attacks on Saddam's chemical, biological, and nuclear weapons programs, set them back. However, since many facilities associated with them had been well hidden before the war began, they were not eliminated as important factors in the region's postwar military balance. Attacks on Iraqi mobile Scud launchers were controversial during and after the war. Air force officers maintained that those strikes diverted too many aircraft from far more valuable targets. However, those criticisms were largely irrelevant. The great Scud hunt "suppressed the Iraqis ability to launch their grossly inaccurate missiles at Israeli and Saudi cities. . . . [I]t was the perception that coalition air forces were making a major effort against the Scuds that prevented Israeli air strikes against the [Iraqis] . . . with potentially dangerous consequences to the coalition's stability."[32]

Air force planners concluded prior to the start of Desert Storm that Iraq's civilian population was vulnerable to air attacks. However, air strikes designed to intimidate Iraqi civilians proved to be as futile as earlier bombing campaigns against noncombatants during World War II, the Korean War, and in Vietnam. Supported by his Republican Guard units and secret police, Saddam retained his iron grip on political power in Iraq. Horner's planners limited targeting of the civilian population's will to psychological operations and the indirect effects of other attacks, such as those directed at the Iraqi power grid. Their effort to spare civilian lives suffered from two important lapses: the Royal Air Force's attack on a bridge at Nasiriyah, and an F-117's bombing of the Al-Firdos bunker. While civilian deaths in both strikes were unintentional, they caused the Bush administration to limit further strikes on Baghdad. Horner and other officers realized that there were few useful targets left there anyway. Ironically, the civilians killed in the Al-Firdos bunker were there because of their political connections to Saddam's regime. But the global public uproar caused by live television coverage of the recovery of their bodies ended all efforts to attack Saddam's control of the Iraqi population.[33]

The second major element of the air campaign focused on the Iraqi army in the KTO. At the outset, General Schwarzkopf set high numerical goals for the coalition's air forces. They agreed to destroy at least 50 percent of the enemy's tanks and artillery pieces before the coalition launched a ground offensive. Although those numerical goals were based on U.S. Army doctrine that a unit that lost 50 percent of anything was combat ineffective, they led to furious arguments between the airmen and soldiers over who nominated targets, how many strikes were to be flown against enemy forces in the KTO versus the strategic air campaign in Iraq, and the effect of the strikes made on the enemy's forces in the field. Those quarrels lasted until the ground campaign was launched. They resumed in the Pentagon and on Capitol Hill with equally great intensity when the postwar budget fights between the armed forces began.

While the centralized, preplanned ATO process worked well during the strategic air campaign against Iraq, it proved to be inadequate when the emphasis shifted to the more mobile targets in the KTO. Driven by the general aim of reducing the combat ability of Iraqi forces, especially Republican Guard units, in the field, and the inadequate flexibility of the ATO process, a new system was developed that divided the operational theater into a series of kill boxes and also included strip alert aircraft, as well as uncommitted ATO sorties. Attacking aircraft were scheduled into the kill-box areas in accordance with priorities and schedules set by Horner's planners in Riyadh. They kept score based upon the number of sorties and tons of bombs dropped on each box. There was little evidence during the early part of the air campaign that those attacks were inflicting much serious damage. Most coalition aircraft in the KTO were not equipped with PGMs, and they flew above the range of Iraqi AAA and handheld missile fire to minimize their own losses.

Initially, many high-altitude B-52 strikes with conventional "dumb" bombs missed their targets because the bombers were using different grid coordinates than the theater planners. In early February, as it became increasingly clear that little damage was being done to Iraqi equipment in Kuwait, Schwarzkopf ordered Horner to use his PGM-equipped F-111s against the enemy army. Those attacks dramatically altered the situation. Air force aircrews loved the "tank-plinking" campaign. However, while the destruction of Iraqi equipment mounted, so did "furious debate between the air planners and the ground commanders as to exactly how much equipment the air attacks were destroying and whether the air campaign was reaching the agreed upon levels of destruction."[34]

Those arguments, based upon different doctrinal conceptions of warfare and parochial service interests, were largely irrelevant. As photographs of hordes of Iraqi soldiers surrendering en masse, some of them to helicopters, later suggested, the enormous and unceasing air campaign destroyed the morale of enemy troops who had to use that equipment. Ironically, as revealed by POW interrogations, the weapon that Iraqi soldiers feared most was the least accurate one employed against them, the B-52. Williamson Murray concluded that, in the final analysis, "it was the psychological impact of air attacks that mattered. . . . As in previous wars it was the imponderables, the unmeasurables that mattered, not the mathematically calculable."[35]

Coalition aircraft also mounted a major interdiction campaign designed to isolate the KTO and strangle the Iraqi army deployed there. The campaign destroyed forty-one major bridges and thirty-one pontoon structures. The enemy had hastily assembled the latter across the Tigris and Euphrates Rivers after the bombing began. Although Saddam's forces "had already stockpiled much equipment and supplies in Kuwait, the combination of destroyed bridges and the unwillingness of truck drivers to drive under the constant observation of Coalition aircraft resulted in the Iraqis losing the capability for offensive operations. As food and other supplies became scarce, so did many defenders, who fled in search of safer areas. By mid-February, intelligence agencies estimated that the Iraqi forces in Kuwait could barely subsist in place, let alone fight."[36]

While his airmen were pounding the enemy around the clock with a massive and multifaceted assault, Schwarzkopf prepared a ground campaign designed to liberate Kuwait and destroy Iraqi forces deployed in southern Iraq. Unlike the situation in Vietnam, American commanders did not underestimate the enemy. Schwarzkopf's ground campaign plan featured a fast flanking move by armored forces into the area between the Iraqi city of Basra and Kuwait, from the desert and oilfields to the west. His preparations were hidden from the enemy by coalition air forces that completely dominated the skies, preventing the Iraqis from conducting effective aerial or ground reconnaissance. To protect the attack's western flank, the U.S. XVIII Airborne Corps would launch an airmobile and mechanized drive all the way to the Euphrates.

To tie down Iraqi forces deployed in the KTO so that VII Corps could destroy the elite Republican Guard divisions deployed in southern Iraq unmolested, simultaneous offensives were planned directly into Kuwait by an Arab corps and the I Marine Expeditionary Force, which consisted of two divisions. In addition, a marine amphibious brigade remained afloat in the Persian Gulf to distract the Iraqis. A second marine amphibious brigade was brought ashore during Desert Storm to reinforce units in the KTO. The fleet provided additional major distractions to the Iraqis with battleship bombardments, air attacks on armed coastal platforms and coastal defensive positions, and the seizure of islands by marines and navy Sea, Air, Land (SEAL) teams. Naval aircraft launched from carriers headed straight for Kuwait's beaches, then turned away at the last minute to stimulate Iraqi reactions. The marines wanted to mount an amphibious assault in Kuwait, but Schwarzkopf had ruled that out early on as unnecessary. He subsequently hardened his opposition to an amphibious assault because he did not want to destroy Kuwait's coastal cities and feared the casualties that an amphibious operation might produce. Besides, he was convinced his ground forces in the KTO were already strong enough to complete the job.[37]

Space-based reconnaissance assets supported the air and ground campaigns. They included six meteorological, three Defense Support Program (DSP), and two commercial satellites. The DSP satellites successfully reported Scud missile launches. However, most of the satellites first had to be reconfigured from their Cold War emphasis on supporting a strategic nuclear exchange between the United States and the Soviet Union. That transition was time-consuming and remained incomplete when the war ended. Weather conditions and oil fires in Kuwait limited the ability of the satellites to obtain targeting and bomb damage assessment data for the coalition forces. Strategic aircraft reconnaissance systems, including the U-2/TR-1 and RC-135 Rivet Joint were of limited value because they were too vulnerable for operations in enemy airspace. Consequently, the coalition turned to tactical reconnaissance aircraft, but those assets proved to be clearly inadequate. Only a handful of air force and Air National Guard RF-4Cs were assigned to the reconnaissance effort. They were augmented by a variety of fighter aircraft, including navy F-14s equipped with photoreconnaissance pods.

To help fill the gap, the Joint Surveillance Target Attack Radar System (JSTARS) E-8 surveillance aircraft and Pioneer unmanned aerial vehicles (UAVs) were used to obtain battlefield surveillance data for commanders. The former were Boeing 707s modified with synthetic aperture radar beneath their fuselages and were capable of tracking vehicles moving on the earth's surface. Flying in Saudi Arabia, they could track moving vehicles and many stationary objects throughout Kuwait and in major portions of southern Iraq. At first, the air force rejected Horner's request to deploy two aircraft to the theater because they were still experimental prototypes taking part in a joint program with the army. However, the service relented under congressional pressure and the aircraft were deployed in time to begin flying missions on January 14, 1991. They provided valuable all-weather ground coverage of the battle area. One of the two aircraft flew each night of the war, passing targeting information to AWACS and airborne command and control aircraft.

Pioneer UAVs flew almost three hundred missions during the war, most of them for the marines. They carried infrared and television equipment, giving them day and night real-time capabilities. Battleships relied on UAVs to serve as their eyes during coastal bombardments and for collecting intelligence on enemy dispositions and fortifications ashore. However, UAVs lacked the range and technical capabilities to conduct large-scale reconnaissance operations.[38]

While the performance of space-based systems in providing intelligence on mobile systems and bomb damage assessment was somewhat disappointing, satellites were absolutely invaluable in their communications, weather, and navigational roles. Sixteen military and five commercial satellites carried approximately 90 percent of intertheater communications. In addition, they were utilized for a substantial but undetermined portion of the intratheater communications. Satellites also supplied enormously useful weather information to coalition airmen. Global Positioning System satellites provided highly accurate navigational data to aircrews, ships, and even ground units once adequate numbers of receiver terminals were provided to forces in the theater.

Nonetheless, David N. Spires emphasized that the Persian Gulf crisis "exposed the Achille's heel of the space program. . . . In effect, the U.S. space launch program continued to reflect a policy of launching [satellites] on schedule, not on demand. It simply could not respond to short notice requests."[39] A postwar analysis of the air war cautioned that "access to space-based sensors and location/navigation systems provided the Coalition with yet another advantage throughout Desert Shield and Desert Storm, a condition that may not necessarily be repeated in future conflicts."[40]

The final act of Desert Storm was played out on the earth, not in space. Although necessary to expel the Iraqis from Kuwait, the coalition's ground offensive turned out to be more of a drive-by shooting than the tough fight General Schwarzkopf had feared when he first arrived in Saudi Arabia. Begun at 4 A.M. on February 24, it was halted by the Bush administration a hundred hours later. A-10s, AV-8s, and attack helicopters had helped pave the way for the advancing ground forces, but heavy artillery, mobile rocket launchers, and tanks played even more important roles. Close air support of rapidly advancing coalition ground forces did not become a major factor because the enemy fled so rapidly and there was an abundance of ground-based firepower available to deal with those who could not escape.

In one of the most dramatic uses of army aviation during the entire war, three hundred helicopters moved troops and equipment of the 101st Airborne Division 110 miles into Iraq on the first day of the ground campaign. On the second day, elements of the division were ferried to the banks of the Euphrates by helicopters. While no more than 33 percent of Iraq's military forces survived the information age blitzkrieg, they were enough to keep Saddam in power, even though he lost Kuwait and its enormous oil revenues. Assured that his foreign enemies would not intervene, the Iraqi dictator launched bloody campaigns after the war to suppress uprisings by minority populations in the northern and southern regions of Iraq. Political leaders and some senior military officers within the coalition considered it unlikely that public opinion would have supported a wider war that included a march on Baghdad to remove him from power. Another consideration dampening any enthusiasm that coalition policy makers may have privately harbored for removing Saddam from power was their consensus that such action would have produced a fragmented and weakened Iraq that could not have played a serious role in offsetting Iranian power in the Persian Gulf region.

Desert Storm was the first war in American history in which ground forces supported aviation. Although ground forces were needed to finish off the Iraqis and occupy ground in the KTO, the air campaign was the dominant element in the coalition's incomplete victory. Although air power "did not fulfill all of its expectations, it ruined the organization of Iraqi strategic military power for the bombing of Iraq's air defense system and military infrastructure came close to meeting General Horner's objectives. . . . The combination of high pilot experience, sophisticated planning, electronic warfare, advanced aircraft technology, state-of-the-art avionics, and precision-guided munitions gave tactical air warfare a new dimension of effectiveness."[41]

The particular circumstances of the Persian Gulf crisis of 1990–91 influenced much of the war's military outcome. The Iraqis made several fundamental miscalculations. They were isolated from any significant outside support. Their former friend and patron, the Soviet Union, would not intervene to help them.

Apparently convinced that the Americans would never risk a large number of casualties by actually fighting for Kuwait, the Iraqis allowed them and their coalition allies to build up a huge military force in the region unmolested. Satellites, reconnaissance aircraft, and remotely piloted vehicles provided Schwarzkopf and Horner with an enormous amount of information, whereas Iraqi forces were denied access to such intelligence once the coalition had deployed significant air power to the Persian Gulf region and Turkey in the fall of 1990.

The war was largely fought in and above the desert, where the coalition's military advantages were magnified. Skeptics remained unconvinced that the victory over Iraq offered conclusive proof that air power had finally arrived as the dominant force in modern warfare. They pointed out that Saddam's forces were vastly overmatched and lacked formidable allies. The coalition's air superiority was never in doubt. Although President Bush contended that the Gulf War allowed America and its armed forces to put Vietnam behind them, that judgment appeared to be premature.[42]

Air power and the rest of the American military forces assembled in the region benefited from the stubbornness and miscalculations of the Iraqi dictator. Donald and Frederick Kagan concluded that Saddam, "as Thucydides said of the Spartans, was a convenient enemy. He was given countless opportunities to withdraw, with his Army, weapons, and country intact. . . . Had he pulled out of Kuwait [before Desert Storm] the United States would have withdrawn its forces, and in a while, his military power would have begun to impose its influence on the region again."[43]

It would have been difficult, if not impossible, for a geographically remote power like the United States to assemble another broad coalition for a war halfway around the world against Iraq. The Kagans also observed: "He was equally convenient in his conduct of the war. Thirty-eight days of devastating bombing changed neither his stubbornness or his military deployments. The bulk of his forces remained dug in facing Saudi Arabia while his enemies went around his right flank and through his debilitated and demoralized front line. In four days his army was smashed and routed, suffering heavy casualties."[44]

Opinion on the Gulf War's outcome was divided. Although understandable in terms of maintaining the wartime coalition and holding down American casualties, President Bush's decision not to topple Saddam by either conquering all of Iraq or pressing on militarily until he was removed from power failed to eliminate the main threat to stability in the region. Desert Storm, as it turned out, was not the opening act of a clear and strong American policy of peacekeeping in the post–Cold War era. "The hasty, confused, and unsatisfactory conclusion of the Gulf War became instead the pattern for a hesitant, confused, and unsatisfactory foreign policy carried on for the rest of the Bush administration and then by its successor," the Kagans stressed. "The uncanny decision to end the Gulf War without overthrowing Saddam Hussein . . . marked the still-birth of . . . [President Bush's] New World Order."[45]

However, the threat to the stability of the Persian Gulf region posed by Saddam Hussein's regime was minimized following Operation Desert Storm. No American lives were lost to Iraq's armed forces after the war ended. Oil tankers and other commercial shipping flowed unmolested through the Gulf. The Bush administration had a clear mandate to expel the Iraqis from Kuwait and return control of that nation to its government while containing Saddam's expansionist impulses. Except for the regime's attacks on minorities in the north and south, Iraq was not convulsed by an orgy of death and destruction that could have accompanied any breakup of the country precipitated by Saddam's violent removal from power. Iran and Iraq did not go to war again. Although hardly a cure-all, America's containment strategy was effective in protecting the nation's vital interests in the Persian Gulf region.

THE NEW WORLD DISORDER

The United States and its allies "were unprepared for the rapid demise of Soviet military and economic power, and in the years after 1991, the major players in the Cold War tried to find a new strategic template that would organize their foreign policy. With the possible exception of China, that template proved elusive in the 1990s."[46] Furthermore, defense spending had fallen by the year 2000 to its smallest share of the nation's gross domestic product since before Pearl Harbor. Nevertheless, America's armed forces were in incomparably better shape than they were in 1939 when the U.S. Army was the nineteenth largest in the world, one-tenth the size of Germany's. American weapons were at least a generation ahead of those of its most formidable potential rivals. Although there had been significant cuts in defense spending since 1985, the nation's military budget for FY 2000 was about 85 percent of its Cold War average in real (i.e., inflation adjusted) terms. Nevertheless, military leaders and their political allies complained that the defense budget was inadequate to sustain America's expanding global commitments.[47]

American policy makers had to grapple with the difficult issues of sizing the armed forces appropriately and deciding when to employ them. General Powell, who served as JCS chairman from October, 1989, to September, 1993, promoted significant changes in U.S. military force structure, deployment patterns, and strategy to deal with the dramatically changing international environment. Powell's proposals, known as the "Base Force," concluded that the threat of a massive global war had evaporated. The new strategic objective was to be able to fight and win two major regional contingencies (MRCs) simultaneously without the help of allies. It was designed to deal with the potential threats to U.S. interests posed by such rogue states as Iran, Iraq, Syria, and North Korea. That strategy ignored the worst nightmare facing military planners: the possibility, however remote, of war with either Communist China or a resurgent Russia. Like Britain, the sole superpower during the interwar period, America appeared to be unwilling or unable to address the implications of armed conflict with either of those nations.[48]

A critical challenge facing senior U.S. officials was deciding when and how to use the armed forces. President Bush ordered a reluctant American military establishment to launch a "war on drugs" in 1989. That effort concentrated on using air and naval assets, working in cooperation with other federal agencies, to interdict the flow of illegal substances into the United States. American ground and air units were also involved in supporting low-level offensive operations against powerful drug cartels in South America. Despite impressive statistics on intercepts and drug seizures, the impact of the costly military interdiction campaign on drug availability and costs in the United States was negligible.

Quite independent of the military's counternarcotics effort, Pres. Bill Clinton announced in 1997 that there had been significant reductions in illegal drug use by Americans. That encouraging news was tempered by the loss of a U.S. Army RC-7 aircraft packed with electronics surveillance gear in the jungles of southern Colombia in the summer of 1999. The crash of the drug surveillance aircraft highlighted the growing U.S. role in Colombia's long civil war. The area where the plane went down was the stronghold of leftist guerrillas who financed much of their insurrection through the sale of illegal narcotics. Opponents of sending American military air assets to Colombia warned that the United States was being sucked into another quagmire like Vietnam. But that historical analogy, while it still exercised a powerful grip on the American imagination, was not necessarily appropriate. Rather than a legacy of the Cold War, the fight against drug trafficking in Latin America seemed to be an example of a broad spectrum of asymmetrical threats to U.S. national security that were emerging at the end of the twentieth century. In addition to illegal drugs, they included computer viruses designed to cripple banking and air control systems, chemical and biological strikes aimed at "soft" civilian targets, and terrorist attacks sponsored by various nongovernmental groups.[49]

Counterdrug operations in Latin America were only the tip of the iceberg with respect to the growing tendency in the 1990s to employ American military forces abroad as the favored instrument of U.S. foreign policy. During the final years of the Bush administration, U.S. and allied air and naval forces were deployed to the Persian Gulf on a more or less permanent basis to enforce UN sanctions and protect the Shiite Muslim minority population in southern Iraq. Air units were also dispatched to Turkey to enforce UN sanctions against Iraq and defend the Kurdish population in the northern portion of that country. The Iraqis attempted on several occasions to reassert their air sovereignty over the no-fly zones, but they provoked intense allied air strikes that forced them to back down.

In October, 1994, Saddam moved two Republican Guard divisions close to the Kuwaiti border. The United States responded by dispatching air combat units and airlifting twelve thousand ground troops into the area. Faced with growing American forces on his doorstep, the Iraqi dictator backed down and withdrew his units. In December, 1998, he declared that the no-fly zones violated Iraqi sovereignty and expelled UN weapons inspectors who were attempting to eliminate his weapons of mass destruction in accordance with the 1991 Gulf War cease-fire agreement. Although additional ground forces and warships were dispatched to the Persian Gulf region, the main U.S. and allied military response consisted of a flurry of fighter and cruise missile attacks on Iraqi targets in what one anonymous government official described "as a tit-for-tat de facto war."[50]

The airborne attackers struck missile sites, AAA batteries, radar sites, and radio towers when the Iraqis fired on U.S. and allied aircraft or even attempted to track them with electronic devices. Retaliation for such incidents often occurred miles away and hours later against different Iraqi installations than the ones that had actually threatened the aircraft. In August, 1999, Pentagon officials reported that the aerial sniping over the northern and southern no-fly zones was costing upward of $1 billion a year. At that point, more than two hundred aircraft, nineteen warships, and twenty-two thousand U.S. troops were participating in those operations. Along with their allies, they had flown ten thousand combat or combat-support sorties while launching over a thousand bombs and missiles against more than four hundred Iraqi targets since December, 1998. However, like the U.S. war on drugs in Latin America and the Caribbean, operations against Iraq were controversial and their impact was difficult to assess. They were reactive and had no long-term strategic objective other than containing Iraq by enforcing the no-fly zones.[51]

The air force made the most extensive and creative use of its reserve components to augment its active force during the 1990s. Elements of Air National Guard and Air Force Reserve units were involved in every major contingency and humanitarian operation after the Persian Gulf crisis in 1990–91, usually on a volunteer basis. Use of that "silent call-up option" avoided politically sensitive mobilizations. Typically, a guard or reserve unit would take responsibility for fulfilling an overseas operational commitment for thirty to

An air force E-3 Sentry Airborne Warning and Control System (AWACS) aircraft lands after completing a mission over Turkey enforcing the United Nations no-fly zone in Iraq to protect Kurdish refugees in the region. The no-fly zone was established after Operation Desert Storm in 1991. (Photo courtesy of the Defense Visual Information Center.)

forty-five days with its aircraft and personnel. Each unit would rotate volunteers overseas for at least fifteen days, a period that corresponded to their annual training requirement, until the entire commitment was fulfilled. Because of their relatively high experience levels and close management of personnel, guard and reserve units were able to employ short rotations effectively despite some initial misgivings by the air force. The opportunity to participate in "real world" operations also provided excellent training for guard and reserve units. In addition, the overseas deployments reinforced the argument that the air reserve components were essential and had to be liberally funded and supplied with modern equipment.

Regardless of the professional expertise of American airmen and the integration of the air reserve components into the active force's operations, critics charged that the U.S. policy on Iraq lacked a viable long-term strategy or realistic objectives. Rear Admiral Eugene Carroll, USN (Ret.), deputy director of the Center for Defense Information, characterized American policy as "almost like a child's game—'I dare you,' 'I double-dare you,' 'Don't put your toe over the line,' 'I'm putting my toe over the line.' It inhibits any progress toward political resolution."[52]

President Bush authorized U.S. forces to begin a major humanitarian relief operation in Somalia in August, 1992. Thousands of people were starving because escalating political violence between rival clans had blocked the efforts of UN relief workers to help them. Air force, Air National Guard, and Air Force Reserve C-130s began flying food and relief supplies from Kenya to the Somalis that month. They were aided by air force C-5s and C-141s as well as RAF and German air force transports. But the violence continued to escalate in Somalia and the UN brought in a Pakistani peacekeeping force to protect the relief supplies. When that move proved ineffective, the UN suspended relief efforts until the clans could be controlled.

In November, Bush agreed to send in American ground forces. An air bridge of long-range transports and tankers quickly moved most of the troops and their supplies to Somalia from bases in the United States and Europe. Bush's successor, Bill Clinton, committed the troops to ending the civil strife and establishing an effective government in that turbulent nation. The effort fell apart and the Americans started heading for the exits when eighteen U.S. soldiers were killed and eighty-four others wounded during a running gun battle in Mogadishu in October, 1993, that received global television coverage. The last American troops left Somalia the following March and chaos returned to that nation. For U.S. military planners and policy makers, the principle lessons of Somalia were the need to stress force protection and a consensus that the success, indeed the very survival, of future operations would be judged by the level of American casualties.[53]

THE LAST SUPPER

The defense industry, plagued by military procurement budgets that plummeted 50 percent within several years of the Soviet Union's collapse, eliminated some three hundred thousand to four hundred thousand jobs. To help adjust to that situation, the Pentagon approved another round of corporate mergers and restructuring. In the spring of 1995, William Perry, President Clinton's secretary of defense, hosted a dinner for top executives, later dubbed "the last supper" by industry insiders. During that get-together Perry had actively promoted the further consolidation of leading arms makers. Boeing bought out McDonnell Douglas and a large portion of Rockwell. Lockheed gobbled up Martin Marietta and some of General Dynamics. Raytheon purchased the defense electronics segments of Hughes and Texas Instruments.

With the demise of the evil empire and the rise of the Internet-based information economy, the old military-industrial complex did not appear to carry

A Kentucky Air National Guard C-130 Hercules operates from a primitive airstrip in Somalia on January 23, 1993. Air Force airlifters played a critical role in moving food and humanitarian relief supplies into that war-ravaged nation during Operation Restore Hope. (Photo by Pam Spaulding courtesy © The Courier-Journal of Louisville, Kentucky.)

quite the same political and economic clout that its critics had warned about during the last few decades of the Cold War. The combined 1999 market value of the top ten defense contractors was less than 25 percent of the Microsoft Corporation. To help compensate for deep cuts in military procurement, the U.S. defense industry rapidly expanded its foreign military sales, replacing the Russians as the world's leader in arms exports. The value of those American arms sales abroad skyrocketed from $20 billion in 1990 to $32 billion by 1992.[54]

Although concerns still lingered about the influence of the military-industrial complex at the end of the twentieth century, it had become a much smaller part of the U.S. economy than during the heyday of the Cold War. Military spending accounted for less than 3 percent of the gross national product in the late 1990s. The aerospace industry sought to adapt to the end of the Cold War by relying more on commercial and foreign sales. Total sales in the civil aircraft sector—including engines and spare parts—amounted to $39 billion in the year 2000. Sales of military aircraft, engines, and parts added up to $33 billion (including $3 billion in exports). Missile and space sales were estimated at $9.7 billion and $32 billion respectively (including $12.6 billion for the military).[55]

The growth of space systems also had a major impact on the industry. In 1990, space-related sales totaled $28.9 billion. The Department of Defense claimed the largest share of that amount with $15.4 billion. Ballistic missiles, which also serve as launch vehicles for space systems, encouraged developments in microcircuitry that have had an enormous impact on American life. The use of semiconductor microchips in the commercial sector of the U.S. economy had been rooted in the development and volume production of those devices for the Minuteman ICBM program.[56]

The success of the aerospace industry's high-technology weapons in Operation Desert Storm and the Soviet Union's demise encouraged foreign sales during the 1990s. The United States also pressed forward with another round of weapons modernization programs following the Cold War in order to maintain its technological advantage over potential adversaries. The new generation of extremely expensive aircraft includes the multiservice Joint Strike Fighter, the air force's F-22 Raptor, F-117A Nighthawk, B-2 Spirit stealth bomber, and C-17 Globemaster III transport, as well as the navy's F/A-18E/F Super Hornet and A-12 stealth attack aircraft, plus the Marine Corps's troubled MV-22 Osprey tilt-rotor transport. Richard Cheney, secretary of defense during the first Bush administration and vice president in the second, canceled the controversial A-12 stealth attack aircraft in 1991 after the navy had already spent some $5 billion on it and had nothing more than engineering studies to show for it. The B-2's estimated price tag of $865 million per aircraft generated tremendous opposition on Capitol Hill. Congress limited production to twenty-one aircraft instead of the 132 originally planned. The skyrocketing costs of new weapons systems, especially electronics, smart munitions, and supporting space equipment, coupled with tighter defense budgets that concentrated on realistic training and current military operations, restricted the procurement of new aircraft in the 1990s. Despite such setbacks, the most sophisticated products of the aerospace industry continue to represent the military might and prestige of the world's most powerful nation.[57]

IMMACULATE DESTRUCTION

Following the end of the Cold War, most of the former communist nations in Eastern Europe pursued peaceful means to establish democratic forms of government, develop capitalist economic systems, and cultivate closer ties with NATO members. Several former Eastern bloc nations even joined the alliance, much to the dismay of the Russians. Yugoslavia, however, followed a radically different path. Marshal Josip Broz Tito had maintained Yugoslavia as a multiethnic communist state independent of the Kremlin's control following World War II.

Following Tito's death in 1980, that Balkan nation had begun to unravel. Some Yugoslav politicians began to cultivate longstanding ethnic and religious tensions as a means of consolidating their own power. In June, 1991, the Yugoslav provinces of Slovenia and Croatia declared their independence. Germany, a historic ally, quickly recognized them as sovereign states. War erupted when the primarily Serbian government of Yugoslavia, led by Slobodan Milošević, tried to reassert control of the breakaway provinces with the aid of Serbian minorities. Bosnia-Herzegovina declared its independence and was recognized diplomatically by the European Community and the United States in March, 1992. Macedonia had already broken away from Yugoslavia. Serb forces shifted their attacks from Croatia to Bosnia-Herzegovina shortly after the latter declared its independence.

Reports of murders, mass rapes, and "ethnic cleansing" led to demands for Western intervention. The spreading chaos in Bosnia led the United Nations to impose an arms embargo on all the warring parties and to dispatch a peacekeeping force to the area to mount a humanitarian relief operation in 1992. However, the UN forces were unable to handle the situation because the competing factions really did not want them to get involved.[58]

After UN peacekeepers secured the Sarajevo airport in Bosnia, air force C-130s initiated a humanitarian relief effort known as Operation Provide Relief in July, 1992. Later, Air National Guard and Air Force Reserve C-130s and air force C-141s briefly joined the operation. The warring factions often fired on the transports from the ring of mountains surrounding Sarajevo. The operation, which lasted until January, 1996, was the longest humanitarian airlift in history. It was responsible for delivering some 180,000 tons of food and supplies to the besieged civilians in Sarajevo. Because of the threats posed by anti-aircraft weapons and the use of aircraft by the different factions in the former Yugoslavia, the UN declared a no-fly zone over Bosnia in October, 1992. The Serbs ignored it and continued their ground campaign in Bosnia. The UN then asked NATO to enforce the no-fly zone in the spring of 1993. The operation, subsequently code-named Deny Flight, began on April 12. Directed from a combined operations center in Vicenza, Italy, the operation primarily involved air force, navy, and Marine Corps fighter aircraft.

Because of post–Cold War reductions in the active force, Air National Guard, and Air Force Reserve fighter, airlift, and tanker units participated in the operation on short voluntary tours of duty. American air units were joined by British, French, Dutch, and Turkish contingents. Supported by tankers and reconnaissance aircraft, the allied fighters flew round-the-clock combat air patrols over Bosnia. Those operations were largely uneventful until February, 1994, when the Serbs shelled a shopping area in Sarajevo. The attack, which killed sixty-eight civilians and wounded more than two hundred more, drew international outrage. Under the threat of air attack, NATO forced the Serbs to withdraw their heavy weapons at least twelve miles from the besieged city. Thereafter, NATO aircraft engaged in a limited number of attacks on Serb aircraft and ground units that violated UN restrictions on the combatants.

Ground fighting continued and escalated in the fall of 1994. Fearing that the situation was spiraling completely out of control, the UN asked for NATO air strikes on Serbian forces. The attacks began on November 21, but UN targeting restrictions hobbled them. The following month, former president Jimmy Carter negotiated an uneasy cease-fire for the troubled region that was broken in May, 1995, when the Croatians recaptured western Slavonia from the Serbs. Chaos returned to the region. When the Serbs shelled another Sarajevo marketplace in August, killing thirty-eight civilians and wounding eighty-five more, NATO initiated a bombing campaign that it had been planning for since the previous December. The intensity of Operation Deliberate Force, which began on August 30, stunned the Serbs. Coupled with victories by an American-trained Croation-Muslim army in western Bosnia, it forced the Serbs to ask for peace. The NATO allies agreed to a temporary bombing halt on September 14 and ended Deliberate Force six days later.[59]

American airmen had relied heavily on precision-guided munitions. Those so-called smart weapons allow warfare to be waged at a distance with far less risk to friendly forces. The result is maximum damage to enemy targets, and limited "collateral" damage to civilian structures. Foreign policy analyst Leslie H. Gelb characterized such high-technology attacks as campaigns of "immaculate destruction."[60] More than two hundred aircraft flew over thirty-five hundred sorties, including 750 strike missions against the Serbs. They delivered more than six hundred PGMs against fifty-five preselected targets before the campaign ended. Air power had helped to bring all sides to the peace table, but achieving a formal cessation of hostilities proved to be difficult. An effective cease-fire was finally instituted in October. The following month, the presidents of Bosnia, Croatia, and Serbia negotiated a peace agreement at Wright-Patterson AFB near Dayton, Ohio. The formal signing ceremony of the Dayton Accords was held in Paris on December 14.

The United Nations turned over operations in Bosnia and Croatia to NATO. The United States joined a multinational ground force that includes British and French troops to keep the peace in Bosnia. They were later joined by a contingent of Russian soldiers. Although the operation was originally scheduled to last only one year, through December 1996, the peacekeepers remain there with no end to their deployment in sight because of fears that fighting will resume if they withdraw. Aircraft based outside Bosnia stand ready to support the NATO and Russian troops there. They are authorized to use force if they so much as perceive a threat to their own security while operating over the occupied area.[61]

Bosnia was only a warm-up for the troubles in Yugoslavia's Kosovo Province. President Milošević had stripped Kosovo of its autonomy and instituted repressive policies there after he came to power in Belgrade during the late 1980s. Although they account for 90 percent of its population, Kosovar Albanians had been removed from most positions of authority by the Yugoslav government. Tensions between the two groups were exacerbated by the fact that the Kosovars are Muslims while the Serbs are Orthodox Christians. In March, 1998, Serbian discrimination turned into systematic, government-sponsored violence against a growing insurgent movement known as the Kosovo Liberation Army (KLA).

Yugoslav security forces began terrorizing the civilian population and then launched an offensive against the KLA, which advocated Kosovo's independence from Yugoslavia. As bodies started to pile up and some Kosovars were forced from their homes, NATO and the international community pressured Milošević to end the repression and violence. Although he agreed to those demands in October, Serb compliance was short-lived. Massacres of civilians and other acts of terrorism by the Serbs soon made it clear that Milošević had initiated a campaign to ethnically cleanse Kosovar Albanians from the province. The day after international negotiations in Paris designed to peacefully resolve the situation collapsed, Serb forces launched an offensive in Kosovo that drove thousands of ethnic Albanians from the province. Some were executed, and many homes were burned.[62]

After last-ditch diplomatic efforts failed to obtain any concessions from Milošević, President Clinton declared on March 23, 1999, that armed force was necessary to halt Serb aggression. The following day, NATO air and naval forces, primarily American, began an assault on Serb targets with bombs, cruise missiles, and precision-guided munitions called Operation Allied Force. Contingency planning for the use of military force had been under way for about a year. From the outset, NATO governments ruled out the use of their own ground forces. The alliance went to extraordinary lengths to avoid any casualties among its own aircrews and minimize enemy civilian deaths. Proposals for a massive initial air attack on "the head of the snake" in Serbia were rejected. Instead, in a strange echo of Vietnam, targets were selected to send carefully calibrated messages to Milošević that aggression would not pay. Politicians in Washington and European capitals, expecting the Serbs to cave in quickly, retained the authority to veto targets. Nevertheless, American military leaders throughout the chain of command expected that two or three days of bombing would destroy Milošević's determination to resist NATO and the international community.[63]

Staff Sergeant Dixie Strom of the Air National Guard's 104th Expeditionary Operations Group assembles a bomb fuse at Trapani Air Base, Sicily, in 1999 during Operation Allied Force, the war for Kosovo. By the last decade of the twentieth century, women had made significant gains in military aviation across a wide variety of occupational specialties from which they had been excluded earlier. (U.S. Force photo by S.Sgt. Chani Devers.)

General Wesley K. Clark, the U.S. Army officer in command of NATO forces, was caught in the middle of the profound contradictions of American policies in the Kosovo crisis. The Pentagon was reluctant to become militarily involved in that situation. Senior civilian officials in the Clinton administration wanted to "exercise great power throughout the world, but do it in a way that caused no (or at least few) American casualties and no larger political problems. It was Clark's fate to run the military side of this unwanted war, fought by an essentially uninterested country, orchestrated by a divided government where the consensus was, at best, extremely flimsy, and, where, once the war started, there would be a complex multinational political command to which he reported."[64]

Undeterred by the initial pinprick attacks, Serbian forces accelerated their campaign to drive ethnic Albanians out of the province. Before the war ended, approximately a million Kosovars fled to neighboring Macedonia, Albania, and

Montenegro. Another unintended consequence of the air war was to transform the Kosovo situation into a vital U.S. national interest. The United States and NATO had staked their credibility on Allied Force's outcome. If the Clinton administration had suddenly reversed course after the bombing began, it could have created a crisis within NATO on the same scale as Suez in 1956. The humanitarian implications of the situation in Kosovo had grown enormously and were reinforced by a critical strategic interest in maintaining America's alliance with Europe.[65]

Despite its inauspicious beginning, Operation Allied Force was a relatively one-sided military contest. The Serbs were isolated diplomatically and militarily. They could not count on their historic Russian ally for any meaningful assistance because of the growing economic and military problems of that struggling democracy. Following U.S. joint doctrine, initial allied attacks had focused on gaining air superiority. Aircraft also bombed Yugoslav military headquarters and barracks in Serbia during the opening phase of Allied Force. The tiny Serb air force was no match for the NATO air forces. Allied airmen quickly destroyed or disabled its small inventory of MiG-29 fighters. Apparently mindful of the rapid destruction of the Iraqi air defense system during the opening phase of Desert Storm, the Yugoslav armed forces seldom turned on their ground-based radars and widely dispersed their SAMs and AAA. Surface-to-air missiles were occasionally fired, but without radar guidance. To avoid fire from small arms, most AAA, and hand-held SAMs, aircraft initially operated above fifteen thousand feet. Although the altitude restriction was later relaxed, NATO aircraft still operated at altitudes that limited their effectiveness against dispersed, mobile Serb army targets deployed in the villages, forests, and mountains of Kosovo.[66]

Earl Tilford observed that, in essence, Milošević's armed forces "adopted a form of air deniability used so effectively by the North Vietnamese three decades ago. But, unlike the North Vietnamese, the Serbs did not aggressively confront NATO air attack. To do so would have put their air defense system in jeopardy. . . . Rather, they employed a kind of 'rope-a-dope' defense, riding out NATO attacks and using their weapons sparingly and only when they had a reasonable chance of success."[67]

The pace of operations during the first three weeks of Allied Force was not particularly intense. An unnamed air force official stressed that "This is not Instant Thunder [the original code name for the air component of Desert Storm]; it is more like Constant Drizzle."[68] About a month into the campaign, NATO was averaging approximately 150 sorties per day compared to the sixteen hundred a day the coalition had flown during Desert Storm. Through mid-April, some 90 percent of the weapons used were PGMs. At the same time, ethnic cleansing had accelerated dramatically and was continuing despite the application of NATO air power.[69]

Just like with Operation Rolling Thunder in Vietnam, NATO target restrictions were gradually relaxed and the pace of the bombing campaign was intensified over time. Additional U.S. warplanes were dispatched to Europe. President Clinton approved a limited mobilization of guard and reserve forces in April. In addition to providing essential logistics, communications, and other ground-based support services, Air National Guardsmen and Air Force Reservists flew attack, tanker, and airlift aircraft during Allied Force. While Yugoslav forces continued rampaging through Kosovo, NATO focused its escalating air attacks on Yugoslavia's industries, oil refineries, electrical power system, and bridges across major rivers, as well as military installations and the economic resources of Belgrade's ruling elite.

During the three weeks following the mobilization of guard and reserve units, the pace of the bombing campaign escalated considerably. Attacks against Serbian forces in Kosovo were increased. In late May, a KLA offensive against the Serb units in Kosovo forced the latter to come out of hiding and concentrate against the rebels. That change in tactics, combined with improved weather conditions, rendered the Serbs far more vulnerable to NATO air attacks. Attacks on Serbia's urban infrastructure, including its electrical grid and water supplies, made civilian life increasingly dangerous and uncomfortable. Although every effort was made to avoid collateral damage, an estimated twelve hundred civilians died as a result of mistaken bombings of nongovernmental vehicles and structures—including the Chinese embassy in Belgrade. After the war ended, NATO estimated that some twelve hundred Serb soldiers and police were killed by the aerial onslaught. The government in Belgrade put that number at approximately six hundred.

While the bombing continued in May, the British government pressed for a NATO ground offensive. But growing opposition to the war in Germany, Italy, and Greece apparently scotched whatever small possibility there may have been to prepare the alliance to exercise that option. On June 3, Milošević , responding to the deteriorating situation in Serbia and Kosovo as well as pressure from foreign envoys, suddenly announced that he was willing to accept an international peace proposal. The scheme called for the restoration of peace in Kosovo, followed by the rapid withdrawal of all forty thousand Serbian military and police personnel. Ethnic Albanian refugees would be allowed to return and the province would retain "substantial autonomy" as part of Yugoslavia. Under a UN flag, U.S. and other NATO troops (later joined by Russian soldiers) would serve as peacekeepers in Kosovo. Milošević accepted those arrangements. The bombing ended on June 10 and Serb forces began their rapid withdrawal from the beleaguered province.[70]

During Operation Allied Force, NATO aircrews flew some thirty-five thousand sorties, including ten thousand combat ones in which approximately twenty-three thousand bombs and missiles were expended. The U.S. Air Force flew the vast majority of them. Its enthusiasts argued that Allied Force "was the first time air power alone had defeated an enemy land army. One U.S. Air Force general claimed that 99.6 percent of the 23,000 bombs dropped on Yugoslavia hit their targets."[71] B-2 bombers based in the United States repeatedly struck Yugoslav targets. For some champions of the air force, Kosovo vindicated Billy Mitchell. Technology appeared to have finally caught up with the dreams and doctrine favored by ardent air power advocates. However, very few destroyed Serb artillery pieces, tanks, or other military vehicles were found in Kosovo after NATO ground forces occupied it.

Air force partisans were not the only individuals to spin the results of the Kosovo War through the lenses of their own ideologies, doctrinal precepts, and organizational interests. Sea power advocates championing the U.S. Navy's organizational interests claimed that "that the 74 aircraft in the *Theodore Roosevelt* battle group air wing accounted for a significantly greater percentage of the targets struck than their small numbers would have otherwise indicated. The 74 aircraft . . . accounted for just 4,270 sorties. . . . Still, they were responsible for the destruction or damage of 447 tactical targets and 88 fixed targets."[72] Naval sources also helpfully informed the public that "The Navy's EA-6B Prowlers were called upon to escort practically every strike package on attack runs—including with F-117A Nighthawk fighters and B-2 Spirit bombers."[73] Cruise missiles were fired from U.S. and British submarines, as well as surface ships operating in the Adriatic Sea.[74]

The marines were more restrained in their public comments since the war for Kosovo was outside their doctrinal emphasis on employing an integrated land-air team. They stressed that their EA-6B Prowlers deployed to Aviano Air Base in Italy before the war began flew over 460 sorties while logging more than twenty-one hundred combat hours and providing critical almost real-time electronic and signals intelligence once Allied Force kicked off. In May, two squadrons of F/A-18D Hornets joined the fray, flying more than two hundred combat sorties.[75]

Army sources suggested that although NATO ground forces did not participate in the war, the KLA offensive in May and allied preparations for a ground campaign had been critical factors in Milošević's decision to withdraw his forces. They were largely mum on why it had taken an extraordinary amount of time to deploy a contingent of attack helicopters to Albania for possible use in the air war and then had restricted them to training activities whose only tangible results were the deaths of several army aviators in crashes. Army attack helicopter assets were not trained and equipped to fight independently of ground units. Most members of the alliance remained steadfastly opposed to a ground campaign, as did many senior U.S. military officers and civilian leaders. In reality, there were no credible preparations for a ground campaign during the Kosovo War.[76] According to *Washington Post* reporter Dana Priest, "the vaunted helicopters came to symbolize everything wrong with the army as it enters into the twenty-first century; its inability to move quickly; its resistance to change; its obsession with casualties; its post–Cold War identity crisis."[77]

The exact reasons why Milošević decided to capitulate remained unclear after the war ended. The growing attacks against military, governmental, and economic targets in Serbia plus those against Yugoslav army and police units deployed in Kosovo clearly affected his decision, although estimates of how badly the Yugoslav army was actually hurt varied widely. The NATO alliance's ability to maintain its solidarity, despite serious misgivings in some member nations, was another major factor. Although the Russians strongly opposed the air war, they refused to intervene diplomatically or militarily on Serbia's behalf. The NATO economic sanctions and Milošević's indictment as a war criminal by an international tribunal may have raised the level of anxiety among the ruling elite in Belgrade. Finally, the inability of Yugoslav forces to completely suppress the KLA and the latter's growing role in the final stages of the war may have influenced the decision in Belgrade to withdraw from Kosovo.[78]

DUELING DOCTRINES

Former senior Reagan administration defense official Lawrence J. Korb observed that the Kosovo War underscored the most difficult challenge facing U.S. national security policy makers "deciding when to use our military forces. Starting with the last days of the Bush administration when the military was deployed to the Persian Gulf on a permanent basis and troops were sent to Somalia, U.S. forces began to be deployed with increasing frequency and became the preferred instrument for implementing U.S. foreign policy. According to some estimates, the U.S. military has been used for unexpected contingency operations about once every nine weeks since the end of the Cold War."[79]

The greater reliance on the armed forces in "operations other than war" was justified by what later became known as the "Clinton Doctrine." In June, 1999, President Clinton told NATO troops in Macedonia: "Whether you live in Africa or Central Europe or any place, if somebody comes after civilians and tries to kill them *en masse* because of their race, their ethnic background or their religion, and it is within our power to stop it, we will stop it."[80] The president apologized in that same speech for his government's failure to halt earlier mass killings in Ruwanda and its sluggishness in responding to the ethnic slaughter in Bosnia.[81]

The Clinton Doctrine was in direct opposition to the ideas of General Powell and other senior U.S. military officers whose professional careers had been shaped by the Vietnam War. Powell had "argued that U.S. troops should be deployed only when three conditions were met: First, our political objective was clear and measurable; second, the country was prepared to use overwhelming force quickly and decisively to advance that objective; and third, military forces would be withdrawn when the objective was accomplished."[82] Officers like Powell did not want to see American troops drawn into anymore Vietnams or Lebanons, where American policy objectives were unclear and the military operated under crippling restrictions. The JCS chairman's position on the use of military force was based upon a speech that Defense Secretary Caspar Weinberger delivered at the National Press Club in November, 1984. To their critics, Weinberger's and Powell's ideas were a formula for almost never using the armed forces in combat.[83]

The Clinton Doctrine was based upon historical analogies with what happened at Auschwitz in 1940 and Sarajevo in 1914. Its fundamental argument was that atrocities against innocent civilians and relatively small regional conflicts could balloon into major wars unless they were dealt with firmly and immediately by the major powers. According to Lawrence J. Korb, it also meant that "the American military could be sent into hostile situations without a specific, vital interest being involved and with the goal of achieving only such amorphous, open-ended objectives as stopping violence or building democracy. . . . [I]f our foreign policy is guided by the Clinton Doctrine, the United States in effect, would become a global policeman and would run the risk of stretching its military thin trying to accomplish virtually impossible goals, such as trying to change the political system of another country."[84]

By the late 1990s, the U.S. armed forces were structured to implement the "Powell Doctrine, which required tank-equipped heavy divisions, blue-water battle groups built around nuclear-powered aircraft carriers, and highly sophisticated combat aircraft, all designed to fight two major theater wars simultaneously against states like Iraq and North Korea. However, they were actually being tasked to implement the Clinton Doctrine, which required lighter, more mobile conventional and special operations forces.

That mismatch created at least three major problems, according to Korb. First, there had been about a 25 percent shortfall in equipment modernization spending from 1995–2000. Defense Department outlays to procure new equipment averaged $45 billion a year during that period. Money that should have been spent on new aircraft, ships, tanks, and advanced technological research was being used on deployments for operations other than war. Second, readiness was suffering. Instead of preparing for major theater wars, the armed forces were spending much of their time and energy in peacekeeping and humanitarian operations. Fighter pilots could not maintain all of their critical wartime skills while flying armed patrols over the Balkans and Iraq. Critical spare parts for aircraft were in short supply. Equipment cannibalization to obtain such items was widespread. Retention of highly skilled personnel in critical fields was an even more worrisome problem. For example, in 1998, only one in ten eligible carrier-based naval aviators accepted incentive bonuses to remain in the service.[85]

THE AMERICAN WAY OF WAR

During the Persian Gulf crisis of 1990–91, air power was the dominant arm of America's military forces. It later made a solo performance in Kosovo. In both episodes, the political results of its application were at best murky. However, since both Iraq and Yugoslavia were politically isolated states that fielded second- or third-class military machines, their defeat by vastly superior coalitions headed by the United States did not offer conclusive proof about the role of American military aviation. In other post–Cold War contingencies, the latter's relevance to vital American national security and foreign policy objectives ranged from critical to marginal, with many gradations in between. In varying degrees, each of the U.S. armed forces had tied their future to military aviation after the Vietnam War. Their varying approaches to the employment of aviation reflected a complex mixture of professional conviction and organizational self-interest.[86]

Air power—spearheaded by cruise missiles and air-refueled fighter-bombers armed with precision-guided munitions—emerged as the primary arm of American military power in the second half of the twentieth century. After the war in Southeast Asia, the armed forces revamped their technology, training, and doctrine to enable the United States and its allies to fight and win a conventional war against the numerically superior forces of the Soviet Union and its Warsaw Pact client states. Plans for this combined arms approach to warfare relied increasingly on interservice cooperation, joint command structures, and advanced technology associated with computers, infrared and radar sensors, and low-observable platforms. A smaller and more consolidated aerospace industry supplied the U.S. armed forces with aircraft, engines, missiles, electronics, and space systems that were decidedly superior to those of America's allies and rivals. Nuclear weapons declined in relative importance as both superpowers sought to increase their own security by negotiating arms control and then arms reduction agreements for those devices and the bombers and missiles that deliver them.

During the final decade of the twentieth century, the U.S. armed forces were compelled to make significant changes because of the Cold War's end, technological advances, and shrinking defense spending. Active duty military strength dropped to approximately 1.4 million personnel, some two hundred thousand below General Powell's original Base Force level, but still very high by historic American peacetime standards. The Defense Department's civilian work force has been cut substantially to a little over 756,000 individuals. In addition, many military installations have been closed or cut back substantially under the politically painful Base Realignment and Closure (BRAC) process. The BRAC commission, an independent body created by Congress with White House support, recommended closing seventy-nine bases in the United States and realigning twenty-six others for a projected savings of $19.3 billion. The Clinton administration pressed for additional rounds of basing closings, but Congress rebuffed it after the president appeared to play politics with several approved base closings during the 1996 election.

Air power became even more attractive to planners and senior policy makers during the 1990s because it appeared to offer an effective way to compensate for significant reductions in conventional ground and naval forces. The navy was forced to gradually reduce John Lehman's never quite realized six-hundred-ship fleet to three hundred vessels. It reoriented its strategic thinking and planning from waging a self-reliant blue-water campaign against the Soviet fleet and attacking key military assets in the Soviet Union to conducting joint and combined littoral warfare around the globe. Carrier aircraft and cruise missiles have played a central role in its overhauled strategic vision.

The air force combined SAC's bombers and TAC's fighters into a new Air Combat Command while handing responsibility for air defense of the continental United States to the Air National Guard. It consolidated its airlift and air-refueling aircraft into a new Air Mobility Command to promote more effective centralized control of those assets. Borrowing a page from the navy, it reorganized itself into ten Aerospace Expeditionary Forces (AEFs) that can deploy quickly to overseas hot spots that unexpectedly pop up. At the same time, those AEFs are designed to spread the burden of existing overseas rotations to longstanding forward deployments like the no-fly zones over Iraq more evenly across the service. This has been especially important because of the extensive cuts in the air force's size. For example, its active duty military manpower shrank from 570,880 in 1989 to 360,590 in 1999. During that same period, its aircraft inventory shrank from 6,971 to 4,413.

The air force promoted a new catch phrase—"Global Reach, Global Power"—to highlight the special characteristics it believes the service contributes to national defense: the speed, range, flexibility, precision, and lethality of modern air power. It was later refined as "Global Presence," a contemporary version of Mitchellite ideas that suggest not only a global war-fighting capacity, but also "power projection" and "virtual presence" capabilities from bases in the continental United States that challenge the established expeditionary roles of the navy and Marine Corps. The service transformed itself into a force composed primarily of fighter aircraft equipped to deliver precision-guided munitions and fielded the world's first stealthy, long-range, high-payload bomber, the Northrop Grumman B-2 Spirit.

After the Persian Gulf crisis of 1990–91, the air force made a concerted effort to integrate space programs into the realm of the war fighter, especially for regional conflicts. Starting with General Horner in 1992, commanders of the air force Space Command were chosen from the operational flying side of the service instead of its technical support organizations. From a doctrinal perspective, the air force was moving away from the notion that all space could do was support war fighters to a growing emphasis on the need to be able to dominate space in the same way that the air is controlled. Guided munitions linked to GPS satellites were used with devastating effectiveness during the Kosovo War. In early January, 2001, a congressionally mandated Space Commission headed by Donald H. Rumsfeld recommended that the air force be designated as DOD's executive agent for space. After Rumsfeld became secretary of defense later that year, he implemented that recommendation despite the continuing opposition of the other armed services, which remain concerned that the air force will not look out for their best interests in space. Many military officers continue to view space as the realm of technocrats rather than warriors. Much remains to be done before space can become a fully integrated element of U.S. military operations. For example, the critical problem of being unable to launch satellites in accordance with operational demands has not been resolved.

Meanwhile, the army cut its force structure from fourteen to ten divisions and continues to struggle to determine how light they should be while remaining able to meet the challenges of global mobility for major theater wars and lesser contingencies. The Marine Corps struggles to obtain sufficient funds to sustain the personnel it needs to man those formations while meeting its forward deployment obligations. In a major departure from Cold War norms, airlift and sealift programs of the joint U.S. Transportation Command received funding increases while the overall defense budget was being cut during the 1990s.

In addition to downsizing, reorienting, and modernizing the armed forces, nuclear arms control remains a major challenge facing American policy makers in the aftermath of the Cold War. Both the United States and Russia maintain awesome nuclear arsenals and formidable means to deliver them on a moment's notice. On July 31, 1991, Presidents George Bush and Boris Yeltsin signed the Strategic Arms Reduction Talks (START) I agreement limiting each side to six thousand strategic nuclear warheads on bombers, submarines, and land-based missiles. They then signed a START II agreement on January 3, 1993, proposing a phased reduction to thirty-five hundred warheads, as well as the elimination of MIRV'd ICBMs. The U.S. Senate ratified START II in January, 1996, and the Russian parliament did the same in April, 2000. In March, 1997, Clinton and Yeltsin signed protocols extending the deadline for START II reductions from January, 2003, to December, 2007. Neither of the treaties restricted the number of warheads that can be stored in reserve.[87]

The sudden and unexpected demise of Ronald Reagan's "evil empire," confronted the United States with a radically changed international environment in which terrorism, communal violence, and international drug trafficking were its greatest challenges. Although air power seemed ill suited to deal with many of those challenges, it became the instrument of choice for senior U.S. government policy makers in many instances because it promised decisive results at a relatively low cost in lives and national commitment. In that respect, it is the quintessential American way of war. According to Eliot Cohen, military aviation's high technology orientation appeals to "the machine-mindedness of a machine-oriented civilization. . . . Air power can indeed overawe opponents, who know quite well that they cannot hope to match or directly counter American air power. . . . Air power may not decide all conflicts or achieve all of a country's political objectives, but neither can land power."[88]

Epilogue

As the United States enters a new millennium, air power has emerged as an indispensable arm of its military forces. In many respects, the central theme of the history of American military aviation has been the continuing struggle to adapt aircraft to the changing operational requirements, doctrines, and competing organizational interests of the armed forces while accommodating evolving national strategies. Only a rich, highly industrialized, and technologically advanced nation like the United States has been able to afford to develop a full spectrum of air power capabilities that reflect the diverse conceptions of military aviation's many possible uses. Those ideas range from infantrymen who saw aircraft as flying scouting platforms and heavy artillery to visionaries convinced that modern air power could win wars relatively quickly without subjecting the United States to bloody ground and naval campaigns.

American air power remains an integral element of an international phenomenon. James L. Stokesbury observed: "at all levels of conflict and in all ways, air power is an element no military force dares ignore. For intelligence, logistics, and tactical support, it is an imperative no modern force can do without. Those low-level or primitive forces not possessing air power must adjust accordingly, must fight by night or live underground, must always beware of the sky."[1] Air power's impact is adversely affected by geographical conditions such as dense jungles and heavily forested mountains as well as poor weapons and training or inappropriate strategy and tactics. Stokesbury cautioned that "in the current world we must all beware of the sky, primitive or not, in the age of the missile, the great bomber, the nuclear standoff. . . . United Airlines asks people to 'fly the friendly skies.' But for much of the time airplanes, and air power, have been in existence, the skies have not been friendly, and air power has not always been a means of bringing people together."[2] This uneasiness and ambivalence about aviation's impact on modern life has permeated many cultures since World War II. That uneasiness was reinforced in a horrific way when terrorists inspired by extremist interpretations of Islam, hijacked four commercial airliners in the United States on September 11, 2001, crashing two of them into the twin towers of New York City's World Trade Center and a third into the Pentagon. The fourth hijacked airliner crashed into a rural area in western Pennsylvania. More than three thousand people were listed as dead or missing as a result of those suicide bombings, making them the deadliest terrorist attacks ever.

The history of American military aviation also underscores the point that technology is not inherently good, evil, or even neutral. It will affect us as circumstances shape it. Technology has no real logic of its own. While technological factors have been extremely important in the development of air power, the organizational interests of the armed forces, their changing doctrines and operational concepts, evolving national strategies, and domestic political and economic interests have played even larger roles.

Aviators have often oversold the airplane's military potential. But they have hardly been alone in that regard. From its inception, many civilians, including top government officials, have expected more of American air power than it could possibly deliver. Starting with Woodrow Wilson's support of a huge aviation program in 1917 to defeat Imperial Germany through Franklin D. Roosevelt's emphasis on building a giant air force in the late 1930s to defend the United States against the rising totalitarian threat, Dwight D. Eisenhower's nuclear-armed New Look strategy to deter Soviet Union aggression in the 1950s, Lyndon B. Johnson's Rolling Thunder bombing campaign against North Vietnam in the 1960s, and the Clinton administration's reliance on air power as its military instrument of choice in the 1990s, they have frequently pinned their hopes on aviation. This pattern has been grounded in a persistent American tendency to seek clear-cut and relatively straightforward answers to complex political and military problems by turning to technology and money while minimizing the shedding of their fellow countrymen's blood. On the surface, it has been a reasonable pattern of behavior for a wealthy and technologically advanced nation to follow. However, although an increasingly lethal tool of national security policy, air power alone often has proven not to be a panacea for resolving all such challenges.

Historically, the exaggerated claims of some air power proponents, both military and civilian, have frequently obscured its real achievements and limitations. Aviation began to play an important supporting role for American ground and naval forces during World War I. Since the United States declared war on Japan and Germany in 1941, it has been inconceivable that the nation's armed forces would either go to war or become involved in lesser contingencies without employing significant aviation resources. Like American Express travelers checks, they cannot leave home without them. If anything has characterized a distinctively American way of war since the Japanese attack on Pearl Harbor, it has been the nation's heavy reliance on the speed, flexibility, and lethality of military aviation in its many forms. This has meant the allocation of enormous resources to developing the capabilities of combat aviation forces. In addition, following World War II, airlift and tanker units emerged as distinctive national assets capable of supporting vital U.S. policy objectives independent of the combat operations of its air, ground, and naval forces. The most prominent examples of that development were the American responses to the Berlin blockade and the 1973 Arab-Israeli war.[3]

Along with professionals, citizen soldiers have been a key element of the American military tradition. In an often-overlooked link with America's militia past, the U.S. armed forces have relied on guardsmen and reservists, as well as wartime volunteers to provide the vast majority of aircrews and support personnel for wartime air forces until the conflict in Southeast Asia. However, because of the huge active duty force that had been built up to prosecute the Cold War and President Johnson's reluctance to resort to a politically risky large-scale mobilization, guardsmen and reservists played a limited role in the Vietnam War. Their main contributions were to provide either organizational cadres or partially trained individuals for wartime expansion, as well as individual volunteers for a variety of tasks during peacetime and in national emergencies for which the active force lacked adequate resources. Although individual augmentees remained important, the emphasis began to shift in the 1960s to providing fully trained air units with modern equipment that were capable of rapid mobilization and immediate deployment to combat zones.

The total force policy in the 1970s and a large infusion of money and modern equipment during the following decade furthered that process. The air force enjoyed a deserved reputation as having made the most effective use of its reserve components. The Air National Guard and Air Force Reserve were well integrated into its planning, budgeting, and training activities. As early as the 1950s, elements of guard fighter-interceptor and reserve airlift units had begun supporting air force peacetime operations on a volunteer basis. This daily operational integration became routine and global by the 1990s. The performance of mobilized guard and reserve fighter, airlift, tanker, special operations, and support units during the Persian Gulf and Kosovo Wars in the 1990s underscored the high level of military proficiency they had achieved.

With substantial reductions in air force personnel and operational units during the 1990s, the air reserve components formed a larger and larger share of the USAF's remaining force structure. They did not shrink nearly as fast or as far as their parent service. By 1998, the Air National Guard had some 108,000 personnel, whereas the Air Force Reserve consisted of about seventy-three thousand. Taken together, the air reserve components accounted for about 33 percent of the total air force, compared with 25 percent in 1988 and 12 percent in the 1960s. They provided almost 40 percent of the service's fighter inventory and 25 percent of its bombers. Consequently, the guard and reserve were frequently called upon to support the air force's global responsibilities—primarily through volunteerism. Not surprisingly, those reserve organizations began to confront growing recruiting, retention, and equipment modernization challenges as their operations tempo increased in the late 1990s.[4]

Although a twentieth-century phenomenon, military aviation has deep cultural, scientific, and technological roots. Men have dreamed about flight since ancient times, but they failed to achieve it until the emergence of hot-air ballooning in France in the late eighteenth century. Early efforts to employ balloons in support of military operations in Europe and North America through the end of the nineteenth century achieved limited success because of their vulnerability to ground fire, limited carrying capacity, and control problems. Even a military genius like Napoleon, who was unwilling or unable to fit balloons into his ideas about warfare, abandoned them. Interacting with politics and national strategic circumstances, organizational culture, doctrine, and bureaucratic interests would shape the development of military aviation even more profoundly than technology.

Technological progress in aviation has fundamentally been a collaborative and cumulative process. Beginning in the late eighteenth century, controlled powered flight by heavier-than-air vehicles appeared to be a more promising path for aviation than balloons. However, it took over a century of scientific experimentation by a number of individuals to develop the technologies critical to achieving that breakthrough. Relying on the best available science and engineering from European and American sources, the Wright brothers perfected and fused those technologies to achieve the first controlled powered flight by an aircraft in 1903. Their triumph at Kitty Hawk, North Carolina, was one of the greatest creative achievements in history.

The progress of American military aviation has been part of an international phenomenon. From the initial work of the Wrights through the theoretical foundations of stealth technology, America and its armed forces benefited enormously from European contributions to aviation. Like technological innovators before and after them, the Wrights entertained utopian dreams that aviation would promote an era of unprecedented international peace and prosperity. When commercial interest in their innovation failed to materialize, they turned to the armed forces. However, the army and navy were slow to recognize the military potential of their frail contraption. Instead, balloons were favored for reconnaissance and artillery-spotting missions by the army's Signal Corps. After the Wrights were rebuffed by the armed forces, it took Pres. Theodore Roosevelt's intervention to gain them an opportunity to demonstrate their invention to army authorities.

Roger Bilstein observed: "The European inheritance, generously acknowledged in other areas of the history of technology, has not been similarly acknowledged in the context of American aerospace history. Having absorbed European contributions, however, American entrepreneurs often adapted and modified them into far more successful applications."[5] The armed forces relied on the aircraft (later aerospace) industry, supported by university and government laboratories, for technological innovation and aircraft production. Military aircraft and engine production requirements in World War I created that industry as an economically significant enterprise grounded in modern science and engineering. With the exception of the Naval Aircraft Factory, which functioned until the 1950s primarily to establish cost yardsticks for aircraft development and production, the military services abandoned the idea of using government arsenals to supply aircraft in the early 1920s. Aviation technology was changing too rapidly to rely on an arsenal system for aircraft development and production. Moreover, military and naval officers grew comfortable working closely with the aircraft industry to design and manufacture increasingly capable equipment. Congress, the White House, and the armed services were also the objects of fierce lobbying by aircraft manufacturers determined to win contracts for their struggling firms and equally determined to choke off any government rivals. Although commercial aviation emerged as a significant market for the industry in the 1930s, military aviation has always been its single most important customer.

During World War I, European military and naval aviators developed through trail and error most of the basic missions of air power that exist to the present day. They included reconnaissance and liaison, air superiority, close air support, interdiction, strategic bombing, and airlift. Under the pressures of combat, the technology of flight made enormous progress. Contrary to many accounts of that period by pioneer aviators and their publicists, there was significant high-level civilian and military support for aviation in both Europe and the United

States. Pilots, especially aces, became heroes in the mass popular culture. Although it got a late start, American aviation progressed rapidly during the war. Like its European counterparts, Yankee air power played a distinctly supporting role to the established ground and naval forces. Observation aviation, which spotted friendly artillery fire and watched for signs of enemy offensives, was its most valuable contribution to the war effort. World War I established the modern American aircraft industry based on modern science and engineering and largely dependent on its military customers. It also created a cadre of enthusiastic army, navy, and marine officers who were dedicated to advancing aviation in the service of their country by applying it to a variety of ideas about the future of warfare.

Throughout the 1920s and 1930s, those officers and their successors worked to either establish sound aviation programs to further the established missions of their branches of the armed forces or, in the case of some army flyers, create a new military service and develop a revolutionary form of warfare based on strategic bombing. Despite American isolationism, meager defense budgets, and strong antimilitary sentiments, the interwar period was a golden age of technological, doctrinal, and organizational innovation for American military aviation. Flyers forged strong alliances with politicians, aircraft and engine builders, scientists and engineers, Hollywood, and the media to promote their competing visions of air power. The aviation arms of the military services promoted and played a primary role in sustaining a strong and progressive aviation industry. Their money and performance requirements played a critical role in promoting the development of modern, prejet aircraft during the "airframe revolution" of that period.

Despite popular images of reactionary admirals and generals who really did not understand air power, many senior leaders in the armed forces recognized its potential and actively encouraged its development. The real issue was who would control it and how it would be employed in the next war. Arguably, the navy was more successful in that regard than the army initially because it pursued the less ambitious objective of integrating aviation into its existing warfighting system. Unlike the army, the sea service was not deeply split between the influential officers who saw it as a revolutionary new form of warfare and those who wanted to subordinate it to the needs of the traditional surface combat forces. With its long history of technological innovation and adaptation, the navy's organizational culture found it easier to incorporate aviation than did the army's. The marines embraced aviation during the interwar period as a means of supporting their emerging amphibious warfare mission. Notwithstanding false starts like the Air Corps's embrace of strategic bombing as a military panacea, the U.S. armed forces and their allies in industry, government, and university laboratories made enormous strides in aviation during the 1920s and 1930s. Their achievements paved the way for the enormous operational success and frightening destructiveness of American military aviation during World War II.

Each major generational leap in aviation technology—the airframe revolution, the emergence of jets and nuclear weapons, and the advent of precision-guided munitions and stealthy aircraft—has encouraged fresh claims that air power has become the decisive force in warfare. But military aviation has neither rendered war obsolete nor eliminated the need for armies and navies, as some of its most ardent champions have predicted. Rather, it has transformed modern warfare. While not changing the fundamental nature of armed conflict between states, it increased the speed, flexibility, scope, and destructiveness of modern warfare. Military aviation has made it possible to launch direct attacks on enemy cities, economies, and civilian populations without the necessity of first defeating their armies and navies. That development contributed significantly to the fact that the twentieth century was the bloodiest in human history. At the operational level, aviation has extended the zone of conflict from the immediate battle zone to the distant rear areas of armies and navies. In some instances, aviation has played the decisive role in individual battles and campaigns such as Midway, Kuwait and Kosovo. Nevertheless, American air power has usually worked best as an integral part of a combined arms approach to warfare. Only one significant aspect of air power, strategic bombing, has dominated civilian attitudes toward military aviation in the United States. Radical advocates like Billy Mitchell had little real impact on the development of air power, but their inflated claims became the yardstick by which it was measured and seemed to fail in the strategic bombing campaigns of World War II. That distorted focus was reinforced by the searing images of Dresden, Hiroshima, and Nagasaki.

Bombing contributed enormously to the economic collapse of Germany and Japan in World War II. However, it did not result in a quick, clear-cut, and relatively cheap victory, as prewar planners and air power advocates had predicted. Rather, it was a battle of attrition that consumed rivers of blood and treasure—especially over the Third Reich. Tactical aviation played an even larger role than strategic bombing for the American armed forces during World War II and ever since. John Buckley emphasized that the development of air power was linked to national strategies. In the case of the United States, he observed that it reflected a "productivist approach to war which symbolized total war more than any other [belligerent], recognizing the need to disable the enemy's industrial output prior to, or in conjunction with ground assault."[6] Buckley added that tactical aviation probably played an even more important role than strategic bombing in the American war effort, noting that "Without aerial control or at least the denial of such power to an enemy, land operations became at least hazardous and at worst untenable."[7]

Air power required the massive mobilization of American scientific, engineering, and industrial resources during World War II. That kind of mobilization for total war is probably a thing of the past. Buckley stressed that "Since 1945, the impact of air power on the conduct and planning of conflict has lessened, largely because mass industrial war has, in effect become obsolete. . . . Nevertheless, air power in conjunction with nuclear weapons played a major part in shaping the Cold War. . . . [W]ar was not made obsolete by nuclear armed air forces, as some have argued, but it has become so potentially destructive that it had to be conducted by other means. When so constrained, air power has been less effective."[8] Buckley was convinced that military aviation had "transformed warfare in the most revolutionary manner. . . . The escalation of war into the skies was a culmination of the drive towards mass industrial warfare, a trend begun a century before as western civilization first started linking economic strength with military capability on an ever increasing scale."[9]

Because of the restraints placed upon its employment and its own inherent limitations, American air power could not secure victory over North Korean and Chinese forces during the Korean War despite maintaining air superiority over the theater of operations. However, it did play a critical role in preventing the communists from winning that war. After active hostilities ceased, the army and air force failed to resolve their differences about how air power would support ground forces in the future. This repeated the pattern of unsatisfactory relationships established between the two services after World War II. Some army aviators began to experiment with helicopters, which had been used for transportation and medical evacuation missions, to provide greater battlefield mobility and direct fire support for soldiers. The marines were convinced that Korea had validated their fundamental ground-air team concepts of warfare. Like the army, they began to explore ways to make greater use of helicopters. During the 1950s, nuclear-armed U.S. air power, especially SAC's bombers, gained an unparalleled position in national strategy but could not be decisive in a tactical or operational sense because of many political, moral, and technical limitations. The tactical air forces tried to turn themselves into a junior version of SAC, and airlift languished. The navy launched a new class of supercarriers armed with jets as platforms for waging nuclear war against the Soviet Union. President Eisenhower's New Look strategy probably deterred a catastrophic war with the Soviet Union, but it left the military services poorly prepared to deal with lesser conflicts like Vietnam. Although American air power achieved notable successes in conjunction with ground forces on the battlefields of South Vietnam, its own technical and operational limitations, plus crippling restrictions placed upon its employment against North Vietnam, contributed to the defeat of the United States and its allies in that conflict.

America's defeat in Southeast Asia stimulated a postwar military renaissance by the U.S. armed forces, including their aviation arms. In order to fight and win against numerically superior Soviet forces, the latter modernized their aircraft, missiles, and electronic systems, instituted far more rigorous combat training programs, and developed new doctrines. Air-refueled fighter-bombers equipped with precision-guided munitions and sophisticated electronic gear emerged from that period as the nation's aerial weapons of choice. For the army and Marine Corps, helicopters provided enormous battlefield mobility and critical direct-fire support, including the ability to destroy enemy armor. The Reagan military buildup provided the resources needed to bring that renaissance to fruition.

Except for World War II, when mass-production techniques were successfully applied, the construction of military aircraft and associated equipment has essentially been a handicraft operation. Beginning in the 1950s, space, missiles, and electronics have emerged as vital segments of the industry's military business. The Cold War's end and dramatic reductions in spending on new weapons have encouraged industry consolidation and a greater emphasis on foreign military sales and coproduction agreements. In the final analysis, American military aviation and the aerospace industry are like a happily married older couple. Their relationship over the years has had its ups and downs, but they depend on each other. They sometimes get cranky and short-tempered, but one could not exist without the other. Like most successful modern marriages, it is a partnership that both sides contribute to and have a strong vested interest in maintaining. The military has usually been the dominant partner because it has been the aerospace industry's most important customer and supplied the operational requirements that have pushed technical development in certain directions much of the time.

Since the end of the Cold War and the Soviet Union's collapse, air power has once again emerged as the military instrument of choice among U.S. civilian policy makers. Its starring role in the Persian Gulf and Kosovo has made it especially attractive to officials seeking a quick and decisive means of achieving national policy objectives with minimum risk to American lives. They do not want the United States to be mired down in another Vietnam-type war. However, the results of America's post–Cold War interventions abroad have been mixed at best. Somalia and Haiti, for example, were primarily ground force operations. Although airlift and tanker forces moved troops and supplies quickly to those troubled nations, it seems unlikely that a vigorous application of aerial firepower could have overcome American policy deficiencies dramatized by the unsatisfactory outcomes of both interventions.

In 1991, U.S. and coalition air power played the leading role in defeating Iraq after it seized Kuwait. Although a ground campaign was necessary to secure the victory, air power played the leading role in winning a war for the first time in American history. Unfortunately, it was an incomplete and unsatisfactory victory. Although the Iraqis were driven out of Kuwait and its oilfields, Saddam Hussein remained in power. He crushed his domestic opposition and continued to menace his neighbors from time to time. Acting largely alone, air power kept him in check using pinprick, tit-for-tat retaliatory strikes, but it could not resolve the fundamental political and security issues that have since plagued the Persian Gulf region. In the Balkans, Pres. Slobodan Milošević briefly held power after losing a series of wars to retain control of breakaway provinces of the Yugoslav federation. Although U.S. and NATO air power stopped the ethnic cleansing in Kosovo and forced the withdrawal of Serbian forces from that troubled Yugoslav province without a land invasion in 1999, ground troops had to secure the troubled victory by occupying it after the war ended. The incomplete and politically disappointing victories over Iraq and Yugoslavia underscore the historic point that air power is not a panacea. Although lethal and increasingly precise in terms of the acquisition and destruction of stationary targets, air power continues to operate within military and diplomatic constraints.

By the end of the twentieth century's final decade, the costs of advanced technologies and the vast training and logistics infrastructure needed to sustain a full spectrum of global air power had become so huge that only the United States could afford them. In some specialized areas, such as stealth and advanced electronic warfare, only the world's lone remaining superpower has been able to pay the cost of full admission to the modern air power club. In the case of critical missions like air superiority, the United States appears to be at least a decade ahead of its nearest rivals. But it remains unclear what roles air power can play in dealing with emerging asymmetrical threats to national security, including urban terrorism, narcotics smuggling, computer hackers and viruses, and weapons of mass destruction smuggled into urban centers by dissident groups.[10]

Although it is difficult to sort out military aviation's influence on American culture and society, it is clear that aviation as a whole has had a significant impact. According to historian Roger Bilstein: "aviation and space flight have become ingrained within the sociological framework of American life. The perception of aerospace patterns shifted during various decades, but the concept of flight had unquestionably become a permanent fixture within the lifestyles and consciousness of the American public. Literature, cartoons, motion pictures, fine art, and music incorporated various aspects of flight."[11]

During the first half of the twentieth century, the American public turned aviation into a "secular creed of progress toward a utopian future, [and] took the achievements of such persons as Orville and Wilbur Wright and converted them into a veritable religion complete with saints, shrines, liturgies, relics, and extravagant visions of aeronautical salvation."[12] However, as Joseph Corn has documented, during and immediately after World War II Americans became increasingly disillusioned with that utopian vision. Instead, they saw the airplane as convenient transportation at its best or as an instrument of mass destruction at its worst.[13] While rejecting aviation as a means of reorganizing society, it continued to exercise a strong but ambivalent influence on popular culture and society.

In an age where the nation's politics and popular culture are heavily influenced by the mass media, air power has had an enormous impact on American perceptions of modern war. John Buckley observed that, from images of a devastated Hiroshima to Vietnamese peasants taunting captured American pilots and burned out Iraqi tanks in Kuwait's desert, the military component of aviation has shaped our "changing perceptions of the role of war and peace in the modern world. . . . [A]ir power and total war were linked as both causes and consequences of each other, shaping and deepening the experience of war in the twentieth century to a degree unknown in modern history."[14]

Aside from the widely accepted conclusion that it will continue to play a crucial role in shaping and implementing the national security policies of the United States, it is difficult to predict the future of American military aviation. Some analysts have suggested that strategic bombers and aircraft carriers represent sunset weapons systems in an era of space satellites and highly accurate missiles that do not have to expose human crews to strong enemy defenses to destroy their targets. The development of remotely piloted aerial vehicles for reconnaissance missions suggests to some that the era of manned combat aircraft may be coming to an end. However, that is a distinctly minority opinion. For many years, military theorists in the former Soviet Union wrote about the value of developing a reconnaissance-strike complex that could locate and destroy earthbound mobile targets on a real-time basis. Emerging space and information systems, as well as precision guidance and low-observable technologies mated to RPVs, could make that a reality in the future. Such systems might employ nonlethal technologies that could disable rather than kill or physically destroy their targets. Some enthusiasts view space as the emerging high ground of warfare and are lobbying to create a new military service focused on that medium. However, serious technological, cost, and treaty limitations will have to be overcome before space can become an active combat arena. In the meantime, air and surface forces will continue to rely on it more and more for intelligence, communications, and weather support. Airlift and tanker forces will likely continue to serve as enormously valuable tools for senior civilian and military officials. The most difficult challenge confronting American military aviation will continue to be determining which technological opportunities the armed forces will pursue and how they will incorporate them into their war-fighting systems.

If we are to prepare for the future, it is necessary to understand the past. There is one ghost from history that is seldom if ever remembered when speculating about America's military future. Count Alfred von Schlieffen, not Vietnam, is the ghost that haunts U.S. military planners and civilian officials at the dawn of the twenty-first century. Schlieffen was a military historian and senior member of the Prussian General Staff who developed a flexible strategic concept for a two-front war against France and Russia in the latter part of the nineteenth century. As refined by his less able successors, the Schlieffen plan, coupled with revolutionary advances in military technology and concentration on perfecting the operational art of warfare, encouraged the conviction that future armed conflicts between modern European powers would be quick, decisive, and relatively bloodless affairs. The tragic error of that opinion, which was widely held by influential European soldiers and statesmen at the start of the twentieth century, became apparent in 1914. Conditioned by the promise and potential of high-technology air power as well as budgetary constraints, current American military planning and national security policy appears to be grounded in its own short-war illusion.[15]

NOTES

CHAPTER 1: BRIGADES OF FLYING HORSES

1. Charles H. Gibbs-Smith, *Aviation: An Historical Survey From Its Origins To The End of World War II*, 1–10; Martin van Creveld, *Technology and War: From 2000 B.C. to the Present*, 183; Roger E. Bilstein, *Flight in America, 1900–1983: From the Wrights to the Astronauts*, 1–4; James L. Stokesbury, *A Short History of Air Power*, 13; Charles H. Gibbs-Smith, *Flight Through the Ages: A Complete, Illustrated Chronology from the Dreams of Early History to the Age of Space Exploration*, 1–14.

2. Gibbs-Smith, *Aviation*, 6–8, 17–41; van Creveld, *Technology and War*, 184–85; Bilstein, *Flight in America*, 4–7; Alfred Goldberg, ed., *A History of the United States Air Force, 1907–1957*, 1; Bilstein, *Flight in America*, 53; Juliette A. Hennessy, *The United States Army Air Arm, April 1861 to April 1917*, 1–12.

3. Robert F. Futrell, *Ideas, Concepts, Doctrine: A History of Basic Thinking in the United States Air Force, 1907–1964*, 8; Edmund Morris, *The Rise of Theodore Roosevelt*, 609, 612; Goldberg, ed., *History*, 1–3, 8; Roy A. Grossnick, *United States Naval Aviation, 1910–1995*, 1; Wayne Biddle, *Barons of the Sky: From Early Flight to Strategic Warfare, the Story of the American Aerospace Industry*, 29–33; Charles DeForest Chandler and Frank P. Lahm, *How Our Army Grew Wings: Airmen and Aircraft Before 1914*, 144–45; Hennessy, *United States Army Air Arm*, 20–21.

4. Chase C. Mooney and Martha E. Layman, *Organization of Military Aeronautics, 1907–1935, (Congressional and War Department Action)*, 2–3; Chandler and Lahm, *How Our Army Grew Wings*, 76–92; Hennessy, *United States Army Air Arm*, 119; Benjamin D. Foulois and Carroll V. Glines, *From the Wright Brothers to the Astronauts: The Memoirs of Major General Benjamin D. Foulois*, 42–52; Charles H. Gibbs-Smith, *A History of Flying*, 217–78; Adolphus A. Greely, *Reminiscences of Adventure and Service: A Record of Sixty-five Years*, 26–100, 120–52, 166–75.

5. Marvin McFarland, ed., *The Papers of Wilbur and Orville Wright*, 2:754–55, 757, 761–63; Chandler and Lahm, *How Our Army Grew Wings*, 142–43; Hennessy, *United States Army Air Arm*, 25–26; Herbert A. Johnson, "The Aero Club of America and Army Aviation, 1907–1916," *New York History* (Oct., 1985) 375–95; Paul Wilson Clark, "Major General George Owen Squier: Military Scientist" (Ph.D. diss., Case-Western Reserve University, 1974), 69, 136–38; Charles J. Gross, "George Owen Squier and the Origins of American Military Aviation," *Journal of Military History* 54, no. 3 (July, 1990): 281–305.

6. Clark, "Major General Squier," 69, 110–20, 133, 136–38; Greely, *Reminiscences*, 162–63, 180–90; Flint O. DuPre, *U.S. Air Force Biographical Dictionary*, 221; Gross, "George Owen Squier," 303–305; Foulois and Glines, *From the Wright Brothers*, 53–54; Chandler and Lahm, *How Our Army Grew Wings*, 150; Hennessy, *United States Army Air Arm*, 26–28.

7. Hennessy, *United States Army Air Arm*, 28, 33; Chandler and Lahm, *How Our Army Grew Wings*, 155; Foulois and Glines, *From the Wright Brothers*, 56, 57; George Owen Squier, "Aeronautics in the United States at the Signing of the Armistice, November 11, 1918," box 6, folder 2, George Owen Squier Papers, U.S. Air Force Academy Library, Colorado Springs, Colo. (hereafter USAFAL), 3; Joseph J. Corn, *The Winged Gospel: America's Romance with Aviation, 1900–1950*, 3.

8. Hennessy, *United States Army Air Arm*, 34; " Report of the Chief Signal Officer," in *U.S. War Department Annual Reports, 1911*, 1:739.

9. Richard P. Hallion, *Test Pilots: The Frontiersmen of Flight*, 37–38; "Report of the Chief Signal Officer," 1911, 1:966; "Report of the Chief Signal Officer," in *U.S. War Department Annual Reports, 1913*, 1:781.

10. Grossnick, *United States Naval Aviation*, 1–3; Archibald D. Turnbull and Clifford L. Lord, *History of United States Naval Aviation*, 1–11; William J. Armstrong, "Aircraft Go to Sea: A Brief History of Aviation in the U.S. Navy," *Aerospace Historian* 25, no. 2 (June, 1978): 79–80; Arthur Hezlet, *Aircraft and Sea Power*, 3.

11. Grossnick, *United States Naval Aviation*, 3–5; Armstrong, "Aircraft Go To Sea," 79–80; Clark G. Reynolds, *Admiral John H. Towers: The Struggle for Naval Air Supremacy*, 28–32; George F. Pearce, "He Did Not Curry Favor," *Aerospace Historian* 30, no. 3 (Sept., 1983): 193; Turnbull and Lord, *History*, 7–17; Hezlet, *Aircraft and Sea Power*, 5–11; Mark Evans and Roy Grossnick, Aviation History Branch, Naval Historical Center, memorandum for Charles J. Gross, Subject: Joint Comments, Sept., 2001, copy in author's possession.

12. Allan R. Millett and Peter Maslowski, *For the Common Defense: A Military History of the United States,* rev. and enl. ed., 336–37; Martin P. Claussen, *Materiel Research and Development in the Army Air Arm, 1914–1945*, 12; Clark, "Major General Squier," 155–58; Turnbull and Lord, *History*, 17; Hezlet, *Aircraft And Sea Power*, 11.

13. Jerome C. Hunsaker, "Forty Years of Aeronautical Research," in *Annual Report of the Smithsonian Institution, 1955*, 243–47; Clark, "Major General Squier," 155–59, 258–59.

14. Futrell, *Ideas, Concepts, Doctrine*, 10; George W. Gray, *Frontiers of Flight: The Story of NACA Research*, 10–13.

15. Hunsaker, "Forty Years," 247–51; Goldberg, ed., *History*, 11; Martin P. Claussen, *Comparative History of Research and Development Policies Affecting Air Materiel, 1915–1944*, 24–25.

16. Russell F. Weigley, *History of the United States Army*, 322; Goldberg, ed., *History*, 4, 6, 8; Turnbull and Lord, *History*, 81; Evans and Grossnick memorandum.

17. Hennessy, *U.S. Army Air Arm*, 45, 47, 53, 62; Chandler and Lahm, *How Our Army Grew Wings*, 206–209; Henry H. Arnold, *Global Mission*, 30–37.

18. Reynolds, *Admiral Towers*, 4–7, 28–29, 56–63; Grossnick, *United States Naval Aviation*, 2–5, 10–11.

19. Reynolds, *Admiral Towers*, 56–63; Peter B. Mersky, *U.S. Marine Corps Aviation, 1912 to the Present*, 2–4; Allan R. Millett and Peter Maslowski, *For the Common Defense: A Military History of the United States of America*, 307.

20. Hennessy, *U.S. Army Air Arm*, 102–103; "Report of the Chief Signal Officer," *U.S. War Department Annual Reports, 1914*, 1:509, 517.

21. Hennessy, *U.S. Army Air Arm*, 131–34, 183–87; Rene J. Francillon, *The Air Guard*, 11–15; Charles J. Gross, *Prelude to the Total Force: The Air National Guard, 1943–1969*, 1–2;

306   ✹   NOTES TO PAGES 19–25

John K. Mahon, *History of the Militia and National Guard*, 146; Rene J. Francillon, *The United States Air National Guard*, 15–17.

22. Goldberg, ed., *History*, 79; Foulois and Glines, *From the Wright Brothers*, 107–10; Arnold, *Global Mission*, 41–42; Hennessy, *U.S. Army Air Arm*, 74; Reynolds, *Admiral Towers*, 77–80; Turnbull and Lord, *History*, 42; Hezlett, *Aircraft and Sea Power*, 22.

23. Herbert A. Johnson, "Seeds of Separation: The General Staff Corps and Military Aviation Before World War I," *Air University Review* 34, no. 1 (Nov.–Dec., 1982): 36–38, 41; Hennessy, *U.S. Army Air Arm*, 72.

24. Donald Smythe, *Guerrilla Warrior: The Early Life of John J. Pershing*, 217–21; Hennessy, *U.S. Army Air Arm*, 145–67; Goldberg, ed., *History*, 10; James L. Crouch, "Wings South: The First Foreign Employment of Air Power by the United States," *Aerospace Historian* 19, no. 1 (Mar., 1972): 27–31.

25. Smythe, *Guerrilla Warrior*, 232–33; Weigley, *History*, 342–54; Walter Millis, *Arms and Men: A Study in American Military History*, 214–26.

26. Weigley, *History*, 348–49; Goldberg, ed., *History*, 10; Hennessy, *U.S. Army Air Arm*, 154–57; George W. Baer, *One Hundred Years of Sea Power: The U.S. Navy, 1890–1990*, 59–63; Turnbull and Lord, *History*, 81; Millett and Maslowski, *For the Common Defense*, 325; William F. Levantrosser, *Congress and the Citizen-Soldier: Legislative Policy-making for the Federal Armed Forces Reserve*, 13; Robert L. Goldich, "Historical Continuity in the U.S. Military Reserve System," *Armed Forces and Society* 7, no. 1 (fall, 1980): 22; Office of History, Headquarters, U.S. Air Force Reserve (hereafter, OH, HQ USAFRES), "A Brief History of the United States Air Force Reserve, 1916–1991," January, 1992, 1; Richard B. Crossland and James T. Currie, *Twice A Citizen: A History of the United States Army Reserve, 1908–1983*, 17–32.

27. Foulois and Glines, *From the Wright Brothers*, 138–41; Hennessy, *U.S. Army Air Arm*, 157; Clark, "Major General Squier," 195–249; Reynolds, *Admiral Towers*, ix–xi, 106–109; Grossnick, *United States Naval Aviation*, 13, 21.

28. Reynolds, *Admiral Towers*, 110; Goldberg, ed., *History*, 10–11; Hennessy, *U.S. Army Air Arm*, 197, 252.

29. Hennessy, *U.S. Army Air Arm*, 197, 252.

30. Baer, *One Hundred Years*, 64; Goldberg, ed., *History*, 13; I. B. Holley Jr., *Ideas and Weapons: Exploitation of the Aerial Weapon by the United States in World War I; A Study in the Relationship of Technological Advance, Military Doctrine, and the Development of Weapons*, 37; James J. Hudson, *Hostile Skies: A Combat History of the American Air Service in World War I*, 2–3; Hennessy, *U.S. Army Air Arm*, 246–48; Turnbull and Lord, *History*, 81–96; Grossnick, *United States Naval Aviation*, 23; Mersky, *U.S. Marine Corps Aviation*, 6–7; Foulois and Glines, *From the Wright Brothers*, 141; Arnold, *Global Mission*, 53; Harry Howe Ransom, "The Air Corps Act of 1926: A Study of the Legislative Process" (Ph.D. diss., Princeton University, 1953), 27–29; Evans and Grossnick memorandum.

31. Turnbull and Lord, *History*, 98–109; Baer, *One Hundred Years*, 64–82; Reynolds, *Admiral Towers*, 111–19, 120–23; Mersky, *U.S. Marine Corps Aviation*, 6; Millett and Maslowski, *For the Common Defense*, 359; William F. Trimble, *Wings For the Navy: A History of the Naval Aircraft Factory*, 19; Lawrence D. Sheely, ed., *Sailor of the Air: The 1917–1919 Letters & Dairy of USN CMM/A Irving Edward Sheely*, 3; Lee Kennett, *The First Air War, 1914–1918*, 206; Grossnick, *United States Naval Aviation*, 23–37; Evans and Grossnick memorandum.

32. Benjamin D. Foulois, "Air Service's Lessons Learned During the Great War," Jan. 29, 1919, box 7, folder 1, Papers of Benjamin Foulois, USAFAL, 2 (hereafter Foulois Papers); Ransom, "Air Corps Act of 1926," 34; Goldberg, ed., *History*, 34; Foulois and Glines, *From the Wright Brothers*, 143.

33. Clark, "Major General Squier," 281–82; Foulois, "Air Service's Lessons Learned," 23; Hudson, *Hostile Skies*, 5; Foulois and Glines, *From the Wright Brothers*, 144–45; Ransom, "Air Corps Act of 1926," 36–37; Gross, "George Owen Squier," 44–50; John F. Shiner, *Foulois and the U.S. Army Air Corps, 1931–1935*, 1–3, 8.

34. Ransom, "Air Corps Act of 1926," 36–37; Foulois and Glines, *From the Wright Brothers*, 145–47; John F. Victory, "Early Aeronautical Research," Speech at Air Research and Development Command (ARDC) Officers' Open Mess, Apr. 24, 1952, Baltimore, box 19, folder 2, John F. Victory Papers, USAFAL. Victory became the first employee of the NACA in 1915. He administered the organization from 1927–58, first as secretary and then as executive secretary. In 1958, NACA became the National Aeronautics and Space Administration (NASA). Victory retired as a special assistant to the NASA administrator in July, 1960.

35. Ransom, "Air Corps Act of 1926," 39–40.

36. Ibid.

37. Ibid., 36, 4043, 49; Foulois and Glines, *From the Wright Brothers*, 147; Goldberg, ed., *History*, 14; Arnold, *Global Mission*, 54.

38. Millett and Maslowski, *For the Common Defense*, 321–24; Hennessy, *U.S. Army Air Arm*, 131–34, 183–87; Francillon, *Air Guard*, 11–15; Gross, *Prelude to the Total Force*, 1–2; Mahon, *History*, 146; Henry Greenleaf Pearson, *A Business Man in Uniform: Raynal Cawthorne Bolling*, 66–84; Militia Bureau, "Annual Report of the Acting Chief of the Militia Bureau, 1916," 26–28; DuPre, *Air Force Biographical Dictionary*, 22.

39. Foulois, "Air Service's Lessons Learned," 3; Hudson, *Hostile Skies*, 13; Gross, *Prelude to the Total Force*, 12; Holley, *Ideas and Weapons*, 56; Foulois and Glines, *From the Wright Brothers*, 150–51; Maurer Maurer, comp. and ed., *The U.S. Air Service in World War I*, vol. 1, *The Final Report and a Tactical History*, 52–53. This history was one of four volumes of documents published by the Office of Air Force History. They were edited versions of the history and "Final Report" of U.S. Army air activities in Europe produced by Col. Edgar S. Gorrell and others for Maj. Gen. Mason M. Patrick, chief of the AEF Air Service. The Air Service published the final report in 1921. Another key document in that series was the "Tactical History" of the AEF's Air Service. Written by Lt. Col. William C. Sherman and a group of other officers in France at war's end, it was published by the Air Service in 1920.

40. Foulois and Glines, *From the Wright Brothers*, 151–53; Charles F. O'Connell Jr., "The Failure of the American Aeronautical Production and Procurement Effort During the First World War" (master's thesis, Ohio State University, 1978), 51–52; Maurer Maurer, comp. and ed., *The U.S. Air Service in World War I*, vol. 2, *Early Concepts of Military Aviation*, 131–33.

41. Hudson, *Hostile Skies*, 31; Maurer, *Early Concepts*, 2:14; Goldberg, ed., *History*, 14, 18; Ransom, "Air Corps Act of 1926," 51–52, 63; Weigley, *History*, 361; Alex Roland, *Model Research: The National Advisory Committee for Aeronautics, 1915–1918*, 1:37–38; Clark, "Major General Squier," 272–73.

42. O'Connell, "Failure," 17.

43. Foulois and Glines, *From the Wright Brothers*, 142–43; Arnold, *Global Mission*, 57;

Hudson, *Hostile Skies,* 6–7; Ransom, "Air Corps Act of 1926," 27–29; Elsbeth E. Freudenthal, *The Aviation Business: From Kitty Hawk to Wall Street,* 37; Glenn L. Martin, "The First Half-Century of Flight in America," *Journal of Aeronautical Sciences* (Feb., 1954): 75. Martin was one of America's pioneer aircraft manufacturers. In 1909 he established one of the first aircraft plants in the United States. His Glenn L. Martin Company, formed in 1929, specialized in bombers and transoceanic flying boats.

44. Benedict Crowell, *America's Munitions, 1917–1918,* 243, 251–52; Theodore M. Knappen, *Wings of War: An Account of the Important Contributions of the United States to Aircraft Invention, Engineering, Development, and Production During the World War,* 33, 39; O'Connell, "Failure," 32–35; Hudson, *Hostile Skies,* 17.

45. Weigley, *History,* 361; Roland, *Model Research,* 1:37–41; Clark, "Major General Squier," 272–80.

46. Crowell, *America's Munitions,* 266–67; Knappen, *Wings of War,* 69–70; O'Connell, "Failure," 77; William Glenn Cunningham, *The American Aircraft Industry: A Study in Industrial Location,* 37.

47. Clark, "Major General Squier," 287–89; Freudenthal, *Aviation Business,* 55; Hewes, *Army Organization,* 36.

48. Goldberg, ed., *History,* 15; Holley, *Ideas and Weapons,* 68–69; 78–79; Ransom, "Air Corps Act of 1926," 57; O'Connell, "Failure," 25–26; Mooney and Laymen, *Military Aeronautics,* 35.

49. Trimble, *Wings for the Navy,* 8–39; Gross, "George Owen Squier," 296–97.

50. Philip M. Flammer, "The Myth of the Lafayette Escadrille," *Aerospace Historian* 22, no. 1 (Mar., 1975): 23; idem., *The Vivid Air: The Lafayette Escadrille,* 5–10, 26, 181–83.

51. Goldberg, ed., *History,* 21–22; John H. Morrow Jr., *The Great War in the Air: Military Aviation from 1909 to 1921,* 271–72; James J. Cooke, *The U.S. Air Service in the Great War, 1917–1919,* 19–21; Hudson, *Hostile Skies,* 51–58.

52. Goldberg, ed., *History,* 21–22; Morrow, *Great War,* 271–72; Cooke, *U.S. Air Service,* 19–21; Hudson, *Hostile Skies,* 51–58.

53. Goldberg, ed., *History,* 22; Shiner, *Foulois,* 9–10; Robert P. White, "Air Power Engineer: MGen. Mason M. Patrick and the Air Force Road to Independence" (paper presented at the Air Force History and Museums Program Symposium, Arlington, Va., May 28, 1997), 8.

54. Goldberg, ed., *History,* 18–21; Morrow, *Great War,* 272; Hudson, *Hostile Skies,* 24–43; Rebecca Hancock Cameron, *Training To Fly: Military Flight Training, 1907–1945,* 107–108.

55. Cooke, *U.S. Air Service,* 25; Goldberg, ed., *History,* 21; Hudson, *Hostile Skies,* 42–43; Samuel S. Whitt, "Frank Lahm: Pioneer Military Aviator," *Aerospace Historian* 19, no. 4 (Dec., 1972): 174–76; Hennessy, *U.S. Army Air Arm,* 236.

56. R. D. Layman, *Naval Aviation in the First World War: Its Impact and Influence,* 10–12, 138–55, 172–79, 191, 200–204; Hezlet, *Aircraft and Sea Power,* 91–101; R. Ernest Dupuy and Trevor N. Dupuy, *The Encyclopedia of Military History: From 3500 B.C. to the Present.* 953–55, 964–67; Turnbull and Lord, *History,* 98–109; Reynolds, *Admiral Towers,* 111–19, 120–23; Mersky, *U.S. Marine Corps Aviation,* 6; Millett and Maslowski, *For the Common Defense,* 359; Trimble, *Wings for the Navy,* 19; Sheely, ed., *Sailor of the Air,* 3; Kennett, *First Air War,* 206; Grossnick, *United States Naval Aviation,* 26–31.

57. Maurer Maurer, comp. and ed., *The U.S. Air Service in World War I,* vol. 4, *Postwar Review,* 313; Goldberg, ed., *History,* 23–24; Stokesbury, *Short History,* 104–107; Hudson, *Hostile Skies,* 1–2.

58. Goldberg, ed., *History*, 23–27; Stokesbury, *Short History*, 106–108; Morrow, *Great War*, 336–40.

59. Ibid.

60. Crowell, *America's Munitions*, 235–37, 243, 250, 254, 291; O'Connell, "Failure," 90–92.

61. Millett and Maslowski, *For the Common Defense*, 352–53; Kennett, *First Air War*, 217–28; Morrow, *Great War*, 338–44; Richard P. Hallion, *Strike from the Sky: The History of Battlefield Air Attack, 1911–1945*, 12–41.

62. Van Creveld, *Technology and War*, 187–88.

63. Ibid., 188.

64. Millett and Maslowski, *For the Common Defense*, 359; Hezlet, *Aircraft and Sea Power*, 94–103; Mersky, *U.S. Marine Corps Aviation*, 7–12; Reynolds, *Admiral Towers*, 119–23; Roger A. Caras, *Wings of Gold: The Story of United States Naval Aviation*, 47–55; Turnbull and Lord, *History*, 144; Basil Collier, *A History of Air Power*, 81; Evans and Grossnick memorandum.

65. O'Connell, "Failure," passim; Crowell, *America's Munitions*, 235–67; Arnold, *Global Mission*, 57; Jacob A. Vander Meulen, *The Politics of Aircraft: Building an American Military Industry*, 1–10; Kennett, *First Air War*, 217–29; Morrow, *Great War*, 344.

CHAPTER 2: A GOLDEN AGE OF INNOVATION

1. E. T. Wooldridge, ed., *The Golden Age Remembered: U.S. Naval Aviation, 1919–1941*, xiii; Millis, *Arms and Men*, 238; van Creveld, *Technology and War*, 187–92, 211–13; Kenneth J. Hagan, *This People's Navy: The Making of American Sea Power*, 259–99; Allan R. Millett, *Semper Fidelis: The History of the United States Marine Corps*, 319–43; Weigley, *History*, 395–96; Ransom, "Air Corps Act of 1926," 75–78, 85.

2. David R. Mets, "Dive-Bombing Between the Wars," *Airpower Historian* 12, no. 3 (July, 1965): 85–86; Bilstein, *Flight in America*, 42–47; Millett and Maslowski, *For the Common Defense*, 368–85; Stokesbury, *Short History*, 116–56.

3. Russell F. Weigley, *The American Way of War: A History of United States Military Strategy and Policy*, 244–45; Millis, *Arms and Men*, 246–48; Ransom, "Air Corps Act of 1926," 89; Stokesbury, *Short History*, 132; Robert W. Love Jr., *History of the U.S. Navy*, 1:534–37; Alfred F. Hurley, *Billy Mitchell: Crusader for Air Power*, 40, 42–45; Ransom, "Air Corps Act of 1926," 128–29; William Mitchell and Townsend F. Dodd, "Recommendations Concerning the Establishment of a Department of Aeronautics," Apr. 17, 1919, box 1, Record Group 18, Army Air Force Records, Series 211 (U-Stencils), National Archives and Records Administration, Washington, D.C., 20–22; Timothy Moy, *War Machines: Transforming Technologies in the U.S. Military, 1920–1940*, 4, 27–30.

4. Moy, *War Machines*, 7–8; Corn, *Winged Gospel*, 11–12; Charles J. Gross, *Militiaman, Volunteer, and Professional: The Air National Guard and the American Military Tradition*, 39–40; Michael S. Sherry, *The Rise of American Air Power: The Creation of Armageddon*, 36–43.

5. Weigley, *History*, 399–403; Ransom, "Air Corps Act of 1926," 140–45, 199; Hurley, *Billy Mitchell*, 47–49; U.S. Congress, House, Hearings Before a Subcommittee of the Committee on Military Affairs, *United States Air Service*, 66th Cong., 2d sess., Dec., 1919–Feb., 1920, passim; Futrell, *Ideas, Concepts, Doctrine*, 17–20; Love, *History*, 1:537.

6. Curtis Alan Utz, "Carrier Aviation Policy and Procurement in the U.S. Navy, 1936–1940" (master's thesis, University of Maryland, 1989), 7; Thomas H. Hone, "Navy Air

Leadership: RADM W. A. Moffett as Chief of the Bureau of Aeronautics" (paper delivered at the joint meeting of the American Military Institute, Air Force Historical Foundation, and Military Classics Seminar, Apr., 1984), 1–2; Turnbull and Lord, *History*, 170; Hezlet, *Aircraft and Sea Power*, 107–108; Grossnick, *United States Naval Aviation*, 59; Bilstein, *Flight in America*, 45–46; Reynolds, *Admiral Towers*, 124–72; Weigley, *American Way of War*, 249; J. Gordon Vaeth, "Daughter of the Stars," *U.S. Naval Institute Proceedings* 99, no. 9 (Sept., 1973): 61–67; Grossnick, *United States Naval Aviation*, 40.

7. Moy, *War Machines*, 7–8; Hurley, *Billy Mitchell*, 40, 49, 60–64; Goldberg, ed., *History*, 29; Weigley, *History*, 400; Shiner, *Foulois*, 17; Gerald T. Cantwell, *Citizen Airmen: A History of the Air Force Reserve, 1946–1994*, 1–22; Arnold, *Global Mission*, 91–94; William F. Trimble, *Admiral William A. Moffett: Architect of Naval Aviation*, 65–88, 274–75; Turnbull and Lord, *History*, 186–92; Love, *History*, 1:538–39.

8. Hurley, *Billy Mitchell*, 56–57, 84; Ransom, "Air Corps Act of 1926," 174; Goldberg, ed., *History*, 31–32; Millett and Maslowski, *For the Common Defense*, 370; Weigley, *History*, 561; Shiner, *Foulois*, 18; Goldberg, ed., *History*, 32.

9. Louis A. Peake, "Major General Mason M. Patrick: Military Aviation Pioneer," *American Aviation Historical Society Journal* 26, no. 3 (fall, 1981): 200–204; Mason M. Patrick, *The United States in the Air*, 89–90; Ransom, "Air Corps Act of 1926," 218; Hurley, *Billy Mitchell*, 68–69.

10. Hurley, *Billy Mitchell*, 89–93; Peake, "General Patrick," 203; Robert McHenry, ed., *Webster's American Military Biographies*, 311; Myron Smith, "Patrick, Mason Mathews," in *Dictionary of American Military Biography*, ed. Spiller, 2:826–29; "Diaries of Mason M. Patrick, Chief of Air Service, 1921–1924," passim, box 6, folders 8 and 9, Foulois Papers.

11. Hurley, *Billy Mitchell*, 101–107; David R. Mets, *Master of Airpower: General Carl A. Spaatz*, 62; Millett and Maslowski, *For the Common Defense*, 368–71; Roger G. Miller, "The U.S. Army Air Corps and the Search for Autonomy" (paper presented at the Air Force History and Museums Program Symposium, Arlington, Va., May 28, 1997), 3; DuPre, *Air Force Biographical Dictionary*, 74–75, 171; "AUSA Leader Cites Limits and Failures of Air Power," *Air Force Magazine*, Apr., 2001, 20.

12. White, "MGen. Mason M. Patrick," 2–5, 12; Patrick, *United States*, 89–93; Peake, "General Patrick," 203; McHenry, ed., *Webster's American Military Biographies*, 311; Smith, "Patrick, Mason Mathews," 826–29; "Diaries of Mason M. Patrick"; Goldberg, ed., *History*, 32–34; Trimble, *Admiral Moffett*, 66–90; Love, *History*, 1:538–39.

13. Aeronautical Chamber of Commerce of America, *The Aircraft Yearbook for 1934*, 114–15; Patrick, *United States*, 98; John B. Rae, *Climb to Greatness: The American Aviation Industry, 1920–1960*, 7; U.S. Army Air Service, *Annual Report of the Chief of the Air Service for the Fiscal Year Ending June 30, 1921*, 31; Mansfield, *Vision*, 42; Goldberg, ed., *History*, 33; Vander Meulen, *Politics of Aircraft*, 2–5, 57–58; White, "MGen. Mason M. Patrick," 12–13, 25–27.

14. Millett and Maslowski, *For the Common Defense*, 371; Ransom, "Air Corps Act of 1926," 338–40; Goldberg, ed., *History*, 36–37; Maurer Maurer, *Aviation in the U.S. Army, 1919–1939*, 441–43; Miller, "U.S. Army Air Corps," 5–6.

15. Millett and Maslowski, *For the Common Defense*, 371; Love, *History*, 1:546; Hezlet, *Aircraft and Sea Power*, 116; Trimble, *Admiral Moffett*, 65–199; Charles M. Melhorn, *Two-Block Fox: The Rise of the Aircraft Carrier, 1911–1929*, 4–5, 33–38; Reynolds, *Admiral Towers*, 176–87; Stokesbury, *Short History*, 132; Turnbull and Lord, *History*, 151–70, 186–92.

16. Graham A. Cosmas, "The Formative Years of Marine Corps Aviation, 1912–1939," *Aerospace Historian* 24, no. 2 (June, 1977): 87–90; Millett, *Semper Fidelis,* 333–35; Mersky, *U.S. Marine Corps Aviation,* 13–19; Evans and Grossnick memorandum.

17. Reynolds, *Admiral Towers,* 126–68; Grossnick, *United States Naval Aviation,* 39; Terry Gwynn-Jones, *Farther and Faster: Aviation's Pioneering Years, 1909–1939,* 182–95.

18. Goldberg, ed., *History,* 34–35; Patrick, *United States,* 115–24; Eugene M. Emme, *Aeronautics and Astronautics. An American Chronology of Science and Technology in the Exploration of Space, 1915–1960,* 10, 17; Gwynn-Jones, *Farther and Faster,* 189–95.

19. Ernest A. McKay, *A World to Conquer: The Story of the First Round-the-World Flight by the U.S. Army Air Service,* passim; Emme, *Aeronautics and Astronautics,* 18; Thomas G. Foxworth, *The Speed Seekers,* 4–5, 16; Gwynn-Jones, *Farther and Faster,* 103–78; Hallion, *Test Pilots,* 88–94; Gibbs-Smith, *Aviation,* 185, 190; Ransom, "Air Corps Act of 1926," 230.

20. Patrick, *United States,* 97; Goldberg, ed., *History,* 29; U.S. Army Air Service, *Annual Report of the Air Service, Fiscal Year 1919,* 55; Freudenthal, *Aviation Business,* 62–63; Harold Mansfield, *Vision: A Saga of the Sky,* 30–31; Howard Mingos, "Birth of an Industry," in *The History of the American Aircraft Industry: An Anthology,* ed. G. R. Simanson, 53.

21. Aeronautical Chamber of Commerce of America, *Aircraft Yearbook for 1934,* 114–15; Patrick, *United States,* 98; Rae, *Climb to Greatness,* 7; U.S. Army Air Service, *Annual Report, 1921,* 31; Mansfield, *Vision,* 42; Goldberg, ed., *History,* 33; Vander Meulen, *Politics of Aircraft,* 2–5, 57–58; White, "MGen. Mason M. Patrick," 12–13.

22. Trimble, *Admiral Moffett,* 65–199; Melhorn, *Two-Block Fox,* 4–5, 33–38; Reynolds, *Admiral Towers,* 176–87; Stokesbury, *Short History,* 132; Turnbull and Lord, *History,* 151–70, 186–92; Utz, "Carrier Aviation Policy," 19; Roland, *Model Research,* 1:88, 93, 98, 113–16; Hunsaker, "Forty Years," 257–59; Gray, *Frontiers of Flight,* 16.

23. Aeronautical Chamber of Commerce of America, *Aircraft Yearbook for 1934,* 114–15; Patrick, *United States,* 98; Rae, *Climb to Greatness,* 7, 58–73; Mansfield, *Vision,* 42; Vander Meulen, *Politics of Aircraft,* 2–5, 57–58; White, "MGen. Mason M. Patrick," 12–13, 25–27; Gibbs-Smith, *Aviation,* 174, 197–204.

24. Melvin Kranzberg and Carroll W. Pursell Jr., eds., *Technology in Western Civilization,* vol. 2, *Technology in the Twentieth Century,* 160.

25. Phillip S. Meilinger, "The Impact of Technology and Design Choice on the Development of U.S. Fighter Aircraft," *American Aviation Historical Society Journal* 36, no. 1 (spring, 1991): 60–69.

26. Aeronautical Chamber of Commerce of America, *Aircraft Yearbook for 1934,* 114–15; Patrick, *United States,* 98; Rae, *Climb to Greatness,* 7, 58–73; Mansfield, *Vision,* 42; Vander Meulen, *Politics of Aircraft,* 2–5, 57–58; White, "MGen. Mason M. Patrick," 12–13, 25–27; Gibbs-Smith, *Aviation,* 174, 197–204; Grossnick, *United States Naval Aviation,* 47.

27. Thomas H. Greer, *The Development of Air Doctrine in the Army Air Arm, 1917–1941,* 36–37; Futrell, *Ideas, Concepts, Doctrine,* 32–33; Doris A. Canham, *Development and Production of Fighter Aircraft for the United States Air Force,* 3, 5–36; Ross G. Hoyt, "Metamorphosis of the Fighter," *Air Force Magazine,* Oct., 1975, 20; Biddle, *Barons of the Sky,* 166–67; Gibbs-Smith, *Aviation,* 180–95.

28. Moy, *War Machines,* 36–39.

29. Irving Brinton Holley Jr., *Buying Aircraft: Materiel Procurement for the Army Air Forces,* 6–42; Rae, *Climb to Greatness,* 84–85; Freudenthal, *Aviation Business,* 118.

30. Utz, "Carrier Aviation Policy," 7–8; Love, *History,* 1:543–45; Grossnick, *United States Naval Aviation,* 47–73, 423; Hezlet, *Aircraft and Seapower,* 120–21, 124–25, 131, 134–35; Grossnick, *United States Naval Aviation,* 81–86; Mets, "Dive Bombing," 86; idem., *Master of Airpower,* 88–89.

31. Utz, "Carrier Aviation Policy," 8–9; Hezlet, *Aircraft and Sea Power,* 112–16; Bilstein, *Flight in America,* 47–48, 130–31; Robin Higham, *Air Power: A Concise History,* 62; Melhorn, *Two-Block Fox,* 24–25; Stokesbury, *Short History,* 135.

32. Hezlet, *Aircraft and Sea Power,* 107–108, 120, 125–26; Bilstein, *Flight in America,* 129; Turnbull and Lord, *History,* 172–73; Trimble, *Admiral Moffett,* 111–40, 264-267; Armstrong, "Aircraft Go to Sea," 84; Grossnick, *United States Naval Aviation,* 84, 89.

33. Kennett, *A History of Strategic Bombing,* 86–88; White, "MGen. Mason M. Patrick," 16–18; Sherry, *Rise of American Air Power,* 51; Miller, "U.S. Army Air Corps," 1–6.

34. Millett and Maslowski, *For the Common Defense,* 383; Shiner, *Foulois,* 44–50; Greer, *Development of Air Doctrine,* 44–75; Wesley Frank Craven and James Lea Cate, eds., *The Army Air Forces in World War II,* vol. 1, *Plans And Early Operations, January 1939 to August 1942,* 46; Miller, "U.S. Army Air Corps," 8–9.

35. Sherry, *Rise of American Air Power,* 54–57; Stokesbury, *Short History,* 151; Jeffery S. Underwood, "The Army Air Corps under Franklin D. Roosevelt: The Influence of Air Power on the Roosevelt Administration, 1933–1941" (Ph.D. diss., Louisiana State University, 1988), 154.

36. Greer, *Development of Air Doctrine,* 36–37, 39–40, 44–47; Futrell, *Ideas, Concepts, Doctrine,* 32–33; Canham, *Development and Production,* 35–36; Hoyt, "Metamorphosis," 20; Metz, *Master of Airpower,* 67–68; Millett and Maslowski, *For the Common Defense,* 383, 384.

37. Foulois and Glines, *From the Wright Brothers,* 229; Futrell, *Ideas, Concepts, Doctrine,* 42; Craven and Cate, *Plans and Early Operations,* 1:30, 46, 60–61, 62; Millett and Maslowski, *For the Common Defense,* 384–85; Arnold, *Global Mission,* 157; Millis, *Arms and Men,* 269; Shiner, *Foulois,* 54–56, 63; Robert W. Krauskopf, "The Army and the Strategic Bomber, 1930–1939," pt. 1, *Military Affairs* 22, no. 2 (summer, 1958): 87.

38. Claire L. Chennault, *Way of a Fighter: The Memoirs of Claire Lee Chennault,* 24. William M. Leary Jr., "Chennault, Claire Lee," in *Dictionary of American Military Biography,* ed. Spiller, 170–71.

39. John F. Shiner, "Foulois, Benjamin D.," in *Dictionary of American Military Biography,* ed. Spiller, 1:345; idem., *Foulois,* 125–27; Vander Meulen, *Politics of Aircraft,* 132–40.

40. Shiner, *Foulois,* 142–45; Clarence H. Danhoff, *Government Contracting and Technological Change,* 26–29; Vander Meulen, *Politics of Aircraft,* 137–40; Foulois and Glines, *From the Wright Brothers,* 233–62; U.S. Congress, House, Committee on Military Affairs, "Investigation of Profiteering in Military Aircraft Under HR 275," HR 2060, 73d Cong., 2d sess., June 15, 1934, 1–3, 12–14; Eugene M. Emme, "The American Dimension," 71; Futrell, *Ideas, Concepts, Doctrine,* 36–37; Goldberg, ed., *History,* 39–40; Miller, "U.S. Army Air Corps," 3.

41. Holley, *Buying Aircraft,* 139–46; Aeronautical Chamber of Commerce of America, *The Aircraft Yearbook for 1936,* 62–65. Goldberg, ed., *History,* 40; Shiner, *Foulois,* 170; Utz, "Carrier Aviation Policy," 28–29.

42. Benjamin S. Kelsey, *The Dragon's Teeth: The Creation of United States Air Power for World War II,* 131

43. Goldberg, ed., *History,* 39–40; Futrell, *Ideas, Concepts, Doctrine,* 36–39; Emme, "American Dimension," 71; Arnold, *Global Mission,* 145–48; Maurer, *Aviation in the Army,* 315–29; DuPre, *Air Force Biographical Dictionary,* 6; John F. Shiner, "The Birth of the GHQ Air Force," *Military Affairs* 42, no. 3 (Oct., 1978): 113–19; Bernard C. Nalty, ed., *Winged Shield, Winged Sword: A History of the United States Air Force,* 1:126.

44. Jean H. Dubuque, *The Development of the Heavy Bomber, 1918–1994,* 15–17; Futrell, *Ideas, Concepts, Doctrine,* 36, 44; Mary R. Self, *History of the Development and Production of USAF Heavy Bombardment Aircraft, 1917–1949,* 18–19; Mansfield, *Vision,* 117–24; James Eastman, "The Development of Big Bombers," *Aerospace Historian* 25, no. 4 (Dec., 1978): 214–15; Gordon Swanborough and Peter M. Bowers, *United States Military Aircraft Since 1908,* 87–96.

45. Futrell, *Ideas, Concepts, Doctrine,* 32; Greer, *Development of Air Doctrine,* 46; Swanborough and Bowers, *U.S. Military Aircraft,* 83–84; James C. Fahey, *Army Aircraft (Heavier-Than-Air), 1908–1946,* 22; Miller, "U.S. Army Air Corps," 10.

46. Goldberg, ed., *History,* 41–43; Futrell, *Ideas, Concepts, Doctrine,* 41–47; Weigley, *History,* 560; U.S. Congress, Senate, Committee on Military Affairs, "To Provide More Effectively for National Defense By Further Increasing the Effectiveness and Efficiency of the Air Corps of the Army of the United States, SR 2131, 74th Cong., 2d sess., May 12, 1936, 1–2; U.S. Congress, House, Committee on Appropriations, "Military Establishment Appropriations Bill for [FY] 1938, Hearings before a Subcommittee of the Committee on Appropriations," 75th Cong., 1st sess., 1937, 516–20, 533.

47. Dubuque, *Development of the Heavy Bomber,* 18; Mansfield, *Vision,* 133–40; Eastman, "Development of Big Bombers," 214–15; Swanborough and Bowers, *U.S. Military Aircraft,* 151.

48. Underwood, "Army Air Corps," 1–191; Miller, "U.S. Army Air Corps," 6–7; Goldberg, ed., *History,* 42–43.

49. Fred Green, "The Military View of American National Policy, 1904–1940," 354–76; Millett and Maslowski, *For the Common Defense,* rev. and enl. ed., 391–92, 396–401, 404–405, 407; Love, *History,* 1:592–93; Hezlet, *Aircraft and Sea Power,* 124–25; Weigley, *History,* 420; Craven and Cate, *Plans and Early Operations,* 1:103–50.

50. Millett and Maslowski, *For the Common Defense,* 387; Underwood, "Army Air Corps," 165–68; Hagan, *This People's Navy,* 284–86; Love, *History,* 607; Weigley, *History,* 420; Turnbull and Lord, *History,* 284–85; Grossnick, *United States Naval Aviation,* 77–96, 423.

51. Millett and Maslowski, *For the Common Defense,* 387; Hagan, *This People's Navy,* 607; Turnbull and Lord, *History,* 284–85; Hezlet, *Aircraft and Sea Power,* 120–21, 131, 134–38, 194–95; Utz, "Carrier Aviation Policy," 31–33; John Major, "The Navy Plans for War, 1937–1941," in *New Interpretations of American Naval History, 1775–1985,* ed. Kenneth J. Hagan, 241.

52. Hezlet, *Aircraft And Sea Power,* 120–21, 131, 134–38, 194–95; Gordon Swanborough and Peter M. Bowers, *United States Navy Aircraft Since 1911,* 181–82; Utz, "Carrier Aviation Policy," 31–33; William M. Leary, "Assessing the Japanese Threat: Air Intelligence Prior to Pearl Harbor," *Aerospace Historian* 34, no. 4 (Dec., 1987): 273, 277; Evans and Grossnick memorandum.

53. Leary, "Assessing the Japanese Threat," 274.

54. Ibid.

55. Ibid., 276–77.

56. Miller, "U.S. Army Air Corps," 7; Bilstein, *Flight in America,* 130–31; Hezlet, *Aircraft and Sea Power,* 120–34; Turnbull and Lord, *History,* 285–303; Millett and Maslowski, *For the Common Defense,* 373, 387; Millett, *Semper Fidelis,* 334–35; Cosmas, "Formative Years," 91–93; Mersky, *U.S. Marine Corps Aviation,* 25–28.

57. Underwood, "Army Air Corps," 196–99; Forrest C. Pogue, "George Catlett Marshall," in *Dictionary of American Military Biography,* ed. Spiller, 2:735; Goldberg, ed., *History,* 43–45; Miller, "U.S. Army Air Corps," 12–14; Futrell, *Ideas, Concepts, Doctrine,* 48–49; Stokesbury, *Short History,* 150—51; Underwood, "Army Air Corps," 215–16, 222; Sherry, *Rise of American Air Power,* 69–75; Richard J. Overy, *The Air War, 1939–1945,* 3.

58. Futrell, *Ideas, Concepts, Doctrine,* 49; Underwood, "Army Air Corps," 214; Millett and Maslowski, *For the Common Defense,* 388–89; Sherry, *Rise of American Air Power,* 76–82; Bilstein, *Flight in America,* 128–29; Miller, "U.S. Army Air Corps," 11; Rae, *Climb to Greatness,* 108–109.

59. Wesley Frank Craven and James Lea Cate, eds., *The Army Air Forces In World War II,* vol. 6, *Men and Planes,* 6:307–308; Reynolds, *Admiral Towers,* 317–18, 323–29; Trimble, *Wings for the Navy,* 205–206; Love, *History,* 1:618–22; Millett and Maslowski, *For the Common Defense,* 395–98; Nalty, ed., *Winged Shield:* 1:165–73; Futrell, *Ideas, Concepts, Doctrine,* 55; Truman R. Clark, *Flood of Victory: The American Logistics Mass In World Wars I And II,* 70.

60. Kenneth Schaffel, *The Emerging Shield: The Air Force and the Evolution of Continental Air Defense, 1945–1960,* 6–36; Craven and Cate, eds., *Men and Planes,* 6:307–308; van Creveld, *Technology and War,* 187–92, 211–13; Daniel T. Kuehl, "RADAR," in *Oxford Companion,* ed. Chambers, 586–87; Thomas S. Snyder, ed., *Air Force Communications Command, 1938–1991: An Illustrated History. Third Edition,* (Scott AFB, Illinois: 1991), 1–3; Carol E. Stokes, "Communications," in *Oxford Companion,* ed. Chambers, 171–72; Grossnick, *United States Naval Aviation,* 22, 82–85, 96; Millett and Maslowski, *For the Common Defense,* 395–96; Nalty, ed., *Winged Shield,* 1:165; Futrell, *Ideas, Concepts, Doctrine,* 55.

61. Reynolds, *Admiral Towers,* 317–18, 323–29; Trimble, *Wings for the Navy,* 205–206; Love, *History,* 1:618–19, 622, 629–31; Millett and Maslowski, *For the Common Defense,* 394–98; Nalty, ed., *Winged Shield,* 1:165; Millett, *Semper Fidelis,* 185–88, 346; Ronald H. Spector, *Eagle Against the Sun: The American War with Japan,* 58–59; Grossnick, *United States Naval Aviation,* 101–103.

62. Reynolds, *Admiral Towers,* 295; Richard Shipman, *Wings at the Ready: 75 Years of the Naval Air Reserve,* 30; Nalty, ed., *Winged Shield,* 1:179–84; Richard G. Davis, *HAP: Henry H. Arnold, Military Aviator,* 21; Francillon, *Air Guard,* 10; Futrell, *Ideas, Concepts, Doctrine,* 50–51; OH, HQ USAFRES, "Brief History," 1; Cantwell, *Citizen Airmen,* 20–21; Memo for the Assistant Chief of Air Staff-1, from Col. Sweetser, Chief, Reserve & National Guard Division, AC/AS-1, Subject: "Progress Report RES-ROTC-NG Affairs," n.d., with attachment: "Composition of Personnel in AAF by Component and Aeronautical Status (As of 25 July 1945)," Archives of the Directorate of Historical Services, Headquarters, Air Force Reserve Command, Robins AFB, Ga.; Shipman, *Wings at the Ready,* 30–31.

63. The Air Corps and the Air Force Combat Command (formerly the GHQ Air Force) were subordinate arms of the USAAF. Within a year, General Marshall made the USAAF a coequal branch of the army with the Ground Forces and the Services of Supply.

64. Nalty, ed., *Winged Shield,* 1:179–84; Davis, *HAP,* 21; Millett and Maslowski, *For the Common Defense,* 393–402; idem., *For the Common Defense,* rev. and enl. ed., 418;

Overy, *Air War*, 62–82, 152–54; Emme, "American Dimension," 78–79; Joel R. Davidson, *The Unsinkable Fleet: The Politics of U.S. Navy Expansion in World War II*, 24–28; Turnbull and Lord, *History*, 322; Hagan, *This People's Navy*, 294–306; Arthur Percy, *A History of U.S. Coast Guard Aviation*, 20–28, Schaffel, *Emerging Shield*, 36–38.

CHAPTER 3: ARMAGEDDON

1. Spector, *Eagle Against the Sun*, xi; Overy, *Air War*, 82–83.
2. Overy, *Air War*, 82–83; Spector, *Eagle Against the Sun*, xi.
3. Roger G. Miller, "Air Transport on the Eve of Pearl Harbor," *Air Power History* 45, no. 2 (summer, 1998): 26–37; Goldberg, ed., *History*, 53; Bilstein, *Flight in America*, 162; "Military Airlift Command," *Air Force Magazine*, May, 1998, 64; Reynolds, *Admiral Towers*, 375; Howard Lee Scamehorn, "American Air Transport and Airpower Doctrine in World War II," *Airpower Historian* 8, no. 3 (July, 1961): 148–50; Roger E. Bilstein, *Airlift and Airborne Operations in World War II*, 1–11; Michael D. Doubler, "Airborne Warfare," in *Oxford Companion*, ed. Chambers, 14–15; van Creveld, *Technology and War*, 195–96.
4. Bilstein, *Flight in America*, 162.
5. Goldberg, ed., *History*, 147; Scamehorn, "American Air Transport," 151; Betty R. Kennedy, ed., *Anything, Anywhere, Anytime: An Illustrated History of the Military Airlift Command, 1941–1991*, 18–23.
6. Scamehorn, "American Air Transport," 148–55.
7. Bilstein, *Airlift and Airborne Operations*, 46–47.
8. Millett and Maslowski, *For the Common Defense*, rev. and enl. ed., 427–32; idem., *For the Common Defense*, 408; Overy, *Air War*, 150; Holley, *Buying Aircraft*, 248–49; R. Elberton Smith, *The Army and Economic Mobilization*, 98–103; Craven and Cate, eds., *Plans and Early Operations*, 1:106–107; Nalty, ed., *Winged Shield*, 1:234–35, 237; Craven and Cate, eds., *Men and Planes*, 6:307, 350–51; Rae, *Climb to Greatness*, 121–22; Thomas H. Hone, "Fighting on Our Ground: The War of Production, 1920–1942," *Naval War College Review* 45, no. 2 (spring, 1992): 93–107.
9. Roger E. Bilstein, *The American Aerospace Industry*, 72–77, 193; Rae, *Climb to Greatness*, 132–37, 141–46; Stephen L. McFarland, *A Concise History of the U.S. Air Force*, 20; Nalty, ed., *Winged Shield*, 1:239; Craven and Cate, eds., *Men and Planes*, 6:320–28, 350–51; Overy, *Air War*, 150; Hone, "Fighting on Our Own Ground," 96; Thomas H. Hone, "Naval Reconstitution, Surge, and Mobilization: Once and Future," *Naval War College Review* 47, no. 3 (summer, 1994): 75; Norman Polmar to author, Aug. 29, 2001.
10. Rae, *Climb to Greatness*, 162–67; Swanborough and Bowers, *U.S. Navy Aircraft*, 402–403.
11. Danhoff, *Government Contracting*, 33–36; Emme, "American Dimension," 78; Theodore C. Von Karman with Lee Edson, *The Wind and Beyond: Theodore Von Karman, Pioneer in Aviation and Pathfinder in Space*, 243–54, 264–66; Craven and Cate, eds., *Men and Planes*, 1:607–608; Millett and Maslowski, *For the Common Defense*, 413–14; Bilstein, *Flight in America*, 164–65; Overy, *Air War*, 187–92; Kuehl, "Radar," 586; Polmar to author.
12. Overy, *Air War*, 138–39; Turnbull and Lord, *History*, 316; Goldberg, ed., *History*, 94–95; Bilstein, *Flight in America*, 161–62; Reynolds, *Admiral Towers*, 375–81; Nalty, ed., *Winged Shield*, 1:251–62; Ann R. Johnson, "The WASP of World War II," *Aerospace Historian* 17, nos. 2 and 3 (summer-fall, 1970): 76–82; Morris J. MacGregor Jr., *Integration of The Armed Forces, 1940–1965*, 58–122; A. R. Buchanan, ed., *The Navy's Air War: A*

Mission Completed, 307–323, 354; Mattie E. Treadwell, *The Women's Army Corps,* 24–45, 113–21, 219–30, 281–95, 765; Kennedy, ed., *Anything, Anywhere, Anytime,* 30–31.

13. Goldberg, ed., *History,* 94–95; Overy, *Air War,* 136–39; Turnbull and Lord, *History,* 316; Reynolds, *Admiral Towers,* 375–82; Nalty, ed., *Winged Shield,* 1:251–62; Johnson, "WASP of World War II," 76–82; Alan L. Gropman, *The Air Force Integrates, 1945–1964,* 4–31; Polmar to author.

14. Millett and Maslowski, *For the Common Defense,* 403–10; Stokesbury, *Short History,* 195–96; Williamson Murray and Allan R. Millett, *A War to Be Won: Fighting the Second World War,* 304–305, 311.

15. DuPre, *Air Force Biographical Dictionary,* 8–10; Richard G. Davis, "Arnold, 'Hap'," in *Oxford Companion,* ed. Chambers, 62; John W. Huston, "Arnold, Henry Harley," in *Dictionary of American Military Biography,* ed. Spiller, 1:42–45.

16. Davis, "Arnold," 62; Huston, "Arnold," 43–44; DuPre, *Air Force Biographical Dictionary,* 9.

17. Millett and Maslowski, *For the Common Defense,* 415; Hagan, *This People's Navy,* 296–97; Eliot A. Cohen and John Gooch, "Failure to Learn: American Antisubmarine Warfare in 1942," *Military Misfortunes: The Anatomy of Failure in War,* (New York: Vintage Books, 1990), 59–62.

18. Millett and Maslowski, *For the Common Defense,* 415–17; Hagan, *This People's Navy,* 296–97; Buchanan, ed., *Navy's Air War,* 40–41; Cohen and Gooch, *Military Misfortunes,* 59–62, 67–68, 74–75; Richard C. Bowman, "Organizational Fanaticism: A Case Study of Allied Air Operations Against the U-Boat During World War II," *Airpower Historian* 10, no. 2 (Apr., 1963): 50–52; A. Timothy Warnock, *The Battle Against the U-Boat in the American Theater,* 2–13; Bernard C. Nalty, "Blimps and Dirigibles," in *Oxford Companion,* ed. Chambers, 80; William F. Althoff, *Sky Ships: A History of the Airship in the United States Navy,* 165–204; Goldberg, ed., *History,* 90; Nalty, ed., *Winged Shield,* 1:208–209; Overy, *Air War,* 71; Hezlet, *Aircraft and Sea Power,* 272–81.

19. Clark Reynolds, "Aircraft Carriers," in *Oxford Companion to American Military History,* 16; Polmar to author; Buchanan, ed., *Navy's Air War,* 41–45; Henry M. Deter, "Development of the Escort Carrier," *Military Affairs* 12, no. 2 (summer, 1948): 79–83. Deter headed the Aviation History Unit in the Office of the Chief of Naval Operations when this article was published.

20. Hezlet, *Aircraft and Sea Power,* 282–87; Baer, *One Hundred Years,* 202–204; Millett and Maslowski, *For the Common Defense,* 416–17; Hagan, *This People's Navy,* 298; Deter, "Development of the Escort Carrier," 83–85; Cohen and Gooch, *Military Misfortunes,* 85, 91; Warnock, *Battle Against the U-Boat,* 13–29; Buchanan, ed., *Navy's Air War,* 40–45; Baer, *One Hundred Years,* 203–204; Polmar to author.

21. Baer, *One Hundred Years,* 204–205.

22. Ibid.

23. Bilstein, *Flight in America,* 133–36; Stokesbury, *Short History,* 196; Grossnick, *United States Naval Aviation,* 121; Nalty, ed., *Winged Shield,* 1:270–79; Overy, *Air War,* 64–65; Buchanan, ed., *Navy's Air War,* 50–56

24. Overy, *Air War,* 68–69; Nalty, ed., *Winged Shield,* 1:270–78; Bilstein, *Flight in America,* 135–36; Overy, *Air War,* 64–69; Daniel R. Mortensen, ed., *Airpower and Ground Armies: Essays on the Evolution of Anglo-American Air Doctrine, 1940–43,* xiii–xvi, 45–82; Millett and Maslowski, *For the Common Defense,* 423; McFarland, *Concise History,* 23–24; Bilstein, *Flight in America,* 136.

25. Benjamin Franklin Cooling, "A History of U.S. Army Aviation," *Aerospace Historian* 21, no. 2 (June, 1974): 102–103; Frederick A. Bergerson, *The Army Gets an Air Force: Tactics of Insurgent Bureaucratic Politics*, 29–37.

26. Millett and Maslowski, *For the Common Defense*, 423–24, 435–36; Nalty, ed., *Winged Shield*, 1:278–80; Stokesbury, *Short History*, 198; Overy, *Air War*, 74–75.

27. Thomas Alexander Hughes, *Overlord: General Pete Quesada and the Triumph of Tactical Air Power in World War II*, 94–102; Millet and Maslowski, *For the Common Defense*, rev. and enl. ed., 444–45; Bilstein, *Flight in America*, 137–38; Nalty, ed., *Winged Shield*, 1:289–92; Stokesbury, *Short History*, 224; Buchanan, ed., *Navy's Air War*, 83–85; Polmar to author.

28. Millett and Maslowski, *For the Common Defense*, 424–26; Bilstein, *Flight in America*, 137–39; Nalty, ed., *Winged Shield*, 1:289–96; Stokesbury, *Short History*, 224; Buchanan, ed., *Navy's Air War*, 83–87; Stephen E. Ambrose, *The Supreme Commander: The War Years of General Dwight D. Eisenhower*, 270–72.

29. Alfred M. Beck, ed., *With Courage: The U.S. Army Air Forces In World War II*, 150–51; Millett and Maslowski, *For the Common Defense*, 437–40; Nalty, ed., *Winged Shield*, 1:284–87; Bilstein, *Flight in America*, 142–47; Stokesbury, *Short History*, 198–201; Overy, *Air War*, 74–75; Polmar to author.

30. Hallion, *Strike from the Sky*, 189; Beck, *With Courage*, 150–51; Millett and Maslowski, *For the Common Defense*, 437–40; Nalty, ed., *Winged Shield*, 1:284–87; Bilstein, *Flight in America*, 142–47; Stokesbury, *Short History*, 198–201; Overy, *Air War*, 74–75.

31. Overy, *Air War*, 75–78; Murray and Millett, *A War to Be Won*, 325–28; Nalty, ed., *Winged Shield*, 1:300–10; Bilstein, *Flight in America*, 143–45; Stokesbury, *Short History*, 229–33; Millett and Maslowski, *For the Common Defense*, 435–40, 446–51; Ambrose, *Supreme Commander*, 349–445.

32. Overy, *Air War*, 76–78; Bilstein, *Airlift and Airborne Operations*, 33–36; Millett and Maslowski, *For the Common Defense*, 449–54; Kennedy, ed., *Anything, Anywhere, Anytime*, 49–51; Nalty, ed., *Winged Shield*, 1:308–309; Edward T. Russell, *Leaping the Atlantic Wall: Army Air Forces Campaigns in Western Europe, 1942–1945*, 15–17.

33. Buchanan, ed., *Navy's Air War*, 93–96; Millett and Maslowski, *For the Common Defense*, rev. and enl. ed., 471.

34. Stokesbury, *Short History*, 233–35; Bilstein, *Flight in America*, 145; Buchanan, ed., *Navy's Air War*, 334; Polmar to author; Murray and Millett, *A War to Be Won*, 599–600; Roger D. Launius, "Air and Space Defense," in *Oxford Companion*, ed. Chambers, 13.

35. Murray and Millett, *A War to Be Won*, 330–31.

36. Stokesbury, *Short History*, 239–40; Bilstein, *Flight in America*, 145.

37. Nalty, ed., *Winged Shield*, 1:309–10, 313–15; Richard G. Davis, "World War II, U.S. Air Operations in: The Air War in Europe," in *Oxford Companion*, ed. Chambers, 832; Millett and Maslowski, *For the Common Defense*, 437–40; Russell, *Leaping the Atlantic Wall*, 30–31.

38. Overy, *Air War*, 90; Spector, *Eagle Against the Sun*, 17, 19.

39. Ibid., xiii, xiv, 118, 143–45; Hagan, *This People's Navy*, 309–10; Baer, *One Hundred Years*, 213–17; Millett and Maslowski, *For the Common Defense*, 432–34; idem., *For the Common Defense*, rev. and enl. ed., 422; Weigley, *American Way of War*, 276; Overy, *Air War*, 92–93; Beck, *With Courage*, 262.

40. Samuel Eliot Morison, *History of United States Naval Operations in World War II*, vol. 3, *The Rising Sun in the Pacific, 1931–April 1942*, 210–14, 257; idem., *History of United States Naval Operations in World War II*, vol. 4, *Coral Sea, Midway and Submarine Ac-*

tions, May 1942–August 1942, 19, 21–64, 90–159; Hagan, *This People's Navy,* 311–14; Spector, *Eagle Against the Sun,* 148–49; Baer, *One Hundred Years,* 212–17; Hezlet, *Aircraft and Sea Power,* 199–201, 220–22; Grossnick, *United States Naval Aviation,* 423.

41. Overy, *Air War,* 92; Hagan, *This People's Navy,* 311–14; Spector, *Eagle Against the Sun,* 176–78; Hezlet, *Aircraft and Sea Power,* 243–49; Stokesbury, *Short History,* 216–18.

42. Overy, *Air War,* 93–94.

43. Millett, *Semper Fidelis,* 364–68; Hagan, *This People's Navy,* 315–17; Spector, *Eagle Against the Sun,* 195; Stokesbury, *Short History,* 219; Millett and Maslowski, *For the Common Defense,* 422.

44. Thomas E. Griffith Jr., *MacArthur's Airman: General George C. Kenney and the War in the Southwest Pacific,* 231–47; Stokesbury, *Short History,* 242.

45. Stokesbury, *Short History,* 233–35, 242–46; Hagan, *This People's Navy,* 317–19; Nalty, ed., *Winged Shield,* 1:330–32; Stokesbury, *Short History,* 242; Joe Gray Taylor, "The American Experience in the Southwest Pacific," in Benjamin Franklin Cooling, ed., *Case Studies in the Development of Close Air Support,* 329; Edward J. Drea, "ULTRA," in *Oxford Companion,* ed. Chambers, 738–39.

46. Nalty, ed., *Winged Shield,* 1:249–50; Hagan, *This People's Navy,* 318; Griffith, *MacArthur's Airman,* 246.

47. Griffith, *MacArthur's Airman,* 246–47; Spector, *Eagle Against the Sun,* 299.

48. Griffith, *MacArthur's Airman,* 234; Millett and Maslowski, *For the Common Defense,* 422–23; Hagan, *This People's Navy,* 318–20; Weigley, *American Way of War,* 280; Millett, *Semper Fidelis,* 378–87; Spector, *Eagle Against the Sun,* 227–28, 244–46; Stokesbury, *Short History,* 219–20, 242; Hezlet, *Aircraft and Sea Power,* 265–66; Taylor, "American Experience," 295–330.

49. Spector, *Eagle Against the Sun,* 276–79.

50. Ibid., 244–46.

51. Hagan, *This People's Navy,* 319–20; Spector, *Eagle Against the Sun,* 257–58; Bilstein, *Flight in America,* 150–51; Hezlet, *Aircraft and Sea Power,* 292–93.

52. Hagan, *This Peoples' Navy,* 320; Spector, *Eagle Against the Sun,* 257–60, 283–84, 290–300; Weigley, *American Way of War,* 283–84; Henry M. Deter, "Tactical Use of Air Power in World War II: The Navy Experience," *Military Affairs* (winter, 1950): 192–98; Polmar to author.

53. Hagan, *This People's Navy,* 321–23; Spector, *Eagle Against the Sun,* 276–79; Millett, *Semper Fidelis,* 405–408; Stokesbury, *Short History,* 243–44; Clark G. Reynolds, *The Fast Carriers: The Forging of an Air Navy,* 79–109; Polmar to author.

54. Overy, *Air War,* 95; Stokesbury, *Short History,* 243–44; Bilstein, *Flight in America,* 151; Weigley, *American Way of War,* 298; Spector, *Eagle Against the Sun,* 302–12; Reynolds, *Fast Carriers,* 204; Hagan, *This People's Navy,* 321–25; Polmar to author.

55. Mansfield, *Vision,* 174–78; Hagan, *This People's Navy,* 325; Spector, *Eagle Against the Sun,* 487–90; Stokesbury, *Short History,* 244–45; Weigley, *American Way of War,* 282; Bilstein, *Flight in America,* 153–54, 156–58; Millett and Maslowski, *For the Common Defense,* 457–58; Overy, *Air War,* 97–98; Bilstein, *Airlift and Airborne Operations,* 38–43; Kennedy, ed., *Anything, Anywhere, Anytime,* 36–42; Beck, *With Courage,* 272–77; Murray and Millett, *A War to Be Won,* 504; Nalty, ed., *Winged Shield,* 1:335–45; Kenneth P. Werrell, *Blankets of Fire: U.S. Bombers Over Japan During World War II,* 225.

56. Millett and Maslowski, *For the Common Defense,* rev. and enl. ed., 464–65; Hagan, *This People's Navy,* 325–26; Spector, *Eagle Against the Sun,* 428–41; Reynolds, *Fast Carriers,*

253–300; Hezlet, *Aircraft and Sea Power,* 303, 313–14; Millett and Maslowski, *For the Common Defense,* 444–45.

57. Spector, *Eagle Against the Sun,* 423; Reynolds, *Fast Carriers,* 51–78, 233–34; Spiller, ed., *Dictionary of American Military Biography,* 3:1032–35.

58. Spector, *Eagle Against the Sun,* 423–24, 511–17, 529–30; Stokesbury, *Short History,* 247; Reynolds, *Fast Carriers,* 211–52; Millett, *Semper Fidelis,* 424–25.

59. Spector, *Eagle Against the Sun,* 480–87; Hagan, *This People's Navy,* 306; Polmar to author.

60. Millett and Maslowski, *For the Common Defense,* 461–62; Spector, *Eagle Against the Sun,* 492–503; Stokesbury, *Short History,* 247–53; Millett, *Semper Fidelis,* 408–409; Werrell, *Blankets of Fire,* 225–26; McFarland, *Concise History,* 38; Polmar to author.

61. Nalty, ed., *Winged Shield,* 1:342–43, 350–60; Werrell, *Blankets of Fire,* 226–30; Spector, *Eagle Against the Sun,* 503–505; Weigley, *American Way of War,* 307; McFarland, *Concise History,* 38–39.

62. Spector, *Eagle Against the Sun,* 536–40; Overy, *Air War,* 95; Weigley, *American Way of War,* 307–309; Hagan, *This People's Navy,* 327; Hezlet, *Aircraft and Sea Power,* 315–18; Werrell, *Blankets of Fire,* 235–38; Millett, *Semper Fidelis,* 408–409; Polmar to author.

63. Millett and Maslowski, *For the Common Defense,* 464–66; Weigley, *American Way of War,* 310–11; Werrell, *Blankets of Fire,* 230–41; DuPre, *Air Force Biographical Dictionary,* 233–34; William Head, "Hiroshima and Nagasaki, Bombings of," in *Oxford Companion,* ed. Chambers, 314–15; Spector, *Eagle Against the Sun,* 544–57; Nalty, ed., *Winged Shield,* 1:355–62, 364–65; Stokesbury, *Short History,* 255–56.

64. Stokesbury, *Short History,* 256; Reynolds, *Fast Carriers,* 379; Werrell, *Blankets of Fire,* 241.

65. Overy, *Air War,* 78–84; Bilstein, *Flight in America,* 158.

66. Murray and Millett, *A War to Be Won,* 334–35.

67. Ibid., 335.

68. Overy, *Air War,* 100.

69. Ibid.

70. Ibid., 101.

71. Overy, *Air War,* 205.

72. Ibid., 206.

73. John Rae, "Wartime Technology and Commercial Aviation," *Aerospace Historian* 20, no. 3 (Sept., 1973): 132.

74. Ibid., 131–36.

75. Ibid., 131, 136.

76. Ibid., 131.

77. Overy, *Air War,* 206.

78. Charles D. Bright, *The Jet Makers: The Aerospace Industry from 1945 to 1972,* 9; Overy, *Air War,* 203–11; Bilstein, *American Aerospace Industry,* 73; Cunningham, *Aircraft Industry,* 98–142; Corn, *Winged Gospel,* 65–66, 138–39.

CHAPTER 4: AN AGE OF LIMITS

1. Mark Clodfelter, *The Limits of Air Power: The American Bombing of North Vietnam,* 12; John Buckley, *Air Power in the Age of Total War,* 1–3, 198–203.

2. Buckley, *Air Power,* 200–202; Alex Roland, "Science, Technology, War, and the Military," in *Oxford Companion,* ed. Chambers, 641.

3. Roland, "Science, Technology, War," 642; Stokesbury, *Short History,* 259; Weigley, *American Way of War,* 366; Millett and Maslowski, *For the Common Defense,* 471–83.

4. Harvey M. Sapolsky, "Equipping the Armed Forces," *Armed Forces and Society* 14, no. 1 (fall, 1987): 116–18; Millett and Maslowski, *For the Common Defense,* 408, 476–82; Weigley, *American Way of War,* 365–75; idem., *History,* 485–501; Stokesbury, *Short History,* 259–60; Love, *History of the United States Navy,* 1:311; Millett, *Semper Fidelis,* 456–64; Richard G. Davis, *The 31 Initiatives: A Study in Air Force-Army Cooperation,* 9; Conrad C. Crane, *American Airpower Strategy in Korea, 1950–1953,* 21–22; Phillip S. Meilinger, *Hoyt S. Vandenberg: The Life of a General,* 125, 128–38; Gross, *Prelude to the Total Force,* 7–21; Cooling, "History," 104; Perry McCoy Smith, *The Air Force Plans for Peace, 1943–1945,* passim; Futrell, *Ideas, Concepts, Doctrine,* 103–105; Richard P. Hallion, *The Naval Air War in Korea,* 3–6; E. T. Wooldridge, ed., *Into the Jet Age: Conflict and Change in Naval Aviation, 1945–1975, An Oral History,* 10; Grossnick, *United States Naval Aviation,* 442, 593.

5. Bilstein, *Flight in America,* 192–95; Meilinger, *Hoyt S. Vandenberg,* 95–102; McFarland, *Concise History,* 44–45; Stokesbury, *Short History,* 259; Nalty, ed., *Winged Shield,* 1:380–81, 415, 426–31, 433; Roger G. Miller, *To Save a City: The Berlin Airlift, 1948–1949,* 1–108; Robin Higham, "Berlin Airlift," in *Oxford Companion,* ed. Chambers, 78.

6. Quoted in Miller, *To Save a City,* 109–10.

7. Stokesbury, *Short History,* 109.

8. Townsend Hoopes, "Forrestal, James V.," in *Oxford Companion,* ed. Chambers, 274–75; Stokesbury, *Short History,* 260.

9. Millett and Maslowski, *For the Common Defense,* 478–79; Stokesbury, *Short History,* 261; Marcelle Size Knaack, *Encyclopedia of U.S. Air Force Aircraft and Missile Systems,* 2:3–4.; Harry R. Borowski, *A Hollow Threat: Strategic Air Power and Containment before Korea,* 4–6, 190–210; idem., "Air Force Atomic Capability from V-J Day to the Berlin Blockade—Potential or Real ?" *Military Affairs* 44, no. 3 (Oct., 1980): 105–10; Jeffrey G. Barlow, "The Navy's View of the 'Revolt of the Admirals'," *Occasional Papers,* ed. Roger R. Trask, no. 1, 17–27; Crane, *American Airpower Strategy,* 19–21; Borowski, "Air Force Atomic Capability," 109; idem., *Hollow Threat,* 194–95; Richard G. Davis, "LeMay, Curtis E.," in *Oxford Companion,* ed. Chambers, 389.

10. Millett and Maslowski, *For the Common Defense,* 476–77; Stephen M. Millett, "The Capabilities of the American Nuclear Deterrent, 1945–1950," *Aerospace Historian* 27, no. 1 (Mar., 1980): 28–30; Meilinger, *Hoyt S. Vandenberg,* 150–57, 160–89; Knaack, *Encyclopedia,* 2:99–157, 205–94; Bilstein, *American Aerospace Industry,* 88–92; idem., *Flight in America,* 180–84; Robert Perry, "Trends in Military Aeronautics, 1908–1976," in Eugene M. Emme, ed., *Two Hundred Years of Flight in America: A Bicentennial Survey,* 150–52.

11. Nalty, ed., *Winged Shield,* 1:115, 412; Richard K. Smith, *Seventy-five Years of In-flight Refueling: Highlights, 1923–1998,* 1–51; Borowski, *Hollow Threat,* 195; Vernon Byrd, *Passing Gas: The History of In-Flight Refueling,* 88–89; *Aerial Refueling Highlights in the Air Force's First Decade, 1947–1957,* 1–16; J. C. Hopkins and Sheldon Goldberg, *The Development of Strategic Air Command, 1946–1986,* 34; "Flight Refueling," *Aviation Week,* Feb. 21, 1949, 17–18, 21.

12. Weigley, *American Way of War,* 368, 370–72, 377–78; Hagan, *This Peoples' Navy,* 331–37; Millett and Maslowski, *For the Common Defense,* 477, 481; Hezlet, *Aircraft and Sea Power,* 326–27; Millett, *Semper Fidelis,* 445–56; Love, *History,* 2:316–18; Jeffrey G.

Barlow, *Revolt of the Admirals: The Fight for Naval Aviation, 1945–1950*, 131–213; idem., "Navy's View," 17–21; Stokesbury, *Short History*, 261; Grossnick, *United States Naval Aviation*, 425; Norman Polmar to author, Oct. 7, 2001.

13. Barlow, "Navy's View," 25.

14. Hallion, *Naval Air War in Korea*, 22–24; Meilinger, *Hoyt S. Vandenberg*, 128–38, 147–48; Herman S. Wolk, "The Quiet Coup of 1949," *Air Force Magazine*, July, 1999, 76–81; Millett and Maslowski, *For the Common Defense*, 481–82.

15. Weigley, *American Way of War*, 378–91; Millett and Maslowski, *For the Common Defense*, 482–87; Meilinger, *Hoyt S. Vandenberg*, 160–89; Hallion, *Naval Air War in Korea*, 26–37; M. J. Armitage and R. A. Mason, *Air Power in the Nuclear Age*, 21–23; Clodfelter, *Limits of Air Power*, 12–15.

16. Thomas C. Hone, "Korea," in *Case Studies in the Achievement of Air Superiority*, ed. Benjamin Franklin Cooling, 453–57; Crane, *American Airpower Strategy*, 23–26, 34–39; Mike Worden, *Rise of the Fighter Generals: The Problem of Air Force Leadership, 1945–1982*, 41; Wayne Thompson and Bernard C. Nalty, *Within Limits: The U.S. Air Force and the Korean War*, 5–7; Marcelle Size Knaack, *Encyclopedia*, 1:8–9.

17. Thompson and Nalty, *Within Limits*, 7; Crane, *American Airpower Strategy*, 24–25; Hallion, *Naval Air War in Korea*, 22–23, 34–37; Hezlet, *Aircraft and Sea Power*, 328–30; Armitage and Mason, *Air Power*, 21–23.

18. Hallion, *Naval Air War in Korea*, 37–44; Allan R. Millett, "Korea, 1950–1953," 345–68; Crane, *American Airpower Strategy*, 24–30; Weigley, *American Way of War*, 385; Thompson and Nalty, *Within Limits*, 15–20.

19. Hallion, *Naval Air War in Korea*, 44–56; Millett, "Korea," 353–68; Weigley, *American Way of War*, 382–85; Thompson and Nalty, *Within Limits*, 15–20; Crane, *American Airpower Strategy*, 27–28.

20. Millett and Maslowski, *For the Common Defense*, 487–88; Weigley, *American Way of War*, 385–90; Hallion, *Naval Air War in Korea*, 57–65, 72–76; William T. Y'Blood, *MiG Alley: The Fight for Air Superiority*, 9–10; D. Clayton James, "MacArthur and the Chinese Intervention in the Korean War, September–December 1950," in *A New Equation: Chinese Intervention into the Korean War, Colloquium on Contemporary History, No. 3*, 5–7; Millett, "Korea," 369–70; Thompson and Nalty, *Within Limits*, 10–15, 20–32; Xiaoming Zhang, "China and the Air War in Korea, 1950–1953," *Journal of Military History* 62, no. 2 (Apr., 1998): 345–46, 349; Crane, *American Airpower Strategy*, 49–50, 53, 68, 83, 85–92, 99, 103, 130, 167–68.

21. Meilinger, *Hoyt S. Vandenberg*, 189; Millett and Maslowski, *For the Common Defense*, 488–92; Weigley, *American Way of War*, 385–90; Crane, *American Airpower Strategy*, 56–59, 70–71; Weigley, *History*, 505–506; Cantwell, *Citizen Airmen*, 87–119; OH, HQ USAFRES, "Brief History," 2; Gross, *Prelude to the Total Force*, 58–59; Shipman, *Wings at the Ready*, 41–43; Lawrence Kapp, *Involuntary Reserve Activations for U.S. Military Operations Since World War II*, 5; Millett, *Semper Fidelis*, 480–81; Reserve Officers Public Affairs Unit 4-1, *The Marine Corps Reserve: A History*, 179; Kapp, *Involuntary Reserve Activations*, 5.

22. James L. Abrahamson, "Economy And War," in *Oxford Companion*, ed. Chambers, 243; Weigley, *History*, 507; Bright, *Jet Makers*, 15, 62–64; E. Clifford Snyder, *History of Aircraft Production Problems during the Air Force Buildup (1950–1954)*, 1:20–23, 29, 34–35; Hagan, *This Peoples' Navy*, 341–43; Millett, *Semper Fidelis*, 505–506; Bilstein, *Flight in America*, 189; Cooling, "History," 104.

23. Bilstein, *Flight in America,* 189; Kennedy, ed., *Anything, Anywhere, Anytime,* 74–75, 77, 80; William M. Leary Jr., *Anything, Anywhere, Anytime: Combat Cargo in the Korean War,* 3–4, 34–35; Smith, *Seventy-five Years,* 33–37; Weigley, *History,* 521–22.

24. Hone, "Korea," 453–504; Y'Blood, *MiG Alley,* 43; Weigley, *American Way of War,* 392–93; Thompson and Nalty, *Within Limits,* 31–36, 46–49; Zhang, "China," 335–52; Gross, *Prelude to the Total Force,* 70; Eduard Mark, *Aerial Interdiction: Air Power and the Land Battle in Three American Wars,* 289–319.

25. Hallion, *Naval Air War in Korea,* 89–100; Millett, *Semper Fidelis,* 502; Millett, "Korea," 371–73, 383–99; Thompson and Nalty, *Within Limits,* 49–50.

26. Stephen E. Ambrose, *Eisenhower: Soldier and President,* 295; Millett and Maslowski, *For the Common Defense,* 501–503; Thompson and Nalty, *Within Limits,* 41–42, 51–60; Hallion, *The Naval Air War in Korea,* 120–36.

27. Millett and Maslowski, *For the Common Defense,* 501–504; Thompson and Nalty, *Within Limits,* 57–58; John Darrell Sherwood, *Officers in Flight Suits: The Story of American Air Force Fighter Pilots in the Korean War,* 8 and n 17; Tara Rigler, "DoD Discoloses New Korean War Casualty Figures," available at http://www.koreanwar.net/dod-03.htm.

28. Hallion, *Naval Air War in Korea,* 190–97, 204–208; Hone, "Korea," 497; Clodfelter, *Limits of Air Power,* 13–22; Millett, "Korea," 395–99.

29. Worden, *Rise,* 42–43.

30. Ibid., 43–45; Crane, *American Airpower Strategy,* 171–75.

31. Worden, *Rise,* 45–46; Hone, "Korea," 497; Crane, *American Airpower Strategy,* 172–75.

32. Hallion, *Naval Air War in Korea,* 190–97, 206; Hezlet, *Aircraft and Sea Power,* 328–30; Millett, "Korea," 396; Millett and Maslowski, *For the Common Defense,* 491; Hagan, *This People's Navy,* 343–52; Baer, *One Hundred Years,* 315–16, 335–40; Smith, *Seventy-five Years,* 47–48; Grossnick, *United States Naval Aviation,* 423, 448–49; Swanborough and Bowers, *U.S. Navy Aircraft,* 202–205, 517; Love, *History,* 2:380–84; Grossnick, *United States Naval Aviation,* 242, 426.

33. Love, *History,* 2:379–82; memorandum for record, June 27, 1997, Subject: "Post World War II Naval Aviation," copy in author's possession, 1–2.

34. Eduard Mark, *Defending the West: The United States Air Force and European Security, 1946–1948,* 36; Millett and Maslowski, *For the Common Defense,* 490–97.

35. Millett and Maslowski, *For the Common Defense,* 490–97; Launius, "Air and Space Defense," 13–14; "USAF Leaders Through the Years," *Air Force Magazine,* May, 1999, 42.

36. Marcelle Size Knaack, *Encyclopedia of U.S. Air Force Aircraft and Missile Systems,* vol. 2, *Post–World War II Bombers, 1945–1973,* 205–92, 351–97; Bilstein, *Flight in America,* 220–26; idem., *American Aerospace Industry,* 92–93; Francillon, *U.S. Air National Guard,* 181–82, 199.

37. Chuck Hansen, *U.S. Nuclear Weapons: The Secret History,* 109.

38. Dwight D. Eisenhower, *Mandate for Change: The White House Years, 1953–1956,* 446; Douglas Kinnard, *President Eisenhower and Strategy Management: A Study in Defense Politics,* 2–10; Ambrose, *Eisenhower,* 321; Weigley, *American Way of War,* 399–404; Millett and Maslowski, *For the Common Defense,* 509–12, 518; Buckley, *Air Power,* 207–208; Hagan, *This Peoples' Navy,* 350; Nalty, ed., *Winged Shield,* 2:74–75; Schaffell, *Emerging Shield,* 169–266.

39. Millett and Maslowski, *For the Common Defense,* 518; Schaffel, *Emerging Shield,* 268; Launius, "Air and Space Defense," 14.

40. Hagan, *This Peoples' Navy*, 346–53; Love, *History*, 1:375–84.

41. Millett, *Semper Fidelis*, 518–26, 534–35.

42. Gross, *Militiaman, Volunteer, and Professional*, 84–88; Abbott A. Brayton, "American Reserve Policies Since World War II," *Military Affairs* (Dec., 1972): 140. Shipman, *Wings at the Ready*, 49–50; Millett, *Semper Fidelis*, 552.

43. Hagan, *This Peoples' Navy*, 354–55; Millett and Maslowski, *For the Common Defense*, 527–28; Worden, *Rise*, 73–74; Buckley, *Air Power*, 202, 207–208; Nalty, ed., *Winged Shield*, 2:144–47, 152–55.

44. Nalty, ed., *Winged Shield*, 2:152–55.

45. Ambrose, *Eisenhower*, 379.

46. Nalty, ed., *Winged Shield*, 2:83–93; Robert J. Watson, *History of the Office of the Secretary of Defense*, vol. 4, *Into the Missile Age, 1956–1960*, 157–201; Hagan, *This People's Navy*, 355; Millett and Maslowski, *For the Common Defense*, 518–19.

47. Worden, *Rise*, 74; Buckley, *Air Power*, 6–11, 199–202; Millett and Maslowski, *For the Common Defense*, 531–36; Michael Beschloss, review of William E. Burrows, *By Any Means Necessary: America's Secret Air War in the Cold War*, *New York Times Book Review*, Dec. 16, 2001, reprinted in "The Early Bird," December, 2001, available at http://ebird.dtic.mil/dec2001; Weigley, *American Way of War*, 441–48; Ambrose, *Eisenhower*, 478.

48. Ambrose, *Eisenhower*, 536,

49. Ibid.

50. Ibid., 536–37.

51. Ibid.

52. Nalty, ed., *Winged Shield*, 2:102; James Kurth, "Military-Industrial Complex," *Oxford Companion*, ed. Chambers, 438–39; Rae, *Climb to Greatness*, 201, 212–13; Melvin Kranzberg, "Science-Technology and Warfare: Action, Reaction, and Interaction in the Post–World War II Era," in *Science, Technology and Warfare: Proceedings of the Third Military History Symposium, USAF Academy, 1969*, 162–65; Bilstein, *American Aerospace Industry*, 95–101.

53. Buckley, *Air Power*, 197–99; Bilstein, *American Aerospace Industry*, 106; James L. Clayton, "Industry and War," in *Oxford Companion*, ed. Chambers, 332.

54. Edgar F. Rains Jr., "Army Combat Branches: Aviation," in *Oxford Companion*, ed. Chambers, 59; DeLyle G. Redmond, "The Role of Attack Helicopters in Conventional War," *U.S. Army Aviation Digest*, Jan., 1972, 7; Lawrence Freedman, "Arms Race: Nuclear Arms," in *Oxford Companion*, ed. Chambers, 44.

55. Buckley, *Air Power*, 222.

CHAPTER 5: COLD WARRIORS

1. Weigley, *American Way of War*, 441–48; Worden, *Rise*, 110–11; Love, *History*, 2:482–85; Richard G. Head, "The Air Force A-7 Decision: The Politics of Close Air Support," *Aerospace Historian* 22, no. 4 (Dec., 1974): 219–24; Bilstein, *American Aerospace Industry*, 101–103; Millett and Maslowski, *For the Common Defense*, 531–36.

2. Millett and Maslowski, *For the Common Defense*, 533–36; Ambrose, *Eisenhower*, 501–502; Freedman, "Arms Race," 44; Weigley, *History*, 538–39, 542–44; William H. Tunner, *Over the Hump*, 287.

3. Tunner, *Over the Hump*, 287; Kennedy, ed., *Anything, Anywhere, Anytime*, 89–115, 122–23; Susan H. H. Young, "USAF Almanac: Gallery of USAF Weapons," *Air Force Maga-*

zine, May, 1998, 148–49, 151–52; Charles J. Gross, *Adapting the Force: Evolution of the Air National Guard's Air Mobility Mission*, 18–19.

4. Worden, *Rise*, 108–10.

5. Millett and Maslowski, *For the Common Defense*, 537; Brayton, "American Reserve Policies," 142; Gross, *Prelude to the Total Force*, 122–42; Shipman, *Wings at the Ready*, 52–54; Mark, *Defending the West*, 38.

6. Millett and Maslowski, *For the Common Defense*, 537–39; Weigley, *American Way of War*, 457–60; Hagan, *This Peoples' Navy*, 355–61; Stokesbury, *Short History*, 276; Nalty, ed., *Winged Shield*, 2:179–80, 233–37; Grossnick, *United States Naval Aviation*, 250; Curtis Alan Utz, *Cordon of Steel: The U.S. Navy and the Cuban Missile Crisis*, 3–46.

7. Stokesbury, *Short History*, 276.

8. Ibid., 276, 277; Weigley, *American Way of War*, 457–60; Millett and Maslowski, *For the Common Defense*, 538; Worden, *Rise*, 133–37.

9. Brian VanDeMark, *Into the Quagmire: Lyndon Johnson and the Escalation of the Vietnam War*, 4–8; John Schlight, *A War Too Long: The U.S. Air Force in Southeast Asia, 1961–1975*, 1–2, 4, 6; Millett and Maslowski, *For the Common Defense*, 544–50; Clodfelter, *Limits of Air Power*, 44; Gross, *Adapting the Force*, 10–12.

10. Millett and Maslowski, *For the Common Defense*, 548–49; Hagan, *This People's Navy*, 364–65; Edward J. Marolda, *By Sea, Air, and Land: An Illustrated History of the U.S. Navy and the War in Southeast Asia*, 48–53; Grossnick, *United States Naval Aviation*, 255, 705.

11. Hagan, *This People's Navy*, 365, Malcom W. Cagle, "Task Force 77 in Action Off Korea," *U.S. Naval Institute Proceedings, Naval Review, 1972* (May, 1972): 68; Edward J. Marolda, *Carrier Operations: The Illustrated History of the Vietnam War*, 13–16.

12. Wayne Thompson, *To Hanoi and Back: The United States Air Force and North Vietnam, 1966–1973*, 33, 35, 37, 40, 46, 49, 57, 143, 196, 269, 275; Millett and Maslowski, *For the Common Defense*, 550–53, 557; Schlight, *War Too Long*, 45–46; Hagan, *This People's Navy*, 363–68; Thomas H. Hone; "Southeast Asia," in *Case Studies . . . Air Superiority*, ed. Cooling, 505–26, 553–56; Love, *History*, 2:524–30; Clodfelter, *Limits of Air Power*, 44–141; Marshall L. Michael III, *Clashes: Air Combat Over North Vietnam, 1965–1972*, 1–4; John D. Sherwood to Charles J. Gross et al., E-mail message, Subject: "Fast Movers: America's Jet Pilots and the Vietnam War Experience," Feb. 3, 2000, copy in author's possession.

13. Sherwood, E-mail, "Fast Movers," 5.

14. Millett and Maslowski, *For the Common Defense*, 529; Bilstein, *Flight in America*, 249; Cooling, "History," 105–106; Bergerson, *Army Gets an Air Force*, 70–81, 104–20; Bruce Palmer Jr., *The 25-Year War: America's Military Role in Vietnam*, 26–27; Cooling, "History," 106–107.

15. Bilstein, *Flight in America*, 251.

16. Ibid., 251–53; Millett and Maslowski, *For the Common Defense*, 554; John J. Sbrega, "Southeast Asia," in *Case Studies . . . Close Air Support*, ed. Cooling, 413–18, 425–27; Schlight, *War Too Long*, 10, 23, 26–31; Worden, *Rise*, 157–59, 174–76; Mark, *Aerial Interdiction*, 336–37; Nalty, ed., *Winged Shield*, 2:269.

17. Curtis Peebles, *High Frontier: The U.S. Air Force and the Military Space Program*, 52–53; David N. Spires, *Beyond Horizons: A Half Century of Air Force Space Leadership*, 147, 169, 170–71.

18. Sherwood, E-mail, "Fast Movers," 1; Bilstein, *Flight in America*, 253; R. L. Schreadly,

"Zumwalt, Elmo R. Jr.," *Oxford Companion,* ed. Chambers, 841; Fred A. Wilcox, "Toxic Agents," ibid., 725.

19. Schreadly, "Zumwalt," 841.

20. Millett and Maslowski, *For the Common Defense,* 554; Hagan, *This People's Navy,* 363–66; Schlight, *War Too Long,* 26–27.

21. Millett and Maslowski, *For the Common Defense,* 555–60; Schlight, *War Too Long,* 28, 33–37, 43–45; Stokesbury, *Short History,* 279–83; Millett, *Semper Fidelis,* 568–86; Gross, *Prelude to the Total Force,* 156–60; idem., *Militiaman, Volunteer, and Professional,* 100; Shipman, *Wings at the Ready,* 54–56; Grossnick, *United States Naval Aviation,* 265.

22. Schlight, *War Too Long,* 53–55, 71; Bilstein, *Flight in America,* 255–56; Millett and Maslowski, *For the Common Defense,* 556–57; Mark, *Aerial Interdiction,* 329–64; Carl Berger, ed., *The United States Air Force in Southeast Asia, 1961–1973,* 121.

23. Berger, ed., *United States Air Force,* 121–35; Marolda, *Carrier Operations,* 16–17, 20–21; Schlight, *War Too Long,* 58–60.

24. Millett and Maslowski, *For the Common Defense,* 561, 571–73; Schlight, *War Too Long,* 87–106; Worden, *Rise,* 195–204; John D. Sherwood, *Fast Movers: America's Jet Pilots and the Vietnam Experience,* 62–63, 67, 84–88, 97–98; Grossnick, *United States Naval Aviation,* 293–94, 311–12, 714; Marolda, *Carrier Operations,* 133–51; Millett and Maslowski, *For the Common Defense,* rev. and enl. ed., 589–93; David E. Michlovitz, "Precision-Guided Munitions," in *Oxford Companion,* ed. Chambers, 556–57.

25. George C. Herring, *America's Longest War: The United States and Vietnam, 1950–1975,* quoted in Schlight, *War Too Long,* 106.

26. Thompson, *To Hanoi and Back,* v–x; Schight, *War Too Long,* 102–108; Millett and Maslowski, *For the Common Defense,* 542–44, 565, 571–73.

27. Palmer, *25-Year War,* 160.

28. Ibid., 160–161; Michael, *Clashes,* 2–4, 285–95; Fred J. Shaw Jr. and Timothy Warnock, *The Cold War and Beyond: Chronology of the United States Air Force, 1947–1997,* 76; Richard P. Hallion, *Storm Over Iraq: Air Power and the Gulf War,* 30–33, 103.

29. Sherwood, *Fast Movers,* 217–19.

30. Ibid., 220.

31. Clodfelter, *Limits of Air Power,* 201, 208.

32. Ibid., 208.

33. Ibid., 210; Worden, *Rise,* 201–204; Hagan, *This People's Navy,* 368; Smith, *Seventy-five Years,* 55–60; Ray L. Bowers, *The United States Air Force in Southeast Asia: Tactical Airlift,* vii–viii, 649–59; Alan L. Gropman, "History and Heroics," *Air Force Magazine,* Apr., 1984, 114; Kennedy, ed., *Anything, Anywhere, Anytime,* 117–54; Smith, *Seventy-five Years,* 55–60; Gross, *Adapting the Force,* 27–30; OH, HQ USAFRES, "Brief History," 6–9.

34. Millett, *Semper Fidelis,* 583–606; Millett and Maslowski, *For the Common Defense,* 554; Cooling, "History," 106–107; Palmer, *25-Year War,* 156; Redmond, "Role of Attack Helicopters," 7.

CHAPTER 6: THE RENAISSANCE OF AMERICAN MILITARY POWER

1. Millett and Maslowski, *For the Common Defense,* 565–67; idem., *For The Common Defense,* rev. and enl. ed., 570–71.

2. Buckley, *Air Power,* 213–14, 217–18; Millett and Maslowski, *For the Common Defense,*

rev. and enl. ed., 607–608, 613–14, 615–19, 627–29, 647–51; Hallion, *Storm Over Iraq,* 27–109.

3. Millett and Maslowski, *For the Common Defense,* rev. and enl. ed., 569.

4. Gross, *Prelude to the Total Force,* 166–67; idem., *Militiaman, Volunteer, and Professional,* 113–15; David Henry Montplaisir, "The Total Force Policy: A Critical Defense Policy Issue" (Ph.D. diss., Catholic University of America, 1985), 105–107.

5. Gross, *Militiaman, Volunteer, and Professional,* 86–87, 99, 115–18, 132; idem., *Adapting the Force,* 26–31; Cantwell, *Citizen Airmen,* 209–11; James B. Deerin, "A Decade of Dedication," *National Guardsman,* May, 1977, 2; Chief, National Guard Bureau, "Annual Review: FY 1977," National Guard Bureau, Historical Services Division, Arlington, Va. (hereafter NGB-HSD), 51.

6. Millett and Maslowski, *For the Common Defense,* 567; McFarland, *Concise History,* 70; Kenneth P. Werrell, "The Weapon the Military Did Not Want: The Modern Strategic Cruise Missile," *Journal of Military History* 53, no. 4 (Oct., 1989): 419–20.

7. Werrell, "Weapon," 420–37.

8. McFarland, *Concise History,* 70; Millett and Maslowski, *For the Common Defense,* 567–68.

9. Buckley, *Air Power,* 209–10.

10. Gross, *Militiaman, Volunteer, and Professional,* 117–18; Nalty, ed., *Winged Shield,* 2:364; Spires, *Beyond Horizons,* 193–205; Leslie Filson, *Sovereign Skies: Air National Guard Takes Command of 1st Air Force,* 2–37, 110–15.

11. Buckley, *Air Power,* 211–13; Worden, *Rise,* 211–27; McFarland, *Concise History,* 73–74; Millett and Maslowski, *For the Common Defense,* 565–73; Davis, *31 Initiatives,* 24–33; McFarland, *Concise History,* 73–74.

12. Worden, *Rise,* 228;

13. Hallion, *Storm Over Iraq,* 74–81.

14. John A. Warden III, *The Air Campaign: Planning for Combat,* 1–9, 128–43; McFarland, *Concise History,* 74.

15. McFarland, *Concise History,* 74.

16. Warden, *The Air Campaign,* 7; McFarland, *Concise History,* 74.

17. Buckley, *Air Power,* 211–13, 217–18; Hallion, *Storm Over Iraq,* 37–45; Bilstein, *Flight in America,* 299–305; Nalty, ed., *Winged Shield,* 2:366–72; Millett, *Semper Fidelis,* 596; Love, *History,* 2:670–80; Young, "USAF Almanac: Gallery of USAF Weapons," *Air Force Magazine,* May, 2000, 136–44.

18. Richard P. Hallion, "AWACS and E-3S," in *Oxford Companion,* ed. Chambers, 66–67; Fact Sheet, U.S. Air Force, no. 88-6, "E-3 Sentry (AWCS)," Mar., 1988, copy in author's possession; Young, "USAF Almanac," 1998, 143.

19. Buckley, *Air Power,* 216.

20. Elmo R. Zumwalt Jr. *On Watch: A Memoir,* 77–152; Hagan, *This People's Navy,* 376–82; Love, *History,* 2:631–38, 678–80; Baer, *One Hundred Years,* 394–417; John Lehman, "He Made the Navy Great Again," *Wall Street Journal,* Jan. 5, 2000.

21. Swanborough and Bowers, *U.S. Navy Aircraft,* 276–79; Love, *History,* 2:681; Bilstein, *Flight in America,* 304–305.

22. Swanborough and Bowers, *U.S. Navy Aircraft,* 276–79; Hallion, *Storm Over Iraq,* 43–46; Millett, *Semper Fidelis,* 611–12; Bilstein, *Flight in America,* 304–305; Historical Office, Office of the Secretary of Defense, "Department of Defense Key Officials, 1947–1995," May, 1995, NGB-HSD, 11; Love, *History,* 2:681–83.

23. Grossnick, *United States Naval Aviation,* 279.

24. Peter Mersky, ed., *U.S. Naval Air Reserve,* 3:23–27.

25. Hallion, *Storm Over Iraq,* 29.

26. Ibid., 30–46.

27. Ibid., 46–51.

28. Ibid., 61–62; Edward J. Marolda and Robert J. Schneller, *Shield and Sword: The United States Navy and the Persian Gulf War,* 27.

29. U.S. Air Force Museum home page, "Lockheed SR-71A," available at http://www.wpafb.af.mil/museum/modern_flight/mf35.htm; Richard Hallion, "Stealth Aircraft," in *Oxford Companion to American Military History,* 678.

30. Ibid.

31. Ibid., 678–79.

32. Ibid.; Young, "USAF Almanac," 2000, 136–37, 141; Ron Dick, "Bomber Aircraft," in *Oxford Companion,* ed. Chambers, 84.

33. Grossnick, *United States Naval Aviation,* 279; Bilstein, *Flight in America,* 305; Millett, *Semper Fidelis,* 596–614; Allan R. Millett, *Semper Fidelis: The History Of the United States Marine Corps,* rev. and enl. ed., 620–23.

34. Bilstein, *Flight in America,* 305; James W. Bradin, *From Hot Air to Hellfire: The History of Army Attack Aviation,* 115–24.

35. Davis, *31 Initiatives,* 23; Redmond, "Role of Attack Helicopters," 7–9, 35; Bradin, *From Hot Air to Hellfire,* 124–26.

36. Frederick A. Bergerson and Jason E. Trumpler, "Helicopters," in *Oxford Companion,* ed. Chambers, 312–13; Bradin, *From Hot Air to Hellfire,* 125–27.

37. Davis, *31 Initiatives,* 23; Bradin, *Hot Air to Hellfire,* 115–31; Frank N. Schubert and Theresa L. Kraus, eds., *The Whirlwind War: The United States Army in Operations DESERT SHIELD and DESERT STORM,* 3–5.

38. Rae, *Climb to Greatness,* 201, 205–11; Bilstein, *American Aerospace Industry,* 160–61; idem., *Flight in America,* 290–91.

39. Bilstein, *American Aerospace Industry,* 168–69.

40. Ibid., 168, 200–201.

41. Hallion, *Storm Over Iraq,* 56; Samuel P. Huntington, "Foreword," in Asa A. Clark, *The Defense Reform Debate: Issues and Analysis,* ix–xi.

42. Huntington, "Foreword," xi.

43. Stokesbury, *Short History,* 285; Nalty, ed., *Winged Shield,* 2:384–88; Walter J. Boyne, "Nickel Grass," *Air Force Magazine,* Dec., 1998, 56.

44. Boyne, "Nickel Grass," 56; Stokesbury, *Short History,* 285–86.

45. Stokesbury, *Short History,* 286.

46. Ibid., 287; Nalty, ed., *Winged Shield,* 2:384–88; Hallion, *Storm Over Iraq,* 62–64; Young, "USAF Almanac," 1998, 148–49, 151; Boyne, "Nickel Grass," 56–59; Smith, *Seventy-five Years,* 63–65; Kennedy, ed., *Anything, Anywhere, Anytime,* 154–62.

47. Nalty, ed., *Winged Shield,* 2:388–90; Boyne, "Nickel Grass," 59; Kennedy, ed., *Anything, Anywhere, Anytime,* 157–68; Hallion, *Storm Over Iraq,* 64.

48. Gross, *Militiaman, Volunteer, and Professional,* 148.

49. Stokesbury, *Short History,* 287; Millett and Maslowski, *For the Common Defense,* rev. and enl. ed., 610–14; Nalty, ed., *Winged Shield,* 2:390–93; Love, *History,* 2:635, 692–700.

50. Hagan, *This People's Navy,* 380–82; Millett and Maslowski, *For the Common Defense,*

578; Baer, *One Hundred Years,* 394–413; "China, People's Republic of," in *The World Almanac and Book of Facts, 2001,* ed. Lori P. Wiesenfeld, 776.

51. Hagan, *This People's Navy,* 380–82; Millett and Maslowski, *For the Common Defense,* rev. and enl. ed., 610–11.

52. Nalty, ed., *Winged Shield,* 2:390–93; Millett and Maslowski, *For the Common Defense,* rev. and enl. ed., 610–14; Douglas Little, "Middle East, U.S. Involvement in," in *Oxford Companion,* ed. Chambers, 436–37; John Whiteclay Chambers II, "Carter, Jimmy," in *Oxford Companion,* ed. Chambers, 105–106; Roger R. Trask, *The Secretaries of Defense: A Brief History, 1947–1985,* 45–49.

53. Millett and Maslowski, *For the Common Defense,* rev. and enl. ed., 615–16; Michael Schaller, "Reagan, Ronald," in *Oxford Companion,* ed. Chambers, 592.

54. Schaller, "Reagan," 592; Millett and Maslowski, *For the Common Defense,* rev. and enl. ed., 615–18; Love, *History,* 2:702; Hagan, *This People's Navy,* 382–85; Buckley, *Air Power,* 213–14.

55. Schaller, "Reagan," 592; Millett and Maslowski, *For The Common Defense,* rev. and enl. ed., 615–18; Love, *History,* 2:702; Hagan; *This People's Navy,* 382–85; Buckley, *Air Power,* 213–14.

56. Hagan, *This People's Navy,* 382–85; Baer, *One Hundred Years,* 418–44; Barbara Brooks Tomblin, "Aegis," in *Oxford Companion,* ed. Chambers, 7.

57. Millett and Maslowski, *For the Common Defense,* rev. and enl. ed., 619–21; McFarland, *Concise History,* 74; Nalty, ed., *Winged Shield,* 2:406–17.

58. McFarland, *Concise History,* 74; Millett and Maslowski, *For the Common Defense,* rev. and enl. ed., 619–21.

59. Ibid., 627.

60. Hagan, *This People's Navy,* 390.

CHAPTER 7: THE EMPIRE STRIKES OUT

1. Thomas A. Keany and Eliot A. Cohen, *Revolution in Warfare? Air Power in the Persian Gulf,* 213.

2. James R. Arnold, "Bush, George," in *Oxford Companion,* ed. Chambers, 97; Millett and Maslowski, *For the Common Defense,* rev. and enl. ed., 627–31.

3. Millett and Maslowski, *For the Common Defense,* rev. and enl. ed., 607–608, 624; Zachary Karabell, "Cold War (1945–91): External Course," *in Oxford Companion,* ed. Chambers, 152.

4. Millett and Maslowski, *For the Common Defense,* rev. and enl. ed., 607; Jan de Weydenthal, "Poland: Inevitable Fall of Communism Began Ten Years Ago," September 13, 1999, Radio Free Europe/Radio Liberty available at http://www.rferl.org/nca/special/10years/Poland1.html; Mark, *Defending the West,* 47; Karabell, "Cold War," 152; Donald Kagan and Frederick W. Kagan, *While America Sleeps: Self-Delusion, Military Weakness, and the Threat to Peace Today,* 269.

5. Millett and Maslowski, *For the Common Defense,* rev. and enl. ed., 607.

6. Ibid., 608.

7. Ibid.; Buckley, *Air Power,* 213–14.

8. Millett and Maslowski, *For the Common Defense,* rev. and enl. ed., 628–29; David Halberstam, *War in a Time of Peace: Bush, Clinton, and the Generals,* 9–23.

9. Ibid., 630–31.

10. Ibid.; Nalty, ed., *Winged Shield,* 2:429–40; OH, HQ USAFRES, "Brief History," 12; "History, ANG, 1986–1991," 131–41.

11. Nalty, ed., *Winged Shield,* 2:440.

12. Ibid.

13. Ibid.; Thomas A. Keaney and Eliot A. Cohen, *Gulf War Air Power Survey: Summary Report,* 1–3; idem., *Revolution in Warfare?* 1–3; Diane T. Putney, "From Instant Thunder to Desert Storm: Developing the Gulf War Air Campaign's Phases," *Air Power History* 41, no. 3 (fall, 1994): 40; Millett and Maslowski, *For the Common Defense,* rev. and enl. ed., 631; Perry D. Jamieson, *Lucrative Targets: The U.S. Air Force in the Kuwaiti Theater of Operations,* 1–2; Gen. Charles A. Horner, USAF (Ret.), to author, E-mail message, Subject: "Review [of the Indispensable Arm]," Sept. 1, 2001, 10:01 A.M., with attachment: "Notes on The Indispensable Arm: A History of American Military Aviation," copy in author's possession.

14. Gross, *Militiaman, Volunteer, and Professional,* 118–19; Nalty, ed., *Winged Shield,* 2:441–43; Michael A. Palmer, *On Course to Desert Storm: The United States Navy and the Persian Gulf,* 1–5, 80–81; Love, *History,* 2:630–35; Daniel Yergin, *The Prize: The Epic Quest for Oil, Money, and Power,* 291, 300, 301, 395–99, 403–404, 427–28, 565, 567, 594–95; Weigley, *History,* 457; James Gormly, "Keeping the Door Open in Saudi Arabia," *Diplomatic History* 4, no. 2 (spring, 1980): 192–200; Dore Gold, *America, the Gulf, and Israel: CENTCOM (Central Command) and Emerging U.S. Regional Security Policies in the Middle East,* 12; William Oliver Turner Jr., "U.S. Arms Sales to Saudi Arabia: Implications for American Foreign Policy" (Ph.D. diss., George Washington University, 1982), 14–25; Anthony H. Cordesman, "Defense Planning in Saudi Arabia," in *Defense Planning in Less-Developed States: The Middle East and South Asia,* ed., Stephanie G. Neuman, 74–78; Henry Kissinger, *The White House Years,* 224–25; Anthony Cordesman, *The Gulf and the Search for Strategic Stability,* 213, 269–340; Acharya Amitav, *U.S. Military Strategy in the Gulf,* 49–53, 63–67, 80–84; Robert P. Hoffa Jr., *The Half War: Planning U.S. Rapid Deployment Forces to Meet a Limited Contingency, 1960–1983,* 107–109, 117–29; Lawrence R. Benson and Jay E. Hines, *The United States Military in North Africa and Southwest Asia Since World War II,* 33, 40; Caspar W. Weinberger, *Fighting for Peace: Seven Critical Years in the Pentagon,* 388; Eliot A. Cohen, director, *Gulf War Air Power Survey,* vol. 3, *Logistics and Support,* 2; idem., *Gulf War Air Power Survey,* vol. 2, *Operations and Effects and Effectiveness,* 3, 17.

15. Nalty, ed., *Winged Shield,* 2:444–45; Mark Clodfelter, "Of Demons, Storms, and Thunder: A Preliminary Look at Vietnam's Impact on the Persian Gulf Air Campaign," *Airpower Journal* 5, no. 4 (winter, 1991): 26; Millett and Maslowski, *For the Common Defense,* rev. and enl. ed., 631–38.

16. Millett and Maslowski, *For the Common Defense,* rev. and enl. ed., 631–38.

17. Marolda and Schneller, *Shield and Sword,* 3–4, 360–64; Grossnick, *United States Naval Aviation,* 364; McFarland, *Concise History,* 75; Millett and Maslowski, *For the Common Defense,* rev. and enl. ed., 631–42; Nalty, ed., *Winged Shield,* 2:442–54; Keany and Cohen, *Revolution in Warfare?* 154–60.

18. Millett and Maslowski, *For the Common Defense,* rev. and enl. ed., 631–38; Gross, *Militiaman, Volunteer, and Professional,* 141–61; OH, HQ USAFRES, "Brief History," 12–18; Cantwell, *Citizen Airmen,* 364–75; Millett, *Semper Fidelis,* rev. and enl. ed., 636–37; John Mueller, *Policy and Opinion in the Gulf War,* (Chicago: University of Chicago Press, 1994), 22, 69, 162–63; "Non-Carrier Based Navy Squadrons that Participated in

Operation Desert Shield and Desert Storm," in Grossnick, *United States Naval Aviation,* 742; Edward Marolda, senior historian, Naval Historical Center, to author, memorandum, Subject: "Ed Moralda Comments on Chapter VII, 'The Empire Strikes Out,' of 'The Indispensable Arm: A History of American Military Aviation,'" Sept., 2001, copy in author's possession.

19. Clodfelter, "Of Demons," 17–31; Putney, "From Instant Thunder," 40–48; Williamson Murray, "Air War in the Gulf: The Limits of Air Power," *Strategic Review* 26, no. 1 (winter, 1998): 28–36; Marolda and Schneller, *Shield and Sword,* 366; Marolda, "Comments on Chapter VII," 2; Horner to author, E-mail message.

20. Murray, "Air War," 29–30; Millett, *Semper Fidelis,* rev. and enl. ed., 636–38; Marolda, "Comments on Chapter VII," 2.

21. Marolda and Schneller, *Shield and Sword,* 367.

22. Ibid.

23. Ibid., p 375.

24. Ibid; Marolda, "Comments on Chapter VII," 2.

25. Marolda and Schneller, *Shield and Sword,* 355–85; Marolda, "Comments on Chapter VII," 2; Grossnick, *United States Naval Aviation,* 364–73, 425–26; Keaney and Cohen, *Gulf War,* 184–85.

26. Millett and Maslowski, *For the Common Defense,* rev. and enl. ed., 632–34.

27. Ibid., 637–638.

28. Ibid., 638.

29. Nalty, ed., *Winged Shield,* 2:458–64; Jamieson, *Lucrative Targets,* 43–44; Marolda and Schneller, *Shield and Sword,* 143, 369–70; Marolda, "Comments on Chapter VII," 2; Murray, "Air War," 32.

30. Nalty, ed., *Winged Shield,* 2:468–69.

31. Murray, "Air War," 30–32; Putney, "From Instant Thunder," 40–48; Horner to author, E-mail message.

32. Clodfelter, "Of Demons," 21; Murray, "Air War," 32–33.

33. Clodfelter, "Of Demons," 24; Murray, "Air War," 33–34; Horner to author, E-mail message.

34. Nalty, ed., *Winged Shield,* 2:456–57; Horner to author, E-mail message; Murray, "Air War," 35–36.

35. Nalty, ed., *Winged Shield,* 2:482–85; Murray, "Air War," 36.

36. Nalty, ed., *Winged Shield,* 2:475–76.

37. Clodfelter, "Of Demons," 26; Millett and Maslowski, *For the Common Defense,* rev. and enl. ed., 638; Marolda, "Comments on Chapter VII," 3.

38. Robert H. Scales, *Certain Victory: The U.S. Army in the Gulf War,* 167–69; Young, "USAF Almanac," 2000, 143; Spires, *Beyond Horizons,* 243–69; Keany and Cohen, *Revolution in Warfare?* 162–64; Marolda, "Comments on Chapter VII," 3.

39. Keaney and Cohen, *Revolution,* 162–63, 211; Spires, *Beyond Horizons,* 243–69.

40. Keany and Cohen, *Revolution,* 211.

41. Nalty, ed., *Winged Shield,* 2:482–85; Schubert and Kraus, eds., *Whirlwind War,* 175, 182; Millett and Maslowski, *For the Common Defense,* rev. and enl. ed., 638–42.

42. Clodfelter, "Of Demons," 27–31; Millett and Maslowski, *For the Common Defense,* rev. and enl. ed., 640–42; Marolda and Schneller, *Shield and Sword,* 381–85; Nalty, ed., *Winged Shield,* 2:484–86; Buckley, *Air Power,* 217–18.

43. Kagan and Kagan, *While America Sleeps,* 253.

44. Ibid.

45. Ibid., 256.

46. Karabell, "Cold War," 152.

47. Lawrence J. Korb "Force Is the Issue," *Government Executive,* Jan., 2000, 31–32; Rick Maze, "Senate to Chiefs: What Took So Long?" *Air Force Times,* Oct. 12, 1998; Rick Maze, "Straight Talk on Readiness," *Air Force Times,* Oct. 12, 1998; "Now Hear This," *Inside the Pentagon,* Dec. 17, 1998, 1; George Piatt, "Defense Raise to Target Specifics," *European Stars and Stripes,* Jan. 10, 1999; Thomas E. Ricks, "Joint Chiefs Say Defense Needs Bigger Raise Than Clinton Plans," *Wall Street Journal,* Jan. 6, 1999; Bradley Graham, "Military: Budget Will Meet Top Needs," *Washington Post,* Jan. 6, 1999; Marlene Cimons, "Clinton Calls for Defense Spending Hike," *Los Angeles Times,* Jan. 3, 1999.

48. Lora S. Jaffe, *The Development of the Base Force, 1989–1992,* 1–14; "Department of Defense Key Officials, 1947–1995," 12, 60; Secretary of Defense Richard B. Cheney, "Report of the Secretary of Defense to the President and the Congress," Feb., 1992, 1; Korb, "Force Is the Issue," 32; Associated Press, "140,000 National Guard, Reserve Jobs Slated for Cuts," *Washington Times,* Mar. 27, 1992; Andy Paztor, "Pentagon Set to Unveil Plan on Reserve Cuts," *Wall Street Journal,* Mar. 26, 1992.

49. Korb, "Force Is the Issue," 32; Millett and Maslowski, *For the Common Defense,* rev. and enl. ed., 648–49; Joshua Hammer and Michael Isikoff, "The Narco-Guerrilla War," *Newsweek,* Aug. 9, 1999; Associated Press, "General Says Billions Spent on Fighting Drugs Ineffective," *Washington Times,* Feb. 17, 1995; Howard LaFranchi, "Drugs Pulling US Into Columbia's War," *Christian Science Monitor,* July 27, 1999; Karen DeYoung, "Columbia's U.S. Connection Not Winning Drug War," *Washington Post,* July 6, 1999, 1; Douglas Farah, "U.S. Widens Columbia Counter-Drug Efforts," *Washington Post,* July 10, 1999; Karen DeYoung, "U.S. Reports Major Rise in Columbian Drug Output," *Washington Post,* Feb. 15, 2000.

50. Nalty, ed., *Winged Shield,* 2:486–90; Korb, "Force Is the Issue," 32; Steven Lee Myers, "With Little Notice, U.S. Planes Have Been Striking Iraq All Year," *New York Times,* Aug. 13, 1999; Roberto Suro, "U.S. Air Raids Over Iraq Become an Almost Daily Ritual," *Washington Post,* Aug. 30, 1999; Chuck Vinch, "Caught Between Iraq and a Hard Place," *European Stars and Stripes,* Sept. 1, 1999; Terry Boyd, "Northern Watch Keeps Tight Reins on Iraq," *European Stars and Stripes,* May 8, 2000, 3.

51. Nalty, ed., *Winged Shield,* 2:486–90; *History, Air National Guard, CY 1992–CY 1994,* 75–87; ibid., *CY 1995–CY 1997,* 80–90; Tamar A. Mehuron, Chart, "Other Than War," *Air Force Magazine,* Mar., 1999, 19; Korb, "Force Is the Issue," 32; Millett and Maslowski, *For the Common Defense,* rev. and enl. ed., 649; Steven Lee Myers, "With Little Notice, U.S. Planes Have Been Striking Iraq All Year," *New York Times,* August 13, 1999; Suro, "U.S. Air Raids"; Vinch, "Caught Between Iraq," 2; Terry Boyd, "Northern Watch," 3.

52. Suro, "U.S. Air Raids," 3; Vinch, "Caught Between Iraq," 2; Gross, *Adapting the Force,* 49–50; Steve Vogel, "Military Matters: Area Reserve Unit Completes a Forgotten—but Risky—Mission Over Iraq," *Washington Post,* May 18, 2000.

53. Nalty, ed., *Winged Shield,* 2:495–96; Millett, *For the Common Defense,* rev. and enl. ed., 649; Mark Bowden, *Black Hawk Down: A Story of Modern War,* passim.

54. Ann Markusen, "Procurement: Aerospace Industry," in *Oxford Companion,* ed. Chambers, 566; Thomas C. Donlan, "Cover Your Contingency: The Defense Industry

Needs Help," *Wall Street Journal,* Mar. 13, 2000; Lawrence F. Skibbie, "Long-Term Remedy Needed for Ailing Defense Industry," *National Defense,* Mar., 2000, 2; Greg Schneider, "U.S. Help Urged for Defense Industry," *Washington Post,* May 18, 2000, E-1.

55. Kurth, "Military-Industrial Complex," 439–40; David H. Napier, director, Aerospace Research Center, "2000 Year-End Review and 2001 Forecast—An Analysis," available at http://www.aia-aerospace.org., 1–2.

56. Bilstein, *American Aerospace Industry,* 168.

57. Ibid., 202-208; Young, "USAF Almanac," 2000, 136–38, 140–41, 148; Frank G. Hoffman, "The U.S. Marine Corps in Review," *U.S. Naval Institute Proceedings* (May, 2000): 90; "Super Hornet Enters Full Rate Production," Department of Defense News Release no. 342-00, June 16, 2000, available at http://defenselink.mil/news/Jun2000/b06162000_bt342-00.html; John Whiteclay Chambers II, "Weaponry, Evolution of," in *Oxford Companion,* ed. Chambers, 794.

58. John Whiteclay Chambers II, "Bosnian Crisis," in *Oxford Companion,* ed. Chambers, 88–89; DOD Report to Congress, "Kosovo/Operation Allied Force After-Action Report," Jan. 31, 2000, 1; Halberstram, *War In A Time of Peace,* 24–46; Nalty, ed., *Winged Shield,* 2:496–500; *History, Air National Guard, CY 1992–CY 1994,* 97–103; ibid., *CY 1995–CY 1997,* 91–102; Dupuy and Dupuy, *Encyclopedia of Military History,* 1270, 1271.

59. Nalty, ed., *Winged Shield,* 2:499–500; Chambers, "Bosnian Crisis," 88–89; *History, Air National Guard, CY 1992–CY 1994,* 101–103; ibid., *CY 1995–CY 1997,* 93–102; Halberstam, *War,* 338–51.

60. Halberstam, *War,* 55–56.

61. Nalty, ed., *Winged Shield,* 2:510–11; Chambers, "Bosnian Crisis," 88–89; *History, Air National Guard, CY 1995–1997,* 97–102.

62. DOD Report to Congress, "Kosovo/Operation Allied Force," 1–3; John Whiteclay Chambers II, "Kosovo Crisis (1999)," in *Oxford Companion,* ed. Chambers, 374–75.

63. Chambers, "Kosovo Crisis," 374–75; DOD Report to Congress, "Kosovo/Operation Allied Force," xvii–xxiv; Earl H. Tilford, "Operation Allied Force and the Role of Air Power," *Parameters* 29, no. 4 (winter 1999-2000): 24–38; Richard J. Newman, "Vietnam's Forgotten Lessons," *U.S. News & World Report,* May 1, 2000, 30–35, 38, 40; Scott C. Truver, "The U.S. Navy in Review," *U.S. Naval Institute Proceedings* 126 (May, 2000): 76–77; Joseph S. Nye Jr., "Redefining the National Interest," *Foreign Affairs,* July/August, 1999, 34–35; Marolda, "Comments on Chapter VII," 4; Halberstam, *War,* 444–80.

64. Halbertam, *War,* 436–38.

65. Chambers, "Kosovo Crisis," 374–75; DOD, Report to Congress, "Kosovo/Operation Allied Force," xvii–xxiv; Tilford, "Operation Allied Force," 24–38; Newman, "Vietnam's Forgotten Lessons," 30–35, 38, 40; Truver, "U.S. Navy," 76–77; "PBS Interview with Lt. Gen. Short," 1–22; Marolda, "Comments on Chapter VII," 4; Halberstam, *War,* 444–80.

66. Tilford, "Operation Allied Force," 24–38; Chambers, "Kosovo Crisis," 374–75; Newman, "Vietnam's Forgotten Lessons," 30–31, 35, 38, 40.

67. Tilford, "Operation Allied Force," 34-35.

68. Ibid., 24–31; Chambers, "Kosovo Crisis," 374–75.

69. Tilford, "Operation Allied Force," 31; Halberstam, *War,* 444–80.

70. Chambers, "Kosovo Crisis," 374–75; Craig R. Whitney, "Bombing Ends As Serbs Begin Pullout," *New York Times,* June 11, 1999; DOD, Report to Congress, "Kosovo/Operation Allied Force," 1–10; James Carroll, "The Truth About NATO's Air War," *Boston Globe,* June 20, 2000; Halberstam, *War,* 444–80.

71. Chambers, "Kosovo Crisis," 374–75; Tilford, "Operation Allied Force," 24.

72. Marolda, "Comments on Chapter VII," 4; Truver, "U.S. Navy," 77.

73. Truver, "U.S. Navy," 77.

74. Marolda, "Comments on Chapter VII," 4.

75. Truver, "U.S. Navy," 77; Hoffman, "U.S. Marine Corps," 85; Tilford, "Operation Allied Force," 34–36.

76. Tilford, "Operation Allied Force," 34–36.

77. Quoted in Halberstam, *War,* 464.

78. Chambers, "Kosovo Crisis," 374–75; Tilford, "Operation Allied Force," 34–38; Truver, "U.S. Navy," 76–77; DOD, Report to Congress, "Kosovo/Operation Allied Force," 10–12.

79. Korb, "Force Is the Issue," 32.

80. Ibid.

81. Ibid.

82. Ibid.

83. Ibid., 32–33; Weinberger, *Fighting for Peace,* 433–45; Nye, "Redefining the National Interest," 22–24; Newman, "Vietnam's Forgotten Lessons," 34, 38.

84. Korb, "Force Is the Issue," 32–33.

85. Ibid., 33.

86. Buckley, *Air Power,* 217–18; Keaney and Cohen, *Revolution,* 222.

87. Millett and Maslowski, *For the Common Defense,* rev. and enl. ed., 648–50; Robert Suro, "For U.S. Aviators, Readiness Woes Are a 2-Front Struggle," *Washington Post,* Feb. 3, 2000; "People," *Air Force Magazine,* May, 2000, 55; "Equipment," *Air Force Magazine,* May, 2000, 66; Deputy Assistant Secretary (Cost and Economics), Assistant Secretary of the Air Force (Financial Management and Comptroller of the Air Force), "Total Aircraft Inventory (TAI) Trends," in "United States Air Force Statistical Digest, Fiscal Year 1999," n.d., Air Force History Support Office, Headquarters, U.S. Air Force, Washington, D.C., 91; Nalty, ed., *Winged Shield,* 2:513–15, 551; Spires, *Beyond Horizons,* 270–84; Rand H. Fisher and Kent B. Pelot, "The Navy Has a Stake in Space," *U.S. Naval Institute Proceedings* (Oct., 2001): 62; Marolda, "Comments on Chapter VII," 4; Bud Jones, review of *Shield and Sword: The United States Navy and the Persian Gulf War,* in *Air Power History* (summer, 2000): 64–65; Department of Defense Home Page, http://www.defenselink.mil/pubs/almanac/, "Personnel as of 30 September 1998," "Weapons Platforms/Systems-Ships as of January 1999," and "General Purpose Forces Highlights," *Defense Almanac;* Daniel Williams, "Putin Wins Vote on START II," *Washington Post,* Apr. 15, 2000; Walter Pincus, "U.S. Plan to Renovate Warheads Stirs Opposition," *Washington Post,* Mar. 26, 2000; David A. Deptula, "Embracing Change," *Armed Forces Journal International,* Oct., 2001, 69; John T. Correll, ed., "Crossroads in Space," *Air Force Magazine,* Mar., 2001, 2; John A. Tripak, "The Space Commission Reports," *Air Force Magazine,* Mar. 2001, 30–35; Commission to Assess United States National Security Space Management and Organization, "Report of the Commission to Assess United States National Security Space Management and Organization," January, 2001, passim, available at http://www.defenselink.mil/pubs/space20010111.html.

88. Buckley, *Air Power,* 217–18; Keaney and Cohen, *Revolution,* 222–23.

1. Stokesbury, *Short History,* 290.
2. Ibid.
3. Keaney and Cohen, *Revolution,* 220–26; James R. Hansen, "Flight and Technology: An Overview," in *1998 National Aerospace Conference: The Meaning of Flight in the 20th Century,* ed. Janet R. Bednarek, 156–57; John A. Tirpak, "The State of Precision Engagement," *Air Force Magazine,* Mar., 2000, 25–30; Elaine A. Grossman, "Airpower Gains in the Doctrine Wars," *Air Force Magazine,* Mar., 2000, 46–47; Smith, *Seventy-Five Years,* 63–65; Michael Grunwald, "Terrorists Hijack 4 Airliners, Destroy World Trade Center; Hit Pentagon; Hundreds Dead," *Washington Post,* Sept. 12, 2001; David Von Drehle, "World War, Cold War Won; Now, the Gray War," *Washington Post,* Sept. 12, 2001.
4. Gross, *Militiaman, Volunteer, and Professional,* passim; Cantwell, *Citizen Airmen,* passim; Gross, *Adapting the Force,* passim; Bruce D. Callander, "Pressures on the Guard and Reserve," *Air Force Magazine,* Nov., 1998, 36–40.
5. Hansen, "Flight and Technology," 156–57; Bilstein, *American Aerospace Industry,* 220.
6. Buckley, *Air Power,* 1–9; Stokesbury, *Short History,* 289–90.
7. Buckley, *Air Power,* 6.
8. Ibid., 220–22.
9. Ibid., 222.
10. Keaney and Cohen, *Revolution,* 220–26.
11. Bilstein, *Flight in America,* 307.
12. W. David Lewis, review of *The Winged Gospel: America's Romance with Aviation, 1900–1950,* by Joseph J. Corn, in *Technology and Culture,* 874.
13. Ibid.
14. Buckley, *Air Power,* 222.
15. Dupuy and Dupuy, *Encyclopedia of Military History,* 821; L. L. Farrar Jr., *The Short War Illusion: German Policy, Strategy, and Domestic Affairs, August–December 1914,* passim.

BIBLIOGRAPHY

Aerial Refueling Highlights in the Air Force's First Decade, 1947–1957. Scott Air Force Base, Ill.: Office of History, Air Mobility Command, 1997.

Aeronautical Chamber of Commerce of America. *The Aircraft Yearbook for 1934.* New York: Aeronautical Chamber of Commerce, 1934.

———. *The Aircraft Yearbook for 1936.* New York: Aeronautical Chamber of Commerce of America, 1936.

Althoff, William F. *Skyships: A History of the Airship in the United States Navy.* Pacifica, Calif.: Pacifica Press, 1990.

Ambrose, Stephen E. *The Supreme Commander: The War Years of General Dwight D. Eisenhower.* Garden City, N.Y.: Doubleday, 1970.

———. *Eisenhower: Soldier and President.* New York: Simon and Schuster, 1990.

Amitav, Acharya. *U.S. Military Strategy in the Gulf.* New York: Routledge, 1989.

Armitage. M. J., and R. A. Mason. *Air Power in the Nuclear Age.* Urbana: University of Illinois Press, 1983, 1985.

Armstrong, William J. "Aircraft Go to Sea: A Brief History of Aviation in the U.S. Navy," *Aerospace Historian* 25, no. 2 (June, 1978): 79–91.

Arnold, General of the Air Force Henry H., (Ret.). *Global Mission.* New York: Harper and Brothers, 1949.

Associated Press. "140,000 National Guard, Reserve Jobs Slated for Cuts." *Washington Times,* March 27, 1992.

———. "General Says Billions Spent on Fighting Drugs Ineffective." *Washington Times,* February 17, 1995.

Baer, George W. *One Hundred Years of Sea Power: The U.S. Navy, 1890–1990.* Stanford, Calif.: Stanford University Press, 1994.

Barlow, Jeffrey G. *Revolt of the Admirals: The Fight for Naval Aviation, 1945–1950.* Washington, D.C.: Naval Historical Center, 1994.

———. "The Navy's View of the 'Revolt of the Admirals'." In *Occasional Papers,* no. 1, ed. Roger R. Trask. Washington, D.C.: Society for History in the Federal Government, 1997.

Beck, Alfred M., ed. *With Courage: The U.S. Army Air Forces in World War II.* Washington, D.C.: Air Force History and Museums Program, 1994.

Bednarek, Janet R., ed. *1998 National Aerospace Conference: The Meaning of Flight in the 20th Century.* Dayton, Ohio: Wright State University, 1999.

Benson, Lawrence R., and Jay E. Hines. *The United States Military in North Africa and Southwest Asia Since World War II.* MacDill Air Force Base, Fla.: History Office, U.S. Central Command, 1987.

Berger, Carl, ed. *The United States Air Force in Southeast Asia, 1961–1973*. Washington, D.C.: Office of Air Force History, 1977.

Bergerson, Frederick A. *The Army Gets an Air Force: Tactics of Insurgent Bureaucratic Politics*. Baltimore: Johns Hopkins University Press, 1980.

Beschloss, Michael. Review of William E. Burrows, *By Any Means Necessary: America's Secret Air War in the Cold War*. In *New York Times Book Review*, December 16, 2001.

Biddle, Wayne. *Barons of the Sky: From Early Flight to Strategic Warfare, the Story of the American Aerospace Industry*. New York: Simon and Schuster, 1991.

Bilstein, Roger E. *Flight Patterns: Trends of Aeronautical Development in the United States*. Athens: University of Georgia Press, 1983.

———. *Flight in America, 1900–1983: From the Wrights to the Astronauts*. Baltimore: Johns Hopkins, 1984, 1987.

———. *The American Aerospace Industry: From Workshop to Global Enterprise*. New York: Twayne, an imprint of Simon and Schuster, 1996.

———. *Airlift and Airborne Operations in World War II*. Washington, D.C.: Air Force History and Museums Program, 1998.

Borowski, Harry R. *A Hollow Threat: Strategic Air Power and Containment before Korea*. Westport, Conn.: Greenwood Press, 1982.

———. "Air Force Atomic Capability from V-J Day to the Berlin Blockade—Potential or Real ?" *Military Affairs* 44, no. 3 (October, 1980): 105–10.

Bowden, Mark. *Black Hawk Down: A Story of Modern War*. New York: Atlantic Monthly Press, 1999.

Bowers, Ray L. *The United States Air Force in Southeast Asia: Tactical Airlift*. Washington, D.C.: Office of Air Force History, 1983.

Bowman, Richard C. "Organizational Fanaticism: A Case Study of Allied Air Operations Against the U-Boat During World War II." *Airpower Historian* 10, no. 2 (April, 1963): 50–53.

Boyd, Terry. "Northern Watch Keeps Tight Reins on Iraq." *European Stars and Stripes*, May 8, 2000.

Boyne, Walter J. "Nickel Grass." *Air Force Magazine*, December, 1998, 54–59.

Bradin, James W. *From Hot Air to Hellfire: The History of Army Attack Aviation*. Novato, Calif.: Presidio Press, 1994.

Brayton, Abbott A. "American Reserve Policies Since World War II." *Military Affairs* 36, no. 4 (December, 1972): 139–44.

Bright, Charles D. *The Jet Makers: The Aerospace Industry from 1945 to 1972*. Lawrence: Regents Press of Kansas, 1978.

Buchanan, A. R, ed. *The Navy's Air War: A Mission Completed*. New York: Harper and Brothers, 1946.

Buckley, John. *Air Power in the Age of Total War*. Bloomington: Indiana University Press, 1999.

Byrd, Vernon. *Passing Gas: The History of In-Flight Refueling*. Chico, Calif.: Byrd, 1994.

Cagle, Malcom W. "Task Force 77 in Action Off Korea." *U.S. Naval Institute Proceedings* 98 (May, 1972): 68–109.

Callander, Bruce D. "Pressures on the Guard and Reserve." *Air Force Magazine*, November, 1998, 36–40.

Cameron, Rebecca Hancock. *Training To Fly: Military Flight Training, 1907–1945*. Washington, D.C.: Air Force History and Museums Program, 1999.

Canham, Doris A. *Development and Production of Fighter Aircraft for the United States Air Force.* Wright-Patterson Air Force Base, Ohio: Historical Office, Air Materiel Command, 1949.

Cantwell, Gerald T. *Citizen Airmen: A History of the Air Force Reserve, 1946–1994.* Washington, D.C.: Air Force History and Museums Program, 1997.

Caras, Roger A. *Wings of Gold: The Story of United States Naval Aviation.* Philadelphia and New York: J. B. Lippincott, 1965.

Carroll, James. "The Truth About NATO's Air War." *Boston Globe,* June 20, 2000.

Chambers, John Whiteclay, II, ed. *The Oxford Companion to American Military History.* Oxford: Oxford University Press, 1999.

Chandler, Charles DeForest, and Frank P. Lahm. *How Our Army Grew Wings: Airmen and Aircraft Before 1914.* New York: Ronald Press, 1943.

Chennault, Claire L. *Way of a Fighter: The Memoirs of Claire Lee Chennault.* New York: G. P. Putnam's Sons, 1949.

"China, People's Republic of." In *The World Almanac and Book of Facts, 2001,* ed. Lori P. Wiesenfeld. Mahwah, N.J.: World Almanac Books, 2001.

Cimons, Marlene. "Clinton Calls for Defense Spending Hike." *Los Angeles Times,* January 3, 1999.

Clark, Paul Wilson. "Major General George Owen Squier: Military Scientist." Ph.D. diss., Case-Western Reserve University, 1974.

Clark, Truman R. *Flood of Victory: The American Logistics Mass in World Wars I and II.* Air Force Logistics Command Historical Study no. 408. Wright-Patterson Air Force Base, Ohio: Office of History, Air Force Logistics Command, 1986.

Claussen, Martin P. *Comparative History of Research and Development Policies Affecting Air Materiel, 1915–1945.* AAF Historical Study no. 20. Washington, D.C.: AAF Historical Division, June, 1945.

—. *Materiel Research and Development in the Army Air Arm, 1914–1945.* AAF Historical Study no. 50. Washington, D.C.: AAF Historical Division, November, 1946.

Clodfelter, Mark. *The Limits of Air Power: The American Bombing of North Vietnam.* New York: Free Press, 1989.

—. "Of Demons, Storms, and Thunder: A Preliminary Look at Vietnam's Impact on the Persian Gulf Air Campaign." *Airpower Journal* 5, no. 4 (winter, 1991): 17–32.

Cohen, Eliot A., director. *Gulf War Air Power Survey.* Vol. 2, *Operations and Effects and Effectiveness.* Washington, D.C.: Department of the Air Force, 1993.

—. *Gulf War Air Power Survey.* Vol. 3, *Logistics and Support.* Washington, D.C.: Department of the Air Force, 1993.

Cohen, Eliot A., and John Gooch. *Military Misfortunes: The Anatomy of Failure in War.* New York: Vintage Books, 1990.

Collier, Basil. *A History of Air Power.* New York: Macmillan, 1974.

Commission to Assess United States National Security Space Management and Organization. "Report of the Commission to Assess United States National Security Space Management and Organization," January, 2001, available at http://www.defenselink.mil/pubs/space20010111.html.

Cooke, James J. *The U.S. Air Service in the Great War, 1917–1919.* Westport, Conn.: Praeger, 1996.

Cooling, Benjamin Franklin. "A History of U.S. Army Aviation." *Aerospace Historian* 21, no. 2 (June, 1974): 102–108.

————, ed. *Case Studies in the Development of Close Air Support.* Washington, D.C.: Office of Air Force History, 1990.

————, ed. *Case Studies in the Achievement of Air Superiority.* Washington, D.C.: Center for Air Force History, 1994.

Cordesman, Anthony. *The Gulf and the Search for Strategic Stability.* Boulder, Colo.: Westview Press, 1984.

————. "Defense Planning in Saudi Arabia." In *Defense Planning in Less-Developed States: The Middle East and South Asia,* ed., Stephanie G. Neuman. Lexington, Ky.: D. C. Heath, 1984.

Corn, Joseph J. *The Winged Gospel: America's Romance with Aviation, 1900–1950.* New York: Oxford University Press, 1983.

Correll, John T., ed. "Crossroads in Space." *Air Force Magazine,* March, 2001, 2.

Cosmas, Graham A. "The Formative Years of Marine Corps Aviation, 1912–1939." *Aerospace Historian* 24, no. 2 (June, 1977): 82–93.

Crane, Conrad C. *American Airpower Strategy in Korea, 1950–1953.* Lawrence: University Press of Kansas, 2000.

Craven, Wesley Frank, and James Lea Cate, eds. *The Army Air Forces in World War II.* Vol. 1, *Plans and Early Operations, January 1939 to August 1942.* Chicago: University of Chicago Press, 1948. Reprint, Washington, D.C.: Office of Air Force History, 1983.

————, eds. *The Army Air Forces in World War II.* Vol. 6, *Men and Planes.* Chicago: University of Chicago Press, 1958. Reprint, Washington, D.C.: Office of Air Force History, 1983.

Crossland, Richard B., and James T. Currie. *Twice A Citizen: A History of the United States Army Reserve, 1908–1983.* Washington, D.C.: Office of the Chief, U.S. Army Reserve, 1984.

Crouch, James L. "Wings South: The First Employment of Air Power by the United States." *Aerospace Historian* 19, no. 1 (March, 1972): 27–31.

Crowell, Benedict. *America's Munitions, 1917–1918.* Washington, D.C.: GPO, 1919.

Cunningham, William Glenn. *The American Aircraft Industry: A Study in Industrial Location.* Los Angeles: Lorrin L. Morrison, 1961.

Danhoff, Clarence H. *Government Contracting and Technological Change.* Washington, D.C.: Brookings Institution, 1968.

Davidson, Joel R. *The Unsinkable Fleet: The Politics of U.S. Navy Expansion in World War II.* Annapolis, Md.: Naval Institute Press, 1996.

Davis, Richard G. *The 31 Initiatives: A Study in Air Force-Army Cooperation.* Washington, D.C.: Office of Air Force History, 1987.

————. *HAP: Henry H. Arnold, Military Aviator.* Washington, D.C.: Air Force History and Museums Program, 1997.

Davis, Vincent. *Postwar Defense Policy and the U.S. Navy, 1943–1946.* Chapel Hill: University of North Carolina Press, 1962, 1966.

Deerin, James B. "A Decade of Dedication." *National Guardsman,* May, 1977, 2–3, 6–9.

Department of Defense, "Kosovo/Allied Force After-Action Report," January, 2000, archives, National Guard Bureau, Historical Services Division, Arlington, Va.

Deptula, David A. "Embracing Change," *Armed Forces Journal International,* October, 2001, 69–71.

Deputy Assistant Secretary (Cost and Economics), Assistant Secretary of the Air Force (Financial Management and Comptroller of the Air Force), "Total Aircraft Inventory

(TAI) Trends," in "United States Air Force Statistical Digest, Fiscal Year 1999," undated, Air Force History Support Office, Headquarters, U.S. Air Force, Washington, D.C.

Deter, Henry M. "Development of the Escort Carrier." *Military Affairs* 12, no. 2 (summer, 1948): 79–90.

———. "Tactical Use of Air Power in World War II: The Navy Experience." *Military Affairs* 14, no. 4 (winter, 1950): 192–200.

DeYoung, Karen. "Columbia's U.S. Connection Not Winning Drug War." *Washington Post,* July 6, 1999.

———. "U.S. Reports Major Rise in Columbian Drug Output." *Washington Post,* February 15, 2000.

Donlan, Thomas C. "Cover Your Contingency: The Defense Industry Needs Help." *Wall Street Journal,* March 13, 2000.

Doubler, Michael D. "Airborne Warfare." In *The Oxford Companion to American Military History,* ed. John Whiteclay Chambers II. Oxford: Oxford University Press, 1999.

Dubuque, Jean H. *The Development of the Heavy Bomber, 1918–1994.* USAF Historical Study no. 6. Maxwell Air Force Base, Ala.: Historical Division, Air University, 1951.

DuPre, Flint O. *U.S. Air Force Biographical Dictionary.* New York: Franklin Watts, 1965.

Dupuy, R. Ernest, and Trevor N. Dupuy. *The Encyclopedia of Military History: From 3500 B.C. to the Present.* 2d rev. ed. New York: Harper and Row, 1986.

Eastman, James. "The Development of Big Bombers." *Aerospace Historian* 25, no. 4 (December, 1978): 211–19.

Eisenhower, Dwight D. *Mandate for Change: The White House Years, 1953–1956.* Garden City, N.Y.: Doubleday, 1963.

Emme, Eugene M. *Aeronautics and Astronautics. An American Chronology of Science and Technology in the Exploration of Space, 1915–1960.* Washington, D.C.: GPO, 1961.

———. "The American Dimension." In *Air Power and Warfare: Proceedings of the Eighth Military History Symposium, United States Air Force Academy, 18–20 October 1978.* Washington, D.C.: Office of Air Force History and U.S. Air Force Academy, 1979.

"Equipment." *Air Force Magazine,* May, 2000, 66.

Etzold, Thomas H. *Defense or Delusion? America's Military in the 1980s.* New York: Harper and Row, 1982.

Fahey, James C. *Army Aircraft (Heavier-Than-Air), 1908–1946.* New York: Ships and Aircraft, 1946.

Farah, Douglas. "U.S. Widens Columbia Counter-Drug Efforts." *Washington Post,* July 10, 1999.

Farrar, L. L., Jr. *The Short War Illusion: German Policy, Strategy, and Domestic Affairs, August–December 1914.* Santa Barbara, Calif.: American Biographical Center-Clio Press, 1973.

Filson, Leslie. *Sovereign Skies: Air National Guard Takes Command of First Air Force.* Tyndall Air Force Base, Fla.: Headquarters, First Air Force, 1999.

Fisher, Rand H., and Kent B. Pelot. "The Navy Has a Stake in Space." *U.S. Naval Institute Proceedings* 127 (October, 2001) L 58–63.

Flammer, Philip M. *The Vivid Air: The Lafayette Escadrille.* Athens: University of Georgia Press, 1981.

———. "The Myth of the Lafayette Escadrille." *Aerospace Historian* 22, no. 1 (March, 1975): 23–28.

Foulois, Benjamin D., and Carroll V. Glines. *From the Wright Brothers to the Astronauts: The Memoirs of Major General Benjamin D. Foulois.* New York: McGraw-Hill, 1968.

Foxworth, Thomas G. *The Speed Seekers.* New York: Doubleday, 1975.

Francillon, Rene J. *The Air Guard.* Arlington, Va.: Aerofax, n.d.

————. *The United States Air National Guard.* London: Aerospace, 1993.

Freudenthal, Elsbeth E. *The Aviation Business: From Kitty Hawk to Wall Street.* New York: Vanguard Press, 1940.

Futrell, Robert F. *Ideas, Concepts, Doctrine: A History of Basic Thinking in the United States Air Force, 1907–1964.* Maxwell Air Force Base, Ala.: Air University Press, 1971, 1974.

Gibbs-Smith, Charles H. *A History of Flying.* New York and London: Butsford, 1953.

————. *Aviation: An Historical Survey from Its Origins to the End of World War II.* London: HMSO, 1970.

————. *Flight Through the Ages: A Complete, Illustrated Chronology from the Dreams of Early History to the Age of Space Exploration.* New York: Thomas Y. Crowell, 1974.

Gold, Dore. *America, the Gulf, and Israel: CENTCOM (Central Command) and Emerging U.S. Regional Security Policies in the Middle East.* Boulder, Colo.: Westview Press, 1980.

Goldberg, Alfred, ed. *A History of the United States Air Force, 1907–1957.* Washington, D.C.: Air Force Association, 1957; reprint, New York: Arno Press, 1974.

Goldich, Robert L. "Historical Continuity in the U.S. Military Reserve System." *Armed Forces and Society* 7, no. 1 (fall, 1980): 9–27.

Gormly, James. "Keeping the Door Open in Saudi Arabia." *Diplomatic History* 4, no. 2 (spring, 1980): 192–200.

Graham, Bradley. "Military: Budget Will Meet Top Needs." *Washington Post,* January 6, 1999.

Gray, George W. *Frontiers of Flight: The Story of NACA Research.* New York: Alfred A. Knopf, 1945, 1948.

Greely, Adolphus A. *Reminiscences of Adventure and Service: A Record of Sixty-Five Years.* New York, Charles Scribner's Sons, 1927.

Green, Fred. "The Military View of American National Policy, 1904–1940." Bobbs-Merrill Reprint H-273. Reprinted from *American Historical Review,* January 2, 1961, 354–76.

Greer, Thomas H. *The Development of Air Doctrine in the Army Air Arm, 1917–1941.* Air Force Historical Study no. 89. Maxwell Air Force Base, Ala.: U.S. Air Force Historical Division, Air University, 1953.

Griffith, Thomas E., Jr. *MacArthur's Airman: General George C. Kenney and the War in the Southwest Pacific.* Lawrence: University Press of Kansas, 1998.

Gropman, Alan L. *The Air Force Integrates, 1945–1964.* Washington, D.C.: Office of Air Force History, 1978.

————. "History and Heroics." *Air Force Magazine,* April, 1984, 114.

Gross, Charles J. *Prelude to the Total Force: The Air National Guard, 1943–1969.* Bolling Air Force Base, D.C.: Office of Air Force History, U.S. Air Force, 1985.

————. *Militiaman, Volunteer, and Professional: The Air National Guard and the American Military Tradition.* Washington, D.C.: Historical Services Division, National Guard Bureau, 1995.

————. *Adapting the Force: Evolution of the Air National Guard's Air Mobility Mission.* Washington, D.C.: Historical Services Division, National Guard Bureau, 1998.

————. *Turning Point: The Air National Guard and the Korean War.* Washington, D.C.: Historical Services Division, National Guard Bureau, 2000.

————. "A Different Breed of Cats: The Air National Guard and the 1968 Reserve Mobilizations." *Air University Review* 34, no. 2 (January-February, 1983): 92–99.

————. "The Birth of the Air National Guard, 1943–1946: A Case Study in Military Institutional Politics." *Military Affairs* 49, no. 2 (April, 1985): 69–74.

————. "George Owen Squier and the Origins of American Military Aviation." *Journal of Military History* 54, no. 3 (July, 1990): 281–305.

————. "Operation Creek Party, 1967–1977." *Air Power History* 46, no. 3 (fall, 1999): 24–35.

Grossman, Elaine A. "Airpower Gains in the Doctrine Wars." *Air Force Magazine,* March, 2000, 46–47.

Grossnick, Roy A. *United States Naval Aviation, 1910–1995.* 4th ed. Washington, D.C.: U.S. Naval Historical Center, 1997.

Grunwald, Michael. "Terrorists Hijack 4 Airliners, Destroy World Trade Center; Hit Pentagon; Hundreds Dead." *Washington Post,* September 12, 2001.

Gwynn-Jones, Terry. *Farther and Faster: Aviation's Pioneering Years, 1909–1939.* Washington, D.C.: Smithsonian Institution Press, 1991.

Hagan, Kenneth J. *This People's Navy: The Making of American Sea Power.* New York: Free Press, 1991.

————, ed. *New Interpretations of American Naval History, 1775–1985.* 2d ed. Westport, Conn.: Greenwood Press, 1984.

Halberstam, David. *War in a Time of Peace: Bush, Clinton, and the Generals.* New York: Scribner, 2001.

Hallion, Richard P. *Test Pilots: The Frontiersmen of Flight.* Garden City, N.Y.: Doubleday, 1981.

————. *The Rise of Fighter Aircraft, 1914–1918.* Annapolis, Md.: Nautical and Aviation, 1984.

————. *The Naval Air War in Korea.* Baltimore: Nautical and Aviation, 1986.

————. *Strike from the Sky: The History of Battlefield Air Attack, 1911–1945.* Washington, D.C.: Smithsonian Institution Press, 1989.

————. *Storm Over Iraq: Air Power and the Gulf War.* Washington, D.C.: Smithsonian Institution Press, 1992.

Hammer, Joshua, and Michael Isikoff. "The Narco-Guerrilla War." *Newsweek,* August 9, 1999, 42–43.

Hansen, Chuck. *U.S. Nuclear Weapons: The Secret History.* Arlington, Va.: Aerofax, 1988.

Hansen, James R. "Flight and Technology: An Overview." In *1998 National Aerospace Conference: The Meaning of Flight in the 20th Century,* ed. Janet R. Bednarek. Dayton, Ohio: Wright State University, 1999.

Head, Richard G. "The Air Force A-7 Decision: The Politics of Close Air Support." *Aerospace Historian* 22, no. 4 (December, 1974): 219–24.

Hennessy, Juliette A. *The United States Army Air Arm, April 1861 to April 1917.* Air Force Historical Study no. 98. Maxwell Air Force Base, Ala.: U.S. Air Force Historical Division, Research Studies Institute, Air University, May, 1958.

Herring, George C. *America's Longest War: The United States and Vietnam, 1950–1975.* 3d ed. New York: McGraw-Hill, 1996.

Hezlet, Arthur. *Aircraft and Sea Power.* New York: Stein and Day, 1970.

Higham, Robin. *Air Power: A Concise History.* New York: St. Martin's Press, 1972.

History, Air National Guard, CY 1992–CY 1994. Washington, D.C.: Historical Services Division, National Guard Bureau, 1995.

————. *History, Air National Guard, CY 1995–CY 1997.* Washington, D.C.: Historical Services Division, National Guard Bureau, 1998.

Hoffa, Robert P., Jr. *The Half War: Planning U.S. Rapid Deployment Forces to Meet a Limited Contingency, 1960–1983.* Boulder, Colo.: Westview Press, 1984.

Holley, Irving Brinton, Jr. *Ideas and Weapons: Exploitation of the Aerial Weapon by the United States in World War I; A Study in the Relationship of Technological Advance, Military Doctrine, and the Development of Weapons.* Hamden, Conn.: Archon, 1971.

―――. *Buying Aircraft: Materiel Procurement for the Army Air Forces.* Special Studies. *U.S. Army in World War II.* Washington, D.C.: Center of Military History, 1964, 1989.

Hone, Thomas C. "Naval Reconstitution, Surge, and Mobilization: Once and Future." *Naval War College Review* 47, no. 3 (summer, 1994): 67–85.

―――. "Fighting on Our Ground: The War of Production, 1920–1942." *Naval War College Review* 45, no. 2 (spring, 1992): 93–107.

―――. "Korea." In *Case Studies in the Achievement of Air Superiority,* ed. Benjamin Franklin Cooling. Washington, D.C.: Center for Air Force History, 1994.

―――. "Southeast Asia." In *Case Studies in the Achievement of Air Superiority,* ed. Benjamin F. Cooling. Washington, D.C.: Center For Air Force History, 1994.

―――. "Navy Air Leadership: RADM W. A. Moffett as Chief of the Bureau of Aeronautics." Paper presented at the joint meeting of the American Military Institute, Air Force Historical Foundation, and Military Classics Seminar, April, 1984.

Hopkins, J. C., and Sheldon Goldberg. *The Development of Strategic Air Command, 1946–1986.* Offutt Air Force Base, Neb.: Headquarters Strategic Air Command, Office of the Historian, 1986.

Hoyt, Ross G. "Metamorphosis of the Fighter." *Air Force Magazine,* October, 1975.

Hudson, James J. *Hostile Skies: A Combat History of the American Air Service in World War I.* Syracuse, N.Y.: Syracuse University Press, 1968.

Hughes, Thomas Alexander. *Overlord: General Pete Quesada and the Triumph of Tactical Air Power in World War II.* New York: Free Press, 1995.

Hunsaker, Jerome C. "Forty Years of Aeronautical Research." In *Annual Report of the Smithsonian Institution, 1955.* Washington, D.C.: GPO, 1956.

Huntington, Samuel P. "Foreword." In Asa A. Clark, *The Defense Reform Debate: Issues and Analysis.* Baltimore: Johns Hopkins University Press, 1984.

Hurley, Alfred F. *Billy Mitchell: Crusader for Air Power.* New York: Franklin Watts, 1964.

Jaffe, Lora S. *The Development of the Base Force, 1989–1992.* Washington, D.C.: Joint History Office, Office of the Chairman of the Joint Chiefs of Staff, 1993.

James, D. Clayton. "MacArthur and the Chinese Intervention in the Korean War, September–December 1950." In *A New Equation: Chinese Intervention into the Korean War, Colloquium on Contemporary History, No. 3.* Washington, D.C.: Naval Historical Center, June 20, 1990.

Jamieson, Perry D. *Lucrative Targets: The U.S. Air Force in the Kuwaiti Theater of Operations.* Washington, D.C.: Air Force History and Museums Program, 2001.

Johnson, Ann R. "The WASP of World War II." *Aerospace Historian* 17, nos. 2 and 3 (summer-fall, 1970): 76–82.

Johnson, Herbert A. "Seeds of Separation: The General Staff Corps and Military Aviation Before World War I." *Air University Review* 34, no. 1 (November–December 1982): 29–45.

―――. "The Aero Club of America and Army Aviation, 1907–1916." *New York History* (October, 1985): 375–95.

Jones, Bud. Review of *Shield and Sword: The United States Navy and the Persian Gulf War.* In *Air Power History* 47, no. 2 (summer, 2000): 64–65.

Kagan, Donald, and Frederick W. Kagan. *While America Sleeps: Self-Delusion, Military Weakness, and the Threat to Peace Today.* New York: St. Martin's Press, 2000.

Kapp, Lawrence. *Involuntary Reserve Activations for U.S. Military Operations Since World War II.* Congressional Research Service Report to Congress. Washington, D.C.: Congressional Research Service, Library of Congress, August 14, 2000.

Keaney, Thomas A., and Eliot A. Cohen. *Gulf War Air Power Survey: Summary Report.* Washington, D.C.: Department of the Air Force, 1993.

———. *Revolution in Warfare? Air Power in the Persian Gulf.* Annapolis, Md.: Naval Institute Press, 1995.

Kelsey, Benjamin S. *The Dragon's Teeth: The Creation of United States Air Power for World War II.* Washington, D.C.: Smithsonian, 1982.

Kennedy, Betty R., ed. *Anything, Anywhere, Anytime: An Illustrated History of the Military Airlift Command, 1941–1991.* Scott Air Force Base, Ill.: Office of History, Military Airlift Command, 1991.

Kennett, Lee. *A History of Strategic Bombing.* New York: Scribner, 1982.

———. *The First Air War, 1914–1918.* New York: Free Press, 1991.

Kinnard, Douglas. *President Eisenhower and Strategy Management: A Study in Defense Politics.* Lexington: University Press of Kentucky, 1977.

Kissinger, Henry. *The White House Years.* Boston: Little, Brown, 1979.

Knaack, Marcelle Size. *Encyclopedia of US Air Force Aircraft and Missile Systems.* 2 vols. Washington, D.C.: Office of Air Force History, 1978.

Knappen, Theodore M. *Wings of War: An Account of the Important Contributions of the United States to Aircraft Invention, Engineering, Development, and Production During the World War.* New York: Putnam, 1920.

Korb, Lawrence J. "Force Is the Issue." *Government Executive,* January, 2000, 31–33.

Kranzberg, Melvin, and Carroll W. Pursell Jr., eds. *Technology in Western Civilization.* Vol. 2, *Technology in the Twentieth Century.* London: Oxford University Press, 1967.

———. "Science-Technology and Warfare: Action, Reaction, and Interaction in the Post–World War II Era." In *Science, Technology and Warfare: Proceedings of the Third Military History Symposium, USAF Academy, 1969.* Washington, D.C.: Office of Air Force History and the U.S. Air Force Academy, 1969.

Krauskopf, Robert W. "The Army and the Strategic Bomber, 1930–1939." Pt. 1. *Military Affairs* 22, no. 2 (summer, 1958): 83–94.

———. "The Army and the Strategic Bomber, 1930–1939." Pt. 2. *Military Affairs* 23, no. 4 (winter, 1959): 208–15.

Kuehl, Daniel T. "RADAR." In *The Oxford Companion to American Military History,* ed. John Whiteclay Chambers II. Oxford: Oxford University Press, 1999.

LaFranchi, Howard. "Drugs Pulling US Into Columbia's War." *Christian Science Monitor,* July 27, 1999.

Layman, R. D. *Naval Aviation in the First World War: Its Impact and Influence.* Annapolis, Md.: Naval Institute Press, 1996.

Leary, William M., Jr. *Anything, Anywhere, Anytime: Combat Cargo in the Korean War.* Korean War Fiftieth Anniversary Commemorative ed. Washington, D.C.: Air Force History and Museums Program, 2000.

———. "Assessing the Japanese Threat: Air Intelligence Prior to Pearl Harbor." *Aerospace Historian* 34, no. 4 (December, 1987): 273–77.

Lehman, John. "He Made the Navy Great Again," *Wall Street Journal,* Jan. 5, 2000.

Levantrosser, William F. *Congress and the Citizen-Soldier: Legislative Policy-making for the Federal Armed Forces Reserve.* Columbus: Ohio State University Press, 1967.

Love, Robert W., Jr. *History of the U.S. Navy.* 2 vols. Harrisburg: Stackpole, 1991, 1992.

MacGregor, Morris J., Jr. Integration of The Armed Forces, 1940–1965. Defense Studies Series. Washington, D.C.: Center of Military History, 1981.

Mahon, John K. *History of the Militia and National Guard.* New York: MacMillan, 1983.

Major, John. "The Navy Plans for War, 1937–1941." In *New Interpretations of American Naval History, 1775–1985,* ed. Kenneth J. Hagan. 2d ed. Westport, Conn.: Greenwood Press, 1984.

Mansfield, Harold. *Vision: A Saga of the Sky.* New York: Duell, Sloan, and Pearce, 1956.

Mark, Eduard. *Aerial Interdiction: Air Power and the Land Battle in Three American Wars.* Washington, D.C.: Center for Air Force History, 1994.

———. *Defending the West: The United States Air Force and European Security, 1946–1948.* Washington, D.C.: Air Force History and Museums Program, 1999.

Markusen, Ann. "Procurement: Aerospace Industry." In *The Oxford Companion to American Military History,* ed. John Whiteclay Chambers II. Oxford: Oxford University Press, 1999.

Marolda, Edward J. *Carrier Operations: The Illustrated History of the Vietnam War.* New York: Bantam Books, 1987.

———. *By Sea, Air, and Land: An Illustrated History of the U.S. Navy and the War in Southeast Asia.* Washington, D.C.: Naval Historical Center, 1994.

———, and Robert J. Schneller. *Shield and Sword: The United States Navy and the Persian Gulf War.* Washington, D.C.: Naval Historical Center, 1998.

Martin, Glenn L. "The First Half-Century of Flight in America." *Journal of Aeronautical Sciences* 21, no. 2 (February, 1954): 73–84.

Maurer, Maurer. *Aviation in the U.S. Army, 1919–1939.* Washington, D.C.: Office of Air Force History, U.S. Air Force, 1987.

———, comp. and ed. *The U.S. Air Service in World War I.* Vol. 1, *The Final Report and a Tactical History.* Washington, D.C.: Office of Air Force History, 1978.

———, comp. and ed. *The U.S. Air Service in World War I.* Vol. 2, *Early Concepts of Military Aviation.* Washington, D.C.: Office of Air Force History, 1978.

———. comp. and ed. *The U.S. Air Service in World War I.* Vol. 4, *Postwar Review.* Washington, D.C.: Office of Air Force History, 1979.

Maze, Rick. "Senate to Chiefs: What Took So Long?" *Air Force Times,* October 12, 1998.

———. "Straight Talk on Readiness." *Air Force Times,* October 12, 1998.

McFarland, Marvin, ed. *The Papers of Wilbur and Orville Wright.* Vol. 2. New York: McGraw-Hill, 1953.

McFarland, Stephen L. *A Concise History of the U.S. Air Force.* Air Force Fiftieth Anniversary Commemorative ed. Washington, D.C.: Air Force History and Museums Program, 1997.

McHenry, Robert, ed. *Webster's American Military Biographies.* Springfield, Mass.: Merriam, 1978.

McKay, Ernest A. *A World to Conquer: The Story of the First Round-the-World Flight by the U.S. Army Air Service.* New York: Arco, 1981.

Mehuron, Tamar A. Chart, "Other Than War." *Air Force Magazine,* March, 1999.

Meilinger, Philip S. *Hoyt S. Vandenberg: The Life of a General.* Bloomington: Indiana University Press, 1989.

———. "The Impact of Technology and Design Choice on the Development of U.S. Fighter Aircraft." *American Aviation Historical Society Journal* 36, no. 1 (spring, 1991): 60–69.

Melhorn, Charles M. *Two-Block Fox: The Rise of the Aircraft Carrier, 1911–1929.* Annapolis, Md.: Naval Institute Press, 1974.

Mersky, Comdr. Peter B., USNR (Ret.) *U.S. Marine Corps Aviation, 1912 to the Present.* Annapolis, Md.: U.S. Naval Institute, 1983.

————, ed. *U.S. Naval Air Reserve.* Vol. 3. Washington, D.C.: Deputy Chief of Naval Operations, Air Warfare, and Commander, Naval Air Systems Command, n.d.

Mets, David R. *Master of Airpower: General Carl A. Spaatz.* Novato, Calif.: Presidio Press, 1988.

————. "Dive Bombing Between the Wars." *Airpower Historian* 12, no. 3 (July, 1965): 85–89.

Michael, Marshall L, III. *Clashes: Air Combat Over North Vietnam, 1965–1972.* Annapolis, Md.: Naval Institute Press, 1997.

Militia Bureau. "Annual Report of the Acting Chief, Militia Bureau, 1916." Washington, D.C.: GPO, 1916.

Miller, Roger G. *To Save a City: The Berlin Airlift, 1948–1949.* Washington, D.C.: Air Force History and Museums Program, 1998.

————. "Air Transport on the Eve of Pearl Harbor." *Air Power History* 45, no. 2 (summer, 1998): 26–37.

————. "The U.S. Army Air Corps and the Search for Autonomy." Paper presented at the Air Force History and Museums Program Symposium, Arlington, Va., May 28, 1997.

Millett, Allan R. *Semper Fidelis: The History of the United States Marine Corps.* New York: Macmillan, 1980.

————. *Semper Fidelis: The History of the United States Marine Corps.* Rev. and enl. ed. New York: Free Press, 1991.

————, and Peter Maslowski. *For the Common Defense: A Military History of the United States of America.* New York: Free Press, 1984.

————. *For the Common Defense: A Military History of the United States.* Rev. and enl. ed. New York: Free Press, 1994.

————. "Korea, 1950–1953." In *Case Studies in the Development of Close Air Support,* ed. Benjamin F. Cooling. Washington, D.C.: Office of Air Force History, 1990.

Millett, Capt. Stephen M., USAF. "The Capabilities of the American Nuclear Deterrent, 1945–1950." *Aerospace Historian* 27, no. 1 (March, 1980): 27–32.

Millis, Walter. *Arms and Men: A Study in American Military History.* New York: G. P. Putnam's Sons, 1956.

Mingos, Howard. "Birth of an Industry." In *The History of the American Aircraft Industry: An Anthology,* ed. G. R. Simanson. Cambridge, Mass.: MIT Press, 1968.

Montplaisir, David Henry. "The Total Force Policy: A Critical Defense Policy Issue." Ph.D. diss., Catholic University of America, 1985.

Mooney, Chase C., and Martha E. Layman. *Organization of Military Aeronautics, 1907–1935 (Congressional and War Department Action).* AAF Historical Study no. 25. Washington, D.C.: AAF Historical Division, 1944.

Morison, Samuel Eliot. *History of United States Naval Operations in World War II.* Vol. 3, *The Rising Sun in the Pacific, 1931–April 1942.* Boston: Little, Brown, 1950.

————. *History of United States Naval Operations in World War II.* Vol. 4, *Coral Sea, Midway and Submarine Actions, May 1942–August 1942.* Boston: Little, Brown, 1959.

Morris, Edmund. *The Rise of Theodore Roosevelt.* New York: Coward, McCann, and Geoghegan, 1979.

Morrow, John H., Jr. *The Great War in the Air: Military Aviation from 1909 to 1921.* Washington, D.C.: Smithsonian, 1993.

Mortensen, Daniel R., ed. *Airpower and Ground Armies: Essays on the Evolution of Anglo-American Air Doctrine, 1940–43.* Maxwell Air Force Base, Ala.: Air University Press, 1998.

Moy, Timothy. *War Machines: Transforming Technologies in the U.S. Military, 1920–1940.* College Station: Texas A&M University Press, 2001.

Mueller, John. *Policy and Opinion in the Gulf War.* Chicago: University of Chicago Press, 1994.

Muir, Malcolm, Jr., "United States Aviation Units Aviation Units Aboard Fast Battleships in World War II: Changing Missions in Midstream," *Aerospace Historian* 27, no. 2 (June, 1980): 95–100.

Murray, Williamson, with Wayne Thompson. *Air War in the Persian Gulf.* Baltimore: Nautical and Aviation, 1995, 1996.

Murray, Williamson, and Allan R. Millett. *A War to Be Won: Fighting the Second World War.* Cambridge, Mass.: Belknap Press, 2000.

Murray, Williamson. "Air War in the Gulf: The Limits of Air Power." *Strategic Review* 26, no. 1 (winter, 1998): 28–38.

Myers, Steven Lee. "With Little Notice, U.S. Planes Have Been Striking Iraq All Year." *New York Times,* August 13, 1999.

Nalty, Bernard C., ed. *Winged Shield, Winged Victory: A History of the United States Air Force.* 2 vols. Washington, D.C.: Air Force History and Museums Program, 1997.

Napier, David H., director, Aerospace Research Center. "2000 Year-End Review and 2001 Forecast—An Analysis," available at http://www.aia-aerospace.org.

Newman, Richard J. "Vietnam's Forgotten Lessons." *U.S. News & World Report,* May 1, 2000, 30–32, 34–35, 38, 40.

"Now Hear This." *Inside the Pentagon,* December 17, 1998.

Nye, Joseph S., Jr. "Redefining the National Interest." *Foreign Affairs* 78, no. 4 (July–August, 1999): 22–35.

O'Connell, Charles F., Jr. "The Failure of the American Aeronautical Production and Procurement Effort During the First World War." Master's thesis, Ohio State University; 1978.

Office of History, Headquarters, U.S. Air Force Reserve, "A Brief History of the United States Air Force Reserve, 1916–1991," January, 1992, Robins Air Force Base, Ga.

Overy, Richard J. *The Air War, 1939–1945.* New York: Stein and Day, 1981.

Palmer, Bruce, Jr. *The 25-Year War: America's Military Role in Vietnam.* Lexington: University Press of Kentucky, 1984

Palmer, Michael A. *On Course to Desert Storm: The United States Navy and the Persian Gulf.* Washington, D.C.: Naval Historical Center, 1992.

Patrick, Mason M. *The United States in the Air.* Garden City: Doubleday, Doran, 1928.

Paztor, Andy. "Pentagon Set to Unveil Plan on Reserve Cuts." *Wall Street Journal,* March 26, 1992.

Peake, Louis A. "Major General Mason M. Patrick: Military Aviation Pioneer." *American Aviation Historical Society Journal* 26, no. 3 (fall, 1981): 200–204.

Pearce, George F. "He Did Not Curry Favor," *Aerospace Historian* 30, no. 3 (September, 1983): 193–99.

Pearson, Henry Greenleaf. *A Business Man in Uniform: Raynal Cawthorne Bolling.* New York: Duffield, 1923.

Peebles, Curtis. *High Frontier: The U.S. Air Force and the Military Space Program.* Washington, D.C.: Air Force History and Museums Program, 1997.

"People." *Air Force Magazine,* May, 2000, 55.

Percy, Arthur. *A History of U.S. Coast Guard Aviation.* Annapolis, Md.: Naval Institute Press, 1989.

Perry, Robert. "Trends in Military Aeronautics, 1908–1976." In *Two Hundred Years of Flight in America: A Bicentennial Survey,* ed. Eugene M. Emme. AAS History Series. Vol. 1. San Diego: American Astronautical Society, 1979.

Piatt, George. "Defense Raise to Target Specifics." *European Stars and Stripes,* January 10, 1999.

Pincus, Walter. "U.S. Plan to Renovate Warheads Stirs Opposition." *Washington Post,* March 26, 2000.

Putney, Diane T. "From Instant Thunder to Desert Storm: Developing the Gulf War Air Campaign's Phases," *Air Power History* 41, no. 3 (fall, 1994): 38–50.

Rae, John B. *Climb To Greatness: The American Aviation Industry, 1920–1960.* Cambridge, Mass.: MIT Press, 1968.

———. "Wartime Technology and Commercial Aviation." *Aerospace Historian* 20, no. 3 (September, 1973): 131–36.

Raines, Edgar F., Jr., *Army Historical Series. Eyes Of Artillery: The Origins Of Modern U.S. Army Aviation In World War II.* Washington, D.C.: Center of Military History, United States Army, 2000.

Ransom, Harry Howe. "The Air Corps Act of 1926: A Study of the Legislative Process." Ph.D. diss., Princeton University, 1953.

Redmond, DeLyle G. "The Role of Attack Helicopters in Conventional War." *U.S. Army Aviation Digest,* January, 1972, 7–9, 35.

"Report of the Chief Signal Officer." In *U.S. War Department Annual Reports, 1911.* Vol. 1. Washington, D.C.: GPO, 1912.

"Report of the Chief Signal Officer." In *U.S. War Department Annual Reports, 1913.* Vol. 1. Washington, D.C.: GPO, 1914.

"Report of the Chief Signal Officer." In *U.S. War Department Annual Reports, 1914.* Vol. 1. Washington, D.C.: GPO, 1915.

Reserve Officers Public Affairs Unit 4-1. *The Marine Corps Reserve: A History.* Washington, D.C.: Division of Reserve, Headquarters, U.S. Marine Corps, 1966.

Reynolds, Clark G. *The Fast Carriers: The Forging of an Air Navy.* New York: McGraw-Hill, 1968.

———. *Admiral John H. Towers: The Struggle for Naval Air Supremacy.* Annapolis, Md.: Naval Institute Press, 1991.

Ricks, Thomas E. "Joint Chiefs Say Defense Needs Bigger Raise Than Clinton Plans." *Wall Street Journal,* January 6, 1999.

Roland, Alex. *Model Research: The National Advisory Committee for Aeronautics, 1915–1918.* Vol. 1. Washington, D.C.: National Air and Space Administration, 1975.

Russell, Edward T. *Leaping the Atlantic Wall: Army Air Forces Campaigns in Western Europe, 1942–1945.* Washington, D.C.: Air Force History and Museums Program, 1999.

Sapolsky, Harvey M. "Equipping the Armed Forces." *Armed Forces and Society* 14, no. 1 (fall, 1987): 113–28.

Scales, Robert H. *Certain Victory: The U.S. Army in the Gulf War.* Washington, D.C.: Office of the Chief of Staff, U.S. Army, 1993.

Scamehorn, Howard Lee. "American Air Transport and Airpower Doctrine in World War II." *Airpower Historian* 8, no. 3 (July, 1961): 148–55.

Schaffel, Kenneth. *The Emerging Shield: The Air Force and the Evolution of Continental Air Defense, 1945–1960.* Washington, D.C.: Office of Air Force History, 1991.

Schneider, Greg. "U.S. Help Urged for Defense Industry." *Washington Post,* May 18, 2000.

Schlight, John. *A War Too Long: The U.S. Air Force in Southeast Asia, 1961–1975.* Washington, D.C.: Air Force History and Museums Program, 1996.

Schubert, Frank N., and Theresa L. Kraus, eds. *The Whirlwind War: The United States Army in Operations DESERT SHIELD and DESERT STORM.* Washington, D.C.: Center of Military History, 1994.

Self, Mary R. *History of the Development and Production of USAF Heavy Bombardment Aircraft, 1917–1949.* Wright-Patterson Air Force Base, Ohio: Historical Office, Air Materiel Command, 1950.

Shaw, Fred J., Jr., and Timothy Warnock. *The Cold War and Beyond: Chronology of the United States Air Force, 1947–1997.* Maxwell Air Force Base, Ala.: Air Force History and Museums Program and Air University Press, 1997.

Sheely, Lawrence D., ed. *Sailor of the Air: The 1917–1919 Letters & Dairy of USN CMM/A Irving Edward Sheely.* Tuscaloosa: University of Alabama Press, 1993.

Sherry, Michael S. *The Rise of American Air Power: The Creation Of Armageddon.* New York: Yale University Press, 1987.

Sherwood, John D. *Officers in Flight Suits: The Story of American Air Force Fighter Pilots in the Korean War.* New York: New York University Press, 1996.

———. *Fast Movers: America's Jet Pilots and the Vietnam War Experience.* New York: Free Press, 1999.

Shiner, John F. *Foulois and the U.S. Army Air Corps, 1931–1935.* Washington, D.C.: Office of Air Force History, 1983.

———. "The Birth of the GHQ Air Force." *Military Affairs* 42, no. 3 (October, 1978): 113–19.

Shipman, Richard. *Wings at the Ready: 75 Years of the Naval Air Reserve.* Annapolis, Md.: Naval Institute Press, 1991.

Simanson, G. R, Editor. *The History of the American Aircraft Industry: An Anthology.* Cambridge: MIT Press, 1968.

Skibbie, Lawrence F. "Long-Term Remedy Needed for Ailing Defense Industry." *National Defense,* March, 2000, 2.

Smith, Perry McCoy. *The Air Force Plans for Peace, 1943–1945.* Baltimore: Johns Hopkins University Press, 1970.

Smith, R. Elberton. *The Army and Economic Mobilization.* The War Department. *U.S. Army in World War II.* Washington, D.C.: Office of the Chief of Military History, 1959.

Smith, Richard K. *Seventy-five Years of In-flight Refueling: Highlights, 1923–1998.* Washington, D.C.: Air Force History and Museums Program, 1998.

Smythe, Donald. *Guerrilla Warrior: The Early Life of John J. Pershing.* New York: Charles Scribner's Sons, 1973.

Snyder, E. Clifford. *History of Aircraft Production Problems during the Air Force Buildup (1950–1954).* Vol. 1. *Air Force Logistics Command Historical Study no. 253.* Wright-Patterson Air Force Base, Ohio: Office of History, Air Materiel Command, 1956.

Snyder, Thomas S., ed. *Air Force Communications Command, 1938–1991: An Illustrated History.* 3d ed. Scott Air Force Base, Ill.: Air Force Communications Command, 1991.

Spector, Ronald H. *Eagle Against the Sun: The American War with Japan*. New York: Vintage Books, 1985.

Spiller, Roger J., ed. *Dictionary of American Military Biography*. 3 vols. Westport, Conn.: Greenwood Press, 1984.

Spires, David N. *Beyond Horizons: A Half Century of Air Force Space Leadership*. Rev. ed. Colorado Springs: Air University Press, 1998.

Stokesbury, James L. *A Short History Of Air Power*. New York: William Morrow and Co., Inc., 1986.

"Super Hornet Enters Full Rate Production." Department of Defense News Release no. 342-00, June 16, 2000, available at http://defenselink.mil/news/Jun2000/b06162000_bt342-00.html.

Suro, Roberto. "U.S. Air Raids Over Iraq Become an Almost Daily Ritual." *Washington Post*, August 30, 1999.

———. "For U.S. Aviators, Readiness Woes Are a 2-Front Struggle." *Washington Post*, February 3, 2000.

Swanborough, Gordon, and Peter M. Bowers. *United States Military Aircraft Since 1908*. Rev. ed. London: Putnam, 1971.

———. *United States Navy Aircraft Since 1911*. London: Putnam Aeronautical Books, 1990.

Thompson, Wayne. *To Hanoi and Back: The United States Air Force and North Vietnam, 1966–1973*. Washington, D.C.: Air Force History and Museums Program, 2000.

———, and Bernard C. Nalty. *Within Limits: The U.S. Air Force and the Korean War*. Washington, D.C.: Air Force History and Museums Program, 1996.

Tilford, Earl H., Jr. "Operation Allied Force and the Role of Air Power." *Parameters* 29, no. 4 (winter, 1999–2000): 24–38.

Tirpak, John A. "The State of Precision Engagement." *Air Force Magazine*, March 2000, 25–30.

Trask, Roger R. *The Secretaries of Defense: A Brief History, 1947–1985*. Washington, D.C.: Historical Office, Office of the Secretary of Defense, 1985.

Treadwell, Mattie E. *The Women's Army Corps*. Special Studies. *U.S. Army in World War II*. Washington, D.C.: Office of the Chief of Military History, 1954.

Trimble, William F. *Wings for the Navy: A History of the Naval Aircraft Factory*. Annapolis, Md.: Naval Institute Press, 1990.

———. *Admiral William A. Moffett: Architect of Naval Aviation*. Smithsonian History of Aviation Series. Washington, D.C.: Smithsonian Institution Press, 1994.

Tripak, John A. "The Space Commission Reports. *Air Force Magazine*, March, 2001, 30–35.

Truver, Scott C. "The U.S. Navy in Review." *U.S. Naval Institute Proceedings* 126 (May, 2000): 76–78, 80, 82.

Tunner, William H. *Over the Hump*. New York: Duell, Sloan, and Pearce, 1964; Reprint, Washington, D.C.: Office of Air Force History, 1985.

Turnbull, Archibald D., and Clifford L. Lord. *History of United States Naval Aviation*. New Haven, Conn.: Yale University Press, 1949. Reprint, New York: Arno Press, 1972.

Turner, William Oliver, Jr. "U.S. Arms Sales to Saudi Arabia: Implications for American Foreign Policy." Ph.D. diss., George Washington University, 1982.

Underwood, Jeffery S. "The Army Air Corps under Franklin D. Roosevelt: The Influence of Air Power on the Roosevelt Administration, 1933–1941." Ph.D. diss., Louisiana State University, 1988.

"USAF Leaders Through the Years." *Air Force Magazine*, May, 1999, 42, 44–46, 48.

U.S. Army Air Service. *Annual Report of the Air Service, Fiscal Year 1919*. Washington, D.C.: Department of War, 1919.

———. *Annual Report of the Chief of the Air Service for the Fiscal Year Ending June 30, 1921*. Washington, D.C.: GPO, 1921.

U.S. Congress, House. "Hearings before a Subcommittee of the Committee on Military Affairs, United States Air Service." 66th Cong., 2d sess., Dec., 1919–Feb., 1920.

———, Committee on Military Affairs. "Investigation of Profiteering in Military Aircraft under HR 275." HR 2060, 73d Cong., 2d sess., June 15, 1934.

———, Committee on Appropriations. "Military Establishment Appropriations Bill for [FY] 1938, Hearings before a Subcommittee of the Committee on Appropriations." 75th Cong., 1st sess., 1937.

Utz, Curtis Alan. *Cordon of Steel: The U.S. Navy and the Cuban Missile Crisis*. The U.S. Navy in the Modern World, no. 1. Washington, D.C.: Naval Historical Center, Department of the Navy, 1993.

———. "Carrier Aviation Policy and Procurement in the U.S. Navy, 1936–1940." Master's thesis, University of Maryland, 1989.

Vaeth, J. Gordon. "Daughter of the Stars." *U.S. Naval Institute Proceedings* 99 (September, 1973): 61–67.

Van Creveld, Martin. *Technology and War: From 2000 B.C. to the Present*. New York: Free Press, 1989.

VanDeMark, Brian. *Into the Quagmire: Lyndon Johnson and the Escalation of the Vietnam War*. New York: Oxford University Press, 1991, 1995.

Vander Meulen, Jacob A. *The Politics of Aircraft: Building an American Military Industry*. Lawrence: University Press of Kansas, 1991.

Vinch, Chuck. "Caught Between Iraq and a Hard Place." *European Stars and Stripes*, September 1, 1999.

Vogel, Steve. "Military Matters: Area Reserve Unit Completes a Forgotten—but Risky—Mission Over Iraq." *Washington Post*, May 18, 2000.

Von Drehle, David. "World War, Cold War Won; Now, the Gray War." *Washington Post*, September 12, 2001.

Von Karman, Theodore C., with Lee Edson. *The Wind and Beyond: Theodore Von Karman, Pioneer in Aviation and Pathfinder in Space*. Boston: Little, Brown, 1967.

Warden, John A., III. *The Air Campaign: Planning for Combat*. Washington, D.C.: Pergamon-Brassey's, 1989.

Warnock, A. Timothy. *The Battle Against the U-Boat in the American Theater*. The U.S. Army Air Forces in World War II. Washington, D.C.: Center for Air Force History, n.d.

Watson, Robert J. *History of the Office of the Secretary of Defense*. Vol. 4, *Into the Missile Age, 1956–1960*. Washington, D.C.: Historical Office, Office of the Secretary of Defense, 1997.

Weigley, Russell F. *History of the United States Army*. New York: Macmillan, 1967.

———. *The American Way of War: A History of United States Military Strategy and Policy*. New York: Macmillan, 1973.

Weinberger, Caspar W. *Fighting for Peace: Seven Critical Years in the Pentagon*. New York: Warner Books, 1990.

Werrell, Kenneth P. *Blankets of Fire: U.S. Bombers Over Japan During World War II*. Washington, D.C.: Smithsonian Institution Press, 1996.

———. "The Weapon the Military Did Not Want: The Modern Strategic Cruise Missile," *Journal of Military History* 53, no. 4 (October, 1989): 419–38.

White, Robert P. "Air Power Engineer: MGen. Mason M. Patrick and the Air Force Road to Independence." Paper presented at the Air Force History and Museums Program Symposium, Arlington, Va., May 28, 1997.

Whitney, Craig R. "Bombing Ends As Serbs Begin Pullout." *New York Times,* June 11, 1999.

Whitt, Samuel S. "Frank Lahm: Pioneer Military Aviator." *Aerospace Historian* 19, no. 4 (December, 1972): 172–77.

Williams, Daniel. "Putin Wins Vote on START II." *Washington Post,* April 15, 2000.

Wolk, Herman S. "The Quiet Coup of 1949." *Air Force Magazine,* July, 1999, 78–81.

Wooldridge, E. T., ed. *Into the Jet Age: Conflict and Change in Naval Aviation, 1945–1975, An Oral History.* Annapolis, Md.: Naval Institute Press, 1995.

———, ed. *The Golden Age Remembered: U.S. Naval Aviation, 1919–1941.* Annapolis, Md.: Naval Institute Press, 1998.

Worden, Mike. *Rise of the Fighter Generals: The Problem of Air Force Leadership, 1945–1982.* Maxwell Air Force Base, Ala.: Air University Press, 1998.

Y'Blood, William T. *MiG Alley: The Fight for Air Superiority.* The U.S. Air Force in Korea. Washington, D.C.: Air Force History And Museums Program, 2000.

Yergin, Daniel. *The Prize: The Epic Quest for Oil, Money, and Power.* New York: Simon and Schuster, 1993.

Young, Susan H. H. "USAF Almanac: Gallery of USAF Weapons." *Air Force Magazine,* May, 1998, 139–62.

———. "USAF Almanac: Gallery of USAF Weapons." *Air Force Magazine,* May, 2000, 136–62.

Xiaoming Zhang. "China and the Air War in Korea, 1950–1953." *Journal of Military History* 62, no. 2 (April, 1998): 335–70.

Zumwalt, Elmo R., Jr. *On Watch: A Memoir.* New York: Quadrangle, 1976.

INDEX

Italicized page numbers refer to photographs.

ABC-1 Staff Agreement, 90, 91
Aberdeen, Maryland, 87
Acheson, Dean, 156
Adriatic Sea, 286
Aegis combat system, 247
Aegis cruisers, 264
aerial bombardment (bombing), 32, 43, 50,
    54–55, 68–69, 111, 195; dive-bombing,
    67; high-altitude, 123, 133; strategic, 3–4,
    6–7, 8, 50, 78, 115–19, 132, 137–38, 150,
    155, 157, 171, 203, 297
Aero Club of America, 17
Aero Reserve Squadron, 27
Aeronautical Chamber of Commerce, 67
aeronautical research. *See* aviation: research
    and development
Aerospace Defense Command, 222
Aerospace Expeditionary Force (AEF), 290
aerospace industry, 236–38, 278–79, 301
Aerostatic Corps, 12
Afghanistan, 9, 242, 251; Russian invasion
    of, 244, 256
Africa, 8, 79
Agent Orange, 204
Agnew, Spiro, 239
air bases: Aviano Air Base (Italy), 286;
    Carswell Air Force Base (N.M.), 152;
    McGuire AFB (N.J.), 240; Offutt Air
    Force Base (Neb.), 150, 209; Rhein-
    Main Air Base (Germany), 220; Trapani
    Air Base (Sicily), *283;* Wright-Patterson
    Air Force Base (Dayton, Ohio), 36. *See
    also* air fields
Air Combat Command, 290
Air Command Solomons
    (COMAIRSOLS), 124, 125

Air Corps Act (1926), 58, 59, 66, 72–73, 75
Air Corps. *See* U.S. Army Air Corps
aircraft (by category): biplanes, 20;
    bombers, 74–75, 78, 171 —dive, 67, 69,
    82, 133 —fighter, 193 —long-range, 193
    —strategic, 158, 193 —torpedo, 82, 107;
    drones/decoys, 265; fighters, 75, 111, 158,
    193; fixed-wing, 166, 199, 201, 202, 235;
    flying boats, 40, 309n.43; floatplanes,
    25, 53; gliders, 12, 14, 15, 99; heavier-
    than-air, 14–16, 296; helicopters
    (choppers), 11, 14, 65, 99, 153, 166, 195,
    199, 201, 216–17, 300; jet, 166, 173, 175;
    monoplanes, 14, 82; ornithopters, 11, 14;
    pushers, 24; rotary-wing, 210, 235;
    trimotors, 61. *See also* lighter-than-air
    craft
aircraft (by name): 707, 190, 226, 270; 747,
    249; A1, 207; A-1 Triad, 21; A3D
    Skywarrior, 153, 174; A-4, 240, 247; A-6
    fighter, 198, 208, 229, 247; A-7 Corsair
    II, 188, 208, 229, 253; A-7B, 230; A-10,
    271; A-10 Warthog, 7; A-10 Thunder-
    bolt II, 225–26; A-12, 279 ; AC-47, 203;
    AC-130, 203, 253; AD Skyraider, 158,
    169; AH-1G Cobra, 235; AH-2 Cobra,
    234; AH-64 Apache, 265; AH-64A
    Apache, 235, 236; AH-65A Cheyenne,
    236; AJ-1 Savage, 153, 174; AJ-2 Savage,
    174; AV-8 Harrier, 228, 234, 271; AV-8A,
    234; AV-8B, 234; B-1, 221, 226; B-1A,
    221; B-1B Lancer, 221; B-2 Spirit, 233,
    279, 286, 291; B-9, 74; B-10, 74; B-17
    "Flying Fortress," 78, 79, *80,* 81, 86, 113,
    113, 114, 226; B-18, 78; B-24, 106, 107,
    113; B-25, 121, 124, 129; B-26, 169, 207;

aircraft, *continued*

B-29 Superfortress, 128–30, 131–32, 133, 134, 136, 149, 152, 158, 159, 161, 162, 170 —Enola Gay, 135, *136;* B-36, 150, *154,* 155; B-47 Stratojet, 151, *154,* 165; B-50, 152 —Lucky Lady II, 152; B-52 Stratofortress, 151, *154,* 165, 174, 176, 203, 209–10, 216, 226, 244, 268; B-52G, 175; B-52H, 175; B-70, 189; Backfire bombers (Soviet), 229; Badger (Soviet), 230; Bear bomber (Soviet), 230; Bison bomber (Soviet), 230; C-5 Galaxy, 190–91, 236, 277; C-5A Galaxy, 188, 240, 241; C-7, 216; C-9B, 259; C-17, jet transport, 241; C-17 Globemaster III, 279; C-47, 147, 166; C-97, 166; C-121 Constellation, 226; C-123, 216; C-124 Globemaster, 166, *192;* C-130 transport, 216, 221, 244, 259, 277, *278,* 280; C-130E Hercules, 190, 203, 244; C-135 Stratolifter, 190; C-141 Starlifter, 190, 216, *231,* 277, 280; C-141A, 190, 240, 241; CH-46, 234; CH-53, 234; CH-53E, 229; CR-3, 62; Constellation, 139; Cougar, 174; DC-3, 64; DC-4, 139; DH-4, 33; E-2C, 230; E-3 Airborne Warning and Control System (AWACS) (aircraft), 226–27, 256, 262, 270; E-3 Sentry, *276;* E-3B AWACS, 258; E-3A, 247, 254; E-8, 270; EA-6B Prowler, 232, 265, 286; EC-121, 177; EF-111A Raven, 232, 265; F-4 Phantom II, 178, 188, *200,* 213, *214,* 229, 234, 240, 269; F-4B, 230; F-4E Wild Weasels, 226, 232; F4U Corsair, 128, *140,* 158, 169, *170;* F-5-L flying boat, 35, 36; F6F Hellcat, 126; F8D, 207; F8U Crusader, 174, 178; F9F Panther, 158, 161, 162; F-14 Tomcat, 188, 229, 229, 233, 237, 247; F-15 Eagle, 225, 237, 254, 256; F-15C, 258; F-15E, 265; F-16 Fighting Falcon, 225, 229, *260;* F-17, 229; F-20 Tigershark, 237; F-22 Raptor, 279; F-51, 159; F-80, 159, 161, 169; F-80 Shooting Star, 158, 159, 161; F-84, 169; F-84E, 152; F-84G, 167; F-86 Sabre, 151, 162, *163,* 167, 168; F-100 Super Sabre, 175, 206, 207; F-102 Delta Dagger, 175;

F-104 Starfighter, 183, *192;* F-105, 199, 201; F-106 Delta Dart, 175, *248;* F-111, 188, 248, 268; F-111A, 226; F-111B, 229; F-117 Nighthawk, 233, 253, *255,* 265, 267; F-177A Nighthawk, 265, 279, 286; FA-18 Hornet, 229, 229, 234, 237; FA-18D Hornet, 286; FA-18EF Super Hornet, 279; FD-1 Phantom, 100; Fireflies, 158; H-16, 35; Il-28 jet bomber, 162, *192;* J-1 blimp, 71; JN-3, 26; Japanese Type 96, 83; KA-3, 216; KA-6, 216; KB-29, 166, 167; KC-97L, 220; KC-135, 216, 240, *260; Kate* (Japanese), 83; L-4, 110, *110;* MH-53J Pave Low, 265; MiGs (Russian), 174, 198–99, 207, 213, *214,* 216, 230; MiG15, 161–62, 167, 168; MiG17, 213; MiG21, 213, 238 MiG29, 284; Model 299, 77–78; MV-22 Osprey, 279; N-1, 35; NC-4 flying boat, *62;* P2V-7 Neptune, 194; P-3, 259; P-3A Orion, 230; P-38 Lightings, 114, 124; P-40, 108, 129, *140;* P-47 Thunderbolt, 7, 114; P-51 Mustang, 114, *114,* 132; PBY "Catalina," 71, 106; Pioneer UAV (unmanned aerial vehicles), 270; R-6 floatplanes, 45; RB-36D Peacemaker, *154;* RC-7, 274; RC-135 River Joint, 269; RF-4C, 269; Ryan FR-1, 100; Ryan XFR-1, 100; SH-2D helicopter, 229; SR-71 Blackbird, 232; Seafires, 158; Stratoliner, 138; T-2 transport, 61; TBD "Devastator," 82; U-2 spy plane, 182, 192; U-2/TR-1, 269; UH-1 Huey helicopter, 201, 202; UH-1B Huey, 235; UH-1D, *202;* UH-60A Black Hawk, 235; UF-1E, 234; V-22A Osprey, 234; *Val* (Japanese), 83; X-1, 152; XP-59A, 100; XP-80, 100; YB-10, 67; YB-12, 67; Zero (Japanese), 126

Aircraft Production Board, 31, 34

Air Defense Command, 222

air defense, 6, 105, 138, 177; systems of, 87–89

air fields: March Field (Calif.), *76;* Henderson Field (Guadalcanal) 123; Kelly Field (Tex.), 39; Langley Field (Vir.), 72, 77, *255;* McCook Field (Ohio) 36; March Field (Calif.), *76;*

Maxwell Field (Ala.), 72; Mitchell Field (Long Island, N.Y.), 80; Scott Field, Ill., 39; Tuskegee Field (Ala.), 102; Wendover Field (Utah), 134; Wright Field (Ohio), 57, 66, 78. *See also* air bases

airlift, 7, 8, 96–97, 104, 105, 219, 295, 297; to Berlin, 147–49; to China, 129–30, 149; humanitarian, 280; to Israel, 240–41; during the Persian Gulf crisis, 258–59; during Vietnam, 195, 201, 216; during World War I, 96–97; during World War II, 137, 150

Air Mobility Command, 290

Air National Guard, 147, 166; and aircraft numbers, 223; and air defense, 290; in Berlin, 192; and Korean War, 159; in Kosovo, 285; in Panama, 253; dispatched to South Vietnam, 206, 220; and humanitarian relief, 280; mobilization of, 164–65; non-mobilization support role, 220–21, 275–76 (*see also* Operation Creek Party; Operation Volant Oak); and operational integration, 179, 195, 259, 295–96; and the Persian Gulf War, 269; units of —Arizona ANG, *260* —Kentucky ANG, *278* —South Carolina ANG, *192* —West Virginia ANG, *245;* women in, *283*

Air Service. *See* U.S. Army Air Service

Air Transport Command (ATC), 96–97, 129

Albania, 282–83, 286

Albuquerque, 151

Allcorn, Ford, *110*

Allen, James, 13, 17

Allies, 26, 40–42, 87; and aircraft from the U.S., 99

Ambrose, Stephen E., 180, 183

American Airlines, 97

American arms sales abroad, 278–79

American Defense Society, 26

American Expeditionary Forces (AEF), 36, 39; Balloon Section, 39; First Army, 38. *See also* U.S. Air Service

American Express, 295

American Volunteer Group, 75

Anderson, George W., 197

Andrews, Frank M., 73, 77, 84

Anglo-American Combined Bomber Offensive, 110, 111, 112, 119

Anglo-American Combined Chiefs of Staff, 104

Ansbach, Germany, 235

Antiballistic Missile (ABM) Treaty. *See* SALT I treaty

antisubmarine warfare (ASW). *See* U.S. Army Air Forces (USAAF): and antisubmarine warfare (ASW); U.S. Navy (the navy): and antisubmarine warfare (ASW)

Antwerp, 117

Anzio landing, 112

Arabian Peninsula, 256–57, 259

Arabian Sea, 262

Arab-Israeli war, 232, 295

Archytas of Tarantum, 11

Ardennes, 117, 119

Armed Forces Reserve Act (1952), 178

Army Appropriations Act, 26, 27

Army National Guard, 192

Army of the Potomac, 13

Army of the Republic of Vietnam (ARVN), 197, 210

Army-Navy Joint Planning Committee, 90

Arnold, Henry H. (Hap), 56–57, 73, 74, 78, 86, 100, 128, 132; and Air Corps reorganization, 92; and air defense systems, 87, 89; and airlift operations, 96–97; and cross-Channel invasion, 103, 108; and disagreement with Franklin Roosevelt, 90; and the navy, 105; and the USAAF, 104

Arthur, Stanley R., 261–62, 263

Atlantic Fleet, 24

Atlantic Ocean, 105, 106, 107, 193

atomic bomb. *See* weaponry: nuclear

Atomic Energy Commission (AEC), 151, 183

atomic fusion, 100

Auschwitz, 288

Australia, 120, 122, 127

Austria, 79

Austria-Hungary, 22

auto industry, 98

Automobile Club of America, 17

aviation (commercial industry): 3, 28, 47, 49, 61, 63–66, 184, 236, 297, 298; and airlift operations, 258; contributions to military war effort, 97–99, 166; impact of World War II on, 139–40; and sales to foreign countries, 184, 237. *See also* aerospace industry

aviation (general): aircraft design, 24, 64–66 —electronic developments, 101 — instrumentation and navigation, 65, 74; —jet engines/propulsion, 99–100, 299–300; —patent issues, 34 —wing warping, 16, 24: and airframe design revolution, 64–66, 82, 298, 299; and American culture, 9, 44, 51, 140; and impact of World War II, 137–41; and research and development, 14, 33, 46, 51, 63–65, 98–99, 151

aviation (military): aerial combat, 40; AirLand Battle doctrine, 109, 224, 246; airmobility, 219, 223; air superiority, 25, 41, 43, 50, 69, 110, 115, 123–24, 137, 168, 171, 203, 224, 272, 297 —as strategy, 225; antisubmarine campaign of, 40, 45; and centralized air tasking orders (ATO), 262–63, 267; and close air support, 160, 169, 172, 178, 203, 204–205, 297; and combat/weaponry, 23, 25, 40, 50, 117 (*see also* weaponry); and command, control, communications, and intelligence (C_3I), 7, 259; as deterrent, 85–86; and direct fire support, 202; doctrine and tactics, 219, 228, 243, 247, 264; and escort duties, 126–28; and flight training, 38–39, 101–102; and ground force support, 37, 41–44, 108; and interdiction, 7, 169, 172, 203, 207, 268, 297; and inter-service relationships, 49, 205, 212, 249, 262, 289; and mechanical/technical support personnel, 39, 50; and medical evacuation, 201; and need for independent air force, 50–51, 72–79; observation/reconnaissance duties of, 6, 25–26, 32, 39, 41–42, 43, 44, 195, 201, 270, 297, 298; and pursuit, 32, 41, 44, 74; and the role of women, 102;

and search-and-destroy, *202,* 205; tactical capabilities of, 150, 223, 224, 227, 299, 300; and technology *v.* turf, 222, 223

aviation (technological advances): aerial refueling, 6, 7, 8, 150, 166, *192,* 216, 217, 218, 240, 258–59, *260,* 264, 265, 301; Airborne Warning and Control System (AWACS), 264 (*see also* aircraft (by name); airborne ground target acquisition systems (JSTARS), 264; electronic countermeasures packages (ECM), 223, 224, 232, 237, 265; parachute, 11; precision-guided munitions, 219, 223, 281, 299 (*see also* missile: precision guided); Norden bombsight, 74; radar technology (*see* radar); radio communication, 31; radio-guided bombs, 101; Rolls Royce-Packard Merlin engine, 114; supersonic speed, 152; target acquisition systems, 219

AWPD-I (plan), 92

Axis coalition, 79, 87, 90, 91, 99

Azores, 30, 45, 61

Bacon, Roger, 11

Badger, Charles J., 23

Baghdad, 264, 265, 271

Baghdad Pact, 177

Bahrain, 255

Baker, Newton D., 28, 31, 32, 33, 77

Baker, Royal N., *163*

Baker Board, 77

Balkan conflict, 4, 9, 112, 302. *See also* Bosnia- Herzegovina; Kosovo; Serbia; Yugoslavia

Baltic Sea, 246

Barlow, Jeffrey G., 155

Base Force proposals, 273

Base Realignment and Closure (BRAC), 290

Basra (Iraq), 269

Battle Force Yankee, 262

Battle Force Zulu, 262, 264

battles: of the Atlantic, 104, 106, 108, 118; of Britain, 91, 101, 126, 130; of the Bulge, 116; of Leyte Gulf, 130–31; of Midway, *122,* 299

Bay of Biscay, 40

Bay of Pigs, 191
Beirut, 248
Belgium, 89
Belgrade, 282, 285
Bell, Alexander Graham, 22
Bell Corporation, 67, 236
Berlin Wall, 252
Berlin, 85, 187; airlift, 8, 147–49, *148;* Crisis of 1962, 191–92, *192;* Soviet blockade of, 147, 295
Bethesda Naval Hospital, 154
Biddle, William P., 24
Big Week, 115
Bilstein, Roger E.: *Fight in America, 1903– 1983,* 6, 201, 297, 302
Bishop, Corlandt, 17
Blanchard, Jean-Pierre, 12
Board of Ordnance and Fortification, 17, 18
Boeing Company, 67, 151, 166, 226, 236, 237
Bolling, Raynal Cawthorne, 24, 32, 37
Bolshevik Revolution, 65
BOMARC air defense missile program, 177. *See also* missile (by category); missile (by name)
bomber gap controversy, 181
Bong, Dick, 140
Boomer, Walter, 261
Bosnia-Herzegovina, 280, 281–82, 288
Bougainville, 125
Boyington, Gregory (Pappy), 140, *140*
Bradley, Omar N., 116, 118
Brazil, 22, 106
Brown, Harold, 229
Brown, Jesse L., *170*
Brown, Wilson, Jr., 121
Buckley, John, 142, 186, 227, 299–300, 303
Bulgaria, 22
Bureau of Aeronautics (navy), 20, 55, 58, 59, 77, 91
Bureau of Construction and Repair, 20
Bureau of Equipment (navy), 20
Bureau of Navigation, 58
Burke, Arleigh, 177
Burma, 129, 144
Bush, George Herbert Walker, 251; and START I agreement, 292; and use of the military —in Kuwait, 263–65 —in Panama, 253–54 —in the Persian Gulf, 260, 266, 271–72, 287 —in Somalia, 277, 287 —in the war on drugs, 274
Bush, Vannevar, 100
Byrd, Richard, 61

Cactus Air Force, 123
Caley, George, 14, 15
Cambodia, 195, 211; bombing of, 208, 210
Canada, 30
Cape May, New Jersey, 45
Caproni, Gianni, 72
Caribbean, 24, 50, 87, 106
Caribbean Defense Command, 84
Carroll, Eugene, 276
Carter, Jimmy: defense spending, 219, 228, 242–44, 256; and the B-1 program, 221, 243; and cease-fire in Bosnia, 281; and national security, 243–44; and nuclear deterrence, 243
Carter Doctrine, 256
Casablanca, 110, 112
Castro, Fidel, 191, 193
Center for Defense Information, 276
Central Intelligence Agency (CIA), 145, 177, 182; and Bay of Pigs invasion, 191
Central Powers, 33
Chambers, John Whiteclay, II, 6
Chambers, Reed, *43*
Chambers, Washington Irving, 20, 21
Chance-Vought Aircraft, Inc., 174
Chanute, Octave, 15, 16, 17
Château-Thierry, 41
Cheney, Richard B., 254, 258, 279
Chennault, Claire Lee, 75, 83, 129, 141
Chiang Kai-shek, 83
Chicago, 50
Chief of Naval Operations (CNO), 157, 177, 227, 261
China, 273; airlift to 129–30, 164; China/ Soviet cooperation, 167; Communist, 156, 158, 180, 274; and intervention in the Korean War, 151, 162, 165; invasion of, 79, 81; and Korean War armistice, 171; and Lend-Lease assistance, 87; Nationalist, 75, 180; and North

China, *continued*
Vietnam, 208, 212; use of airbases in, 129; use of air power against, 73, 85; visit by Nixon to, 243
China Air Task Force, 75
China-Burma-India theater, 128–30, 149
Chinese People's Liberation Army Air Force (PLAAF), 167
Chinese People's Volunteers, 162
Chosin Reservoir (Korea), 163, *170*
Churchill, Winston, 103, 108, 110, 130, 143
citizen-soldiers, 27, 49, 53, 91, 206, 295. *See also* guard and reserve forces
Civil Reserve Air Fleet (CRAF), 241, 258
Civil War, 13, 27
Clark, Mark W., *170*
Clark, Paul Wilson, 22
Clark, Wesley K., 283
Clay, Lucius D., 147, 192
Clayton, James L., 185
Clinton Doctrine, 287–88
Clinton, Bill, 274, 277, 285, 287, 292, 294; and Bosnia/Kosovo, 282–84
Coast Artillery, 23
Coast Guard, 70, 92–93; and Operation Husky, 111; women in, 102
Codfelter, Mark, 215
Coffin, Howard, 31–32, 33
Cohen, Eliot A., 250, 292
Cold War, 144, 152, 217; arms race, 142, 185–86, 221, 237; and Cuban missile crisis, 193, *194;* end of, 219, 252; and Middle East crisis (1973), 238; and nuclear weapons, 222, 300; and U.S. military build up, 173–77, 221, 246; and U.S. military superiority, 182, 211
Collier, Basil, 4
Cologne, *113*
Colombia, 274
Columbus, New Mexico, 26
combat training programs, 219, 223, 225, 231
Combined Bomber Offensive. *See* Anglo-American Combined Bomber Offensive
Consolidated Aircraft Corporation, 46, 71
Convair Corporation, 155, 175
Coolidge, Calvin, 71
Coral Sea, 121

Corn, Joseph: *The Winged Gospel,* 6, 141, 303
Council of National Defense, 27
Craig, Malin, 78, 79
Crissy, Myron, 23
Croatia, 280, 281
Crouch, Thomas: *The Bishop's Boys,* 4
Cuba, 187, 191, 247; blockade of, 193; missile sites in, 192
Cunningham, Alfred A., 24, 45, 46, 59
Curtiss, Glenn H., *21*, 22, 23, 34, 35, 45, 85
Curtiss Aeroplane Company, 24, 34, 66
Curtiss-Wright Corporation, 67
Czechoslovakia, 79, 84

Dawn Patrol (movie), 51
Dayton, Ohio, 36, 57
Dayton-Wright Aeroplane Company, 34
D-Day, 115, 118, 133
Deeds, Edward, 33
Defense Intelligence Agency, 188
Defense Reorganization Act (1958), 182
Defense Supply Agency, 188
de Mille, Cecil B., 51
Denfeld, Louis E., 155
Denmark, 89
Dern, George H., 77
Desert Storm. *See* military operations: Desert Storm
de Seversky, Alexander P.: *Airpower: Key to Survival,* 4
Dhahran (Saudi Arabia), 255
Diego Garcia, 254, 256
Dien Bien Phu (Vietnam), 179, *194*
Distant Early Warning (DEW) line, 175
Dominican Republic, 20, 60
Dönitz, Karl, 104, 107
Doolittle, James H. (Jimmy), 63, 121, 140
Douglas Aircraft Company, 61, 67, 236
Douglas, Donald W., 78, 85, 139
Douhet, Giulio, 72
Dresden, 117, 299
Duc Pho (Quang Ngai Province) (Vietnam), *202*
Dutch East Indies, 144

Eaker, Ira C., 78, 113
Eastman, Joseph, *43*

Egypt, 238, 240–41
XVIII Airborne Corps, 269
Eighth Air Force, 113, *114*
Eighth Army, 160, 161, 162, 163, 164
82nd Airborne Division, 258
Einstein, Albert, 134
Eisenhower, Dwight D., 109, 111, 115, 116,
    187; and international unrest, 179–80,
    195; and New Look strategy, 294, 176–
    79, 223, 300; and military-industrial
    complex, 183–85, 189; and nuclear
    deterrence, 171, 172, 179, 182, 183
Elbe River, 119
Ellyson, Theodore G., 23
Elmer (Benedictine monk), 12
Ely, Eugene, 20, *21*
England, 6, 45
English Channel, 12, 45, 88, 108
Ethiopia, 73, 85
Euphrates River, 268, 269, 271
Europe, 30

Fahd ibn 'Abd al-'Aziz al-Saud (King
    Fahd), 254
Fairchild Company, 225
Far East Air Forces (FEAF), 157–58, 168,
    170; Bomber Command, 169
Fechet, James E., 73–74
Federal Aviation Commission, 77
Federal Republic of Germany, 149. *See also*
    Germany
Felt, Harry D., 197
Fickel, Jacob E., 23
Fifth Air Force, 164, 168, 170
Fifth Fleet, 128
Fighter Mafia, 225
Fighter Weapons School (Top Gun), 213
Firmen, Armin, 11
1st Aero Squadron, 26, 41
1st Air Brigade, 41
1st Cavalry Division (Airmobile), 201, *202*
1st Marine Air Wing (MAW), 163, 165, 168,
    169, *200*, 204
1st Marine Division, 161, 163, *170*
1st Marine Expeditionary Force, 269
555th Tactical Fighter Squadron, *214*
Fischer Body Company, 34

Fleet, Reuben H., *46*
Fleet Marine Force, 127, 128, 145, 169
Flying Tigers, (movie), 141
Flying Tigers, 129, *140*
Foggia (Italy), 112
Fokker, Anthony, 61
Ford, Gerald, 242
Ford Motor Company, 188
Foreign Corrupt Practices Act (1977), 237
Formosa, 130, 133
Forrestal, James V., 145, 149–50, 152, 153, 154
Fort Knox, Ky., 75, 87
Fort Rucker, Ala., 200
Foss, Joe, 140
Foulois, Benjamin D., *19*, 30, 38, 72, 75, 76,
    78
Fourteenth Air Force, 75
4th Fighter Wing, *163*
France, 40, 226, 303; and aviation research,
    22, 33, 296; and the Berlin airlift, 147;
    flight training in, 38–39; and French/
    American cooperation, 40, 45, 112; and
    German invasion, 89; in Southeast Asia,
    179, 194–95; as supplier of aircraft, 257;
    and war with Germany, 82, 86, 115; and
    war in Yugoslavia, 280
Franco-Prussian War, 14
French Indochina. *See* Indochina
French Revolution, 12
Fulton, Mo., 143

Gaddis, John Lewis, 149
Gates, Thomas S., 181
Gelb, Leslie H. , 281
General Dynamics Corporation, 185, 225,
    229, 277
General Headquarters Air Force (GHQ Air
    Force), 77, 78–79, 315n.63. *See also* U.S.
    Air Force (USAF): Combat Command
Geneva Accords, 195
Germany, 78, 80, 137, 294, 295; and airborne
    warfare, 96; and the aircraft industry, 22,
    98–99; Allied bombing of, 112, 115, 117,
    299; and Allied destruction of transporta-
    tion system, 116–17, 138; and annexation
    of Sudetenland, 84; and the Ardennes
    counteroffensive, 119; and Axis coalition,

Germany, *continued*
79; and bombing of Britain, 117; and
forces in the Mediterranean, 111; and
humanitarian air support, 277; and
invasion —of Poland, 81, 86 —of the
Soviet Union, 91, 92, 117; and NATO
forces in Kosovo, 285; and radar
research, 88; and regional aggression,
82, 89; reunification of, 252; submarine
threat of, 29–30, 104–105, 110
Gibbs-Smith, Charles H.: *Aviation: An
Historical Survey from Its Origins to the
End of World War II,* 4
Giffard, Henri, 13
Gilbert Islands, 127
Glenn L. Martin Company, 67, 309n.43
Global Positioning System (GPS). *See*
satellites: Global Positioning System
(GPS)
Gnome engine, 24
Golan Heights, 238
Goldwater-Nichols Reorganization Act
(1986), 249, 261
Gorbachev, Mikhail, 251–52
Gordon Bennett air race, 62
Göring, Hermann, 44
Grande Armée, 12
Great Britain, 22, 82, 226, 274; and the
aircraft industry, 98–99; and air power
strategy, 85, 137; acquires the AWACS,
226; and the Berlin airlift, 147; declares
war on Germany, 86; flight training in,
39; and lend-lease assistance, 87; and
NATO forces in Kosovo, 285; and naval
air bases, 30; and radar research, 88; and
troop withdrawal, 254, 255; and war in
Yugoslavia, 280
Great Depression, 59, 62, 64, 66, 77, 79
Great Marianas Turkey Shoot, 128
Greece, 143, 285
Greely, Adolphus W., 17
Grenada, 247
Gross, Robert, 78
Grumman Corporation, 126, 174, 229
Guadalcanal, 122
Guam, 157, 158, 216
Guantanamo Bay (Cuba), 23

guard and reserve forces: and airlift to
Israel, 241; augmentation units of, 230;
mobilization —of 1961, 192 —of 1968,
206 —of 1990, 259, 260 —of 1999, 285;
and the New Look strategy, 178–79;
and silent call-up, 275–76; and total
force policies, 295; and war in Yugosla-
via, 280
Guatamela, 177
Gulf Cooperation Council, 263
Gulf of Mexico, 105, 106
Gulf of Sidra, 248
Gulf of Tonkin, 196–97, *198,* 216
Gulf of Tonkin Resolution, 196

Hagan, Kenneth, *This People's Navy,* 4
Haiphong Harbor, 208
Haiti, 20, 50, 60, 250, 301
Hallion, Richard, 94, 232
Halsey, William F. (Bull), 59, 107, 141; and
carrier command, 59; on New Guinea,
125; and war in the Pacific, 121, 124, 126–
28, 130
Hanoi, 195, 196, 197, 205, 206, 257
Hansell, Haywood S., Jr., 132
Havens, Beckwith, 24
Hawaii, 74, 93, 127
Hawker (British aircraft firm), 234
Hell's Angels (movie), 51
Helm, William H., 13
Heron, S. D., 66
Herring, George C., 210
Hertz, Heinrich, 87
Higham, Robin: *Airpower,* 3
Himalayas, 129
Hirohito, 135–36, *136*
Hiroshima, 135, 150, 299, 303
Hitler, Adolf, 79, 84, 86, 87, 91, 261; declares
war on U.S., 93, 97
Ho Chi Minh, 195, 205, 206, 209
Ho Chi Minh Trail, 207
Holland, 89
Holley, Irving B., Jr.: *Ideas and Weapons,* 5
Hollywood (film industry), 298
Hoover, Herbert, 79
Horn of Africa, 244
Horner, Charles A., 291; and air campaign

in the Persian Gulf, 261–62, 266–67, 270–72; and naval forces 263, 265
House Armed Services Committee, 190
Howell, Clark, 77
Hudson, James J.: *Hostile Skies,* 5
Huerta, Victoriano, 25
Hughes Aircraft Corporation, 235, 277
Hump airlift, 129, 149
Hungary, 179
Hungnam (Korea), 163
Huntington, Samuel P., 237–38
Hurley, Alfred F.: *Billy Mitchell,* 5
Hürtgen Forest, 116
Hussein, Saddam al-Tikriti, 264, 302; and American Military aid, 254; chemical, biological, and nuclear weapons of, 266; and economic sanctions against, 258, 260; elimination of, 261, 266, 271, 273; mistakes of, 272; and regional threats of, 275; and use of the Republican Guard, 257
Huston, John W., 104

Icarus, 11
Iceland, 92, 106
Identification Friend or Foe (IFF), 162
Inchon (Korea), 161
India, 129
Indian Ocean, 193, 254
Indochina, 93, 144, 194–95, 254. *See also* Cambodia; Laos; Vietnam
interservice cooperation, 249, 289
Iran, 177, 242, 257, 273, 274; and terrorists, 249; U.S. support of, 255, 256
Iran-Iraq War (1980–88), 227, 256, 273
Iraq, 250, 274, 288, 289, 301–302; and destruction of air defense systems, 265; and invasion of Kuwait, 254; and the no-fly zone, 275, 290; at war, 250, 257–60, 264, 271–73
Ireland, 45, 106
Iron Curtain, 143
Irwin, Noble, 30
Islam, 294
Israel, 238–40; and threat of Iraq, 267
Israeli Air Force, 238
Italy, 5, 22, 45, 81, 103, 168; and Axis

coalition, 79; invasion of, 110–12; lack of military success against, 130–31; and NATO forces in Kosovo, 285
Iwo Jima, 132–33, 135

Japan, 78–81, 87, 90, 91, 137, 299; and the aircraft industry, 98–99, 122, 128; and attack at Pearl Harbor, 93, 99, 140, 295; bombing of, 129, 133; and Combined Fleet of, 131; and invasion —of China, 81 —of the Philippines, 123; and naval expansion, 82–83; and reserve patrol units, 230; and submarine threat, 107; surrender of, 135; U.S. defense of, 157–59, 168
Japanese Imperial Navy, 83
Johns Hopkins University, 18
Johnson, Harold, K., 201
Johnson, Louis, 154, 155, 156, 173
Johnson, Lyndon B., 196, 212, 213, 295; and escalation of military involvement, 197, 206; expectations of for role of air power, 294; and graduated response strategy, 196; and the guard/reserves, 259; and negotiations with North Vietnam, 207; and Great Society program, 196
Joint Army-Navy Technical Aircraft Committee, 30, 32
Joint Force Air Component Commander (JFACC), 261, 262, 264
Joint Operations Center (JOC), 160
Joint Strategic Planning Staff, 181
Joint Surveillance Target Attack Radar System (JSTARS), 264, 270. *See also* radar
Joint Task Force (JTF) Proven Force, 265–66
Jolo (Philippines), 20
Joy, Turner C., 158

Kagan, Donald, 272–73
Kagan, Frederick, 272–73
Keely, Oakley G., 61
Kelsey, Benjamin S., 77
Kelso, Frank B., II, 261
Kenly, William L., 37–38
Kennan, George F., 144

Kennedy, George C., 123–24, 125
Kennedy, John F., 183, 187, 217; and flexible response, 187, 189, 190–92; and support of South Vietnam, 195
Kennett, Lee: *The First Air War, 1914–1918,* 4
Key West, Fla., 153
Khe Sanh, 205
Khmer Rouge, 210
Khomeini, Ayatollah Ruhollah, 244
Khrushchev, Nikita, 191, 192, 193
Kill Devil Hill, N.C., 16
Kim Il Sung, 156
Kimpo (Korea), 158
King, Ernest J., 77, 107, 120, 127, 130; as advocate for naval air power, 105, 126, 130; and Bureau of Aeronautics, 77; and carrier command, 59, 131
Kissinger, Henry, 215, 240
Kitty Hawk, N.C., 13, 296
Korb, Lawrence J., 287, 288
Korea, 156, 223
Korean War, 100, 147, 153, 167, 185, 254, 300; armistice, 171, 180; beginnings of, 157–58; and China, 151; post-war analysis and implications of, 172–76, 227; and U.S. bombing, 158, 169–70
Kosovo Liberation Army (KLA), 282, 285, 286, 287
Kosovo War, 7, 282–84, *283,* 289, 291, 296, 299, 301–302
Kremlin, 157
Kriegsmarine, 104
Kuter, Lawrence C., 180
Kuwait, 254, 256–57, 263, 299, 301–302, 303; crisis, 257–59, 265; the Kuwait Theater of Operations (KTO), 264, 267
Kyushu, 135

Lafayette Escadrille, 36, 40
LaGuardia, Fiorello H., 50
Lahm, Frank P., 39
Laird, Melvin, 220, 223
Lajes, Azores, 240, 241
Lakehurst, New Jersey, 50, 54
Langley, Samuel Pierpont, 15, 16–8, 19, 22
Langley Memorial Aeronautical Laboratory, 22, 63

Laos, 195, 203, 206, 207, 211–12, 216
Lawrence Aero Engine Corporation, 66
League of Nations, 49
Lebanon, 190, 214, 238
Le Croisic NAS (France) 40
Lehman, John F., Jr., 214, 246–47, 290
LeMay, Curtis E. 129, 141; and aerial refueling, 152; and air assault in Vietnam, 197, 201; and airlift in China, 129; and the B-29 bombing campaign, 132–34; and the Berlin blockade, 147; and nuclear superiority, 191; and SAC command, 150–51, 158, 164
Lend-Lease Act, 87
Lenoir, Jean Joseph Étienne, 14
Leonardo da Vinci, 11
Lewis, Isaac N., 23
Leyte, 130–31
Libia, 248, 249
lighter-than-air craft: airships (rigid), 71 — *Akron,* 71 —*Macon,* 71; balloons, 12–13, 24, 39, 41, 44, 296, 297; ; blimps, 53, 71, 105; dirigibles, 17, 49, 50; zeppelins, 6
Lilienthal, Otto, 15
Lilley, Leonard W., *163*
Lindbergh, Charles A., 9, 51–52, *52,* 85, 141
Lisbon, 61, *62*
Lockheed Aircraft Corporation, 100, 185, 233, 236, 237; acquires Martin Marietta, 277
Lod International Airport (Israel), 231
Lord, Clifford D. (coauthor): *History of United States Naval Aviation,* 4
Louisiana, 109
Love, Robert, 229
low observable aircraft. *See* radar
Lowe, James F., *163*
Lowe, Thaddeus S. C., 13
Luftwaffe, 101, 119, 138; and the Battle of Britain, 91; defeat through attrition, 110, 115; as threat, 101, 109, 111, 113–14; and war role, 81, 85–86
Luxembourg, 89
Luzon, 130, 131

MacArthur, Douglas, 74, 75, 93, 120, 128, 130, 136; and Korean conflict, 157–58,

161–63, 166; and Medal of Honor, 120; on New Guinea, 123, 125; relieved of command, 164

MacArthur-Pratt agreement, 75

McDonald, David L., 197

McDonnell Aircraft Corporation, 178, 236

McDonnell Douglas Corporation, 185, 225, 229, 234, 236, 237, 277

Macedonia, 280, 283, 287

McNair, Lesley J., 116

McNamara, Robert S., 187, 188, 191, 212; and air mobility units, 201; and military manpower, 189; and nuclear weapons, 189; and retaliatory air strikes, 196

Macready, John A., 61

Magic (decrypted radio messages), 123

Malaya, 144

Malesbury Abbey, 12

Manchuria, 79, 167

Manhattan Project, 134

Mao Tse-tung, 156, 162

Marconi, Guglielmo, 89

Mariana Islands, 128, 130, 132

Marine Aviation Reserve, 60, 179

Marine Corps Reserve, 165, 208, 259

Marne-Champagne campaign, 41

Marolda, Edward J. (coauthor): *Shield and Sword*, 6, 264

Marrs, Theodore, 220

Marseille, 116

Marshall Islands, 121, 127, 128

Marshall Plan, 144

Marshall, George C., 103, 105, *106*, 120, 126, 144, 315n.63; and advocate of military air power, 84, 92; and invasion of Europe, 103; and guard/reserve units, 146–47; and joint command, 107

Martin Marietta Corporation, 277

Martin, Glenn L., 78, 309n.43

Maryland, 239

M.A.S.H. (television series), 166

Maslowski, Peter (coauthor): *For the Common Defense*, 4

Massachusetts Institute of Technology (MIT), 63

Matsu (island), 180

Mauz, Henry M., 261, 262

Mediterranean, 105, 108, 110, 126, 137, 166, 228, 248

Meir, Golda, 240

Meissner, James, *43*

Menoher, Charles T., 56

Meuse-Argonne offensive, 42

Mexican civil war, 25

Mexican revolution, 20

Mexican War, 13

Mexico, 25, 26

Microsoft Corporation, 278

Middleberg, Va. 56

Midway Island, 121, 124, 128

Military Air Transport Service (MATS), 166, 190, *192*

Military Airlift Command (MAC), *231*, 240, 241, 242, 258

military operations: Allied Force, 8, 282, *283*, 284–85, 286; Anvil, 116; Coronet Oak, 221; Creek Party, 220; Deliberate Force, 281; Deny Flight, 280; Desert Shield, *255*, 258, 259, 262, *263*, 270; Desert Storm, 8, *255*, 259, *260*, 262, 264, 265, 269, 270, 271, 272, 273, *276*, 279, 284; Flaming Dart, 196; Husky, 111; Instant Thunder, 284; Just Cause, 253; Linebacker, 208; Linebacker II, 210, 213, 215, 257; Market-Garden, 116; Nickel Grass, 231, 240, 241; Overlord, 115, 116; Provide Relief, 280; Restore Hope, *278;* Rolling Thunder, 197, 198–99, 207, 208, 212, 213, 285, 294; Strangle, 168–69; Torch, 108; Urgent Fury, 247–48; Volant Oak, 220

military planning/strategy, 80–81

military spending, 9

military vehicles: M1 Abrams tank, 235; M2 Bradley vehicle, 235

military-industrial complex, 278

militia. *See* citizen-soldier; National Guard

Millett, Allan R.: *For the Common Defense* (coauthor), 4; *Semper Fidelis*, 4; *A War to be Won* (coauthor), 5, 103

Milošević, Slobodan, 280, 282, 284–87, 302

Mindanao, 20

missile (by category): air-launched cruise

missile, *continued*

missile (ALCM), 221, 226; air-to-air, 229, 230 —advanced medium range air-to-air (AMRAAM), 230–32; antiballistic missile (ABM) program, 189 (*see also* SALT I treaty; SALT II treaty); ballistic, 237, 279 —intercontinental (ICBM), 181–82, 193, 221, 223, 244, 292 — submarine-launched (SLBM), 181, 193; cruise, 181, 221, 265, 286 —resistance to adopt, 221–22; high-speed antiradiation missile (HARM), 232; multiple, independently targeted warhead (MIRV), 221, 222, 292; precision guided missiles (PGMs), 209, 215, 224, 249, 262, 268, 284, 301 (*see also* weaponry: precision guided munitions); short-range attack (SRAM), 226; surface-to-air (SAM), 177, 180–81, 189, 192, 198, 207, 214, 216, 223, 232, 235, 238, 257, 265, 284; tube-launched, optically sited, wire-guided (TOW), 209, 235

missile (by name): AIM-120, 230, 232; AIM-4 Falcon, 230; AIM-54, 230, 232; AIM-7 Sparrow, 230, 232; AIM-9 Sidewinder, 230, 232; Atlas, 181; Hellfire (helicopter-launched, fire-and-forget), 235, 236; MX, 226, 246; Minuteman, 279; Nike, 177; Patriot, 235; Paveway, 209; Phoenix, 229, 231; Scud, 257, 265, 266–67, 269; Tomahawk, 265; Walleye, 209; Silkworn, 262

missile defense (warning) systems, 222, 247

Mitchell, William "Billy," 5, 46, 49, 59, 104, 145, 147; as advocate for independent air force, 50–51, 52, 54–55, 58, 72, 73; and aerial reconnaissance program, 30; civilian exploits of, 61, 88; contributions of, 56–57; and 1st Army command, 41–42; and friction within the Air Service, 36–38; and the importance of air power, 150, 176, 225, 250, 286, 299

Moffett, William A., 5, 55, 57–58, 59, 60, 61; and integration of aviation into the navy, 67–69, 71; and support of commercial aviation industry, 63–64

Mogadishu, 277

Montenegro, 284

Montgolfier, Jacques-Étienne, 12

Montgolfier, Joseph-Michel, 12

Montgomery, Bernard Law, 116

Moore, Royal N., Jr., 261, 263

Morocco, *110*

Morrow, John H., Jr.: *The Great War in the Air,* 5

Moscow Institute of Radio Engineering, 233

Moy, Timothy, 51

Munich crisis (1938), 84, 86

Murray, Williamson (coauthor): *A War to Be Won,* 5, 103

Murray, Williamson, 103, 268

Mustin, Henry C., 20, 25

Nagasaki, 135, *136,* 150, 299

Nalty, Bernard: *Winged Shield, Winged Sword,* 6, 247

nape-of the-earth (NOE) flying technique, 235

Naples, 111

Napoleon, 12, 296

Nasiriyah, 267

National Academy of Sciences, 100

National Advisory Committee for Aeronautics (NACA), 22, 34, 35, 63, 66, 100, 152, 308n.34

National Aeronautical and Space Administration (NASA), 237, 308n.34

National Defense Act: of 1916, 26, 27; of 1920, 53, 54

National Defense Research Committee, 100

National Guard Association, 147

National Guard, 24–25, 27, 178; and manpower mobilization, 26, 89; and pilots, 51; as reserve combat force, 146; source of the citizen-soldier, 53; and Total Force, 220; Missouri, 52. *See also* Air National Guard

National Military Establishment, 145, 155. *See also* U.S. Department of Defense (DOD)

National Press Club, 288

National Recovery Administration (NRA), 81

National Security Act: of 1947, 145; of 1949, 155

National Security Council (NSC), 145, 176, 180; Memorandum 68, 156

National Security League, 26

national security, 144–46, 303; and arms control, 219, 221, 291; and biological, chemical, nuclear threat, 302; and electronic terrorism, 302; and illegal narcotics, 274, 302; and nuclear deterrence, 145, 219, 243; and role of air power, 3, 9, 294; and terrorism, 302

Naval Air Reserve, 165, 229–30

Naval Air Transport Service (NATS), 96–97

Naval Board of Construction, 19

Naval Expansion Act, 81

Naval Forces Far East, 158

Naval Intelligence Command's Strike Projection Evaluation Research group (SPEAR), 265

Naval Reserve Act of 1939, 91

Naval Reserve, 259

Naval War College, 67

Nellis AFB, Nevada, 213

Netherlands, 280

New Britain, 125

New Deal, 76

New Guinea, 124, 125

New Mexico, 134

New York, 61, 294

New Zealand, 127

Newport, R.I., 153

Ngo Dinh Diem, 195–96

Nguyen Van Thieu, 209

Nicaragua, 60

Nimitz, Chester W., 120, 125, 126, 127, 128, 130, 131

XIX Tactical Air Command, 118

94th Aero Squadron, *43*

Ninth Air Force, 118

IX Tactical Air Command, 118

Nixon Doctrine, 218, 219

Nixon, Richard M., 207, 213, 215; and China, 243; and Defense spending, 242; and the Middle East crisis, 239–41; and Vietnamization program, 208

Noriega, Manuel, 253

Normandy, 115–16, 118

North Africa, 103, 108–12, 137; and air-ground teams, 116, 118

North American Air Defense Command (NORAD), 177. *See also,* Aerospace Defense Command

North American Aviation Corporation, 67, 114, 151

North Atlantic Treaty Organization (NATO), 144, 279; and the Berlin blockade, 149; and Bosnia/Kosovo, 280–87, 302; forces of, 192, 223–26, 234–35, 243–44, 246–47, 256; French participation in, 194; and Korea, 164; and the Middle East airlift, 240; and Nixon Doctrine, 218; and nuclear weapons, 173, 176; and the Reagan Doctrine, 246–47; and weapons reduction, 252

North Korea, 156–59, 161, 206, 258, 274, 288, 300. *See also* Korea

North Korean People's Army (NKPA), 159, 161

North Sea, 246

North Vietnam. *See* Vietnam: North Vietnam

North Vietnamese Army (NVA), 203, 205, 206, 208, 209, 210

Northern Bombing Group, 45

Northrop Company, 233, 237

Northrop, Jack, 78

Norway, 89

Norwegian Sea, 246

nuclear forces, 194

nuclear weapons. *See* weaponry; nuclear weapons

O'Ryan, John, 25

Office of Scientific Research and Development (OSRD), 100–102

Office of the Secretary of Defense (OSD), 156

Okinawa, 133, 135, 157, 171

Olds, Robin, *214*

157th Fighter-Interceptor Squadron, *192*

101st Airborne Division, 271

104th Expeditionary Operations Group, *283*

Organization of Petroleum Exporting
Countries (OPEC), 241
Ostie, Ralph A., 83
Otto & Daimler, 14
Overholser, Denys, 233
Overy, Richard J.: *The Air War, 1939–1945,* 5,
95, 138, 140

Pacific Air Forces, 180
Pacific Ocean, 105, 193
Packard, 34
Palestine Liberation Organization (PLO),
238
Pan American Airlines, 249
Panama Canal Zone, 30, 253
Panama Canal, 70, 74, 80, 84
Panama, 221, 250, 253–54
Panmunjom, Korea, 170
Papal Nuncio, 253
Paris, 282
Park Avenue Armory, 24
Parris Island, S.C., 59
Parsons, Herbert, 17
Pathet Lao forces, 207, 210, 212
Patrick, Mason M., 5, 38, 40, *60,* 61;
contributions of, 56–58; and operations
v. research, 66; and separate air force,
72–73, 77; and support of commercial
aviation industry, 63–64
Pearl Harbor, 130; attack on, 93, 97, 131, 135,
137, 140
Penaud, Alphonse, 14
Pennsylvania, 294
Pensacola, Fla., 28, 50
Pentagon, 150, 162, 169, 179, 294
People's Republic of China, 180, 243
People's Republic of Kampuchea, 210
Perry, William, 277
Pershing, John J., 26, 36–38, 40, 41, 42, 46, 56
Persian Gulf War, 4, 7, *260,* 296, 301–302;
and the contribution of satellites, 227,
291; petroleum interests in, 254–261;
tactics of, 262–73, 289
Persian Gulf, 9, 263; defense of, 244. *See also*
Persian Gulf War
Philippines, 20, 74, 87, 93, 120, 130, 144, 157
Philippine Sea, 128

Piper Aircraft Corporation, 109
Plymouth (England), *62*
Poland, 81, 252
Polish Communist Party, 252
Polk, James H., 235
Polmar, Norman, 127
Portugal, 240
Potomac River, 16
Powell, Colin, 252, 266, 273, 288, 290
Powell Doctrine, 288
POWs (prisoners of war), 171, 203, 210
Pratt, William V., 74
precision engagement. *See* aviation
(technological advances): precision-
guided munitions; missile; precision
guided
Priest, Dana, 287
prisoners of war. *See* POWs (prisoners of
war)
Puerto Rico, 24
Pulitzer air race, 62
Pusan (South Korea), 157, 159, 160, 161
Pyongyang (North Korea), 158

Qadhafi, Muammar, 248
Quantico, Vir., 59–60
Quemoy (island), 180
Qwesada, Elwood R., (Pete), 118

Rabaul, 125–26, 127
radar, 73, 87–88, 100, 105, 126, 232, 257; IFF
radar, 227;; radar-directed antiaircraft
artillery (AAA), 198, 207, 223, 232, 235,
257, 268, 284. *See also* Joint Surveillance
Target Attack Radar System; stealth
technology
Rae, John B.: *Climb to Greatness,* 4, 139
Rainbow (war plans), 90; Rainbow 5, 81, 90
Raytheon, 277
Reagan, Ronald, 219, 221, 243, 251, 292; and
clandestine war, 248–49; and military
build up, 244, 246–49, 256, 301
recruitment issues, 220; draft (conscription),
219, 244; volunteerism, 219, 242
Red Flag training program, 213, 225
Red Sea, 262, *263,* 263
Reed, Albert C., *62*

Reed, Joseph M., 68
Reeves, Joseph Mason, 70
Republic Aviation, 199
Republican Guard (Iraqi), 257, 267, 269, 275
Republican Party, 120
Reserve Military Aviator, 27, 38
Reserve Officers Training Corps (ROTC),
    27
Reynolds, Clark G.: *Admiral John H.
    Towers,* 5
Rhee, Syngman, 156, 268
Rhineland, 79
Rhine River, 116
Rhone River, 116
Ribot, Alexander, 30
Richardson, James O., 93
Rickenbacker, Edward V. (Eddie), 9, 42, *43,*
    44, 85, 141
Rickover, Hyman G., 228
Ridgway, Matthew B., 164, 166, 170, 183
Risner, Robinson, *163*
Riyadh, 254, 256, 261, 268
rocketry research/development, 101. *See also*
    missile
Rockwell International, 277
Rodgers, John, 23
Rogers, Buck, 51
Rohrbach, Adolph, 65
Roland, Alex, 143
Rome, 112
Roosevelt, Franklin D., 59, 75, 77, 176; and
    airmail contracts, 75–77, *76;* and global
    unrest, 78, 79, 81; and the Joint Chiefs
    of Staff, 145; and MacArthur, 130; and
    military build up, 89–93, 98, 107; and
    nuclear weapons, 134; and neutrality,
    87; and the role of air power, 176, 294;
    as Assistant Secretary of the Navy, 34;
    and support of the Air Corps, 85–86;
    and World War II, 108, 110, 120
Roosevelt, Theodore, 120; and military
    romanticism, 246; and strong defense,
    26; and support of aviation, 15, 17–18,
    19, 297
Royal Air Force (RAF), 3, 6, 72, 81, 86; and
    the Battle of Britain, 91; and the Berlin
    airlift, *148;* and escort missions, 118;

Fighter Command of, 130; and German
    submarine threat, 104, 106; and
    humanitarian aid air support, 277; and
    Operation Overlord, 115; in Persian Gulf
    War, 267; and radar research, 88, 101, 126;
    and support from U.S. marines, 45; and
    use of night attacks, 112; and use of
    offensive air power, 109, 115, 118
Royal Canadian Air Force, 223
Royal Flying Corps (Canada), 40
Royal Navy, 82; Air Service, 72; and carrier
    missions, 53, 111, 116, 126, 158; and
    German submarine threat, 29, 40, 45, 87,
    104–105; and Operation Husky, 111; and
    postwar weakness, 153
Royal New Zealand Air Force, 123, 124
Rumsfeld, Donald H., 291
Russia, 22, 179, 274, 279, 303; and nuclear
    weapons, 292; and Persian Gulf war, 264
Ryan Aeronautical Corporation, 52, 100
Ryan, John B., 20, 35

Sadat, Anwar, 241–42
Saddam. *See* Hussein, Saddam al-Tikriti
Saigon, 196, 197, 210
Saint-Lô, 118
Saint-Mihiel, 41–42
Salerno, 111
SALT I treaty, 222
SALT II treaty, 226, 246
San Diego, 25, 50, 59–60, 61, 68
San Francisco Bay, 70
Sarajevo, 288
Sarajevo airport, 280
satellites: Defense Support Program (DSP),
    269; Global Positioning System (GPS),
    227, 270, 291; modernization of, 219, 291;
    Navstar, 227; Project Corona, 182; Samos
    project, 182; space surveillance/reconnais-
    sance, 6, 182, 203–204, 222, 269, 270;
    warning systems, 222
Saudi Arabia, 226–27, 255–56, 258; military
    air power, 256
Schlessinger, James, 254
Schlieffen, Alfred von, 304
Schlieffen plan, 303
Schlight, John, 204

Schmued, Edgar, 114

Schneider Trophy Race, 62

Schneller, Robert J., Jr. (coauthor): *Shield and Sword*, 6, 264

Schwarzkoph, H. Norman, 261, 266, 267, 268, 271, 272

Schweinfurt, Germany, 114

Scotland, 249

Scott, Riley, E., 23

Sea Frontier, 105

Sea, Air, Land (SEAL) teams, 269

Selfridge, Thomas, 18

Seminole War, 13

Seoul, Korea, 158

Serbia, 280, 281–82, 302

VII Corps, 269

Seventh Fleet, 261

Seversky Corporation, 67

Shah of Iran, 244, 256

Sheepshead Bay, 23

Shepherd, Lemuel C., Jr., 178

Sherman, Forrest P., 157, 173

Sherwood, John D., 199, 214–15

Shiite Muslims, 275

Shiner, John F.: *Foulois and the Army Air Corps, 1931–1935*, 5

ships (U.S.): *Essex*, 193; *New Jersey*, 54; *United States*, 153; USS *America*, 263, 264; USS *Birmingham*, 20, *21;* USS *Constellation*, 196; USS *Coral Sea*, 208; USS *Eisenhower*, 258; USS *Enterprise*, 81, *122*, 174; USS *Forrestal*, 174, *198;* USS *Franklin D. Roosevelt*, *239;* USS *Hornet*, 121; USS *Independence*, 247, 258; USS *John F. Kennedy*, *263*, 264; USS *Kearny*, 92; USS *Langley*, 67, 69; USS *Lexington*, 69; USS *Leyte*, *170;* USS *Long Island*, 107; USS *Maddox*, 196; USS *Midway*, 264; USS *Mississippi*, *263;* USS *Missouri*, 136; USS *Normandy*, *263;* USS *Pennsylvania*, 20, *21;* USS *Philippine Sea*, *263;* USS *Preble*, *263;* USS *Pueblo*, 206; USS *Ranger*, 70, 108, 110, *110*, 230, 264; USS *Reuben James*, 92; USS *San Jacinto*, *263;* USS *Saratoga*, 69, 70, *263*, 264; USS *Theodore Roosevelt*, 264, 286; USS *Thomas S. Gates*, *263;* USS

Ticonderoga, 196; USS *William V. Pratt*, *263;* USS *Wright*, 54; USS *Yorktown*, 81; USS *Valley Forge*, 158; *Virginia*, 54

ships (foreign): HMS *Triumph*, 158 (British); *Hosho* (Japanese), 82; *Ostfriesland* (German), 54; *Rex* (Italian), 79, *80*

ships (by category) battleships, 83, 121, 126; carriers (flattops, supercarriers), 53, 82, 83, 119, 121, 126, 128, 150, 178, 216, 227, 228, 243, 262 —*Essex*-class, 126, 153, 158, 165, 174, 228 —*Forrestal*-class, 155 — *Independence*-class, 126 —*Midway*-class, 153, 166 —nuclear-powered, 228–29; cruisers, 83, 126; destroyers, 126; Landing Ship Tank (LST), 111; submarines, 131–32, 134 —German U-boats, 20–30, 40, 45, 104–107, 110, 121, 137 —Polaris, 181 —Trident nuclear, 244

Sicily, 103, 110–12, 248

Sikorsky, Igor, 65, 99

Sikorsky Aircraft, 236

Sims, William S., 30, 40, 46, 67

Sinai Peninsula, 241, 244

Single Integrated Operational Plan (SIOP), 182

Six-Day War (1967), 238

Sixth Army, 131

Slovenia, 280

Smith, C. R., 97

Smithsonian Institution, 15

Solomon Islands, 120, 121, 122, 124–26

Somalia, 250, 277, *278*, 301

South America, 80, 86

South Korea, 168, 206, 244

South Vietnam. *See* Vietnam: South Vietnam

Southeast Asia Treaty Organization (SEATO), 177, 195

Soviet Union, 8, 9, 158, 294, 300; and airborne warfare, 96, 223; and the aircraft industry, 99; and appeasement, 79; and the Berlin blockade, 147, 149; and the Berlin Wall, 252; and China/ Soviet cooperation, 162, 166, 167; collapse of, 250, 273; and the Cuban Missile crisis, 191–93; and détente, 243,

244; and invasion —of Afghanistan, 256 —of Czechoslovakia, 144 —of Poland, 86; invaded by Germany, 91; and Iraq, 271; and lend-lease assistance, 87; and the Middle East crisis (1973), 238, 241; and military advances, 180–81; and military build up, 227; and North Vietnam, 208, 212; and the Reagan administration, 246; as supplier of aircraft, 257; and war with Japan, 134. *See also* Cold War

Spaatz, Carl A., 70–71, 75

Space Commission, 291

Spain, 73, 79, 85, 230

Spanish-American War, 26

Spector, Ronald H.: *Eagle Against the Sun,* 5, 119, 125

Speer, Albert, 119

Sperry, Lawrence, 65

Spires, David N., 270

Spruance, Raymond, 128

Sputnik, 182, 183

Squier, George Owen, *31;* as advocate of aviation program, 30, 32; as advocate for technological resources, 28; and army study of aeronautics, 17–18, 20, 22; and the Signal Corps, 35, 36–37

St. Paul, Minn., 39

Stalin, Joseph, 91, 134, 147, 149, 171, 191

Star Wars. *See* Strategic Defense Initiative (SDI) (Star Wars)

stealth technology, 219, 226, 232–33, 244, 246, 296, 299, 302

Stilwell, Joseph W., 129

Stimson, Henry L., 109, 151

Stokesbury, James L.: *A Sort History of Airpower,* 5, 293–94

Straits of Messina, 111

Strategic Air Command (SAC), *154,* 172, 220; and air defense, 177, 181, 221–23; on heightened alert, 241; and rearmament program, 175; and Tactical Air Command, 173; under the command of LeMay, 150–51; and the use of bombers, 176, 203, 209, 222, 224, 300

Strategic Arms Reduction Talks (START) I, 292

Strategic Arms Reduction Talks (START) II, 292

Strategic Defense Initiative (SDI) (Star Wars), 244

Stratemeyer, George E., 157

Strike Warfare Training Center, 214

Strom, Dixie, *283*

submarines. *See* ships (by category): submarines

Suez Canal, 238, 240, 254, 284

Sullivan, John, 155

Syria, 238, 274

Tactical Air Command (TAC), 173, 222

Tactical Air Control Center (TACC), 160

Taebeck Mountains, 162, 163

Taft, William Howard, 17, 22

Taiwan, 180

Taiwan Straits crisis, 190

Tam Ky (Vietnam), *200*

Tampico (Mexico), 25

Tarawa (atoll), 127

Task Force 77, 158, 159, 168, 169, 196

Taylor, Thorn C., *43*

Tedder, Arthur W., 115, 117

Tegel airport, 147

Teheran, 244

Tel Aviv, 240

Tempelhof Airport, 147

X Corps, 161, 162, 163, 169

Tenth Fleet, 107

Texas, 25

Texas Instruments, 277

Texas Tower radar platforms, 177

Thailand, 216

Third Fleet, 128

3rd Marine Air Wing (Reinforced), 261, 263

Third Reich, 110, 299

38th Parallel, 156, 161, 163, 168, 170

332d Fighter Group, 112

Thucydides, 272

Tibbets, Paul W., Jr., 134, 135

Tigris River, 268

Tilford, Earl, 284

Tinian, 134, 135

Tito, Josip Broz, 279–80

Tizard, Henry, 101

Tokyo, 83, 157, 161
Tokyo Bay, 136
Torrijos, Omar, 253
Total Force, 220, 259
Toul, France, 41
Towers, John H., 20, 23, 46; and air
    combat unit, 40; as career aviator, 59;
    and German submarine threat, 29–30;
    and reservists, 91; and role of naval
    aviation, 25, 28, 131; transatlantic flight,
    61
Training and Administration of Reserves
    (TAR) program, 179
Treaty of Versailles, 49, 79
Trenchard, Hugh M., 72
Trimble, William F.: *Admiral William A.
    Moffett*, 5
Troop Carrier Command, 96
Truman, Harry S., 134, 135, 143; and Korea,
    161; and the military budget, 153, 155,
    175; and military build up, 156, 157, 164,
    173, 187; and nuclear weapons, 151; and
    unification of the armed forces, 147, 149
Tunisia, 109
Tunner, William H., 129, 147
Turkey, 143, 179, 258, 264, 265, 272, *276*,
    280
Turnbull, Archibald D. (coauthor): *History
    of United States Naval Aviation*, 4
Tuskegee airmen, 103
12 O'Clock High (movie), 141
Twentieth Air Force, 128
XX Bomber Command, 128
XXI Bomber Command, 128, 132

U.S. Aeronautic Reserve, 20
U.S. Air Force (USAF), 145, 257; and
    aircraft numbers, 223; airlift capabilities
    of, 190; and the Berlin airlift, 147, *148;*
    and centralized close air support, 160,
    169, 204; Combat Command, 290,
    315n.63; and disagreement with the
    Kennedy administration, 191; in Kosovo
    conflict, 286; and missile development,
    181; Space Command of, 222, 291
U.S. Air Force Reserve, 147; airlift units of,
    259, 285; and humanitarian relief, 179,

275–76, 280; mobilization of, 164; and
    operational rotation, 220; and opera-
    tional integration, 295–96
U.S. Army (the army), 13, 267; and
    appropriations, 29, 31–32; and aviation,
    16–18, 22, 27, 40–41, 75, 298 (*see also*
    American Expeditionary Forces); and
    ballooning, 17; and close air support,
    169; and cross-Channel invasion, 108;
    Engineering Division, 36; Enlisted
    Reserve Corps, 26; General Board of, 69;
    General Staff of, 29, 54, 58, 75, 77; and
    ground forces, 109–10, 315n.63; impact of
    World War II on, 137–41; and manpower
    mobilization, 26; Office Reserve Corps
    of, 26; and post—Cold War strength,
    273; and Services of Supply, 315n.63;
    Signal Corps, 17, 26 27, 34, 88, 297 —
    Aeronautical Division, 17 —Aviation
    Section, 22 28, 29, 30, 35, 38 —
    Specification No. 486, 18; Special Forces
    (Green Berets), 190; and war in the
    Pacific, 120; War Plans Division of, 84
U.S. Army Air Corps, 5, 58, 67, 70, 96, 298,
    315n.63; and airmail contracts, 75–76, 77;
    and the citizen-soldier, 91; and coastal
    defense, 74–75, 78; funding of 58–59, 73,
    81, 86; and lack of trained personnel, 86,
    91; and land-based air attacks, 74;
    renamed, 92; Tactical School of, 72, 73
U.S. Army Air Forces (USAAF), 56, 92, 99,
    100, 101, 104, 255, 315n.63; and air
    superiority, 123; and antisubmarine
    warfare (ASW), 105–108, 137; blacks in,
    102–103, 112; Aviation Engineers of, 124–
    25; and bombing campaign, 112–4, 115–
    17; and centralized command, 109, 119;
    and cross-Channel invasion, 108; and
    escort missions, 118; 509th Composite
    Group, 134; impact of World War II on,
    137–41; and light aircraft, 109–10, *110;*
    and Operation Overlord, 115; pilot
    combat/training rotation of, 121; and
    postwar role, 146; struggle for indepen-
    dent air force status, 72–79, 145; tactical
    doctrines of, 123, 137, 168; and use of
    signal intelligence, 123; women in, 102

U.S. Army Air Service, 36–42, 44, 54, 66; and air defense, 87; and the AWPD-1, 92; in disarray, 56; Engineering Division of, 63; renamed, 58. *See also* U.S. Air Corps; American Expeditionary Forces

U.S. Army Corps of Engineers, 257

U.S. Army Reserve, 26, 192

U.S. Asiatic Fleet, 83

U.S. Central Command (CENTCOM), 257, 258

U.S. Congress, 145, 155, 249; and defense budget issues, 220, 273; and national security policy, 218–19; and neutrality, 79, 87; and military build up, 90; and military procurement, 64–66

U.S. Department of Defense (DOD), 145, 155; reorganization of, 187; and weapons acquisition, 185, 222, 236, 288

U.S. Department of the Navy, 155

U.S. Joint Chiefs of Staff (JCS), 104, 150, 183; and air assault in Vietnam, 197, 201; authority of, 249; and the Berlin airlift, 147; chairman of, 155; and MAC, 241; and military build up, 156, 165; and military cutbacks, 252; and nuclear weapons, 135, 153, 158, 164, 180; and Powell as chairman, 273; and system of military negotiation, 145; and war in the Pacific, 121, 128, 131, 133

U.S. Marine Air Station (Yuma MAS, Ariz.), 214

U.S. Marine Corps (marines), 7, 24, 29, 30, 44, 83, 89; and amphibious assault capability, 145, 153, 154, 233, 269; and aviation, 59, 99, 122, 127, 298; blacks in, 102; and decentralized close air support, 160, 169, 178, 204–205; impact of World War II on, 137–41; marine fliers of, 50, 60; and navy/marine command, 132; and operations in —Guadalcanal, 122 —Luzon, 131 —Saudi Arabia, 258; 3d Battalion, 5th Marine Regiment, *200;* and use of helicopters, 166, 178, 301; women in, 102

U.S. Military Academy (West Point), 18, 72

U.S. Military Assistance Command, Vietnam (MACV), 197, 205

U.S. Naval Academy (Annapolis), 20, 24, 28

U.S. Naval Air Station (NAS): Fallon NAS (Nev.), 214; Miramar NAS (Calif.), 213; Rockaway NAS, (N.Y.), 61, *62*

U.S. Navy (the navy): and antisubmarine warfare (ASW), 105–108, 137, 228, 229; and atomic weapons, 154; and aviation, 18, 19–21, 22–24, 27, 29–30, 35–36, 40, 45–46, 67–71, 90, 99, 298 —as auxiliary support, 132 —as patrol force, 53 —for reconnaissance, 53; and the Berlin airlift, *148;* blacks in, 102; Bureau of Aeronautics, 49–50; Construction Battalions, 124 and decentralized close air support, 160, 169; and escort missions, 116; and funding, 53, 54, 59; on Guadalcanal, 122; and impact of World War II, 137–41; and logistics, 127, 130; and Navy Department, 55; Naval Aircraft Factory (NAF) of, 35, 63, 297; and navy/marine command, 132; Naval Flying Corps, 53; Naval Reserve Flying Corps, 28, 91 —"First Yale Unit," 28; Office of the Chief of Naval Operations, 28; Patrol Squadron, 18, 194; and postwar role, 146, 153; Seabees, 124–25; and shipbuilding program, 27, 90; and the Victory Program, 91; and World War I, 29–30

U.S. Senate, 292

U.S. State Department, 156, 180

U.S. Transportation Command, 291

U.S. Veterans Administration, 204

U.S. War Department, 17, 25, 27, 33, 53, 58, 73, 145; and aircraft procurement programs, 76; and Air Service, 35, 36; and Bureau of Aircraft Production (BAP), 35; and Division of Military Aeronautics (DMA), 35; and doctrine FM 100-20, 109; and foreign military contracts, 66; and funding, 55; General Staff of, 31–32; and policy toward blacks, 102

U-boats. *See* ships (by category): submarines —German U-boats

Ufimtsev, Pytor, 233

Ultra, 105, 109
Underwood, Jeffrey S.: *The Wings of Democracy, 1933–1941*, 5
Union Army, 13
United Airlines, 293
United Nations Command (UNC), 157, 158, 161, 164, 168–72
United Nations, 157, 252; in Bosnia, 280–87; in Iraq, *276;* peace keeping force, 241, 280 (*see also* United Nations Command); relief workers, 277; sanctions, 258, 274–75; Security Council, 264
Universal Military Training and Service Act (UMT) (1951), 178

Valkyries, 11
Van Creveld, Martin, 44
Vandenberg, Hoyt S., 151, 157, 158
Venice, 13
Veracruz, Mexico, 25
Verdun, 115
Vicenza, Italy, 280
Victory, John F., 308n.34
Victory Program, 92
Vienna, 191
Vietcong, 195, 197, 205
Vietminh, 179, 194, 195
Vietnam War, 7, 29, 300; and affect on postwar U.S. military, 223, 227, 243, 259, 289; Easter offensive of, 208, 209; and commercial aerospace industry, 235; Eleven-Day War, 215; and guard/reservists, 295; and policy restrictions for aviators, 199; success of air power, 211–17; Tet offensive, 206, 216; and U.S. defense spending, 185; and the use of defoliants, 204. *See also* Vietnam
Vietnam, 195; North Vietnam, 195, 258, 294; air defense systems of, 212–13; bombing of, 197–98, 212, 215; South Vietnam, 195, 216
Villa, Pancho, 26
Vinson, Carl, 81
Vinson-Trammel Act, 81
V-J Day, 143, 144, 146

Vladivostok Accords, 222
VMF-214 Black Sheep squadron, *140*

Wagner, Herbert, 65
Walcott, Charles D., 22
Warden, John, 224–25
Warsaw Pact, 176; countries, 243, 246; forces, 223–24, 235; and weapons reduction, 252
Washington Naval Conference, 82
Washington Post, 287
Washington, George, 144
Watergate scandal, 239
weaponry: biological, 258; chemical, 257, 258; inventory/loss of, 242; modernization, 219, 221, 223, 242, 279, 289–92 —costs of, 288; nuclear weapons, 9, 134–35, *136*, 142, 150–53, 164, 174, 249, 289, 299–300 —hydrogen bombs, 175 —tactical, 223, 243; delivery systems for, 173, 176, 221; precision-guided munitions, 9, 216 (*see also* missile); procurement of, 188–89; simulated combat testing of, 231; for terror, 117 —kamikaze flights, 131, 133–34, 135; and test-ban treaty, 194
Weeks, John W., 56
Wehrmacht, 111, 117
Weigley, Russell F.: *The American Way of War,* 4; *History of the United States Army,* 4
Weinberger, Caspar, 244, 288
Werrell, Kenneth P., 136, 221
West Point. *See* U.S. Military Academy (West Point)
Westmoreland, William C., 197, 205, 206, 261
Weyland Otto P., 118
Wheeler, Earle G., 201
White House, 145
White, Robert P.: *Major General Mason M. Patrick and the Fight for Air Service Independence,* 5
Whiting, Kenneth, 40
Wilhelm II, 29
Wilson, Woodrow, 33, 35; expectations of for role of air power, 176, 294; orders the study of aviation, 22; and Treaty of

Versailles, 49; and war with —
Germany, 29–32, 42 —Mexico, 25–26
Wings (movie), 51
Women Accepted for Voluntary Emergency
Service (WAVES), 102
Women Airforce Service Pilots (WASP), 102
Women's Army Auxiliary Corps (WAAC),
102
Women's Army Corps (WAC), 102
Worden, Michael, 172, 191
Works Projects Administration (WPA), 81
World Trade Center, 294
World War I, 5, 22, 25–26, 30, 32, 33, 34; and
role of aircraft, 36–47, 64, 295, 297, 298
World War II, 50, 63, 71, 87–94, 293, 299–
301; and bombing (*see* aerial bombard-
ment); and global airlift (*see* airlift); and
U.S. air power, 95

World War III, 142
Wright brothers, 4, 13, 14, 17, 18, 20, 23, 24,
296, 297; training by, 39, 104
Wright, Orville, 3, 15–6, 18, *19,* 19, 20, 303
Wright, Wilbur, 3, 15–6, *19,* 303
Wright-Martin, 34

Yalu River, 161, 162, 163, 168
Yanamoto, Isoroku, 124
Yarnell, Harry E., 83
Yeager, Charles E., 152
Yellow Sea, 158
Yeltsin, Boris, 292
Yom Kippur War, 8, 238–42
Yugoslavia, 250, 279–80, 302

Zuckerman, Solly, 115
Zumwalt, Elmo, 204, 227–28, 254

CHARLES J. GROSS, who holds a Ph.D. in military history from The Ohio State University, has worked as a U.S. Air Force civilian historian and is currently the chief of the Air National Guard history program. He has written numerous studies for the air force and Air National Guard and has contributed widely to service and scholarly journals. He served on active duty in the U.S. Air Force from 1964 to 1969 and retired as a colonel in 1994 after a long career in the Air Force Reserve and the Air National Guard.

ISBN 1-58544-255-0

9 781585 442553   90000